COMPANION ENCYCLOPEDIA
OF ARCHAEOLOGY

COMPANION
ENCYCLOPEDIA
OF ARCHAEOLOGY

EDITED BY

GRAEME BARKER

Volume 2

London and New York

First published 1999
by Routledge
11 New Fetter Lane, London EC4P 4EE

29 West 35th Street, New York, NY 10001

© 1999 Routledge

Typeset in Ehrhardt by
RefineCatch Limited, Bungay, Suffolk
Printed and bound in Great Britain by
Butler and Tanner Ltd, Frome and London

British Library Cataloguing in Publication Data
A catalogue record for this book is available from the British Library

Library of Congress Cataloging-in-Publication Data
Companion encyclopedia of archaeology / edited by Graeme Barker
p.   cm.
Includes bibliographical references and index.
(alk. paper)
1. Archaeology – Encyclopedias.   I. Barker, Graeme.
CC70.C59   1999   98–7621
930.1 – dc21   CIP

ISBN 0–415–06448–1 (set)
0–415–21329–0 (vol. 1)
0–415–21330–4 (vol. 2)

CONTENTS

VOLUME 1

PART I: ORIGINS, AIMS AND METHODS

16

PRODUCTION AND EXCHANGE IN HISTORICAL ARCHAEOLOGY

John Moreland

The view we must adopt regarding these Melanesian peoples ... is very different from the view which is normally taken. They have an extra domestic economy and a highly developed exchange system, and are busier commercially than French peasants and fishermen have been for the past hundred years. They have an extensive economic life and a considerable trade that cuts across geographical and linguistic boundaries. They replace our system of sale and purchase with one of gifts and return gifts ...

Thus we see that a part of mankind, wealthy, hard-working and creating large surpluses, exchanges vast amounts in ways and for reasons other than those with which we are familiar from our own societies.

(Mauss 1967: 30–31)

UNDERSTANDING HISTORICAL ECONOMIES

The economy in the past?

At the beginning of the second volume of his magisterial and comprehensive history of *Civilization and Capitalism*, Fernand Braudel considered the functioning of the economy. For him it consisted 'at first sight' of two areas – production and consumption. However, 'between these two worlds slides another, as narrow but as turbulent as a river, and like the others instantly recognizable: exchange, trade, in other words the market economy' (Braudel 1982: 25). The economy thus consists of 'three worlds' – production, exchange (circulation), consumption. This same triad formed the basis of Marx's analysis of the emergence and development of capitalism (Marx 1973: 83–100).

Figure 16.1 Market scene in Tononicapán Western Highlands, Guatemala. Photograph: P. Chiles.

For Braudel, 'the market' spelt 'liberation, openness, access to another world' (Braudel 1982: 26) (Fig. 16.1). Through participation in the market, through access to the goods offered there, the world of the early modern European peasant was linked to the wider world which was at that time being revealed. Through 'the market' 'the traditional, the archaic and the modern and the ultra-modern' were conjoined (Braudel 1982: 26).

The problem we have to face in writing of production and exchange in historical archaeology, however, is to what extent the three worlds of Braudel's economy can be discerned in the 'traditional' and in 'archaic' societies. Both Marx and Braudel were analysing the emergence and functioning of one particular form of economy – capitalism.

Although it is true that we can speak of production, exchange and consumption in all societies, can we assume that they took the same form in all societies? that the relationship between them was the same – production for exchange through the market? that they can (or should) be separated analytically? that 'the economy' can be studied in and of itself? We could surely argue that to make these assumptions is to impose on the world of the pre-capitalist past the values, mores and *mentalité* of the present. If we (unconsciously) make such an imposition, could we not argue that we must fail to understand the past, and the role of production and exchange in that past? Might we not be better to heed the words of Karl Polanyi when he said that

we must rid ourselves of the ingrained notion that the economy is a field of experience of which human beings have necessarily always been conscious . . . The crystallization of the concept of economy was a matter of time and history.

(Polanyi 1957: 74)

Might we not better consider a pre-capitalist past in which those activities which we see as 'economic' were not separate from, but embedded in, the other structures of society?

The expansion of the European powers to conquer and dominate the rest of the world from the late fifteenth century to the early twentieth resulted in dramatic changes in the lives of the conquered peoples. Not only did the Europeans bring their own technologies and diseases which contributed to the decimation of the indigenous populations of the Americas (McNeill 1976; Wright 1992), they also brought their particular way of seeing the natural world and their ideas about people's relationship with that world. Gradually they imposed those ideas on others.

The basis of the production of all material goods, and therefore of their exchange, is the natural world, the world of nature. In the accounts of sixteenth- and early seventeenth-century visitors to North America, we get a very particular image of the landscape, an image which reflects a Europeanized perspective on the world of nature.

> Most of the early explorers sought to discover what Richard Hakluyt had called 'merchantable commodities' in his classic *Discourse Concerning Western Planting* in 1584. These were the natural products which could be shipped to Europe and sold at a profit in order to provide a steady income for colonial settlements.
>
> (Cronon 1983: 20)

This perception of the world of nature as a source of commodities stemmed partly from a view widely held in Europe that 'the world had been created for man's sake and that other species were meant to be subordinate to his needs and wishes' (Thomas 1984: 17). When Europeans encountered peoples who did not see and use the natural world in the same way, the reaction was one of 'baffled contempt' (Thomas 1984: 21). To people whose systems of production and exchange were based on landscapes of ordered fields and domesticated animals, and who were imbued with notions of the God-given superiority of human beings, the Native American use of their landscape rendered them barely human (if at all) and unfit to possess the land. Because the Indians, in the course of their hunting activities 'do but run over the grass, as do also the foxes and wild beasts', Robert Cushman in 1621 declared that the land was 'spacious and void' and therefore free for English taking (Cronon 1983: 56; see also Jennings 1975). This was one aspect of the general 'myth of emptiness' which was used to justify the expropriation of native lands: 'the colonized had no property rights to . . . land because they had no concept of property rights in land' (Blaut 1993: 25).

The purpose of the above discussion has been to illustrate the fact that the relationship between man and the natural world which was prevalent in Europe at the time of the 'voyages of discovery' was not natural, in the sense that it was not inherent in all human beings. It had emerged in a particular place, at a particular point in time. In other parts of the world, at other times in the past, the relationship between man and the natural world was different. The rationale behind production and exchange would also therefore have been different. In these worlds, people would have produced and exchanged 'for reasons other than those with which we are familiar from our own societies' (Mauss 1967: 31). To understand these worlds we cannot use the logic of capitalism.

The theme of 'production and exchange in historical archaeology' must, of course, be concerned with the development and spread of capitalism. In fact, there are those archaeologists, usually American, who argue (in my view erroneously) that historical archaeology is the archaeology of the 'modern world', 'the time when colonialism, Eurocentrism, capitalism, and modernity all come together' (Orser 1996: 86), or indeed 'the archaeology of capitalism' (Deagan 1994: 16–23; see also Deetz 1977: 5; Leone and Potter 1988: 19), but many pre-capitalist societies existed 'in history' (see below, p. 649; for a further critique of this view, see Moreland, forthcoming). The questions we have to consider are: How are we to understand the logics of production and exchange in pre-capitalist, historical societies? In what ways did these logics differ from those of capitalist societies? How did they react to and interact with the spread of capitalism? We can only begin to address questions of such magnitude in this chapter, but we have to start by considering how we can gain an insight into worlds so different from our own.

Anthropology, production and exchange

Given that we are seeking to understand pre-capitalist as well as capitalist societies, might we not argue that a study of those societies encountered by anthropologists would give us insights into the pre-capitalist, historical world? This has indeed been argued by many archaeologists and historians. At the turn of the twentieth century, Sir Baldwin Spencer wrote:

> Australia is the present home and refuge of creatures, often crude and quaint, that have elsewhere passed away and given place to higher forms. This applies equally to the Aboriginal as to the platypus and kangaroo. Just as the platypus . . . reveals a mammal in the making, so does the aboriginal show us, at least in broad outline, what early man must have been like before he learned to read and write, domesticate animals, cultivate crops and use a metal tool. It has been possible to study in Australia human beings that still remain on the culture level of men of the Stone Age.
>
> (cited in Bahn 1996: 181; see also Trigger 1989: 143)

The attitudes expressed here represent a version of the 'theory of our contemporary ancestors' which asserts that 'as we move farther and farther away from civilized Europe, we encounter people who, successively, reflect earlier and earlier epochs of history and culture' (Blaut 1993: 16). Oriental cultures were condescendingly venerated because they contained 'the eternal in its present'. 'In other words, contemporary India was not truly contemporary, but showed Europe its own past' (Dirlik 1996: 102, fn. 16). The eternal in the Indian present was the world we had lost through the rupture caused by capitalism. We could rediscover for ourselves the supposed values of that lost world, and understand our own past, through a study of the Indian (and other non-European) presents.

The same Eurocentric views are made much more explicit in the work of some evolutionary anthropologists (Marcus and Fischer 1986: 17). Perhaps the clearest expression was given by Marshall Sahlins in 1963 (although it must be emphasized that his later work (Sahlins 1974, 1987, 1995) demonstrates a much more sophisticated understanding of the relationship between the West and the peoples encountered by anthropology):

> the native peoples of Pacific islands . . . present to anthropologists a generous scientific gift; an extended series of experiments in cultural adaptation and evolutionary development . . . From Australian aborigines, whose hunting and gathering activities duplicate in outline the cultural life of the later palaeolithic, to the great chiefdoms of Hawaii, where society approached the formative levels of the old Fertile Crescent civilizations, almost every phase in the progress of primitive culture is exemplified.
>
> (Sahlins 1963: 285)

It would appear then, from these perspectives, that to understand the logic of production and exchange in the pre-capitalist world (prehistoric and historic) anthropology provided a key. Particularly influential for archaeologists was Elman Service's typology of bands > tribes > chiefdoms > early states (Service 1971; see Fig. 12.2). Chiefdoms and early states began to appear in profusion in archaeologists' discussions of early historic societies. Service's typology is explicitly adopted by Richard Hodges in his analysis of the production and exchange systems operative in north-western Europe in the early Middle Ages (Hodges 1982: 26–27); Klavs Randsborg uses chiefdoms, early states and secondary states as analytical concepts around which to hang his discussion of the Viking Age in Denmark (Randsborg 1980: 7–10, 167–69); we have complex chiefdoms in the European Iron Age (Champion and Champion 1986; Collis 1984: 18–19) and in early North America (Peebles 1987; Steponaitis 1978; Renfrew and Bahn 1991: 155–56).

In terms of production and exchange, these chiefdoms are supposed to have been organized around the principle of redistribution. As we have seen in Chapter 15, this was one element in the typology of exchange systems developed by Karl Polanyi (1957). It is useful in so far as it provides us with a logic for the organization of production and exchange 'other than those with which we are familiar from our own societies' (Mauss 1967: 31). However, this appreciation must be set against the fact that it seems capable of application to societies from the late Neolithic onwards. Real understanding of the historical communities labelled 'chiefdoms' or 'early states' is denied through the assertion of identity – they are all chiefdoms; they all operate through redistribution:

> Identity is always the primordial term. Although each documented chiefdom . . . is distinct from any other chiefdom . . . , in an evolutionary framework these differences become subsumed and relegated as secondary or contingent.
>
> (Shanks and Tilley 1987: 149)

So rather than providing a key to the understanding of the different logics of production and exchange in pre-capitalist historical communities, evolutionary frameworks, like the one just discussed, deny such difference through the imposition of another form of identity. However, before we conclude this discussion of anthropology and its impact on our understanding of pre-capitalist, historical economies we must return to Marcel Mauss, for he provided archaeologists with an alternative logic for the organization of production and exchange – the Gift.

Mauss and the Gift

Writing originally in 1925, Mauss argued that Man had only recently become 'an economic animal . . . a machine, a calculating machine' (1967: 74); before this transformation into *homo economicus*, exchanges involved

> not exclusively goods and wealth, real and personal property, and things of economic value. They exchange rather courtesies, entertainments, ritual, military assistance, women, children, dances, and feasts; and fairs in which the market is but one element and the circulation of wealth but one part of a wide and enduring contract.
>
> (Mauss 1967: 3)

For Mauss, 'the exchanges of archaic societies . . . are *total social movements* or activities. They are at the same time economic, juridical, moral, aesthetic, religious, mythological and socio-morphological phenomena. Their meaning can therefore only be grasped if they are viewed as a complex concrete reality' (Evans-Pritchard 1967: vii). This is an important insight and is one developed by some of the anthropologists I have already discussed. In pre-capitalist societies, production and exchange were not only (or even) 'economic' activities. They were part of the total fabric of society. When the Quebec Eskimo killed a reindeer they were not merely performing an economic activity – 'from the hunters' point of view their slaughter and consumption is an integral and necessary part of the creative cycle of renewal' (Ingold 1986: 250). It is only with capitalism (and perhaps not even fully there – Mauss 1967: 2; Hodder 1986: 30; Samson 1991: 88), that the 'economy' becomes disembedded from the other structures of society (Polanyi 1957; Sahlins 1974; Goelier 1977). Mauss argued that many 'embedded' exchanges took place through the medium of *the gift*.

Mauss argued that gift exchange was characterized by three obligations – the obligation to give; the obligation to receive; and the obligation to repay (1967: 37–41). The giving of gifts to others demonstrates the power of the donor. The receiving of gifts puts the recipient in the 'moral debt' of the donor, creating a relationship of subordination. Hence the obligation to repay. Failure to repay, at the appropriate time and in an appropriate manner, reproduces the social relationship of subordination. It was impossible to avoid getting into 'social debt' by refusing a gift, since normally refusal resulted in loss of face and social subordination. (The above is a very brief summary of Mauss's arguments on gift exchange, supplemented by the discussions of Gregory (1982) and Gosden (1989).)

This system, although different from ours, was not inferior. It provided the logic for some of the most extensive movements of products in the non-capitalist world – e.g. the Trobriand Island system (Mauss 1967: 18–31).

Mauss constructed his picture of gift exchange on the basis of the study of a few societies, most of them on the Pacific rim. Despite this, he argues that the concept of gift exchange as a means of structuring society was 'not merely local' (Mauss 1967: 16). Its greater applicability in time and space is supported by the quotation from *Hávamál*, an Icelandic saga, with which he begins his book: 'A man ought to be a friend to a friend and repay a gift with a gift'; by the fact that the French historian Paul Veyne used a variation of the concept to explain substantial 'economic' exchanges in the Greek and Roman world (Veyne 1990); and by the fact that archaeologists and historians have found it useful as a heuristic device in their interpretation of prehistoric and early historic societies (see for example Balzaretti 1992; Geary 1994; Gosden 1989; Hauken 1991; Wickham 1992). Might 'the Gift' then provide us with an 'alternative' logic for the organization of production and exchange in pre-capitalist, historical societies?

Gifts and commodities

In recent years substantive critiques of the concept of the gift have emerged (see, for example, Sahlins 1974: 149–83). In particular, the notion of the morally-binding force of the gift has been called into question. It will be remembered that the exchange of gifts created social relationships. For Mauss, the focus was on the construction of these relationships, not on the objects exchanged (except in so far as the objects were thought to contain 'the spirit of things', 'a spiritual power' *'hau'* (Mauss 1967: 8–9; Vestergaard 1991: 97–99; Samson 1991). Here the contrast is with the societies 'with which we are familiar', where exchange is an impersonal process, mediated through the anonymity of money and the market (Mauss 1967: 93–94; Evans-Pritchard 1967: ix). In gift-giving societies, exchange, as part of the total social fabric, creates and reproduces *personal* relationships: '[w]ithout exchange social life, social communication, would not be' (Vestergaard 1991: 98). In our societies, exchange creates relationships between *things*.

In his recent book *Entangled Objects: Exchange, Material Culture and Colonialism in the Pacific*, Nicholas Thomas (1991: 15) summarizes the perceived differences between exchange in capitalist and non-capitalist societies as follows (see also Geary 1994: 216):

Commodities	*Gifts*
Alienable	Inalienable
Independence	Dependence
Quantity (price)	Quality (rank)
Objects	Subjects

He points out that the difference between 'the gift' and 'the commodity' is so great that one can be seen as the inverse of the other. He argues that we have constructed the concept of the gift, not from the dispassionate observation of the process in action, but on the basis of our perception of the (im)morality of exchange in our own society (see also Rowlands 1994: 2).

There is a tendency in the writing of history and anthropology to see capitalist, industrial society as devoid of the humanity which is the essence of the small-scale societies which we reconstruct for the past (Thomas 1991: 10). This 'ideology of primitivism', this dissatisfaction with the world we live in, encourages us to emphasize the differences between it and the world of 'the others', to the extent that their world becomes the desired antithesis of our own. Such 'constructed idylls' can be found in some of the earliest ethnohistorical works (for an eighteenth-century view of the Kahnawake in north-east America, see Demos 1996: 150), and can be traced at least as early as the description of the Germans presented to the Romans by Tacitus in the first century AD.

Nicholas Thomas suggests that, although the Gift may have been the basis for exchange and social reproduction in some societies, some of the time, Mauss over-generalized from his particular case studies, and we have subsequently developed Mauss's images to construct a desired-for world of simplicity, morality, and humanity – a world closer to nature.

What recent work (archaeological, historical and anthropological) has made clear is that, even when gift exchange can be demonstrated, it was not always the only system of exchange in operation, nor did it always function in the socially cohesive fashion proposed by Mauss, nor was money the 'subversive threatening force' which it has been presented as (Bloch and Parry 1989; Carsten 1989; Rowlands 1994; and Samson 1991 for details).

What has to be made clear is that there are no 'pristine' societies in which we can disinterestedly observe pre-capitalist systems of production and exchange to use as models for the historical past. The worlds of anthropology have been linked to that of capitalism since the inception of the discipline and they have profoundly influenced each other. In fact it can be (and has been) argued that anthropology is not the disinterested observation, recording, and analysis of the people encountered in the process of colonialism, but was itself an active participant in the imperialist process (Said 1994, [1978] 1995). At the same time as the land and rights of the indigenous peoples of the world were being removed by the imperialists, their culture and traditions were being appropriated by anthropologists and historians as models for the European past (see pp. 640–42). We can draw three conclusions from all of this which are of direct relevance to our attempts to reconstruct pre-capitalist, historical economies.

First, our vision of anthropology and ethnohistory has been too simple. A consequence of this is that the imposition of models drawn from these disciplines onto the more distant past results in our under-playing the complexity of production and exchange activities. As a reaction to the iniquities and immorality of capitalism, we have constructed monolithic worlds of reciprocity, redistribution and gift exchange. We should understand that such monoliths can rarely have existed and realize that no society in the past was constructed on the basis of a single mode of production or exchange (Rowlands 1994; Wickham 1984).

Second, we must appreciate that the 'entanglement with capitalism' has produced the historically specific societies which anthropologists have observed, and which archaeologists and historians have used as the basis for analogies. We can see that the development and spread of 'dominant' systems of production and exchange in historical periods can radically transform all aspects of society and economy in formerly 'independent' worlds. The spread of capitalism is the most obvious, and most pervasive, example. Numerous studies have now been devoted to showing how, from the sixteenth century onwards, the expansion of the European powers and their modes of organizing production and exchange profoundly altered the social structure, economy, and *mentalité* of societies in Africa, America, Australasia, and the Far East (among many others, see Dincauze and Hasenstab 1989; Wolf 1982; Brenner 1988; Rowlands 1979; Deagan 1983).

What is clear from these studies, however, is that, whenever capitalism came into contact with other modes of organizing production and exchange, the 'native' forms did not just disappear. Just because capitalism became the dominant mode does not mean that it was adopted wholesale and without modification by non-European societies. The interaction between the capitalist and the non-capitalist modes of production and exchange produced hybrid economies and, as Carol Smith has pointed out as a result of her study of Guatemalan peasants, in some cases the interaction could alter the form of the dominant mode itself (Smith 1984).

Third, we can argue that the capacity to interact with and transform 'native' economies is not a unique feature of capitalism. There have been other world empires and world economies – to use the phraseology of Wallerstein (1984: 147–58) – whose dominant mode of production must have had an impact on the economies of the societies with which they came into contact. One thinks immediately of the Roman empire and its transformation of the structure of the economy in, for example, the province of Britannia (see, amongst others, Millett 1990; for northwest Europe generally see Hedeager 1992). However, we can also refer to the impact of Islamic silver, and general contacts with the Middle East, on the structure of society in early medieval Denmark (Randsborg 1980), and in a slightly different mode we should note the relationships between the Middle East, India, and China fostered by the fact of trade across the Indian Ocean:

> The Indian Ocean itself created a . . . kind of unity through the long-distance trade and the great urban emporia. The free port and the trading city of caravan routes represented the essence of many different civilisations, a distillation of a multitude of geographical images.
>
> (Chaudhuri 1990: 147)

In the Americas, Randy McGuire has charted the impact of Mesoamerican contact on the thirteenth-century Anasazi, in the south-western United States (McGuire 1989).

Nicholas Thomas has argued that 'there should be a movement of perspective from economic abstractions to historical forms' (1991: 16). In other words, we should cease imposing the constructs of western anthropological thought and concentrate on analysing the specifics of exchange relations and their impact on particular historical communities (Geary 1994: 218; see Sahlins 1987 for a fine example of how this can be done).

We can only appreciate the historical specificity of past historical economies if we study them in all the detail that the combination of the archaeological and the historical record allows (Thomas 1991: 16). The non-capitalist economic categories proposed by Mauss, Polanyi and others may be useful as heuristic devices, as foils for developing our ideas about the nature of production and exchange in particular societies, but they only obscure our vision when they are *imposed* on the past as reified conceptual categories. Before we turn to look at the complexities which analyses of real, historical production and exchange systems reveal, we must consider two 'institutions' which both partially differentiate such systems from those encountered by anthropologists and partially define the former as entities in their own right: money and writing.

Money and writing

Money stored value, and helped to foster the growth of long-distance markets. Writing stored rights and obligations, and helped to create a larger store of knowledge, a system of laws, and a market in cultural skills and values. Their operation was mutually reinforcing, since both money and writing are systems of impersonal, symbolic exchange . . . Writing and money were two powerful agents of communication and control . . .

(Hopkins 1991: 157)

As with many of the terms we use in the human sciences, money and writing at first sight appear easily understandable – they are things with which we are familiar, recognizable aspects of the modern world. However, such understanding is illusory. Definitions of money and of writing, which apply across time and space, have proved difficult to produce (see, for example, McKitterick 1990; Goody 1968; Stock 1983 for literacy; Dalton 1977; Hodges 1988 for money). I do not intend to try to produce such definitions here. Equally I do not intend to try to differentiate the 'money-like' things and the 'writing-like' things recorded by anthropologists, from the coins and documents which we will encounter in the text below (although some references to such differences will appear) (see Mauss 1967: 93–4; Dalton 1977; Gregory 1982; Sahlins 1974: 277–314 for 'money-like things'; Hooker 1990 for texts and 'text-like' things). Here I want to consider briefly the 'function' of these institutions in historical economies.

Money is held by some to be one of the defining characteristics of complex historical economies. Fernand Braudel wrote that 'the operation of the money supply can be seen as an instrument, a fundamental and regular phenomenon of any moderately developed commercial life' (Braudel 1981: 436). It was a powerful force in the creation, transformation, and reproduction of those economies, since the development of media through which all exchange could be conducted enhanced the speed of exchange and the quantity of goods involved. Anthony Giddens argues that money makes possible the circulation of exchange values across vast areas of time and space. In addition it permits the storage of wealth on a massive scale (Giddens 1981: 116–17). As such, a consideration of money would be central to any understanding of production and exchange activities in historical economies.

The role of writing in the organization of production and exchange activities is less self-evident, but no less important (Fig. 16.2). Giddens has argued that the use of writing was more important than technological change in the generation of surplus, since writing allowed greater control of knowledge about the production process (Giddens 1981: 94–95). The full implications of writing for society in general, and for systems of production and exchange in particular, have been spelt out by Jack Goody:

The importance of writing lies in its creating a new medium of communication between

Figure 16.2 Writing and the market – Mexico City. Photograph: P. Chiles.

men. Its essential service is to objectify speech, to provide language with a material correlative, a set of visible signs. In this material form speech can be transmitted over space and preserved over time . . . The range of human intercourse can now be greatly extended both in time and space. The potentialities of this new instrument of communication can affect the gamut of human activity, political, economic, legal and religious. In the administrative sphere, complex bureaucratic organizations are directly dependent upon writing for the organization of their activities, especially financial. It provides a reliable method for transmitting information between the centre and the periphery . . .

So too in the organization of long-distance trade and estate agriculture: it is writing that assists with the calculation of profit and loss.

(Goody 1968: 1–2; see also Giddens 1979: 200–4)

Goody argues that, even in its earliest manifestations (Fig. 16.3), writing was directly implicated in the production and exchange activities of complex economies (see Maisels 1990; Nissen 1986; Larsen 1988; Hallo 1979 for *cuneiform* and production in early Mesopotamia; Chadwick 1990 and Halstead 1992 for *Linear B* and ancient Crete; Baines 1983 for hieroglyphs and ancient Egypt).

Where it exists, there is generally an integral link between writing, production and exchange. This is true even when the use of writing is restricted to a small élite – as it generally was up until (and even beyond) the invention of the printing press (Eisenstein 1979). In societies with 'restricted literacy', writing and the word were frequently linked to the Gods and the supernatural, and therefore to 'power' (Bowman and Woolf 1994). This was not only true of the 'religions of the Book' – Christianity, Judaism and Islam (Goody 1986: 1): a similar link has also been argued for Roman paganism (Beard 1991), ancient Egypt (Baines 1983, 1989), the Minoan palaces on Crete (Cherry 1986), and for early medieval Sri Lanka (Goody 1986: 59–61). Writing, through its connections with the élite and the Gods, legitimated the social relationships which lay behind many of the production and exchange activities of the historical past. This connection added to the power which writing endowed on élites by virtue of its capacity to list, record and transmit information across time and space. As such, even the illiterate became entangled in the tentacles of writing (Hopkins 1991).

So far I have been speaking in generalities about the 'function' and power of money and writing to affect the operation of systems of production and exchange in historical economies. But as with the anthropological analogies which I discussed above, it is important not to reduce the analysis of past economies to the level of 'sameness' through the uncritical application of these generalities to the whole of

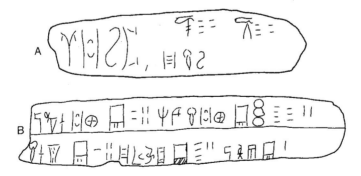

Figure 16.3 Ancient texts and production – Knossos tablets recording (A) fifty rams and fifty ewes, and (B) different kinds of cloth. Source: Chadwick 1976.

the historical past. It is now time to turn from these 'economic abstractions' and consider some 'historical forms' (Thomas 1991: 16). In doing so, I hope to use the insights derived from the generalized discussions of the anthropology of 'pre-capitalist' societies, money and writing, to uncover the complexities of historical economies and to understand them in their own terms rather than as simplified worlds we have lost. In each of the studies below, I shall examine the 'historical forms' as entities in their own right, but also as exemplars of the kind of complexity which we might expect to find in all historical economies.

RECONSTRUCTING HISTORICAL ECONOMIES

Money and morality in the medieval world

A mere handful of men – unending emptiness stretching so far west, north, and east that it covers everything . . . clearings here and there, wrested from the forest but still only half-tamed; shallow pitiful furrows that wooden implements drawn by scrawny oxen have scratched on the unyielding soil; . . . huts of stone, mud, or branches clustered in hamlets surrounded by thorn hedges and a belt of gardens; sometimes inside the palisade that shields it, a chieftain's dwelling, a wooden hangar, granaries, the slaves' sheds and the cooking hearth some ways off to the side; sparsely scattered towns, the mere whitened skeletons of Roman cities invaded by rural nature, . . . near them a few dozen huts that house the vinegrowers, weavers and blacksmiths, all the domestic craftsmen who make ornaments and arms for the garrison and the local bishop; two or three Jewish families who lend a little money on pledge; trails, the long lines of men at portage, flotillas of small boats on every waterway . . .

Such is the Western world in the year 1000 . . . it seems rustic, very poor and defence-less. A wild world ringed round by hunger. Its meagre population is in fact too large.

(Duby 1981: 3)

This was the image of the western world in the early Middle Ages, and of the systems of production and exchange which sustained it, which prevailed until recently. It is an image which fits well with perceptions of degradation and ruin following the demise of complex social systems (see Renfrew 1979; Tainter 1988). Production is at the level of bare subsistence; technology is fighting a losing battle with a combative Nature; craft production is limited and controlled by the élite living in the decayed remains of once splendid Roman cities. Trade is small scale and conducted only with difficulty. There appear to be two 'economies' – that of the self-sufficient or autarkic peasant, struggling to wrest a living from nature; and that of the bishop linked to a wider world through 'flotillas of small boats' and the loans of Jewish merchants.

However, even before this highly pessimistic account of the early Middle Ages was written, archaeology was providing the documentation for another story. Excavations across north-western Europe were revealing evidence for organized villages and planned landscapes, for palatial and ecclesiastical complexes; much of this recent evidence is summarized by Hamerow (1994) and Randsborg (1991). Together, archaeology and history have been documenting fairly complex systems of agricultural production (Astill and Grant 1988).

More surprisingly (but only in terms of the 'catastrophist' bent of much previous history writing), archaeologists had been bringing to light the remains of a series of coastal settlements (emporia) with abundant evidence for long distance trade. It had been a commonplace of historical interpretation of the early Middle Ages that the movement of goods over long distances had been reduced to minimal levels. However, as long ago as 1939 the excavations of the Sutton Hoo ship burial demonstrated the long distance movement of goods from the Mediterranean to Britain – the Anastasias dish and the Coptic bowls for example (Bruce-Mitford 1975–83). (For the location of Sutton Hoo and other sites mentioned in this section, see Fig. 16.4.) The discovery of a sixth- to seventh-century north Indian Buddha at Heglö in Sweden shows more wide-ranging contacts (illustrated in Graham-Campbell 1994: 33). The analysis of pottery from the west of Britain has shown the persistence of long distance contacts with the East Mediterranean throughout late Antiquity (Fulford 1989; Thomas 1993: 93–96).

Most significantly, the excavations of the numerous west European emporia (coastal trading sites) in the period since the Second World War have demonstrated a dramatic increase in the range of contacts and the movement of goods in the eighth and ninth centuries (see Clarke and Ambrosiani 1991; Hodges 1982; Hodges and Hobley 1988). More often than not, analogies drawn from anthropology, and specifically concepts of gift exchange, were used to account for such movements (Hodges 1982, especially pp. 52–56; Jones 1993). In addition, control over this exchange was seen as one of the principal bases for power in many early medieval kingdoms, and the trade itself was seen as 'directional' between the elite trading partners in participating kingdoms (Hodges 1982: 54). What is especially significant about emporia such as that at *Hamwic* (Saxon Southampton) is that it was part of a 'world system' of production and exchange. Through trading links with other emporia in Holland (Dorestad), Denmark (Ribe and Hedeby), Sweden (Birka), and Russia (Staraya Ladoga), connections were created which linked the kingdoms of western Europe with the Near and Far East, and which supplied the European élites with exotic products such as the Buddha found at Heglö (for this 'world' system see Graham-Campbell 1994; Hodges 1982; Hodges and Whitehouse 1983).

More recent results suggest that it was not just low-volume, high-prestige goods which were being traded at this time. Recent historical research has begun to investigate the movement of the 'everyday' goods which must have constituted the majority of traded products at the local and regional levels (for example, Blair 1994; Everitt 1986; Hooke 1989; Kelly 1992). However, it is also now clear that ordinary

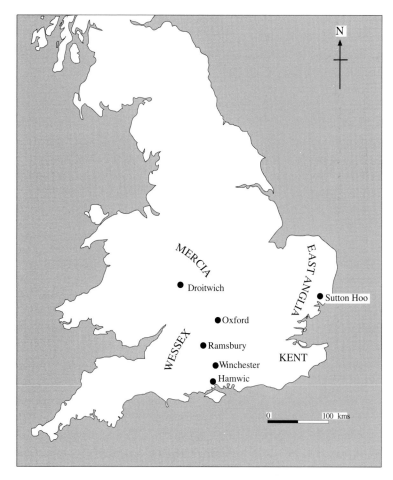

Figure 16.4 Exchange in early medieval England – location of sites mentioned in the text.
Source: J. Moreland. Drawn by D. Miles-Williams.

produce could be moved over quite long distances. An analysis of the weed seeds from the Dutch emporium of Dorestad has demonstrated the importation of grain in the eighth and ninth centuries (van Zeist 1990), while the movement of bulk staples has also been noted in the Baltic at a slightly later date (Randsborg 1980: 100). John Blair has argued for the continued importance of the long distance movement of salt from the Droitwich region in the early Middle Ages (Blair 1994: 84–87). Chemical analyses of the interior surfaces of pottery from Saxon South-ampton show the presence of olive oil (Evans 1988). Archaeozoological evidence suggests that the Danish emporium of Hedeby was being supplied with meat from rural settlements, like that at Elisenhof some 50 km to the south (Randsborg 1980: 57–59), and that the region around the English emporium of Hamwic (Saxon

652

Southampton) was supplying the population with the meat for their stews (Bourdillon 1988: 180; 1994), and flour for their bread (Fowler 1982: 276). (From now on I will focus mainly on the evidence from Anglo-Saxon England, and particularly the site of Hamwic.)

It would now appear that the emporia were not solely concerned with long-distance trade. In the past, archaeological attention was focused on the exotic material found on the emporia sites, as evidence for the postulated significance of long-distance 'directional trade between elites' (Hodges 1980, and 1982: 56–60). More recently, an analysis of the pottery from Hamwic has shown that locally made coarse wares dominated the assemblage (82 per cent of the total – Timby 1988: 73), perhaps indicating that our perspective on the nature of the Anglo-Saxon economy, and on the role of long-distance trade in prestige goods within it, has been coloured by the presence of a small number of items of exotic material culture.

The evidence from the emporia is now being reassessed and it is clear that at, for example, Hamwic, Dorestad, and Hedeby (Denmark), the production of craft goods was a major activity (Fig. 16.5) (Brisbane 1988; Morton 1992; Randsborg 1980; van Es 1990). At Hamwic there is direct or indirect evidence for

> iron working (mostly smithing, but perhaps also smelting), copper-alloy working, lead working, gold working (including mercuric gilding), bone and antler working, wool processing, textile production, leatherworking, glass working . . . woodworking, and butchery.
>
> (Brisbane 1988: 104)

From the evidence of the production facilities, the amount of waste produced and the objects themselves, it is clear that this production was above and beyond the needs of the community. Production *and* exchange of 'craft goods' are clearly involved, and control over the production of craft goods is now seen as a critical factor in the reproduction of power relations (Hodges 1989: 70; more generally, see Gosden 1989).

Finally, we must briefly consider the fact that small silver coins (*sceattas*) have been found on many of the sites of the eighth century in England. I cannot discuss their origins or evolution in any detail (see Grierson and Blackburn 1986: 164–89, 266–95; Hodges 1989: 71–79). All we need to note here is that they are frequently found on emporia sites and that there is some evidence that at least some of them may have been produced there (Hodges 1989: 83; Jensen 1991: 11). They are also found in association with craft production activities (Fenwick 1984). We should also note that, although many more have been found in the last few years, primarily by metal detectors (Blair 1994: 84), the numbers known are still counted in the low thousands. In addition, it is perhaps important that these 'coins' were struck in silver, and only in silver.

Figure 16.5 Houses and production in Hamwic. © J. Hodgson.

Archaeology has moved us a long way from a 'rustic, very poor and defenceless world'. But we would also appear to have contrasting pictures, with several 'economies'. On the one hand we have the evidence for long-distance trade in 'prestige goods', explained by many in terms of a version of Maussian gift exchange; then we have the provisioning of settlements like Hamwic with the raw materials for subsistence and craft production; we have craft production which, although focused on emporia, was not restricted to them (Carr *et al.* 1988; Haslam 1980); we have the association between *sceattas*, exchange, and craft production; and finally we have the agricultural production of the vast majority of the population, living and working from villages and hamlets spread throughout the landscape of England. How were these systems of production and exchange linked? What was the underlying logic of the system? Was there in fact a single logic, a single early medieval economy?

More than usual, we should be wary of assuming a single overarching structure for the economies of early medieval north-west Europe since, socially and politically, the region was extremely fragmented. However, given the presence of *sceattas* across much of north-western Europe and the discovery of 'foreign' *sceattas* at sites like Hamwic (Fig. 16.6), might we not see this coinage as evidence for the re-

Figure 16.6 Sceatta from Hamwic. © Southampton City Council.

emergence of a monetary, commercialized economy? Might not coinage have been the medium through which the economies of this period were articulated? If so what was the role of the putative gift exchange and what was the relationship between this, the 'money economy' and the ubiquitous system of agricultural production and exchange? Here we have to consider the detail of the archaeological and historical evidence.

In his discussion of the *sceatta* coinage, D. M. Metcalf (1984) presents his arguments in terms which are unambiguously 'modernist'. Thus he argues that

> These scarce early coins seem to be relatively more plentiful as continental finds than their output in relation to the succeeding primary series would have led us to expect. In monetary terms the pattern is one of contacts between Kent and the Thames estuary and the Rhine mouths, and quite possibly a net drift of coin from south eastern England to the Continent; that is to say, England may have run a small *balance-of-payments deficit*, which was inimical to a net drift of coin in the other direction, namely towards the English midlands.
>
> (Metcalf 1984: 30, emphasis added)

In essence, Metcalf is suggesting that *sceattas* were coins used in a monetary economy. He implies that his argument is supported by the number of coins which he assumes to have been in existence. He estimates that some 2–3 million coins may have been produced in some of the *sceatta* series, while the coinage of Offa, the late eighth-century king of Mercia, should be numbered in tens of millions (Metcalf 1965). Here we see an Anglo-Saxon economy in which production and exchange are structured through money and the market, much like today. Presumably gift exchange is epiphenomenal in such a system.

Some support for the idea that we should be talking about a commercialized economy is to be found in the historical sources. In a study of documents recording the sale of land in Anglo-Saxon England, James Campbell notes that in the late seventh century, Abbot Haedda paid 500 *solidi* to Ethelred, king of Mercia, for a piece of land (Campbell 1989: 27). This, and other documents, would seem to confirm that that most precious of commodities – land – could be alienated from the kin group through the medium of coinage. But before we go any further we should note what the rest of this document says. Campbell continues as follows:

> Before the chink of coin has died from our ears it [the text] goes on to explain what is meant by 500 *solidi*; *id est*, it says, twelve beds, namely feather mattresses and elaborate pillows together with muslin and linen sheets as is customary in Britain; also a slave, with a slave girl; also a gold brooch and two horses with wagons.
>
> (Campbell 1989: 29)

This apparently transparent transaction begins to look less like a straightforward commercial sale, and should caution us against too literal a reading of other written sources which might seem to imply commercialized exchange (see Jones 1993: 664 for other examples; and Bloch 1965: 66–67 for a general discussion).

The archaeological evidence is also not as straightforward as it appears. We cannot doubt the existence of silver coins from the late seventh century, but we can question the numbers postulated and the interpretation presented by Metcalf. First we should consider the numbers of coins in circulation. Metcalf's figures are based on a formula used to estimate the volume of coins of Queen Elizabeth I (1558–1603), which involves multiplying the number of dies used by the number of coins which *may* have been minted from any one die. Metcalf argues that up to 10,000 coins could have been produced from one die, and that no less than 150 obverse dies would have been used. This results in millions of coins produced (Metcalf 1965). However, as several observers have pointed out, it might not be appropriate to apply the figures for coin production in the sixteenth century, a period when we see the beginnings of the emergence of the 'modern world system', to the economies of early medieval England. Thus Hodges argues that in the eighth century it is as likely that one *sceatta* was struck from a die as 10,000 (1982: 115). Although we cannot give precise figures for the number of *sceattas* struck and put into circulation, the comparatively low numbers (*c.* 127) found at major sites like Hamwic (Saxon Southampton) suggest that we should be talking in terms of tens of thousands rather than millions (for the number of *sceattas*, see Metcalf 1988: 15). This must affect our perception of the efficacy of these 'coins' as media of exchange and as providing a logic for the overall economy. It is perhaps worth noting that '[t]he foreign sceattas found in Hamwic would have been sufficient . . . to requite the damage to only five or six ox horns: and all the Dark Age coins [from Hamwic] would have been a payment for only twenty ox horns' (Morton 1992: 66).

In this context we must also consider the fact that these coins were made of silver, and only of silver; there were no other denominations. Although the silver content of the coins fluctuated (Hodges 1982: 113, fig. 28), they cannot be regarded as small change (for the comparative value of early tenth-century coins, see Whitelock 1955:

388, n. 37, 6.2). It is doubtful, therefore, that they were involved in many ordinary market transactions. The discovery of these coins on certain classes of site – emporia, ecclesiastical and royal settlements, hill top 'fair' sites – does link them with exchange, perhaps with the 'closed sphere of foreign trade' (Hodges 1989: 76), but their comparatively low numbers, their distribution, and their occurrence in a single (high value) denomination all suggest that they were not the only, or even the most important, medium of exchange. They coexisted and articulated with other forms and it is to a short consideration of these that we must now turn.

It is evident that much production in the early Middle Ages was focused on the provision of objects for use as gifts, even if it is now also clear that such gifts were produced and acquired in circumstances very different from the 'primitivist' ones envisaged by Georges Duby (see p. 650; Geary 1994). Gifts may have been given and exchanged at all levels of society. The texts give us some hints as to what may have been exchanged at the highest levels. The 'belt and Hunnish sword' which we are told the Emperor Charlemagne sent to King Offa of Mercia can be seen as a gift from the ruler of one country to the ruler of another (Whitelock 1955: 781–82, n. 197). The gold rings specified in charters of the ninth century should equally be seen as aristocratic gifts (Campbell 1989: 27). We have already noted Mauss's quotation from the *Hávamál* ('a man ought to be a friend to a friend and repay a gift with a gift' (Mauss 1967: xiv), and Stephen White has written on 'gifts to saints' in eleventh- and twelfth-century France (White 1988). Equally, there can be little doubt that, although the *sceattas* did not function like modern coins and that the Anglo-Saxon economy was not a monetary economy, these coins had some connection with systems of craft production and long-distance trade. As importantly, we always have to remember that most production and exchange took place in the context of relations of dependency between lord and tenant, relations which would have been mediated through custom and tradition and not through money.

Having recognized the multiplicity of ways in which production and exchange might have been structured in the early Middle Ages, and having down-played the role of coinage as a structuring mechanism, we again have to face the crucial question as to how they were articulated

We should begin by noting that emporia like Hamwic seem to have been set up and controlled by kings. These kings also owned estates worked by peasants who delivered renders. John Blair has argued that some of the cattle consumed at Hamwic may have been supplied from as far away as the Upper Thames valley, with salt travelling even greater distances. It is perhaps significant that Hamwic-type *sceattas* have been found in the Upper Thames region (Blair 1994: 82–89).

Estates will have produced more than agricultural produce. The eighth-century settlement at Ramsbury in Wiltshire may have been part of a royal estate, and the archaeological evidence suggests that one of its principal activities may have been the production of iron (Haslam 1980). German lava quern stones found at

Ramsbury may originally have been imported through Hamwic, travelling to Ramsbury partly by the same route (in reverse) postulated by Blair for salt and cattle (Haslam 1980: 56).

It is possible that the people of Hamwic were supported by peasant renders to the *villa regalis* (the royal centre) which we know existed there, and that they used the renders from estates like Ramsbury to produce craft items. These items may then have been exchanged (as gifts?) at the regional and perhaps international level (the letter from Charlemagne to Offa also mentions cloaks and 'black stones' – presumably quern stones), to reproduce social relations in a way similar to that proposed by Mauss. More prestige items, like the late eighth- or early ninth-century Anglo-Saxon embroideries from Maaseik in Belgium, were gifts between the secular and ecclesiastical élites of north-west Europe (Budny 1984). They may have been traded through the emporia, but they were probably made elsewhere – in the case of the embroideries, an ecclesiastical context is most likely. Whatever the case, their production rested on the basis of an economic infrastructure dominated by relations of peasant dependency. If we can summarize this complex situation, it would seem that production and exchange among the élites were dominated by gift exchange, but at more basic levels renders of food and services were predicated on relationships of subordination and dependency.

Coinage was used, in a way we do not yet understand, to link the systems of craft production and that of long-distance trade. As such, it should be connected both with the sphere of prestige goods exchange and with peasant production. Although we do not fully understand the nature of this connection, we can be sure that, at this stage in the development of the Anglo-Saxon economy, money did not provide the overall rationale for the operation of the system (for a partial explanation, see Jones 1993: 661–63). To argue that it did is to ignore the evidence for the *mores* and values of the period which all point to the personalized nature of exchange.

The Anglo-Saxon economy of the eighth century was one in which 'economic' activities were still structured through personal relations rather than through the mechanism of the market. In that respect, it bears a strong resemblance to aspects of the economy of the late Roman empire, where, argues C. R. Whittaker '[a] good deal . . . of produce was moved internally, as it were, between domainal estates. Ausonius moved wine by cask from his Garonne estate to another of his estates at Saintes . . . just as Gregory transported timber to Rome from his papal estates in Bruttium' (1983: 171). This observation is supported by Averil Cameron, who suggests that

> [w]hile . . . a landlord might well become involved in production and engage in long-distance transport, both might take place within an exchange system involving either simply his own estates, or those of himself and his friends; this is less an economic activity than a patronal relationship.
>
> (Cameron 1993: 89)

It must be emphasized that I am not here offering support for an autarkic early Middle Ages. I am not here talking about 'l'économie domaniale fermée' (Devroey 1984: 570), a closed manorial economy where all production and exchange took place within the bounds of estates. I am arguing that it is a mistake simply to assume that there were whole periods of the past in which only a *single* system of production and exchange operated. We have to envisage a network of relationships which linked the peasant in the Upper Thames valley, the lord in his villa, the craft producer at Hamwic, the king at Winchester or one of his other palaces; and a web of connections which linked this system with others – organized along the same lines or not – stretching across the North Sea into the Baltic and from there as far as the silver mines of the Far East.

We also have to remember that this was not a static situation. The texts and the archaeology all point to the growing importance of coinage from the ninth century onwards. In addition, the documentary evidence suggests that the transfer of land from one person to another, and outside kin relations, became more frequent at the same time, and that the documents were themselves a fundamental part of the process (see Kelly 1990; for the importance of texts in the process, see Moreland 1992). However, it is likely that most production and exchange remained socially 'embedded' throughout the Anglo-Saxon period. Money and the market were condemned by ecclesiastics right through the medieval period, and the clamour of the Church against the market reached its height at exactly the time (the thirteenth century) when we know that 'the market' was making real inroads into traditional means of production and exchange (Le Goff 1988). However, as Le Goff says, '[o]ne economic system replaces another only after it has passed through a long and varied obstacle course' (Le Goff 1988: 93), and the evidence for the eighth and ninth centuries suggests that the obstacle course from gift and render to monetary exchange had not yet been completed. As the next section describes, archaeological evidence from Morocco suggests that the process was still not completed by the beginning of the modern world.

Morocco in a world system

Qsar es-Seghir is situated on the southern shores of the Straits of Gibraltar which separate Spain and Morocco. This location, at the crossroads of the Islamic and Western worlds, and controlling the entrance to and exit from the Mediterranean basin, made it a site of some importance in the developing world systems of the late medieval period (Fig. 16.7). The archaeology and history of the settlement are now well known due to the research carried out by Professor Charles Redman and his colleagues, and much of what follows is based on that work (Redman 1986).

The settlement appears to have been founded in the eighth century AD as a small fort, with an associated village, designed to provide a focus for the movement of Islamic troops to and from Spain. Although the Islamic invasions of Europe provided the settlement with its original rationale, it only developed as a major settlement in the late twelfth century (Redman 1986: 235). Between the eleventh and the fourteenth centuries, Qsar es-Seghir may have been one of a series of coastal entrepôts funnelling the products of long-distance trade from sub-Saharan Africa into Spain (Redman 1986: 25). It reached a zenith in the fourteenth century, but the changing military, religious and economic circumstances of the following century resulted in major transformations in the fortunes of Qsar es-Seghir.

The town was conquered by the Portuguese in 1458, part of the more general *Reconquista* of Islamic territory by the kings of Spain and Portugal. However, this *Reconquista* cannot be seen as motivated purely by religious zeal. The world was at a crucial juncture. What has become known as the 'modern world system' was in its early stages of development (Wallerstein 1974) and this development needed infrastructural support. As Redman (1986: 33) notes:

> Europe was in need of increasing amounts of gold to fuel the growing monetary economy of the era and raw materials for productive industries. The major source for the gold was sub-Saharan Africa, and the traders and trading cities that brought it to the Europeans were those in North Africa. Clearly, to control these trading centres would give a European power tremendous advantages in the growing monetary economy.
>
> (Redman 1986: 33)

The historical and archaeological evidence indicates that, with the Portuguese conquest the settlement was isolated from the surrounding countryside (Redman 1986: 11). At the same time the Portuguese, and other European kingdoms, had begun to exploit the new trade routes opened up by the 'voyages of discovery' (see Wolf 1982). The products of sub-Saharan trade via Morocco became less important to the growing European economies and Qsar es-Seghir was abandoned in 1550.

The excavations at Qsar es-Seghir recovered thirty coins from the levels of Islamic occupation. Of these about two-thirds were high denomination silver or gold. Both the numbers and the type of coins stand in marked contrast to those discovered in the later Portuguese levels. Here were found over two thousand coins, mostly small denomination copper issues (Redman 1986: 208). This suggests that the two communities (Islamic and Portuguese) used fundamentally different trading principles. Redman argues that the comparative scarcity of coins in the Islamic community means that '[t]he Muslims must have been able to deal with merchants on personal accounts, suggesting a community where everyone was acquainted and trusted', whereas an indication of a 'less co-operative situation in the Portuguese period was the abundance of coins at that time' (1986: 246). In essence, Redman is here using the coins as indicators of the shift from a community in which much exchange would have been carried out without the use of coinage, instead being

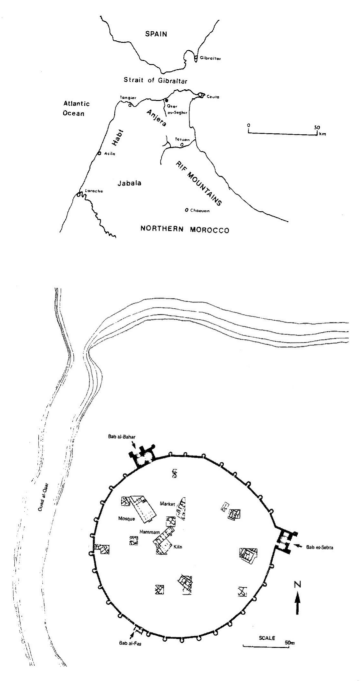

Figure 16.7 The medieval settlement of Qsar es–Seghir, Morocco: location map (above) and site plan (below). Source: Redman 1986.

mediated through personal, and/or kin relationships (we should remember that most of the Islamic coins were of very high denominations, useless for everyday economic activities), to one where coinage was used to mediate exchange relationships between both strangers and kin. He argues that this points to a more competitive and a more individualistic community in the Portuguese period; a community which was among the 'first spearheads of a world expansionist movement that was rapidly making Portugal a world power' (1986: 247).

The 'Embarrassment of Riches': Holland in the seventeenth century

Holland in the seventeenth century was 'the most formidable capitalism the world had yet seen' (Schama 1987: 323). From a region threatened with inundation by the sea, Holland had amassed an Empire and had come to dominate much of world trade (for the archaeology of this trade, see Gawronski 1990). The fruits of this trade produced what Simon Schama has called an 'Embarrassment of Riches': Dutch society in the seventeenth century was phenomenally wealthy. At the same time Calvinism was the most pervasive and powerful religious belief. The Dutch therefore faced the dilemma produced by the accumulation of wealth and the damnation which was the promised consequence of the building up of worldly goods.

One of the strangest, and at the same time most illuminating, episodes of Dutch history in this 'Golden Age' occurred between 1636 and 1637 and has been called the 'great tulip mania' (Schama 1987: 350). Tulips originated in Turkey, and in the early decades of the seventeenth century their production and trade were in the hands of specialists. By the 1630s the market had expanded, and by 1634 the desirability of the tulip, especially rare varieties, had grown so rapidly that what we would call 'futures trading' had begun to take place. By 1637 the inevitable collapse took place. This, however, is not the point of relating this story. For this, we have to go back to 1636, to the height of the mania. In that year, at the same time as 'futures trading' was taking place:

> [a] quarter of a pound of White Crowns . . . were bought for fl. 525 to be paid on delivery together with four cows paid at once. A one-pound Centen was paid for by fl. 1,800 and immediate transfer of a 'best shot coat, one old rose noble and one coin with a silver chain to hang around a child's neck' . . . In all likelihood it was a farmer who paid fl. 2,500 for a single Viceroy in the form of two *last* of wheat and four of rye, four fat oxen, eight pigs, a dozen sheep, two oxheads of wine, four tons of butter, a thousand pounds of cheese, a bed, some clothing and a silver beaker.
>
> (Schama 1987: 358)

These sales reveal the 'strangeness' of this phenomenon. That such an apparently humble item should be sold for such vast sums is strange enough to us. However, that strangeness is compounded when we look again at the objects exchanged. 'Futures trading' was taking place at the same time as farm produce (in large quantities) was being exchanged for tulips. This does not seem to be economic activity concomitant with Holland's status as 'the most formidable capitalism the world had yet seen' (Schama 1987: 323). However, it does make the point that even in this very 'advanced' economy, money was not necessarily the only medium of exchange. These were exceptional circumstances to be sure, but the fact that such exchanges could still take place shows that at least the *mentalité* behind such exchanges persisted.

It would be no exaggeration to say that in this respect the Dutch were closer to the morality of the Middle Ages than that of the modern world. The warnings of the ministry and the magistracy about the dangers of the wealth generated by Holland's overseas trade stemmed from the abhorrence of 'riches acquired without labour' (Schama 1987: 347), and were a strong echo, across the centuries, of Thomas of Chobham's thirteenth-century condemnation of usury:

> The usurer wants to make a profit without doing any work, even while he is sleeping, which goes against the precepts of the Lord, who said 'By the sweat of your face shall you get bread to eat' [Gen. 3:19].
>
> (quoted in Le Goff 1988: 42)

In the thirteenth century, exceptions to the universal and unambiguous condemnation of usurers to damnation were being 'discovered'. Amongst these was the development of the concept of Purgatory, a 'half-way house' between Heaven and Hell to which the sinner was condemned for a limited period (for a full discussion, see Le Goff 1984), and an increased emphasis on the notion of contrition. According to Le Goff, the development of the concept of Purgatory was important not just for the soul but for the development of the economic system. He writes that

> Purgatory was just one of the complicitous winks that Christianity sent the usurer's way during the thirteenth century, but it was the only one that gave him unrestricted assurance of Paradise. Purgatory was *hope* . . . The hope of escaping Hell, thanks to Purgatory, permitted the usurer to propel the economy and society of the thirteenth century ahead towards capitalism.
>
> (Le Goff 1988: 92–93)

The transformation in medieval attitudes to money may indeed have engendered changes in conceptions of labour and trade which helped the transition to capitalism (as well as allowing the usurer to eventually enter Paradise) but, as we have seen, remnants of such thought could still be found in seventeenth-century Holland, 'the most formidable capitalism the world had yet seen' (Schama 1987: 323) and, if we believe Nicholas Thomas, Maurice Bloch and Jonathan Parry, they persist in the writings of anthropologists today.

Conclusion: 'Gnawing it out' in the heart of England

In 1942 Walter Rose published his memories of childhood in Buckinghamshire in the 1870s and 1880s (Reed 1990: 85). He recalled that

> [a] large part of the trade within the village was carried out on a system called gnawing it out – a method something like the primitive trade by barter in days before coin came into general use. The butcher having had his cart repaired by the wheelwright, rather than part with ready cash, expected the wheelwright to run up a bill for meat in settlement.
>
> (cited in Reed 1990: 85)

This was in the heart of England. This was the time when the British Empire was at its height, when the products of Empire filled British warehouses and when British colonial administrators ran one of the biggest economic and political systems the world had ever seen. In Buckinghamshire they were still 'gnawing it out'.

The point here is not to produce an exceptional example to show the strangeness of the past. Rather, I have been trying to argue that, at all periods of the past, modes of structuring production and exchange coexisted and interacted. The butcher and the wheelwright in this example may well have been 'gnawing it out', but they still had coins in their pockets with which they would rather not part for the purposes of this kind of exchange. However, they were still connected to, and participated in, the wider regional, national, and international systems of production and exchange. Pre-capitalist forms of exchange could coexist and articulate with capitalist forms in nineteenth-century Buckinghamshire, just as exchange through coinage coexisted with the personalized systems of production and exchange in the early Middle Ages. We shall always fail to understand the complexity of the situation, and the lived reality of the historical past, if we impose singular categories such as 'gift-exchange', 'capitalism', 'pre-capitalist', 'tributary', on that past. Only archaeology and history can provide us with the level of detail which we need if we are not to submerge the people of the past under the 'sameness' of a capitalist present or an undifferentiated 'otherness' derived from anthropology.

REFERENCES

Astill, G. and Grant, A. (eds.) (1988) *The Countryside of Medieval England*, Oxford: Blackwell.

Bahn, P. (ed.) (1996) *The Cambridge Illustrated History of Archaeology*, Cambridge: Cambridge University Press.

Baines, J. (1983) 'Literacy and Egyptian society', *Man* 81: 572–99.

Baines, J. (1989) 'Communication and display: the integration of early Egyptian art and writing', *Antiquity* 63: 471–82.

Balzaretti, R. (1992) 'Trade, industry and the wealth of king Alfred', *Past and Present* 136: 142–50.

Beard, M. (1991) '*Ancient literacy* and the function of the written word in Roman religion', in J. Humphreys (ed.) *Literacy in the Roman World*, Journal of Roman Archaeology, Supplementary Series 3, Ann Arbor: University of Michigan Press: 35–58.

Blair, J. (1994) *Anglo-Saxon Oxfordshire*, Stroud: Alan Sutton Books.

Blaut, J. M. (1993) *The Colonizer's Model of the World. Geographical Diffusionism and Eurocentric History*, New York: The Guildford Press.

Bloch, M. (1965) *Feudal Society*, London: Routledge and Kegan Paul.

Bloch, M. and Parry, J. (eds) (1989) *Money and the Morality of Exchange*, Cambridge: Cambridge University Press.

Bourdillon, J. (1988) 'Countryside and town: the animal resources of Saxon Southampton', in D. Hooke (ed.) *Anglo-Saxon Settlements*, Oxford: Blackwell: 177–95.

Bourdillon, J. (1994) 'The animal provisioning of Saxon Southampton', in J. Rackham (ed.) *Environment and Economy in Anglo-Saxon England*, Research Report 89, London: Council for British Archaeology: 120–25.

Bowman, A. K. and Woolf, G. (eds) (1994) *Literacy and Power in the Ancient World*, Cambridge: Cambridge University Press.

Braudel, F. (1981) *The Structures of Everyday Life: The Limits of the Possible* (Volume 1 of *Civilization and Capitalism 15th–18th Century*), London: Fontana.

Braudel, F. (1982) *The Wheels of Commerce* (Volume 2 of *Civilization and Capitalism 15th–18th Century*), London: Fontana.

Brenner, E. (1988) 'Sociopolitical implications of mortuary ritual remains in 17th century native southern New England', in M. Leone and P. Potter, Jr. (eds) *The Recovery of Meaning: Historical Archaeology in the Eastern United States*, Washington: Smithsonian Institution Press: 147–81.

Brisbane, M. (1988) 'Hamwic (Saxon Southampton): an 8th century port and production centre', in R. Hodges and B. Hobley (eds) *The Rebirth of Towns in the West AD 700–1050*, Research Report 68, London: Council for British Archaeology: 101–8.

Bruce-Mitford, B. (1975–83) *The Sutton Hoo Ship-Burial*, London: British Museum Publications (3 volumes).

Budny, M. (1984) 'The Anglo-Saxon embroideries at Maaseik: their historical and art-historical context', *Academie voor Wetenschappen, Letteren en schone Kunsten van België* 45: 57–133.

Cameron, A. (1993) *The Mediterranean World in Late Antiquity, A.D. 395–600*, London: Routledge.

Campbell, J. (1989) 'The sale of land and the economics of power in early England: problems and possibilities', *Haskins Society Journal* 1: 23–37.

Carr, R. D., Tester, A. and Murphy, P. (1988) 'The middle Saxon settlement at Staunch Meadow, Brandon', *Antiquity* 62: 371–77.

Carsten, J. (1989) 'Cooking money: gender and symbolic transformation of means of exchange in a Malay fishing community', in M. Bloch and J. Parry (eds) *Money and the Morality of Exchange*, Cambridge: Cambridge University Press: 117–41.

Chadwick, J. (1976) *The Mycenaean World*, Cambridge: Cambridge University Press.

Chadwick, J. (1990) 'Linear B', in J. T. Hooker (ed.) *Reading the Past: Ancient Writing from Cuneiform to the Alphabet*, London: British Museum Publications: 137–96.

Champion, T. and Champion, S. (1986) 'Peer polity interaction in the European Iron Age', in C. Renfrew and J. Cherry (eds) *Peer Polity Interaction and Socio-Political Change*, Cambridge: Cambridge University Press: 59–68.

Chaudhuri, K. (1990) *Asia before Europe: Economy and Civilization of the Indian Ocean from the Rise of Islam to 1750*, Cambridge: Cambridge University Press.

Cherry, J. (1986) 'Polities and palaces: some problems in Minoan state formation', in C. Renfrew and J. Cherry (eds) *Peer Polity Interaction and Socio-Political Change*, Cambridge: Cambridge University Press: 19–46.

Clarke, H. and Ambrosiani, B. (1991) *Towns in the Viking Age*, Leicester: Leicester University Press.

Collis, J. R. (1984) *The European Iron Age*, London: Batsford.

Cronon, W. (1983) *Changes in the Land. Indians, Colonists and the Ecology of New England*, New York: Hill and Wang.

Dalton, G. (1977) 'Aboriginal economies in stateless societies', in T. Earle and J. Ericson (eds) *Exchange Systems in Prehistory*, New York: Academic Press: 191–212.

Deagan, K. (1983) *Spanish St. Augustine: The Archaeology of a Colonial Creole Community*, New York: Academic Press.

Deagan, K. (1994) 'People with history: an update on historical archaeology in the United States', *Journal of Archaeological Method and Theory* 1 (1): 5–40.

Deetz, J. (1977) *In Small Things Forgotten. The Archaeology of Early American Life*, New York: Anchor Books.

Demos, J. (1996) *The Unredeemed Captive. A Family Story from Early America*, London: Papermac.

Devroey, J.-P. (1984) 'Un monastère dans l'économie d'échanges', *Annales E.S.C.* 39: 570–89.

Dincauze, D. and Hasenstab, R. (1989) 'Explaining the Iroquois: tribalization on a prehistoric periphery', in T. Champion (ed.) *Centre and Periphery: Comparative Studies in Archaeology*, London: Unwin Hyman: 67–87.

Dirlik, A. (1996) 'Chinese history and the question of Orientalism', *History and Theory* 35: 96–118.

Duby, G. (1981) *The Age of Cathedrals: Art and Society, 980–1420*, London: Croom Helm.

Eisenstein, E. (1979) *The Printing Press as an Agent of Change: Communications and Cultural Transformations in Early Modern Europe*, Cambridge: Cambridge University Press.

Evans, J. (1988) 'The organic residues', in P. Andrews (ed.) *Southampton Finds, Volume 1: The Coins and Pottery from Hamwic*, Southampton: Southampton City Museums: 123–24.

Evans-Pritchard, E. (1967) 'Introduction', in M. Mauss, *The Gift: Forms and Functions of Exchange in Archaic Societies*, New York: Norton: v–x.

Everitt, A. (1986) *Continuity and Colonisation. The Evolution of Kentish Settlement*, Leicester: Leicester University Press.

Fenwick, V. (1984) 'Insula de Burgh: excavations at Burrow Hill, Butley, Suffolk 1978–81', *Anglo-Saxon Studies in Archaeology and History* 3: 35–54.

Fowler, P. (1982) 'Farming in the Anglo-Saxon landscape: an archaeologist's view', *Anglo-Saxon England* 9: 263–80.

Fulford, M. (1989) 'Byzantium and Britain: a Mediterranean perspective on post-Roman Mediterranean imports in western Britain and Ireland', *Medieval Archaeology* 33: 1–6.

Gawronski, J. (1990) 'Sunken Dutch East Indiamen as a subject of underwater archaeological and historical research', in J. Besteman, J. Bos and H. Heidinga (eds) *Medieval Archaeology in the Netherlands: Studies Presented to H. H. van Regteren Altena*, Assen: Van Gorcum: 299–314.

Geary, P. (1994) 'Sacred commodities: the circulation of medieval relics', in P. Geary, *Living with the Dead in the Middles Ages*, Ithaca: Cornell University Press: 194–218.

Giddens, A. (1979) *Central Problems in Social Theory*, London: Macmillan.

Giddens, A. (1981) *A Contemporary Critique of Historical Materialism*, London: Macmillan.

Godelier, M. (1977) 'The concept of "social and economic formation": the Inca example', in M. Godelier, *Perspectives in Marxist Anthropology*, Cambridge: Cambridge University Press: 63–69.

Goody, J. (1968) 'Introduction', in J. Goody (ed.) *Literacy in Traditional Societies*, Cambridge: Cambridge University Press: 1–26.

Goody, J. (1986) *The Logic of Writing and the Organisation of Society*, Cambridge: Cambridge University Press.

Gosden, C. (1989) 'Debt, production, and prehistory', *Journal of Anthropological Archaeology* 8: 355–87.

Graham-Campbell, J. (ed.) (1994) *Cultural Atlas of the Viking World*, Abingdon: Andromeda.

Gregory, C. (1982) *Gifts and Commodities*, Cambridge: Cambridge University Press.

Grierson, P. and Blackburn, M. (1986) *Medieval European Coinage*, Cambridge: Cambridge University Press.

Hallo, W. (1979) 'God, king, and man at Yale', in E. Lipinski (ed.) *State and Temple Economy in the Ancient Near East* I, Leuven: Departement Oriëntalistiek: 99–112.

Halstead, P. (1992) 'The Mycenaean palatial economy: making the most of the gaps in the evidence', *Proceedings of the Cambridge Philological Society* 38: 57–86.

Hamerow, H. (1994) 'The archaeology of rural settlement in early medieval Europe', *Early Medieval Europe* 3: 167–79.

Haslam, J. (1980) 'A middle Saxon iron smelting site at Ramsbury, Wiltshire', *Medieval Archaeology* 24: 1–68.

Hauken, A. D. (1991) 'Gift exchange in early Iron Age Norse society', in R. Samson (ed.) *Social Approaches to Viking Studies*, Glasgow: Cruithne Press: 105–12.

Hedeager, L. (1992) *Iron-Age Societies: From Tribe to State in Northern Europe 500 B.C.–A.D. 700*, Oxford: Blackwell.

Hodder, I. (1986) *Reading the Past*, Cambridge: Cambridge University Press.

Hodges, R. (1980) *The Hamwih Pottery; the Local and Imported Wares from Thirty Years' Excavations and their European Context*, Research Report 37, London: Council for British Archaeology.

Hodges, R. (1982) *Dark Age Economics: The Origins of Towns and Trade A.D. 600–1000*, London: Duckworth.

Hodges, R. (1988) *Primitive and Peasant Markets*, Oxford: Blackwell.

Hodges, R. (1989) *The Anglo-Saxon Achievement: Archaeology and the Beginnings of English Society*, London: Duckworth.

Hodges, R. and Hobley, B. (eds) (1988) *The Rebirth of Towns in the West AD 700–1050*, Research Report 68, London: Council for British Archaeology.

Hodges, R. and Whitehouse, D. (1983) *Mohammed, Charlemagne and the Origins of Europe*, London: Duckworth.

Hooke, D. (1989) 'Early medieval estate and settlement patterns: the documentary evidence', in M. Aston, D. Austin and C. Dyer (eds) *The Rural Settlements of Medieval England*, Oxford: Blackwell: 9–30.

Hooker, J. T. (ed.) (1990) *Reading the Past: Ancient Writing from Cuneiform to the Alphabet*, London: British Museum Publications.

Hopkins, K. (1991) 'Conquest by book', in J. Humphreys (ed.) *Literacy in the Roman World*, Journal of Roman Archaeology Supplementary Series 3, Ann Arbor: University of Michigan Press: 133–58.

Ingold, T. (1986) 'Hunting, sacrifice and the domestication of animals', in T. Ingold, *The Appropriation of Nature*, Manchester: Manchester University Press: 243–76.

Jennings, F. (1975) *The Invasion of America: Indians, Colonialism, and the Cant of Conquest*, New York: W. W. Norton and Co.

Jensen, S. (1991) *The Vikings of Ribe*, Ribe: Den Antikvariske Samling.

Jones, S. R. H. (1993) 'Transaction costs, institutional change, and the emergence of a market economy in later Anglo-Saxon England', *Economic History Review* 46: 658–78.

Kelly, S. (1990) 'Anglo-Saxon lay society and the written word', in R. McKitterick (ed.) *The Uses of Literacy in Early Medieval Europe*, Cambridge: Cambridge University Press: 36–62.

Kelly, S. (1992) 'Trading privileges from eighth century England', *Early Medieval Europe* 1: 3–28.

Larsen, M. (1988) 'Introduction: literacy and social complexity', in J. Gledhill, B. Bender and M. Larsen (eds) *State and Society: The Emergence and Development of Social Hierarchy and Political Centralisation*, London: Unwin Hyman: 173–91.

Le Goff, J. (1984) *The Birth of Purgatory*, Chicago: University of Chicago Press.

Le Goff, J. (1988) *Your Money or Your Life: Economy and Religion in the Middle Ages*, New York: Zone Books.

Leone, M. and Potter, P. (1988) 'Introduction: issues in historical archaeology', in M. Leone and P. Potter (eds.) *The Recovery of Meaning. Historical Archaeology in the Eastern United States*, Washington, DC: Smithsonian Institution Press: 1–22.

McGuire, R. (1989) 'The greater Southwest as a periphery of Mesoamerica', in T. Champion (ed.) *Centre and Periphery: Comparative Studies in Archaeology*, London: Unwin Hyman: 40–66.

McKitterick, R. (1990) 'Introduction', in R. McKitterick (ed.) *The Uses of Literacy in Early Medieval Europe*, Cambridge: Cambridge University Press: 1–10.

McNeill, W. H. (1976) *Plagues and People*, New York: Anchor Books.

Maisels, C. (1990) *The Emergence of Civilisation: From Hunting and Gathering to Agriculture, Cities and the State in the Near East*, London: Routledge.

Marcus, G. and Fischer, M. (1986) *Anthropology as Cultural Critique. An Experimental Moment in the Human Sciences*, Chicago: University of Chicago Press.

Marx, K. (1973) *Grundrisse*, London: Penguin.

Mauss, M. (1967) *The Gift: Forms and Functions of Exchange in Archaic Societies*, New York: Norton.

Metcalf, D. M. (1965) 'How large was the Anglo-Saxon currency?', *English History Review* 18: 475–82.

Metcalf, D. M. (1984) 'Monetary circulation in Southern England', in D. Hill and D. Metcalf (eds) *Sceattas in England and on the Continent*, British Archaeological Reports, British Series 128, Oxford: BAR: 27–69.

Metcalf, D. M. (1988) 'The coins', in P. Andrews (ed.) *Southampton Finds, Volume 1: The Coins and Pottery from Hamwic*, Southampton: Southampton City Museums: 15–59.

Millett, M. (1990) *The Romanization of Britain: An Essay in Archaeological Interpretation*, Cambridge: Cambridge University Press.

Moreland, J. (1992) 'Restoring the dialectic: settlement patterns and documents in medieval central Italy', in B. Knapp (ed.) *Archaeology, Annales, and Ethnohistory*, Cambridge: Cambridge University Press: 112–29.

Moreland, J. (forthcoming) 'Review of C. Orser *A Historical Archaeology of the Modern World* and M. Johnson *An Archaeology of Capitalism*', *Northeast Historical Archaeology*.

Morton, A. (1992) *Excavations at Hamwic: Volume 1*, Research Report 84, London: Council for British Archaeology.

Nissen, H. J. (1986) 'The archaic texts from Uruk', *World Archaeology* 17 (3): 317–34.

Orser, C. (1996) *A Historical Archaeology of the Modern World*, New York: Plenum Press.

Peebles, C. (1987) 'Moundville from 1000–1500 AD', in R. D. Drennan and C. A. Uribe (eds) *Chiefdoms in the Americas*, Lanham: University of America Press: 21–41.

Polanyi, K. (1957) 'The economy as instituted process', in K. Polanyi, C. Arensberg and H. Pearson (eds) *Trade and Markets in Early Empires*, Glencoe, Ill.: Free Press: 243–69.

Randsborg, K. (1980) *The Viking Age in Denmark*, London: Duckworth.

Randsborg, K. (1991) *The First Millennium A.D. in Europe and the Mediterranean*, Cambridge: Cambridge University Press.

Redman, C. L. (1986) *Qsar es-Seghir: An Archaeological View of Medieval Life*, New York: Academic Press.

Reed, M. (1990) '"Gnawing it out": a new look at economic relations in nineteenth century rural England', *Rural History* 1: 83–94.

Renfrew, C. (1979) 'Systems collapse as social transformation: catastrophe and anastrophe in early state societies', in C. Renfrew and K. Cooke (eds) *Transformations: Mathematical Approaches to Culture Change*, London: Academic Press: 481–506.

Renfrew, C. and Bahn, P. (1991) *Archaeology: Theories, Methods and Practice*, London: Thames and Hudson.

Rowlands, M. (1979) 'Local and long distance trade and incipient state formation on the Bamenda Plateau', *Paideuma* 25: 1–19.

Rowlands, M. (1994) 'From "the Gift" to market economies: the ideology and politics of European Iron Age studies', in K. Kristiansen and J. Jensen (eds) *Europe in the First Millennium B.C.*, Sheffield: J. R. Collis Publications: 1–5.

Sahlins, M. (1963) 'Poor man, rich man, Big Man, Chief: political types in Melanesia and Polynesia', *Comparative Studies in Society and History* 5: 285–303.

Sahlins, M. (1974) *Stone Age Economics*, London: Tavistock.

Sahlins, M. (1987) *Islands of History*, London: Tavistock.

Sahlins, M. (1995) *How 'Natives' Think. About Captain Cook for Example*, Chicago: University of Chicago Press.

Said, E. (1994) *Culture and Imperialism*, London: Vintage.

Said, E. ([1978] 1995) *Orientalism. Western Conceptions of the Orient*, London: Penguin.

Samson, R. (1991) 'Economic anthropology and the Vikings', in R. Samson (ed.) *Social Approaches to Viking Studies*, Glasgow: Cruithne Press: 87–96.

Schama, S. (1987) *The Embarrassment of Riches: An Interpretation of Dutch Culture in the Golden Age*, London: Fontana.

Service, E. (1971) *Primitive Social Organization. An Evolutionary Perspective*, New York: Random House.

Shanks, M. and Tilley, C. (1987) *Social Theory and Archaeology*, Oxford: Polity.

Smith, C. (1984) 'Local history in global context: social and economic transitions in western Guatemala', *Comparative Studies in Society and History* 26: 193–228.

Steponaitis, V. P. (1978) 'Location theory and complex chiefdoms', in B. D. Smith (ed.) *Mississippian Settlement Patterns*, New York: Academic Press: 417–54.

Stock, B. (1983) *The Implications of Literacy: Written Language and Models of Interpretation in the Eleventh and Twelfth Centuries*, Princeton: Princeton University Press.

Tainter, J. (1988) *The Collapse of Complex Societies*, Cambridge: Cambridge University Press.

Thomas, C. (1993) *Tintagel. Arthur and Archaeology*, London: Batsford.

Thomas, K. (1984) *Man and the Natural World: Changing Attitudes in England 1500–1800*, London: Penguin.

Thomas, N. (1991) *Entangled Objects: Exchange, Material Culture and Colonialism in the Pacific*, Cambridge, Mass.: Harvard University Press.

Timby, J. R. (1988) 'The middle Saxon Pottery', in P. Andrews (ed.) *Southampton Finds Volume 1: The Coins and Pottery from Hamwic*, Southampton: Southampton City Museums: 73–122.

Trigger, B. (1989) *A History of Archaeological Thought*, Cambridge: Cambridge University Press.

van Es, W. A. (1990) 'Dorestad Centred', in J. Besteman, J. Bos and H. Heidinga (eds) *Medieval Archaeology in the Netherlands: Studies Presented to H. H. van Regteren Altena*, Assen: Van Gorcum: 151–82.

van Zeist, W. (1990) 'The palaeobotany of early medieval Dorestad: evidence of grain trade', *Proceedings of the Koninklijke Nederlandse Akademie van Wetenschappen* 93: 335–48.

Vestergaard, E. (1991) 'Gift-giving, hoarding, and outdoings', in R. Samson (ed.) *Social Approaches to Viking Studies*, Glasgow: Cruithne Press: 97–104.

Veyne, P. (1990) *Bread and Circuses: Historical Sociology and Political Pluralism*, Harmondsworth: Allen Lane/Penguin.

Wallerstein, I. (1974) *The Modern World System I: Capitalist Agriculture and the Origins of the European World-Economy in the Sixteenth Century*, New York: Academic Press.

Wallerstein, I. (1984) *The Politics of the World Economy: the States, the Movements and the Civilizations*, Cambridge: Cambridge University Press.

White, S. (1988) *Custom, Kinship and Gifts to Saints: The* Lauditio Parentum *in Western France, 1050–1150*, Chapel Hill: University of North Carolina Press.

Whitelock, D. (ed.) (1955) *English Historical Documents, Volume 1*, London: Eyre and Spottiswoode.

Whittaker, C. R. (1983) 'Late Roman trade and traders', in P. Garnsey, K. Hopkins and C. R. Whittaker (eds) *Trade in the Ancient Economy*, London: Chatto and Windus: 163–80.

Wickham, C. (1984) 'The other transition: from the ancient world to feudalism', *Past and Present* 103: 3–36.

Wickham, C. (1992) 'Problems of comparing rural societies in early medieval western Europe', *Transactions of the Royal Historical Society* (Sixth Series) 2: 221–46.

Wolf, E. (1982) *Europe and the People without History*, Berkeley: University of California Press.

Wright, R. (1992) *Stolen Continents. The Indian Story*, London: Pimlico.

SELECT BIBLIOGRAPHY

The anthropology of production and exchange has been the subject of much discussion in the past. Sahlins (1974) must still be an essential starting point. More recent thinking on the notion of gift-exchange is presented by Thomas (1991), while archaeological approaches are summarized in Renfrew and Bahn (1991: 307–8). It is still worth consulting Mauss's original essay on 'The Gift' (1967) for some of the nuances of his argument. Production and exchange in the early Middle Ages in north-west Europe is best analysed by Hodges (1989);

for the other case studies cited, it is best to refer to the original publications: Redman (1986) and Schama (1987). More general pictures (but based on a wealth of detail) of production and exchange in the early modern world are produced in the magisterial works by Braudel (1981, 1982) and Wolf (1982).

POPULATION DYNAMICS

Fekri A. Hassan

Thus my little ones will speak of me,
As long as they travel in life's path
An Omaha song

INTRODUCTION

Population dynamics are inexorably linked to cultural events, as is clearly shown by pronounced demographic transformations accompanying major cultural transitions. In archaeology, the emergence of an interest in the cultural processes that have shaped our archaeological past (Childe 1936) fostered an examination of aspects of prehistoric populations related to subsistence and settlements. A particular emphasis was placed on estimating population size and density, as in the pioneer syntheses by Howells (1960) and Cook (1972). In 1968, Lewis Binford introduced population increase as a possible mechanism in the transition from hunting-gathering to agriculture, blasting a new trail of archaeological inquiry on the role of population growth in major cultural transitions (see Chapter 21). *Population Growth: Anthropological Implications* (Spooner 1972) set the stage for further avenues of future investigations, including a convergence with the studies undertaken by physical anthropologists interested in the lifespan and vital statistics of prehistoric populations (Vallois 1960). The pioneer work by J. L. Angel was extremely influential: his emphasis on the relationship between palaeodemography, palaeoecology, and health (Angel 1975) highlighted the importance of the study of palaeopathology as a means of assessing the relationship between health, disease and the fertility and mortality of ancient populations.

Palaeodemography, as used first by Acsádi and Nemeskéri (1957), Brothwell (1971) and Angel (1975) refers to the estimates of the biological population parameters from a study of skeletal remains. Such estimates include fertility rates and mortality rates, population structure, and life expectancy. With an increasing interest in the role of demographic variables in prehistory, and as a consequence of my early work on population growth during the Neolithic, *Demographic Archaeology* (Hassan 1981) presented a comprehensive overview of this budding field. In addition to encompassing the sister field palaeodemography, demographic archaeology deals with the use of archaeological, ecological, historical, and ethnographic data to estimate the size and density of local and regional populations, population growth rates, patterns and rates of population dispersal and migrations. These archaeo-demographic data are utilized to explore the links between population dynamics and cultural events in prehistoric and pre-industrial societies.

During the last two decades, population studies in archaeology have shown that our understanding of social history can never be fully achieved without a full awareness of population dynamics. Social processes are a result of actions by human communities: the numbers, composition, and density of a community, as well as its variability in time and space, are crucial for comprehending the cultural pool of ideas, artefacts, and language. Moreover, no clear understanding of human evolution, population expansion and diffusion can be achieved without a determination of the growth rates, the relationship between resources and population movements and innovation, and the rates and patterns of population dispersal. The major transitions in the history of humanity are definitely associated with characteristic demographic parameters (M. Cohen 1995). Demographers often refer to *the* Demographic Transition, the change in population parameters in the wake of industrialization (Weinstein 1976; Wrigley 1971; Zelinsky 1979). However, there have been other major transitions, notably those following the emergence of our immediate ancestors (*Homo sapiens sapiens*), the advent of agriculture, and the establishment of towns and cities. The ingenuity and social organizational skills of modern humans created the potential to cope with natural scarcities and enable fertility to increase, promoting a relatively fast increase in world population.

Agriculture created new opportunities, promoting an increase in population size and density as well as the emergence of modes of social organization that in turn became a major incentive for both agrarian developments and economic growth. The emergence of the first cities created an unprecedented demographic situation that fostered the elements of our contemporary civilization. Before cities, the emergence of a cultural landscape crowded (relatively speaking) with large permanent communities, enabled regional differentiation and the development of fairly independent political units, thus establishing the foundation of state societies. Cities and agrarian states developed at different rates and tempos in different regions, creating a flux of people and ideas. Next to settled farming, nomadic pastoralists with their own demographic profiles interacted with settled farmers, causing major historical changes in the distribution and pattern of world populations.

In spite of regional variations in demographic conditions and short-term temporal fluctuations, world population as a whole has followed a course of population increase with varying rates since the inception of agriculture. At times, world population growth slowed down. There are also occasions when numbers were dramatically reduced. The dynamics of demographic transitions and social change are fascinating, and the exploration of the role of population in social affairs provides a corrective to historical theories that are divorced from the lives of ordinary people who make and change history. The number, density, and distribution of world populations influence production, markets, warfare, and politics (Thomlinson 1965). Both historical demography and demographic archaeology are essential for exploring the long-term dynamics of population and social change.

Our present concern for population and development (Cassen 1994; J. E. Cohen 1995) is an echo of human voices that are at least as old as 1600 BC, when overpopulation was feared in Mesopotamia (J. E. Cohen 1995: 5). The study of the archaeology of human populations provides us with a sharper view of our present and helps us reflect on the future. From an archaeological perspective, the recent reduction of infant and child mortality and the prolongation of life expectancy in industrial nations, and the incredible numbers of people now alive, and the explosive rate of population growth in many para-industrial countries, are simultaneously astounding and alarming. Are we facing a time bomb? Has it already exploded? Or is all this talk of overpopulation an exaggerated doomsday vision? In this contribution I hope to sketch out the outstanding aspects of our demographic ancestry and explore the links between population dynamics and culture in the long prelude to the present. Inevitably in this topic, empirical data are still scanty and often misleading, and we can only hope to make plausible accounts of the past guided by the primary principles that structure population dynamics.

POPULATION PARAMETERS

The dynamics of a population may be described in terms of spatial or temporal variability. The spatial patterning of a population (for example, density, aggregation, dispersal, migrations, size hierarchy) are often included under the rubric of 'population geography'. Most population studies, however, are concerned with changes in the size and composition of a population through time. Temporal change in the number of a group is a function of three variables: number of births (fertility), number of deaths (mortality), and number of migrants (Newell 1989; Pressat 1972). A population will increase if the number of births and/or immigrants exceeds the number of deaths, and will decline if the number of deaths is persistently greater than the number of births and/or immigrants. This simple model becomes rather complicated when we consider that the numbers of births, deaths, and immigrants are in turn related to many variables such as age at marriage, sex ratio, age-specific fertility and mortality, disease, diet, and child-spacing practices. These variables are in turn related both to natural and cultural factors that vary from one population to another, and are also subject to historical change.

To estimate these parameters for past populations, information is obtained from the study of human skeletal remains and archaeological data (see Chapter 7). Palaeodemographic analysis of skeletal remains depends on the ageing and sexing of bones, as well as on certain assumptions about the stability of the population (Acsádi and Nemeskéri 1970; Brown 1995; Gage and Mode 1993; Horowitz *et al.* 1988; Howell 1976, 1986, 1992; Johansson and Horowitz 1986; Konigsberg and Frankenberg 1992; Sattenspiel and Harpending 1983; Saunders *et al.* 1992; Weiss 1973, 1976; Weiss and Smouse 1976). This type of analysis was criticized by Bocquet-Appel and Masset (1982), creating an ongoing debate (Jackes 1992; Konigsberg and Frankenberg 1994; Roth 1992; Saunders *et al.* 1992).

In addition to estimates based on the study of palaeodemographic analysis from skeletal series and by analogy from ethnographic cases, computer simulations may provide additional insights (Buikstra *et al.* 1986; Dyke and MacCluer 1975; Roth *et al.* 1984). Independently, all of these sources are not likely to provide accurate estimates of population parameters. Nevertheless, cross-checking data from different sources and different contexts can provide a basis for judging the adequacy of demographic inferences in archaeology. One notable example is the synthesis by Jaffe (1992) of the population history of Amerindians. Jaffe compiled, gleaned, and synthesized data from disparate and far-flung sources: archaeological and palaeo-demographic 'guesstimates', census data, and historical accounts. In addition, he developed separate life tables for those Amerindians who practised agriculture and those who did not.

Archaeologists utilize settlement data (for example: Rice and Culbert 1990; Roche 1983; Zorn 1994), mortuary data, food remains, and artefacts, to determine the size, density, and growth of prehistoric populations (Hassan 1981), subject to certain assumptions and by reference to ethnographic analogues. Schlanger (1988) and Schlanger and Wilhusen (1990) presented not only a credible estimation of population growth and immigration in south-western Colorado, but also provided an insightful analysis of the fit between climatic change and population history. The contributors to *Precolumbian Population History in the Maya Lowlands* (Rice and Culbert 1990) provide an impressive display of the application of archaeological methods to develop the population history and population size of urban centres.

Historical data are also used to generate population data (for example, Broshi 1979; Russell 1958). The combination of data culled from palaeodemography, demographic archaeology and historical demography provides a basis for making certain inferences on ancient populations. The validity and adequacy of any explanations of population dynamics in the past rest both on the reliability of the estimates of primary population indexes, the logical coherence of the theoretical assumptions, and consistency of the data and the structures of explanation within the existing body of knowledge.

POPULATION GROWTH POTENTIALS

Were hunter-gatherers often at the brink of extinction besieged by diseases, food scarcity, and accidents, their numbers controlled by their short life and high infant mortality? Was their mobility the cause of low fertility, so that as soon as they settled down they began to show higher fertility rates? These questions and current debates concerning the determinants and controls of the rates of population growth before and after the transition to agriculture may be clarified by a consideration of the population growth potential of pre-industrial populations. This may be based on a determination of the length of the reproductive span and the 'natural' birth interval. With a long reproductive period and short live birth intervals, we should expect fertility to be high. The number of female live births that survive to child-bearing age and of females living until menopause will determine the reproductive potential of a population.

Women and men in prehistoric times died fairly young (Table 17.1; Fig. 17.1). The average age at death for adults was between 32 and 40 years (Angel 1972, 1975); women, in general, died a few years younger, and also reached menarche at a much older age than females in industrial societies, so the reproductive period was relatively short. With no cultural interference, the time interval between successive births (natural births interval) is about twenty-eight months (Barrett 1972).

Table 17.1 Average age at death for adults (15 or older)

Australopithecines	28 yr	Roman (Imperial)	40
Homo erectus	>30	Byzantine	38
Early *Homo sapiens*	33	Medieval	35
Upper Palaeolithic	32	Middle Ages (England)	33
Homo sapiens		Turkish	31
Epipalaeolithic (Natufian)	33	1687–91 (Breslau)	33.5
Neolithic (Çatal Hüyük)	32	Before 1789 (US)	35.5
Hunter-gatherers (historic)	41	1838–54 (England and Wales)	40.9
Early Bronze Age	34	1900–2 (US)	49.2
Late Bronze Age	39	1946 (US)	66.7
Mycenaean	36	1961–5 (Sweden)	73.6
Early Iron Age	39		

Sources: Data from Angel (1972, 1975), Pressat (1972).

676

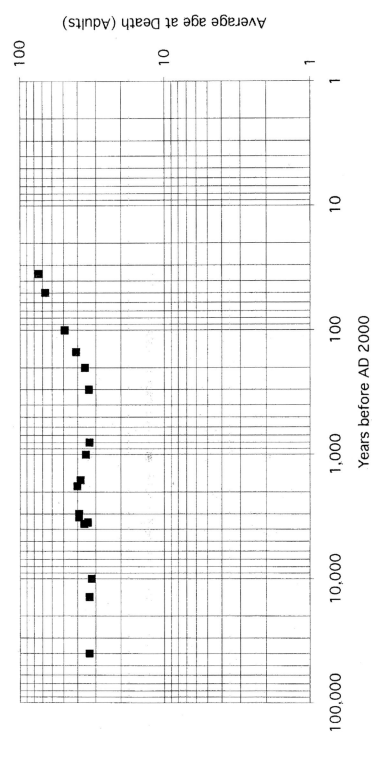

Figure 17.1 Average age at death for prehistoric and historic populations. Note a dramatic change beginning about 100 years ago. The recent high values are for industrial populations. Average ages at death for people in rural communities are still low. Source: F. Hassan.

Under prehistoric conditions, many children died before reaching adulthood: estimates range from 40–50 per cent of all born infants. However, even under these conditions a population can grow as fast as 1–2 per cent. This rate, however, is often reduced because the child-spacing period observed among most hunter-gatherers and farmers in non-industrial settings is between three and four years. In many contemporary agricultural (non-industrial) populations, as among Punjabi women, the age at marriage is about 17–19, and the end of the reproductive span is at about 34–37 years (Nag 1962). These women show a total fertility of 7.5, and rates of 1.5 per cent to 3 per cent are common among such populations in many parts of the world. In the traditional bands of the !Kung, often considered somewhat as analogues to prehistoric foragers, females have menarche at 16.5, first birth at 19.5, and long lactations of 42 months. The mean age at final birth is 34.4 years. A person expects to live 34 years from birth. Of all infants born, only 59 per cent survive to age 20 (Howell 1979). The number of live births per female is 4.20, which compares favourably with a range of 4.14 to 4.7 for the !Kung (Harpending 1976). Simulations by Howell (1979) reveal that a range of annual growth rates from −0.045 per cent to +0.047 per cent among the !Kung may be due to random variations.

CULTURAL PRACTICES AND POPULATION DYNAMICS

The dynamics of population growth are closely linked with diet, health, disease, and social norms and values. The social values are, in turn, linked with subsistence and economy, but the link is neither unidirectional nor necessarily harmonious. This is especially true in complex societies consisting of different socio-economic groups who may have different moral or social attitudes towards procreation or population controls. They may also have different political and economic interests.

In general, a model of population dynamics must take into consideration two factors: first, conditions that influence people regardless of their values or decision criteria (such as epidemics, or changes in food abundance due to climatic resources) and second, the family – the fundamental unit of reproduction. The family makes decisions concerning marriage and family planning. Their decisions may be made on the basis of the social and economic benefits of children relative to the cost of rearing children given the parents' expectations. The costs may be both economic and non-economic – social and psychological. Economic costs include the costs of food, clothing, sheltering, education, and health care, which may negatively affect the family's standard of living and the family savings and investments.

In many rural communities the desired size of a completed family (the number of surviving children in a family whose mother has completed her child-bearing period) is large, with a special preference towards males. Continuity of family name,

678

support in old age, as well as a large labour force and social power, are perceived to be advantages associated with a large family. As long as there are work opportunities and as long as the cost to raise children is low, the preference towards a large family may persist.

CARRYING CAPACITY

Carrying capacity has become one of the fundamental notions in archaeological discussions of ancient populations (Chapman 1988; Dewar 1984; Hayden 1975). In general, the usage of the concept, first developed by ecologists, was linked with the potential number of people that can be supported given existing food resources. Carrying capacity, as used by ecologists, refers to the maximum population that can be supported in a given area under given conditions. The concept, however, is problematic, and must be applied with major modifications to human populations (Hassan 1981). First, we must acknowledge the role of human populations in changing economic conditions and so lifting or depressing carrying capacity. In addition, the term should be considered in a temporal dimension, with a consideration for changes in yield from subsistence activities subject to natural or cultural causes. Moreover, the number of people that can be sustained depends on the rates of consumption – not only of food resources, but also of other resources regarded as essential for a desirable standard of living. We must also consider the fluidity of spatial boundaries, as well as the changeable size and composition of the group, especially among hunter–gatherers.

The major modes of subsistence – foraging, farming, pastoralism, fishing, sea-mammal hunting, and modern agro-business – are all characterized by differences not only in carrying capacity but also in the *potential* to increase carrying capacity, and in the yield, quality, seasonality, concentration, storability, and spatio-temporal fluctuations of resources. For any subsistence regime, the amount of yield that can support people depends on resources of labour, management, knowledge, and technology. In modern farming conditions, it also depends on fossil fuels and other sources of energy and capital. In addition to major developments in technology, from using a chopping-tool to extract more meat from a carcass to genetically improving cultigens, changes in population respond also to the change in the labour requirements brought about by a transition from one mode of subsistence to another. Demands for a large labour force, as in farming communities, not only encourage greater fertility but also encourage the aggregation of groups in larger units. With a concentration of resources and higher yields, people can also reside permanently in villages.

One of the major difficulties with carrying capacity in archaeology is 'operationalization'. Hayden (1975), for example, points out that it is difficult to calculate carrying capacity, and that the variability and cyclical nature of resources are not taken into consideration. Dewar (1984) suggests that carrying capacity is a conflation of functions for potential resources and technology, and a measure of the upper limit for population density. He also argues that it is difficult to demonstrate that human populations are density-dependent. The application of the concept of carrying capacity will continue to be a subject of debate and controversy, but it is important to realize that the concept is not applicable to human populations without significant overhauling. It is also essential to note the following considerations: the roles of diet, labour, and technology in defining the productive potential of a population; people do not respond culturally to a hypothetical long-term mean, but to variations that are within their knowledge domain; response by a human population to an environment is not limited to certain kinds of food but to a wide range of resources depending on economic expectations and standard of living; regulation of human population, and indeed many other animal populations, is neither solely nor strictly determined by factors related to population density relative to a presumed level of production; and models of 'economic rationality' and 'economic optimization' may not be the most appropriate in populations with limited knowledge and goals different from those prevailing in market economies.

POPULATION REGULATION

The potential for rapid population increase under natural conditions among hunter-gatherers, even with high infant mortality and short life expectancy, leads us to consider the means by which prehistoric populations would have been kept sufficiently low to explain the extremely low population density by the end of the Pleistocene before the adoption of agriculture. It has also been proposed that prehistoric populations were automatically regulated by a long breast-feeding period, suppressing the ability of the female to conceive (Wood 1990). Prolonged lactation, however, is not sufficient to regulate the population to the desired socio-economic levels. Nevertheless, frequent breast-feeding and late weaning must have extended the child-spacing period, thus relatively dampening fertility. Prolonged lactation provides infants with adequate nutrition and protection from diarrhoea-producing bacteria. Mother's milk also reduces the risk of respiratory infection (Kent 1987: 616). Children also receive more care and attention than they would otherwise if there are too many other children of similar age.

The long period of child-spacing cannot be viewed as an effective regulatory mechanism, because it does not eliminate the stochastic increase and decline of a population that characterizes small populations. Other expedient controls are necessary to regulate the population in order to maintain an adequate standard of living. Accordingly, it is important to consider population regulation in Antiquity as a result of decisions based on perceptions of either an undesirably large population or an insufficient population size. Lacking an overall view of the population as a whole and a centralized management of fertility and mortality, decisions are likely to have been made by individuals and families on the basis of cues related to their own conditions. The cues for an excessive population increase can be reflected in an increase in the ratio of dependants to producers (more children than they can feed), an increase in the number of children (interfering with the woman's ability to gather food, undertake domestic activities, and care for other children), or any other cues related to diet, work, and acceptable levels of social welfare.

Population regulation could be achieved through a variety of behavioural controls, such as abstinence, celibacy, delayed or restricted marriage, reducing the frequency of coitus, the practice of *coitus interruptus*, contraceptives, induced sterility, abortion, infanticide, or preferential homicide (Harris and Ross 1987). Data on legal abortions, for example, suggest 260–450 such abortions per 1,000 live births (Peters and Larkin 1979). Abortions are also very common among non-industrial groups and are regarded as a universal practice (Harris and Ross 1987). Nurge (1973: 12) suggested that the rate of abortion during the Pleistocene may have amounted to 10–25 per cent. Infanticide, a common practice among all human populations, is presumed to have been widely practised in prehistoric times (Harris and Ross 1987).

The checks on population can be subdivided into those that have an immediate impact on the extant population size and composition, such as abortion, infanticide, and homicide, and those that would have a delayed effect, such as marriage rules, timing and frequency of coitus, contraceptives, induced sterility, and induced morbidity. They may also be subdivided in terms of their efficacy. One can argue that, under severe conditions of population/resource imbalance, infanticide is likely to be the most efficacious and speedy mechanism to prevent an additional increase in group size. The alternatives are highly disruptive to social order, and include high morbidity, indiscriminate infant mortality, violence and aggression, as well as sexual aberrations (Welinder 1979: 54).

Regulation of a population is not to be equated with deliberate population checks. The practice of a prolonged child-spacing period is a regulatory mechanism even if it is practised to safeguard the health of the mother or the survival of existing children. Poor health during periods of scarcity, or as a result of poverty in a system of inequality, influences many population parameters. In addition, when a population is fixed to a certain level with minor or wild oscillations (as, for example, during the Pleistocene or in the ancient civilizations), a model of population equilibrium is sometimes hypothesized (Wrigley 1971). Over hundreds or thousands of years, with the prevalence of specific conditions of fertility and mortality, the population grows, declines, or remains stationary within a certain range. Before and after the prevalence of such conditions, cultural change will bring about changes in the factors influencing fertility and mortality. As long as such conditions prevail, a new 'platform' will be reached. We may thus view the population history of humankind in terms of phases or situations of certain fertility and mortality parameters that are markedly different.

HUMAN EVOLUTION AND POPULATION GROWTH

It was believed at one time that early human populations were malnourished, ridden by disease, and hardly capable of survival, but recent investigations of the skeletal remains of prehistoric peoples, archaeological sites, simulations, as well as studies of contemporary hunters and gatherers, have revealed that early human populations were, in general, much better off than previously believed (M. Cohen 1995). It is also evident now that such populations were potentially capable of producing more children than were required for replacement and that they practised birth control. However, population growth during the Pleistocene was drastically lower than the current world population growth rate.

In general, the size of early hominid populations was exceedingly small in comparison with the present human population. The early populations of *Homo sapiens sapiens* were also comparatively small. Deevey (1960) estimated the size of populations during the Lower Palaeolithic, Middle Palaeolithic, Upper Palaeolithic, and Mesolithic as 0.125, 1, 3.34, and 5.32 million, respectively. Birdsell (1972) provided estimates for the Lower Palaeolithic, Middle Palaeolithic, and Upper Palaeolithic of 0.4, 1.0, and 2.3 million. In 1981, I recalculated the probable density and distribution of the populations and arrived at estimates of 0.4, 0.8, 1.2, 6, and 8–9 million for Basal Pleistocene, Lower Palaeolithic, Middle Palaeolithic, Upper Palaeolithic and Mesolithic/Epipalaeolithic populations respectively (Hassan 1981: 198–99).

The overall trend of world population growth shows an increase from a few millions by the end of the Pleistocene to about 100 million by 2500 BP and about 230 million by 200 BC (Table 17.2; Fig. 17.2). From 200 BC to AD 1000 the world population fluctuated between 200 and 250 million, with no appreciable gain over 1,200 years! A spurt of increase after AD 1200 and again after AD 1500 led to an increase to 545 million by AD 1650. The world population then began to soar, with a noticeable acceleration in growth rate leading to a total population approaching a billion in the early part of the nineteenth century. Within the span of the following two centuries, the world population achieved an all-time record high of population growth rate approaching 2 per cent after 1975. In 1994, as representatives from world nations gathered in Cairo to debate population issues, the world population had reached 5.66 billion.

By comparison with the historical rates of increase, and particularly the growth rates during the last two centuries, the Palaeolithic growth rates, and even the

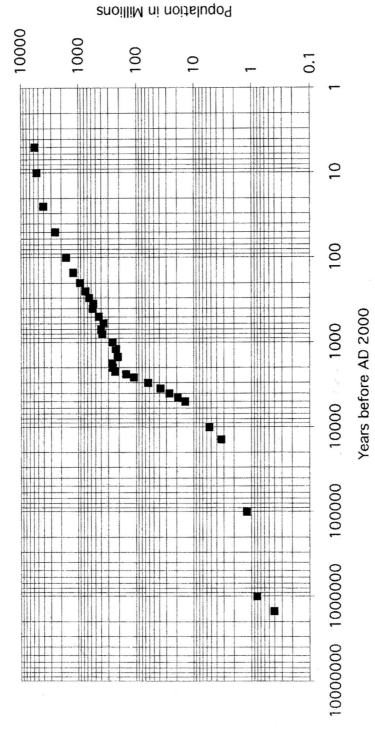

Figure 17.2 Global human population increase in the past 10,000,000 years. Note that the scale is log-log (logarithmic scale for both population and time). Source: F. Hassan.

Table 17.2 General trend of world population

Period	World population (in millions)	Growth rate (% per year)	Doubling time (in years)
Basal Pleistocene	0.4		
1,500,000 BP	0.8	0.00007	1,000,000
100,000 BP	1.2	0.00054	140,000
140,000 BP	3.3	0.0039	18,000
8000 BC	5.3	0.0088	8,000
3000 BC	14	0.032	2,000
2500 BC	19	0.061	1,000
2000 BC	27	0.070	1,000
1500 BC	38	0.068	1,000
1000 BC	62	0.098	700
600 BC	110	0.143	480
400 BC	153–162	0.164–0.194	420–350
200 BC	225–231	0.193–0.176	420–390
1 AD	252	0.211–0.043	330–1,600
200 AD	257	0.010	7,000
500 AD	207	−0.05	
800 AD	224	0.026	3,850
1000 AD	253–265	0.061–0.084	800–450
1200 AD	360–400	0.153–0.229	450–300
1300 AD	360–432	0–0.074	⇒900
1400 AD	350–375	−0.139 to −0.028	
1500 AD	425–461	0.0194–0.206	3,500–485
1600 AD	545–578	0.226–0.248	300–280
1650 AD	545	0	
1700 AD	610–680	0.225	308
1750 AD	720–770	0.251–0.332	275–200
1800 AD	900–954	0.43–0.446	160–155
1850 AD	1,200–1,241	0.525–0.575	130–120
1900 AD	1,625–1,633	0.55–0.606	125–115
1950	2,513–2,516	0.874	80
1975	4,075	1.93	36
1990	5,292–5,333	1.74	40
1995	5,700	1.49	47

'explosive' growth rates of early agricultural societies, are practically negligible: average annual rates are calculated as of 0.0054 per cent during the Middle Palaeolithic, 0.011 per cent during the Upper Palaeolithic (Hassan 1981: 200), and 0.064–0.0152 per cent for the Upper Palaeolithic (Groube 1996: 102). On the basis of the growth rates during the Neolithic in the Near East, the world population during that period has been estimated at 50 million, climbing to this figure as a result of a growth rate estimated at about 0.1 per cent (Carneiro and Hilse 1966; Hassan 1981: 221). In the light of more recent estimates of world population between 3000 BC and the present by Livi-Bacci (1992), Eckhardt (1992) and Kremer (1993), the global figure of 50 million for the Neolithic is apparently too excessive. These estimates provide an average (global) annual growth rate during the early Neolithic of 0.03 per cent (Fig. 17.3).

Undoubtedly, the global average annual growth rates mask short-term and regional variations. The fastest growth rates during the early agrarian cultures, as in the Near East, were on average as high as 0.1 per cent. Peak rates after 3000 BC within the context of agrarian state societies were probably as high as 0.35–0.59 per cent (Blanton 1972). The increase in world population associated with the spread of agriculture altered both the natural and cultural landscape: hunter-gatherers and foragers were absorbed in the tide of agrarian expansion, or either isolated or pushed into marginal agricultural land. Foragers also developed diversified economic patterns which included elements of food production and technology. The numbers of hunter-gatherers are difficult to establish, because in places they might have been subjected to diseases brought about by contact with farming communities. However, symbiosis with farmers and food exchanges could have led to an increase in the population size of others. Nevertheless the total number of foragers is not likely to have exceeded 6–10 million.

In addition to variations on a regional scale, great variations must have also prevailed among small local populations. Given that prehistoric population units were in the range of 400–1,000 persons (20–500 females), consisting of several bands of 25–50 persons each, stochastic variations are likely to have led to frequent episodes of high population growth alternating with others of no growth or depopulation (Wobst 1974). Naturally, this must have been more so for the small bands, necessitating constant demographic flux to maintain the appropriate size of the workforce and to secure mates for marriageable adults.

In addition, fluctuations in the abundance, quality, and distribution of natural resources are likely to have influenced the yield that could be extracted, as well as the size, mobility, and the territorial range of the population. It is thus inevitable that a population would have to engage in inter-population interactions to even out the random fluctuations affecting individual situations. Sometimes, however, the situation could not be remedied by inter-population demographic rearrangements of work mates and spouses, or even whole groups (by processes such as internal migration, external migration, flux, or dispersal), especially when adjacent populations underwent synchronous conditions of population increase, depopulation, or a fall in the productivity or quality of resources. Accordingly, fertility dampening practices and infanticide during episodes of regional population increase were as advantageous as a relaxation of population checks when the threat of depopulation was imminent.

There must also have been another complicating factor: the nature of chaotic dynamic systems, in which a slight change in the initial conditions can lead to unexpected major variations in the outcome (May 1976). Experimenting with the impact of variations in the population growth rate on the outcome of population

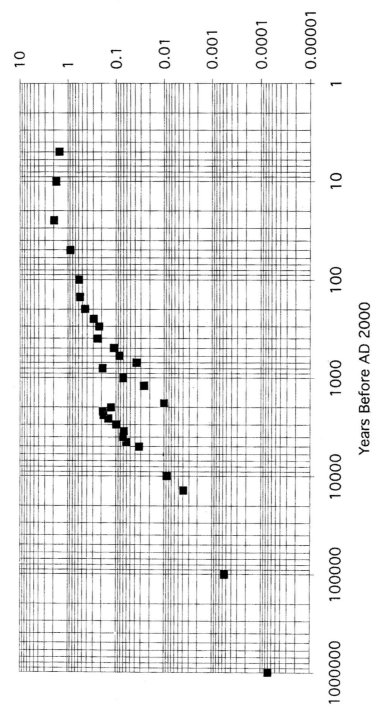

Figure 17.3 Changes in global population growth rates showing that population growth followed a non-linear pattern, with key transitions marked by slowing down or lack of growth following episodes of rapid increase.

growth using a logistic curve, May discovered that raising the parameter changed not just the quantity of the outcome but also its quality. When the parameter was low, his simple model settled at a steady state. When the parameter was high, the population would break apart and would oscillate between two alternating values. With higher values, more splitting is observed, and at yet higher values the system becomes chaotic, and the population visits many different values.

Small groups are prone to marked random variations, compounded by the erratic fluctuations of the environment, especially those at a scale that could not be recognized and understood by Pleistocene foragers. Jorde and Harpending (1976) suggested that, as people develop mechanisms to cope with short-term fluctuations, they may render themselves less stable in the face of long-term phenomena. Worse still, economic set-backs might have precipitated further fluctuations as, for example, when infanticide influences the sex ratio (the number of females relative to males) and population structure. Stochastic variations may also lead to severe imbalance in the sex ratio. Simulations reveal aberrant sex ratios (as high as 195), which are liable to throw the marriageable generation out of balance because of the lack of suitable mates (Bocquet-Appel and Masset 1982: 331). The Pleistocene demographic system was most likely chaotic, with non-linear growth patterns. Population flux, exogamy, migrations, fluid territoriality, and flexible group composition were necessities for overcoming the changing size and structure of regional population. As a by-product of this demographic solution, which ultimately leads to the transmission of genes, ideas, and artefacts from one region to another, we have evolved into a single species with a universal aptitude for culture and with fundamental similarities, in spite of the vast territories we occupy.

The interaction of human populations during periods of migration may in some cases have been disadvantageous to one of the groups, especially between groups with different economies and disease regimes. Such encounters include the impact of colonizing farmers on indigenous foragers, the interactions between pastoralists, foragers, and farmers, as well as the better known example of the impact of the spread of modern populations into territories occupied by foragers and other tribal populations.

In the remainder of this chapter I explore the possible demographic patterns of human populations during the successive cultural stages of human evolution. This will shed more light on the population history of humanity and the linkage between population dynamics and culture change.

PLEISTOCENE FORAGERS

Throughout the Pleistocene, from the appearance of *Homo habilis* to the advent of agriculture, several developments can be assessed from a demographic perspective.

The emergence of these practices may or may not have been directly related to population regulation, but, in as much as they were a part of the dynamic demographic system, they must be considered in attempting to understand population growth rates during the Pleistocene.

The Basal Pleistocene

During the Basal Pleistocene, the earliest hominids were most probably faced with severe problems resulting from food procurement difficulties, inadequate diet, and defence against predators. The situation was aggravated by the long period of infant dependence, which was likely to have posed a heavy nutritional load on nursing mothers, an additional workload, and the burden of carrying the infants during the movement of the troop or band. The birth of 'immature neonates' and the low fat and protein of the mother's milk meant that the breast must be always available and, hence, that the mother had to carry the infant while foraging. Nursing on demand was also likely to have kept early hominids from ovulating during at least a two-year period following birth, thus prolonging the birth interval to 3–4 years. This birth interval is comparable to the 3.5–4.5 years for gorillas (Sussman 1972).

However, with a long child-spacing period, the likelihood of greater maternal drain subjected the females to greater health hazards. The burdened females, as well as the helpless infants, were also likely to be more vulnerable to predation and less effective in securing meat. Meat would have to be obtained from either scavenging or hunting. Scavenging, the most likely practice for obtaining meat at the time (see Chapter 20), would have exposed the females and their infants to competing carnivores. Bipedalism would have also made it difficult for infants to cling to the mother. Nevertheless, bipedal locomotion freed the hands of women to carry an infant and engage in other activities, and allowed males to carry food to a sheltered location (Klein 1989: 181). In addition to the rise of group solidarity and bonding between males and females, the ability to store fat in the body, the potential to have intercourse unhindered by oestrus, and the enlargement of breasts, provided factors that might have increased fertility through increasing food yield available per capita, especially for pregnant or nursing females. This, in turn, increased the frequency of coitus, as well as increasing the ability of a female to cope with the burden of child rearing. The chances of infants surviving to child-bearing age were improved. A prolongation of the reproductive span could have been a key variable in enhancing the reproductive success of the Australopithecines. Equally effective would have been a reduction in the child-spacing period, but this would have increased female morbidity and mortality, thus ultimately lowering the growth rate.

Finds outside of Africa of one to two million years ago indicate that dispersal out of Africa may have occurred as an outcome of budding-off and dispersal during episodes of population increase as a response to climatic fluctuations, or just as a result of random walk. Population dispersal occurred perhaps in waves, reflecting both peaks of population increase resulting from the chaotic dynamics of the population system and as a result of improved ecological conditions in response to climatic changes. Parent populations with no option for further dispersal would have had either to yield to natural checks or deliberate behavioural controls. Given that infanticide was already common among primates, it is not unlikely that it was practised by early hominids as necessity dictated.

A significant development that would have had a strong influence on early hominid populations was a greater investment in a few offspring by females and males in a biological family and by the social group. This strategy may be referred to as a 'strong K-strategy' or even a 'Super K-strategy'. A K-strategy is preferred when environmental conditions are stable. A strong K-strategy would thus require stabilization of the environment. The emergence of a strong K-strategy might thus have been closely linked with an increasing ability to procure food of high quality, to protect females and infants, and to achieve a social organization that bonded males and females/infants, as well as one that ensured a basis for a durable social organization. Undoubtedly a human-like brain, the ability for complex learning, and an advanced level of communication (even if it were by signs) would have been tremendous advantages (see Chapter 18). Intelligence and better sensory–motor coordination would have facilitated tool-making and improved diet.

The Middle Pleistocene

The appearance of tools about 2.5 million years ago, as well as evidence of food sharing at about that time, attests to the emergence of genetic and cultural traits that were to lead to better food-procurement practices. More effective and sophisticated tools, as well as the widespread use of fire, were to emerge later in association with *Homo erectus*. With these biological and cultural traits, we can assume better control of the environment as well as greater abilities for behavioural population controls.

With increasing encephalization (the increase in brain size from 700 to 1,000 cc), gestation is not likely to have increased beyond that of the Australopithecines, or the gorillas for that matter. If the foetus gestated longer, the head would become too large at delivery to pass through the birth canal. If the head did pass, it might cause trauma or perhaps lead to the death of the mother. A selection for immature neonates placed still greater selective advantage for mothers who invested their newborn with care and a social organization that included male parental care and group solidarity. Midwifery might have become a traditional behavioural trait, because it would have reduced neonate mortality and female death during child birth (see also Harpending *et al.* 1990 on parental care and mortality).

The spatial distribution of *Homo erectus* and the stone tools of the Acheulian tradition associated with *Homo erectus* suggest expansion into India, Burma, Thailand, Malay, China, Java, central Spain, southern France and Hungary during the early Pleistocene, and farther north during the Middle Pleistocene (Klein 1989). The earliest human populations lived in open grasslands or parklands. In the course of human evolution, people moved into other biomes. Initially human dispersal and migrations probably took place in familiar habitats or in corridors of hospitable biotopes, perhaps at times of climatic amelioration. Further expansion into northern latitudes, as well as into arid habitats, during the later part of the Middle Pleistocene was associated with increasing use of fire and greater hunting and organizational skills (Dennell and Roebroeks 1996; Roebroeks and van Kolfschoten 1995; and see Chapter 19). The temperate environment, with its low winter and night temperature, might have led to an added stress on females. Seasonal scarcity of food may have reduced body fat proportions. In addition, poorer diet combined with cold stress and infections may have increased female morbidity, delayed menarche, and interrupted ovulation and menstruation. These factors would have also caused a higher infant mortality.

In spite of these difficulties, the greater care of neonates and mothers, an advanced brain, and more than two million years of cultural tradition, provided the basis for better food procurement, adequate shelter, and effective protection from predators and enemies. Age at death climbed to an average in excess of thirty years, perhaps approaching the 33–37 years characteristic of contemporary hunter-gatherers (Acsádi and Nemeskéri 1970: 146). Selection for late onset of first reproduction to perhaps twelve years would have benefited the females, who would have had a chance to mature physically before being subjected to the heavy demands of child-bearing and nursing. A late entry to motherhood and domestic home activities would have allowed the female to become properly socialized and trained, especially if we assume that monogamous marriage arrangements may have emerged by that time.

The Late Pleistocene

The Late Pleistocene was a period of major transformation in human biology, involving the disappearance of archaic *Homo sapiens* and Neanderthals and the emergence of modern *Homo sapiens sapiens* or near-modern humans in Africa between 130,000 and 50,000/40,000 years ago (Klein 1989). The spread of modern humans sometime between 60,000 and 40,000 years ago led to the demise of earlier populations and the homogenization of human populations into a single species.

Within a span of 10,000 years, the Neanderthal populations were replaced or absorbed into modern humans.

Average age at death of adults was about 33–34.5 years (Hassan 1981: 101; Weiss 1973). The Neanderthals attained old age, as we know it now. The long-term average population growth rate among the Neanderthals and early *Homo sapiens* rose dramatically compared with that of *Homo erectus* populations, perhaps in the magnitude of seven to eight times the previous long-term average rate. The estimated world-wide average long-term rate during the Middle Palaeolithic was perhaps about 0.0005 per cent, compared with an estimate of 0.00007 per cent for the Lower Palaeolithic. Given that the increase in longevity was probably not much higher than that of *Homo erectus*, it is possible that greater survival of infants to child-bearing age was the most significant factor behind the dramatic rise in population growth rate in the long run. The greater survival of children might have been related to advanced midwifery (Trevathan 1987: 224–29), greater group support of infants, better genetic and cultural adaptive responses to cold environments, advanced cognitive abilities, and a fully developed language. The greater survival of children might have overcompensated for further retardation of menarche to fifteen to sixteen years (see p. 678). According to Trinkaus and Tompkins (1990), the degree of the shift in longevity and other aspects of the life cycle from late Archaic humans like the Neanderthals and modern humans, was modest. Klein (1989) notes the various injuries sustained by the Neanderthals, as well as the evidence for substantial help and care from their comrades.

The emergence of *Homo sapiens sapiens* was associated with still greater average long-term growth rate than that of earlier populates, perhaps again seven or eight times the rate during the Middle Palaeolithic. The average age at death does not seem to have been much higher than that of the Neanderthals (about 34 years), and we must hypothesize that the assumed increase in population growth rate was a function of greater success in coping with population and resource stochastic fluctuations. One of the successful strategies was the continued dispersal into new lands.

At the beginning of the Late Pleistocene, modern or near-modern human populations ventured farther north into the cold steppes of the Ukraine, the Iranian Plateau, Turkmenia, and Uzbekistan in Asia, and into central Germany and southern Poland in Europe. They also expanded into Australia, where a recent examination of radio-carbon and TL dates, in the light of U/Th dating of coral reefs, has led Chappell *et al.* (1996) to suggest that the luminescence-based age of 50–60,000 is the best available estimate of the age of human presence in Australia; an even earlier date is also suggested by recent discoveries. Human colonization of the Americas is well attested by 12,000 BP, but may have been preceded by initial infiltrations between 25,000 to 20,000 years ago, and perhaps earlier according to some scholars (Taylor *et al.* 1996). The expansion into North America was fairly rapid: Haynes (1969) estimates an average annual growth rate of 0.08 per cent from the increase in the number of sites. At such a rate, an initially small population would have required about 10,000 years to saturate North America (Hassan 1981: 202). If the movement was not a result of population increase and expansion, but a leap-frog movement by small, mobile groups, the rate of dispersal would have been much faster.

The improvement in the adaptive success of the human population emerging during the Middle Palaeolithic was enhanced by the rapid increase in the size of the world population. By the end of the Pleistocene, about 3 million individuals spread over much of the space currently occupied, consisting of 3,000–6,000 local population units in different habitats and with various degrees of partial isolation and contact. Geographic separation allowed for regional cultural differences to appear. However, interpopulation gene flow was sufficiently effective for maintaining the unity of a single species. The increase in the number of people represented an increase in the number of potential innovations. With language and some sort of notational book-keeping, an information revolution was achieved (see Chapters 18 and 20). Pooling information allowed the exploitation of a wide range of resources. The exploitation of aquatic resources, small game animals, and cereal grasses, as well as the widespread usage of food-processing devices ranging from grinding stones to smoking fish, together with adequate storage, were the basis for expanding the carrying capacity and a relatively rapid rate of population growth as in certain parts of western Europe, estimated at 0.1–0.13 per cent by Constandse-Westermann and Newell (1984).

EARLY FARMING POPULATIONS

The most remarkable achievement in the history of human population was the emergence about 10,000 years ago of the ability to manipulate the productivity of natural resources, allowing large human groups to settle in permanent communities close to each other in a pattern that has radically altered both the natural and the human landscape (Cowan and Watson 1992; Harris 1996a; and see Chapter 21). In his overview of the current evidence for agricultural origins, Harris (1996b, 1996c) provides a model of evolutionary stages marked by an increasing dependence on domesticated plants and greater sophistication of farming practices. He also favours linking the emergence of agriculture in south-west Asia, and very possibly also east Asia, with the widespread climatic and vegetation changes that occurred at, and immediately after, the transition from the terminal Pleistocene to the early Holocene (see also: Hassan 1981; Henry 1989; McCorrison and Hole 1991). Matthews *et al.* (1995) also explore the global climatic conditions at the time of agricultural origins, and Hillman (1996) provides a cogent argument for the role of climatic–environmental changes starting at 15,000 years ago in increasing the gross yield of potential starch-protein staples.

A hitherto unexplored factor associated with global postglacial warming has recently been put forward by Groube (1996), who suggests that the warming was a bonanza for many temperature and humidity micro-organisms that utilize part of the human body for food or reproduction (such as *vivax* malaria). Populations close to zero growth either settled to increase fertility, or moved away from infested regions. With sedentism, they began to intensify the food quest from specific resources that ultimately led to food production. This theory suffers from lack of empirical support and does not explain why sedentism, which would make communities more vulnerable, would have been adopted. It also does not provide a mechanism for the transition from foraging to farming. The emergence of agriculture has also been attributed to population pressure (see Sanderson (1995) for a recent endorsement of that model), coevolutionary changes (Rindos 1984), and ecological stress (Harris 1977). The population pressure model has been dismissed by Cowgill (1975) and Hassan (1981). The coevolutionary model has been criticized by Blumler (1996). Nevertheless, Sanderson (1995) rejected all models in favour of the population pressure model.

More recently, the transition to agriculture has been characterized as the result of rapid, discrete, responses to severe and abrupt climatic events (Gasse and van Campo 1994; Hassan 1996). By 14,000 years ago, postglacial warming began a series of climatic changes that were crucial in upsetting previously established glacial regimes of atmospheric circulation. Populations situated in arid and semi-arid regions in climatically unstable zones were particularly vulnerable to seasonal and spatial unpredictability (see Hassan 1977, and Hassan 1981: 214). One of the critical events was a severe episode of cold climate known as the Younger Dryas about 11,500 radio-carbon years ago (Hillman 1996; Matthews *et al.* 1995), the first of a series of such spells that each lasted less than a century, at about 10,000, 8,500, and 7,500/6,000 years ago. These short-term severe variations, associated with dramatic increases in inter-annual variability, prompted modes of actions that previously might only have been used occasionally and as a matter of necessity because they were not compatible with a mobile and 'free' foraging-hunting ethos: intensively utilizing particular wild grasses that were high yielding and storable, and managing certain animal species, leading to coevolutionary changes that increased the dependence of people on specific resources and vice versa. These changes coincided with demographic developments such as congregation of large groups in seasonal and permanent settlements. An increase in the size of the family was due to labour shortage at the times of sowing and harvesting, which provided opportunities for productive child labour. Relaxation of population controls, coupled with the effects of unpredictable climatic events and failures of agricultural production, are likely to have led to dispersal and relocation.

The transition from hunting-gathering to agriculture represents a major population change within a short time interval, from a low, relatively inelastic, ceiling of population, to another state of dynamic growth, which not only allowed larger populations but also sustained the acceleration in the rate of population growth during the end of the Pleistocene. Birth rates perhaps as high as 0.1 per cent in agrarian zones were matched by slower rates elsewhere, until the spread and intensification of agriculture led to a global annual rate exceeding 0.1 per cent after 1000 BC: by that time, the world was between ten and twenty times the world at the eve of the agricultural revolution. Thereafter, and as a consequence of improvements in agricultural production, the world today is populated by more than 6 billion people. The ability to feed this vast number of people and sustain other economic gains is a testimony to the tremendous potential of agriculture as a subsistence pursuit.

Carr-Saunders (1922: 216–17), and later Sussman (1972), attributed the relatively rapid growth following agriculture to the effect of *sedentary* residence on shortening the child-spacing interval. Handwerker (1983) strongly dismisses the link between sedentariness and higher fertility and suggests that the 'demand for children did not appreciably affect fertility and does not account for variation in fertility among settled agricultural populations' (1983: 19).

The correlation between higher fertility and sedentism is probably not causal. A long child-spacing period among foragers is not simply a function of foraging mobility (Cashdan 1985): it seems to be primarily a response to heavy workloads, the young age of mothers increasing the effect of maternal drain on their health, the lack of baby foods, and the hazards of child-bearing (Hassan 1981: 223). The transition to agriculture provided 'a definite economic motive to enlarging the size of the family unit and the size of the labour pool' (Hassan 1981: 224). The increase in population concomitant with the advent of agriculture was a function of the change in socio-economic conditions, favouring slight relaxation of the controls damping fertility without too much prolongation of the child-spacing period. The availability of weaning foods could have reduced the nutritional cost of children. The impact of the diet on survivorship and age at menarche was most probably negligible, but the cereal diet may have increased infant mortality (Hassan 1981: 224).

The causes of the increase in human population coincident with the emergence of food production have also been explored recently by Pennington (1996), who draws upon findings that indicate substantial increase in the survival of children as populations switch from nomadic to sedentary lives. Given a schedule of mortality and fertility, a projection of life tables shows that moderate increases in child survival rates have more substantial effects on population growth than mortality at later ages. Higher child survival rates may be so critical that even a reduction in life expectancy at birth of more than a decade can occur without a reduction in population growth rate. However, the basis for Pennington's projection is flawed, since the ethnographic example used for analogy is based on the !Kung Bushmen of the northern Kalahari desert in Botswana, where a reduction in child mortality was a function of increased access to milk, which was not the case among early farmers. Nevertheless, an increase in child survival in such early agricultural communities, as posited by Pennington, was more likely a result of relaxing population controls even as infant mortality rates increased.

Demographic conditions following the transition to agriculture were closely linked to changes in diet, work activities, labour requirements, food quality and abundance, storage, and health. Mark Cohen (1995, with references) posits that infection and infectious disease observable on bone seem to increase as human settlements increase in size and permanence. A case study by Kent (1987) shows that the sedentary environment can lead to the contamination of mother's milk by transmitted viral and bacterial infections. Mothers transmitted infectious agents to their infants causing diarrhoeal diseases. Kent argues that a high rate of infant death (50–60 per cent of all infant death) from diarrhoeal diseases in agrarian communities would have been a result of aggregation and sedentary residence rather than poor diet.

A combination of crowded, sedentary residence, combined with poor diet, would have been particularly disadvantageous. M. Cohen (1995) suggests that early farmers were less well nourished than their ancestral hunter-gatherers, but comparison of Harris lines in hunting-gathering populations and early farmers indicates that the lines are more common in hunter-gatherers. This probably suggests that early farmers were *less* prone to spells of biological stress, because the frequency of Harris lines suggests seasonal stress or episodes of famines and feasting. A full study of the palaeopathology of a sample of aboriginal Australians (Webb 1995) revealed that the Harris lines as well as dental enamel hypoplasia and *Cribra orbitalia* are common, comparable with those of early farmers in North America. The evidence suggests that males were more prone to childhood stress and that they were more likely to recover, possibly due to a cultural preference which favoured male children.

Contrary to M. Cohen's (1989, 1995) suggestion that health declined with the advent of farming and associated sedentism and large population size, Wood *et al.* (1992) argue that the reverse is possible. Using the same data, they suggest that lesions indicate healthy individuals who recovered, whereas those who died because of poor health are not likely to show healing lesions. Although such a debate may continue until ancillary evidence is marshalled, it appears that a discussion of health cannot be solely based on a partial record of certain diseases from skeletal remains. Models of ancient disease should be constructed with a clear understanding of the cultural context and the natural environment. Crowding, contact with 'strangers' in trading communities, division of labour between the sexes and gender status, social hierarchy and differential access to high quality food, health care, differences in workload and exposure – all are clearly factors that came in the wake of agriculture. These factors are likely to have influenced health and mortality. Archaeological proxies for such cultural factors must be obtained in conjunction with bio-anthropological data. It may also be important to note that the segments of population buried among farmers may not be representative of the masses of farmers, but of those who had burial privileges, which was certainly the case among the early state societies.

The emergence of cultivation and animal husbandry was also associated with marked dislocation of populations and dispersal from the source areas. In some situations, symbiotic relationships existed between foragers who persisted in areas marginal to pastoralism or agriculture. Other major population movements in later prehistory and classical Antiquity were associated variously with: the sedentarization of pastoralists and later fusion with agricultural communities; conquests of agrarian polities by organized nomadic pastoralists; forced relocation of farming populations by powerful states; colonization of distant regions by military force; and relocation motivated by better economic opportunities. In the most recent period of human evolution, the motivations for territorial expansion or migrations have not necessarily been related to subsistence, but rather to the standard of living set by an élite in societies with a hierarchical social organization.

Examination of the landscape and the distribution of Neolithic sites in Europe has led van Andel and Runnels (1995) to present a model of migration in discrete steps with time lapses in between. This model is a modification of an earlier model by Ammerman and Cavalli-Sforza (1984: 6) which assumed a continuous spread in a wave driven by steady population growth. The new model does not depend on population increase, since there is no evidence of high population density or crowding in south-eastern Europe. The implication of the model is that migrants were small in numbers and that they are likely to have mingled with the indigenous foraging populations. The peopling of Europe raises interesting questions concerning the possibility of using genetics to discern prehistoric and historical population movements and regional variations (Cavalli-Sforza 1994, 1996). Although one must guard against racial abuses of population studies (see Evison 1996, with references to critics of the applications of genetics in archeology), genetic data are sources of information that, together with linguistic, archaeological, and historical data, are likely to clarify prehistoric population geography. In a joinder to the contribution by Cavalli-Sforza, Renfrew (1996) cautions against the uncritical application of molecular genetic data to linguistic and historical phenomena.

EARLY STATE SOCIETIES

Early state societies consisted of local communities connected in a large population agglomerate, bound together by an administrative cadre of officials who legitimated their power by religious ideology, and – as warranted – by coercion (Chapter 23).

The total population of an early state was a function of the number of communities that could be strung together as well as the size of local communities. The size of local communities was, in turn, a function of agricultural productivity. Under pre-industrial agricultural technology, agricultural productivity was relatively low, with modern records of food production which were only exceeded in post-medieval times. Low agricultural yields supported people at a density of less than ten persons per square kilometre to more than a hundred persons per square kilometre, with perhaps an average of 10–25 persons per square kilometre in the earliest farming communities. In general, these communities rarely farmed an area more than 5 kilometres from their settlement; more often, the farming area was within 1–2 kilometres, an area of 1–4 square kilometres. The minimal population units in an early state may thus have consisted of a few families in a hamlet, or 25–100 persons in small villages. Larger village size was possible with greater productivity and a larger farming area: estimates of prehistoric villages from Mesoamerica range from 15–50 people to 114–285 people.

A number of villages and hamlets in a single valley or a region with access to each other, may form a polity, a village chiefdom. Such an alliance may have been motivated by the need to overcome fluctuations in yield that may have affected villages differentially as a result of variations in rainfall, pest infestations, or other unforeseen causes in farming practices. The number of communities that can be amalgamated together was a function of access and transport. Since most transport before modern times was by foot, pack animals, or boats, the distance travelled within a reasonable time was relatively short. With an average travel distance of 10–20 kilometres per day, a strip of land 80–100 kilometres long (and say 10 kilometres wide) could be traversed in a week or less. A human carrier can carry a load of 20–30 kilograms for a distance of about 20 kilometres a day (Blanton *et al.* 1981: 248), compared with the 150–200 kilograms that can be carried the same distance by a donkey. A carrier will consume about 0.44–0.55 kilograms of food per day, so for a return trip of two weeks one way (a distance of 240 kilometres), the carrier would need 14 kilograms, or more than 50 per cent of the load. To be 'cost-effective', the distance should be within the range allowing the delivery of about 70 per cent of the load. The earliest petty states may have thus covered relatively small areas. With an average of 10–25 persons per square kilometre, the population of the villages forming the polity may have been between 8,000 and 25,000 persons in an area of 800–1,000 square kilometres.

With good coordination, consisting of central storage and redistribution of grain to communities facing food shortages, a higher population density could be supported. Also, with accumulating agricultural experiences, more yields could be obtained. In addition, certain communities in favoured localities would have higher yields that could support as many as 40 persons per square kilometre. Such a density could have made possible a population of 32,000 and up to 40,000 persons in an area of 800–1,000 square kilometres. Petty states in Mesoamerica and Predynastic Egypt were fairly limited in their territorial range, covering areas between around 100 to 400 square kilometres. The consolidation of several regions in late Predynastic Egypt created units that covered 1,200–1,600 square kilometres, with as many as 20,000 to 30,000 people. The unification of Egypt led to the establishment of a state covering about 30,000 square kilometres.

Empires after 1500 BC (Chapter 24) controlled vast areas: the Harappan civilization, for example, covered an area of approximately 5.5 million square kilometres. Imperial expansion was facilitated both by advances in water transport and construction of roads. The Inca empire, which covered five times the area of Europe between AD 1100 and 1400, was linked together by a 16,000-kilometre network of highways. Estimates of the size of empires by Taagepera (1978) and Eckhardt (1992), recently reviewed by Sanderson (1995), indicate that there were three stages; from 3000 to 600 BC, 600 BC to AD 1600, and after AD 1600. During the first phase, the Egyptian empire in 1500 BC was one square megametre (one square megametre = 386,000 square miles), compared with 0.45 of a square megametre in China at 1000 BC. Persia controlled an empire of 5.5 square megametres around 600 BC. By AD 1300, China had an empire as large as 15 square megametres.

A large population provides both economic and political power. The ratio of workers in a pre-industrial population ranges from 40–70 per cent of the population. A unit that manages to achieve a population unit with as many as 40,000 people will have as many as 16,000 to 28,000 workers. The population will also include 10–15 per cent male adults that can be mobilized as warriors, amounting to as many as 4,000 to 6,000 warriors. If all adult males were 'drafted', that would provide perhaps as many as 10,000 warriors. Large kingdoms with as many as 1–2 million people could easily amass armies of 20,000–40,000 warriors, about 15–25 per cent of all adult males. States that manage to control such a large population (equivalent to the size of Egypt during the Old Kingdom), other factors being equal, could conquer and dominate smaller states. Large states can also afford to lose large numbers of warriors that can be replaced by warriors from other provinces.

Areas with naturally high productivity were more likely to achieve higher population density than others. This accounts for the rise of many early state societies in river valleys, such as the Tigris and Euphrates, the Nile, the Indus, and the Yangtze and the Hwang Ho. The rivers also provided the potential for water transport, as well as a better overland transport network than mountainous or plateau areas. Certain settings and historical factors thus created a favourable environment for the emergence of people under state organization. In Mesoamerica, about 35 million people occupied an area of 1 million square kilometres. In China, the population is estimated at 60 million in AD 180 and 200 million in AD 1585. In Egypt, with a much smaller agricultural area (roughly 30,000 square kilometres), the population is estimated at 1.2 million during the Old Kingdom (third millennium BC) and 3.2 million in Hellenistic times (Hassan 1993). By comparison, the population of the Roman empire is estimated at 54 million.

Population and power were thus closely linked since the beginning of farming and political coordination of neighbouring villages. The groups that managed to achieve a political union were far more powerful than other scattered villages and could, under suitable conditions, manage to extend their control over them. The synchronous emergence of polities may also lead to conflicts and competition. Motivations for extending political control over a large area is a function of the inherent unpredictability of agricultural production. The larger a group, the greater the amount that can be saved to redistribute in times of need. However, an increase in the size of population leads to an increase in administrators who are entrusted with collecting and storing food in communal storage facilities. This leads to an increase in 'overhead', especially since administrators manage to subsist because of the power they control at a higher standard of living than peasants. Greater security is also maintained by improving transportation, by investing in pack animals, and by boat building. In addition, with accumulation of grain and wealth, the need for defence increases. Investment in temples and priests, as well as in gifts to provincial chiefs and headmen, is also necessary to bind the group in a 'national' unity and to mitigate against revolts and schism. There is also a need for a police force to coax those who defect in paying tribute to comply. Disputes likely to emerge in a large population where accounts become important require clerks, scribes, and judges. Accordingly, as a state grows bigger, the cost of its operation rises precipitously. At a certain point, the cost of running the affairs of the state outpaces the amount of tribute that can be extracted from the region under control. Military expansion follows. The process is repeated until, finally, the cost of controlling territory rises beyond returns, as a function of transport cost and the military as well as administrative force required to keep outlying regions under check. The expansion of states is also motivated by incidence of drops in yield due to natural disasters and mismanagement, in part, of land fertility due to soil erosion or salinization (Conrad and Demarest 1984; Tainter 1988; and see Chapter 25).

The formation of a state was also inexorably linked with greater demands for increasing yield from village communities. Technological advances were limited and were not likely to have led to a major increase in productivity until after post-medieval times, with the application of chemical fertilizers, pesticides, herbicides, mechanized farming, use of fossil fuels and other forms of energy, modern

699

irrigation, genetic improvement of cultigens, and modern storage methods. Increasing yield was based on expanding the area cultivated and increasing the yield from areas cultivated by labour-intensive practices, such as weeding, water-lifting, hoeing, ploughing, and so on. Families were thus faced with the need to increase the number of children as a means of meeting the labour demands placed upon them by high taxation. In the Valley of Oaxaca, for example, population increase in the piedmont area during Monte Alban I was a consequence of urban administrative demands (Blanton *et al.* 1981: 223–24).

As a result of labour demands, an ethos emphasizing large family size and preference for males (for heavy farm labour) became dominant. Larger families placed additional burdens on mothers, who had to cope with a large number of children in addition to the chores associated with farming. Heavy taxation and tribute also reduced families to a state of misery and poverty, which was commonly associated with high infant mortality, poor health, and malnutrition.

The emergence of state societies (Chapter 23) was associated not only with the regional integration of many local communities, but was also characterized by the emergence of a major distinction between villages and the settlements where administrators and state officials resided. These settlements included relatively more people than the neighbouring villages, had a relatively higher population density, and included amenities associated with wealth and power. These settlements were called towns and cities and were often characterized by a temple or a fort. Towns generally included a few thousand people, while cities in early civilizations attained populations of as many as 40,000 people. In general, pre-industrial capital cities consisted of 20,000 to 40,000, with many other cities with little more than 10,000 and perhaps only 5,000 people (Sjoberg 1960: 83). In Mesopotamia, Ur had 24,000–34,000 inhabitants, Lagesh 19,000, Umma 16,000, and Khafaje 12,000. In the Indus valley, Mohenjo-Daro and Harappa probably contained a population of 20,000 (Piggott 1950). The population of Tell el-Amarna in Egypt has been estimated at between 20,000 and 29,000 (Kemp 1981: 97), and Thebes in 1300 BC was a city of 20,000–40,000 people (Hassan 1993).

A survey of the size of the largest cities since 2250 BC (Sanderson 1995) reveals that about 40,000 persons was the minimum size of the largest cities until AD 1300. In 650 BC, the largest cities consisted of about 120,000 persons. The maximum size increased to a range from 400,000 to 700,000 between AD 100 and AD 1500. However, the maximum population of Rome in the late sixth century BC is estimated at 35,000–50,000 (Cornell 1995: 204–7): census data of 103,000–152,000 adult male citizens for 508–392 BC 'can on no account be genuine' (Cornell 1995: 208) – it might refer to the total population of Rome and its territories.

The size of towns and cities was limited by low agricultural productivity, the limitations on the speed and load of transport, and the lack of professional armies. The emergence of professional soldiers in a later stage of state societies associated with investment in fast, military ships led to the rise of ancient empires in the Near East, Persia, Greece, and Italy. The territorial expansion allowed large cities to emerge. Cities also became larger by attracting or forcing farmers to reside within the city limits in order to secure access to food, to reduce cost, and to minimize the threat of siege or reduction of tributes. Teotihuacán in Mesoamerica increased from 15,000 to 125,000 people in the Middle Classic Period by the displacement of rural settlements to the city. Lowland Maya cities included urban cores ranging from 13,000 to 60,000 people, with smaller centres consisting of 1,500–10,000 persons (Rice and Culbert 1990). Large cities were thus more the exception than the rule. This situation prevailed until manufacture and trade in Europe allowed cities to expand. During the twelfth century, Milan may have had as many as 80,000 people, of whom 20,000 were artisans. Most city-states, however, consisted of smaller populations: Pisa, for example, consisted of 10,000 people. In medieval times, Cairo had 25,000 inhabitants.

The estimation of the population of cities in archaeology is often based on ethnographic analogy. Early estimates provide figures between 200 and 300 persons per hectare. Sumner (1989) provided estimates of 66–293 persons per hectare in Near Eastern settlements. Russell (1958: 64–66) provides estimates of 160 persons per hectare for ancient Pompeii, 250–350 persons per hectare for Imperial Rome, and 200 persons per hectare for Constantinople in the fifth century AD. For ancient walled cities in Palestine, Broshi (1979) suggests that as many as 400–500 persons per hectare were crowded within the city walls. However, before estimating population sizes of early cities from ethnographic analogies of so many people per unit of space, we should have information on three factors: the density of houses; the percentage of non-living space; and the area actually occupied at any given time. A good example of this approach is the work by Kemp (1981) at Tell el-Amarna: using archaeological data he estimates a density of 60–75 persons per hectare.

Modern urbanization, after AD 1650 (Fig. 17.4), has been associated with industry and commerce, whereas early urbanization was based on manufacture or trade under the patronage of the king or the temple. Manufactured goods were for the state functionaries, to be awarded by the head of the state. The expansion of manufacture and trade in later times was not only related to advances in technology, but also to the breakdown in the monopoly of manufacture and trade by divine kings, allowing many individuals to engage in such activities and raising the number of consumers by allowing commoners to have access to luxury goods. However, some early states generated income for the élite through manufacture and trade: in Teotihuacán, for example, it is presumed that one-third of the population consisted of craft specialists. Commercialization during the Post-classic period in Mesoamerica was apparently linked with weak state control and the appearance of an autonomous and self-regulating economy after the collapse of the powerful governments (Blanton et al. 1981: 251).

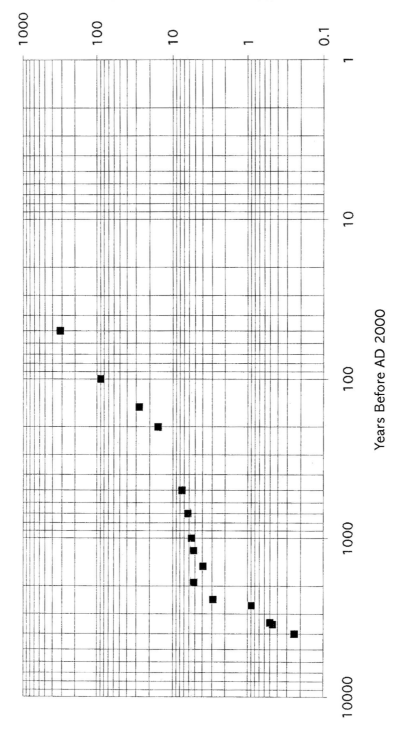

Urban World Population of Cities
>100,000 in Millions

Years Before AD 2000

Figure 17.4 Urban population of cities >100,000 in millions over the last 4,000 years.

Many cities began as cult centres, as places identified with ancestral homes, settlements of a prestigious lineage, or trade loci. Agricultural potential in the immediate vicinity of the city may be high or low because the growth of a city depends primarily on food imports from tribute, taxation, or trade (Herbert and Thomas 1990). The enlargement of population units in early state societies was associated with a hierarchy of settlements of different sizes. Capital cities maintained access to the rural area through large towns serving as urban centres of administrative regions. These towns, in turn, were surrounded by a cluster of smaller towns or large villages that served as local markets for local produce and administrative posts. The capitals were, in some cases as in Uruk, many times larger than any town, in a pattern known as primate distribution. In other cases, distribution of settlement size followed a log-normal or rank-size distribution in which settlements were only slightly larger than the next smaller settlement.

The urban population in early state societies was a very small proportion of the total population. In fact, this was the case until modern urbanization: as late as 1790, the urban population of the USA was no more than 5.1 per cent of the total population (Thomlinson 1965: 21). In pre-industrial societies, the urban population was often about 5 per cent, and rarely as high as 8–10 per cent of the population (Sjoberg 1960: 83).

The size of a city clearly varied according to political and economic conditions. Ancient Jerusalem varied from a town of 2,000 inhabitants at the time of David (965 BC) to 53,000 at the time of Justinian (AD 565) (Broshi 1975). The major expansion of the city coincided with the Roman and Byzantine empires. In Egypt, a population of 2.1 million during the New Kingdom had an urban population of about 150,000, with forty-four provincial towns, each with an average of 2,000–3,000 people and a national capital with about 30,000 people (Hassan 1993).

CONCLUSION

To gain even a partial vision of the demographic conditions of prehistoric peoples is a daunting task. Painstaking analysis of settlement areas, density of settlements, frequency of artefacts, and food remains, provide a possibility of making some reasonable estimates in the light of our knowledge of contemporary foragers and pre-industrial peoples. Important information is also adduced from ageing and sexing skeletal remains and investigations of ancient diseases – palaeopathology (Chapter 7). Not without problems, palaeodemographic studies provide approximate measures of the development, longevity, and fertility of ancient populations. Population studies in archaeology (including palaeodemography, demographic archaeology, and historical demography) have provided a wealth of information over the last three decades, but much remains to be done. We are still in need of more reliable methods to provide better proxies of the demographic profiles of prehistoric peoples. We also need to develop models of prehistoric mortality and fertility that do not suffer from a close adherence to models developed within a western, industrial context.

Simulations and a closer consideration of stochastic oscillations may provide a deeper understanding of population dynamics. Based on uniform demographic principles with attention to the structure of proximate, intermediate and distal causes and the mode of causality, simulations of individual life cycle for groups in dynamic cultural and natural contexts promise to provide answers to some vexing questions (see Mangel and Tier (1993) on the dynamics of metapopulation with demographic stochasticity and environmental catastrophes). Such dynamic, open-ended, micro-models with unexpected random variables create mathematical nightmares, but we may be consoled by the elegance of the simple principle under-lying such hellish complexity. Prehistoric populations were probably far from being discrete, stationary, and stable. This was in part due to the foraging mode of existence that prevailed for millions of years. However, the biological changes in hominid evolution enabling the rearing of children in a protective social context and the ability to overcome scarcities and overcrowding through dispersal, migration, technological, social, and ideological means, are the greatest demographic feat of humanity.

Although we can trace our biological ancestry to more than three million years ago, our current cultural milieu has been shaped by forces that were set into motion in the wake of the adoption of farming and herding communities between 10,000 and 6,000 years ago. We can hardly imagine a world with no more than 3–5 million people as the stock of our crowded world with more than 6 billion on all con-tinents. Through the lens of history, it is difficult to see beyond a world already populated with hundreds of millions living in cities and governed by states with mighty rulers and powerful magnates. Yet this history is radically different from the state of affairs that prevailed in the deep, prehistoric past. As our immediate ances-tors climbed the evolutionary ladder, they were progressively more successful in enhancing the number of the newborn who survived to child-bearing age. The increase was imperceptible and subject to severe natural and cultural checks. Death claimed a large percentage of infants and children. The life of adults was fairly short, with little improvement in the average age at death (32–33 years) from the Middle Pleistocene to the Neolithic. A few lived well into their sixties. Women died on average about four years younger than their mates. They lived in small groups in larger mating pools, with marked spatial mobility and fluidity in size and composition. Mortality rates were high and the size of families was small. Fertility was controlled to maintain an exceedingly low rate of population increase.

The relationship between our foraging ancestors and resources is intricate, but the concept of 'carrying capacity' is often used to estimate how many people can be supported over a long period of time. This concept, however, is only useful if we take into consideration the role of human ingenuity in overcoming food shortages, their ability to disperse, and their capacity to regulate their numbers so that they can remain at a safe level below frequent oscillations in the natural yield of resources. Nevertheless, severe, natural fluctuations beyond the social memory of a group may place them at severe risk. Outbreaks of disease or simply stochastic variations can cause occasional depopulation or overpopulation. The intrinsic ability to increase at a fairly rapid rate was instrumental when groups were threatened by extinction. At the same time, cultural checks were necessary to maintain a fairly healthy population. It is likely that *Homo sapiens sapiens* increased at a faster rate than their predecessors and engaged in a variety of social, technological, and cultural innovations by the end of the Pleistocene. This may be in part a result of their cognitive capabilities, but it might have also been a function of regionalization and a free flow of ideas amongst contiguous groups creating a dynamic intellectual environment.

The first steps towards managing plants and animals at the end of the Pleistocene were rapidly followed by a series of steps that ultimately led to agrarian, settled communities and nomadic pastoralists. This marked a new cultural setting, with a new demographic order, characterized by high regional densities which allowed large populations to reside within fairly small areas. These aggregates formed the nucleus of state societies.

The emergence of the state had in turn a major influence on the demographic landscape. In many cases, towns and cities emerged as density spikes with anomalously large populations. Initially only hosting a few hundreds, the early cities soon mushroomed into hundreds of thousands, but with a fairly basic maximum size of 20,000 to 40,000 before the modern megalopolis became commonplace. The states were organizational polities that through time fostered social, ideational, technological, and economic changes that not only delineated the shape of civilization as we know it, but also created an environment for an expansion of world population hitting the 100 million mark by 600 BC. The early state, however, was based on great inequalities. The fundamental basis of state aggrandizement was human labour. The larger the working labour force, the greater the revenues to the governing élite. There was rarely ever a shortage of land. Moreover, various innovations increased productivity. A pronatal ethos, combined with warfare and other means to secure slaves and serfs, placed a heavy burden on women. As the source of offspring, women became an economic commodity. However, the greater need for male labour in intensive agriculture and as fodder for war did not do much to enhance the social status of women.

There were no major improvements in life expectancy in the early civilizations, with an average age at death for adults of 36 years (31–40 years) – in fact, it was not until after 1840 that the average age at death for adults increased gradually towards its modern value in industrial nations. However, growth rates became progressively higher, except for a few interludes due to dramatic natural or cultural checks.

The advent of agriculture introduced new diseases, as people provided a resident host for infectious diseases. Epidemics became more common and virulent. Paradoxically, with greater productivity, only a small percentage have had the privilege of a decent diet and the pleasures of civilization. In the meantime, the cost of high productivity and the impact of billions of people on the habitats of the earth are causing a noticeable strain. The problem is not so much one of numbers but of ecological stewardship and global economy. To wave the threat of 'overpopulation', or continue to reiterate the pro-birth policies encoded in early agrarian state ideologies, is short-sighted (Hern 1990). Nine months after Hitler came to power in 1934, his ruthless suppression of abortion led to a sudden rise of birth rate at 4 points per 1,000 (Pressat 1971: 116). Policies that still adhere to a view of having more people as a means of increasing state power and the labour force ignore the economics and politics of the present. The population dilemma lies today in the divergence between the objectives of the state and the family. In addition, there is a legacy of a pronatalist ethos that has victimized women in the past. Ironically, women were valued only as 'mothers'. Women are also caught in the cycle of poverty related to population growth. Greater demands on natural resources lead to environmental degradation, which leads the poor to depend on child labour to maintain a living; this contributes to population growth, which in turn contributes to greater poverty (Dasgupta 1995).

Industrialization benefiting from the colonial possessions not only created an array of desirable consumer goods but also more effective means of increasing agricultural yield. Either in order to improve one's station in life, or to evade punishment or murder, more children were procured to fuel the industrial machine. Most of this increase was not a result of better health conditions, but primarily a consequence of reducing or eliminating cultural population controls. Where health 'improvements' were made, they were mostly in reducing infant mortality. Many women in many Third World countries still die at a tender age as did their grandmothers hundreds of years ago.

In attempting to piece together the demographic past of humanity, archaeologists highlight our modern predicament and lead us to question pet theories and sacrosanct beliefs shaped by our modern historical experiences. We may not be able to make any valid long-term projections, since the trends of demographic change are non-linear or predictable, but we can gauge the role of various forces that shape the demographic landscape. We have never been at the mercy of nature from the day we generated a spark of fire, and our ingenuity as a species has been remarkable. Archaeological insights into our common demographic past provide a corrective to our stereotypical view of the 'nasty, brutish and short' lives of our ancestors and an antidote to our short-sighted view of population dynamics from recent historical contexts.

ACKNOWLEDGEMENTS

I am indebted to all my colleagues who have laboured to bring a better understanding of the demography of pre-industrial and non-industrial nations, and who still struggle to find appropriate methods for the study of this unwieldy subject. I am particularly grateful to those who have shared and challenged their ideas. The list is too long, but I wish to mention J. L. Angel, Steve Polgar, Mark Cohen, Marvin Harris, Warren Hern and B. Chiarrili. I am also thankful to Teri L. Tucker and Dido Clark for their help in shaping the final version of this work.

REFERENCES

Acsádi, G.-Y. and Nemeskéri, J. (1957) 'Paläodemographische probleme am biespiel des frühmittelichen Gräberfeldes von Halimba-Cseres, Kom. Veszpréml Ungarn', *Homo* 8: 133–37.

Acsádi, G.-Y. and Nemeskéri, J. (1970) *History of Human Life Span and Mortality*, Budapest: Akademia Kiado.

Ammerman, A. J. and Cavalli-Sforza, L. L. (1984) *The Neolithic Transition and the Genetics of Population in Europe*, Princeton, N.J.: Princeton University Press.

Angel, J. L. (1972) 'Ecology and population in the eastern Mediterranean', *World Archaeology* 4: 88–105.

Angel, J. L. (1975) 'Paleoecology, paleodemography and health', in S. Polgar (ed) *Population, Ecology and Social Change*, The Hague: Mouton: 167–90.

Barrett, J. C. (1972) 'A Monte Carlo simulation of reproduction', in W. Brass (ed.) *Biological Aspects of Demography*, London: Taylor and Francis: 11–30.

Binford, L. R. (1968) 'Post-Pleistocene adaptations', in S. R. Binford and L. R. Binford (eds) *New Perspectives in Archeology*, New York: Aldine: 313–41.

Birdsell, J. B. (1972) *Human Evolution*, Chicago: Rand McNally.

Blanton, R. E. (1972) 'Prehispanic adaptation in Ixtapalapa', *Science* 175: 515–18.

Blanton, R. E., Kowalewski, S. E., Feinman, G. M. and Finsten, L. M. (1981) *Ancient Mesoamerica: a Comparison of Change in Three Regions*, New York: Cambridge University Press.

Blumler, M. A. (1996) 'Ecology, evolutionary theory and agricultural origins', in D. Harris (ed.) *The Origins and Spread of Agriculture and Pastoralism in Eurasia*, London: University College London Press: 25–50.

Bocquet-Appel, J.-P. and Masset, C. (1982) 'Farewell to paleodemography', *Journal of Human Evolution* 11: 321–33.

Boserup, E. (1965) *The Conditions of Agricultural Growth*, London: Allen and Unwin.

Broshi, M. (1975) 'La population de l'ancienne Jérusalem', *Revue Biblique* 82: 5–14.

Broshi, M. (1979) 'The population of Western Palestine in the Roman-Byzantine period', *Bulletin of the American Schools of Oriental Research* 236: 1–10.

Brothwell, D. R. (1971) 'Paleodemography', in W. Brass (ed.) *Biological Aspects of Demography*, London: Taylor and Francis: 111–30.

Brown, J. (1995) 'On mortuary analysis – with specific reference to the Saxe–Binford research program', in L. A. Beck (ed.) *Regional Approaches to Mortuary Analysis*, New York: Plenum Press: 3–26.

Buikstra, J., Konigsberg, L. and Bullington, J. (1986) 'Fertility and the development of agriculture in the Prehistoric Midwest', *American Antiquity* 51: 528–46.

Carneiro, R. L. and Hilse, D. (1966) 'On determining the probable rate of population growth during the Neolithic', *American Antropologist* 68 (1): 179–81.

Carr-Saunders, A. M. (1922) *The Population Problem*, London: Oxford University Press.

Cashdan, E. A. (1985) 'Natural fertility, birth spacing, and the "First Demographic Transition"', *American Anthropologist*: 87: 651–56.

Cassen, R. (1994) *Population and Development: Old Debates, New Conclusions*, Oxford: Transactions Publishers.

Cavalli-Sforza, L. L. (1994) *The History and Geography of Human Genes*, Princeton, N.J.: Princeton University Press.

Cavalli-Sforza, L. L. (1996) 'The spread of agriculture and nomadic pastoralism: insights from genetics, linguistics and archaeology', in D. Harris (ed.) *The Origins and Spread of Agriculture and Pastoralism in Eurasia*, London: University College London Press: 51–59.

Cavalli-Sforza, L. L., Mennozzi, P. and Piazza, A. (1994) *The History and Geography of Princeton (NJ)*, Princeton, N.J.: Princeton University Press.

Chapman, J. (1988) 'Putting pressures in population: social alternatives to Malthus and Boserup', in J. L. Blintliff and G. Davidson (eds.) *Conceptual Issues in Environmental Archaeology*, Edinburgh: Edinburgh University Press: 291–300.

Chappell, J., Head, J. and Magee, J. (1996) 'Beyond the radiocarbon limit in Australian archaeology and Quaternary Research', *Antiquity* 70: 543–52.

Childe, V. G. (1936) *Man Makes Himself*, London: Watts.

Cohen, J. E. (1995) *How Many People Can The Earth Support?*, New York: Norton and Company.

Cohen, M. (1977) *The Food Crisis in Prehistory*, New Haven: Yale University Press.

Cohen, M. (1989) *Health and the Rise of Civilization*, New Haven: Yale University Press.

Cohen, M. (1995) 'Prehistoric patterns of hunger', in L. F. Newman (ed.) *Hunger in History*, Oxford: Blackwell: 56–97.

Cohen, M. and Armelagos, G. (eds) (1984) *Paleopathology at the Origins of Agriculture*, Orlando: Academic Press: 56–97.

Conrad, G. W. and Demarest, A. A. (1984) *Religion and Empire: The Dynamics of Aztec and Inca Expansion*, Cambridge: Cambridge University Press.

Constandse-Westermann, T. S. and Newell, R. R. (1984) 'Human biological background of population dynamics in the western European Mesolithic', *Proceedings of the Koninklijke Nederlandse Akademie van Wetenschappen*, Series B, 87 (2): 139–223.

Cook, S. F. (1972) *Prehistoric Demography*, McCaleb Module in Anthropology, Reading, Mass.: Addison-Wesley.

Cornell, T. J. (1995) *The Beginnings of Rome*, London: Routledge.

Cowan, M. and Watson, P. J. (1992) *Origins of Agriculture*, Washington, DC: Smithsonian Institution Press.

Cowgill, G. (1975) 'Population pressure as a non-explanation', in A. C. Swedlund (ed.) *Population Studies in Archaeology and Biological Anthropology*, Society for American Archaeology, Memoir No. 30, *American Antiquity* 40 (2): 127–31.

Dasgupta, P. S. (1995) 'Population, poverty and the local environment', *Scientific American*, February: 26–31.

Deevey, E. S. (1960) 'The human population', *Scientific American* 203: 195–204.

Dennell, R. and Roebroeks, W. (1996) 'The earliest colonization of Europe: the short chronology revisited', *Antiquity* 70: 535–42.

Dewar, R. E. (1984) 'Environmental productivity, population regulation, and carrying capacity', *American Anthropologist* 86: 601–13.

Divale, D. J. (1972) 'Systematic population control in the Middle Palaeolithic and Upper Palaeolithic: inferences based on contemporary hunter-gatherers', *World Archaeology* 4 (2): 222–37.

Dyke, B. and MacCluer, J. (1975) *Computer Simulation in Human Population Studies*, New York: Academic Press.

Eckhardt, W. (1992) *Civilizations, Empires, and Wars: A Quantitative History of War*, Jefferson, N.C.: McFarland.

Evison, M. P. (1996) 'Genetics, ethics, and archeology', *Antiquity* 70: 512–14.

Gage, T. B. and Mode, C. (1993) 'Some laws of mortality: how well do they fit?', *Human Biology* 65: 445–61.

Gasse, F. and van Campo, E. (1994) 'Abrupt post-glacial climate events in West Asia and North Africa monsoon domains', *Earth and Planetary Science Letters* 1256: 435–36.

Groube, L. (1996) 'The impact of diseases upon the emergence of agriculture', in D. Harris (ed.) *The Origins and Spread of Agriculture and Pastoralism in Eurasia*, London: University College London Press: 101–40.

Handwerker, W. (1983) 'The first demographic transition: an analysis of subsistence choices and reproductive consequences', *American Anthropologist* 85: 5–27.

Harpending, H. (1976) 'Regional variation in !Kung populations', in R. B. Lee and I. DeVore (eds) *Kalahari Hunter-Gatherers*, Cambridge, Mass.: Harvard University Press: 241–55.

Harpending, H., Draper, P. and Pennington, R. (1990) 'Cultural evolution, parental care, and mortality', in A. Swedlund and G. Armelagos (eds) *Health and Disease in Transitional Societies*, South Hadley, Mass.: Bergin and Garvey: 241–55.

Harris, D. (1977) 'Alternative pathways towards agriculture', in C. Reed (ed.) *Origins of Agriculture*, The Hague: Mouton: 179–243.

Harris, D. (ed.) (1996a) *The Origins and Spread of Agriculture and Pastoralism in Eurasia*, London: University College London Press.

Harris, D. (1996b) 'Introduction: themes and concepts in the study of early agriculture', in D. Harris (ed.) *The Origins and Spread of Agriculture and Pastoralism in Eurasia*, London: University College London Press: 1–9.

Harris, D. (1996c) 'The origins and spread of agriculture and pastoralism in Eurasia: an overview', in D. Harris (ed.) *The Origins and Spread of Agriculture and Pastoralism in Eurasia*, London: University College London Press: 557–73.

Harris, M. and Ross, E. B. (1987) *Death, Sex, and Fertility: Population Regulation in Preindustrial and Developing Societies*, New York: Columbia University Press.

Hassan, F. A. (1977) 'The dynamics of agricultural origins in Palestine: a theoretical model', in C. Reed (ed.) *Agricultural Origins*, The Hague: Mouton: 589–609.

Hassan, F. A. (1981) *Demographic Archaeology*, New York: Academic Press.

Hassan, F. A. (1993) 'Town and village in ancient Egypt: ecology, society and urbanization', in T. Shaw, P. Sinclair, B. Andah and A. Okpoko (eds) *The Archaeology of Africa: Food, Metals and Towns*, London: Routledge: 551–69.

Hassan, F. A. (1996) 'Abrupt Holocene climatic events in Africa', *Proceedings of the 10th Congress of the Pan African Association for Prehistory and Related Studies, Harare*: 83–89.

709

Hayden, B. (1975) 'The carrying capacity dilemma', in A. C. Swedlund (ed.) *Population Studies in Archaeology and Physical Anthropology*, Society for American Archaeology, Memoir No. 30, *American Antiquity* 40 (2), Part 2: 11–21.

Haynes, C. V. Jr. (1969) 'The earliest Americans', *Science* 166: 709–15.

Henry, D. O. (1989) *From Foraging to Agriculture: the Levant at the End of the Ice Age*, Philadelphia: University of Pennsylvania Press.

Herbert, D. T. and Thomas, C. J. (1990) *Cities in Space, City as Place*, London: David Fulton Publishers.

Hern, W. M. (1990) 'The politics of choice: abortion as insurrection', in W. P. Handwerker (ed.) *Births and Power: Social Change and the Politics of Reproduction*, Boulder: Westview Press: 127–45.

Hillman, G. (1996) 'Late Pleistocene changes in wild plant-foods available to hunter-gatherers of the northern Fertile Crescent: possible prelude to cereal cultivation', in D. Harris (ed.) *The Origins and Spread of Agriculture and Pastoralism in Eurasia*, London: University College London Press: 159–203.

Hoffman, L. W. and Hoffman, M. L. (1973) 'The value of children to parents', in J. W. Fawcett (ed.) *Psychological Perspectives on Population*, New York: Basic Books:

Horowitz, S., Armelagos, G. and Wachter, K. (1988) 'On generating birthrates from skeletal populations', *American Journal of Physical Anthropology* 76: 189–96.

Howell, N. (1973) 'The feasibility of demographic studies in "anthropological" populations', in M. Crawford and P. Workman (eds.) *Methods and Theories of Anthropological Genetics*, Albuquerque: University of New Mexico: 249–62.

Howell, N. (1976) 'Toward a uniformitarian theory of human paleodemography', *Journal of Human Evolution* 5: 25–40.

Howell, N. (1979) *Demography of the Dobe !Kung*, New York: Academic Press.

Howell, N. (1986) 'Demographic anthropology', *Annual Review of Anthropology* 15: 219–46.

Howell, N. (1992) 'Village composition implied by a paleodemographic life table: the Libben Site', *American Journal of Physical Anthropology* 59: 263–69.

Howells, W. W. (1960) 'Estimating population numbers through archaeological and skeletal remains', in R. F. Heizer and S. F. Cook (eds) *The Application of Quantitative Methods in Archaeology*, Viking Fund Publications in Anthropology No. 28, Chicago: Quadrangle Books: 158–59.

Jackes, M. (1992) 'Paleodemography: problems and techniques', in S. R. Saunders and M. A. Katzenberg (eds) *Skeletal Biology of Past Peoples: Research Methods*, New York: Wiley–Liss: 189–224.

Jaffe, A. J. (1992) *The First Immigrants from Asia: A Population History of the North American Indians*, New York: Plenum Press.

Johansson, S. R. and Horowitz, S. (1986) 'Estimating mortality in skeletal populations. Influence of the growth rate upon the interpretation of levels and trends during the transition to agriculture', *American Journal of Physical Anthropology* 71: 233–50.

Jorde, L. B. and Harpending, H. C. (1976) 'Cross-cultural analysis of rainfall and human birth rates: an empirical test of a linear model', in R. H. Ward and K. M. Weiss (eds) *The Demographic Evolution of Human Populations*, New York: Academic Press: 128–38.

Kemp, B. J. (1981) 'The character of the south suburb at Tell el-'Amãrna', *Meteillungen der Deutschen Orient-Gesellschaft zu Berlin* 113: 81–97.

Kent, S. (1987) 'The influence of sedentism and aggregation on porotic hyperstosis and anaemia: a case study', *Man* (N.S.) 21: 605–36.

Klein, R. (1989) *The Human Career, Human Biological and Cultural Origins*, Chicago: University of Chicago Press.

Konigsberg, L. W. and Frankenberg, S. R. (1992) 'Estimation of age structure in anthropological demography', *American Journal of Physical Anthropology* 89: 235–56.

Konigsberg, L. W. and Frankenberg, S. R. (1994) 'Paleodemography. "Not quite dead"', *Evolutionary Ecology* 3: 92–105.

Kremer, M. (1993) 'Population growth and technological change: one million BC to 1990', *Quarterly Journal of Economics* 108 (3): 32–35.

Livi-Bacci, M. (1992) *A Concise History of World Population* (translated by Carl Ibsen), Oxford: Blackwell.

McCorrison, J. and Hole, F. (1991) 'The ecology of seasonal stress and the origins of agriculture in the Near East', *American Anthropologist* 93: 46–69.

Mangel, M. and Tier, C. (1993) 'Dynamics of metapopulations with demographic stochasticity and environmental catastrophes', *Theoretical Population Biology* 44 (1): 1–31.

Matthews, R. D., Anderson, R., Chen, S. and Webb, T. (1995) 'Global climate and the origins of agriculture', in L. F. Newman (ed.) *Hunger in History: Food Shortage, Poverty, and Deprivation*, Oxford: Blackwell: 27–55.

May, R. M. (1976) 'Simple mathematical models with very complicated dynamics', *Nature* 261: 459–67.

Nag, M. (1962) *Factors Affecting Fertility in Non-industrial Societies: a Cross-Cultural Study*, New Haven, Conn.: Human Relations Area Files Press.

Newell, C. (1989) *Methods and Models in Demography*, Chichester: Wiley

Nurge, E. (1973) 'Abortion in the Pleistocene', Paper presented at the Ninth Congress of Anthropological and Ethnological Sciences, Chicago.

Pennington, R. L. (1996) 'Causes of early human population growth', *American Journal of Physical Anthropology* 99 (2): 259–74.

Peters, G. L. and Larkin, R. P. (1979) *Population Geography*, Dubuque, Ia.: Kendall/Hunt.

Piggott, S. (1950) *Prehistoric India*, Harmondsworth: Penguin Books.

Pressat, R. (1971) *Population*, Baltimore: Penguin Books.

Pressat, R. (1972) *Demographic Analysis*, Chicago: Aldine.

Renfrew, C. (1996) 'Language families and the spread of farming', in D. Harris (ed.) *The Origins and Spread of Agriculture and Pastoralism in Eurasia*, London: University College London Press: 70–92.

Rice, D. S. and Culbert, T. P. (eds) (1990) *Precolumbian Population History in Maya Lowlands*, Albuquerque: University of New Mexico Press.

Rindos, D. (1984) *The Origins of Agriculture: An Evolutionary Perspective*, Orlando, Fla.: Academic Press.

Roche, D. (1983) 'Population estimates from settlement area and number of residences', *Journal of Field Archaeology* 10: 187–92.

Roebroeks, W. and van Kolfschoten, T. (eds) (1995) *The Earliest Occupation of Europe. Proceedings of the European Science Foundation Workshop at Tautvel (France), 1993*, Leiden: Leiden University Press.

Roth, E. A. (1992) 'Applications of demographic models to paleodemography', in S. R. Saunders and M. A. Katzenberg (eds) *Skeletal Biology of Past Peoples: Research Methods*, New York: Wiley–Liss: 175–88.

Roth, E. A., Ray, A. K. and Mohanty, B. (1984) 'Computer simulation of an Indian tribal population', *Current Anthropology* 25: 347–49.

Russell, J. C. (1958) 'Late ancient and medieval population', *Transactions of the American Philosophical Society* 48 (3): 1–152.

Sanderson, S. K. (1995) *Social Transformations: a General Theory of Historical Development*, Oxford: Blackwell.

Sattenspiel, L. and Harpending, H. (1983) 'Stable populations and skeletal age', *American Antiquity* 48: 489–98.

Saunders, S. R., Fitzgerald, C., Rogers, T., Dunbar, C. and McKillop, H. (1992) 'A test of several methods of skeletal age estimation using a documented archaeological sample', *Canadian Society of Forensic Sciences Journal* 25: 97–117.

Schlanger, S. (1988) 'Patterns of population movement and long-term population growth rates in southwestern Colorado', *American Antiquity* 53: 773–93.

Schlanger, S. and Wilhusen, R. W. (1990) 'Local abandonments and regional conditions in the North American Southwest', in C. Cameron and S. Tomka (eds) *The Abandonment of Settlements and Regions: Ethnoarchaeological and Archaeological Approaches*, Cambridge: Cambridge University Press: 85–98.

Sjoberg, G. (1960) *The Preindustrial City: Past and Present*, Glencoe, Ill.: Free Press.

Spooner, R. (ed.) (1972) *Population Growth; Anthropological Implications*, Cambridge, Mass.: MIT Press.

Storey, R. (1992) *Life and Death in the Ancient City of Teotihuacan: A Modern Paleodemographic Synthesis*, Tuscaloosa: University of Alabama Press.

Sumner, W. M. (1989) 'Population and settlement area: an example from Iran', *American Anthropologist* 91: 631–41.

Sussman, R. W. (1972) 'Child transport, family size, and increase in human population during the Neolithic', *Current Anthropology* 13: 258–59.

Swedlund, A. C. and Armelagos, G. J. (1976) *Demographic Anthropology*, Dubuque, Ia.: Wm. C. Brown Company.

Taagepera, R. (1978) 'Size and duration of empires: systematics of size', *Social Science Research* 7: 108–27.

Tainter, J. A. (1988) *The Collapse of Complex Societies*, New York: Cambridge University Press.

Taylor, R. E., Vance Haynes, C. Jr. and Stuiver, M. (1996) 'Clovis and Folsom age estimates: stratigraphic context and radiocarbon calibration', *Antiquity* 70: 515–25.

Thomlinson, R. (1965) *Population Dynamics*, New York: Random House.

Trevathan, W. (1987) *Human Birth: an Evolutionary Perspective*, New York: Aldine.

Trinkhaus, E. and Tompkins, R. L. (1990) 'The Neanderthal life cycle: the possibility, probability, and perceptibility of contrasts with recent humans', in C. J. DeRousseau (ed.) *Primate Life History and Evolution*, Monographs in Primatology 14, New York: Wiley and Sons: 153–89.

Ubelaker, D. (1984) 'Prehistoric human biology of Ecuador: possible temporal trends and cultural correlations', in M. Cohen and G. Armelagos (eds) *Paleopathology at the Origins of Agriculture*, Orlando, Fla.: Academic Press: 491–513.

Vallois, H. V. (1960) 'Vital statistics in prehistoric population as determined from archaeological data. Quantitative methods in archaeology', in R. F. Heizer and S. F. Cook (eds) *The Application of Quantitative Methods in Archaeology*, Viking Fund Publications in Anthropology No. 28, Chicago: Quadrangle Books: 186–222.

van Andel, Tjeerd H. and Runnels, C. N. (1995) 'The earliest farmers in Europe', *Antiquity* 69: 481–500.

Webb, S. (1995) *Palaeopathology of Aboriginal Australians: Health and Disease across a Hunter-Gatherer Continent*, Cambridge: Cambridge University Press.

Weinstein, J. A. (1976) *Demographic Transitions and Social Change*, Morristown, N.J.: General Learning Press.

Weiss, K. M. (1973) *Demographic Models for Anthropology*, Society for American Archeology, Memoir No. 27, *American Antiquity* 38 (2), Part 2.

Weiss, K. M. (1976) 'Demographic theory and anthropological inference', *Annual Review of Anthropology* 5: 351–81.

Weiss, K. M. and Smouse, P. E. (1976) 'The demographic stability of small human populations', in R. H. Ward and K. M. Weiss (eds) *The Demographic Evolution of Human Populations*, New York: Academic Press: 59–73.

Welinder, S. (1979) *Prehistoric Demography*, Lund: Acta Archaeologica Lundensia.

Wobst, H. M. (1974) 'Boundary conditions for palaeolithic social systems: a simulation approach', *American Antiquity* 39 (2): 147–78.

Wolf, E. R. (1982) *Europe and the People without History*, Berkeley: University of California Press.

Wood, J. W. (1990) 'Fertility in anthropological populations', *Annual Review of Anthropology* 19: 211–42.

Wood, J. W., Milner, G. R., Harpending, H. C. and Weiss, K. M. (1992) 'The osteological paradox. Problems of inferring prehistoric health from skeletal samples', *Current Anthropology* 33 (4): 343–70.

Wrigley, E. A. (1971) *Population and History*, New York: McGraw-Hill.

Zelinsky, W. (1979) 'The demographic transition: changing patterns of migration', in IUSSP, *Population Science in the Service of Mankind*, Liège: Ordina.

Zorn, J. R. (1994) 'Estimating the population size of ancient settlements: methods, problems, solutions and a case study', *Bulletin of the American School of Oriental Research* 295: 31–48.

SELECT BIBLIOGRAPHY

Basic palaeodemographic approaches are well presented in the classic work by Acsádi and Nemeskéri (1970). Pressat (1972) and Newell (1989) provide the fundamental principles of formal demographic analysis. Howell (1986) gives a useful review of anthropological demography. Cohen's *Health and the Rise of Civilization* (1989) is a readable, exhaustive survey of the relations between diet, disease and population. *Demographic Archaeology* (Hassan 1981) presents a comprehensive approach to population studies in archaeology with an exposition of palaeodemographic and archaeological methods, as well as explanations of the role of population dynamics in culture change. Swedlund and Armelagos (1976) is an excellent, brief introduction to demographic processes, demographic studies in anthropology, and palaeodemographic studies. The field of demographic anthropology is also reviewed by Howell (1986), who discusses methodological as well as theoretical issues, and presents an overview of population problems in archaeology.

18

COGNITION
Thought, ideas and belief

Steven Mithen and Nigel Spivey

INTRODUCTION

Just as we wish to know how people lived in the past, we also wish to know what they thought, and how they thought. Indeed, it is difficult to address questions of subsistence, trade and social organization without some understanding of the manner in which people in the past viewed their world. While archaeologists have long asked such questions, the late 1980s saw a concerted move towards the development of a 'cognitive archaeology' (Renfrew 1982; Renfrew and Zubrow 1994). This cannot boast the theoretical and field studies which developed from the move towards a 'social archaeology' twenty years previously, but its consequences for the discipline are likely to be as profound. At present, however, cognitive archaeology is a rather disparate body of work, varying markedly in its content and approaches. This is understandable, since trying to infer the nature and contents of, for example, the minds of prehistoric people from the stone tools, broken bones and potsherds of the archaeological record is certainly a daunting, optimistic, and some might say foolhardy task. And even if such inference seems successful, what results might it yield when carried over into a literate era of history – when, arguably, a cognitive record has been in some way directly inscribed or 'scripted'? Undaunted, this chapter sketches the nature of cognitive archaeology for two very different time periods, with very different databases: the Palaeolithic, and classical Greece.

For early prehistory, during which the archaeological record monitors not only cultural but also biological evolution, the major concern of a cognitive archaeology must be with the evolution of the human mind: when did the architecture of the modern mind evolve? This question has to be addressed with the often sparse data from the palaeolithic record, dominated by stone tools and, in the later Palaeolithic, faunal assemblages. For later prehistory, the focus shifts to how cognitive architecture – uniform in its essence across all living people – has led to the development of different concepts and ways of viewing the world. Ideology becomes a central concern: how different ideologies develop and their role in social, economic and political organization (Miller and Tilley 1984). The study of human burial plays a major role in this, partly due to the dominance of the burial record during many periods of later prehistory and its direct connection with past ideology (Hodder 1982; Shanks and Tilley 1982; Thomas 1988). These studies, which must be embraced within a cognitive archaeology, have been termed symbolic and structural archaeology and have formed a major part of the post-processual critique (Hodder 1982, 1990). Another example of relevant research in later prehistory is Bradley's work on the relationship between rock art and the perception of landscape in Britain (Bradley 1991).

Not surprisingly, the character of cognitive archaeology changes significantly when we are dealing with periods for which we have written documents as well as material remains. The significance of written records in changing the nature of cognitive archaeology can be seen in the study of hunter-gatherer rock art. When an ethnohistorical record of the mythology and social organization of a hunter-gatherer group is available, archaeologists are able to make very detailed interpretations of rock art traditions, as for instance in Australia (Haskovec and Sullivan 1989; Morphy 1989) and southern Africa (Lewis-Williams 1982). These show how many of the images in these traditions have complex interpretations and intimate links with ideology and a symbolic construction of the world. However, when similar interpretations are imposed upon prehistoric art, the results are unconvincing, such as the claim that many abstract marks in upper palaeolithic art are 'entoptic' phenomena seen by shamans in a state of trance (Lewis-Williams and Dowson 1988). A cognitive approach to prehistoric art clearly has to take on a different guise, not inferior to that when ethnographic data is available, but simply different.

The roots of cognitive archaeology lie both within and outside the discipline. With respect to the former it arises from the failure of the processual archaeology of the 1970s to address cognitive issues, and indeed its inability to do so due to the constraints of theory and method it imposed upon itself (see Chapter 2). Equally, however, it has arisen from the failure of the post-processual critique: while this pointed to a series of important failings in processual archaeology, such as its lack of concern with individual action, symbols and historical process (Hodder 1985), it failed to provide an alternative that maintained a credible 'scientific' approach, becoming dominated by an unrestrained subjectivity lacking a concern to connect theory with data (for example, Shanks and Tilley 1987). Cognitive archaeology seeks to maintain the scientific credibility of processual archaeology, while addressing issues of cognition and symbolic behaviour as had been raised by the post-processualists.

It is no coincidence that the development of cognitive archaeology has occurred at a time when related disciplines have also become more concerned with cognition. There has been much renewed interest in the issues of language, consciousness, and creativity in psychology and philosophy in recent years, partly stimulated by the development of artificial intelligence (Boden 1990; Corballis 1992; Dennett 1992; Donald 1991). Indeed, it is only in the past two decades that the discipline of cognitive science has arisen (Gardner 1987) and the impact of this is being felt through many disciplines. Cognition is beginning to play a more prominent role in the study of animal behaviour, often with an implicit goal of contributing to our understanding of human cognition (Bryne and Whitten 1988; Cheney and Seyfarth 1990; Griffin 1981, 1982; Humphrey 1976). More recently a distinct sub-discipline of 'evolutionary psychology' has emerged (Barkow *et al.* 1992). This makes explicit reference to the Pleistocene environments within which the human mind evolved. Significant progress on understanding the modern mind is likely to arise from an integration of this 'evolutionary psychology' and 'cognitive archaeology', as has been attempted by Mithen (1996). What is readily apparent, however, is that the emergence of a cognitive archaeology is part of a multidisciplinary trend to address the nature of the human mind, rather than just a particular sub-area of the discipline of archaeology.

THE EVOLUTION OF THE HUMAN MIND: PRE-MODERN HUMANS

Language, intelligence, and consciousness are frequently invoked to differentiate humans from other animal species. None of these is easy to define and each is (arguably) represented in many animal species, particularly primates. In humans, however, these cognitive processes are extraordinarily complex and intertwined: they may be different in kind, rather than degree, to those found in other species.

Before we consider the archaeology, it is important to establish that we should not see the evolution of the human mind as an upwardly progressive process beginning with the proverbial Neanderthal incapable of thought and ending in the supposed cognitive pinnacle of our fine minds of today. There is a great temptation to see the cognition of early hominid species as *inferior* versions of our own. This is a mistaken approach: comparative psychology has demonstrated that intelligence is a multivariate phenomenon. Some bird species, for example, can perform specific cognitive feats which are far beyond the capacity of primates, humans included. Cognition, just as much as physiology, should be seen as fitting an organism for a particular way of life, and, while inter-specific comparisons can be made, value judgements are of limited worth. However, while we should avoid seeing the minds

716

of our hominid ancestors as simply watered-down versions of our own, we can nevertheless assume that an evolutionary pathway exists. Evolution works by building upon existing structures: indeed, some argue that we can see in the modern mind vestiges of the distinctive cognitive processes of our ancestors (for example, Donald 1991).

A second important point is that, when we talk about the evolution of the human mind, it is unclear what this means. There are two schools of thought on this issue. One might be called the 'big bang' school, in that they see the mind as one general-purpose information processor, with intimate connections between all the distinctly human cognitive processes (for example, Piaget 1960). The other might be termed the 'cognitive creep' school: this views the mind as a series of modules, each evolved for a specific task (for example, Cosmides and Tooby 1987), or for there to be different types of intelligences, such as those for language, mathematics and music (Gardner 1983). This views the mind not as a 'general-purpose computer' but as having evolved to solve a specific suite of problems faced by hominids in their evolutionary environments. Others take a mixture of these approaches: Fodor (1983), for example, sees a general-purpose central system, but with a series of 'encapsulated' input or perceptual processes. One implication of modular approaches is that different aspects of the human mind are likely to have evolved at different times. As this chapter describes, the archaeological data from the Palaeolithic appears to provide greater support to the gradual creep rather than big bang theory of cognitive evolution.

The fossil evidence provides limited information concerning the evolution of the human mind. The most useful is that concerning brain enlargement, which has been a continuous process during human evolution (Stringer 1984). Two points should be noted. First, while brain size among mammals is related to body size, the enlargement in the hominid brain outstrips that which can be accounted for by increasing body size alone (Martin 1983). Second, the major phase of brain enlargement occurred early in human evolution: *Homo erectus*, appearing at *c.* 1.8 million years ago (hereafter MYA), had a cranial capacity that was 80 per cent that of modern humans. However, while the fossil record allows us to trace the expansion, and to some extent the structure, of the hominid brain, we need to turn to the archaeological record to speculate upon the character of hominid minds. For our early ancestors this record is dominated by stone tools. Drawing inferences about prehistoric cognition from such material is fraught with difficulties, and few specialists agree about the implications of particular industrial traditions (e.g. Dibble 1989; Gowlett 1984). Some of the most controversial data are the earliest, the lower Pleistocene stone industries from East Africa which first appear at *c.* 2.5 MYA.

Oldowan technology: ape, human or neither?

The most important assemblages of these early stone tools come from Beds I and II at Olduvai Gorge and were termed by Mary Leakey (1971) 'the Oldowan Industry'. It is generally assumed that these artefacts were manufactured by *Homo habilis*, although there is no reason why contemporary australopithecine species may not also have been tool-makers (Susman 1991; and see also Chapter 20). Oldowan artefacts, and those of similar date from Koobi Fora and Shungura (Isaac 1984), are usually simple 'tools' resulting from direct percussion on basalt, quartz and limestone (Fig. 18.1).

A critical issue is whether 'types' are present within the Oldowan, and if they are, how they should be interpreted. Archaeologists use the notion of type to refer to an artefact that has been made to a distinct pattern. The existence of types is often taken to imply the ability to form mental templates which may, in turn, imply abilities to form linguistic categories. Similarly the presence of types has been taken to suggest an ability to share mental concepts between individuals, again implying that language may be present (Chase 1991). Mary Leakey suggested that 'types' did exist within the Oldowan, and used terms such as choppers, discoids and polyhedrons to describe recurring artefact morphologies (Leakey 1971).

However, experimental knapping has challenged this view by showing that the recurring artefact shapes arise due to two principal factors: the shape of the original nodule and the intensity of the flaking (Potts 1988; Toth 1985); much of the variability was also due to the effects of the raw material used (Isaac 1984; Stiles 1991; Toth 1985). The 'types' Leakey identified were a product of archaeological classification rather than intended products of hominid stone knappers. In this light, it has been argued that the cognitive processes implicated by Oldowan artefacts are equivalent to those employed by chimpanzees when they produce tools such as

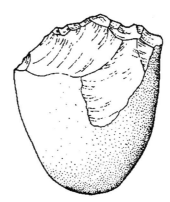

Figure 18.1 Oldowan chopper, the classic tool made by *H. habilis*, produced by removing one or more flakes from a single face of a basalt nodule. Source: S. Mithen 1996.

718

termite sticks (Wynn and McGrew 1989). However, this extreme position probably underestimates the level of technical skill and consequently the required cognitive processes required to coordinate perception and motor actions in stone knapping (Gowlett 1986).

The artefacts themselves may not be the most informative source of data about hominid cognition. The distribution of artefacts in the early Pleistocene landscapes suggests behaviour and thought which are different from those observed or inferred among modern apes. At many East African sites there is evidence that raw materials were transported substantial distances before they were knapped and discarded (Hay 1976; Isaac 1978, 1984; Leakey 1971). The comparison between experimentally knapped and real lithic assemblages has shown that partially worked cores were also transported around the landscape (Toth 1985). The Olduvai sites are particularly interesting in this respect, since they indicate that different types of raw material were transported over different distances.

Artefact transport over such distances has not been observed in any non-human primate: the furthest chimpanzees appear to transport stone artefacts is 500 metres (Boesch and Boesch 1983). Potts (1988) has argued that much of this artefact transport, particularly of unworked nodules, was to create stone tool caches to use when scavenging carcasses – occasions when ready access to sharp flakes would have been essential to minimize exposure time to competing scavengers such as hyenas. Consequently, while the manufacture of Oldowan tools may have required cognitive processes no different to those possessed by modern apes, the manner in which these tools were used may reflect a different, perhaps more human, type of cognition, indicating that hominids were engaged in considerable planning of subsistence activities involving the anticipation of the future use of tools.

Homo erectus and the Acheulian

At *c.* 1.4 MYA a new artefact form appears in the archaeological record – the handaxe: bifacially worked implements, often pear-shaped in form, often finished by a series of very fine thinning flakes (Fig. 18.2). They form the central element of Acheulian industries found not only in Africa but also in large parts of Europe and Asia, indicating that *Homo erectus* was the first hominid to disperse out of Africa. Though mainly associated with *H. erectus*, they continued to be manufactured and used by archaic *H. sapiens*, such as Neanderthals, down to 40,000 or so years ago.

Adapting the theories of Piaget regarding the mental development of children, Wynn (1989) has argued that the appearance of these bifaces indicates a much more 'human-like' cognition than the Oldowan industries. Piaget identified a series of cognitive stages in children from sensiormotor to pre-operational to operational thought. Wynn suggested that, as Oldowan artefacts display the minimum degree

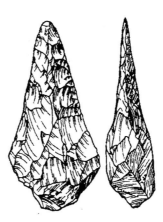

Figure 18.2 Acheulian handaxe. Handaxes first appeared 1.4 million years ago, and up until 100,000 years ago are found very widely in Africa, Asia and Europe. They come in all shapes and sizes, but frequently have a highly symmetrical form, clearly implying the existence of a mental template in the mind of the knapper and requiring considerable planning in their execution. Source: S. Mithen 1996.

of spatial competence, their makers had only reached the cognitive level of pre-operational thought, as possessed by young children and apes; by contrast, the symmetry of early bifaces, and the fact that flake removal was often geared to the production of an end product, indicated to him more advanced spatial competence, implying an early stage of operational thought, substantially different to those of apes. He further argued that by 300,000 years ago bifaces display additional spatial concepts which suggest that fully modern operational thought had developed. The most important feature of the later Acheulian bifaces, according to Wynn, is their symmetry in three dimensions; the removal of each flake had to maintain symmetry in all three dimensions, a complex cognitive and motor action task.

Wynn's analysis of bifaces is elegant, and his conclusion that fully modern thought had arisen by 300,000 years ago provocative, but the content and value of this conclusion are highly questionable. His analysis is built on the notion that ontogeny recapitulates phylogeny, which can be held with little confidence (Gould 1977), whilst Piaget's scheme is solely descriptive and does not engage with a Darwinian approach, which is the only paradigm for understanding human evolution. It is also intuitively unconvincing that 300,000 years ago hominid cognition was of the same type as modern humans, implying that the appearance of art, ritual, big game hunting, colonization and rapid culture change, all of which occurred much later in human evolution, had no implications for the evolution of the human mind.

While the use and significance of spatial concepts in the production of bifaces can be questioned, it is certainly the case that such knapping required advanced sensiormotor skills. A biface is often the end product of a long sequence of actions, involving blank production, initial bifacial shaping, thinning and final shaping, processes which may also involve several different types of hammer stone, each appropriate for a specific task. Mithen (1996) believes that such skills reflect a discrete 'technical intelligence' in the mind of *Homo erectus*; others have argued that such skills derive from the same neurological structure that produces language, recognizing analogies between the production of speech and complex stone tools (Corballis 1992; Falk 1980; Holloway 1969). Such claims have been countered, however, since they fail to draw a sufficiently robust connection between inferred tool behaviour and language (Chase 1991; Wynn 1991). Donald (1991) has marshalled substantial evidence to show that sensiormotor skills and language are cognitively independent: for example, people who suffer from aphasia (loss of linguistic capacities) do not appear to have their motor skills impaired.

However, while stone tools may not provide evidence for language, they certainly do not demonstrate that language was absent. Here we must be careful to differentiate language from speech. Fossil evidence suggests that it was only with *Homo sapiens sapiens* that the vocal tract was so developed that a sufficiently wide range of vocalizations was possible to allow spoken language (Lieberman 1989). Yet *Homo erectus* may well have had language in the form of gestures. This has long been thought of as the root for the evolution of spoken language. Donald (1991) has noted that a 'mimetic' capacity – that is, representation via gesture – is maintained in those who suffer cognitive pathologies preventing spoken language, and suggests that this was the principal means of communication for *Homo erectus*.

There is a greater likelihood that types are present within Acheulian industries than among the Oldowan. In southern England, for example, handaxes come in a variety of shapes and sizes and archaeologists have been quick to classify them into types such as 'pointed', 'ovate' and 'ficrons' (for example, Roe 1981). These types certainly fall on a continuum (Dibble 1989), and raw material variability is likely to have played a substantial role in creating morphological variability. There are, however, three types of evidence that hominids within particular societies 'chose' to make bifaces according to an arbitrary (that is, non-functional) design. First, many artefacts show delicate flaking to create a specific morphology: the resulting shape is not just an unintended consequence of the knapping process. This is particularly evident from the rare sites which provide *in situ* knapping debitage, such as Boxgrove and Caddington (Bradley and Sampson 1978; Roberts 1986). Second, many assemblages are very heavily dominated by one specific type (for example, points in the Middle Gravels of the Barnfield Pit at Swanscombe, and ovates in the Upper Loam: Wymer 1968), and it is difficult to understand how these could have formed unless knapping had been geared to such ends. Third, while the same basic biface form is found throughout much of the Old World, there are regional differences that cannot be attributed to raw material availability and functional variation (Wynn and Tierson 1990).

Experimental tool use (Jones 1980; Toth 1985) and microwear studies (Keeley 1980; Keeley and Toth 1981) have suggested that bifaces were general-purpose tools, and consequently these types are unlikely to reflect artefacts made in specific shapes for specific purposes. Similarly, due to the likely absence of symbolic capacities of *H. erectus*, the types cannot be thought of as symbols, for example to identify ethnicity. The most likely explanation is simply that they reflect traditions of artefact manufacture within particular societies, acquired by social learning, as can be the case amongst different groups of chimpanzees (McGrew *et al.* 1979). The imposition of form within such traditions is most appropriately described as 'isochrestic style' (Sackett 1982); that is, the imposition of form without the intention to communicate (Chase 1991).

This presence of such persistent traditions of tool morphology suggests that social learning may have been intense and that *H. erectus* possessed an extremely important cognitive capacity: imitation. This can be seen most clearly in Acheulian assemblages which have handaxes showing remarkable similarities, such as those from the Wolvercote Channel in Oxfordshire (Tyldesley 1986). The presence of imitative capacities among *H. erectus* marks a very important step in cognitive evolution. Monkeys and apes probably have very limited capacities of imitation (Tomasello 1990; Visalberghi and Fragaszy 1990), whereas these are a critically important cognitive skill among modern humans, upon which much of child development and the acquisition of culture are based (Meltzoff 1988; Yando *et al.* 1978). Imitation was probably a means by which juvenile hominids acquired social and ecological knowledge.

In the light of the general-purpose nature of lower palaeolithic stone tools, it is unlikely that the acquisition of technical skills provided a selective pressure itself for the evolution of imitation, but once this capacity had arisen, it appears to have had a considerable influence on technology, leading to entrenched traditions. This would only have happened in those contexts in which social interaction was sufficiently intense to allow imitation of toolmaking to take place: in the industries from forested interglacial environments, such as the Clactonian and Taubachien (Valoch 1984; Wymer 1988), the lack of tool types and limited technical skill probably reflect the low degree of social learning due to small hominid group size and limited social cohesion (Mithen 1994).

H. erectus was the first hominid species to colonize large parts of the Old World, being present in south-west Asia by 1.8 MYA, and with immediate descendants (probably *H. Heidelbergensis*) in Europe after 1 MYA. This reflects the colonization and exploitation of a wide range of environmental zones, and in particular an ability to cope with high latitudes in which seasonality would have been marked and a dependency on animals required (Dennell 1983, and Chapter 20; Gamble 1986;

Turner 1992). The ability to exploit such a diverse set of environmental types may imply a complex suite of cognitive processes to allow the scheduling of behaviour with seasons, the use of fire, cooperative subsistence activity such as the search for frozen carcasses, and a flexible social organization (Dennell 1983; Gamble 1987). However, while such complex behaviour and cognition have been claimed, there is little direct evidence (Villa 1991). There is, for instance, only one kind of special activity site documented for the Middle Pleistocene – butchery sites; there are no known workshop sites, 'base camps', specialized hunting camps, or settlements known to have been restricted to a single season. While fire must have been essential for survival in northern latitudes, and traces are frequently found on Middle Pleistocene sites, there is no known case of organized activities around a fireplace. Reconstructions of substantial structures at Terra Amata have been shown to be false (Villa 1983). Communal hunting is directly implied by just one known site, the elephant and rhinoceros assemblages at La Cotte on the island of Jersey (Scott 1980), which are most likely to derive from a cliff-fall hunting strategy. Unfortunately, most faunal assemblages, such as from Hoxne, Swanscombe and Torralba, are too poorly preserved to allow inference of foraging strategies (Stopp 1988; Villa 1990, 1991).

Although the detail of such strategies cannot be inferred, the simple fact that these early humans were surviving in glacial environments with a limited technological repertoire implies that they relied on a detailed knowledge of their landscape and potential prey. Studies of modern hunter-gatherers, such as the Inuit and the !Kung, demonstrate that these people are superb naturalists. It is most likely that *H. erectus* and all early humans had similar understanding and knowledge of the natural world. Mithen (1996) attributes them with a distinct 'natural history intelligence'.

Levallois technology and the Mousterian

From *c*. 250,000 years ago, many industries become dominated by tools made on flakes, with bifaces becoming a minor component, if present at all; in south-west Europe and the Near East, such assemblages from the Later Pleistocene are often associated with Neanderthals and labelled Mousterian industries. In many of these assemblages the Levallois technique becomes dominant, a knapping method by which large flakes with predetermined size and shape were removed from a core which had been specially prepared. Some have argued that this technique marks a cognitive advance involving planning the development of the core, but this was probably no greater than that involved in biface manufacture – indeed the technique can be seen as a natural development of the process of thinning bifaces.

The issue of type arises once again with the Mousterian. One of the largest classes of Mousterian artefact is the scraper, a retouched flake. In a classic study, Bordes (1961a) developed a complex typology of such scrapers, seventeen different types, which he thought of as representing different conceptual entities for the Neanderthal flint knapper. Since different assemblages were composed of different frequencies of scraper types, he suggested that these were derived from distinct ethnic groups, each with their particular way of manufacturing scrapers (Bordes 1961b), implying that Neanderthals had an essentially modern type of cognition (Dibble 1989). However, recent research has suggested that a very large part of the variability may be attributed to the intensity of resharpening and variability in raw materials (Dibble 1987; Rolland and Dibble 1990).

Nevertheless, there are other features of the archaeological record associated with Neanderthals that may suggest additional features of cognition to those possessed by *H. erectus*: most notably, Neanderthals may have practised intentional burial, although there are substantial methodological problems in identifying such burials (Bar Yosef *et al.* 1992; Rak *et al.* 1994). The cognitive implications of intentional burial may involve belief in an afterlife, mythology and symbolic thought, though the lack of clear examples of grave-goods with these burials (Chase and Dibble 1987), unlike those of modern humans, warns against such interpretations. The presence of engraved or painted objects in middle palaeolithic contexts would also substantially advance the case that Neanderthals had the capacity for symbolic thought, and numerous claims have been made (Bednarik 1992; Marshack 1989). However, there are no cases of representational art, and few, if any, of the abstract marks recorded are other than the unintentional products of other activities, such as cutting vegetables on a bone or stone support (Chase and Dibble 1987, 1992). However, it is clear from the archaeological record that Neanderthals and earlier hominids were collecting and using pigments, notably iron and manganese oxide, perhaps for body painting.

There are possible indicators of increasing intellectual sophistication amongst pre-modern humans, and the evidence for the development of rather advanced social intelligence characterized by the ability to create and pursue complex social relationships. Nevertheless, probably the most significant feature of pre-modern hominids is the extraordinary stasis in technological development throughout the lower, middle and early part of the later Pleistocene, particularly in the light of the extraordinary developments that then occurred with the transition to the Upper Palaeolithic *c.* 50,000–35,000 years ago. The widespread distribution of *H. erectus* and archaic *H. sapiens* in diverse environments, from North Wales (Green 1984) to the Cape of southern Africa (Keller 1973), suggests that, just as with any primate (Dunbar 1988), there would have been a considerable degree of variability in social organization. Such variability is likely to have included large groups in environments such as the glacial environments of northern Europe (Gamble 1987; Mithen

1994), and an advanced level of social intelligence would have been necessary for the maintenance of such groups.

In summary, one interpretation of the mind of *H. erectus* and archaic *H. sapiens* is that this consisted of a series of discrete intelligences – those for making tools, interacting with the natural world, and living in complex social groups, and perhaps also for language. But these intelligences do not seem to have interacted together in the characteristic manner of a modern human mind (Mithen 1996; Fig. 18.3).

THE EVOLUTION OF THE MODERN HUMAN MIND: *H. SAPIENS SAPIENS*

H. sapiens sapiens first appears in the archaeological record at *c.* 100,000 BP in southern Africa and the Near East, when Neanderthals and other archaic *H. sapiens* species were widespread in many areas of the world; but by 30,000 BP it appears that *H. sapiens sapiens* was the only surviving hominid species. While there are major controversies with the evidence (Lindley and Clark 1990; Mellars 1989; Mellars and Stringer 1989), the fossil record and studies of mtDNA and nuclear DNA in living populations suggest that *H. sapiens sapiens* may have had one local origin, probably in Africa between 400,000 and 200,000 years ago, and then dispersed throughout the globe to replace archaic populations. The contribution of the archaic populations to the gene pool of modern humans is a matter of contention (Smith 1991).

It is also debatable whether or not the anatomical changes defining biologically modern humans, which included notably altered cranial morphology, also represented a major change in cognition. Against all our expectations from evolutionary theory, it appears that the behaviour of the earliest modern humans (that is, prior to *c.* 50,000 BP) was not substantially different to that of the archaic populations. In the caves of Skhul and Qafzeh in the Near East we have well-preserved specimens of early *H. sapiens sapiens* dating to *c.* 95,000 BP associated with a Mousterian technology dominated by Levalloisian flakes, apparently of precisely the same nature and used for the same tasks as those of the Neanderthals (Bar-Yosef 1989; Shea 1989). A similar lack of behavioural change in spite of anatomical change appears to occur in southern Africa (Klein 1989). Whilst this may be due to failings in the archaeological record, for example in evidence for the exploitation of plant resources differentiating a *H. sapiens sapiens* from a Neanderthal lifestyle, at present we are usually unable to identify any differences in behaviour, and consequently cognition, between the earliest *H. sapiens sapiens* and archaic populations, except in very rare instances. For example, at Katanda in Zaire, bone harpoons have been found which date to 90,000 years ago (Yellen *et al.* 1995), and which are similar to those of the European Upper Palaeolithic.

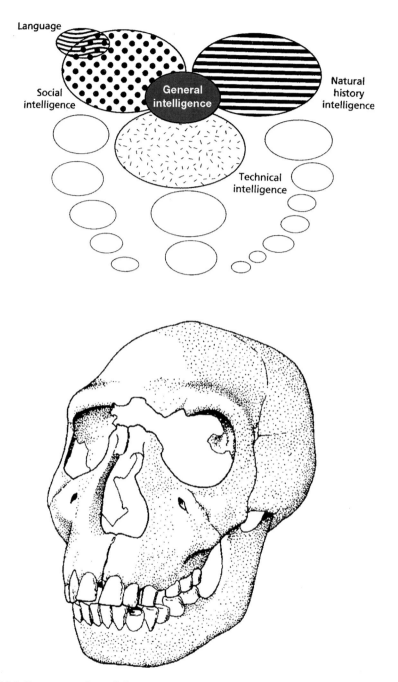

Figure 18.3 Reconstruction of the early human mind. This illustration suggests that early humans had a very different type of cognition from that of modern humans: while they could think in essentially modern ways about making tools (technical intelligence), the natural world (natural history intelligence), and social interaction (social intelligence), they were unable to integrate their ways of thinking and knowledge in these various domains. Although a linguistic capacity may have been present, this was restricted to the social domain, for the communication of social information. The skull depicts that of the *H. erectus* specimen known as Nariokotome boy, dating to 1.6 million years old. (See also Figure 19.6.) Source: S. Mithen 1996.

It is not until c. 50,000 BP, the middle/upper palaeolithic transition, that we find widespread changes in the archaeological record that may reflect the appearance of a fully modern cognition: the appearance of new technologies and of symbolic artefacts; increased rates of culture change; and the colonization of arid regions (Mellars 1973, 1989; White 1982). Whether these developments signify a real break in cultural/cognitive evolution, or just a change in the manner in which archaeologists describe and interpret their material, is hotly debated (Lindley and Clark 1990).

The middle/upper palaeolithic transition is most clearly defined in western Europe, where it appears to correlate directly with the replacement of Neanderthals by *H. sapiens sapiens*. At c. 40,000 BP a new archaeological 'culture' appears, the Aurignacian, which seems to have developed first in the Near East and then spread westwards across Europe. The Aurignacian is characterized by a concentration of blade technology, a series of distinct artefact types such as carinate scrapers and split bone points, and body ornaments such as beads and bracelets (Bordes 1968; Mellars 1989, 1991). Although no fossil remains have been found with the earliest Aurignacian, it is assumed to have been created by *H. sapiens sapiens*. There appears to have been a period of a few thousand years of overlap in western Europe between Neanderthals and *H. sapiens sapiens*, during which time Mousterian industries take on certain attributes of the Upper Palaeolithic (for example the Chatelperronian and Uluzzian), perhaps reflecting a process of acculturation as Neanderthals attempted to imitate the new technologies (Harrold 1989).

The last Neanderthal fossils date to c. 30,000 BP: it appears that Neanderthals were unable to compete with biologically modern humans for resources such as large game. This has been seen as reflecting cognitive differences between the two hominid types (Mellars 1991) allowing modern humans to hunt more efficiently, cope with environmental fluctuations, and attain greater behavioural flexibility. It cannot be doubted that after 35,000 BP biologically modern *Homo* had language, due to the extensive use of visual symbolism in the form of cave art and sculptures (see Davidson 1991), as discussed below. Indeed, some argue that the development of modern language is the root of all the changes that constitute the upper palaeolithic transition (Mellars 1991).

This is a very enticing argument. Certainly we should not doubt that hominids with language will behave very differently, and leave a very different archaeological record, from hominids without language: spoken language not only facilitates communication but also may make fundamental changes in the manner in which individuals think. But perhaps the major change is that language acts to integrate the minds of all individuals into a single network. An analogy with computers is helpful here: the most powerful computers are those which allow parallel processing, the simultaneous execution of a series of related tasks. The presence of language within a hominid community can be thought of as linking minds into one large parallel-processing computer, not only increasing the efficiency with which problems could be solved but also fundamentally changing the types of problems that could be tackled.

The transition to the Upper Palaeolithic is less clearly defined in the Near East and Africa and indeed in regions of Europe away from south-west France. On a global scale, the transition to modern humans and to modern patterns of behaviour presents a complex spatial and temporal mosaic: the apparent correlation between hominid type and culture in south-west France is the exception rather than the rule. This suggests that the developments in this region at *c.* 35,000 BP cannot be explained simply in terms of the arrival of *H. sapiens sapiens*, but must also concern adaptation to the particular glacial environments of the northern latitudes. Indeed, many date the explosion in visual symbolism not to 35,000 but to 20,000 BP, where it is clearly related to changing environmental conditions rather than hominid cognition (Mithen 1990), although this is coming under challenge from new AMS radio-carbon dates of cave paintings (Chauvet *et al.* 1996). In most parts of the world art remains a rare phenomenon during the Palaeolithic, but 'modern' behaviour and thought can be inferred from other types of developments: in particular we see at 50,000 BP, or soon afterwards, the colonization of the final parts of the globe, notably Australasia, Siberia and ultimately the New World. The colonization of such areas with low density, diversity and predictability of resources is likely to have only been possible after fully modern human cognitive capacities had evolved. According to Mithen (1996) this involved the integration of previously isolated intelligences (Fig. 18.4).

The first art and the art of memory

While the rock art of Australia may well date to initial colonization at 55,000 BP, the earliest dated tradition we have at present is the upper palaeolithic art of western Europe starting at *c.* 35,000 BP (Fig. 18.5). This art provides the most eloquent testimony that by this date all elements of a fully modern cognition had evolved (Davidson and Noble 1989): the cave paintings from Lascaux, Altamira, Niaux and the many other decorated caves must surely relate to a mythological world and an ideology that is now lost to us and, in that the animals depicted were those the people hunted, they suggest that the natural world was now viewed in cultural terms – the ice age hunters lived in a culturally created symbolic world.

We can interpret this art in terms of myth and attempt to reconstruct the symbolic world of the hunters (see, for example, Leroi-Gourhan 1968), but without written documents or oral history this is unlikely to be profitable research: the symbolic meanings of the cave paintings are lost to us forever. However, we can

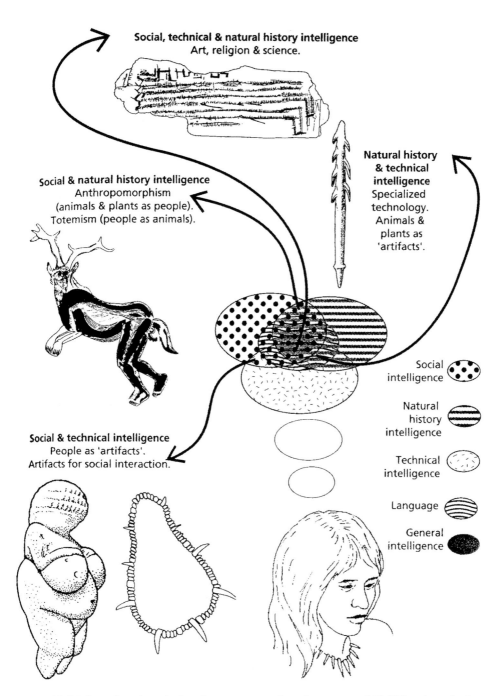

Social, technical & natural history intelligence
Art, religion & science.

Natural history & technical intelligence
Specialized technology. Animals & plants as 'artifacts'.

Social & natural history intelligence
Anthropomorphism (animals & plants as people). Totemism (people as animals).

Social & technical intelligence
People as 'artifacts'. Artifacts for social interaction.

Social intelligence

Natural history intelligence

Technical intelligence

Language

General intelligence

Figure 18.4 The cultural explosion that appears to have begun at *c*. 100,000 and reached a peak *c*. 40,000 years ago is attributed here to a new-found cognitive ability to integrate the multiple intelligences of the early human mind; it resulted in new ways of thinking which lie at the root of art, science and religion in the modern world. Source: S. Mithen 1996.

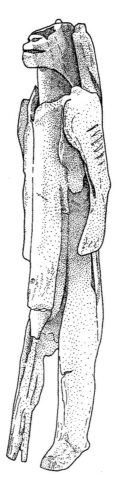

Figure 18.5 The lion/man statue from Hohlenstein-Stadel, southern Germany, *c.* 30–33,000 years old. Height 28 cm. Source: S. Mithen 1996.

analyse this art from a more functional perspective that views it as a means to store, transmit and recall information. Donald (1991) has coined the term 'external symbolic storage' to refer to this type of material culture which marks a major change in the character of human cognition. The value of such external storage should be immediately familiar to us by our use of libraries, and increasing reliance on electronic storage of information; indeed, some early artefacts may be directly comparable, such as the Taï Plaque with its complex series of incisions (Marshack 1991; Fig. 18.6). The range and complexity of the cognitive tasks we can address by using external information stores are of a radically different order of magnitude than if we can only rely on the information that can be stored in human minds. Palaeolithic

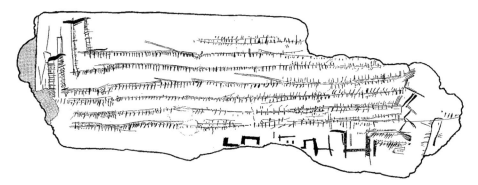

Figure 18.6 Engraved bone plaque from Grotte du Taï, Drôme, France. Length 8.8 cm. Source: S. Mithen 1996, with permission of A. Marshack.

art therefore marks the reversal of the process that began early in prehistory, of ever-increasing demands on human memory and information-processing capacities (Donald 1991).

For many art traditions, the information being stored may be purely symbolic, but in other cases, ecological knowledge may also be stored within the art, and this is likely to be the case for the Upper Palaeolithic. If we examine the imagery of the cave paintings and mobiliary art in detail, we can identify a series of references to the processes by which hunter-gatherers acquire information from their environments, such as by following tracks, inspecting spoor and watching the behaviour of animals, particularly bird life (Mithen 1988a, 1990). These references probably acted as cues to the recall of information from episodic memory (that containing information about past events, rather than more general knowledge which is stored in procedural memory). Hunter-gatherers are always acquiring information and storing it in long-term memory (see Mithen 1990: chapter 3); the problem they face, as with all people, is the recall of relevant information when a particular problem arises. Upper palaeolithic art, with its series of recall cues, is likely to have facilitated such information retrieval, probably at times of substantial change in hunting strategies (Mithen 1988b, 1990).

This approach, as with other functional approaches to the art (Gamble 1982; Jochim 1983) does not deny its aesthetic and symbolic qualities, nor its immense creative achievement (Mithen 1991a), but a study of the creative processes involved in this art is poorly developed. There is a general view that 'creativity' is outside of scientific study, being a mystical process that cannot be explained other than by referring to individual genius. As cognitive archaeology develops, this is likely to change as archaeologists begin to integrate new work in computational psychology, such as that on creativity (Boden 1990), into their theory-building and interpretations.

Rationality, emotion and hunter-gatherer foraging

The study of subsistence has long been a major concern of palaeolithic archaeologists, principally due to the preservation of faunal assemblages that inform about prehistoric hunting strategies, but archaeologists are now beginning to invoke various cognitive processes to replace the behaviourist/functionalist approaches such as those of the Cambridge 'palaeoeconomy' school (Higgs 1975). Such cognitive approaches can be briefly illustrated by considering the subsistence practices of those ice age hunters who created the cave paintings in south-west Europe.

The diversity of game in the faunal assemblages (Delpech 1983; Straus and Clark 1986) makes it clear that these hunters faced choices about which animals to hunt and how they should be exploited: for instance, in many areas and periods there were large migratory herds of reindeer to ambush (Spiess 1979), as well as a range of other large game such as bison, horse and red deer. In addition, there was a range of smaller game. Salmon fishing in the rivers running to the Atlantic may have been particularly productive (Jochim 1983). Individuals and groups of foragers had to make choices between these alternatives, formulate goals, and then plan how these would be attained. Often such planning would have involved acquiring information and developing joint plans with other groups. Moreover, this decision-making would often have taken place under conditions of considerable uncertainty: the hunters were living in environments which had substantial, and to some extent unpredictable, fluctuations in resources across time and space. Consequently, they not only had to make plans, but also contingency plans if the targeted resources were insufficient in number or maybe simply failed to appear.

It was by decision-making in conditions of uncertainty that hunting plans were made and executed, and it was these, in turn, that led to the creation of the large faunal assemblages from cave sites in south-west France. To focus on decision-making, planning, and rationality, however, must not be taken to imply that the cognitive archaeology of prehistoric hunting views people as inhuman information-processing machines: two cognitive features which intuitively appear opposed to rationality would have been central to such decision-making – creativity and emotion. Creativity plays an essential role in planning and decision-making, particularly in conditions of uncertainty when hunters regularly have novel situations bearing similarities to past events but also having unique elements. Consequently, new hunting plans cannot be a simple repeat of those used on previous occasions but require ingenious solutions to novel distributions of resources.

Similarly, we need to view prehistoric hunters as having the full range of human emotions and refer to these in our interpretations of past behaviour. Feelings such as delight, anger, sadness, and so on act as a management system for the control and processing of information. Imagine a prehistoric hunter deciding whether to search for deer in the woodland with other hunters, or to gather molluscs on the seashore.

732

To make a perfectly rational decision, the hunter would need to acquire and process a mass of information about the pros and cons of each resource: the costs, benefits and risks of its exploitation, the reliability of this information, the actions of other hunters and so on. Without any emotion, and with unconstrained rationality, the hunter would starve while acquiring and processing the infinite amount of potentially relevant information, but if we allow him emotion, this quest for perfect rationality will be inhibited and he will choose one course of action rather than another (Mithen 1991b).

In short, as archaeologists adopt a more cognitive approach to prehistoric subsistence by becoming concerned with planning and decision-making, they also achieve a more humanistic vision of the past. A prehistory in which we discuss the role of human creativity and emotion is ultimately more satisfying and appropriate than one in which such cognitive processes – which we know to be essential to our own behaviour – are not invoked. The critical point, however, is that by bringing these into our interpretations we can avoid renouncing a 'scientific' approach to the past by drawing on recent work in cognitive science, which has shown how cognitive processes such as creativity and emotion are indeed amenable to scientific study (de Sousa 1987; Oatley and Johnson-Laird 1987).

COGNITIVE ARCHAEOLOGY IN THE AGE OF PLATO?

We now make a quantum jump in chronology, to classical Greece. And immediately we face a serious question of applicability. After all, many modern philosophers would basically agree with A. N. Whitehead's characterization of the history of Western philosophy as 'a series of footnotes to Plato' (Whitehead 1929: 153). When the structures of the Lyceum, the school created by Plato's successor Aristotle, were revealed in Athens early in 1997, the Western press saluted the event as a sort of intellectual home-coming. So there is a problem here for anyone seeking to pursue the 'archaeology of mind' (Renfrew 1982) into the ambit of classical Greece. It seems impudent to use the objects of archaeology as a means of understanding cognitive development in a society which gave rise to Plato and the Academy, to Aristotle and the Lyceum. What possible light can archaeological remains shed upon the Greek mind, when the literary record is so generous and (if we accept Whitehead's dictum) fundamental?

The enduring tradition of Platonic studies can readily delude us that our mentality is hardly foreign from that of a Greek in the fifth century BC: which explains the sort of jocular handbooks of Greek society such as H. D. F. Kitto's *The Greeks* (first published in 1951; still in print, and popular amongst students), with its engaging air of complete at-homeness with Greek institutions, and its fluent *apologia* for violence, misogyny and economic exploitation in classical Athens. Anyone who shares the Kitto familiarity with the Greek mind will have no problem with the material remains of classical Greece: Kitto salutes classical Greek art and architecture for its 'consuming intellectualism'. (By comparison, the products of Minoan art are nugatory, and the structures of pre-Hellenic Knossos are 'chaotic': Kitto 1951: 25–26.)

The investment of rationality in Greek art and architecture is done so regularly that it would be futile to start listing instances: it is easier to recall the incident described by E. R. Dodds, introducing *The Greeks and the Irrational*, where a young man standing in front of the Elgin Marbles confesses that his response to 'this Greek stuff' is killed by its overbearing 'rationality' (Dodds 1951: 1; see also Vidal-Naquet 1986: 252). Following Nietzsche's basic schism between 'Apolline' rationality and 'Dionysiac' irrationality in the ancient Greeks, Dodds and others have endeavoured to reassure us that the Greeks were less intimidating in their commitment to rationality than we might imagine. The result is not coherent: it seems to put schizophrenia on an almost ethnic scale, whilst it also sets a trap for the would-be archaeologist of mind. Which half of the presumed 'Greek mind' is going to betray itself in the archaeological record: the 'emotional', or the 'rational'? According to some cognitive scientists, the question should never arise (de Sousa 1987).

The extent of the historical problem is nicely illustrated by an anecdote of European antiquarianism. In the Fitzwilliam Museum in Cambridge there is the upper part of a colossal caryatid (Fig. 18.7). Its original Greek site was Eleusis, and the statue was first recorded and identified as Ceres (Demeter) by Sir George Wheeler (Wheeler 1676: 428). Another scholar-tourist, Edward Dodwell, reported the statue in 'its full glory, situated in the centre of a threshing-floor', and tells us that the farmers of Eleusis village 'were impressed with a persuasion that their harvests were the effect of her [that is, Demeter's] bounty' (Dodwell 1819, I: 583). Previous attempts by French antique-hunters to remove the statue had failed; having been dragged to the port, the statue, according to the locals, had flown back to her proper place. It was E. D. Clarke who eventually got Demeter from Eleusis to Cambridge (via shipwreck off Beachy Head) in return for the gift of a telescope to the Turkish administrators and some bribery involving the village priest (Clarke 1803; Otter 1824: 505).

This is a poignant episode, and it raises an important question about the archaeology of mind when applied to museum objects. Our natural response is more or less akin to Clarke's: to imagine that a statue ensures agricultural success is the sign of a 'savage' or 'irrational' mentality. At best, we spare the peasants of Eleusis some romantic sympathy: we may dwell on 'the misty glory which the human imagination sheds around the hard material realities of the food supply' (Frazer 1912: vii). But it is worth pondering the durability of Demeter's cult at Eleusis. The sanctuary and its functions were supposedly ended in AD 396, when Alaric the Goth invaded Greece, so why were Eleusinian farmers still lighting lamps on festival days to the statue of Demeter in AD 1800? Frazer's answer may be predicted: the farmers revere

Figure 18.7 Upper part of a colossal caryatid (basket carrier) from Eleusis. Marble, second century AD. Reproduction by permission of the Syndics of the Fitzwilliam Museum, Cambridge.

the statue because they have yet to discover phosphates; the cult of Demeter is a surrogate for scientific understanding; the magic continues pending the advent of rationality; and so the foundation and development of the sanctuary of Eleusis may be roughly regarded as sustained 'error'.

As Anthony Snodgrass (1984) has pointed out, however, despite our familiarity with Greek sanctuaries as archaeological sites we know surprisingly little about how sanctuaries such as the Athenian Acropolis, Olympia and Delphi actually functioned with regard to their cult practices. The excuse for our ignorance has been given as 'the fact that Greek sanctuaries operated in a way which produced relatively little stratification' (Snodgrass 1984: 227), but there is surely more to it than that. Greek temples are taken to be models of control, regulation, order: the 'orders' of Greek temple architecture were reckoned in the eighteenth century to have developed from the huts of savages; the same orders are regarded by some modern architects and their regal mentors as the ultimate signs of reasonable (or 'God-given') design. Turned into town halls (Leeds) or schools (Edinburgh High) or museums (the British), Greek temples become the circumstances of modern rationality. Who would ever believe that the inner sanctum of the Temple of Apollo at Delphi contained an enclosure in which a woman crouched on top of a tripod, inhaled vapours from a crack in the ground, and went into an inspired fit; or (more incredibly) that representatives from Greek city-states took serious political decisions on the basis of such epileptic ravings?

Most archaeological material from sanctuaries is put into museums, and once inside a museum an object is easily stripped of its cult significance. It requires a massive leap of imagination to envisage a sanctuary like Olympia as it properly was, cluttered with statues, dedications and votive offerings. Pausanias picked his way through a jungle of images at Olympia in the second century AD; and a century of German excavations has revealed an Olympia rich with potential information about cult practices. To an early seventh-century BC stratum belong thousands of bronze and terracotta animals; in the sixth and fifth centuries BC, *tropaia* – tithes of booty offered to Zeus by victorious city-states – were popular; and from the mid-fifth century BC, athletic dedications proliferate. Olympia developed into a sanctuary that hosted, according to Pausanias, some seventy different cults.

We fancy ourselves familiar with the Olympic Games, but we remain unsympathetic to the implications of a running track dominated by a temple, and we might have trouble in understanding the images of the Olympic sanctuary if we did not have Pausanias (V.21) telling us, for example, that the statues of Zeus wielding a thunderbolt have a generic name (*Zanes*), representing the penitence of athletes caught cheating in the Games. All the same, most of the cults mentioned by Pausanias have yet to be identified; hardly surprising, when one of the veteran excavators admits that no one has yet explained the relationship of religious observances and athletic competitions at Olympia (Mallwitz 1988).

This is the problem with the archaeology of mind when applied to classical Greece. It is not a lack of material, stratified or otherwise, but rather a lack of will. There is no reason why the material remains of a classical Greek sanctuary should not be analysed according to the same archaeological and anthropological methods as outlined by Renfrew for the prehistoric site of Phylakopi (Renfrew 1985). Indeed, we ought to be at a great advantage when, for example, the priestly offices at Delphi are filled by characters as divulgative as Plutarch. But Greek rationality is at stake. Greek behaviour at sanctuaries displays features of something we would want to call 'pre-logical thinking', or 'primitive mentality' – or, to risk using their ambivalent own word, *deisidaimonia* ('respect for the gods' or 'superstition') – and as such, certain distinctions we hold dear begin to seem blurred. What is 'Greek' and what is 'barbarian' becomes blurred; what is 'rational' and 'irrational' becomes blurred; and we can no longer be sure of that old logic which equates 'science' with 'civilization'.

The misleading effects of a *mentalité* approach to classical Greece have been exposed by Geoffrey Lloyd (Lloyd 1990). As he shows, drawing the line between 'science' and 'magic' is not as easy as we think. The historian of science collects the writings of Hippocrates and his followers, and salutes the birth of 'clinical' or 'scientific' medicine in the fifth century BC; the archaeologist charts the extraordinary growth, from the fifth century BC onwards, in *Asklepeia*, sanctuaries to the healing god Asklepios, from Athens (420 BC) to Rome (293 BC). Some antipathy can be demonstrated between the Hippocratic practitioners of 'scientific' medicine and their rivals, the faith-healers: but the archaeology of the Asklepios cult suggests that it cannot be polarized as purely psychosomatic. Stelai at the Asklepeion on the island of Cos (the home of Hippocrates) were said by the first-century AD geographer Strabo (XIV.2.19) to carry records of Hippocratic or 'clinical' cures; surviving stelai from other sanctuaries of Asklepios certainly show that the marvels of divine healing could be tempered with proper physiological advice (Edelstein 1945).

Plato's attitude to the 'primitive mentality' of sanctuaries like Delphi is well known. He was perfectly aware of potential hocus-pocus from the mantic quarters of Greek cult practice (*Laws* 908d), but was nevertheless prepared to weave into community life a continuous thread of regular religious observances, in which the *manteis*, or prophets, are fully involved (*Laws* 828b). We do not know how Plato regarded the sort of cult which Clarke found lingering at Eleusis in 1801, but it has been pointed out that the terminology of the Eleusinian Mysteries is metaphorically used in some of Plato's arguments, and it seems likely that he would not have disparaged the value of a statue entrusted with agricultural fertility.

Few Western philosophers have tackled the problems posed by 'irrationality' in the age of Plato, but one exception is Wittgenstein, in his comments on Frazer's *Golden Bough* (Wittgenstein 1979). It is well known that Wittgenstein was profoundly irritated by some aspects of English culture, and his marginalia to Frazer are often more astringent than necessary ('Frazer cannot imagine a priest who is not basically an English parson of our times with all his stupidity and feebleness' – Wittgenstein 1979: 5e); but we can accept the principle Wittgenstein is stating, which is that the treatment of magical and religious notions as mistakes or stupidities (*Dummheiten*) may itself be wrong-headed. The identification and isolation of a 'savage mentality' as a misunderstanding of the physical world are wrong; Frazer's readings of ancient and comparative ritual seem cruder than the rituals themselves; and there is one central factor to be reckoned with – more psychological than anthropological – which is that 'man is a ceremonious animal' (Wittgenstein 1979: 7e).

The implication is that cognitive archaeology is as valid for the age of Plato as it is for the Palaeolithic. In fact, for those trying to understand Greek art and architecture, some process of cognitive archaeology is not only legitimate but also necessary, if anything beyond straight stylistic classification is to be achieved.

Kouroi and 'the Greek Revolution'

The archaeology of mind, as we have seen, has been scarcely pursued beyond the chronological margins of prehistory; yet Colin Renfrew's original rubric for the application of such an archaeology signalled not only the Aegean as an area ripe with possibilities, but also 'early Greek civilization' as offering a particular example of 'symbol systems' in operation (Renfrew 1982: 25). According to Renfrew, the free-standing and life-sized male statues known as *kouroi* ('youths': Fig. 18.8) display a stylistic uniformity that allows them to serve as symbols of interaction between the independent city-states (or 'peer polities') of the Aegean during the sixth century BC (see also Renfrew 1986: 11–12). Standardized, schematic statues may clearly be valuable as symbols; indeed, their symbolic value is dependent precisely upon their schematic features. If the statues failed to conform to expected

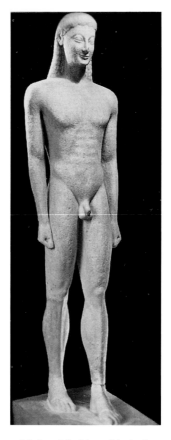

Figure 18.8 Kouros (youth) from Melos. Marble, mid-sixth century BC. © National Archaeological Museum, Athens.

738

schemes, then the shared message implied by the shared style would get lost or confused. So it is easy enough to accept Renfrew's idea that the *kouroi* communicate a common ideology of 'Greekness' amongst the autonomous city-states.

However, what happens when the *kouroi* apparently lose their schematic features? In the stylistic classification of these statues (Richter 1970), the last *kouros* is reckoned to belong to the early fifth century BC; thereafter, free-standing and life-sized male statues no longer show the predictable features which have symbolic value. We arrive at the moment which art historians have dubbed with various terms, all of them dramatic – 'emancipation' (Loewy 1907), 'the great awakening' (Gombrich 1972: 46–64), 'the Greek Revolution' (Gombrich 1960: 99–125; Spivey 1996: 17–53) – when Greek artists turned away from schematic forms or 'memory-pictures' (Loewy 1907) and began working from the direct motive of imitating 'nature'.

This leads us to put an important gloss on Renfrew's use of the 'uniformity' of the *kouroi*. The statues have been chronologically ordered: though 'standardized', they can be perceived as changing over time. The earliest are dominated by geometric forms for limbs, muscles and so on; the latest are naturalistic. Regional distinctions are not easy to define because, amongst the artists of the Greek city-states, 'the progression in anatomical knowledge was amazingly uniform' (Richter 1972: 4). Indeed, the stylistic evidence may well support what the literary tradition subsequently tells us, that Greek artists were peripatetic and took commissions from whichever city-state was offering. This does not affect Renfrew's point: but the logical result is that, sooner or later, the archaeologist of mind is challenged by a lack of uniformity, obvious patterns, standards or schemata in the material record.

Before tackling the consequences of fading schemata, it is worth pointing out that to credit the Greeks of the fifth century BC with a unique 'awakening' in art-historical terms is not to foist upon them some retrospective judgement. Greek artists knew they were leaving the sleep of 'memory-pictures' or patently schematic forms. That is why one Athenian vase-painter, *c*. 510 BC, inscribed one of his red-figured pots with a sporting taunt to a fellow-painter, daring him to accomplish the same skills of naturalistic representation (Boardman 1975: 33); that is why competitive tenders were invited for the decoration of classical temples and sanctuaries (Boardman 1985: 36); that is why anecdotes about illusionistic skills and tricks proliferate about classical artists (Kris and Kurz 1979); and that is why, over a century later, Plato gives this estimate of the Egyptians: 'if you inspect their paintings and reliefs on the spot, you will find that the work of ten thousand years ago – I mean the expression not loosely but in all precision – is neither better nor worse than that of today; both exhibit an identical artistry' (*Laws* 656d).

For Plato, the predictability of Egyptian art was a virtue, a sign of good legislation. Egyptian artists were, in his eyes, entirely subordinate to the Pharaohs for whom they worked. He exaggerated the point, of course: sculptured figures of the

Egyptian Predynastic period (before 3100 BC) are by no means identical with the Late Dynastic period (which is the Egypt Plato knew in the fourth century BC). But it is true that within the iconography of Egyptian 'court art' we can recognize symbols of power which hardly alter over thousands of years, and the style of representation admits amazingly little variation. The Pharaohs of Plato's time, struggling to maintain Egypt's unity against external forces, may have exaggerated this traditionalism. But it is there: a system of symbols entirely suitable for government, based on the concept that Pharaoh was a god and 'the champion of the cosmic order' (Lloyd 1983: 288). Thus Pharaoh with the body of a lion; Pharaoh with a bull's tail; Pharaoh with a sun disc over his head – these are hieroglyphs of divine power, messages whose cognitive value was guaranteed for successive millennia by an enduring system of dynastic rule.

The archaeological record of such schematic art readily lends itself to analysis of autocratic ideologies, or amalgamations of secular and religious authority (Larsen 1979: 295–390). Lord Curzon's well-known comment on the reliefs of the palaces of the Persian kings at Persepolis – 'all the same, and the same again, and yet again' (Curzon 1892, 2: 194) – is easily translated into the cognitive implications of those reliefs. The rulers occupying the buildings decorated by the reliefs had vast armies at their command. The repetition of the figures indicates size; the homogeneity of the figures indicates subordination. And since Persepolis was founded by the same Persian kings who sought to extend their rule over Greece in the first half of the fifth century BC, it is tempting to compare art styles at Persepolis with art styles at Athens. Can it be argued that the 'emancipation' from schematic forms at Athens in the fifth century BC pertains to a society free from autocratic rule? Is there then such a thing as an 'archaeology of democracy'?

The cognitive mapping of classical Athens

In the opening chapter of his *History of the Peloponnesian War*, the historian Thucydides makes the following observation on Athens and Sparta as cities. Imagine, he says, that Sparta became a deserted city, and that you went to visit it: you would never guess that Sparta had been a major power – not only in the Peloponnese but in the Aegean ambit generally – because Sparta as a city 'is not regularly planned and contains no temples or monuments of great magnificence, but is simply a collection of villages'. By contrast, the hypothetical visitor to a deserted Athens 'would conjecture from the eye that the city had been twice as powerful as it in fact is'.

This section of Thucydides' history, written towards the end of the fifth century BC, is sometimes called his 'Archaeology', and archaeologists ought to take note of his observation on the potentially misleading remains of Greek cities. It might well

740

be understood as a caution not to proceed with the analysis of power systems from material remains, or even as a deterrent to attempting an archaeology of mind within classical contexts. Alternatively, it could be argued that the absence of extravagant buildings in Sparta properly reflects aspects of Spartan ideology. However Thucydides' point is taken, we are left with the fact that he, an Athenian of the late fifth century BC, is aware of the value of ideological expression in material terms. His literary testimony constitutes one source for our understanding of the genesis and operation of democracy at Athens: but it is not alone. Ancient Athens was 'a city of images' (Bérard 1989): the images are further testimonies. In other words, the archaeologist should be able to assist in the definition of the Athenian democratic ideology.

Considered in terms of urban form, Athens was more than 'a city of images': it was a city rich in what urban planners call 'imageability'. Imageability is defined as 'that quality in a physical object which gives it a high probability of evoking a strong image in any given observer' (Lynch 1960: 9). Thucydides was evidently aware that the urban form of Athens was 'imageable' on a grandiose scale; and just as he told his readers that his history would last 'for ever', so some of the monuments of classical Athens survive as potent images of 'order', political maturity, and so on. The Acropolis still rises above modern Athens as a highly visible landmark; and the principal temple upon the Acropolis, the Parthenon, has a recent history of serving as the prototype for modern civic and 'democratic' buildings. The recontextualization of such images may be useful: for if we can recognize the cognitive processes whereby we connect, say, a particular statue in New York harbour with 'Liberty', then it will help us understand similar processes suggested by the archaeological record of classical Athens.

Athens was an organic city. In the mid–fifth century BC it could be described as 'wheel-shaped' (*trochoeideos*: Herodotus, *Histories* VII.140), and to those tracing the organic development of this 'wheel', it is clear that in a gradual fashion, the city's hub shifted from the Acropolis to the Agora (inadequately translated as 'marketplace': as we shall see, its functions went far beyond those of commercial exchange). The Acropolis as a rock was always prominent topographically; but the cognitive significance of its landmark qualities demonstrably altered over several centuries. In the Bronze Age, the rock was the basis of a Mycenaean palace, massively fortified in the late thirteenth century BC. This was large enough to provide shelter for perhaps several thousand people in times of danger; otherwise, it was royal accommodation, and monumentally dominated an outlying area of nucleated settlements.

The stratification of subsequent development on the Acropolis is notoriously difficult to define, but the Mycenaean palace yielded to a temple, and then a series of temples; the archaeology can be coloured with stories of the seizure of this area first by tyrants, then by invading Persians. But below the Acropolis, at the end of the seventh century BC, we see what was once a cemetery becoming the focus of palpably 'civic' development: a large quadrangle was cleared, rectangular buildings erected on its west side, and further structures – including a fountain-house and a large walled enclosure – were added during the sixth century BC. Between 500 and 100 BC the remaining three sides of the square were filled: and the area is archaeologically recognizable as the centre of the city (Fig. 18.9). Arterial roads converge upon it, and most of the buildings can be assigned their central civic purposes – not only from literary references but also from the finds of several decades of American excavations. Thus, for example, there were small water-clocks for the timing of speeches; allotment machines for impartial selection of members of juries; publicly stamped sets of crockery, for meals served to senators at public expense; and so on.

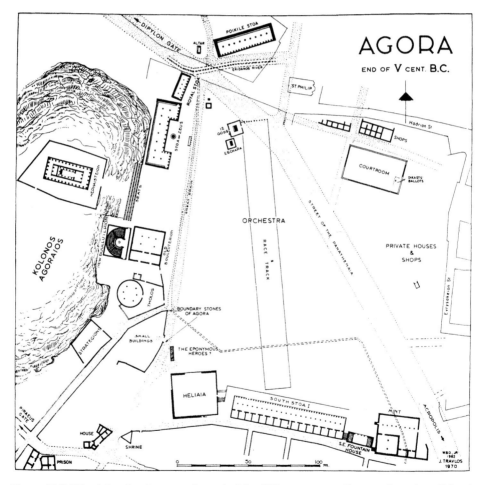

Figure 18.9 The Athenian Agora at the end of the fifth century BC. Source: American School of Classical Studies at Athens: Agora Excavations.

Even without the assistance of literary testimony, an imaginative archaeologist could recognize the protocols of democracy in these objects.

The development of the Agora was not at the cost of the Acropolis, but the public perception of the Acropolis changed: it was an elevated place, but not occupied by temporal rulers. Our knowledge of the Athenian religious calendar is not profound in its detail, but we do know that festival days punctuated many days of many months of the year: and the impression of civic life dominated by cult observances is precisely what we would get from the classically developed Acropolis. It became an area compact with altars, temples, shrines and places of potential taboo; and the rite of passage involved in entering that area was emphasized by the erection, in the 430s BC, of monumental gateways (*Propylaea*). It was no longer a place of royal residence: in the sixth century BC the Peisistratid tyrants may have lived up there (although one building along the west side of the Agora has been tentatively identified as a 'palace' of the Peisistratids), but in the fifth century BC the business of government was clearly accommodated around the Agora.

The ideological consequences of this are clear only when comparisons are made. The Persian kings who built Persepolis adhered to the stock design of oriental monarchies: government offices clustered around the king's (divine) presence in a complex of palaces. The Hellenistic dynasts of Pergamon in Asia Minor installed themselves in palaces adjacent to temples on top of a terraced citadel. The Roman emperor Augustus put up a temple to Apollo on Rome's Palatine Hill, and his own house next to it, so that it was not easy to define where the residence of Apollo ended and the residence of Augustus began. Tyrannies, oligarchies, monarchies and dictatorships take the high ground: the level is for democracy, whose institutions are topographically – and typically – more 'accessible'.

The ordering of urban space along preconceived ideas is often described as a Greek 'invention', and ascribed to Hippodamos of Miletus. One part of Athens – or rather, the harbour town which served Athens, the Piraeus – is reckoned to have been planned by Hippodamos, in the mid-fifth century BC; otherwise, the city lacks the sort of orthogonal or zoned layout which is the Hippodameian hallmark. This is to be expected: though some classical minds dreamed of laying out a geometrically ideal city (Aristophanes, *Birds* 905–1009; Plato, *Laws* 705a–e), in practice this tended to be possible only in situations of artificial 'development', as in the case of the Athenian-inspired colony of Thurii in southern Italy planted as a replacement to the ruined Sybaris. There is, in some of the literary records, almost an inverted snobbery about the lack of Egyptian or Near Eastern-style order in the domestic quarters of Athens, so we are bound to look at the details of areas of public activity if we want information about prevailing ideologies.

Here, the concept of 'the Greek Revolution' needs qualification. It is true that art at Athens in the fifth century BC displays, in its best-known museum pieces (the sculptures of the Parthenon, for example), the sort of non-schematic characteristics which excite our admiration. And, as we maintained above, it is also the case that both artists and their public were conscious of innovations in representation – 'the shock of the new' is a concept by no means confined to the art of our own era. However, it is important to remember the context in which the 'virtuoso' painters, sculptors and architects of classical Athens worked: an essential conservatism in terms of architectural types; an essential homogeneity in the materials used for building; and the retention, for key junctures of public activity, of patently archaic schemata.

The conservatism of the classical temple 'orders' needs no special illustration, but it is worth explaining the extent of other 'orders'. The most curious of these to modern minds is the Herm. *Hermai* – rectangular shafts decorated with male genitalia and the head of the god Hermes on top – hardly change in their design between the sixth century BC and the second century AD. Hundreds of these images stood in Athens, marking entrances of shrines and private houses, and sometimes doubling as victory monuments. The Agora excavations have yielded many examples (Harrison 1965), some of them bearing signs of the mass vandalism which took place one night in 415 BC in what was interpreted as a plot to overthrow democracy (Thucydides VI.26). These statues were germane to orientation within the city. Their regular features (the erect phallus a symbol of luck; the bearded Hermes, of course, the deity of safe passage) remained unchanged: in every sense of the expression, you knew where you were with the Herms.

Likewise, there is no artistic 'revolution' in the Hekataia, the statues of a triple-headed, triple-bodied goddess regularly placed at crossroads or junctions of three roads. Sculptors engaged to carve such images never attempted to alter their style. Without street names, or even gridded streets, people relied upon schematic forms as landmarks, and it was the very archaistic force of such images that gave them their value as signposts. The entrances to the Agora, too, were marked by 'speaking stones': *perirrhanteria*, or lustral basins, of the sort usually associated with temples, were placed there, implying a pseudo-religious purification procedure before entering the business of public life; and the extent of the Agora area was marked by *horoi*, or boundary-stones. These inscribed stones are found elsewhere in the city: they told you when you were on the margins of an area with special status such as a fountain, a shrine, or a burial area (especially necessary in the Kerameikos quarter of the city, where potters worked close by a large cemetery), and the formula of the inscription invests the stone itself with semiotic duties. *Horos eimi tes agoras*: 'I am the boundary of the Agora', declares the stone. It is, like the lustral basins, a feature of near-sacred demarcation.

The survival of archaic images within their city furnished the Athenians with perhaps the most distinctive feature of their political culture: a powerful sense of the past, expressed in an accumulation of commemorative images. Students of Greek art are inclined to underestimate this: faced with the theory that the Parthenon Frieze (carved *c*. 440 BC) commemorated a victory over the Persians at

Marathon in 490 BC (Spivey 1996: 123–51), it is the time-lag of fifty years that seems incredible. But the distance between Athenian citizens and their heroic past was kept short by regular cognitive association of the city with its fixed images.

The best example of this association is provided by a well-known statue group called 'The Tyrannicides', commemorating the murder of Hipparchus, one of the sons of the tyrant Peisistratos, in 510 BC, by two men called Harmodius and Aristogeiton. A hero cult developed, centred around their statue in the Agora; only Roman copies of this have survived (Fig. 18.10), together with a series of iconographic references. The statue may have been placed in the Agora originally because the assassination itself had, according to the historians, taken place at one

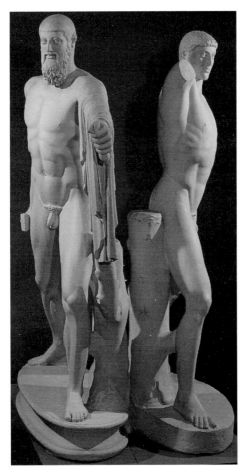

Figure 18.10 'The Tyrannicides', Harmodius and Aristogeiton; cast of a Roman marble copy of a bronze group originally set up in Athens *c*. 470 BC. Source: Museum of Classical Archaeology, Cambridge.

of the shrines there, but subsequently it was simply part of the general architecture of democracy in that area of the city. Its message was essentially a testament to the democratic ideology of classical Athens: the power (*kratia*) of the people (*demos*) to rid themselves of autocrats.

Classical scholars have long debated the meaning of Athenian 'democracy'. But as far as popular perception goes, the images and memorials of fifth-century Athens provide enduring models for modern liberal constitutions. The idea that classical Greek art is owed to a democratic constitution is as old as J. J. Winckelmann (Winckelmann 1764: I.4.130–33). Sir Alfred Zimmern refined and reaffirmed the point: 'we owe the Parthenon sculptures not merely to the genius of Phidias but also to the genius of the social system which knew how to make use of him' (Zimmern 1922: 368). Yet very little has been done, beyond easy assertions of environmental determinism, to study the cognitive connections between ideology and material remains in fifth-century Athens. Isaiah Berlin, a self-styled 'historian of ideas', is issuing a challenge to archaeologists when he asks: 'how much do we know about Athens – the *mentalité*, or the ways of life, in the days of Socrates or Plato or Xenophon? We scarcely know what Athens looked like – did it look like Beirut or a Zulu kraal?' (Jahanbegloo 1992: 26). As we have seen, the picture of classical Athens is not quite so unfocused that the city cannot be distinguished from a Zulu kraal, but Berlin has identified a genuine problem. It is not that the Greeks failed to rationalize their art and architecture, but simply an accident of survival that their treatises on such matters are no longer available for us to consult. We have the opportunity to pick up their material remains – their theories 'reified', in effect – and attempt to reconstruct the thinking behind them.

CONCLUSION

It was the anthropologist Franz Boas who stressed that the mind of early man could never be described as 'primitive' in the sense of being underdeveloped or unsophisticated, either rationally or emotionally (Boas [1927]1955). And it is another anthropologist, Ellen Dissanyake, who has argued for a constant in human development: that art is central to human evolutionary adaptation, and therefore that *Homo aestheticus* is a precursor of *Homo sapiens sapiens* (Dissanyake 1992). In this chapter we have yoked together two fields of archaeological study that are usually kept apart, but which indeed share, or ought to share, these anthropological premises. The mental equipment of those who peopled the Upper Palaeolithic was basically the same as that belonging to the inhabitants of classical Athens. To draw up some sort of absolute progress chart of cognitive 'development' is therefore a misguided enterprise. We should rather be trying to assess historically what cognitive skills were required in a given social situation. We do not need to be structuralists as such (that is, to believe that there are innate human aptitudes for recognizing 'structures' or principles in language, myth, symbols and so on), but we should accept the existence of 'cognitive universals': patterns of thinking common to all who possess the human mind. Archaeologists have been slow to appreciate the possibilities of approaching the material record in search of those cognitive patterns. The caricature of modern tradition is the excavator who, coming across some strange and apparently unidentifiable structure or object, shrugs it off as 'ritual' and has no more to do with it. There are, as we have tried to indicate here, good reasons for adopting a more positive attitude.

REFERENCES

Bar-Yosef, O. (1989) 'Geochronology of the Levantine Middle Palaeolithic', in P. Mellars and C. Stringer (eds) *The Human Revolution: Behavioural and Biological Perspectives in the Origins of Modern Humans*, Edinburgh: Edinburgh University Press: 589–610.

Bar-Yosef, O., Vandermeersch, B., Arensburg, B. *et al.* (1992) 'The excavation in Kebara cave, Mount Carmel', *Current Anthropology* 33: 497–550.

Barkow, J., Cosmides, C. and Tooby, J. (1992) *The Adapted Mind*, Oxford: Oxford University Press.

Bednarik, R. (1992) 'Palaeoart and archaeological myths', *Cambridge Archaeological Journal* 2: 27–43.

Bérard, C. (ed.) (1989) *A City of Images*, Princeton: Princeton University Press.

Boardman, J. (1975) *Athenian Red Figure Vases: the Archaic Period*, London: Thames and Hudson.

Boardman, J. (1985) *Greek Sculpture: the Classical Period*, London: Thames and Hudson.

Boas, F. ([1927]1955) *Primitive Art*, New York: Dover.

Boden, M. (1990) *The Creative Mind: Myths and Mechanisms*, London: Weidenfeld and Nicolson.

Boesch, C. and Boesch, H. (1983) 'Optimisation of nut-cracking with natural hammers by wild chimpanzees', *Behaviour* 83: 265–86.

Bordes, F. (1961a) *Typologie du Paléolithique Ancien et Moyen*, Bordeaux: Publications de l'Institut de Préhistoire de l'Université de Bordeaux.

Bordes, F. (1961b) 'Mousterian cultures in France', *Science* 134: 803–10.

Bordes, F. (1968) *The Old Stone Age*, London: Weidenfeld and Nicolson.

Bradley, B. and Sampson, C. G. (1978) 'Artefacts from the Cottages site', in C. G. Sampson (ed.) *Palaeoecology and Archaeology of an Acheulian Site at Caddington, England*, Dallas: Southern Methodist University: 83–137.

Bradley, R. (1991) 'Rock art and the perception of landscape', *Cambridge Archaeological Journal* 1: 77–101.

Byrne, R. and Whitten, A. (eds) (1988) *Machiavellian Intelligence: Social Expertise and the Evolution of the Intellect in Monkeys, Apes and Humans*, Oxford: Oxford University Press.

Camp, J. M. (1986) *The Athenian Agora*, London: Thames and Hudson.

Chase, P. (1991) 'Symbols and palaeolithic artefacts: style, standardization and the imposition of arbitrary form', *Journal of Anthropological Archaeology* 10: 193–214.

Chase, P. and Dibble, H. (1987) 'Middle palaeolithic symbolism: a review of current evidence and interpretations', *Journal of Anthropological Archaeology* 6: 263–96.

Chase, P. and Dibble, H. (1992) 'Scientific archaeology and the origins of symbolism; a reply to Bednarik', *Cambridge Archaeological Journal* 2: 43–51.

Chauvet, J.-M., Deschamps, E. B. and Hillaire, C. (1996) *Chauvet Cave: The Discovery of the World's Oldest Paintings*, London: Thames and Hudson.

Cheney, D. L. and Seyfarth, R. M. (1990) *How Monkeys See the World*, Chicago: University of Chicago Press.

Clarke, E. D. (1803) *Testimonies of Different Authors Respecting the Colossal Statue of Ceres etc.*, Cambridge.

Corballis, M. (1992) *The Lopsided Ape: Evolution of the Generative Mind*, Oxford: Oxford University Press.

Cosmides, L. and Tooby, J. (1987) 'From evolution to behaviour: evolutionary psychology as the missing link', in J. Dupre (ed.) *The Latest on the Best: Essays on Evolution and Optimality*, Cambridge, Mass.: MIT Press: 277–306.

Curzon, G. N. (1892) *Persia and the Persian Question*, London.

Davidson, I. (1991) 'The archaeology of language origins – a review', *Antiquity* 65: 39–48.

Davidson, I. (1992) 'There's no art – to find the mind's construction – in offence', *Cambridge Archaeological Journal* 2: 52–57.

Davidson, I. and Noble, W. (1989) 'The archaeology of perception: traces of depiction and language', *Current Anthropology* 30: 125–55.

Delpech, F. (1983) *Les Faunes de Paléolithigue Supérieur dans le Sud Ouest de la France*, Paris: Centre National de la Recherche Scientifique.

Dennell, R. (1983) *European Economic Prehistory*, New York: Academic Press.

Dennett, D. (1992) *Consciousness Explained*, London: Penguin Press.

De Sousa, R. (1987) *The Rationality of Emotion*, Cambridge, Mass.: MIT Press.

Dibble, H. (1987) 'The interpretation of middle palaeolithic scraper morphology', *American Antiquity* 52: 109–17.

Dibble, H. (1989) 'The implications of stone tool types for the presence of language during the Lower and Middle Palaeolithic', in P. Mellars and C. Stringer (eds) *The Human Revolution: Behavioural and Biological Perspectives in the Origins of Modern Humans*, Edinburgh: Edinburgh University Press: 415–32.

Dissanayake, E. (1995) *Homo Aestheticus*, Washington, DC: University of Washington Press.

Dodds, E. R. (1951) *The Greeks and the Irrational*, Berkeley: University of California Press.

Dodwell, E. (1819) *A Classical and Topographical Tour through Greece*, London.

Donald, M. (1991) *Origins of the Modern Mind*, Cambridge, Mass.: Harvard University Press.

Dunbar, R. I. M. (1988) *Primate Social Systems*, London: Croom Helm.

Falk, D. (1980) 'Language, handedness and primate brains: did the Australopithecines sign?', *American Anthropologist* 82: 72–78.

Fodor, J. (1983) *The Modularity of Mind*, Cambridge, Mass.: MIT Press.

Frazer, J. G. (1912) *Spirits of the Corn and the Wild* I, London: Macmillan (*The Golden Bough* VII).

Gamble, C. (1982) 'Interaction and alliance in palaeolithic society', *Man* (N.S.) 17: 92–107.

Gamble, C. (1986) *The Palaeolithic Settlement of Europe*, Cambridge: Cambridge University Press.

Gamble, C. (1987) 'Man the shoveler: alternative models for Middle Pleistocene colonization and occupation in northern latitudes', in O. Soffer (ed.) *The Pleistocene Old World*, New York: Plenum Press: 81–98.

Gardner, H. (1983) *Frames of Mind: The Theory of Multiple Intelligences*, London: Heinemann.

Gardner, H. (1987) *The Mind's New Science: A History of the Cognitive Revolution*, New York: Basic Books.

Gibson, K. (1991) 'Tools, language and intelligence: evolutionary implications', *Man* 26: 255–64.

Gombrich, E. H. (1960) *Art and Illusion*, London: Phaidon.

Gombrich, E. H. (1972) *The Story of Art*, London: Phaidon.

Gould, S. (1977) *Ontogeny and Phylogeny*, Cambridge, Mass.: Harvard University Press.

Gowlett, J. (1984) 'The mental abilities of early man: a look at some hard evidence', in R. Foley (ed.) *Human Evolution and Community Ecology*, London: Academic Press: 167–92.

Gowlett, J. (1986) 'Culture and conceptualisation: the Oldowan–Acheulian Gradient', in G. Bailey and P. Callow (eds) *Stone Age Prehistory*, Cambridge: Cambridge University Press: 243–61.

Green, H. S. (1984) *Pontnewydd Cave*, Cardiff: National Museum of Wales.

Griffin, D. R. (1981) *The Question of Animal Awareness* (2nd edition), Los Altos, Calif.: Kaufmann.

Griffin, D. R. (ed.) (1982) *Animal Mind – Human Mind*, Berlin: Springer Verlag.

Harrison, E. (1965) *The Athenian Agora, XI: Archaic and Archaistic Sculpture*, Princeton: American School of Classical Studies at Athens.

Harrold, F. (1989) 'Chatelperronian and early Aurignacian in western Europe: continuity or discontinuity', in P. Mellars and C. Stringer (eds) *The Human Revolution: Behavioural and Biological Perspectives in the Origins of Modern Humans*, Edinburgh: Edinburgh University Press: 677–713.

Haskovec, I. P. and Sullivan, H. (1989) 'Reflections and rejections of an Aboriginal artist', in H. Morphy (ed.) *Animals into Art*, London: Unwin Hyman: 57–74.

Hay, R. (1976) *The Geology of Olduvai Gorge*, Berkeley: University of California Press.

Higgs, E. S. (ed.) (1975) *Palaeoeconomy*, Cambridge: Cambridge University Press.

Hodder, I. (ed.) (1982) *Symbolic and Structural Archaeology*, Cambridge: Cambridge University Press.

Hodder, I. (1985) 'Post-processual archaeology', in M. Schiffer (ed.) *Advances in Archaeological Method and Theory 8*, New York: Academic Press: 1–25.

Hodder, I. (1990) *The Domestication of Europe*, Oxford: Basil Blackwell.

Holloway, R. L. (1969) 'Culture, a human domain', *Current Anthropology* 10: 395–412.

Humphrey, N. (1976) 'The social function of intellect', in P. P. G. Bateson and R. A. Hinde (eds) *Growing Points in Ethology*, Cambridge: Cambridge University Press: 303–17.

Isaac, G. I. (1978) 'The food-sharing behaviour of proto-human hominids', *Scientific American* 238: 90–108.

Isaac, G. I. (1984) 'The archaeology of human origins: studies of the Lower Pleistocene in East Africa', *Advances in World Archaeology* 3: 1–87.

Jahanbegloo, R. (1992) *Conversations with Isaiah Berlin*, London: Peter Halban.

Jelinek, A. (1982) 'The Tabun Cave and palaeolithic man in the Levant', *Science* 216: 1369–75.

Jochim, M. (1983) 'Palaeolithic cave art in ecological perspective', in G. Bailey (ed.) *Hunter-Gatherer Economy in Prehistory*, Cambridge: Cambridge University Press: 212–19.

Jones, P. (1980) 'Experimental butchery with modern stone tools and its relevance for palaeolithic archaeology', *World Archaeology* 12: 153–65.

Keeley, L. (1980) *Experimental Determination of Stone Tool Uses: A Microwear Analysis*, Chicago: Chicago University Press.

Keeley, L. and Toth, N. (1981) 'Microwear polishes on early stone tools from Koobi Fora, Kenya', *Nature* 203: 464–65.

Keller, C. M. (1973) *Montagu Cave in Prehistory*, Berkeley: University of California Press.

Kitto, H. D. F. (1951) *The Greeks*, Harmondsworth: Penguin.

Klein, R. (1989) 'Biological and behavioural perspectives on Modern Human origins in southern Africa', in P. Mellars and C. Stringer (eds) *The Human Revolution: Behavioural and Biological Perspectives in the Origins of Modern Humans*, Edinburgh: Edinburgh University Press: 529–46.

Kris, E. and Kurz, O. (1979) *Legend, Myth and Magic in the Image of the Artist*, New Haven and London: Yale University Press.

Larsen, M. T. (1979) *Power and Propaganda: A Symposium on Ancient Empires*, Copenhagen: Akademisk Forlag.

Leakey, M. (1971) *Olduvai Gorge, Vol. 3, Excavations in Beds I and II*, Cambridge: Cambridge University Press.

Leroi-Gourhan, A. (1968) *The Art of Prehistoric Man in Western Europe*, London: Thames and Hudson.

Lewis-Williams, J. D. (1982) 'The economic and social context of Southern San rock art', *Current Anthropology* 23: 429–49.

Lewis-Williams, J. D. and Dowson, T. A. (1988) 'The signs of all times: entoptic phenomena in upper palaeolithic art', *Current Anthropology* 29: 201–45.

Lieberman, P. (1989) 'The origins of some aspects of human language and cognition', in P. Mellars and C. Stringer (eds) *The Human Revolution: Behavioural and Biological Perspectives in the Origins of Modern Humans*, Edinburgh: Edinburgh University Press: 391–413.

Lindley, J. M. and Clark, G. A. (1990) 'Symbolism and modern human origins', *Current Anthropology* 31: 233–57.

Lloyd, A. B. (1983) 'The Late Period, 664–323 BC', in B. G. Trigger and B. J. Kemp (eds) *Ancient Egypt: A Social History*, Cambridge: Cambridge University Press: 279–364.

Lloyd, G. E. R. (1990) *Demystifying Mentalities*, Cambridge: Cambridge University Press.

Loewy, E. (1907) *The Rendering of Nature in Early Greek Art*, London: Constable.

Lynch, K. (1960) *The Image of the City*, Cambridge, Mass.: MIT Press.

McGrew, W. C., Tutin, C. and Baldwin, P. (1979) 'Chimpanzees, tools, and termites: cross-cultural comparisons of Senegal, Tanzania, and Rio Mini', *Man* 14: 185–214.

Mallwitz, A. (1988) 'Cult and competition locations at Olympia', in W. Raschke (ed.) *The Archaeology of the Olympics*, Madison: University of Wisconsin Press: 79–109.

Marshack, A. (1972) *The Roots of Civilisation*, London: Weidenfeld and Nicolson.

Marshack, A. (1989) 'Early hominid symbol and evolution of the human capacity', in P. Mellars and C. Stringer (eds) *The Human Revolution: Behavioural and Biological Perspectives in the Origins of Modern Humans*, Edinburgh: Edinburgh University Press: 457–98.

Marshack, A. (1991) 'The Tai Plaque and calendrical notation in the Upper Palaeolithic', *Cambridge Archaeological Journal* 1: 25–61.

Martin, R. D. (1983) *Human Brain Evolution in an Ecological Context*, New York: American Museum of Natural History.

Mellars, P. (1973) 'The character of the middle/upper palaeolithic transition in southwest

France', in C. Renfrew (ed.) *The Explanation of Culture Change*, London: Duckworth: 255–76.

Mellars, P. (1989) 'Major issues in the emergence of modern humans', *Current Anthropology* 30: 349–85.

Mellars, P. (1991) 'Cognitive changes and the emergence of modern humans in Europe', *Cambridge Archaeological Journal* 1: 63–76.

Mellars, P. and Stringer, C. (1989) *The Human Revolution: Behavioural and Biological Perspectives in the Origins of Modern Humans*, Edinburgh: Edinburgh University Press.

Meltzoff, A. N. (1988) 'Homo imitans', in T. R. Zentall and B. G. Galef (eds) *Social Learning: a Comparative Approach*, Hillsdale N.J.: Erlbaum Press: 319–42.

Miller, D. and Tilley, C. (eds) (1984) *Ideology, Power and Prehistory*, Cambridge: Cambridge University Press.

Mithen, S. (1988a) 'Looking and learning: upper palaeolithic art and information gathering', *World Archaeology* 19 (3): 297–327.

Mithen, S. (1988b) 'To hunt or to paint? Animals and art in the Upper Palaeolithic', *Man* 23: 71–95.

Mithen, S. (1989) 'Evolutionary theory and post-processual archaeology', *Antiquity* 63: 483–94.

Mithen, S. (1990) *Thoughtful Foragers: A Study of Prehistoric Decision Making*, Cambridge: Cambridge University Press.

Mithen, S. (1991a) 'Ecological interpretations of palaeolithic art', *Proceedings of the Prehistoric Society* 57 (1): 103–14.

Mithen, S. (1991b) 'A cybernetic wasteland? Rationality, emotion and mesolithic foraging', *Proceedings of the Prehistoric Society*, 57 (2): 9–14.

Mithen, S. (1994) 'Technology and society during the Middle Pleistocene', *Cambridge Archaeological Journal* 4: 3–33.

Mithen, S. (1996) *The Prehistory of the Mind*, London: Thames and Hudson.

Morphy, H. (1989) 'On representing Ancestral Beings', in H. Morphy (ed.) *Animals into Art*, London: Unwin Hyman: 144–60.

Oatley, K. and Johnson-Laird, P. (1987) 'Towards a cognitive theory of emotions', *Cognition and Emotions* 1: 1–29.

Otter, W. M. (1824) *Life and Remains of the Rev. E. D. Clarke*, London: J. F. Dove.

Piaget, J. (1960) *The Psychology of Intelligence*, Totowa, N.J.: Littlefield, Adams and Co.

Potts, R. (1988) *Early Hominid Activities at Olduvai*, New York: Aldine de Gruyter.

Price, L. (1954) *Dialogues of Alfred North Whitehead*, London: Riehardt.

Rak, Y., Kimbel, W. H. and Hovers, E. (1994) 'A Neanderthal infant from Amud cave', *Journal of Human Evolution* 26: 313–24.

Renfrew, C. (1982) *Towards an Archaeology of Mind*, Cambridge: Cambridge University Press.

Renfrew, C. (1985) *The Archaeology of Cult: the Sanctuary at Phylakopi*, London: Thames and Hudson.

Renfrew, C. (1986) 'Introduction: peer polity interaction and socio-political change', in C. Renfrew and J. F. Cherry (eds) *Peer Polity Interaction and Socio-Political Change*, Cambridge: Cambridge University Press.

Renfrew, C. and Zubrow, E. (eds) (1994) *The Ancient Mind*, Cambridge: Cambridge University Press.

Richter, G. M. A. (1970) *Kouroi* (3rd edition), London: Phaidon.

Roberts, M. (1986) 'Excavations of the lower palaeolithic site at Amey's Eartham pit, Boxgrove, west Sussex', *Proceedings of the Prehistoric Society* 52: 215–45.

Roe, D. (1981) *The Lower and Middle Palaeolithic Periods in Britain*, London: Routledge and Kegan Paul.

Rolland, N. and Dibble, H. L. (1990) 'A new synthesis of middle palaeolithic variability', *American Antiquity* 55: 480–99.

Sackett, J. R. (1982) 'Approaches to style in lithic archaeology', *Journal of Anthropological Archaeology* 1: 59–112.

Scott, K. (1980) 'Two hunting episodes of middle palaeolithic age at La Cotte de Saint-Brelade, Jersey (Channel Islands)', *World Archaeology* 12: 137–52.

Shanks, M. and Tilley, C. (1982) 'Ideology, symbolic power and ritual communication: a reinterpretation of neolithic mortuary practices', in I. Hodder (ed.) *Symbolic and Structural Archaeology*, Cambridge: Cambridge University Press: 129–54.

Shanks, M. and Tilley, C. (1987) *Reconstructing Archaeology: Theory and Practice*, Cambridge: Cambridge University Press.

Shea, J. J. (1989) 'A functional study of the lithic industries associated with hominid fossils in the Kebara and Qafzeh caves, Israel', in P. Mellars and C. Stringer (eds) *The Human Revolution: Behavioural and Biological Perspectives in the Origins of Modern Humans*, Edinburgh: Edinburgh University Press: 611–25.

Singer, R. and Wymer, J. (1982) *The Middle Stone Age at Klasies River Mouth in South Africa*, Chicago: Chicago University Press.

Smith, F. (1991) 'The Neanderthals: evolutionary dead ends or ancestors of modern people?', *Journal of Anthropological Research* 47: 219–38.

Snodgrass, A. M. (1984) 'The ancient Greek world', in J. Bintliff (ed.) *European Social Evolution: Archaeological Perspectives*, Bradford: University of Bradford: 227–33.

Spiess, A. E. (1979) *Reindeer and Caribou Hunters: An Archaeological Study*, New York: Academic Press.

Spivey, N. J. (1995) 'Bionic statues', in A. Powell (ed.) *The Greek World*, London: Routledge: 442–59.

Spivey, N. J. (1996) *Understanding Greek Sculpture*, London: Thames and Hudson.

Stiles, D. (1991) 'Early hominid behaviour and culture tradition: raw material studies in Bed II, Olduvai Gorge', *The African Archaeological Review* 9: 1–19.

Stopp, M. (1988) 'A Taphonomic Analysis of the Hoxne Site Faunal Assemblages', University of Cambridge, Unpublished M.Phil. thesis.

Straus, L. G. and Clark, G. A. (1986) *La Riera: Stone Age Hunter-Gatherer Adaptations in Cantabrian Spain*, Tucson: University of Arizona Press.

Stringer, C. (1984) 'Human evolution and biological adaptation', in R. Foley (ed.) *Human Evolution and Community Ecology*, London: Academic Press: 55–84.

Susman, R. L. (1991) 'Who made the Oldowan tools? Fossil evidence for tool behaviour in Plio-Pleistocene hominids', *Journal of Anthropological Research* 47: 129–51.

Thomas, J. (1988) 'The social significance of the Cotswold–Severn burial practices', *Man* (N.S.) 23: 540–59.

Tomasello, M. (1990) 'Cultural transmission in tool use and communicatory signalling of chimpanzees', in S. Parker and K. Gibson (eds) *Language and Intelligence in Monkeys and Apes: Developmental Perspectives*, Cambridge: Cambridge University Press: 274–311.

Toth, N. (1985) 'The Oldowan reassessed: a close look at early stone artefacts', *Journal of Archaeological Science* 12: 101–20.

Turner, A. (1992) 'Large carnivores and the earliest European hominids; changing determinants of resource availability during the Lower and Middle Pleistocene', *Journal of Human Evolution* 22: 109–26.

Tyldesley, J. (1986) *The Wolvercote Channel Handaxe Assemblage: a Comparative Study*, Oxford: British Archaeological Reports, British Series 152.

Valoch, K. (1984) 'Le Taubachien, sa géochronologie, paléoécologie et sa paléoethnologie', *L'Anthropologie* 88: 193–208.

Vidal-Nacquet, P. (1986) *The Black Hunter*, Baltimore: Johns Hopkins University Press.

Villa, P. (1983) *Terra Amata and the Middle Pleistocene Archaeological Record from Southern France*, Berkeley: University of California Press.

Villa, P. (1990) 'Torralba and Aridos: elephant exploitation in Middle Pleistocene Spain', *Journal of Human Evolution* 19: 299–309.

Villa, P. (1991) 'Middle Pleistocene prehistory in southwestern Europe: the state of our knowledge and ignorance', *Journal of Anthropological Research* 47: 193–217.

Visalberghi, E. and Fragaszy, D. (1990). 'Do monkeys ape?', in S. Parker and K. Gibson (eds) *Language and Intelligence in Monkeys and Apes: Developmental Perspectives*, Cambridge: Cambridge University Press: 247–73.

Whallon, R. (1989) 'Elements of culture change in the Later Palaeolithic', in P. Mellars and C. Stringer (eds) *The Human Revolution: Behavioural and Biological Perspectives in the Origins of Modern Humans*, Edinburgh: Edinburgh University Press: 433–54.

Wheeler, G. (1676) *Journey into Greece*, London: William Cademan.

White, R. (1982) 'Rethinking the middle/upper palaeolithic transition', *Current Anthropology* 23: 162–92.

Whitehead, A. N. (1929) *Process and Reality*, Cambridge: Cambridge University Press.

Winckelmann, J. J. (1764) *Geschichte der Kunst des Altertums*, Dresden.

Wittgenstein, L. (1979) *Bemerkungen über Frazers Golden Bough* (Remarks on Frazer's Golden Bough) (ed. R. Rhees), Retford: Brynmill Press.

Wymer, J. (1968) *Lower Palaeolithic Archaeology in Britain as Represented by the Thames Valley*, London: John Baker.

Wymer, J. (1988) 'Palaeolithic archaeology and the British Quaternary sequence', *Quaternary Science Reviews* 7: 79–98.

Wynn, T. (1989) *The Evolution of Spatial Competence*, Urbana: University of Illinois Press.

Wynn, T. (1991) 'Tools, grammar and the archaeology of cognition', *Cambridge Archaeological Journal* 1: 191–206.

Wynn, T. and McGrew, W. C. (1989) 'An ape's view of the Oldowan', *Man* (N.S.) 24: 383–98.

Wynn, T. and Tierson, F. (1990) 'Regional comparison of the shapes of later Acheulian handaxes', *American Anthropologist* 92: 73–84.

Yando, R., Seitz, V. and Zigler, E. (1978) *Imitation: A Developmental Perspective*, Hillsdale, N.J.: Lawrence Erlbaum Assoc.

Yates, F. M. (1966) *The Art of Memory*, London: Routledge.

Yellen, J. E., Brooks, A. S., Cornellissen, E. *et al.* (1995) 'A middle stone age worked bone industry from Katanda, upper Semliki valley, Zaire', *Science* 268: 553–56.

Zimmern, A. (1922) *The Greek Commonwealth* (3rd edition), Oxford: Clarendon Press.

Zvelebil, M. (1986) 'Postglacial foraging in the forests of Europe', *Scientific American* (May): 86–93.

SELECT BIBLIOGRAPHY

There has been a massive surge of interest in the evolution of human cognition during the last decade, with contributions coming from archaeologists, anthropologists, psychologists and philosophers; one work that has tried to integrate material from these disciplines is Mithen (1996). R. Byrne, *The Thinking Ape* (Oxford: Oxford University Press, 1995), provides an excellent review of the chimpanzee mind and its implications for the early stages of human cognitive evolution. Three very useful collections of papers which are dominated by studies of early cognition are P. Mellars and K. Gibson, *Modelling the Early Human Mind* (Cambridge: McDonald Institute, 1996), J. Maynard-Smith, *The Evolution of Social Behaviour: Patterns Among Primates and Man* (London: Proceedings of the British Academy, 1996), and T. Ingold and K. Gibson, *Tools, Language and Cognition in Human Evolution* (Cambridge: Cambridge University Press, 1993). *Gossip, Grooming and the Evolution of Language* by R. Dunbar (London: Faber, 1996) provides a provocative theory for the evolution of language and includes a useful summary for changes in the dimensions of the human brain during evolution. Studies of early stone tools which focus on their cognitive implications include Wynn (1989).

For classical Greece, some consideration of 'Hellenization' is essential before turning to the archaeological themes discussed here: F. M. Turner, *The Greek Heritage in Victorian Britain* (Yale: Yale University Press, 1981), is a good introduction to the study of classical paradigms in Western culture, and see also M. Bernal, *Black Athena* (London: Free Association Press, 1987). J. G. Frazer's *The Golden Bough* and his *Commentary on Pausanias* (London: Macmillan, 1898) remain highly useful; for a review of Frazer's current standing, see P. Burke (1986) 'Strengths and weaknesses of the history of *mentalités*', *Journal of the History of European Ideas* 7: 439–51. On the aesthetic consequences of the Greek belief in animated art, see Spivey (1995). For the archaeology of Athenian democracy, see Camp (1986) on the American excavations of the Agora, and for the planning of classical Greek cities see W. Hoepfner and E.-L. Schwandner, *Haus und Stadt im Klassischen Griechenland* (Munich: Deutsche Kunstverlag, 1986), and W. Schuller (ed.), *Demokratie und Architektur* (Munich: Deutsche Kunstverlag, 1989).

Part III

WRITING
ARCHAEOLOGICAL
HISTORY

19

HUMAN EVOLUTION

Andrew T. Chamberlain

INTRODUCTION

Humans, like all other biological species, have an evolutionary history. The evidence for human evolution is found in the fossil and archaeological records and in the detailed similarities between modern humans and their closest relatives among living animals, the primates. The fossil record consists of the mineralized remains of bones and teeth with occasional preservation of the outlines of soft tissues, such as fossilized footprints. Fossils provide most of our information about the earlier, extinct species of humans which preceded the 'anatomically modern' humans that make up the world's population today. The emergence of uniquely human characteristics, such as upright posture, bipedal locomotion, increase in brain size and specialization of the hand, can be investigated by studying these fossils and identifying the changes that have occurred in human skeletal anatomy. Dating of the fossil record establishes the sequence and rate at which these evolutionary changes have occurred.

Although there are many palaeontological sites that have yielded human fossils, most of these sites have produced only fragmentary remains of one or a few individuals. The fossil record for the earliest humans is still surprisingly incomplete compared with the record for other groups of terrestrial mammals. The earliest humans occupied habitats and had a mode of life similar to primates, and like modern monkeys and apes the early humans would have made up only a small proportion of the animal species occupying their environment: in the modern East African savannah ecosystem, for example, primates constitute less than one per cent of the large mammal biomass production.

Humans share many anatomical, physiological, and behavioural similarities with prosimians, monkeys and apes, and these animals are classified together in the order Primates. Biological classification is hierarchical, reflecting the fact that the similarities between animal species define a nested pattern of affinity: similar species are grouped into a genus (plural = genera), similar genera into a family, and so on. This hierarchy is the result of the divergence, or 'cladogenesis', of lineages which occurs when new species are formed. After divergence, the separate lineages of descendants can no longer exchange genetic material, and the combined influence of differential selection pressure and genetic drift will eventually ensure that the species acquire differences in appearance and behaviour.

Modern humans are classified as the species *sapiens* in the genus *Homo*. It is impossible to observe directly the behaviour and genetic structure of early humans, but their fossilized remains differ in appearance (morphology) from modern humans to such an extent that they are classified in different species and sometimes in different genera from ourselves. Palaeontologists recognize and define fossil species by applying the principle of uniformitarianism. The members of a species are individually variable in their appearance, and yet there are usually morphological discontinuities ('gaps') that separate the members of one species from those of another. Palaeontologists make the quite reasonable assumption that fossil species should show approximately the same amount of variation as modern species, and therefore they do not as a rule classify very different fossils in the same species, nor do they create new species solely to account for small differences that are more plausibly interpreted as within-species variation. Of course, with only bones and teeth to work on, it is quite possible that the palaeontologist will not be able to recognize species that were identical in their skeletal anatomy while differing in non-fossilizable features such as coat colour, chromosome number or reproductive behaviour. There is therefore a tendency to underestimate the number of species that are represented by fossils (Foley 1991; Groves 1989; Tattersall 1986), but this practice is preferable to inventing species solely on the basis of minor individual differences.

At present there are about ten separate species recognized in the human fossil record, most of which are are grouped into two genera, *Australopithecus* and *Homo*. Some palaeontologists place the 'robust' australopithecines in a separate genus called *Paranthropus*, and recently an early australopithecine species has been placed in the distinct genus *Ardipithecus* (see p. 774). There has been considerable discussion about the distinction between *Australopithecus* and *Homo* but, as a general rule, species of *Australopithecus* differ from members of the genus *Homo* in having teeth that are large and brains that are small in relation to these animals' overall body size. There has also been debate about the defining features of the family Hominidae, into which *Australopithecus* and *Homo* are grouped. Although the earliest forms of *Australopithecus* were adapted to bipedalism, they were quite primitive in their cranial structure, and are difficult to distinguish from some fossils of Miocene apes.

It is therefore convenient to adopt an evolutionary definition of the Hominidae as the group containing all taxa (that is, species and genera) that are more closely related to *Homo sapiens* than to any other living primate. In other words this is the clade that includes all descendants of the lineage that diverged from the African apes in the late Miocene about eight million years ago (Fig. 19.1). The late divergence of the African apes and humans, which is responsible for their close genetic similarity, has led some authors to group *Australopithecus* and *Homo* into the subfamily Homininae. These same authors use the term Hominidae for the group containing both humans and African apes, but in this chapter the expressions 'hominid' and 'humans' refer exclusively to the clade whose sole living representative is *Homo sapiens*.

PRIMATES AND HUMANS TODAY

Primates are a group of mammals that diverged from other mammalian orders in the early Tertiary era, after the demise of the dinosaurs at about *c.* 65 million years ago. Living non-human primates are confined to the tropical and subtropical areas of the world, and since many species prefer arboreal habitats, most primates are further restricted to forest and woodland biomes. The living primates are classified into a primitive group called the prosimians and a more derived group that includes the monkeys of South and Central America (the New World monkeys or platyr-rhine primates) and the apes and monkeys of Africa and Asia (the catarrhine primates). Most of the prosimian primates are small, solitary nocturnal animals with an insectivorous diet, such as the bush-babies in Africa and the lorises and tarsiers in Asia, but on the island of Madagascar the prosimians diversified and include larger-bodied diurnal and social species. A much more primitive group of animals that is sometimes included within the primates, the Plesiadapiformes, became extinct and are known only from fossils dating to the early part of the Tertiary.

Primates are adapted to live and find their food in the three-dimensional world of the tropical forests. Their senses of vision and touch are more developed than their hearing and smell, and all primates have forward-facing eyes and the ability to grasp objects between the thumb and the rest of the hand. Unlike other arboreal animals such as squirrels, primates cling to supports by grasping with hands and feet rather than using claws. In fact, primate claws have evolved into nails that protect the sensitive touch pads on the tips of the fingers and toes. The inner surfaces of the hands and feet of primates are covered in ridged 'friction skin' (dermatoglyphs, or finger and palm prints) that enhances the grip and provides extra sensitivity when assessing the texture and resilience of touched objects. When travelling quadruped-ally, primates support more of their body weight on the hind limbs than the fore-limbs, and they usually contact the ground with the soles of their feet (plantigrade

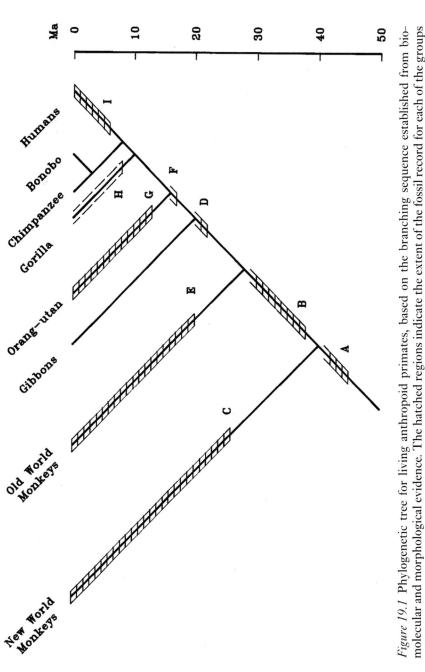

Figure 19.1 Phylogenetic tree for living anthropoid primates, based on the branching sequence established from biomolecular and morphological evidence. The hatched regions indicate the extent of the fossil record for each of the groups of living primates. Fossil evidence for the first appearance of these lineages is as follows: A. Anthropoids (*Algeripithecus*, *Eosimias*); B. Catarrhines (*Aegyptopithecus*, *Propliopithecus*); C. Platyrrhines (*Branizella*, *Tremacebus*, *Dolichocebus*); D. Hominoids (*Proconsul*); E. Cercopithecoids (*Victoriapithecus*); F. Great Apes (*Afropithecus*); G. Pongines (*Sivapithecus*); H. ?Gorillines (*Samburu Hills*); I. Hominids (*Australopithecus*). Dates in millions of years ago (Ma). Source: A. T. Chamberlain.

locomotion) rather than just their toes (digitigrade locomotion). When they cease moving they often adopt a more upright posture that frees the hands for manipulative tasks.

Primate diets are comprised of fruits (including seeds and nuts); other plant items such as foliage, flowers, twigs and resins; and animal prey (mainly insects and other invertebrates, although some primates also pursue and eat small vertebrates). The larger-bodied primates tend to consume a greater proportion of food items with low nutritional value, while the smallest primates tend to include a more substantial amount of insects in their diet. Dietary specialization is reflected in the structure of the teeth and jaws. Fruit-eating primates have large strong front teeth for penetrating the hard outer layers of fruits and seeds, and enlarged premolars that serve to maximize the available grinding surfaces in the mouth. Leaf-eating primates have small front teeth and develop sharp cutting ridges on their chewing teeth. These primates also have large and elaborate digestive tracts that encourage the fermentation of structural carbohydrates that would otherwise be difficult to digest. Insectivorous primates have relatively tall, pointed-cusped, teeth that serve to hold and crush their insect prey. Unlike other insectivorous mammals, primates capture insects by grasping them in one or both hands, an action which requires precise hand–eye coordination.

Primate social groups are stable, cooperative structures in which the members recognize each other individually and can distinguish each other's kinship relationships. Compared with most other mammals, the social bonds between individuals in a primate group are strong, and movement of animals between groups is relatively uncommon. Social interactions in a group are strongly influenced by the pattern of dominance relations among individuals. The facility for individual recognition leads to the development in some primate species of sophisticated social behaviour, including the formation of coalitions and friendships and the occurrence of deliberate social manipulation and deception. Group sizes range from solitary, through monogamous pairs with dependent offspring, to large groups with multiple breeding males. In most primate species the males, on maturing, leave the group in which they were born, with the result that closely related females form the core of the social group. Chimpanzees are exceptional in that females transfer out of their natal group, and related males form the affiliative core of the group.

Compared with other mammals of similar body size, primates have relatively long gestation periods and usually give birth to one or at most two offspring at a time. Young infants are highly dependent on parental care and are carried by their parents for the first few months of life. Growth to sexual maturity is slow and lifespans are often relatively long, providing enhanced opportunities for social learning. Immature primates copy or are passively guided, rather than instructed, by other group members in their acquisition of survival skills, unlike human societies in which teaching is universal.

The Hominoidea is the taxonomic group containing the apes and humans. The hominoids comprise relatively few species today, but were much more diverse in both numbers of species and geographic range during the Miocene epoch. Hominoids are predominantly frugivorous, having broad incisor and molar teeth, and are adapted to climbing and suspensory patterns of movement in the trees. Their forelimbs are relatively long and the shoulder and wrist joints have enhanced mobility, permitting the hand to grasp supports that have different orientations and heights above the head. In this way they contrast with the monkeys, which are more strictly quadrupedal in locomotion. The gibbons, also known as the lesser apes, are small-bodied hominoids that have a specialized mode of arboreal locomotion – 'brachiation', or arm-swinging. They are classified in two genera: *Hylobates* and *Symphalangus*. The living great apes comprise the Asian orang-utan (*Pongo pygmaeus*) and the African apes, which include three species: the gorilla (*Gorilla gorilla*), chimpanzee (*Pan troglodytes*) and bonobo or 'pygmy' chimpanzee (*Pan paniscus*). The African apes are closely related both genetically and morphologically to modern humans, and the chimpanzees in particular are often used as structural and behavioural models for early hominids.

LOOKING AT THE PAST

Fossils and dating

The word fossil means 'something dug up from the ground', but in palaeontology it has a more restricted meaning: the petrified remains of an organism. Fossil fuels do not qualify as fossils in the strict sense because they are not identifiable at the organismal level, and bodies preserved in bogs or in frozen ground are tanned or mummified rather than fossilized. The expression 'sub-fossil' is sometimes used to denote the remains of organisms that have commenced but not completed the process of fossilization. During fossilization the soft tissues of the animal are usually lost through decay, while the hard parts of the skeleton are altered by 'diagenesis', the combined effect of temperature, pressure and chemical reactions in the ground. Diagenesis, which is also responsible for the conversion of soft unconsolidated sediments into hard rocks, modifies skeletal tissues through recrystallization, permineralization and replacement. The mineral crystals originally present in living calcified tissues (which include shells, antlers, bones and teeth) are unstable under the changing conditions of burial, and these minerals tend to recrystallize. In some burial environments the original mineral in the skeleton is dissolved away and replaced by new mineral growth, while porous media such as spongy bone or plant tissues can be partially replaced or impregnated by new minerals (permineralization). 'Trace fossils' are the fossilized remains of animal

762

behaviour such as tracks, burrows and coprolites. Some of the earliest hominid remains, the human footprints discovered at Laetoli in Tanzania, are trace fossils.

The following circumstances provide ideal conditions for fossilization: (1) *rapid burial*, which reduces damage caused by carnivores, by abrasion during water transport, and by the exposure to the sun and wind; (2) *lacustrine or marine environments*, in which continuous sedimentation occurs, reducing the likelihood of reworking of sediments and erosion of fossil-bearing layers; the fine-grained embedding matrix provided by lake sediments also reduces the oxygen content and preserves fine surface detail on the fossil; (3) *slightly alkaline ground water*, such as occurs in calcareous deposits, gives the best preservation of bone and teeth (acid water tends to dissolve the mineral component of the skeleton).

Fossils can be dated in the same way as archaeological finds: either by direct dating or indirectly by determining the time of deposition of the sediments in which they are buried. Absolute dating methods monitor the progression of physical or chemical processes that are slow and regular in time, and are not influenced by the conditions of burial (see Chapter 5). Radio-carbon dating is applicable to the youngest parts of the fossil record, but is effectively limited to organic samples or biogenic carbonates that date to less than 50 ka (50,000 years ago). Potassium-argon dating is suitable for volcanic sediments from 50 ka to many millions of years old. Uranium series dating can be applied to chemically precipitated calcium carbonates and is therefore useful for dating limestones, travertines and stalagmitic deposits in caves. This method conveniently overlaps the radio-carbon and potassium-argon ranges and is suitable for samples up to about 500 ka. Fission-track dating, electron spin resonance (ESR), thermoluminescence (TL) and optically stimulated luminescence (OSL) are different procedures for measuring the accumulated energy from radioactive decay that is stored in crystalline materials; these methods can be applied to lithic artefacts, sediment grains and bones and teeth.

Other important approaches to dating are the methods that allow correlations to be established between the stratigraphies of different fossil sites. When sediments and volcanic rocks are deposited they acquire a magnetization as small magnetic particles in the rock align themselves with the earth's magnetic field. The polarity of the earth's field has reversed many times during the last 10 million years, with the most recent change occurring at about 700 ka. Knowledge of the direction of magnetization of a sample helps to limit the range of possible dates assigned to it. A more finely subdivided chronostratigraphy is provided by the deep ocean oxygen isotope record, which tracks the variation in the ratio of the stable isotopes ^{18}O and ^{16}O in fossil microfauna in deep sea sediments. During periods of cold climate (such as glacials) more precipitated water, and hence more of the lighter isotope ^{16}O, is locked up in glaciers and polar ice caps, thereby raising the marine concentration of ^{18}O. In some parts of the world volcanic eruptions are sufficiently large to spread thin ash layers over very large areas. Individual ash layers can be identified in a sedimentary sequence by their unique chemical composition or 'fingerprint'. A sample of the ash layer is analysed, and the amounts of different major and trace elements provide the signature of a particular volcanic eruption, which can be correlated between the different sites at which it was deposited. The patterns of evolutionary change in lineages of animals are the basis of biostratigraphic dating, which has been used, for example, to date Middle Pleistocene sites in Europe (van Kolfschoten 1990).

Molecular evidence

The phylogenetic relationships and evolutionary histories of organisms can be determined from the analysis of large complex biomolecules: proteins and DNA. Proteins form a major and diverse component of living tissue, being used as structural materials, as transporting molecules (such as haemoglobin, an oxygen-carrying molecule) and as enzymes that act as highly efficient catalysts in biochemical processes. Proteins are large, chain-like, molecules built up out of sub-units called amino acids. There are twenty different amino acids and they can be linked together in any combination, the precise order or sequence being specified by the organism's DNA. The sequence of amino acids determines the protein's physical properties and chemical activity.

The DNA molecule is an even larger double-chain molecule. The longitudinal strands of the double-chain are made from alternating phosphate and sugar sub-units, and the strands are connected between their sugar sub-units by cross-linked pairs of bases. Each cross-link consists of one of two possible pairs of bases, adenine with cytosine or guanine with thymine, but these pairs can be orientated either way round, so there are four possible arrangements at each cross-link position in the DNA molecule. The sequence of base pairs along the DNA molecule determines the amino acid sequence of the organism's proteins, with successive groups of three DNA base-pairs coding for one particular amino acid in a protein molecule. Other parts of the DNA sequence control the growth and development of the organism, and the activities within the organism's cells. As with proteins, the number of possible combinations of DNA base pairs is virtually limitless, but the DNA molecule has a further property. The double-chained molecule can be separated into two single chains by splitting the cross-linked base pairs, and then each chain can serve as a template for the synthesis of a new copy of the opposite chain. Thus DNA not only carries the information that determines protein structure but also can replicate itself, an action that is essential in reproduction when copies of DNA are passed between generations.

Although each individual has a unique DNA sequence, members of a single species are quite similar in their DNA. The most variable parts of the DNA molecule are the sequences of 'junk' DNA which do not appear to code for structural proteins. Sequence differences of about 0.1 per cent are found between human individuals in these parts of the genome, allowing individuals to be 'fingerprinted' by determining their unique base-pair sequences. Differences between individuals belonging to separate but closely related species, for example between a chimpanzee and a human, average just a few per cent in the variable parts of the DNA molecule. The measurement of sequence differences between species provides a way of reconstructing the evolutionary pathways by which they have diverged from a common ancestral species. After two lineages become separated, the DNA (and protein) sequences of the species tend to diverge, as random genetic mutations accumulate in the lineages with each successive generation. Most of the DNA from cell nuclei is non-coding, so most of the mutations that occur in the DNA will neither benefit nor disadvantage the organism and will therefore be passed on to succeeding generations. The rate of this 'neutral' evolution of DNA depends on the properties of the organism, such as efficiency of DNA repair during replication and average generation length, rather than on external factors that could be influenced by the environment. Therefore the differences that accumulate between the DNA molecules of a pair of species are roughly proportional to the length of time that has elapsed since the species diverged from their common ancestor.

Protein and DNA comparisons have been used to construct a well-corroborated sequence of branching among the main groups of living higher primates (Fig. 19.1). The branching pattern can be converted into a 'molecular clock' for determining the time of individual branching events by calibrating at least one speciation event using reliably dated fossil evidence. The molecular phylogeny for the primates has been calibrated at two points, by the fossil evidence for the emergence of the cercopithecoid (Old World Monkey) lineage at 25–35 MYA (million years ago), and by a date for the origin of the lineage leading to the orang-utan, which diverged from the African ape and human lineage before 13 MYA but probably not earlier than 17 MYA. One prediction of this molecular clock is that humans diverged from the African apes in the late Miocene, less than 10 MYA and perhaps as recently as 7 MYA.

Genetic investigations have also been made of living human populations, using a range of different gene frequency and DNA sequence data (Cavalli-Sforza *et al.* 1994; Richards *et al.* 1996; Stoneking 1993). The evidence from these studies suggests that modern humans had a single place of origin, most probably in Africa and around 100–150 thousand years ago, rather than evolving from the regional variants of earlier Pleistocene hominids found in Africa, Europe and Asia.

EARLY PRIMATES

Primates originated in the early Tertiary era at a time when other mammalian orders were rapidly diversifying following the extinction of the dinosaurs at the end of the Cretaceous. During the earliest part of the Tertiary, the Palaeocene (66–55 MYA), the Atlantic Ocean was beginning to widen (Fig. 19.2). North America and Europe were still sufficiently close to permit terrestrial animals to move between these continents, but South America, Africa and India were island continents separated by deep seas from Eurasia and North America. The earliest primates were small, structurally generalized and probably insectivorous and nocturnal animals, and it is exceedingly difficult to distinguish their fossils from those of other contemporary small mammals. One group of 'quasi-primates' that was present in North America and Europe from the early Palaeocene is the Plesiadapiforms (Rose 1994). These animals were very common and diverse, with many species and genera classified into up to six families, and they comprise up to 40 per cent of the mammal species at some North American fossil sites. Their teeth are sharp cusped, indicating a largely insectivorous diet, but they lack virtually all the structural features that define later primates such as forward-facing eyes, increased brain size, an ossified post-orbital bar on the skull, grasping foot, and nails rather than claws on the digits. It is possible that modern primates originated from within this group, but one family of Plesiadapiforms, the Paromomyids, has been shown to be related to colugos ('flying lemurs') rather than to true primates, and the relevance of Plesiadapiforms in early primate evolution is uncertain (Cartmill 1992).

By the end of the Palaeocene most of the Plesiadapiforms had become extinct, and the first true primates had begun to appear. Until recently little was known about early Tertiary primates in Africa. The teeth of the fossil primate *Altiatlasius*, found at Adrar Mgorn in Morocco and dating to the late Palaeocene, suggest that it may be an early representative of the omomyids, one of the major groups of Eocene primates (Rose 1994).

The Eocene (55–36 MYA) was a time of global warming, when the tropical climatic conditions favourable to modern forms of primates became widespread in the northern hemisphere. The early Eocene mammalian faunas of Europe and North America were similar to each other, but continental drift during the Eocene led to a widening of the North Atlantic, which increasingly restricted faunal exchange between the continents. The main primate groups of the Eocene, the adapids and the omomyids, were equivalent in their structure and adaptations to modern prosimians. The adapids resembled modern lemurs, though with longer body and tail (Fig. 19.3), and they were heavier and had longer snouts than the omomyids, which more closely resemble modern tarsiers and galagos.

There is considerable debate about whether the first fossil representatives of the Anthropoid primates (monkeys and apes) evolved in Africa or in Asia during the

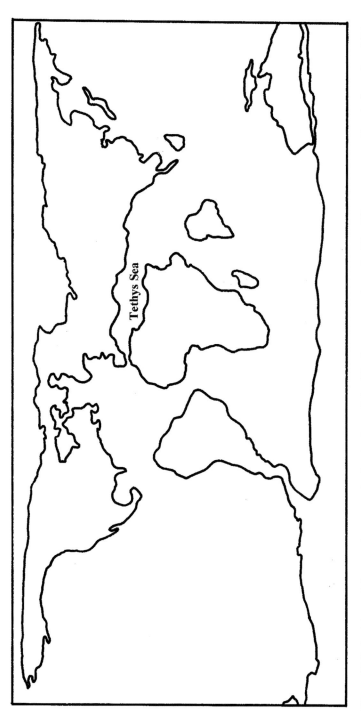

Tethys Sea

Figure 19.2 Position of the continents at the beginning of the Tertiary, approximately 60 million years ago. South America, Africa and India were separated by a continuous seaway from Eurasia and North America. Source: Smith *et al.* 1981.

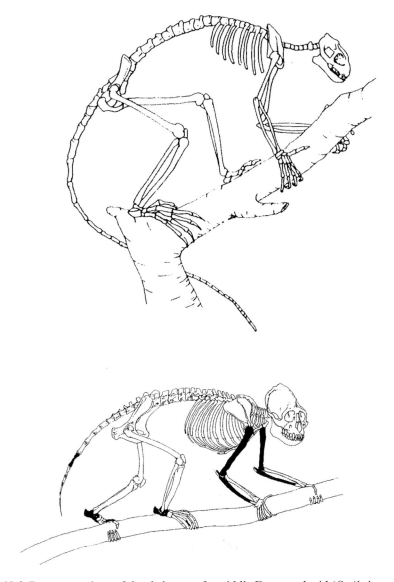

Figure 19.3 Reconstructions of the skeletons of a middle Eocene adapid (*Smilodectes*, above) and an early Oligocene propliopithecid (*Aegyptopithecus*, below). Source: Fleagle 1988.

early part of the Eocene. At Glib Zegdou in Algeria, the fossil teeth of an Early or Middle Eocene (about 45 MYA) primate called *Algeripithecus* have been discovered (Godinot and Mahboubi 1992). This primate, though much smaller than living African monkeys, resembles later African fossils such as the Oligocene monkey *Aegyptopithecus* in the detailed shape of its teeth. Of similar age is a primitive anthropoid called *Eosimias*, recovered from Late Middle Eocene deposits in Shanxi, China (Beard *et al.* 1996). Anthropoid primate fossils have also been found in Late Eocene deposits in Burma and Thailand at sites dating to about 40 MYA. The fossils are *Pondaungia* and *Amphipithecus* from Burma, and *Siamopithecus* from Krabi in Thailand (Chaimanee *et al.* 1997). Compared to adapids and omomyids, the early anthropoids had deeper jaws and more rounded cusps to their cheek teeth (bunodonty), indicating that they were incorporating a larger proportion of hard foods in their diet.

In the Oligocene (36–25 MYA), plate tectonic movements brought the continents into approximately their present-day arrangement, although North and South America were still separated by a deep-water seaway. Rapid global cooling in the early part of the Oligocene may have been triggered by changes in ocean currents and increased polar glaciation following the separation of the continents of South America and Australia from Antarctica. Nearly all primates became extinct in Europe and North America at this time, leaving the tropical latitudes of Africa, Asia and South America as centres of primate evolution.

In Africa, an extensive and diverse early Oligocene fossil primate fauna has been found at the Fayum in Egypt, a site that has been dated by palaeomagnetic methods to 36–33 MYA (Simons 1995). This site has produced fossils of two prosimian species, two groups of ancestral catarrhine primates (the parapithecids and the propliopithecids), and the oligopithecids, which are primitive anthropoids (Simons and Rasmussen 1994). The Fayum parapithecid species belong to the genera *Apidium*, *Parapithecus*, *Qatrania* and *Simonsius*, and range in body size from 300 to 3,000 g. The teeth of these primates show that they were predominantly frugivorous. The propliopithecids, which include the genera *Propliopithecus* and *Aegyptopithecus*, were larger in body size and had teeth that more closely resembled those of the Miocene apes, although their skeletons were adapted for arboreal quadrupedal locomotion as in other monkeys, rather than climbing and suspension as in modern apes (Fig. 19.3). The oligopithecids, which include the genera *Catopithecus*, *Oligopithecus* and *Proteopithecus*, have the same dental formula as Old World monkeys and apes, but in other respects their teeth resemble those of the Eocene adapids. They are therefore viewed as primitive ancestral anthropoids.

The earliest fossil primates in South America date to the late Oligocene (MacFadden 1990). It is not yet known whether these Oligocene primates migrated from North America or from Africa: either route would have required rafting across extensive bodies of water, since South America was still isolated from the other continents at this time (Fig. 19.4). But the global cooling which reached its greatest extent in the middle of the Oligocene also lowered sea levels, reducing the length of the water crossing and perhaps creating a series of island stepping stones in the shallower areas of the equatorial Atlantic Ocean. The Oligocene primates *Branizella* from Bolivia and *Tremacebus* and *Dolichocebus* from Argentina resemble

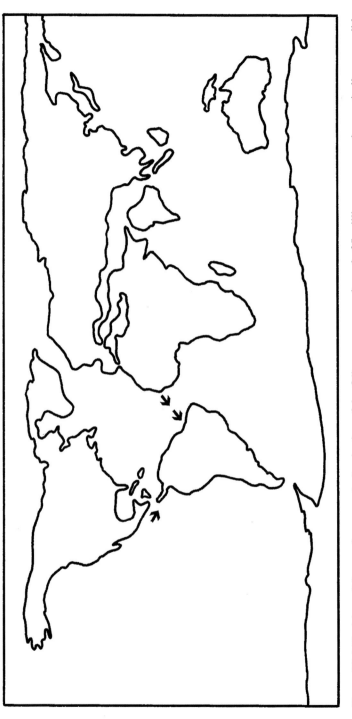

Figure 19.4 Position of the continents at the beginning of the Oligocene, approximately 35 million years ago. Arrows indicate possible routes by which anthropoid primates colonized South America. Source: Smith *et al.* 1981.

the early anthropoids of the Fayum in Africa, which is the only other continent with fossil anthropoids at this period. Subsequently the Oligocene primates evolved into the diverse spectrum of New World primates that now occupy the forested regions of South and Central America.

EVOLUTION OF APES

A large time interval separates the early Oligocene anthropoids of the Fayum and the next oldest catarrhine primates, which are found in the Early Miocene (25–16 MYA) in East Africa. At some point during this interval, the apes (Hominoidea) diverged from the other catarrhine primates (Fig. 19.5). The apes differ from the catarrhine monkeys in having expanded skulls, broader incisors and molars, reduced differences between the premolars, deeper jaws, an absent tail and a series of modifications of the limb bones. The forelimb shows increased flexibility at the shoulder, elbow and wrist joints, while the hindlimb has increased hip and ankle mobility. These are adaptations for the wider range of climbing and suspensory postures that are used by apes.

In the Early Miocene, the global climate was warmer than in the preceding

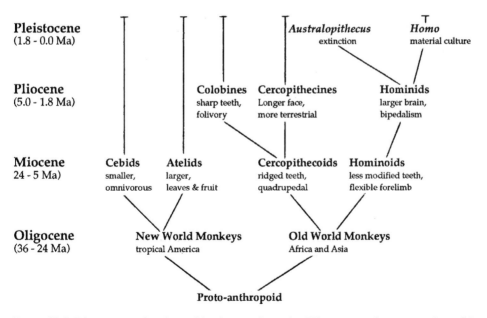

Figure 19.5 Divergence of anthropoid primates from the Oligocene to the present day, with an indication of the major morphological adaptations in each lineage; dates in millions of years ago (Ma). Source: A. T. Chamberlain.

771

Oligocene, and the expanding forests of Africa were populated by an abundant and diverse range of primitive apes. In the Middle Miocene (16–11 MYA), the African/ Arabian continental plate made contact with Eurasia, closing the Tethys Sea (whose remnants form the present day Mediterranean and Caspian Seas) and allowing the northward emigration of African land mammals into Eurasia. The changes in ocean circulation, together with continuing uplift of the Himalayan mountains, led to cooler and drier conditions prevailing in Africa in the Middle Miocene, although true grassland habitats did not predominate in the East African landscape until the late Miocene (11–5 MYA).

The early Miocene fossil sites of East Africa are associated with volcanic lavas and tuffs that erupted from volcanoes along the developing rift valley system. The volcanic layers allow the fossils to be dated radiometrically to between 22 and 16 MYA. Although today this region has a semi-arid climate, in the Early Miocene there was a continuous moist tropical forest extending right across East Africa to the Indian Ocean coast. Fossils of up to six species of ape have been found at a single site, showing that the apes were much more diverse than in present-day Africa. The early Miocene apes probably occupied some of the niches which were subsequently exploited by monkeys, which have come to far outnumber the apes in present-day Africa. The large-bodied (>15 kg) early Miocene apes belong to the genera *Proconsul*, *Rangwapithecus* and *Afropithecus*, while a series of smaller-sized (<10 kg) apes belong to the genera *Micropithecus*, *Nyanzapithecus*, *Simiolus* and *Turkanapithecus*. These taxa had predominantly frugivorous diets, with the exception of *Rangwapithecus* and *Nyanzapithecus*, which were specialized folivores.

During the Middle Miocene, most of the early Miocene ape genera disappear in Africa, but they are replaced at sites such as Fort Ternan, Maboko and Ngorora by a new genus, *Kenyapithecus*. Unlike the early Miocene apes, this genus had robust jaws and thick enamel on its teeth, indicating a dietary shift towards harder foodstuffs. *Kenyapithecus*, which was once classified together with *Ramapithecus* as a hominid (thick enamel is a characteristic of early hominids), was thought to be adapted to open country habitats, but palaeoenvironmental studies of Fort Ternan, a *Kenyapithecus* locality dating to 14 MYA, show that closed forest or woodland was present at this site. *Kenyapithecus* is now thought to be an early representative of the lineage leading to great apes and humans. Closed humid forests also characterized the palaeoenvironment at Berg Aukas in Namibia, where a fossil jaw of the middle Miocene hominoid *Otavipithecus* has recently been recovered (Conroy *et al.* 1993).

Although primates are virtually absent from Europe and Asia in the Early Miocene, a diverse range of catarrhine primates occupied these continents in the Middle and Late Miocene. Several distinct taxonomic families of apes have been identified in the Eurasian Miocene fossil record. The dryopithecids were large (20–40 kg) frugivorous apes, including *Dryopithecus* from Europe and *Lufengpithecus* from China. A partial skeleton of *Dryopithecus laietanus* found at Can Llobateres in

Spain shows that the species was adapted to below-branch arboreal locomotion similar to that seen in the present-day orang-utan (Moyà-Solà and Köhler 1996). The pongids (which include the modern orang-utan *Pongo pygmaeus*) are represented by the fossil genera *Sivapithecus* and *Gigantopithecus*. The pongids are all large apes, with body weights ranging from about 40 kg in small species of *Sivapithecus* to as much as 300 kg in the appropriately named *Gigantopithecus*. *Oreopithecus*, which is represented only by a single species from sites in northern Italy, was a large folivorous catarrhine primate that is currently placed in the Hominoidea in its own family, the oreopithecids. *Graecopithecus* (= *Ouranopithecus*), represented by late Miocene fossils from northern Greece, shows some close similarities to the living African apes, and this genus may therefore be a close relative of the hominids (De Bonis and Koufos 1994). Two additional genera from China, *Dionysopithecus* and *Platydontopithecus*, are unlike the other Eurasian apes and may be representatives of the proconsulids, a family containing mainly early Miocene African taxa.

Fossil remains from Pakistan and Turkey of the hominoid genus *Sivapithecus* have teeth with relatively thick enamel, and their skulls show several similarities to the modern orang-utan with which they are grouped in the family Pongidae. The genus *Ramapithecus*, once thought to be an ancestral hominid, is now also included within the genus *Sivapithecus*.

EARLY HOMINIDS: *AUSTRALOPITHECUS*

Two lines of evidence support an African origin for hominids. First, the primates that are most closely related to hominids are the chimpanzee, bonobo and gorilla, which are endemic to Africa. Among living primates closely related genera and species tend to occupy adjacent geographical areas, and this implies that the divergence of the African ape and hominid lineages may have occurred in Africa. Second, all hominid fossils that have been found outside Africa are no earlier than the terminal Pliocene (1.8 MYA), whereas fossils assigned to the extinct hominid genus *Australopithecus* are present in East Africa from about 6 MYA (Table 19.1).

The oldest fossil hominid yet discovered is a lower jaw from Lothagam in Kenya. This fossil was found in sedimentary deposits between volcanic layers with radiometric dates of 3.8 and 8.5 MYA: faunal correlations between Lothagam and other dated fossil sites show that the jaw is about 5.6 MYA, and is thus late Miocene in age. In contrast with the sparse late Miocene fossil record, there are many Pliocene fossil sites in Africa, and at least a dozen of these have yielded early hominids from the time interval between 6 and 3 MYA (Table 19.1). Several of these fossils have been attributed to *Australopithecus afarensis*, a species that is best known from the samples recovered at Laetoli in Tanzania and Hadar in Ethiopia. The fossil limb bones

Table 19.1 The earliest fossil evidence for hominids in Africa; dates in millions of years ago (MYA)

Date (MYA)	Site	Specimen	Taxonomic attribution
3.0–3.4	Bahr el Ghazal, Chad	KT 12/H1 mandible	*Australopithecus bahrelghazali*
3.2	Hadar, Ethiopia	AL 288–1 'Lucy' skeleton	*Australopithecus afarensis*
3.4	Omo, Ethiopia	Omo 20–1886 tooth	*Australopithecus*
3.6	Laetoli, Tanzania	LH 4 mandible	*Australopithecus afarensis*
3.9	Allia Bay, Kenya	ER 20432 mandible fragment	*Australopithecus anamensis*
<4.0	Maka, Ethiopia	MAK VP 1.1 femur	*Australopithecus afarensis*
4.0	Belohdelie, Ethiopia	BEL VP 1.1 cranial fragments	*Australopithecus afarensis*
4.0–4.2	Fejej, Ethiopia	FJ 4 SB 1,2 teeth	*Australopithecus afarensis*
4.1	Kanapoi, Kenya	KP 29281 mandible	*Australopithecus anamensis*
>4.2	Chemeron, Kenya	BC 1745 humerus	*Australopithecus*
4.4	Aramis, Ethiopia	ARA-VP-1/129 mandible	*Ardipithecus ramidus*
4.9	Tabarin, Kenya	TH 13150 mandible	*Australopithecus*
5.6	Lothagam, Kenya	LT 329 mandible	*Australopithecus*

from Hadar and the fossilized hominid footprints at Laetoli provide clear evidence of bipedalism in *Australopithecus afarensis*, although this species also retained some anatomical adaptations for arboreal locomotion, including relatively long arms and curved foot bones. A small sample of early Pliocene fossils has been attributed to newly discovered species of australopithecine, including *Australopithecus anamensis* (Leakey *et al.* 1995), *Australopithecus bahrelghazali* (Brunet *et al.* 1995) and *Ardipithecus ramidus* (White *et al.* 1994).

The immediate ancestors of hominids were large-bodied hominoids that were adapted for climbing and suspending themselves below arboreal supports. Among the living hominoids, the adults usually move quadrupedally when on the ground, but they also occasionally adopt bipedal postures. Chimpanzee infants learn to walk bipedally before they walk quadrupedally, but in doing so they need to grasp supports with their hands in order to maintain their balance (Doran 1992). Amongst primates, true bipedalism is unique to hominids and a large number of separate anatomical and physiological modifications is implicated in the change from habitual quadrupedal to bipedal locomotion. This implies that bipedalism must

have provided considerable advantages in energy saving or in enhanced reproductive success for the earliest hominids.

When a bipedal animal is walking, it consumes less energy than a quadruped of
the same body size – although this advantage is reversed at higher speeds. Long-
distance bipedal walking might have provided scavenging opportunities (from being
able to follow herds of migrating animals), or alternatively it could have enhanced
the ability of early hominids to provision sedentary individuals who were caring for
dependent infants. However, the degree of sexual dimorphism in early hominids
(see p. 776) is inconsistent with the monogamous group structure required if provisioning is to be a successful evolutionary strategy. It is more probable that early
hominids foraged in large groups, exploiting low density or scattered resources in
grassland habitats. Under these circumstances, the adoption of an upright bipedal
posture can assist thermoregulation in equatorial latitudes by reducing the heat
load from incident solar radiation in the middle of the day. Further advantages in
reducing thermal stress would have been provided by the higher wind speeds and
lower air temperature and humidity away from the ground surface, particularly if
the early hominids, like modern humans, had little body hair. A naked skin allows
for more efficient heat dissipation, particularly when supplied with abundant sweat
glands (Wheeler 1992).

Traditionally, the species of *Australopithecus* have been categorized as 'gracile' or
'robust', a distinction that originated in the recognition of significant differences in
tooth size between fossils of *A. africanus* and *A. robustus* from South Africa. The
distinction, though convenient, is misleading for several reasons. First, all australopithecine species have robust jaws and cheek teeth that are relatively large compared with those of other primates of similar body size (McHenry 1984). Second,
although they possessed large jaws and had skulls that were reinforced against the
stresses generated by their powerful chewing muscles, australopithecine species had
small 'petite' bodies (McHenry 1991) and were substantially lighter in weight than
modern chimpanzees (Table 19.2). Finally, the distinction describes a temporal
trend rather than a taxonomic classification – the 'gracile' species *A. afarensis* and
A. africanus are early forms, whereas *A. aethiopicus*, *A. boizei* and *A. robustus* (the
'robust' australopithecines) evolved more recently and were contemporaneous with
the earliest forms of the genus *Homo* (Table 19.3). Some researchers place the
'robust' australopithecine species in the genus *Paranthropus*, reflecting the likelihood that they form a monophyletic group (Strait *et al.* 1997). However, the phylogeny of the australopithecines as a whole is unclear, and in many publications both
the robust and the gracile forms are classified together in the genus *Australopithecus*.

Fossils of *Australopithecus* were first discovered in the 1920s, 1930s and 1940s in
breccias at the sites of former limestone caves in the Transvaal Province of South
Africa. The remains of *A. africanus* were found at Taung, Sterkfontein and Makapansgat, and those of *A. robustus* at Kromdraai and Swartkrans. Recent excavations

Table 19.2 Estimated body weights of *Australopithecus*, Chimpanzee (*Pan troglodytes*) and humans

Species	Female weight	Male weight	Species average	Dimorphism (M/F)
A. afarensis	29	45	37	1.55
A. africanus	30	41	35	1.37
A. boisei	34	49	41	1.44
A. robustus	32	40	36	1.25
Pan troglodytes	40	54	47	1.35
Homo sapiens	53	65	59	1.23

Note: All weights are in kg. The estimated body weights of fossil species are based on hindlimb joint dimensions, using modern human regression formulae for predicting weight from joint size (McHenry 1992).

Table 19.3 First and last appearances of hominid species *

Taxon	First appearance (MYA)	Last appearance (MYA)	Maximum geographical range
A. anamensis	4.1	3.9	E. Africa
A. afarensis	4.2	2.8	E. Africa
A. africanus	3.1	2.3	S. Africa
A. aethiopicus	2.6	2.3	E. Africa
A. boisei	2.3	1.4	E. Africa
A. robustus	1.9	1.2	S. Africa
H. rudolfensis	2.4	1.8	E. Africa
H. habilis	1.9	1.6	E. Africa
H. erectus/ H. ergaster	1.75	0.1	Africa, Asia
H. heidelbergensis	0.7	0.1	Africa, Asia, Europe
H. neanderthalensis	0.25	0.035	Asia, Europe
H. sapiens	0.1	—	World-wide

Note: * Dates for hominid species known only from a single locality (*A. bahrelghazali* and *A. ramidus*) are given in Table 19.1.

at Swartkrans and Sterkfontein have added to the large collections of over a thousand hominid fossils recovered from these sites, and in 1992 a cave site at Gladysvale, 10 kilometres east of the Sterkfontein valley, yielded hominid teeth that may represent *A. africanus*. In East Africa fossils of *A. boisei* were first discovered at Olduvai Gorge, Tanzania, in 1959, with subsequent identifications of the same species at Peninj in Tanzania, Omo in Ethiopia and at Chesowanja, Koobi Fora and West Turkana in Kenya. *A. aethiopicus* is an earlier and in some respects more primitive species of robust australopithecine that predates *A. boisei* in East Africa (Walker *et al.* 1986).

The early species *A. afarensis* and *A. africanus* were relatively small-brained hominids, with a primitive (ape-like) pattern of cranial cresting and a prominent (prognathic) face with large projecting incisor teeth. Although they were clearly adapted for upright posture and bipedal locomotion, these species retained the upwards-directed shoulder joints, relatively long forelimbs, curved hand and foot bones, and mobile ankle joints characteristic of an arboreal ancestry. The large samples of fossils available from sites such as Hadar in Ethiopia and Sterkfontein in South Africa show that there were substantial differences in size between adult individuals belonging to *A. afarensis* and *A. africanus*. These differences are interpreted as sexual dimorphism, and the estimated sex differences in body weight of the fossil species are a little higher than in modern chimpanzees (Table 19.2), though somewhat less than is found in the strongly dimorphic apes the gorilla and orang-utan.

In *A. boisei* and *A. robustus* the jaws, cheek teeth, and chewing muscles were massively developed and the face was elongated in a vertical rather than a forward direction. The incisor and canine teeth of these species were reduced in size, suggesting a dietary shift in favour of food resources that required less preparation with the anterior teeth, while the increased dimensions of their premolar and molar teeth maximized the surfaces available for grinding hard food items. Reconstructions of the diet of *Australopithecus* have relied on analogy with other savannah-dwelling animals and with modern human hunter-gatherers living in tropical environments. One popular comparison is with the gelada baboon (*Theropithecus*), which evolved reduced anterior and enlarged cheek teeth as an adaptation to seasonal dependence on grass seeds and plant rhizomes. Others have suggested that early hominids exploited a carnivorous diet, acquired through scavenging or hunting. These hypotheses have been tested through recent studies of tooth microwear, and trace element and stable isotope analyses of hominid fossils. Microscopic images of the wearing surfaces of hominid teeth reveal pits and scratches caused by abrasive particles in the diet. The microwear seen on the teeth of *Australopithecus* resembles that observed on the teeth of frugivorous primates such as mandrills, chimps and orang-utans. Of course, these studies cannot determine whether the hominid diet also included food items which produce little abrasive wear. Measurement of the levels of strontium and stable carbon isotopes in fossils of *Australopithecus robustus* suggests that this species did not consume an exclusively herbivorous diet: some animal tissues must have been ingested as a significant component of the diet of *A. robustus*.

EARLY HOMINIDS: ORIGINS OF *HOMO*

Global shifts in climate and vegetation, associated with the onset of polar glaciation at about 2.5 MYA, led to evolutionary changes in the terrestrial faunas of sub-Saharan Africa (Vrba 1995). Grassland habitats expanded at the expense of forests as temperatures and rainfall were reduced, and dramatic extinctions of forest-adapted mammalian species occurred. At East African hominid sites, the palynological record shows a shift from closed canopy to open woodland conditions at this time, and it is possible that these environmental changes led to the extinction of earlier forms of *Australopithecus*. The earlier hominids were replaced by species better adapted to the drier conditions, and amongst these new species were the earliest representatives of the genus *Homo*.

Homo is distinguished from *Australopithecus* by two principal features: the relative enlargement of the brain, and a progressive reduction in the size and anterior projection of the jaws and teeth (Tobias 1991). Hominid fossils from several sites in eastern and southern Africa have been attributed to *Homo habilis* and to the related species *Homo rudolfensis*. *Homo habilis* was defined in 1964 after fossils of a large-brained hominid were discovered at Olduvai Gorge, Tanzania, dating to between 1.85 and 1.6 MYA. The type specimen, OH 7, is a juvenile cranium with part of the lower jaw together with a few hand bones. The brain volume of OH 7 is 674 cm^3, well above the maximum of the range of cranial capacity in *Australopithecus*. The sample of *Homo habilis* fossils from Olduvai Gorge also includes a partial skeleton, OH 62, which was discovered in 1986.

A series of fossils, including the relatively complete cranium ER 1470 from Koobi Fora in Kenya, dating to 1.9–1.8 MYA, has been assigned to the species *Homo rudolfensis* (Wood 1992). At Chemeron in Kenya, a cranial fragment discovered in 1967 and now dated to 2.4 MYA has been proposed as the earliest known specimen of *Homo* (Hill *et al.* 1992). Of similar age are a mandible of *Homo rudolfensis*, recovered from deposits dated biostratigraphically to approximately 2.4 MYA at Uraha in Malawi (Schrenk *et al.* 1993), and a fossil jaw of *Homo* from deposits dated to 2.33 MYA at Hadar in Ethiopia (Kimbel *et al.* 1996). Early forms of *Homo* have also been found at Sterkfontein and Swartkrans in South Africa (Table 19.4).

The fossil sites that have yielded skeletal remains of *Homo habilis* and *H. rudolfensis* have also produced evidence of stone tool manufacture or use. The earliest dated stone tools have been found at Gona, Hadar, and Omo in Ethiopia, and at Lokalalei on the west shore of Lake Turkana in Kenya. At Gona, cores and flakes of Oldowan type were found *in situ* in sediments dated to between 2.5 and 2.6 MYA (Semaw *et al.* 1997). At a nearby site in Hadar, Ethiopia, similar stone tools have been dated to 2.3 MYA (Kimbel *et al.* 1996). Small quartzite artefacts have been excavated from deposits dated to between 2.3 and 2.4 MYA at Omo, Ethiopia. At Lokalalei the artefacts, which were recovered from sediments dated to 2.3 MYA, consisted of many crude cores made on lava cobbles together with a few flakes (Kibunjia 1994). The artefacts found at these sites show a similar degree of flaking skill to that seen at the younger Oldowan sites in Olduvai Gorge, but the cores are less reduced and the flakes are unretouched. Although it is likely that *Homo habilis* and *H. rudolfensis* were tool users, studies of fossil hand bones have shown that

Table 19.4 Fossil crania and mandibles allocated to species of early *Homo*

Species and fossil sites	Cranial remains	Mandibular remains
Homo habilis		
Olduvai, Tanzania	OH 6, 7, 13, 14, 16, 24, 52, 62	OH 7, 13, 37, 62
Koobi Fora, Kenya	ER 1478, 1805, 1813, 3735	ER 1501, 1502, 1805
Homo rudolfensis		
Koobi Fora, Kenya	ER 1470, 1590, 3732, 3735, 3891	ER 819, 1482, 1483, 1801, 1802
Uraha, Malawi	—	UH 501
Homo (indeterminate species)		
Chemeron, Kenya	BC 1	—
Koobi Fora, Kenya	ER 164, 807, 1593, 7330	ER 1506, 1811, 3734, 3950
Hadar, Ethiopia	AL 666-1	—
Omo, Ethiopia	L 894-1	Omo 75-14, Omo 222-2744
Sterkfontein, S. Africa	Sts 19, Stw 53, SE 255, SE 1508, 1579, 1937, 2396	
Swartkrans, S. Africa	SK 23, 847, SKW 3114	SK 45

Australopithecus possessed similar anatomical features and may have been capable of holding objects with the same degree of precision as *Homo*. The fossil remains of 'robust' species of *Australopithecus* are frequently found at the same sites as *Homo habilis*, and it is therefore not possible to exclude *Australopithecus* as a potential maker or user of stone tools.

Average cranial capacity of *Homo habilis* (640 cm^3) is substantially greater than that of *Australopithecus* (species averages range from 410 cm^3 in *A. afarensis* to 530 cm^3 in *A. robustus*), and the increase in brain size is not accounted for by the small differences in body size between *Australopithecus* and early *Homo*. In hominids, the shape of the brain conforms closely to the inner surface of the cranial vault, because the cranial bones are literally moulded over the surface of the brain as it expands rapidly during the early years of post-natal growth. The shape and size of the brain of a fossil skull can be reconstructed by taking latex impressions of the endocranial cavity (in a few hominid skulls a natural endocast is formed during fossilization by sediments hardening inside the cranial cavity). Studies of endocasts show that the brain of *Homo habilis* was enlarged mainly in the frontal and parietal lobes of the cerebral hemispheres. Some details of the left frontal lobe in *Homo habilis* suggest strong development of Broca's area, a region of the brain involved in speech production in modern humans. The other important region of the brain involved in language comprehension is Wernicke's area, partly located on the inferior parietal lobule. The parietal region is another well-developed part of the brain in *Homo habilis* (Tobias 1987).

HOMO ERECTUS

Whilst *Homo habilis* and *Homo rudolfensis* retained many similarities with *Australopithecus*, *Homo erectus* more closely resembles *Homo sapiens* in some parts of its skeletal anatomy. In 1984 a skeleton of *Homo erectus* was found at Nariokotome on the west shore of Lake Turkana in Kenya, a site dated to 1.6 MYA (Walker and Leakey 1993). The skeleton, which has been given the specimen number WT 15000, is the most complete early hominid ever found (Fig. 19.6). Although the skeleton is not fully grown (dental development indicates an age of about 12 years), it belonged to an individual whose stature was between 1.6 and 1.7 metres, weighed about 55 kilograms and had limb proportions within the modern human range of

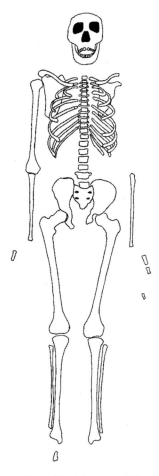

Figure 19.6 Homo erectus skeleton from Nariokotome, West Turkana, Kenya. (After Walker and Leakey 1993.) Source: A. T. Chamberlain. (See also Figure 18.3.)

variation. The cranial capacity of WT 15000 (900 cm^3) is greater than *Homo habilis*, although the increase may be explained in part by the greater body size of *Homo erectus*.

Homo erectus is the hominid that dominates the Lower and early Middle Pleistocene, first appearing in Africa and Asia at about 1.8 MYA and possibly persisting in East Asia to as recent a date as 50 Ka (Swisher *et al.* 1996). The first fossils of *Homo erectus* were found at Trinil, Java, in the 1890s by Eugene Dubois, a Dutch palaeontologist. Dubois coined the species name '*erectus*' because the leg bones showed evidence of upright posture and bipedal locomotion. Subsequent finds in the 1920s at Zhoukoudian, China, and at other sites in Java confirmed the widespread occurrence of the species in Asia (Table 19.5). Although the Indonesian and Chinese fossils were originally placed in the separate genera *Meganthropus*, *Pithecanthropus* and *Sinanthropus*, the close similarities between the fossils from the Asian sites and their clear affinities with other species of *Homo* allow them all to be assigned to the single species *Homo erectus*.

Homo erectus fossils have been found at sites in eastern, northern and southern Africa. The species first appears in the lower part of the KBS member at Koobi

Table 19.5 Dates for *Homo erectus* and *Homo ergaster* sites in Africa and Asia in millions of years ago (MYA)

Africa		Asia	
Site	Date (MYA)	Site	Date (MYA)
Algeria		*China*	
Tighenif	0.6	Chenjiawo	0.65
		Gongwangling	0.75–1.0
Ethiopia		Hexian	0.15–0.20
Konso Gardula	1.4–1.5	Longgupo	2.0–1.8
Melka Kunture	1.0	Yuanmou	0.5–0.6
		Yunxian	?0.3–0.5
Kenya		Zhoukoudian	0.23–0.50
Koobi Fora	1.6–1.8		
Lainyamok	0.7	*Georgia*	
West Turkana	1.6	Dmanisi	?1.6
South Africa		*Israel*	
Swartkrans	1.0–1.5	Ubeidiya	1.4
Tanzania		*Java*	
Olduvai Gorge	0.7–1.2	Modjokerto	1.8
		Ngandong	0.03
		Trinil	1.0
		Sambungmachan	0.04
		Sangiran	1.66
		Vietnam	
		Lang Trang	0.4–0.5

Fora, Kenya, dated to just over 1.75 MYA. *Homo erectus* replaces and does not overlap in time with earlier species of *Homo* at Koobi Fora, but the species *Australopithecus boisei* survives alongside *Homo erectus* in East Africa until about 1.4 MYA. In north-western Africa, several Middle Pleistocene hominid sites have been found along the coastline of Algeria and northern Morocco. The earliest of these sites, Tighenif in Algeria (formerly known as Ternifine), dates to about 0.6 MYA. The specimens from Tighenif comprise mandibles, teeth and a parietal bone, and they show close similarities to the Asian *Homo erectus* fossils. In South Africa, the mandible SK15 from Member 2 at Swartkrans, tentatively dated to between 1.0 and 1.5 MYA, may represent the first arrival of *Homo erectus* in that region.

Morphological differences between early African *Homo erectus* and later Asian examples of the species have led some to argue for the separation of the early African material as a distinct species, *Homo ergaster*. Whether these differences are important enough to merit taxonomic segregation is an unresolved issue (Turner and Chamberlain 1989). The type specimen of *Homo ergaster* is a lower jaw ER 992 from Koobi Fora, Kenya. Bernard Wood has placed this specimen together with the crania ER 3733, ER 3883 and the skeleton WT 15000 in *Homo ergaster* on the grounds that the crania have primitive features that are lost in Asian *Homo erectus* (Wood 1991).

The main distinguishing characteristics of *Homo erectus* are confined to the cranium. The lower jaw, teeth and postcranial bones of *Homo erectus* are well differentiated from those of *Homo habilis* and *Homo rudolfensis*, but there is considerable overlap in these skeletal parts between *Homo erectus* and later forms of *Homo* (see pp. 783–88). The skull of *Homo erectus* shows several distinctive features, including a long, low braincase with maximum width located across the temporal bones and a sharply angled occipital bone at the back of the skull. The prominent browridge forms a straight bar of bone above the eye sockets, and there is noticeable thickening of the skull vault bones along the midline (metopic and sagittal keeling), as well as on the occipital bone and at the lower posterior corner of the parietal bone (occipital and angular torus). Cranial capacities range from 800 to 1,250 cm³, but values above 1,100 cm³ are only found in *Homo erectus* in the Middle Pleistocene specimens from Ngandong and Zhoukoudian.

Homo erectus has often been associated with the Acheulian stone tool industry, a lithic technology typified by its substantial proportion of large bifaces. However, the earliest fossils of *Homo erectus* in Africa predate the first appearance of Acheulian tools by several hundred thousand years, and Acheulian tools first appear in Europe in association with archaic forms of *Homo sapiens* at about 0.5 MYA. At *Homo erectus* sites in eastern Asia, Acheulian artefacts are absent, and instead there is evidence for simpler core and flake technologies being used at Sangiran in Java (Sémah *et al.* 1992) and at Zhoukoudian in China (Zhang 1985).

Localized distributions of baked sediments and burnt stones at some lower palaeolithic sites have been interpreted as human control and use of fire. The earliest such evidence was found at Chesowanja, Kenya, where pieces of baked clay were found in association with faunal remains and Oldowan stone tools in sediments dated to 1.4 MYA. Similar finds have been made at Lower Pleistocene sites including Koobi Fora, Kenya, and at Gadeb (Locality 8E) and the Middle Awash river valley in Ethiopia. It is difficult to prove that these occurrences represent deliberate controlled use of fire, and, in the absence of evidence for hearths, alternative explanations such as natural bush fires or volcanic activity cannot be excluded (James 1989).

Absolute dating of *Homo erectus* fossils has shown that the species had a time-span of well over one million years. The species was eventually replaced in Africa and Asia by 'archaic' forms of *Homo sapiens* after 0.5 MYA. *Homo erectus* has been cited as an example of 'evolutionary stasis' (Rightmire 1990). According to the 'punctuated equilibrium' model, evolutionary change can be episodic, with rapid changes appearing during the initial formation of a new species but the species then undergoing few changes until a subsequent speciation event occurs. Early *Homo erectus* fossils from Lower Pleistocene sites in Africa have been compared with later specimens to determine whether features such as tooth size and cranial capacity change with time. A moderate increase in cranial capacity does seem to characterize the younger fossils, most of which are from Asia, but others have argued that this reflects a taxonomic difference between the earlier forms attributable to *H. ergaster* and the later and predominantly Asian fossils which represent *H. erectus*.

Fossil evidence for hominid occupation of Europe is sporadic until the early part of the Middle Pleistocene, and there is no clear evidence for the presence of *Homo erectus* in Europe. Although archaeological evidence hints at possible Lower Pleistocene migration of hominids to Europe, the earliest securely dated fossil hominids in Europe have been found in deposits dating to 780 Ka at the site of Atapuerca in Spain (Carbonell *et al.* 1995; see also Chapter 20). Although the Atapuerca hominids cannot be distinguished with certainty from *Homo erectus*, they have been allocated provisionally to *Homo heidelbergensis*, a species of 'archaic' *Homo sapiens*. A hominid cranium of similar age was found in 1994 at Ceprano in Italy (Ascenzi *et al.* 1996). The cranium has advanced traits that are not characteristic of *H. erectus*, and like the Atapuerca sample it most probably represents an early form of *H. heidelbergensis*.

'ARCHAIC' *HOMO SAPIENS*

Homo heidelbergensis

The category 'archaic' *Homo sapiens* was formerly used to refer to Middle and Upper Pleistocene fossils of the genus *Homo* that had developed the cranial capacity of *Homo sapiens* while retaining primitive features such as thick cranial bones, large faces and jaws and robust limb bones. In some taxonomic schemes these fossils were classified under several different subspecies of *Homo sapiens* such as *Homo sapiens neanderthalensis* and *Homo sapiens rhodesiensis*. In zoology, a subspecies refers to a discrete, morphologically distinct variety that occupies a limited geographical region within the total range of the species. Modern human variation is geographically continuous (clinal) and there are therefore no discrete subspecies of living humans. With the exception of Neanderthals (classified here as a distinct species *Homo neanderthalensis*), the Middle Pleistocene sample of 'archaic' *Homo sapiens* from Africa, Asia and Europe also forms a homogeneous group that does not exhibit well-defined geographical variation. These hominids, which are clearly distinct from modern humans, are therefore placed in the species *Homo heidelbergensis* (named after the lower jaw from Mauer, near Heidelberg), rather than as subspecies of modern humans.

Homo heidelbergensis is distinguished by its combination of primitive characters retained from a *Homo erectus*-like ancestor and advanced characters that are shared with the Upper Pleistocene species *Homo neanderthalensis* and *Homo sapiens*. *Homo heidelbergensis* is therefore an appropriate ancestor for the hominids of the Upper Pleistocene. Cranial capacity in *Homo heidelbergensis* ranges from 1,000 cm^3 to 1,400 cm^3. Brain enlargement, especially in the parietal and occipital areas, led to increased cranial height, increased parietal bone curvature and a less sharply angled occipital bone. There is some reduction in skull robustness, although larger specimens retain strong brow ridges and thick cranial vault bones. The face is less projecting than in earlier forms of *Homo* and there are the beginnings of the development of a chin at the front of the lower jaw.

The fossil remains of *Homo heidelbergensis* are known from a large number of sites in Africa, Europe and Asia (Table 19.6). Many of these sites have only been dated approximately, but they show that *Homo heidelbergensis* first appeared in Africa and Europe at about 0.5 MYA (the Atapuerca and Ceprano finds suggest a possible earlier appearance in southern Europe). The earliest dates for *Homo heidelbergensis* in Asia are a little later in time, consistent with the late survival of *Homo erectus* in China (Grün *et al.* 1997) and in Indonesia (Swisher *et al.* 1996). Some authors have argued that the Middle Pleistocene crania from China are intermediate between Asian *Homo erectus* and modern Chinese (Li and Etler 1992). In Europe, the fossil hominids from the later part of the Middle Pleistocene begin to show features that are typical of *Homo neanderthalensis*. The occipital bones of the crania from Swanscombe in England and Biache in France closely resemble those of Upper Pleistocene specimens of *Homo neanderthalensis*.

Fossils of *Homo heidelbergensis* are associated at some sites with Acheulian tools and at other sites with core/flake industries. At Bilzingsleben in Germany, fragments of hominid skull bones and teeth have been found on a lower palaeolithic

Table 19.6 Middle Pleistocene fossils attributed to *Homo heidelbergensis*;
dates in millions of years ago (MYA)

Country	Site	Date (MYA)
Africa		
Ethiopia	Bodo	0.6
	Omo Kibish 2	?0.1
Kenya	Baringo	0.3–0.5
	Eliye Springs	?0.1–0.2
Libya	Haua Fteah	0.1–0.15
Morocco	Jebel Irhoud	?0.1–0.2
	Rabat	0.15–0.2
	Sale	0.4
	Sidi Abderrhaman	0.3–0.4
	Thomas	0.3–0.4
S. Africa	Cave of Hearths	?0.2–0.4
	Elandsfontein	?
	Florisbad	?0.1–0.15
	Saldanha	0.2–0.3
Tanzania	Ndutu	0.2–0.4
	Ngaloba	0.1–0.15
Zambia	Kabwe	0.1–0.2
Asia		
China	Dali	0.2–0.25
	Jinniu Shan	0.3
	Maba	0.1–0.2
India	Narmada	?0.2
Europe		
Azerbaijan	Azykh	?0.3–0.4
France	Arago	0.4
Germany	Bilzingsleben	0.4
	Mauer	0.5
	Steinheim	0.2–0.25
Greece	Apidima	?0.2–0.3
	Petralona	0.25
Hungary	Verteszollos	0.2
Italy	Castel de Guido	?0.3
	Cava Pompi	?0.4
	Ceprano	0.7
Spain	Atapuerca (Dolina)	0.8
United Kingdom	Boxgrove	0.5

occupation site dating to about 0.35 MYA. The hominid remains have been likened
to *Homo erectus* (Mania *et al.* 1994), but recent discoveries show that they lack some
diagnostic *H. erectus* features and they are classified here as *Homo heidelbergensis*. In
an excavated area of more than 1,000 m², accumulations of stone and animal bones
were revealed at Bilzingsleben as well as hearths and areas where stone and bone
tools were manufactured or used. The stone tools are mainly cobble hammer stones

and small retouched flakes of chert, while large scrapers, cleavers and picks were fashioned from flakes of elephant long bones.

Homo neanderthalensis

The Neanderthals (*Homo neanderthalensis*) occupied western Asia and most of Europe from before 130 ka to 35 ka. This period includes the end of the last interglacial and most of the last (Würm, Weichselian or Devensian) glaciation, and was therefore a time of environmental extremes in the northern hemisphere. The earliest fossils to be attributed to *Homo neanderthalensis* are from later Middle Pleistocene sites in western Europe dated from about 0.25 MYA (Table 19.7; see also Fig. 19.7) and it is possible that the species originated from or is closely related to *Homo heidelbergensis*.

Distinctive traits of *Homo neanderthalensis* are found in the skull and the limb bones. The brain, which is often larger than in modern humans, has small frontal lobes but is expanded particularly in the occipital region, giving a spherical appearance to the rear of the skull. The face is vertically elongated and the middle of the face is dominated by the large nose and prominent upper jaw, which are set in front of swept-back cheek bones. The limbs have relatively short distal segments (forearms and lower legs), but the bodies of the Neanderthals were powerfully built with large joints and prominent muscle markings on the bones. Body weights and stature have been estimated as averaging 65 kg and 169 cm in males, 50 kg and 160 cm in females. Neanderthals also have long, thin, pubic bones at the front of the pelvis. This feature is related to the different orientation of their pelvis, with the hip joints facing more sideways and less forwards than in modern human skeletons (Rak and Arensburg 1987).

Table 19.7 Middle Pleistocene fossils attributed to *Homo neanderthalensis*; dates in millions of years ago (MYA)

Country	Site	Date (MYA)
Britain	Pontnewydd	0.2
	Swanscombe	0.4
France	Biache	0.1–0.2
	Fontechevade	0.1–0.2
	La Chaise	0.1–0.15
	Lazaret	0.1–0.2
	Montmaurin	0.1–0.2
Germany	Ehringsdorf	0.2
	Reilingen	?0.2–0.4
Italy	Saccopastore	0.12
Spain	Atapuerca (Sima)	0.12–0.3

O-isotope Stage	Magnetic Polarity	Geological Stage	Date (ka)	Principal Hominid Sites
1		Holocene (Flandrian)	0 - 12	
2		Late Weichselian	12 - 24	
3		Middle Weichselian	24 - 59	1st appearance of modern humans in Europe
4		(Middle Devensian)	59 - 71	
5		Early Weichselian	71 - 120	Grotta Guattari, La Chaise
5e		Eemian (Ipswichian)	120 - 128	Bourgeois-Delaunay, Saccopastore
6		)	128 - 186	Biache, Fontechevade, Lazaret
7		) Saalian (Wolstonian)	186 - 245	Ehringsdorf, Petralona, Pontnewydd, Steinheim, Vcrteszollos
8		)	245 - 303	
9		)	303 - 339	
10		) Holsteinian (Hoxnian)	339 - 362	
11		)	362 - 423	Arago, Bilzingsleben, Swanscombe
12		Elsterian (Anglian)	423 - 478	
13		)	478 - 524	Boxgrove, Mauer
14		)	524 - 565	
15		)	565 - 620	
16		) Cromerian Complex	620 - 659	
17		)	659 - 689	
18		)	689 - 726	
19		)	726 - 736	
20		)	736 - 763	
21		) Bavelian/Menapian	763 - 790	Atapuerca (Dolina)
22		)	790 - 810	
23		)	810 - 890	
24		)	890 - 920	
25		)	920 - 960	

Figure 19.7 Oxygen isotope stages, European glacials and interglacials and absolute dates from 960,000 years ago (ka) to the present day. Shaded intervals (odd-numbered oxygen isotape stages) represent warm periods. The chronological positions of some of the main early hominid sites in Europe are also shown. Source: A. T. Chamberlain.

The fossil evidence for *Homo neanderthalensis* is more complete than the record for earlier hominid species, partly because the more recent fossils are generally better preserved but also because some skeletons of *Homo neanderthalensis* were deposited through deliberate burial. The remains of *Homo neanderthalensis* are often associated with Mousterian tools, but the distribution of Mousterian artefacts extends well beyond the known range of Neanderthal fossils, and in western Asia Mousterian is associated with early fossils of *Homo sapiens*. Late Neanderthal remains at the French sites of St Césaire (dated to 36,000 years ago) and Arcy-sur-Cure (dated to 34,000 years ago) are associated with early upper Palaeolithic (Chatelperonian) rather than Mousterian artefacts (Hublin *et al.* 1996; Mercier *et al.* 1991).

The distribution of pathological changes in Neanderthal skeletons provides some insights into their behaviour. Injuries to the skeleton (fractures) were common, and their distribution suggests that they were acquired during subsistence activities such as resource procurement rather than as a result of inter-personal violence. Arthritis is also common, supporting the contention that Neanderthal skeletons were habitually subjected to high physical stress. The anterior teeth often show advanced wear. By analogy with modern hunter-gatherers, the teeth were probably used in non-dietary activities such as bark-stripping, sharpening or retouching tools, and gripping objects while they were being worked.

While the origins of *Homo neanderthalensis* are obscure, their abrupt disappearance from the fossil record in western Europe at 34,000 years ago is suggestive of replacement rather than absorption or hybridization with *Homo sapiens*. In central and eastern Europe, the earliest *Homo sapiens* fossils appear at about 36,000 years ago and are indirectly associated with the appearance of Aurignacian stone tools. These earliest modern humans in Europe retain some archaic features, but do not show any evidence of having inherited uniquely Neanderthal features of the skull or limb bones. Similarly, temporal trends towards modern human morphology are not seen within *Homo neanderthalensis*. The earlier Neanderthals of south-western Asia are more generalized in their skeletal anatomy, with the later 'classic' Neanderthals of western Europe showing increased projection of the middle of the face and the development of more marked features of the postcranial skeleton.

ORIGINS OF MODERN HUMANS

The origin of anatomically modern humans is of great interest because, in investigating the most recent stages of human evolution, the fossil evidence for the origins of *Homo sapiens* can be integrated with genetic and morphological studies of variation among different populations of living humans. Two divergent paradigms that synthesize this evidence in opposing ways have emerged in the last decade (Brauer and Smith 1992; Mellars and Stringer 1989; Trinkaus 1989).

One paradigm views the regional or racial differences among present-day human populations as originating in the pre-existing Lower or Middle Pleistocene populations of *Homo erectus* and *Homo heidelbergensis* that occupied the same regions. According to this 'regional continuity' paradigm, the evolutionary changes that led to the emergence of modern *Homo sapiens* occurred at different rates in different regions of the world, leading to variation in the times of appearance of the first modern humans in the fossil record. The importance of gene flow (the spread of advantageous genes among and between populations) is emphasized as a mechanism for maintaining the cohesion of the species during the gradual transition from archaic to modern forms.

In contrast, the 'replacement' or 'out of Africa' paradigm emphasizes the genetic and morphological homogeneity of modern *Homo sapiens*. The close similarities between modern human populations are explained as a consequence of their descent from one main population that originated recently in a single region of the world, most probably Africa or south-western Asia. This population (in effect, a new species) then migrated outwards, replacing pre-existing populations of archaic hominids with little or no significant assimilation or hybridization. Geographical differences among present-day *Homo sapiens* populations are presumed to have originated after the arrival of the migrating populations in their final regions. Contrasting predictions of the two models are given in Table 19.8.

Table 19.8 Predictions of the 'Regional Continuity' and 'Out of Africa' models

Predictions of the Regional Continuity (multi-origin) model	*Predictions of the Out of Africa (single origin) model*
1 Present-day geographic patterns were established in the Middle Pleistocene.	Present-day patterns were only established at the end of the Pleistocene.
2 Large differences between modern populations, especially peripheral groups.	Small differences between modern populations.
3 Morphological characters of modern regional populations are found in Middle Pleistocene fossils in each region.	Modern regional characters only characterize Middle Pleistocene fossils in the centre of origin (i.e. in Africa)
4 Transitional or intermediate fossils are found in all major regions.	Transitional fossils are only found in Africa.
5 There is no consistent geographic sequence to the appearance of modern *Homo sapiens*.	The appearance of modern *Homo sapiens* occurs in the sequence (a) Africa, (b) south-west Asia, (c) other regions.

Anatomical evidence

All living humans belong to a single species, 'anatomically modern' *Homo sapiens*. The species can be defined by unique features of its skeleton: *Homo sapiens* possesses a short, high, cranial vault with a domed frontal bone and arched parietals. The skull and jaws lack prominent reinforcing structures such as brow ridges or mandibular tori, although there is a prominent bony chin. The nasal region is not projecting. The postcranial bones are more gracile than in other species of *Homo*, and skeletal development and maturation are extended compared with other hominids.

The oldest examples of *Homo sapiens* are from sites in Africa and south-western Asia. Hominid remains from the African sites have modern-looking, lightly constructed limb bones but still retain some archaic features in the skull, such as moderately prominent brow ridges and large teeth and jaws. In South Africa, the cave sites at Border Cave, Die Kelders and Klasies River Mouth were occupied by early *Homo sapiens* between 120,000 and 50,000 years ago. In eastern and north-western Africa, early modern *Homo sapiens* are also present from about 100,000 years ago. In Ethiopia, the Omo Kibish 1 skeleton is dated to between 130,000 and 100,000 years ago, and at Dar es Soltan in Morocco, *Homo sapiens* remains dating to between 50,000 and 70,000 years ago have been found. Early *Homo sapiens* sites in south-western Asia include Qafzeh and Skhul, both dated to between 80,000 and 100,000 years ago. The hominid skeletons from these sites have gracile limb bones and modern pelvises, contrasting with Neanderthal remains from the adjacent sites of Kebara and Tabun. The cranial remains from Qafzeh and Skhul have well-developed brow ridges and projecting jaws, but they lack the midfacial and nasal projection that is characteristic of Neanderthals.

The period between 60,000 and 30,000 years ago witnessed the rapid spread (or emergence?) of *Homo sapiens* across Asia and Australasia. Early appearances in Asia occur at Niah Cave in Borneo, perhaps as old as 40,000 years ago, and *Homo sapiens* fossils from Lake Mungo in Australia have been dated to between 35,000 and 45,000 years ago; much earlier archaeological evidence for hominid occupation of northern Australia, dating to before 100,000 years ago, has recently been reported by Fullagar *et al.* (1996). In China, the sites of Liujiang and Zhoukoudian (Upper Cave) date to between 15,000 and 20,000 years ago. In Europe, the first evidence of anatomically modern *Homo sapiens* is dated to about 35,000 years ago and is associated with the appearance of Aurignacian stone tools. The first European *Homo sapiens* are sometimes referred to as Cro-Magnons, after the hominid fossils recovered from the rock shelter of Cro-Magnon, near Les Eyzies in France.

During the coldest phase of the last ice age, there was a lowering of global sea levels by up to 130 metres. Land connections emerged between Asia and America in the shallow seaway between the Chukot Peninsula at the eastern tip of Asia and the westernmost part of Alaska. The lowest sea levels occurred at about 20,000 years

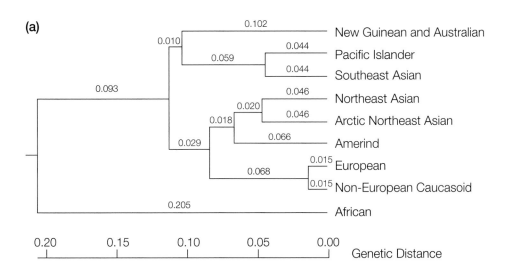

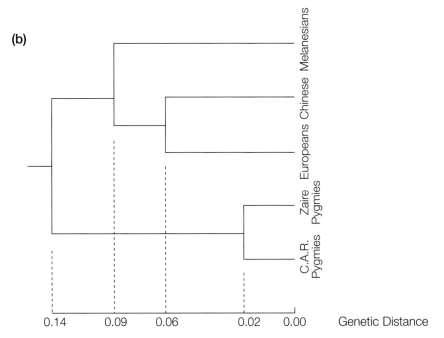

Figure 19.8 (a) Genetic tree constructed from summary genetic distances between living modern human populations; the genetic distances (in F_{ST} units) are calculated from the incidence of classical genetic markers including blood groups, cell surface antigens and protein polymorphisms. (b) Genetic tree constructed from population comparisons of 80 nuclear DNA polymorphic markers. Approximate genetic distances (Nei's distances) are shown for the principal divergence events. Source: L. L. Cavalli-Sforza *et al.* 1994.

ago, and it is possible that *Homo sapiens*, known to be present in North Asia, crossed for the first time into Alaska. Migration into the rest of the North American landmass would have had to overcome potential obstacles presented by the extensive terrestrial ice sheets that covered North America. At the end of the last ice age, global warming and glacial recession at about 11,000 years ago led to rapid expansion of *Homo sapiens* into the rest of continental America.

Biomolecular and genetic evidence

Genetic investigations of living populations of *Homo sapiens* using a range of different gene frequency and nucleotide sequence data offer strong support for the hypothesis that modern humans had an African origin. Most studies confirm that genetic diversity is greatest in Africa, and that genetic distances between African and non-African populations are large. Figure 19.8(a) represents the sequence of divergence of living populations as given by genetic distances based on a large number of classical genetic markers, and Figure 19.8(b) shows the divergence based on analysis of variable regions of nuclear DNA. Both sources of evidence show that after a primary split between African and non-African populations, a more recent subdivision occurred between Australasian and North Asian/Caucasoid (European) groups. These trees show modern Caucasoids as being most closely related to North Asians, but other evidence suggests that Caucasoid populations may have originated from an admixture of Asian and African populations.

The time of origin of human genetic material can be estimated by measuring the divergence between populations with known migration dates (in order to do this, the assumption must also be made that the relevant part of the genome is changing at a constant evolutionary rate). For example, divergence within groups that populated Papua New Guinea must have occurred after the first human colonization of the region, which took place about 60,000 years ago. When the calculated rate of evolution in mitochondrial DNA among New Guineans is applied to other populations of *Homo sapiens*, it gives a best estimate of 130,000 years ago (with 95 per cent confidence intervals of 60–420,000 years ago) for the origin of modern human mitochondrial DNA. This result implies that it is unlikely that modern humans originated from more than one of the Middle Pleistocene hominid populations, since the latter would have diverged much earlier than 400,000 years ago.

REFERENCES

Aiello, L. and Dean, C. (1990) *An Introduction to Human Evolutionary Anatomy*, London: Academic Press.

Ascenzi, A., Biddittu, I., Cassoli, P. F., Segre, A. G. and Segre-Naldini, E. (1996) 'A calvarium of late *Homo erectus* from Ceprano, Italy', *Journal of Human Evolution* 31: 409–23.

Beard, K. C., Tong, Y., Dawson, M. R., Wang, J. and Huang, X. (1996) 'Earliest complete dentition of an anthropoid primate from the Late Middle Eocene of Shanxi Province, China', *Science* 272: 82–85.

Bilsborough, A. (1992) *Human Evolution*, London: Chapman and Hall.

Brauer, G. and Smith, F. H. (eds) (1992) *Continuity or Replacement. Controversies in Homo sapiens Evolution*, Rotterdam: Balkema.

Brunet, M., Beauvilain, A., Coppens, Y., Heintz, E., Moutaye, A. H. E. and Pilbeam, D. (1995) 'The first australopithecine 2,500 kilometres west of the Rift Valley (Chad)', *Nature* 378: 273–75.

Carbonell, E., Bermúdez de Castro, J. M., Arsuaga, J. L. *et al.* (1995) 'Lower Pleistocene hominids and artifacts from Atapuerca-TD6 (Spain)', *Science* 269: 826–30.

Cartmill, M. (1992) 'New views on primate origins', *Evolutionary Anthropology* 1: 105–11.

Cavalli-Sforza, L. L., Menozzi, P. and Piazza, A. (1994) *The History and Geography of Human Genes*, Princeton: Princeton University Press.

Chaimanee, Y., Suteethorn, V., Jaeger, J.-J. and Ducrocq, S. (1997) 'A new Late Eocene anthropoid primate from Thailand', *Nature* 385: 429–31.

Conroy, G. C. (1990) *Primate Evolution*, New York: Norton.

Conroy, G. C., Pickford, M., Senut, B. and Mien, P. (1993) 'Diamonds in the desert: the discovery of *Otavipithecus namibiensis*', *Evolutionary Anthropology* 2: 46–52.

De Bonis, L. and Koufos, G. D. (1994) 'Our ancestors' ancestor: *Ouranopithecus* is a Greek link in human ancestry', *Evolutionary Anthropology* 3: 75–83.

Doran, D. M. (1992) 'The ontogeny of chimpanzee and pygmy chimpanzee locomotor behavior: a case study of paedomorphism and its behavioral correlates', *Journal of Human Evolution* 23: 139–57.

Dunbar, R. I. M. (1994) *Primate Social Systems* (2nd edition), London: Chapman and Hall.

Fleagle, J. G. (1988) *Primate Adaptation and Evolution*, San Diego: Academic Press.

Fleagle, J. G. and Kay, R. F. (eds) (1994) *Anthropoid Origins*, New York: Plenum.

Foley, R. A. (1991) 'How many species of hominid should there be?', *Journal of Human Evolution* 20: 413–27.

Foley, R. (1995) *Humans Before Humanity*, Oxford: Blackwell.

Fullagar, R. L. K., Price, D. M. and Head, L. M. (1996) 'Early human occupation of northern Australia: archaeology and thermoluminescence dating of Jinmium rock-shelter, Northern Territory', *Antiquity* 70: 751–53.

Gamble, C. (1993) *Timewalkers: The Prehistory of Global Colonization*, Stroud: Sutton.

Godinot, M. and Mahboubi, M. (1992) 'Earliest known simian primate found in Algeria', *Nature* 357: 324–26.

Grine, F. E. (ed.) (1988) *Evolutionary History of the 'Robust' Australopithecines*, New York: Aldine de Gruyter.

Groves, C. P. (1989) *A Theory of Primate and Human Evolution*, Oxford: Clarendon Press.

Grün, R., Huang, P.-H., Wu, X., *et al.* (1997) 'ESR analysis of teeth from the palaeo-anthropological site of Zhoukoudian, China', *Journal of Human Evolution* 32: 83–91.

Hill, A., Ward, S., Deino, A., Curtis, G. and Drake, R. (1992) 'Earliest *Homo*', *Nature* 355: 719–22.

Howells, W. W. (1993) *Getting Here: The Story of Human Evolution*, Washington, DC: Compass Press.

Hublin, J.-J., Spoor, F., Braun, M., Zonneveld, F. and Condemi, S. (1996) 'A late Neanderthal associated with upper palaeolithic artefacts', *Nature* 381: 224–26.

James, S. R. (1989) 'Hominid use of fire in the Lower and Middle Pleistocene', *Current Anthropology* 30: 1–26.

Johanson, D. C. and Edgar, B. (1996) *From Lucy to Language*, New York: Simon and Schuster.

Jones, S., Martin, R. and Pilbeam, D. (eds) (1992) *The Cambridge Encyclopedia of Human Evolution*, Cambridge: Cambridge University Press.

Kibunjia, M. (1994) 'Pliocene archaeological occurrences in the Lake Turkana Basin', *Journal of Human Evolution* 27: 159–71.

Kimbel, W. H., Walter, R. C., Johanson, D. C., *et al.* (1996) 'Late Pliocene *Homo* and Oldowan tools from the Hadar Formation (Kada Hadar Member), Ethiopia', *Journal of Human Evolution* 31: 549–61.

Klein, R. G. (1989) *The Human Career*, Chicago: Chicago University Press.

Leakey, M. G., Feibel, C. S., McDougall, I. and Walker, A. (1995) 'New four-million year-old hominid species from Kanapoi and Allia Bay, Kenya', *Nature* 376: 565–71.

Li, T. and Etler, D. A. (1992) 'New Middle Pleistocene hominid crania from Yunxian in China', *Nature* 357: 404–7.

MacFadden, B. J. (1990) 'Chronology of Cenozoic primate localities in South America', *Journal of Human Evolution* 19: 7–21.

McHenry, H. M. (1984) 'Relative cheek–tooth size in *Australopithecus*', *American Journal of Physical Anthropology* 64: 297–306.

McHenry, H. M. (1991) 'Petite bodies of the robust australopithecines', *American Journal of Physical Anthropology* 86: 445–54.

McHenry, H. M. (1992) 'Body size and proportions in early hominids', *American Journal of Physical Anthropology* 87: 407–31.

Mania, D., Mania, D. and Vlcek, E. (1994) 'Latest finds of skull remains of *Homo erectus* from Bilzingsleben (Thuringia)', *Naturwissenschaften* 81: 123–27.

Martin, R. D. (1990) *Primate Origins and Evolution: a Phylogenetic Reconstruction*, Princeton: Princeton University Press.

Meikle, W. E., Howell, F. C. and Jablonski, N. G. (eds) (1996) *Contemporary Issues in Human Evolution*, San Francisco: California Academy of Sciences.

Mellars, P. and Stringer, C. (eds) (1989) *The Human Revolution. Behavioural and Biological Perspectives on the Origins of Modern Humans*, Edinburgh: University of Edinburgh Press.

Mercier, N., Valladas, H., Joron, J.-L., *et al.* (1991) 'Thermoluminescence dating of the late Neanderthal remains from Saint-Césaire', *Nature* 351: 737–39.

Moyà-Solà, S. and Köhler, M. (1996) 'A *Dryopithecus* skeleton and the origins of great-ape locomotion', *Nature* 379: 156–59.

Napier, J. R. and Napier, P. H. (1985) *The Natural History of the Primates*, Cambridge: Cambridge University Press.

Nitecki, M. H. and Nitecki, D. V. (eds) (1994) *Origin of Anatomically Modern Humans*, New York: Plenum.

Rak, Y. and Arensburg, B. (1987) 'Kebara 2 Neanderthal pelvis: first look at a complete inlet', *American Journal of Physical Anthropology* 73: 227–31.

Richard, A. (1985) *Primates in Nature*, New York: Freeman.

Richards, M., Côrte-Real, H., Forster, P., *et al.* (1996) 'Palaeolithic and neolithic lineages in the European mitochondrial gene pool', *American Journal of Human Genetics* 59: 185–203.

Rightmire, G. P. (1990) *The Evolution of Homo erectus*, Cambridge: Cambridge University Press.

Rose, M. D. (1994) 'The earliest primates', *Evolutionary Anthropology* 3: 159–73.

Schrenk, F., Bromage, T. G., Betzler, C. G., Ring, U. and Juwayeyi, Y. M. (1993) 'Oldest *Homo* and Pliocene biogeography of the Malawi Rift', *Nature* 365: 833–36.

Sémah, F., Sémah, A.-M., Djubiantono, T. and Simanjuntak, H. T. (1992) 'Did they also make stone tools?', *Journal of Human Evolution* 23: 439–46.

Semaw, S., Renne, P., Harris, J. W. K. *et al.* (1997) '2.5-million-year-old stone tools from Gona, Ethiopia', *Nature* 385: 333–36.

Simons, E. (1995) 'Egyptian Oligocene primates: a review', *Yearbook of Physical Anthropology* 38: 199–238.

Simons, E. L. and Rasmussen, T. (1994) 'A whole new world of ancestors: Eocene anthropoideans from Africa', *Evolutionary Anthropology* 3: 128–39.

Smith, A. G., Hurley, A. M. and Briden, J. C. (1981) *Phanerozoic Paleocontinental World Maps*, Cambridge: Cambridge University Press.

Smuts, B. B., Cheney, D. L. and Seyfarth, R. M. (eds) (1987) *Primate Societies*, Chicago: University of Chicago Press.

Stoneking, M. (1993) 'DNA and recent human evolution', *Evolutionary Anthropology* 2: 60–73.

Strait, D. S., Grine, F. E. and Moniz, M. A. (1997) 'A reappraisal of early hominid phylogeny', *Journal of Human Evolution* 32: 17–82.

Stringer, C. and Gamble, C. (1993) *In Search of the Neanderthals*, London: Thames and Hudson.

Swisher, C. C., Curtis, G. H., Jacob, T., Getty, A. G. and Suprijo, A. (1994) 'Age of the earliest known hominids in Java', *Science* 263: 1118–21.

Swisher, C. C., Rink, W. J., Antón, S. C., *et al.* (1996) 'Latest *Homo erectus* of Java: potential contemporaneity with *Homo sapiens* in Southeast Asia', *Science* 274: 1870–74.

Szalay, F. and Delson, E. (1979) *Evolutionary History of the Primates*, New York: Academic Press.

Tattersall, I. (1986) 'Species recognition in palaeontology', *Journal of Human Evolution* 15: 165–75.

Tattersall, I. (1993) *The Human Odyssey: Four Million Years of Human Evolution*, New York: Prentice-Hall.

Tattersall, I. (1995) *The Fossil Trail: How We Know What We Think We Know About Human Evolution*, New York: Oxford University Press.

Tattersall, I., Delson, E. and Van Couvering, J. (eds) (1988) *Encyclopedia of Human Evolution and Prehistory*, New York: Garland.

Tobias, P. V. (1987) 'The brain of *Homo habilis*: a new level of organisation in cerebral evolution', *Journal of Human Evolution* 16: 741–61.

Tobias, P. V. (1991) *Olduvai Gorge, Volume 4. The Skulls, Endocasts and Teeth of Homo habilis*, Cambridge: Cambridge University Press.

Trinkaus, E. (ed.) (1989) *The Emergence of Modern Humans. Biocultural Adaptations in the Later Pleistocene*, Cambridge: Cambridge University Press.

Turner, A. and Chamberlain, A. T. (1989) 'Speciation, morphological change and the status of African *Homo erectus*', *Journal of Human Evolution* 18: 115–30.

van Kolfschoten, T. (1990) 'The evolution of the mammal fauna in the Netherlands and the Middle Rhine area (western Germany) during the late Middle Pleistocene', *Mededelingen Rijks Geologische Dienst* 43: 1–69.

Vrba, E. S. (1995) *Paleoclimate and Evolution, with Emphasis on Human Origin*, New Haven: Yale University Press.

Walker, A. and Leakey, R. (eds) (1993) *The Nariokotome Homo erectus Skeleton*, Cambridge, Mass.: Harvard University Press.

Walker, A. C., Leakey, R. E. F., Harris, J. M. and Brown, F. H. (1986) '2.5-Myr *Australopithecus boisei* from west of Lake Turkana', *Nature* 322: 517–22.

Wanpo, H., Ciochon, R., Yumin, G., *et al.* (1995) 'Early *Homo* and associated artefacts from Asia', *Nature* 378: 275–78.

Wheeler, P. E. (1992) 'The influence of the loss of body hair on the water budgets of early hominids', *Journal of Human Evolution* 23: 379–88.

White, T. D., Suwa, G. and Asfaw, B. (1994) '*Australopithecus ramidus*, a new species of early hominid from Aramis, Ethiopia', *Nature* 371: 306–12.

Wood, B. A. (1991) *Koobi Fora Research Project IV: Hominid Cranial Remains from Koobi Fora*, Oxford: Clarendon Press.

Wood, B. A. (1992) 'Origin and evolution of the genus *Homo*', *Nature* 355: 783–90.

Wu, X. and Poirier, F. E. (1995) *Human Evolution in China: a Metric Description of the Fossils and a Review of the Sites*, New York: Oxford University Press.

Zhang, S. (1985) 'The early Palaeolithic of China', in R. Wu and J. W. Olsen (eds) *Palaeoanthropology and Palaeolithic Archaeology in the People's Republic of China*, Orlando: Academic Press: 147–86.

SELECT BIBLIOGRAPHY

Good introductions to the ecology and classification of living primates are Napier and Napier (1985) and Richard (1985). Smuts *et al.* (1987) is a versatile source book of information on primate social behaviour, while Dunbar (1994) provides a more advanced approach to behavioural adaptations in primates. Comprehensive accounts of the evolution of primates are provided in student textbooks by Fleagle (1988) and Conroy (1990), and at a more advanced level by Szalay and Delson (1979), Groves (1989) and Martin (1990). Introductory accounts of human evolution include Klein (1989), Bilsborough (1992), Gamble (1993), Howells (1993), Stringer and Gamble (1993), Tattersall (1993, 1995), Foley (1995) and the excellently illustrated Johanson and Edgar (1996). More comprehensive details can be found in Tattersall *et al.* (1988) and Jones *et al.* (1992). Recent advanced reviews of early hominids are Grine (1988), Rightmire (1990), Tobias (1991), Wood (1991), Walker and Leakey (1993), Wu and Poirier (1995) and Meikle *et al.* (1996), the latter work providing updates on some current debates. Aiello and Dean (1990) is an anatomical textbook that focuses on the bones, teeth and musculature of the great apes and fossil hominids. The fossil and molecular evidence for the origins of anatomically modern *Homo sapiens* is discussed by Mellars and Stringer (1989), Trinkaus (1989), Brauer and Smith (1992) and Nitecki and Nitecki (1994), and a comprehensive analysis of global variation in modern human gene frequencies is provided by Cavalli-Sforza *et al.* (1994). Important new discoveries of fossil hominids are frequently announced in the journals *Nature* and *Science*, with detailed anatomical descriptions subsequently being published in specialist journals such as the *American Journal of Physical Anthropology* and the *Journal of Human Evolution*. The journal *Evolutionary Anthropology* provides news reports and up-to-date reviews of current research on topics relating to human evolution.

20

HUNTER-GATHERER SOCIETIES

Robin Dennell

INTRODUCTION

One consequence of the voyages of Columbus and subsequent navigators was that Europeans increasingly encountered hunter-gatherers in Africa, the Americas and, later, Australia. This contact prompted a number of questions: Who were they? Where had they come from? Were they descended from Adam, or had they been created separately? Did they have souls? Why didn't they practise agriculture? Had Europeans once been hunter-gatherers? And what, if anything, could Europeans learn by observing these peoples? Before the nineteenth century, these questions were not answered by direct, historical and archaeological evidence, but by speculations and conjecture. Whereas Hobbes (1651) memorably dismissed their lives as 'solitary, poor, nasty, brutish and short' because they lacked both the restraints and comforts of civilization, Rousseau (1722) idealized them as living in uncorrupted innocence. Increasingly, throughout the eighteenth century, contemporary hunter-gatherers were seen as representing a 'primitive' stage of human development, and one that Europeans had long escaped by developing first agriculture, and later, metallurgy, writing and civilization. Unsurprisingly, these views sat comfortably with suggestions that European 'Caucasians' – a term first coined in the 1780s – were more advanced than 'inferior' races, notably Negroids and Australian Aborigines, many of whom also happened to be hunter-gatherers. Notions of the racial, economic and social inferiority of non-European hunter-gatherers were also highly compatible with European involvement in slavery, and the establishment of European colonial settlements in hunter-gatherer territories.

If contemporary hunter-gatherers were supposed to be 'primitive' peoples whose development lagged far behind that of Europeans, where had they come from? How long had they been like that? And how ancient was hunting and gathering as a way of life? Answers to those questions became clearer by the mid-nineteenth century once two conditions had been met. The first was the recognition by antiquarians that chipped and flaked stone implements from various parts of Europe had been made deliberately and were not thunderbolts or the result of chance geological flaking. Moreover, some of these artefacts were similar to stone tools used by hunter-gatherers in various parts of the world, and could therefore have been used by Europeans when they too were hunters. By the 1830s, for example, Sven Nilsson felt able to describe the material culture of 'the primitive inhabitants of Scandinavia' in terms of analogies between the stone tools found in Scandinavia and those still used by natives in places such as Tierra del Fuego.

The discovery of the Palaeolithic – or the Old Stone Age – grew out of the fusion of this 'comparative ethnography' with the discovery of unambiguous stone tools in secure geological contexts. In 1796, Frere had cautiously suggested that some stone tools from Hoxne – now a well-known lower palaeolithic site in Suffolk, England – may have been older than the earth; that is, more than the 6,000 years of the Biblical chronology (see Chapter 1; Fig. 1.6). Excavations in caves by the likes of Esper in Germany, Schmerling in Belgium, MacEnery in southern England, Tournal and de Saussure in France, had produced evidence, that in hindsight seems unambiguous, of stone tools in ancient deposits, and associated with the remains of extinct animals. This evidence was often dismissed, however, and often by the excavators themselves, on the grounds that either the stone tools might have been introduced from later levels, or that the deposits in which they were found were not demonstrably ancient (see Daniel 1964: 42). The year 1859 is often quoted as the turning point in the acceptance of human antiquity, not least because it coincided with the publication of Darwin's *Origin of Species*, which did so much to foster the idea of gradual evolution over immense periods of time.

Eighteen fifty-nine was also the end of an era in that it marked the death of Brunel, arguably the greatest Victorian civil engineer: we should remember that the Railway Age not only shrank the world by making it so much easier for geologists, antiquarians and millions of others to travel, but also created much of the evidence of human antiquity by its insatiable demands for gravel ballast, and by the cutting of innumerable geological sections during the construction of railway lines. Thus in 1859, three eminent Victorian geologists – Falconer, Prestwich and Evans – went by train to inspect the evidence of an obscure French customs official, Boucher de Perthes, who had collected large numbers of stone tools from gravel pits along the river Somme in northern France, and claimed they were ancient, and associated with the remains of extinct animals. (These tools are now known as Abbevillian and Acheulian, after the localities where they were found, and the Acheulian in particular is still used to describe lower palaeolithic assemblages from large areas of Europe, Africa, the Near East and India.) Prestwich and his colleagues confirmed his evidence, as well as that collected by the vicar William Pengelly, who had found stone tools beneath a stalagmitic layer in Kent's Cavern in south-west England that are now recognized as middle palaeolithic, and 40–100,000 years old. Thereafter, geology became the foundation of palaeolithic studies in its ability to demonstrate and calibrate human antiquity.

PALAEOLITHIC STUDIES 1859–1959

Once human antiquity had been convincingly demonstrated to most critics' satisfaction, the subsequent century was largely taken up with mapping this antiquity in space and time. By 1914 a recognizable picture of human antiquity had emerged by painstaking stratigraphic observations in excavations and sections. Geologists were also aided by the discovery that the earth's climate had often been considerably colder than today during the time-span of human evolution. Evidence of reindeer, woolly rhinoceros and mammoth from south-western France, for example, or of glaciers that had once covered much of Scandinavia and the British Isles, indicated the existence of at least one 'Ice Age' during the Palaeolithic. Animal remains from cave and riverine deposits were particularly important in showing the prevailing type of climate, and this in turn helped distinguish between 'warm' and 'cold' phases of the remote past, and so allowed geologists to develop a chronological framework by recognizing, for example, an 'Age of Reindeer' and an 'Age of Hippopotamus'. (As we shall see later, faunal remains from palaeolithic sites are used very differently today.)

Nineteenth-century palaeolithic archaeologists relied heavily on notions of evolution and progress as inherent features of the past: if man had evolved like any other animal, so he had also 'progressed' from a 'lower' to a 'higher' level of existence, and such developments would be reflected in the type of tools that were made. Stone tools could therefore be assigned an approximate relative age by their inferred 'crudeness' or 'sophistication'. Again, analogies with known hunter-gatherers continued to be crucial. Stone tools found in Europe that resembled those made by peoples deemed to be very primitive – notably the Tasmanian and Tierra del Fuegean aborigines – were regarded as very ancient, whilst those resembling the artefacts used by more 'advanced' peoples, such as the Eskimo, were regarded as much younger.

In general, cave sites provided most evidence for what is now seen as the Middle and Upper Palaeolithic in Europe, and river deposits were the main source for the Lower. Much of the key nineteenth-century work occurred in France, from which many of the terms still in use were derived. One key piece of work was by two wealthy amateurs, Lartet and Christy, who excavated several cave sites in south-west France that were occupied by people who often hunted reindeer when the climate was considerably colder than today. (These sites, such as Aurignac, Cro-Magnon, and Les Eyzies, are now recognized as Upper Palaeolithic, dating to 30–15,000 BC.) Following the pioneering work of Boucher de Perthes on riverine deposits, others showed that the Acheulian and Abbevillian could be divided into a number of types, defined in terms of skill of manufacture, and thus their relative antiquity. By the 1870s, de Mortillet, one of the most eminent archaeological publicists of the time, could declare in the Paris Exhibition of 1867 the triumphal statement of 'le Loi du Progrès de l'Humanité, le Loi du Développement Similaire, et l'Haute Antiquité de l'Homme' as demonstrated proofs from palaeolithic archaeology.

If the initial demonstration of human antiquity was achieved by British scholars, its study was thereafter dominated by the French until well into the post-war period. The most exciting discoveries probably took place in the ten years or so before the First World War. Particular landmarks were the excavations at the caves of La Ferrassie and La Chapelle-aux-Saints in south-west France, which produced complete skeletons of Neanderthals, and their artefacts, now recognized as Mousterian, after the nearby cave of Le Moustier. Similar and equally important discoveries were also made at the cave of Krapina, Croatia, even though their importance was overshadowed by the French discoveries. It was these that underpinned most subsequent debate, and the public perception of Neanderthals as stocky, stooped and primitive (see Chapter 19).

The discovery of palaeolithic cave art was probably one of the most dramatic discoveries of the late nineteenth century. Engraved and decorated objects had been discovered earlier, but were totally eclipsed by the discovery of painted murals of bison, reindeer and mammoth in the caves of northern Spain, the Pyrenees and south-western France. Despite much initial scepticism that representational art could be so ancient, the evidence was accepted by 1914. A key figure here was the Abbé Breuil, whose meticulous copies and records, often made under the most uncomfortable of conditions, firmly established the authenticity, range and skills of palaeolithic artists through a series of detailed monographs. Breuil probably contributed more to the study of the Palaeolithic than anyone else this century. His 1912 paper on the Upper Palaeolithic replaced de Mortillet's earlier and simpler scheme with a sequence for the upper palaeolithic cultures of south-west France that set the agenda for most subsequent studies. In a major study of the Lower Palaeolithic (Breuil and Kozlowski 1931) he recognized eleven stages of the Acheulian in terms of stratigraphy and typology, and this scheme pervaded similar studies elsewhere in Europe and throughout Africa and India.

If the French dominated studies of palaeolithic archaeology, its climatic and geological framework was established by German scholars. By the 1880s, they had also recognized that the Ice Age had been interspersed by warmer 'interglacial' periods when the climate was more like today. In 1909, two German geologists,

Penck and Bruckner, published their *Die Alpen im Eiszeitalter* (The Alps in the Ice Ages), in which they argued that there had been four major glaciations during the Pleistocene (the most recent geological period and the one in which humans evolved). Each was named after a local river of southern Germany, and, conveniently for generations of students, Penck and Bruckner established the practice of naming the oldest glaciation in a region with a name beginning with a letter near the start of the alphabet. Consequently, in terms of decreasing age, the four major Alpine glaciations that occurred during the Palaeolithic were known as Günz, Mindel, Riss and Würm.

Penck and Bruckner's work provided palaeolithic archaeologists with a series of pegs on which to hang their palaeolithic cultures. For example, most of the lower palaeolithic Acheulian was later dated to the Mindel–Riss interglacial, the Mousterian to the early part of the last (Würm) glaciation, and the Upper Palaeolithic to its latter part. It was also so influential on Pleistocene geology for the next sixty years that it deserves further attention. After the 1914–18 war, researchers in other areas found evidence of four major glaciations, in areas formerly glaciated, and four 'pluvials' – or cool, wet episodes – in regions nearer the equator. Consequently, a 'Grand Synthesis' of regional glaciations and pluvials was established, each with four cold events, named in alphabetical order. Common to many of these schemes was the assumption that first, the early Pleistocene had been pre-glacial; second, that glaciations had tended to be short; and third, that each began and ended gradually. By implication, our ancestors had not had to contend with hostile climates until comparatively late in their evolution, and even then, glaciations had been relatively short, and with a very gradual transition to and from interglacial conditions. As noted below, a very different picture has emerged since the 1970s.

Although prehistoric archaeology first developed in western Europe in the first half of the nineteenth century, it soon ceased to be a monopoly of those areas. The first monograph on the vertebrate palaeontology of India appeared as early as 1845, and the antiquity of the Palaeolithic there was recognized as early as the 1860s. In many areas, palaeolithic investigations were developed within a few years of colonial rule, particularly by the French and British. The 'Golden Age' of colonial archaeology was probably during the 1920s and 1930s, when the foundations of stone age studies were firmly established over much of Africa, India, south-east Asia and the Near East (see Dennell 1990). The major exception was Australia, where little significant archaeological work occurred until its Pleistocene record was discovered in the 1960s.

In Africa and Asia, the Palaeolithic was investigated by Europeans, inheriting and developing a framework that had been developed in Europe. Given that archaeological cultures were seen as equivalent to geological ages, this was not surprising, as a culture found in Europe should be expected in Africa or Asia, just as the Miocene is. Thus the Aurignacian was recognized in areas as remote as

East Africa, whereas it is now seen as local to Europe only. The recognition that archaeological cultures were not universal stages of development, but discrete, localized entities, soon encouraged the development of local terminologies, albeit often within the broader framework of the Lower, Middle and Upper Palaeolithic that stemmed from European discoveries. Even this framework has now largely disappeared in areas where it was formerly prevalent, such as Africa and India, where an Early, Middle and Late Stone Age (abbreviated as the ESA, MSA, and LSA respectively) are seen as more appropriate.

There has always been a fundamental difference between the study of the Palaeolithic and Mesolithic in Europe and the Near East, and their counterparts in the Americas, Africa and Australasia. In Europe, the Palaeolithic ended some 10,000 years ago at the end of the last ice age, and the Mesolithic was followed by the Neolithic by 5,000 years ago over much of Europe. That is to say, hunting and gathering largely disappeared as a dominant lifestyle in Europe thousands of years ago, and so for Europeans it is very much 'ancient history', and removed from them by two or three thousand years of written history and often by as much again of non-literate agrarian history. (The same is even more true, of course, of the Near East.) In other areas, Europeans confronted hunters and gatherers directly, and the Stone Age in Australasia, and much of Africa, Amazonia and North America often effectively ended with their arrival. In those situations, hunters and gatherers were very much in the present, and could be studied directly, not just in terms of their material culture but also in terms of their kinship systems, language, religious attitudes and ideology. Ethnography and social anthropology were thus integrated with prehistoric archaeology in those areas to a much greater extent than in Europe.

PALAEOLITHIC STUDIES FROM THE 1960s

Palaeolithic studies changed profoundly during and after the 1960s. The main reasons usually quoted are the refinement of dating techniques, and the development of new ones; a comparable revolution in studies of past climatic change; and major changes in the ways that archaeologists approached the past. Other factors were also involved: cheaper air travel in the 1970s made overseas fieldwork more practical, and international conferences more accessible; conversely, higher labour costs increasingly meant that archaeologists had to excavate smaller areas in much greater detail.

Two dating techniques – carbon-14 and potassium-argon (K/A) – did much to free palaeolithic archaeologists from the need to focus primarily upon chronology. Neither was an invention of the 1960s: radio-carbon dating, for example, had been used since Libby's pioneering work in the 1940s, and K/A dating since the 1930s. However, these were initially of use respectively on very young (under 10,000 years) and very old (over 10 million years) materials. As they improved, so radio-carbon could be used reliably on materials as old as 30–50,000 years ago, and K/A on volcanic deposits under a million years old. As a result, both the earliest and latest parts of human evolution and stone age societies could be dated, even though there remained an uncomfortable gap between 50,000 and 500,000 years that is only now being plugged. 'Guesstimates' could now be replaced by realistic, verifiable estimates. One immediate reward was that the time-span of human evolution was considerably enlarged: even in the 1940s, authorities such as Louis Leakey and Arthur Keith believed that the whole of human evolution had been crammed into the last million years, whereas thirty years later we find it easy to accept that the first toolmaking hominids lived over 2 million years ago, and the earliest bipedal hominids were walking upright some 2 million years before that (see Chapter 19). A second gain lay in the type of deposits that could now be dated. As seen earlier, riverine deposits and caves had been the main sources of evidence, simply because they contained sufficiently long geological records to allow the construction of local sequences. Open-air sites usually preserved better evidence of *in situ* activities, but were often impossible to date before the refinement of C14 and K/A. Dating techniques have since been considerably enhanced by the development of other methods, such as palaeomagnetism, thermoluminescence (TL), optical saturation luminescence (OSL), electron-spin resonance (ESR), uranium-thorium (U-Th) and other isotopic techniques (Aitken 1990; and see Chapter 5).

Radio-carbon dating in particular had an immense effect in internationalizing studies of ancient hunter-gatherers. A good example is Australia, the stone age archaeology of which had been largely ignored on the grounds that the aborigines were 'an unchanging people, living in an unchanging environment', and therefore unworthy of study. This prejudice was reinforced by the belief that Australia was not colonized until the postglacial conditions in the last 10,000 years. Due to radio-carbon dating, it now has a Pleistocene past extending back at least 60,000 years (Roberts, Jones and Smith 1994) – that is to say, it was colonized by sea when Neanderthals were still living in south-west France. Likewise, we now know that Melanesian islands 200 miles offshore were colonized some 30,000 years ago (Allen *et al.* 1989); and that the Americas had been colonized by 10,000, and perhaps 30,000 years ago. All this proves more than that something is 'older' than something else: it means that each region can now establish its own prehistory, independent of discoveries and prejudices of other regions.

Perhaps the profoundest impact of radio-carbon and other dating techniques upon the study of prehistoric hunter-gatherers has been in the way that stone tools and animal remains associated with stone tools can be studied. As noted earlier, typological studies of stone tools were initially vital for building chronological frameworks. These efforts were often supplemented by the analysis of animal remains to show the prevailing climatic conditions, and/or the approximate age of a deposit by the type of animal. The advent of absolute dating techniques over the last thirty years has largely (but by no means entirely) freed archaeologists from the need to concentrate on chronology, and enabled them to look instead at other questions such as: how were tools made and used?; why were they discarded?; how long did they last?; which members of a group might have made and used them? Or what types of animals were hunted, or scavenged?; which parts of the carcass were preferred?; at what time of year were they killed?; was meat shared? (if so, amongst whom, and by whom?); and how was it used? (eaten fresh, stored?); were skins used, or only the meat and bone?

A revolution of comparable magnitude to that brought about by radio-carbon occurred through isotopic studies of deep-sea sediments. Put briefly, minute marine organisms called foramifera have shells of calcium carbonate (the building-stuff of chalk), compiled from sea-water and carbon-dioxide. As these creatures live, they absorb the prevailing isotopic composition of the water around them, which in turn depends on the prevailing salinity, itself dependent upon the amount of freshwater locked up on the earth's surface as ice and snow. The isotopic composition of these creatures thus gives an indirect account of the prevailing climate. When these creatures die, their remains fall from whatever depth of water they inhabited when alive to the sea bed. Ocean floor sediments thus contain a record of the earth's climate, and moreover it is generally a record that is far more continuous and undisturbed than any sequence on land (Imbrie and Imbrie 1979).

Analyses of these sediments have shown a radically different view of climatic change during human evolution from that developed on land by Penck and Bruckner, and their successors (Fig. 19.7). The 'Magic Four' glaciations of the Pleistocene have now been replaced by at least twenty over the last 2.5 million years; these often began and ended abruptly, and glaciations probably dominated 90 per cent of the last 2 million years. However, substantial problems still exist in relating this new, global picture to the older, regional sequences derived from the classic fourfold glacial model. Many key sites between 50,000 and 500,000 years old are still dated by reference to the old chronological framework, now known to be obsolete, because they are too old to be dated by C14 and too young for K/A. These problems will eventually be resolved through the development of new dating techniques, but anomalies are likely to remain for many years to come.

The 1960s also marked the eclipse of the French domination of palaeolithic studies by American ideas (Villa 1991). As part and parcel of the New Archaeology, palaeolithic archaeologists shifted their focus from the development of cultures and their components through time to the behaviour of individual groups, and the interrelationships of their technology, social organization and environment. This in turn fostered a more closely integrated, interdisciplinary approach. In British circles, this approach grew out of the Cambridge palaeoeconomic approach developed by Graham Clark in the 1950s (Clark 1952), and Eric Higgs in the 1970s (Higgs

1975). American developments were always more deeply rooted in anthropology than in Europe, and owed much to the galvanizing influence of Lewis Binford in forcing attention away from descriptions of archaeological cultures to analyses of how their components interacted with each other and the environment (see, for example: Binford 1983; Binford and Binford 1966).

CURRENT SOURCES AND APPROACHES

In the 1990s, archaeologists investigating prehistoric and especially Pleistocene hunter-gatherers have an enormous array of techniques (potentially) at their disposal. The dating of a site or deposit can often be delegated to a laboratory; the prevailing climate is often known in far greater detail than could be imagined a few decades ago; and improved techniques for retrieving and recording material from excavations have greatly increased the quantity and quality of data. How then are hunter-gatherers studied, and what are the main sources of evidence?

Whereas most earlier work on stone tools focused attention on a small number of distinctive types (or '*type fossiles*') that were chronologically significant, the emphasis now is on the total assemblage, including the parts that may have been waste, or the by-products of making and re-using stone tools. Assemblages are often categorized into percentages of each type to facilitate comparison with others. The French, in particular, brought this approach to a high level of refinement through the work of François Bordes and his successors, and have often used recurrent patterns to designate regional subvariations or subperiods of archaeological cultures. However, this approach is not without problems: the type of stone used, and modifications to stone tools before they were discarded have to be considered, and it is rarely appropriate to very early stone technologies as few tools were of a standard shape, or to areas such as Australia, where hunter-gatherers survived with very few formal tool types (Dibble and Rolland 1992).

Other researchers have stressed more the context in which assemblages were used, modified and discarded. American researchers have been particularly active in this respect, due in no small part to the work by Lewis Binford, who did much to focus attention on studying assemblages in terms of seasonal need, planning depth, raw material availability, and cultural framework. One approach he and others have used is to relate stone tool assemblages to the types of large mammal remains associated with them, on the grounds that much of the tool-kit used by hunters would have been used for obtaining and processing meat, as well as other parts of the carcass. Another major development in stone tool studies is through use-wear – the traces of wear caused by a tool being used for a specific task. This line of research was pioneered in Russia by Semenov (1964), and by Lawrence Keeley (1980) in the USA. This has produced some major surprises in that often the perceived function of a stone tool as a 'knife' or 'scraper', for example, is not confirmed by its use-wear. Often, stone flakes categorized as 'waste' were in fact used as tools. This brings into question the extent to which our perceptions of hunter-gatherer tool-form and tool-use are conditioned by our own western, twentieth-century perceptions. As a result, archaeologists are now more wary about describing stone tools in terms of function ('handaxe', 'scraper', and so on) until the use is confirmed independently, and meanwhile prefer to describe stone tools in terms of their shape, and how they were flaked.

In well-preserved and carefully excavated sites, it is sometimes possible to refit pieces of flaked stone. Although tedious to do, these studies can help elucidate whether stone tools were made or merely modified on a site, which parts of a site were used for stone-working, and even the numbers of people who may have been involved (see, for example, Cahen and Keeley 1980; de Loecker 1994). They can also provide valuable information on the amount of post-depositional disturbance that took place after the material was discarded (Villa 1983).

As with stone tools, large mammal remains are no longer used just for establishing a chronological framework. Information is now usually compiled on not only which types of, and how many, animals are present, but which anatomical elements are most often preserved, which parts were removed, the age at which an animal died, and how animal skeletons were broken and/or cut during and after the dismemberment of a carcass.

Although 'off-the-peg' analogies are clearly inappropriate, ethnographic studies can show us a great deal about hunter-gatherer behaviour, even if much of it is cautionary. For example, they provide a reminder of how impoverished our evidence is for hunting and gathering – a few stone tools, some bones and, if lucky, a few scraps of plant debris. Only rarely – as in waterlogged sites – is the organic component of their material culture preserved in the way of nets, traps, canoes, spears, bows, arrows, baskets and skins. Evidence of plant foods is likewise similarly impoverished. Ethnographic studies also indicate the complexities of hunter-gatherer life in terms of decisions and customs over who does what, and how choices are made and implemented. Study of the 'structure' of their decision-making, and means of effecting these decisions in terms of the social organization and technology, can also help in the generation of hypotheses about the types of archaeological residues that may be predicted from different types of activities and circumstances. In the same way, we can learn an immense amount from primatologists about the way apes behave (McGrew 1992), but without turning early hominids into just another type of chimpanzee.

CONCEPTUAL AND METHODOLOGICAL PROBLEMS

The term 'hunter-gatherer' is often used to describe the subsistence of our predecessors from the time when they first learnt to make stone tools (and thereby left an archaeological record) some 2.5 million years ago to the advent of agriculture in the last few thousand years. This time-span presents three major difficulties to those studying the prehistory of subsistence.

Problems of definition: hunting and gathering as a way of life

Gathering, the less contentious of these two terms, implies the collection but not cultivation of plant foods. As plant foods are rarely directly evidenced before the end of the last ice age their role is often more assumed than demonstrated. 'Hunting' is more problematic, as it implies the deliberate, premeditated, killing of animals, as opposed to the scavenging of carcasses of animals that died naturally or were killed by other predators. In behavioural terms, the two are very different, and require very different skills. Archaeologically, however, they are hard to tell apart from the scraps of bone and teeth that occasionally survive in undisturbed archaeological contexts. In the very remote past, scavenging may well have been more important than hunting, and one current major debate is whether 'hunting' is a comparatively recent phenomenon in our evolutionary history (see, for example, Binford 1989).

A related problem concerns the relative importance of meat to plant foods in the hunter-gatherer (or scavenger-gatherer) diet, and the time spent obtaining them. Large brains require high intakes of protein, and our teeth and digestive system are those of an omnivore. Meat is often assumed to have been more important than plant foods in early hominid diet, not least because the remains of large mammals survive much better archaeologically than those of plants. The image of 'Man the Hunter' as deeply rooted in human evolution has also been powerful, partly due to a male bias (thankfully less evident these days) amongst ethnographers in documenting the activities of contemporary hunters, who also tended to be male. It came as a major surprise in the 1960s to learn that the !Kung Bushmen of the Kalahari obtain 90 per cent of their food from plants, even though their hunting was regarded as a high-status (and usually male) activity (Lee 1979). Many ethnographically documented societies are better categorized as gatherer-hunters than hunter-gatherers, and the same may well hold true of the past. In global terms, the importance of meat to human diet generally decreases towards the equator, and diets composed overwhelmingly of meat tend to be located in Arctic regions. The 'hunting' of large mammals as the main means of procuring food may have been not only a comparatively recent phenomenon, but one confined to cold areas where plant productivity is low.

807

Additionally, the hunting and/or scavenging of large mammals and the gathering of plant foods were not the only options open to early hominids for acquiring food. This applies especially to the acquisition of animal protein. In accounts of human evolution, *carnivory*, or meat-eating, has been emphasized far more than *faunivory*, the eating of animal protein (McGrew 1992: 209). However, large herbivores are not the only source of animal protein: small mammals such as rodents, birds, eggs, reptiles and even insects (such as termites) may also have been eaten by early hominids, not least because none is especially dangerous to catch or likely to be scavenged. Unpalatable though it might be to envisage our earliest ancestors eating mice, lizards, frogs, tortoises, eggs and insects, those may have been more commonly eaten than large mammals. We should not assume early hominids ignored them merely because prehistorians have done so.

How does the archaeological record for prehistoric subsistence relate to the fossil hominid record?

The answer to this question has to be: very tenuously indeed for the most part. First, it is often unclear which type of hominid created the archaeological record: this point applies particularly to the earliest African evidence prior to 1.5 million years ago, but also to the last glaciation in Europe and south-west Asia before 30,000 years ago, as both Neanderthals and anatomically modern humans may have been responsible (see Chapter 19).

Second, even if we know which type of hominid did create the archaeological record, its evolutionary relationship to us is usually unclear and/or contentious. We cannot therefore assume an unbroken thread that somehow links us to those hominids living 50,000, 500,000 or 2 million years ago. The prehistory of hominid subsistence is not one of 'progress' from simple to complex, from primitive to advanced, from crude to sophisticated, or from 'less' to 'more' human. These views were inherent in nineteenth-century accounts, and still haunt many present studies, but human behaviour 2 million years ago – or even 100,000 years ago – was not just a 'simpler' and more 'primitive' version of what is seen today: it was fundamentally different because it was performed by creatures that are now extinct and might not even be directly ancestral to us. Hominid behaviour prior to *Homo sapiens sapiens* has to be studied in its own right, and not as something that becomes inexorably and inevitably more 'human' through time, or, for that matter, less chimpanzee-like. Even after 30,000 years ago, when *H. sapiens sapiens* became the only type of hominid in the world, the diversity of human cultures evidenced today and in the recent past should warn us against simple generalizations. Similarly, enough is now known of the diversity of chimpanzee behaviour to caution us against generalizing about the ape-like 'pre-human' condition.

Third, the behaviour of extinct hominid species probably changed through time: the behaviour of *Homo erectus*, for example, is unlikely to have been static over a million years (especially if it colonized two new continents in that time), even if its anatomy may have been remarkably constant. For that reason alone, it is not especially useful to structure discussions of palaeolithic subsistence in terms of a particular type of hominid.

How does the archaeological record for palaeolithic subsistence relate to artefactually defined periods?

Again, the answer has to be: very weakly indeed. The main units of the Palaeolithic (Lower, Middle and Upper) were initially defined for chronological purposes by the presence of handaxes, prepared cores and blades respectively. None of these helps define human or hominid diets and subsistence strategies, however useful they may have been at the time. The Lower Palaeolithic covers at least 2 million years, from the hominids of the late Pliocene of Africa to those living in Africa, and over much of Asia and Europe some 250,000 years ago. The Middle Palaeolithic has no clear beginning and an extremely contentious end around 35,000 years ago, and those who study the subsistence of the last glaciation would do well to avoid being dragged into palaeontological arguments over whether or not Neanderthals became extinct. The Upper Palaeolithic is little more uniform than the preceding Middle and Lower Palaeolithic once the widespread use of blade tools has been noted. An additional limitation of terms such as Middle and Upper Palaeolithic is that they are very local, and inapplicable outside Europe, the Near East and North Africa.

For these reasons, syntheses of palaeolithic subsistence should attempt to be independent of both the fossil taxa identified by physical anthropologists, and the chronological units initially devised by those who studied stone tools. Such syntheses also need to take account of the major gaps and weaknesses of the archaeological record. Here, four major units are tentatively identified.

The first is one of *tool-assisted omnivory*. This term is intended to summarize the evidence for the earliest hominids, prior to about 1.5 million years ago, and possibly confined to Africa. The second, between 0.5 and 1.5 million years ago, is what this writer would summarize as '*The Big Unknown*' (not unlike Glynn Isaac's famous 'Muddle in the Middle'), as its main concerns are when (and even if) hominids left Africa, and when and how they colonized Asia and Europe. The third is evidenced by at least 500,000 years ago, and can be described as *hunting for immediate consumption*. In the last 25,000 years or so, *hunting with the option of deferred consumption* appears to be the most useful way of summarizing the main developments in Europe at least, where the best evidence obtains.

TOOL-ASSISTED OMNIVORY

As described in Chapter 19, the earliest known hominids, from *c.* 4.5 million years ago, are derived from the Rift Valley in East Africa and later from various cave systems in South Africa (Fig. 20.1). The oldest stone tools are those around 2.5 million years old from the Kadar Gona, Ethiopia (Semaw *et al.* 1997). Slightly younger ones have been found at Koobi Fora, but the best known ones are those from Olduvai Gorge, where they were found associated with both *Homo habilis* and *Australopithecus boisei*. It has usually been argued that *habilis* was the only tool-maker, but recent discoveries of hand bones at Swartkrans Cave in southern Africa suggest that *Paranthropus* (including *A. boisei*) may also have made stone tools (Susman 1987, 1988). This would not be surprising, as chimpanzees can both make and use tools made from wood, leaves and occasionally stone (McGrew 1992), and orang-utans (Wright 1972) and some monkeys (Westergaard and Suomi 1995) can also flake stone. If, as seems reasonable, chimps and humans have inherited these skills from a common background, then tool-making may well pre-date both humans and chimpanzees, and thus be older than when they diverged over 6 million years ago (Westergaard and Suomi 1995). What we may be detecting after 2.5 million years is the onset of localized artefact discard, rather than the advent of stone tool-making.

Investigations into the subsistence of late Pliocene hominids share many features with a courtroom drama. The 'victims' were numerous dead animals, represented either as individual carcasses (such as the elephant at DK1, Olduvai, or the hippo at the Hippo-Artefact Site, Koobi Fora) or, more commonly, as a few bones and teeth of several animals. *H. habilis* has been the usual 'suspect': 'Nutcracker Man' or *A. boisei* was readily dismissed as, at most, a feeble-minded and largely vegetarian bystander because of its small brain and large chewing teeth. The stone tools found in the same context as the animal bones were seen as incriminating evidence that *habilis* had killed and butchered the animals in its quest for meat: it had, in short, the means, motive and opportunity. In an earlier but similar investigation, Raymond Dart (1949) inferred that the 2.5–3.0-million-year-old australopithecines found in the cave deposits at Makapansgat in South Africa had hunted several types of animals, including carnivores, and had even used an 'osteodontokeratic' culture of animal bones, teeth and horns as tools, long before stone was used.

The key assumption in these investigations was that there was a *causal* association between the non-hominid animal remains, the hominid remains themselves (whether *Australopithecus africanus* or *H. habilis*) and, in the East African case, the stone tools. The seemingly common-sense proposition that the association of stone tools and animal remains indicated that hominids had hunted was most clearly expressed by Glynn Isaac (1978). His synthesis rested on the evidence of his own team at Koobi Fora as well as that which Mary Leakey (1971) had meticulously

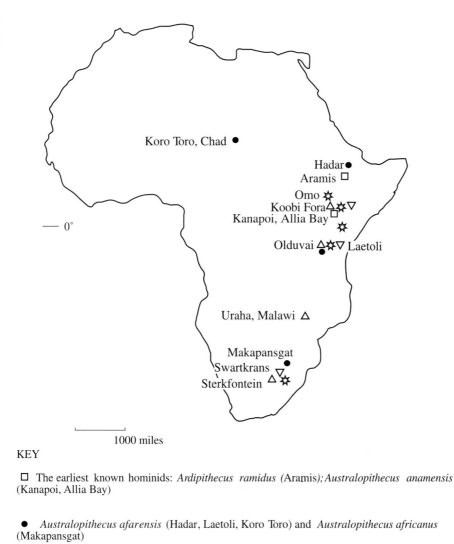

KEY

☐ The earliest known hominids: *Ardipithecus ramidus* (Aramis); *Australopithecus anamensis* (Kanapoi, Allia Bay)

● *Australopithecus afarensis* (Hadar, Laetoli, Koro Toro) and *Australopithecus africanus* (Makapansgat)

� Stone tools older than 1.6 million years: Koobi Fora, Olduvai, the Omo Valley and Swartkrans

▽ *Paranthropus* or *Australopithecus robustus:* Koobi Fora, Olduvai, Swartkrans

△ early *Homo: H. habilis* (Olduvai, possibly Koobi Fora and Sterkfontein); *H. rudolfensis* (Koobi Fora, Uraha)

Figure 20.1 Principal localities of African hominids. 1. The earliest-known hominids *Ardipithecus ramidus* (Aramis) and *Australopithecus anamensis* (Kanapoi, Allia Bay); 2. *Australopithecus afarensis* (Hadar, Laetoli, Koro Toro) and *Australopithecus africanus* (Makapansgat); 3. stone tools earlier than 1.6 million years (Koobi Fora, Olduvai, the Omo valley, Swartkrans); 4. *Paranthropus* or *Australopithecus robustus* (Koobi Fora, Olduvai, Swartkrans); 5. early *Homo* (Olduvai, possibly Koobi Fora and Sterkfontein); *H. rudolfensis* (Koobi Fora, Uraha). Source: R. Dennell; drawn by D. Miles-Williams.

assembled at Olduvai. Her excavations had shown different types of sites: some contained large amounts of flaked stone and animal remains; others had a large amount of flaked stone but few animal remains; and others contained numerous animal remains but only a few stone artefacts.

At the time, the interpretation of this material seemed straightforward, and was similar to that routinely given to other, much younger, palaeolithic sites in Africa, Europe and Asia. Those sites with the remains of a few large animals and only a few stone tools were explicable as butchery sites, where animals were killed or scavenged, and from which parts of the carcass were removed for eating elsewhere. Sites with large amounts of bone and stone were explained as home bases, where members of a hunting group (assumed to be the males) took meat that could be shared with the rest of the group, and particularly with the females and their offspring. One site at Olduvai (DK) in Bed I even had the remains of what was interpreted as a hut, where hominids slept at night (Leakey 1971: 24). Other sites with much stone but little bone were seen as 'workshop sites', where stone tools were made, and perhaps some meat consumed whilst doing so.

This model had several implications on early human behaviour, particularly that of *Homo habilis*, the probable maker of the Oldowan assemblage. Above all, it implied that *habilis* was already behaving in a recognizably 'human' manner 2 million years ago: there was already a sexual division of labour, whereby males hunted and females gathered; a basic family unit, in which males provisioned their female partners and young; meat was already a major part of early hominid diet, and this was acquired by hunting rather than by scavenging. As importantly, home bases were already integral parts of pre-human behaviour in providing foci where hominids ate, slept and cooperated together. A logical and obvious consequence of this model was that if *Homo habilis* was behaving in this way 2 million years ago, then so too were later hominids.

As already stated, the basic assumption of this approach was that there was a *causal* relationship between the stone tools and animal bones: both were found together because hominids had used one to process the other. But was this necessarily the case? Could this association have been merely *casual*? Suppose the stone tools and animal remains had been deposited independently of each other, and by different agencies? In what amounted to a retrial of *H. habilis* and *A. africanus*, and their current acquittal of all charges of systematic hunting and food-sharing, much attention was paid to the association of stone tools and faunal remains. One major starting point was Brain's (1981) reassessment of the evidence from the South African australopithecine caves such as Swartkrans. His work was part of a growing interest in taphonomy – the processes by which fossil and archaeological material is accumulated and buried. Brain paid close attention to the type of debris left by carnivores such as leopard after their feeding, to the types and age-groups of animals that they prefer, and to the parts of the skeleton that most commonly survive. In effect, he overturned Dart's (1949) earlier verdict that the australo-pithecines had been skilled hunters. In Brain's view, these had not been the hunters but the hunted: the remains of their skeletons amongst those of other animals indicated only that they too had been eaten by a non-hominid carnivore.

A second major starting point came from Lewis Binford, who engendered a lively and occasionally heated debate on how the East African early hominid localities had formed. He argued that a causal relationship between stone tools and animal remains had to be demonstrated, not assumed (Binford 1977). He further argued that such associations might have been entirely casual, in that that there was no clear evidence that hominids had accumulated the animal remains. In some cases, stone tools and animal remains could have been mixed together by stream action as a kind of 'fluvial jumble'. If so, the stone tools would have been derived from elsewhere, or during other activities not associated with meat procurement.

Others tested specific parts of the data on which Isaac's model depended – often encouraged by Isaac himself, whose own views developed considerably. Much attention was paid to which parts of animal skeletons were present (Blumenschine 1986; Bunn and Kroll 1986) to see if the debris at these early hominid sites was markedly different from that found at non-hominid feeding and denning localities. Evidence was also sought for cut-marks and tooth-marks as indicators of whether hominids or other carnivores modified bone debris. Both were often evidenced, and in some cases, as at Koobi Fora, the superposition of cut-marks over carnivore tooth-marks (and sometimes vice versa) indicated that both were involved (Gamble 1981). A further weakness of Isaac's original model was the length of time represented by these accumulations. Typically, present-day hunter-gatherer sites are very short term, and leave far less debris than the 'home bases' supposedly evidenced at Olduvai. Studies of the length of time for which bone was exposed before burial indicate that these early sites were often used repetitively, perhaps over several years (Potts 1986).

A decade or more of hard questioning has left very little of Isaac's (1978) and Mary Leakey's (1971) original model intact. The emerging consensus is that *Homo habilis* is far less 'human' than first thought: there is no clear evidence for hunting, let alone food sharing; the dietary importance of meat may have been overestimated; bone marrow may have been at least as important as meat; scavenging may have been more important than hunting; and carnivores probably played a large part in the accumulation of the bone at these localities. Furthermore, the 'home bases' were probably palimpsests of several different activities carried out intermittently under a large area of tree-cover (Kroll 1994) by different kinds of hominids and other carnivores. The role of primates such as baboons – commonly found at some Olduvai localities – in modifying some of these assemblages is another area of uncertainty. Even the hut at site DK at Olduvai now seems to have been a natural feature, resulting from surface weathering of the underlying lava (Potts 1988: 28).

Archaeologists have thus had to accept that these earliest of archaeological sites do not lend themselves to any single, simple, explanation (Fig. 20.2). *Homo habilis* and its contemporaries probably did not live in nuclear families at a home base, or share out the meat that males had hunted and the plant foods that females had gathered. They may instead have fed in sexually discrete groups, and consumed much of their food at or near the place where it was found. Much if not most of the protein in their diet might have derived from insects, eggs, small mammals and reptiles, particularly given the problems of competition with and dangers from carnivores such as hyenas, dogs, lions and leopards. Early *Homo* and *Paranthropus* may also have scavenged off each other, in the same way that lions, hyenas and other predators regularly deprive each other of prey. Like apes and unlike modern humans, it is also likely that they ate and slept in different places, and seldom used one place for more than short periods of time (Sept 1982). It is also probable that much of their time – especially at night, their time of maximum danger – was still spent in trees: Susman and Stern's (1982) analysis of the hands and feet of *H. habilis* suggest it still retained an arboreal capability.

Nevertheless, these hominids were clearly targeting large carcasses, even if the few preserved might represent abnormal feeding events and not their primary source of food. They probably scavenged rather than hunted large animals, and used their technology to 'raid' carcasses so that parts could be removed quickly and taken elsewhere before other carnivores arrived. Smaller animals could have been killed and consumed nearby, in much the same way as some chimpanzees do (Boesch and Boesch 1989), and without leaving any significant archaeological debris. Unlike modern humans, it is also likely that they targeted bone marrow, and thus utilized the non-fleshy parts of carcasses that are normally left by carnivores such as lion or cheetah. Another strong probability is that they avoided direct competition with larger carnivores by, for example, concentrating their feeding activities into the mid part of the day, when the larger carnivores are normally resting (Wheeler 1992).

As stated earlier, proto-human behaviour has to be studied in its own right, and not merely as a crude precursor of what we see today. The lesson from the last decade's reassessments is that hominids of the Plio-Pleistocene behaved in a unique manner that is not seen today among humans, chimpanzees or any other ape. The implications of these reassessments have been far-reaching upon virtually all studies of later hominids. If Plio-Pleistocene hominids were not recognizably 'human' in that they did not hunt, share food, and use home bases, when did these features emerge? Can we assume that they were characteristic of hominids a million years ago, or even 100,000 years ago? At present, these uncertainties have not been resolved, and many former landmarks of the Middle and Upper Pleistocene have become ambiguous, if not discredited, indicators of proto-human hunting. One example is Olorgesaillie in Kenya. This Acheulian site is probably around 900,000

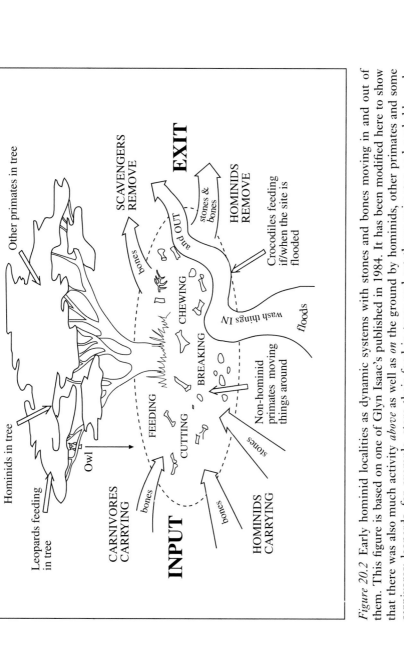

Figure 20.2 Early hominid localities as dynamic systems with stones and bones moving in and out of them. This figure is based on one of Glyn Isaac's published in 1984. It has been modified here to show that there was also much activity *above* as well as *on* the ground by hominids, other primates and some carnivores: leopards, for example, store their food in trees and eat there; primates and probably early *Homo* would have slept above ground level, and may also have consumed food there. On the ground other primates such as baboons might have moved stones and bones around; and if the area was by a lake and flooded in the wet season, crocodiles might also have fed there. In short, these are very 'busy' locations, and sorting out what hominids (*Homo* as well as *Paranthropus*) did is still far from clear. Source: R. Dennell; drawn by D. Miles–Williams.

years old, and has often been interpreted as an example of communal hunting of baboons by *H. erectus* (Shipman *et al.* 1981), but it seems more likely that the baboon and other bones accumulated independently of the stone tools (Binford 1977).

THE BIG UNKNOWN: IN OR OUT OF AFRICA?

One of the most contentious arguments in palaeoanthropology is about when hominids first colonized Asia and Europe (Fig. 20.3). The long-standing view is that *H. erectus* first appeared in East Africa about 1.7–1.8 million years ago, but did not leave Africa until around a million years ago (Rightmire 1991). The site of Ubeidiya, Israel, which may be 1.0–1.4 million years old (Tchernov 1989), is often quoted as the oldest outside Africa. What has never been adequately explained is why the alleged dispersal of *H. erectus* beyond Africa was not accompanied by any major change in technology, anatomy or subsistence; nor was there any discernible climatic or environmental 'window of opportunity' that allowed *H. erectus* to move beyond its African homeland around a million years ago. Equally puzzling is why, once it occupied eastern Asia, *H. erectus* abandoned the Acheulian, bifacial technology that had proved so successful in Africa, Europe and south-west Asia. As will be seen shortly, an alternative view is that hominids had already colonized Asia and perhaps Europe by 2 million years ago (Tattersall 1997). A third possibility is that, if *A. afarensis* already occupied the African grasslands by 3 million years ago (Brunet *et al.* 1995), hominids could have colonized the adjacent Asian grasslands long before 2 million years ago (Dennell 1997).

The timing of the first colonization of Asia and Europe is absolutely critical to studies of prehistoric subsistence as well as to the broader theme of human evolution. By 500,000 years ago, hominids were able to survive in an immense variety of environments, from northern Europe to southern Africa, and from west Africa to northern China and south-east Asia. This alone means that they must have had a wide variety of successful subsistence strategies. What is not known at present is whether hominids possessed the same degree of adaptability a half million, a million, or even 2 million years earlier.

The lack of clear, unambiguous evidence for hominids outside Africa before a million years ago partly reflects the small amount of palaeoanthropological fieldwork in the Asian landmass in the last fifty years, but also results from problems over the context, identification, and dating of finds. Stone artefacts on their own are rarely accepted as sound evidence by hominid palaeontologists; in any case (and as noted already), *Homo* is probably not the only creature that has made simple stone tools in the last few million years. Hominid palaeontologists also have their own disagreements over whether a fossil fragment belonged to a hominid: Orce, Spain,

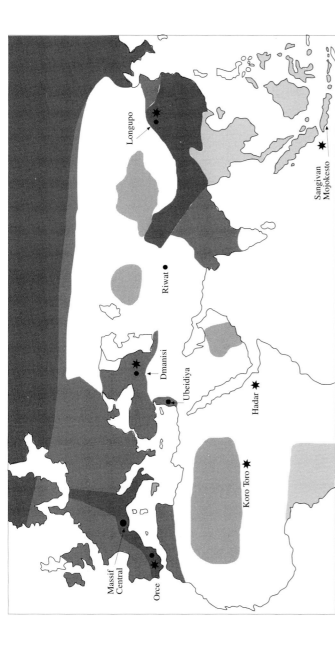

Figure 20.3 Out of Africa – the case for an early departure. The map shows those sites in Eurasia that figure most in claims that hominids left Africa well before 1 million years ago. The prevailing vegetation is taken from the reconstruction by Dowsett *et al.* (1994) of late Pliocene conditions around 3 million years ago. Note that in the late Pliocene, there was no Saharan desert barrier to cut Africa off from Asia, and grasslands (the assumed preferred habitat of early hominids) then extended from west Africa to northern China. If Lucy's contemporaries had already colonized the grasslands of Africa there was nothing to stop them from heading north and east towards China. Reprinted from Dowsett *et al.* 'Joint investigation of the Middle Plioceneclimate I: PRISM Palaeoenvironmental reconstructions', *Global and Planetary Change*, 9: 169–95 (1994), with kind permission of Elsevier Science – NL, Sara Burgerhartstraat 25, 1055 KV Amsterdam, The Netherlands. Adapted by D. Miles-Williams.

and Longgupo, China, are two recent examples where the alleged 'hominid' might be something different (see Dennell and Roebroeks 1996). Uncertainties also arise over the geological or archaeological context of a find: these are especially acute in the case of the Indonesian hominid remains, which most authorities regard as only *c.* 1.0–1.2 million years old, *contra* a recent claim that the oldest may be as much as 1.8 million years old (Swisher *et al.* 1994). Likewise, the mandible from Dmanisi, Georgia (Gabunia and Vekua 1995), may have come from the infilling of an animal burrow dug into earlier deposits, and thus may be somewhat younger than 1.8 million years old. However, it is worth remembering that virtually every major European and African hominid and archaeological locality beyond the range of radio-carbon dating (that is, >50,000 years old) has had its own dating problems: as most of us know from personal experience, good dates are hard to come by!

Much smoke but little evident fire thus obscures our view of when hominids first inhabited Asia and Europe. If they were inhabiting a 7,000-mile-wide expanse from southern Spain to Indonesia by 1.8 million years ago (or earlier), they do not appear to have ventured more than 35 degrees north of the equator, and this may indicate that they were constrained by the length of daylight for locating, obtaining, and processing food during the winter, irrespective of body type, climate, or type of environment.

Sadly, there is little first-class archaeological evidence between 1.5 and 0.5 million years ago that provides more than a minimal view of how *H. erectus* survived. As noted already, the 900,000-year-old site of Olorgesaillie, Kenya, is most unlikely to indicate the mass-slaughter of baboons; sadly, the 700,000-year-long sequence from Upper Bed II to IV at Olduvai (Leakey and Roe 1994) is largely one of stream channels, the contents of which have been too coarsely sorted to indicate how stone tools and animal remains are found in the same geological context. In the absence of good evidence, assessments of how *H. habilis* (in the wide sense) behaved at Olduvai and Koobi Fora have cast a very long shadow over the way hominids may have behaved thereafter. When *H. habilis* was thought to have been a skilled hunter, so too was *H. erectus*; now that *H. habilis* is seen as a largely opportunistic scavenger, there is an understandable temptation to see *H. erectus* in the same light.

However, its larger brain and body must have required a greater intake of protein, and a higher proportion of this might well have been derived from animal meat. A greater degree of cooperative behaviour may also have been needed to ensure the survival of their offspring, assuming that these had a longer period of post-natal helplessness than those of *H. habilis*. *H. erectus* is also likely to have been a ground-dwelling creature, and thus able to deal with nocturnal predators; fire-reddened clay at the 1.5-million-year-old cave-site of Swartkrans, South Africa (Brain and Sillen 1988), and the 1.2-million-year-old site of Chesowanja, Kenya (Gowlett *et al.* 1981) may indicate that the usefulness of fire as a deterrent to predators was already appreciated, even if it was not routinely used until the

Middle Pleistocene (James 1989). These conjectures aside, the quality of the African evidence between 1.5 and 0.5 million years ago needs to improve enormously if we are to see *H. erectus* in its own terms and not in those of its predecessor. Likewise, we need much more evidence from Asia before we can be sure when they were last absent from that continent.

HUNTING FOR IMMEDIATE CONSUMPTION

The earliest European evidence

If we leave aside the uncertainties of when (or even if) hominids first left Africa, the earliest unambiguous evidence for the deliberate, planned hunting and butchery of large mammals comes from northern Europe and dates to around 500,000 years ago (Fig. 20.4). The key evidence comes from two sites, and has been found only since 1995.

The first is the site of Boxgrove in southern England, which has been painstakingly investigated over the last fifteen years (Roberts 1986; Roberts, Stringer and Parfitt 1994). This is an Acheulian site, characterized by the use of bifacial handaxes, and dated on faunal and stratigraphic grounds to *c.* 500,000 years ago, making it one of the earliest sites in northern Europe. The archaeological layers lie in fine sands at the base of a former 60-metre-high cliff that was destroyed by the advance of the Anglian glaciation. Preservation is truly remarkable: most of the flints are as fresh as if they'd been knapped yesterday, and many are still in their original position and can be refitted to show the shape of the original flint nodule. Many bone fragments have not only cut-marks but also microscopic pieces of flint still embedded in them. What Boxgrove shows unambiguously is a number of butchery events, in particular of horse and rhino. These carcasses had been defleshed in an unhurried, systematic manner with the use of handaxes (as confirmed by wear analysis); experiments by a professional butcher on a deer carcass show that these handaxes, held between finger and thumb, are superlative defleshing tools (Mitchell, pers. comm.). In 1995, a horse scapula was found that had a circular perforation consistent with the impact of a thrown spear (BBC *Horizon* 1995).

The second and perhaps even more remarkable site is that of Schöningen in Germany. This is an open-cast brown-coal mine, containing peats and muds dated *c.* 380–400,000 years old that have produced numerous fresh flints and animal remains, many with cut marks (Thieme and Maier 1995). Wooden artefacts have also been found: these include a double-ended spear 0.8–1 metre long that was probably used at close quarters, and, recently, three superb complete throwing spears over 2 metres long and comparable in shape and proportion to a modern

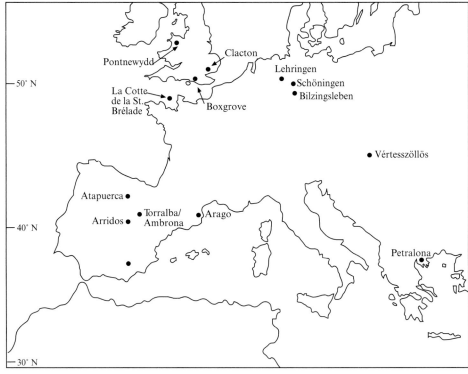

Figure 20.4 Major lower palaeolithic sites in Europe. Source: R. Dennell; drawn by D. Miles-Williams.

javelin (Fig. 20.5). Each was made from the trunk of spruce trees about 30 years old; the front, thrown-end, of these spears was made from the harder wood at the trunk base; and as in modern javelins, the centre of gravity was about one-third of the length from the tip to ensure stability in flight (Thieme 1997). Whilst the roughly contemporaneous spear-tip from Clacton, England has been interpreted as a digging stick or even a snow-probe for locating frozen carcasses (Gamble 1987), there can be no doubt from the size, shape, and craftsmanship of the Schöningen examples that these were throwing spears for killing large animals (Dennell 1997).

This evidence has to be seen in the context of the earliest colonization of Europe. If we leave aside various contentious claims that hominids were in Europe well before a million years ago, the oldest European evidence about which there appears to be reasonable agreement is the TD6 horizon at Atapuerca, Spain, dated palaeomagnetically to >780,000 years ago (Carbonell *et al.* 1995). If this dating is confirmed by faunal evidence, it would suggest that southern Europe was colonized (probably via the Dardanelles) well before northern Europe (Dennell and

Figure 20.5 Spear from Schöningen. Photograph: H. Thieme.

Roebroeks 1996). Intriguingly, the associated lithic assemblage is not Acheulian, but has more in common with the Oldowan; and the hominid remains have cut-marks and the same breakage features as the other animal remains. Whether this shows a ritual intake of human flesh, extreme nutritional stress, or a remarkably indiscriminate diet, remains to be established.

Atapuerca lies at 42° north; the oldest sites in northern Europe, such as Boxgrove, are at 51° north, and thus experience considerably more severe winters than southern Europe. Not only is food scarcest in winter, but the time available to locate, obtain and process it is also severely constrained by the short daylight hours. Even so, the hominids discarding handaxes at Pontnewydd Cave, northern Wales, 200,000 years ago were doing so at 53° north (Green 1981), which is more or less the furthest north that hominids operated before 30,000 years ago. The evidence from Boxgrove and Schöningen is the clearest evidence yet that by 380–500,000 years ago, hominids had acquired the ability to survive winter shortages in northern Europe by hunting large mammals year-round. What remains to be seen is whether earlier hominids possessed the same abilities.

Until recently, the evidence for big-game hunting in the European Lower Palaeolithic has been largely ambiguous and/or relatively recent: at Arridos, Spain, there is clear evidence for the butchery of elephants *c.* 300,000 years ago (Villa 1990), and at La Cotte St Brelade, Channel Islands, for driving rhinoceros and elephant over a cliff edge and then butchering them *c.* 130–200,000 years ago (Scott 1980). However, the faunal remains from earlier sites that were once thought to evidence big-game hunting (for example, of elephant and horse at Torralba/Ambrona,

821

Spain) are in disturbed contexts, small and/or in poor condition, and thus do not clearly indicate hunting, or, for that matter, scavenging (see Villa 1990).

Boxgrove and Schöningen will force a major revision of our assessments of lower palaeolithic subsistence in Europe. In the last fifteen years, the tendency has been to argue against earlier claims of big-game hunting in the European Lower Palaeolithic, and in favour of scavenging and some degree of opportunistic hunting (see, for example, Binford 1989). This caution has been understandable given the taphonomic complexity of many of these sites, and the probable degree of post-depositional disturbance. In contrast, Boxgrove and Schöningen have performed the same service for lower palaeolithic archaeology that the Hubble telescope has for astronomy. As importantly, they also provide a base-line for assessments of later European hominids, notably Neanderthals.

Bilzingsleben, Germany, is also highly relevant as perhaps the best example to date of a European lower palaeolithic living site (Mania 1990). It lay on the edge of a small lake, and is dated as c. 380–400,000 years old. It was perhaps occupied for only 20–30 years, and contains an enormous amount and variety of flaked stone and animal remains, many of which have cut-marks. Bone was also used to make tools, and one piece even has what seems to be a patterned series of marks that are hard to relate to butchery. Although the taphonomic aspects of the site are not fully clear, the spatial clustering of material is suggestive of work areas and structures.

The last glaciation

Both the quality and quantity of archaeological and human skeletal evidence improve considerably after 100,000 years ago. Discussions of this period are dominated by evidence from Europe and the Near East, and usually couched in terms of the 'Neanderthal debate' over whether or not Neanderthals became extinct or evolved into modern humans.

As with earlier periods, the evidence for subsistence is often difficult to interpret. Most of the evidence comes from caves, which have complex sedimentological histories, and were commonly used by animals other than humans. Many ungulate remains in such caves could have been taken by non-human predators such as hyena or wolf. At some sites in western Europe, the remains of bears and Mousterian stone tools were once interpreted as evidence of some kind of bear cult, but might simply indicate that some bears died whilst hibernating in caves that were used by Neanderthals in the summer. Even when it is reasonably certain that animal remains resulted from Neanderthals' activities, the usual problems arise in distinguishing scavenging from hunting by, for example, the type of animal, parts of the skeleton and/or type of damage to bones that are present. A good example are the Mousterian assemblages from the Grotte Vaufrey, France, which Binford (1988) regarded as the outcome of scavenging, but which Grayson (1994) argued were not.

Nevertheless, the ambiguities of much of this data should not obscure the point that systematic, planned hunting is evidenced in Europe 500,000 years ago, and so there is no need to suppose that Neanderthals lacked that basic ability, even if the details are unclear in many individual cases. Unlike their predecessors they may have used stone projectile points that were probably hafted onto a spear for stabbing prey at short distances (Boëda *et al.* 1996; Shay 1988). Nevertheless, meat was probably obtained in several ways: scavenging may have been necessary at times, and males and females (and different age groups) may have targeted different types of prey and used different methods. For example, Stiner (1994) has argued that early Neanderthals in Latium, Italy, scavenged head parts prior to 55,000 years ago, but thereafter ambushed large, prime-age animals. Each strategy seems to have relied on different ways of using stone: before 55,000 years ago the emphasis was on provisioning individuals, and thereafter on provisioning places in preparation for hunting.

Two other features of the European and Near Eastern evidence stand out. The first is that life was rough, tough and brief. There is no evidence of sewn clothing, and so Neanderthals must have survived glacial winters with little more than skin cloaks and the occasional fire. Every adult male Neanderthal skeleton found to date has evidence of repeated and sustained injury, especially to the shoulders, head and forearms: their nearest American counterparts today are rodeo riders (Trinkhaus and Zimmerman 1982). In the Neanderthals' case, the most likely cause of injury was in killing large animals at close range. Notwithstanding these injuries, many survived, most notably the Shanidar 1 individual, with multiple (and probably repeated) trauma to his head, shoulder, forearm and legs, and the 'old man' of La Chapelle-aux-Saints, who was crippled with arthritis and scarcely able to chew his food (Trinkhaus 1985). These examples are perhaps the earliest known of altruism.

Second, all the evidence to date points to the *immediate* consumption of food. There is no evidence that Neanderthals or their contemporaries prepared large amounts of meat for winter consumption by filleting, drying and/or smoking, or used any sort of storage facility. Hominids undoubtedly had the ability to hunt large animals, but must also have had to demonstrate that ability in areas such as northern Europe throughout the winter under conditions of low temperatures and short days.

The Neanderthal debate

As commented above, discussions of this period are dominated by the Neanderthal debate. There is little doubt that Neanderthals led different lives from later populations in all sorts of ways: in addition to the violent nature of their lives and their lack of storage technologies, there were many other things that they did not do, such as trapping small animals, fishing, burying their dead with elaborate grave-goods, wearing sewn clothes, carving elaborate tools from bone, antler or ivory, living in substantial structures, painting animal images, carving figurines and so on. However, all this appears to be equally true of their contemporaries, including those regarded as 'anatomically modern' in Africa and the Near East. In other words, the absence of all these features in the European and Near Eastern Mousterian is irrelevant to whether or not Neanderthals became extinct, as no other population possessed them either. It is up to those arguing that Neanderthals were replaced by incoming groups of humans (currently thought to have derived from Africa) to explain why the innovations seen in the Upper Palaeolithic, that supposedly gave modern humans the advantage over Neanderthals, were not evidenced in other areas beforehand.

HUNTING WITH THE OPTION OF DEFERRED CONSUMPTION

At some time after 35,000 years ago, humans appear to have exercised the option of deferring the consumption of what they hunted. Numerous European examples from the late glacial show the large-scale killing and processing of herbivores, notably reindeer and horse. These are migratory and live in large herds; not coincidentally, the best known sites such as Dolni Vestonice in the Czech Republic lie near where these are likely to have crossed rivers on their autumn and spring migrations. Processing technologies probably included the large-scale filleting of carcasses, followed by drying, smoking, and storage. Reliance on these kinds of preservative technologies has to go hand-in-hand with food-procuring strategies that can harvest key resources when they are most abundant – typically the autumn cull of migratory herds. This in turn requires very precise knowledge of where these are likely to be, and the means to kill large numbers of them very quickly. Perhaps significantly, there were improvements in the late glacial in the techniques used for killing animals: spear-throwers by the late glacial, ivory spears at Sungir in Russia at 23,000 BP, and even boomerangs in Poland by 20,000 BP (Valde-Nowak *et al.* 1987). Other changes include the trapping of fur-bearing animals such as arctic hare; sewing needles after 21,000 BP indicate the first use of sewn clothing and were probably accompanied by more careful and elaborate ways of tanning and curing skins. Cooking techniques also improved: the first stone-lined hearths at Abri Pataud (31,000 BP) are early examples, and thereafter common. Residential structures were also larger and better made, most notably those from eastern Europe.

Open-air European sites show often considerable advances over earlier constructions. Particularly good examples come from eastern Europe, where sites are preserved under loess (wind-blown dust that originated from the outflows of glaciers). Some of these sites indicate large structures, though their size may have been increased through solifluxion, and overestimated by archaeologists. Even so, many were substantial constructions that may have served as winter bases, or even as year-round settlements by some of the inhabitants (see, for example, Soffer 1985). Some of these structures may have had a ceremonial function. One notable example is from Mezherich in the Ukraine, where remains of a group of igloo-type huts were found, made of mammoth tusks and bones that had been arranged in a geometric pattern and painted.

The most visible change, and the one that attracts most public attention, is the representational art, whether engraved, painted or carved. Much of it is found in deep recesses of caves (doubtless facilitating its preservation), and most of it dates from well after 30,000 BP. It is also sporadic: most is in south-west France and northern Spain; other cave-rich areas, such as the Apennines, Italy, and south-east Europe, have none. So too with the portable, or mobiliary art: the enormous amount at Gönnersdorf, Germany, and none at many others. Brian Hayden (1993) links the occurrence of representational art and evidence for personal display (for example in the procurement of exotic items for personal ornamentation) to those environments (such as south-west France) that were rich enough to sustain the large-scale accumulation and storage of food. Others such as Mithen and Spivey (Chapter 18) link it to an information system that stored knowledge about the animals so crucial to a group's survival. For others, art served as a mechanism to facilitate the maintenance of social networks over large and sparsely inhabited territories via the scheduling of feasts and ceremonies. In all these scenarios, the art is deeply embedded in the procurement of food.

Datasets for the last part of the ice age from other parts of the world show long traditions of groups who lived by gathering and hunting, and in a manner that is recognizable today. Beyond Europe, the best are probably from the Near East, southern Africa and India. One of the most graphic examples is from the now defunct lakes of New South Wales, where aboriginal groups camped around the shores, harvesting and hunting numerous types of mammals, birds, fish, reptiles and plants (Lourandos 1987). Evidence from the Cape Province of South Africa shows similar groups, apparently exploiting a wide range of resources in a scheduled manner, and also maintaining a rich artistic tradition (see, for example, Deacon 1984).

The colonization of Australasia, the Americas and Siberia

Three continents and a substantial part of a fourth were colonized during the last glaciation (Fig. 20.6). The first people to reach Australia did so by 60,000 years ago

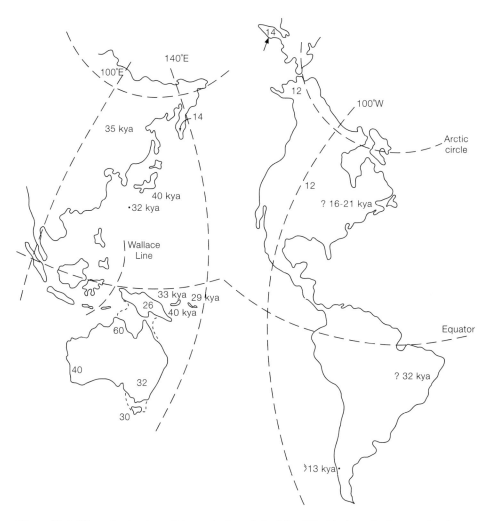

Figure 20.6 The colonization of Australasia and the New World; dates in thousands of years ago (kya). Source: R. Dennell.

(Roberts, Jones and Smith 1994) after crossing at least 60 miles of open sea between Indonesia and the landmass of Australia and New Guinea, then joined by the lowering of sea levels. By 30,000 years ago, some of the Pacific Islands were settled by voyages up to 120 miles across open sea (Allen *et al.* 1989). The other two were the Americas, probably reached via Siberia. This part of Asia may have been colonized around 39,000 years ago, according to recent C14 dating of animal bones associated with upper palaeolithic-type assemblages (Goebel and Aksenov 1995): however, this is at the limit of C14 dating, and the dated bones lack cut-marks and need not therefore have been of animals killed by humans.

When and from where the Americas were colonized still remains unclear. Those favouring an early date point to Meadowcroft in Pennsylvania, at 24,000 BP, to the cave of Pedra Fuerada in Brazil, occupied perhaps as early as 32,000 BP (but see Meltzer *et al.* 1994), and the site of Monte Verde in Chile, occupied 13,000 years ago (Dillehay 1984). Some still argue that the Americas were not colonized until the very end of the last ice age, around 10,000–12,000 years ago. It is of course possible that there was more than one episode of colonization, and possibly from more than one source. Whilst Amerindians probably derive from north-east Asia, it is odd that the earliest archaeological evidence is presently from South America rather than Alaska, the likely point of entry. Although North America could have been reached on foot across what are now the Bering Straits, the main obstacles lay in Siberia. The south-east part was occupied by 35,000 years ago, but the bitterly cold north-eastern part was too severe for humans until *c.* 14,000 years ago (Gamble 1993).

What does this coarse-grained information tell us about human subsistence strategies? And why was Australia colonized long before the Americas? The answer may lie in the issue of food storage. The colonization of Australia and New Guinea from the Asian mainland required a simple type of sea-craft; once ashore, humans could have survived without the need to store foods for long periods of the year. In contrast, the colonization during the last glaciation of north-east Siberia, and of the Americas via the Bering land-bridge, was possible on foot, but survival was impossible without the ability to store large amounts of food for consumption during the long and bitterly cold winters. For this reason, it is improbable that the Americas were colonized before food storage was in general use elsewhere in Eurasia.

The end of the last ice age

Momentous climatic changes some 10,000 years ago brought to an end the last ice age and ushered in the present interglacial (also variously termed the Holocene or Postglacial). The ice sheets that had covered much of Canada, Scandinavia, the British Isles and other large areas of the world retreated, and in many cases disappeared altogether. As a result of the melting of several million square miles of ice, sea levels rose by perhaps a hundred metres. An area the size of western Europe that had formed Beringia, the land-bridge between Siberia and Alaska, was inundated. Australia, New Guinea and Tasmania became separated, as did Europe from the British Isles.

The changes on land were no less dramatic. Areas previously glaciated became available for colonization, particularly Canada, Alaska, Britain and Scandinavia. Areas adjacent to former ice-sheets and glaciers also changed. In time, tundra was replaced by birch forest, and eventually by deciduous species such as oak. The fauna also changed: red deer, roe deer, pig and aurochs (the wild cow) displaced reindeer in much of northern Europe. Some animals such as musk-ox became locally extinct, and others such as mammoth, woolly rhinoceros and cave lion died out altogether. In coastal areas of western and northern Europe, shellfish such as oysters and mussels colonized waters that were previously too intemperate, or inaccessible. Similar types of changes affected the northern United States and Canada.

The net result of all these environmental changes over much of temperate and northern Europe and North America was a considerable increase in plant biomass, of which many seeds, nuts, fruits, and berries were seasonally useful food items for humans. Aquatic resources such as fish, shellfish and sea-mammals were also more common and widely used. Many of these foods, such as shellfish, nuts or seeds, came in small 'packages', and would have required considerable energy and time to process, or to consume in sufficient amounts. Nevertheless, human societies world-wide were rarely slow in developing bows and arrows for shooting individual (and often small) animals; nets, lines, hooks, harpoons and weirs for catching fish; or grinding equipment for processing plant foods (Fig. 20.7).

The types of adaptation to postglacial conditions depended much on where people were. In areas far from glaciated areas, changes were often slow and minor: often, the same sites and resources were used in much the same way as before, and there is no major break between the end of the Palaeolithic and the onset of the Mesolithic. In areas of major environmental change, such as northern Europe, the distinction is seen more easily. Different stone and bone tools were needed, and, unsurprisingly, the first European stone axes and adzes appear in the Mesolithic in northern Europe. (The earliest examples are from Australia, around 20,000 years ago.) Different subsistence strategies were also required. The enormous late glacial herds of reindeer and horse were succeeded by less gregarious animals such as red deer, roe deer and pig that were less easy to target in dense vegetation. A wider range of plant foods was also available, as well as river and sea resources, whether shellfish, fish or birds. In many parts of the world there was a shift towards exploiting a wider range of smaller resources. A good example is the prevalence of shell middens in areas such as northern Europe, Japan, southern Africa and Australia, where considerable amounts were collected during the summer months. (These middens, or mounds of discarded shells, can be several metres thick, and are highly visible both ethnographically and archaeologically. Their size can easily give a misleading impression of the dietary importance of shellfish, which probably formed less than 10 per cent of the total annual diet.) Plant foods such as nuts were also used. All these smaller packages require processing, and often the first grinding equipment is found.

A considerable amount is known of those hunters and gatherers who lived in the postglacial before the appearance of farming communities. One of the best known areas is north-west Europe, partly because of the amount of research done there, but also through excellent preservation in peat bogs and on shorelines. The range of material evidence is often outstanding: boats, paddles, nets, traps, fish lines, huts and a whole range of perishable items that only rarely survive. In Eurasia these often show what could be called 'forest foraging' or even 'forest farming' (Zvelebil 1986). Environmental evidence indicates that areas of forest were managed by controlled burning as a way of encouraging rejuvenation, and thereby raising ground level biomass for animals to feed on, and creating areas where the location of game was more predictable. Evidence from shell middens shows that these were summer resources, probably gathered whilst other more lucrative activities such as fishing or hunting were carried out. In some areas, settlements were probably permanent. One example is Lepenski Vir in Serbia by the Danube, where stone-built houses were inhabited by a community that obtained much of its food from the Danube, supplemented by animals taken inland. Sites in western Russia show similarly stable communities, using hazelnuts, fish, game and so on.

Assessments of the Mesolithic in areas such as northern Europe have changed substantially over thirty years. For much of this century, mesolithic peoples were seen as evidence of decline and even degeneration. This prejudice was partly due to the seemingly sad contrast between the highly visible art of the late Palaeolithic and its apparent absence in the Mesolithic, and partly due to nineteenth-century prejudices of Europeans towards the hunter-gatherers they encountered – and often displaced – in Australia, southern Africa and America. A more realistic assessment is that the postglacial hunter-gatherer societies of northern Europe, Eurasia, and their counterparts in North America, Australia and Africa were among the most numerous and successful hunter-gatherers that have ever lived.

CONCLUSION

This review has attempted to impose some structure on the large and frustratingly incomplete mass of archaeological and palaeontological evidence for different kinds of hominids over the last 3 million years, and, ultimately, on all continents except Antarctica. In doing so, it has had to identify major groupings that are as useful for studying subsistence as fossil taxa are for palaeontologists, or artefactually defined periods were for the prehistorians of the last century. Four such periods have been tentatively identified.

The first encompasses the earliest tool-making hominids. Whilst these ate the meat of large mammals, it is too early to state confidently whether this was their main source of animal protein, how often it was the outcome of premeditated hunting, and the extent to which early hominid omnivory was critically dependent

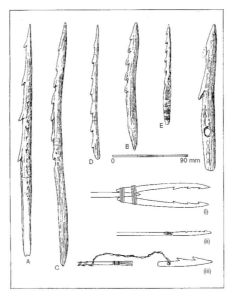

Some of the antler barbed points from Star Carr, Yorkshire. The constructions show how these could have been used as i) prongs for a fishing spear, ii) an arrowhead, or iii) a harpoon.

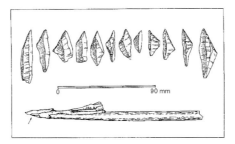

Some microliths, again from Star Carr. These were used as replaceable parts in other tools, such as spears, harpoons, or an arrow, as shown in an example from Sweden.

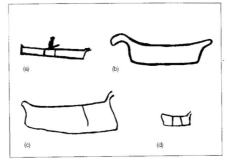

These Norwegian rock carvings remind us that mesolithic peoples used boats, either framed with skins, or made from tree trunks. Wooden paddles are also known from northern Europe.

Figure 20.7 Surviving items of mesolithic technology. At first sight, these do not look particularly impressive or effective. However, microliths could be used as replaceable parts of arrows and knives; and larger pieces of stone were used for scrapers and axes. Simple tools of bone, antler, wood, leather and various fibres enable their users to hunt, trap and fish; to prepare skins, furs and netting to fell trees, and dig for plant foods; and make a wide range of wooden items, varying in size from arrow-shafts to boats. Source: Smith (1991) *Late Stone Age Hunters* (London: Routledge).

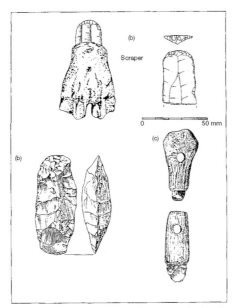

Some larger stone tools, from the mesolithic site of
Thatcham, Berkshire. The scraper (top) and axe or
adze (bottom) were probably set in a bone or antler
haft, as suggested here.

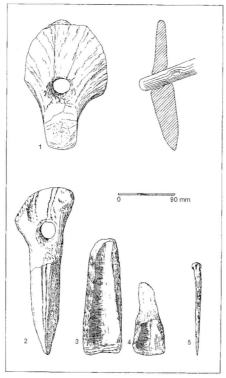

Some typical, simple mesolithic bone and antler
tools; two mattocks from elk antler (1,2); two
scrapers from long-bones of wild cattle; and (3) a
bodkin, made from an elk bone.

upon the use of stone tools. The dense fog enveloping the subsistence behaviour of *H. erectus*, and whether or not it left Africa 1 million years ago or much earlier, impedes any useful discussion of hominid subsistence between 1.5 and 0.5 million years ago, and constitutes a second, and hopefully temporary, unit of study. Thereafter, recent evidence shows two major developments around 500,000 years ago. The first is that hominids extended their range in Europe to at least 53° north, beyond which they rarely ventured until after 25,000 years ago. The second is that by now they could hunt and butcher large animals, and without undue interference from large carnivores. The recent discoveries from Schöningen, Germany, show the sophistication of the spears they used; Boxgrove, England, also indicates that hominids also went prepared with their handaxes (or defleshing tools), and the antler hammers used to knap more if needed. It is tempting to link the colonization of northern Europe with these hunting skills; however, too little is known about the subsistence of *Homo erectus* before 500,000 BP to allow much certainty over this issue.

These earliest north Europeans, Neanderthals, their anatomically modern human contemporaries, and perhaps even some of their successors, are linked by the ability to hunt large animals, to survive in climates considerably colder than today's, and by the probability that almost all food was consumed shortly after it was obtained. In Europe at least, it is the ability to store food when it is plentiful, for consumption when it is scarcest, that was the most distinctive innovation. This development, probably in place by 25,000 years ago, was accompanied by improved abilities to hunt (probably by trapping) fur-bearing animals; at least some sewn clothing; more carefully constructed hearths; and a major reduction in the incidence of bone injuries. It was perhaps also related to the development of painted art and personal ornamentation as an adjunct to the accumulation and storage of food.

Despite an enormous amount of research in the last twenty years, Europe remains the best documented area in the world in terms of the evidence less than 500,000 years old. Yet other areas are no less important. South Africa is a major one that is also the southern hemisphere's equivalent of southern Europe, and also has a far longer archaeological record. Detailed comparisons of the two areas might indicate whether long-term patterns in subsistence override regional variants defined by artefact types or the presence/absence of Neanderthals. Another important and fascinating area is Australia, which also offers a healthy antidote to Europocentrism. One pertinent reminder is that 18,000 years ago, in the coldest part of the last ice age, the aboriginal Tasmanians were the most southerly inhabitants in the world, living within sight of glaciers but with one of the simplest tool-kits ever devised (Kiernan *et al.* 1983): whatever else they may have been, the cave art and elaborate tool-kits of the Magdelanian were not environmentally determined. What both show is that the range of responses human groups could and did make to their environments by 18,000 years ago was no less than the variety of environments which had been colonized by that time.

Finally, the mesolithic and other postglacial hunter-gatherers have been treated as essentially similar to early, late palaeolithic, groups in their ability to hunt and to store foods if needed. This is not to denigrate the distinctiveness of any of these societies, or to downplay the importance of many postglacial innovations, including the development and adoption of farming. Rather, through a telescope scanning a 3-million-year expanse of landscape, these are minor compared to the option of deferring the consumption of food, which is arguably one of the most defining features of *Homo sapiens sapiens*.

REFERENCES

Aitken, M. J. (1990) *Science-based Dating in Archaeology*, London and New York: Longman.

Allen, J., Gosden, C. and White, P. (1989) 'Human Pleistocene adaptations in the tropical island Pacific: recent evidence from New Ireland, a Greater Australian outlier', *Antiquity* 63: 548–61.

Binford, L. (1977) 'Olorgesaillie deserves more than the usual book review', *Journal of Anthropological Research* 33: 493–502.

Binford, L. (1983) *In Pursuit of the Past*, London: Thames and Hudson.

Binford, L. (1988) 'Étude taphonomique des restes fauniques de la Grotte Vaufrey', in J.-P. Rigaud (ed.) *La Grotte Vaufrey à Cénac et St. Julien (Dordognes): Paléoenvironments, Chronologie et Activités Humaines*, Paris: Mémoires de la Société Préhistorique Française 19: 213–90.

Binford, L. (1989) 'Searching for camps and missing the evidence?', in O. Soffer (ed.) *The Pleistocene Old World*, New York: Plenum: 17–31.

Binford, L. and Binford, S. (1966) 'A preliminary analysis of functional variability in the Mousterian of Levallois facies', *American Anthropologist* 68: 238–95.

Blumenschine, R. J. (1986) 'Carcass consumption sequences and the archaeological distinction of scavenging and hunting', *Journal of Human Evolution* 15: 639–59.

Blumenschine, R. J. and Cavallo, J. A. (1992) 'Scavenging and human evolution', *Scientific American* 267: 90–96.

Boëda, E., Connan, J., Dessort, D., Muhesen, S., Mercier, N., Valladas, H. and Tisnérat, N. (1996) 'Bitumen as a hafting material on Middle Palaeolithic artefacts', *Nature* 380: 336–38.

Boesch, C. and Boesch, H. (1989) 'Hunting behavior of wild chimpanzees in the Tai National Park', *American Journal of Physical Anthropology* 78: 547–73.

Bordes, F. and Sonneville-Bordes, D. (1970) 'The significance of variability in Palaeolithic assemblages', *World Archaeology* 2 (1): 61–73.

Brain, C. K. (1981) *The Hunters or the Hunted? An Introduction to African Cave Taphonomy*, Chicago: University of Chicago Press.

Brain, C. K. and Sillen, A. (1988) 'Evidence from the Swartkrans cave for the earliest use of fire', *Nature* 336: 464–66.

Breuil, H. (1912) 'Les subdivisions du paléolithique supérieur et leur significance', *Congrès International d'Anthropologie et d'Archéologie Préhistoriques. Compte Rendue, session 14,* Geneva: 165–238.

Breuil, H. and Kozlowski, L. (1931) 'Étude de stratigraphie paléolithique dans le nord de la France, la Bélgique et l'Angleterre – la vallée de la Somme', *L'Anthropologie* 41: 449–88.

Brunet, M., Beauvillain, A., Coppens, Y., Heintz, E., Montaye, A. H. E. and Pilbeam, D. (1995) 'The first australopithecine 2,500 kilometres west of the Rift Valley (Chad)', *Nature* 378: 273–75.

Bunn, H. and Kroll, E. M. (1986) 'Systematic butchery by Plio/Pleistocene hominids at Olduvai Gorge, Tanzania', *Current Anthropology* 27: 431–52.

Cahen, D. and Keeley, L. (1980) 'Not less than two, not more than three', *World Archaeology* 12 (2): 166–80.

Carbonell, E., Bermúdez de Castro, J. M., Arsuaga, J. L., Díez, J. C., Rosas, A., Cuença-Bescós, G., Sala, R., Mosquera, M. and Rodríguez, X. P. (1995) 'Lower Pleistocene hominids and artefacts from Atapuerca-TD6 (Spain)', *Science* 269: 826–29.

Clark, J. G. D. (1952) *Prehistoric Europe: The Economic Basis*, Cambridge: Cambridge University Press.

Daniel, G. (1964) *The Idea of Prehistory*, London: Penguin.

Dart, R. (1949) 'The predatory implemental technique of Australopithecus', *American Journal of Physical Anthropology* 7: 1–38.

Deacon, J. (1984) 'Later Stone Age people and their descendants in southern Africa', in R. G. Klein (ed.) *Southern African Prehistory and Paleoenvironments*, Rotterdam: Balkema: 221–328.

de Loecker, D. (1994) 'On the refitting analysis of Site K: a middle palaeolithic findspot at Maastricht-Belvédère (The Netherlands)', *Ethnographisch Archaölogische Zeitschrift* 35: 101–17.

DeMenocal, P. B. (1995) 'Plio-Pleistocene African climate', *Science* 270: 53–59.

Dennell, R. W. (1990) 'Progressive gradualism, imperialism and academic fashion: lower palaeolithic archaeology in the 20th century', *Antiquity* 64: 549–58.

Dennell, R. W. (1997) 'The world's oldest spears', *Nature* 385: 767–68.

Dennell, R. W. (1998) 'Grasslands, tool-making, and the earliest colonization of south Asia: a reconsideration', in M. Petraglia and R. Korrisetar (eds) *Early Human Behaviour in Global Context: The Rise and Diversity of the Lower Palaeolithic Record*, London: Routledge: 284–303.

Dennell, R. W. and Roebroeks, W. (1996) 'The earliest colonisation of Europe: the short chronology revisited', *Antiquity* 70: 535–42.

Dennell, R. W., Rendell, H. and Hailwood, E. (1988) 'Early tool-making in Asia: two-million-year-old artefacts in Pakistan', *Antiquity* 62: 98–106.

Dibble, H. L. and Rolland, N. (1992) 'On assemblage variability in the Middle Palaeolithic of western Europe: history, perspectives and a new synthesis', in H. L. Dibble and P. Mellars (eds) *In the Middle Palaeolithic: Adaptation, Behavior and Variability*, Philadelphia: The University Museum, University of Pennsylvania: 1–28.

Dillehay, T. D. (1984) 'A late ice-age settlement in southern Chile', *Scientific American* 251 (4): 100–9.

Dowsett, H., Thompson, R., Barron, J., Cronin, T., Fleming, F., Ishman, S., Poore, R., Willard, D. and Holtz, T. Jnr (1994) 'Joint investigations of the Middle Pliocene climate I: PRISM palaeoenvironmental reconstructions', *Global and Planetary Change* 9: 169–95.

Gabunia, L. and Vekua, A. (1995) 'A Plio-Pleistocene hominid from Dmanisi, East Georgia, Caucasus', *Nature* 373: 509–12.

Gamble, C. (1981) 'Scratches on the palaeolithic record', *Nature* 291: 533–34.

Gamble, C. (1987) 'Man the Shoveller: alternative models for Middle Pleistocene colonisation and occupation in northern latitudes', in O. Soffer (ed.) *The Pleistocene Old World: Regional Perspectives*, New York: Plenum: 81–98.

Gamble, C. (1993) *Timewalkers*, Stroud: Alan Sutton.

Gargett, R. (1989) 'Grave shortcomings: the evidence for Neanderthal burial', *Current Anthropology* 30: 157–90.

Goebel, T. and Aksenov, M. (1995) 'Accelerator radiocarbon dating of the initial Upper Palaeolithic in southeast Siberia', *Antiquity* 69: 349–57.

Gowlett, J. A., Harris, J. W. K., Walton, D. and Wood, B. A. (1981) 'Early archaeological sites, hominid remains, and traces of fire from Chesowanja, Kenya', *Nature* 294: 125–29.

Grayson, D. (1994) 'The evidence for Middle Palaeolithic scavenging from Couche VIII, Grotte Vaufrey (Dordogne, France)', *Journal of Archaeological Science* 21: 359–75.

Green, S. (1981) 'The first Welshman: excavations at Pontnewydd', *Antiquity* 55: 184–96.

Hayden, B. (1993) 'The cultural capacities of Neanderthals: a review and re-evaluation', *Journal of Human Evolution* 24 (2): 113–46.

Higgs, E. S. (ed.) (1975) *Palaeoeconomy*, Cambridge: Cambridge University Press.

Imbrie, J. and Imbrie, K. P. (1979) *Ice-Ages: Solving the Mystery*, London: Macmillan.

Isaac, G. L. (1978) 'The food-sharing behavior of protohuman hominids', *Scientific American* 238: 90–108.

Isaac, G. L. (1984) 'The archaeology of human origins: studies of the Lower Pleistocene in East Africa', in F. Wendorf and A. Close (eds) *Advances in Old World Archaeology*, Vol. 3, New York: Academic Press: 1–87.

James, S. R. (1989) 'Hominid use of fire in the Lower and Middle Pleistocene', *Current Anthropology* 30 (1): 1–26.

Johanson, D. C., Taieb, M. and Coppens, Y. (1982) 'Pliocene hominids from the Hadar Formation', *American Journal of Physical Anthropology* 57: 373–402.

Keeley, L. H. (1980) *Experimental Determination of Stone Tool Uses*, Chicago: University of Chicago Press.

Kiernan, K., Jones, R. and Ransom, D. (1983) 'New evidence from Fraser Cave for glacial age man in south-west Tasmania', *Nature* 301: 28–32.

Kroll, E. (1994) 'Behavioral implications of Plio-Pleistocene archaeological site structure', *Journal of Human Evolution* 27: 107–38.

Kuhn, S. L. (1995) *Mousterian Lithic Technology: An Ecological Perspective*, Princeton: Princeton University Press.

Leakey, M. D. (1971) *Olduvai Gorge. Vol. 3. Excavations in Beds I and II, 1960–1963*, Cambridge: Cambridge University Press.

Leakey, M. D. and Roe, D. A. (1994) *Olduvai Gorge. Vol. 5. Excavations in Beds III, IV and the Masek Beds, 1969–1971*, Cambridge: Cambridge University Press.

Leakey, M. G., Feibel, C. S., McDougall, I. and Walker, A. (1995) 'New four-million-year-old hominid species from Kanapoi and Allia Bay', *Nature* 376: 565–71.

Lee, R. B. (1979) *Kalahari Hunter-Gatherers: Men, Women and Work in a Foraging Society*, Cambridge, Mass.: Harvard University Press.

Lourandos, H. (1987) 'Pleistocene Australia: peopling a continent', in O. Soffer (ed.) *The Pleistocene Old World: Regional Perspectives*, New York: Plenum: 147–65.

McGrew, W. (1992) *Chimpanzee Material Culture*, Cambridge: Cambridge University Press.

Mania, D. (1990) *Auf den Spuren des Ur-Menschen: die Funde von Bilzingsleben*, Berlin: Deutscher Verlag der Wissenschaften.

Meltzer, D. J., Adovasio, J. M. and Dillehay, T. D. (1994) 'On a Pleistocene human occupation at Pedra Furada, Brazil', *Antiquity* 68: 695–714.

Penck, A. and Bruckner, E. (1909) *Die Alpen im Eiszeitalter*, Leipzig: Tauchnitz.

Potts, R. (1986) 'Temporal span of bone accumulations at Olduvai Gorge and implications for early hominid foraging behavior', *Paleobiology* 12: 25–31.

Potts, R. (1988) *Early Hominid Activities at Olduvai*, New York: Aldine de Gruyter.

Rightmire, P. (1991) 'The dispersal of *Homo erectus* from Africa and the emergence of more modern humans', *Journal of Anthropological Research* 51: 107–14.

Roberts, M. (1986) 'Excavation of the Lower Palaeolithic site at Amey's Eartham Pit, Boxgrove, West Sussex: a preliminary report', *Proceedings of the Prehistoric Society* 52: 215–46.

Roberts, M. B., Stringer, C. B. and Parfitt, S. A. (1994) 'A hominid tibia from Middle Pleistocene sediments at Boxgrove, UK', *Nature* 369: 311–13.

Roberts, R. G., Jones, R. and Smith, M. A. (1994) 'Beyond the radiocarbon barrier in Australian prehistory', *Antiquity* 68: 611–16.

Roe, D. (1995) 'The Orce Basin (Andalusia, Spain) and the initial palaeolithic of Europe', *Oxford Journal of Archaeology* 14: 1–12.

Schrenk, F., Bromage, T. G., Bernier, C. G., Ring, U. and Juwayeyi, Y. M. (1993) 'Oldest *Homo* and Pliocene biogeography of the Malawi Rift', *Nature* 365: 833–36.

Schrire, C. (1980) 'An enquiry into the evolutionary status and apparent identity of San hunter-gatherers', *Human Ecology* 8 (1): 9–32.

Scott, K. (1980) 'Two hunting episodes of Middle Palaeolithic age at La Cotte de la St.-Brelade, Jersey', *World Archaeology* 12 (2): 137–52.

Semaw, S., Renne, P., Harris, J. W. K. *et al.* (1997) '2.5-million-year-old stone tools from Gona, Ethiopia', *Nature* 385: 333–36.

Semenov, S. A. (1964) *Prehistoric Technology*, London: Cory, Adams and McKay.

Sept, J. M. (1982) 'Was there no place like home?', *Current Anthropology* 33: 187–207.

Shay, J. J. (1988) 'Spear points from the middle Palaeolithic of the Levant', *Journal of Field Archaeology* 15: 441–50.

Shipman, P., Bosler, W. and Davis, K. L. (1981) 'Butchering of giant Geladas at an Acheulean site', *Current Anthropology* 22 (3): 257–68.

Soffer, O. (1985) *The Upper Palaeolithic of the Central Russian Plain*, London: Academic Press.

Stiner, M. (1994) *Honor among Thieves: A Zooarchaeological Study of Neandertal Ecology*, Princeton: Princeton University Press.

Susman, R. L. (1987) 'Who made the Oldowan stone tools?', *Journal of Anthropological Research* 47 (2): 129–51.

Susman, R. L. (1988) 'Hand of Paranthropus robustus from Member 1, Swartkrans: fossil evidence for tool behavior', *Science* 240: 780–81.

Susman, R. L. and Stern, J. T. (1982) 'Functional morphology of *Homo habilis*', *Science* 217: 931–34.

Swisher, C. C. III, Curtis, G. H., Jacob, T., Getty, A. G., Suprijo, A. and Widiasmoro (1994) 'Age of the earliest hominids in Java, Indonesia', *Science* 263: 1118–21.

Tattersall, I. (1997) 'Out of Africa again . . . and again?', *Scientific American* 276 (4): 46–53.

Tchernov, E. (1989) 'The age of the Ubeidiya Formation', *Israeli Journal of Earth Sciences* 36: 3–30.

Thieme, H. (1997) 'The oldest throwing spears in the world: Middle Pleistocene hunting weapons from Schöningen, Lower Saxony, Germany', *Nature* 385: 807–10.

Thieme, H. and Maier, R. (1995) *Archäologische Ausgrabungen im Braunkohlentagebau Schöningen*, Hannover: Verlag Hahnsche Buchhandlung.

Toth, N. (1993) 'Pan the tool-maker: investigations into the stone tool-making and tool-using capabilities of a Bonobo (*Pan paniscus*)', *Journal of Archaeological Science* 20 (1): 81–92.

Toth, N. and Schick, K. D. (1986) 'The first million years: the archaeology of proto-human culture', in M. B. Schiffer (ed.) *Advances in Archaeological Method and Theory 9*, Orlando: Academic Press: 1–96.

Trinkhaus, E. (1985) 'Pathology and the posture of the La Chapelle-aux-Saints Neanderthal', *American Journal of Physical Anthropology* 67: 19–41.

Trinkhaus, E. and Zimmerman, M. R. (1982) 'Trauma among the Shanidar Neanderthals', *American Journal of Physical Anthropology* 57: 61–76.

Valde-Nowak, P., Nadachowski, A. and Wolsan, M. (1987) 'Upper Palaeolithic boomerang made of a mammoth tusk in south Poland', *Nature* 329: 436–38.

Villa, P. (1983) 'Terra Amata and the Middle Pleistocene archaeological record of southern France', *University of California Publications in Anthropology* 13: 1–303.

Villa, P. (1990) 'Torralba and Aridos: elephant exploitation in Middle Pleistocene Spain', *Journal of Human Evolution* 19: 299–309.

Villa, P. (1991) 'Middle Pleistocene prehistory in south-western Europe: the state of our knowledge and ignorance', *Journal of Anthropological Research* 47: 193–217.

Vrba, E. S. (1985) 'Early hominids in southern Africa: updated observations on chronological and ecological background', in P. Tobias (ed.) *Hominid Evolution Past, Present and Future*, New York: Alan Liss: 195–200.

Wanpo, H., Ciochon, R., Yumin, G., Larick, R., Qiren, F., Schwarcz, H., Yonge, C., de Vos, J. and Rink, W. (1995) 'Early *Homo* and associated artefacts from Asia', *Nature* 378: 275–78.

Westergaard, G. C. and Suomi, S. J. (1995) 'A simple stone tool technology in monkeys', *Journal of Human Evolution* 27: 399–404.

Wheeler, P. E. (1992) 'The thermoregulatory advantages of large body size for hominids foraging in savannah environments', *Journal of Human Evolution* 23: 351–62.

White, T. D., Suwa, G. and Asfaw, B. (1995) 'Corrigendum: *Australopithecus ramidus*, a new species of early hominid from Aramis, Ethiopia', *Nature* 375: 88.

Wright, R. V. S. (1972) 'Imitative learning of a flaked stone technology', *Mankind* 8: 296–306.

Zvelebil, M. (1986) 'Postglacial foraging in the forests of Europe', *Scientific American* 254 (5): 86–93.

SELECT BIBLIOGRAPHY

Although there is a huge literature relevant to discussions of subsistence over the time-span of human evolution, there are no recent syntheses that focus on hominid and early human subsistence on a global scale, and most of the information is scattered throughout an enormous number of books and journals. As starting points, I would recommend the following as basic building blocks: the titles are self-explanatory, and each provides good overviews of various aspects of palaeoanthropology. A. Bilsborough, *Human Evolution* (London: Blackie Academic and Professional, 1992); J. Diamond, *The Rise and Fall of the Third Chimpanzee* (London: Vintage, 1992); C. Gamble, *The Palaeolithic Settlement of Europe* (Cambridge: Cambridge University Press, 1986) and *Timewalkers: The Prehistory of Global Colonisation* (Bradford: Alan Sutton, 1994); R. G. Klein, *The Human Career* (Chicago: Chicago University Press, 1989); and C. Stringer and C. Gamble, *In Search of the Neanderthals* (London: Thames and Hudson, 1994). There is also much useful information in *The Cambridge Encyclopedia of Human Evolution*, edited by S. Jones, R. Martin, D. Pilbeam and S. Bunney (Cambridge: Cambridge University Press, 1992). Two especially thought-provoking books are *Chimpanzee Material Culture* by W. C. McGrew (Cambridge: Cambridge University Press, 1992) and *The Hunters or the Hunted?: An Introduction to African Cave Taphonomy* by C. K. Brain (Chicago: University of Chicago Press, 1981).

21

EARLY AGRICULTURAL
SOCIETIES

Peter Bogucki

TRANSITIONS TO AGRICULTURE

The successful shift from a subsistence economy based wholly on foraging to one based primarily on food production was one of the most significant developments in the existence of the genus *Homo*. For several million years, human beings had obtained their diet first from scavenging, then from hunting, fishing, and collecting. Within approximately the last 10,000 years, markedly different subsistence economies based on cultivated plants and, in many areas, domesticated animals, have replaced hunting and gathering around the world. When viewed from this perspective, the origin and dispersal of food production took place very rapidly. Within these last ten millennia, however, the process of domestication or adoption of domesticates occurred at varying time-scales based on local environmental, economic, and social conditions.

The origins and dispersal of food production have attracted the attention of researchers for several decades and have come to be a major focus of archaeological research. Much of this research has been concentrated on the areas and periods in which plants and animals were first domesticated from indigenous wild species. Some (for example, Minnis 1985) have used the term 'pristine domestication' to refer to such situations in which the human control and manipulation of a species are sufficient to cause phenotypic changes for the first time. A considerably less-developed research orientation is the study of the adoption of domesticated plants and animals and the techniques of agriculture and animal husbandry by populations who did not domesticate the species themselves, as well as the spread of populations practising agriculture into areas where it had been hitherto unknown. As Minnis (1985: 309) points out, such cases have been more frequent and more

839

widespread than the instances of pristine domestication, and he uses the term 'primary crop acquisition' to describe them.

Early views of the transition held that it was an inevitable development on the road to civilization. Yet more thoughtful analyses of this shift in the last three decades have shown that it was not that simple. Much of our understanding of the ramifications of the change from foraging to farming comes from comparative ethnological studies of the remaining hunter-gatherer and incipient agricultural populations on the face of the earth. These studies have shown that foragers have some economic and social options that are not open to farmers and that farmers have other options not open to foragers. For instance, foragers have the option of mobility to respond to local environmental variation, while farmers are tethered to their fields. Foragers often have access to a range of food resources, while agriculture and grazing may reduce the variability in an ecosystem and reduce the number of dietary options. On the other hand, the concentration of food resources made possible by agriculture and animal husbandry can open up social options for exchange and alliances that may be limited for hunter-gatherers. The study of the transition to agriculture, then, attempts to identify the reasons why hunter-gatherers, either by choice or by necessity, found that the advantages of an economic system involving food production outweighed the options available to them as foragers.

THE ORIGINS OF AGRICULTURE

Approaches to the origins of food production in archaeology can be divided into two research orientations, each of which relies upon the other. The first includes both the methodological focus on the recovery of data relating to the phenotypic characteristics of seeds and bones that reflect the changes associated with human control and manipulation and the modelling of the sequence of these changes. In the last thirty years, the development of recovery techniques for small-scale remains, particularly seeds, has exponentially enlarged the corpus of data on early agriculture. Specialists in botanical and faunal analysis are now readily incorporated into archaeological research projects specifically to ask questions about the types of plants and animals used by inhabitants of archaeological sites, rather than to provide a species list appended to a report. New techniques, often involving microscopy and other technical methods of analysis, have been introduced. For instance, in the late 1970s the study of phytoliths, accelerator mass spectrometer (AMS) radio-carbon dating, and the analysis of bone for trace elements and stable isotopes were virtually unknown, while today they are frequently used to ask questions about the origins of food production in various parts of the world. As a result, archaeologists, archaeobotanists, and archaeozoologists have been able to trace the sequence of changes in relations between humans and plant and animal communities with progressively finer resolution.

The other aspect of the study of the transition to agriculture is the modelling of the process by which foraging populations first began to control and manipulate plants and animals. The goal of such studies is to identify the causal links in the sequence of agricultural origins that had the effect of transforming human societies by leading humans to turn from foraging to farming. Clearly this undertaking involves the generation and testing of hypotheses and the reconciliation of often-contradictory evidence. Although it has proved impossible to isolate an unequivocal cause for the transition from foraging to farming, archaeologists have no shortage of theories which provide a variety of reasons for this change.

Seeds of domestication

In 1971, Harlan identified three main centres of pristine domestication within which the major complexes of domesticated plants and animals which transformed prehistoric society were first established (Fig. 21.1). These are the Near East (emmer and einkorn wheat, barley, peas, lentils, sheep, and goats), northern China (millet and rice), and Mesoamerica (beans, chillies, maize, and gourds). To Harlan's three localized centres of domestication can be added one more which has come to light in the last fifteen years. In eastern North America, Smith (1989) has argued for the presence of an independently developed complex of domesticates that includes squash, sump-weed or marsh-elder, sunflower, and chenopod. In addition to these focal points in which pristine domestication was part of a complex transformation of society, Harlan also identified three larger, non-localized, regions in which domestication of a number of species of plants and animals also occurred. In South America, the potato and several camelid species became critical resources for highland populations, while in the lowlands manioc became a staple food. In the northern half of Africa, sorghum and possibly millet and cattle were early domesticates. Finally, there is the broad region of south-east Asia and the Pacific islands in which a complex of tree and root crops was managed, cultivated, and domesticated.

Within most of these localized centres and diffuse regions, an extraordinary amount of research has occurred in the last thirty years to document the initial appearance of domesticated species. The techniques for the recovery, identification, analysis and interpretation of botanical and faunal remains have been improved markedly. Whereas in the late 1960s there had been only a handful of individuals around the world with expertise in these materials, now there is an expanded cohort of researchers who have developed the necessary skills in identification and analysis for many additional species. To this broadened research base, the technique of radio-carbon dating using an accelerator mass spectrometer was added during the

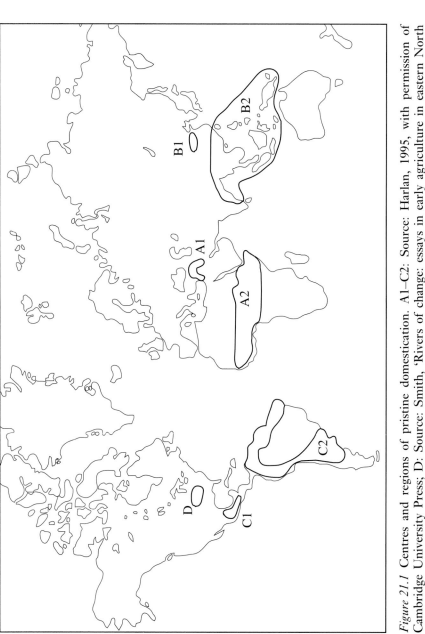

Figure 21.1 Centres and regions of pristine domestication. A1–C2: Source: Harlan, 1995, with permission of Cambridge University Press; D: Source: Smith, 'Rivers of change: essays in early agriculture in eastern North America', *Science*, 246: 1566–71, 1992. Adapted by D. Miles-Williams.

1980s. While this method is still expensive and not universally applied, it has enabled the dating of very small (under 5 mg) samples such as individual seeds or small fragments of animal bones. Much of the evidence for early plant domestication in eastern North America, for instance, rests on AMS dating.

Figure 21.2 offers a simplified chronology of early plant and animal domestication in the above centres and broader regions, though it must be stressed that it is impossible to summarize the current state of knowledge of the complexity of the process, particularly in terms of phylogenetics. The reader is best referred to several recent summaries which should form the baseline for knowledge for some time (for example: Clutton-Brock 1989; Crabtree 1993; Gebauer and Price 1992; Harlan 1995; Harris and Hillman 1989; Price and Gebauer 1995; Smith 1995; Watson and Cowan 1992; Zohary and Hopf 1993). Groups of archaeobotanists and archaeozoologists meet with regularity, and there is normally a major revelation at each of these gatherings.

Taking one step back from the seeds and bones themselves, it is important to consider the process of domestication, first by describing it and then by looking for factors that caused it. Rindos (1984) has proposed a typology of three different sorts of domestication, which he terms 'incidental', 'specialized', and 'agricultural'. Incidental domestication occurs when humans become the agents by which a species is removed from its native habitat and, in some sense, protected and exploited in its new setting. Specialized domestication is an outgrowth of incidental domestication in which humans begin to exhibit conscious and directed behaviour to propagate wild species and to begin to depend on them. Agricultural domestication involves the appearance of behaviour which completely transforms and alters the relationship between hitherto-wild species and humans by controlling the ecology and evolution of the domesticated taxa. Harvesting, seed selection and storage, weeding and removal of competitors, and tillage are all characteristic of agricultural domestication. In Rindos's view, while the origin of domesticated species is important, the more important transformation that occurs in the origins of agriculture is the change that is wrought in the ecosystem, specifically the relationships and interdependencies between plants, animals, and humans.

Ford (1985), writing from the perspective of the prehistory of the south-western United States, takes a somewhat different approach to the sequence of domestication. He distinguishes somewhat sharply between 'foraging' and 'food production' as the poles of the domestication continuum, while dividing the latter into stages of 'cultivation' and 'domestication'. Cutting across these stages of food production are a succession of methods, which Ford characterizes as 'incipient agriculture', 'gardening', and 'field agriculture', within which is a progressively more elaborate set of human activities, ranging from tending through tilling, transplanting, and sowing, to plant breeding.

An elaboration of the above sequences has been presented by Harris (1989), with

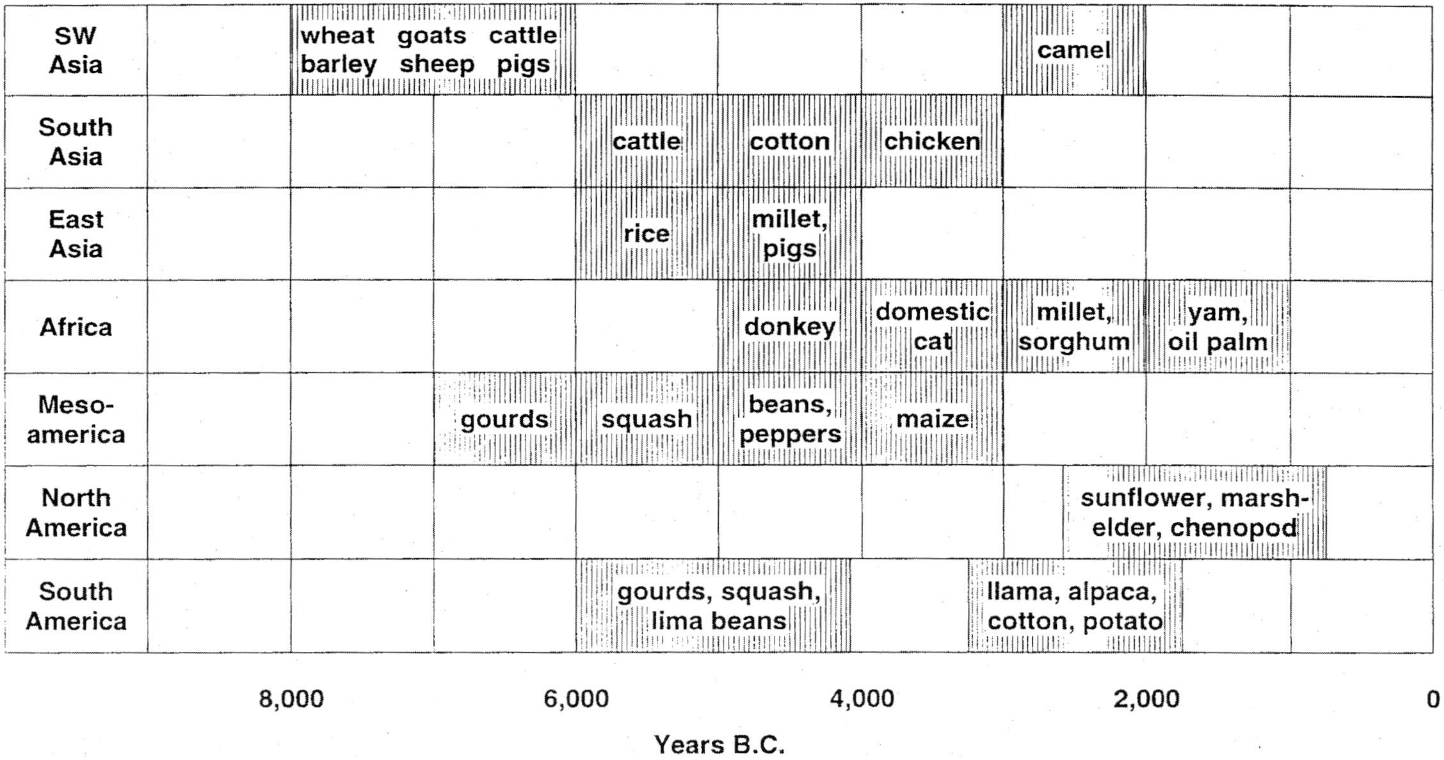

Figure chart — "A simplified chronology of plant and animal domestication" (Years B.C.)

Region	8,000 – 0 B.C. (domesticates)
SW Asia	wheat goats cattle, barley sheep pigs; camel
South Asia	cotton; chicken
East Asia	rice; millet, pigs
Africa	cattle; donkey; domestic cat; millet, sorghum; yam, oil palm
Meso-america	gourds, squash; beans, peppers; maize
North America	sunflower, marsh-elder, chenopod
South America	gourds, squash, lima beans; llama, alpaca, cotton, potato

Figure 21.2 A simplified chronology of plant and animal domestication. After Price and Feinman 1993: 127, with changes to reflect recent advances in dating after B. Smith 1995 and Harlan 1995.

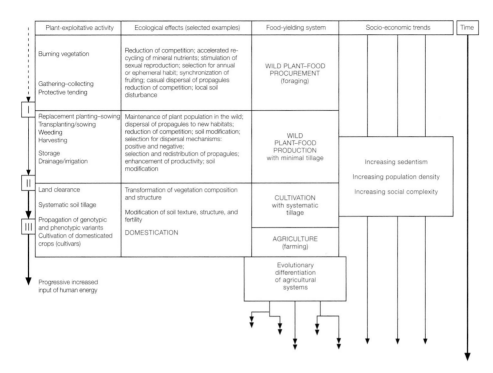

Figure 21.3 Evolutionary sequence describing the origins of cultivation; the Roman numerals at the left indicate thresholds at which a significant increase in energy investment is hypothesized to have occurred. Source: after D. R. Harris 1989, Fig. 1.1.

the addition of several thresholds in which the input of energy into food procurement and production was stepped up (Fig. 21.3). Harris begins with foraging, to include such activities as controlled burning of vegetation, gathering, and protective tending. Food production, in Harris's view, begins with the first leap in energy input, involving sowing, weeding, harvesting, storage, and drainage/irrigation (yet with minimum of tillage). At this point, the plants being used are still phytogenetically wild. The second step up in energy input comes with the transformation of the environment through land clearance and systematic tillage. Finally, the third step, marked with another jump in energy investment, is the propagation of specific variants of the plants being used; namely, the actual domestication of the cultigens. It is at this point, in Harris's model, that agriculture truly begins, with the establishment of true agro–ecosystems.

The schema of Rindos, Ford, and Harris refer largely to plant domestication. With the study of animal domestication, more emphasis has been placed on the characteristics that mark the appearance of domestic forms rather than the shifts in human cultural activities that led up to domestication. An important universal characteristic of the development of animal domestication, which differentiates it clearly from plant domestication, is the shift from the importance of the *dead* animal for its meat alone to the selective propagation of the *living* animal (Meadow 1984, 1989) as a part of a breeding population. Another key difference between animal and plant domestication is that animal populations exhibit social behaviour which conditions their interaction with humans. The behavioural characteristics of the animals that were domesticated in prehistory vary widely, and as a result the sequence of domestication is also variable. The result is that there is greater consideration given to local patterns rather than to models that have global applicability, as well as to models that emphasize the interplay with the local progression of plant domestication (for example, Hole 1984). In general, there is a clear sense that the process of animal domestication was relatively quicker than with plants, with the more important aspect being its subsequent differentiation of emphases in animal husbandry and the products it yielded.

Evolutionary sequences such as those presented above *describe* rather than *explain* the progression of human cultural activities that culminate in domestication and agriculture: they do not provide the causal factors that move the process from one stage to the next. In other words, why did humans add weeding, harvesting, and storage to their earlier foraging activities and then proceed to clear land, till the soil, and propagate specific variants of edible plants? Why did they begin to control and breed herd animals like sheep and goats? Archaeologists have proposed a number of different models for the reliance of human populations on domesticated plants and animals, which are discussed in the following section.

Causes of food production

Once the question shifted from 'how' did food production develop to 'why', anthropological archaeologists began to try to identify causal factors which resulted in a shift from economies based on foraging to ones based on cultivation and livestock. In doing so, they develop models which seek to explain, not simply describe, this process. 'Explanation' implies a search for causation, and the models that archaeologists develop to explain the transition to food production involve an attempt to identify factors which caused societies to make this change. Some models try to isolate single factors, while others propose an interplay of several. It would be impossible to do justice here to all of the models that have been proposed, especially in the last twenty-five years, and this section will attempt simply to illustrate the variation in explanations that have been put forward.

In the first decades of this century there was relatively little attempt made to explain the origins of agriculture. As was often the case, the first real attempt to seek causality in the transition to food production was advanced by V. Gordon Childe, who proposed his 'desiccation' or 'oasis' theory in 1928. Childe suggested that global warming and desiccation at the end of the last ice age led to the concentration of humans, plants, and animals in circumscribed locations, such as oases, and the sheer 'propinquity' or proximity of these species led to the establishment of human control over the eventual domesticates. The difficulty was that available evidence indicated a stable climate, without widespread desiccation, during the period in question between 15,000 and 10,000 years ago. Childe's theory was later overtaken by the view of Braidwood (for example, Braidwood 1960), who suggested that food production in the Old World emerged in certain 'nuclear zones' in the arc of the Taurus and Zagros mountains of the Near East known as the Fertile Crescent. Again, the mere proximity and familiarity of humans with the suite of emmer, einkorn, barley, sheep and goat would have led to the establishment of relations of control and manipulation which resulted in domestication. The advantages of domesticated plants and animals would have been so obvious that this would have become the dominant subsistence strategy in short order.

In the late 1960s there was a shift in anthropological thinking away from a belief in the inherent superiority or attractiveness of agriculture as an economic strategy. Instead, there emerged a prevalent belief that foraging was a successful and stable way of life and that humans would not have taken on the drudgery and risks of agriculture unless they were under duress. None the less, it was clear that in the last 10,000 years virtually all the world's population had made this transition, and the search for the factors which would have compelled humans to make it was intensified. Since 1968, there have been many different theories of the origins of food production that have been proposed, but they can be grouped under several convenient rubrics. Barbara Stark, in a review of the origins of food production in the New World, has identified three main types of models used by archaeologists to trace the transition to food production (Stark 1986), which she terms 'push' models, 'pull' models, and 'social' models (Fig. 21.4). This typology of models is also germane to the study of the origins of food production in the Old World.

'Push' models are by far the most commonly encountered in the archaeological literature. They tend to highlight the presumed duress which would have driven humans to adopt the time-consuming and risky business of food production. Such models, including those proposed by Binford (1968), Flannery (1969), and Cohen (1977) among others, are based on imbalances between population and resources and human populations acting under conditions of stress. Population growth, in an elaboration of the position taken by Boserup (1965), is often regarded as the main 'motor' which propels the sequence of causal relationships, with climatic change often introduced as the trigger which causes a sudden imbalance in the system. Other elements in such models are the emergence of sedentism and the diversification of resource use among terminal hunter-gatherers. As Henry (1989) points out, the main source of variation among the 'push' models is the sequence in which

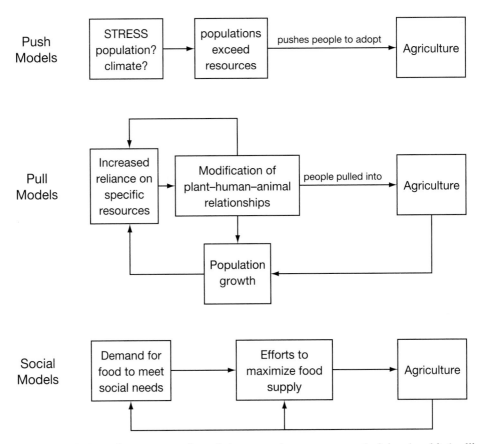

Figure 21.4 Schematic representation of the general arguments underlying 'push', 'pull' and 'social' models of the transition to agriculture. Source: P. Bogucki.

these three key elements are ordered. They are attractive in that the characteristics of sedentism, diversification of resources, and population growth can often be plausibly, if not necessarily conclusively, inferred from archaeological data.

An early example of a 'push' model was that of Binford (1968), who proposed that in certain coastal regions of the world, such as the Levant, populations that relied on rich marine resources grew in size. These populations increased to the point at which they were forced to spill over into adjacent inland zones which were not so richly endowed, also perhaps pushed by a hypothesized rise in sea levels at the close of the Pleistocene. In these marginal zones, these spillover populations needed to increase the resource base artificially, and they did so by sowing wild seeds of grasses like wheat and barley taken from the optimal zones. There is, however, no evidence of large late Pleistocene populations supported by aquatic resources in these regions, so Binford's model has remained unsupported, yet it is important in that it introduced demographic pressure as a causal factor in the discussion of agricultural origins.

Flannery (1969) proposed a model of agricultural origins in the Near East which incorporated many of the elements of Binford's scheme. He argued that, beginning about 20,000 BC, populations in the Near East began to broaden their subsistence base to include all sorts of previously underused plant and animal species – what he termed a 'broad spectrum' pattern. Human populations in certain optimal zones of the Fertile Crescent, where there were large natural populations of wild wheat, barley, sheep and goat, grew to the point where they exceeded the capacity of these regions to support them. At this point, about 8000 BC, they spilled over into adjacent marginal zones, whereupon cultivation began as an attempt to produce artificial stands of cereals 'as dense as those in the *heart* of the "optimum" zone' (Flannery 1969: 81). At this point, phytogenetic changes in the cereals, such as the toughening of the rachis, set in to reinforce the human efforts. Still, harvests were uneven, and the domestication of sheep and goat was an effort to 'bank' food in an attempt to buffer the lean years. Flannery's model was seen as very compelling, and although some have made amendments to it (for example: Hassan 1977; Smith and Young 1972), it remained the basis for the genre of 'push' models of agricultural origins in south-western Asia throughout the 1970s. Attempts have been made to extend the population pressure hypothesis of agricultural origins world-wide (Cohen 1977), but the absence of compelling evidence from many regions has led many archaeologists to be sceptical of it as a universal explanation.

More recently, a certain dissatisfaction with single-factor 'push' models has set in, particularly due to the fact that demonstrating stress or inferring it from population growth is elusive. Moreover, it began to seem clear that the earliest sites with documented plant cultivation and animal husbandry were not in 'marginal zones' but rather in the most productive parts of the Levant. Recent models (McCorriston and Hole 1991; Moore 1982, 1989) have tended to emphasize the interplay of a variety of factors, including changing environments, demography, the foraging economy, settlement patterns, and social organization. The differences among them tend to be the factor which receives the heaviest weight. Moore (1982, 1989), for instance, emphasizes the change to a more sedentary form of settlement which increased pressure on local plant and animal resources. McCorriston and Hole (1991), on the other hand, stress the role of environmental change, as manifested in increased seasonal variation and the drying of lake basins. The increased prominence given to climatic change in many recent models indicates that Childe's speculations of the early twentieth century were not entirely wide of the mark.

Some archaeologists are not comfortable with isolating a source of 'stress' which compelled populations to shift from foraging to farming and have developed so-called 'pull' models, although these are somewhat rarer in the archaeological literature. In such models, the precursors of domesticated plants and animals are inferred to have had certain characteristics which drew human groups to rely more heavily on them than on alternative resources. The increased use of such resources then led to dependence on them to the point that it was impossible to return to the previous patterns of plant and animal exploitation. In such models, population growth continues to play a role, but it functions more as the force that prevents a group from reverting to an earlier pattern of resource use that maintained population at a lower level.

In highland Mesoamerica, Kent Flannery proposed one of the earliest 'pull' models in 1968. He argued that the foraging bands of upland Mesoamerica practised a tightly scheduled seasonal pattern of plant and animal exploitation. Subtle genetic changes in particular plants, especially beans and eventually maize, made them more attractive to foragers, who spent more time collecting them. This upset the tight schedule, leaving the foragers no option but to cultivate the plants on which they had focused in order to maintain their yields. Although it has been refined somewhat over the last two decades (for example, Flannery 1986), this model presents an attractive explanation of the beginnings of cultivation in Mesoamerica, although recent research results may revise our understanding of early agriculture in this region in the near future. For example, the transition from foraging to farming societies was long believed to be very gradual, based on radiocarbon dates of *c.* 5000 BC for maize cobs in the Tehuacan Valley and the eventual appearance of maize-based agricultural villages *c.* 2000 BC. Recent AMS dates, however, indicate that maize domestication may have occurred later, *c.* 3500–3000 BC (Fritz 1994).

Henry (1989) has developed a 'pull' model for agricultural origins in the Near East. He proposed that there were two key points in the process of agricultural origins in the Levant. The first occurred around 12,500 years ago, in which a worldwide increase in temperature promoted long-term settlement and necessitated a shift from what Henry calls 'simple' foraging to 'complex' foraging in the Levant, in which a variety of high-yield resources were exploited, including wild cereals. Restraints on population growth were relaxed. About 2,000 years later, this complex foraging system collapsed, possibly as the result of a second climatic change. The foragers had two options. In the highly productive areas of the Levant, where the highest populations were, they began to cultivate cereals (which, Henry believes, they had known how to do for some time, but had not needed to), while in the marginal areas they reverted to a simpler foraging system.

In 'social' models, factors beyond population growth generate demand for resources, leading to the intensification of subsistence pursuits and ultimately to food production. Among some human groups, it is hypothesized, there existed a need to increase the amount of food available to meet social demands for exchange, bridewealth, distribution for status, and alliance formation. The high productivity of certain potential domesticates led to a concentration on them for this purpose and ultimately to their domestication. The evidence to support 'social' models is quite elusive and requires crossing a wider inferential gap than for 'push' and 'pull' models. None the less, they should not be discounted simply because it is difficult to find direct support for them.

A recent 'social' model for the origins of food production is that of Hayden (1992), which he terms the 'competitive feasting' model. Hayden points out that most hunter-gatherers occupying fluctuating environments share food, and hence there is no incentive to invest time and effort in producing extra, since only others will benefit. In resource-rich areas, however, in which there was adequate food to relax such collective sharing, conditions may have arisen for competition as ambitious individuals staged competitive feasts to gain control over labour and loyalty. The need to generate large amounts of desirable foods in order to stage such competitive feasts stimulated cultivation, which represented no great discovery for foragers who were well aware of seeds and their propagation. Hayden proposes his model without strict geographical reference, suggesting that it may be applicable to both the New World and Old World alike. Similarly, Runnels and van Andel (1988) have argued that in the eastern Mediterranean agriculture may have arisen as a result of a need to produce surplus commodities for trade or to support craftsmen who made goods for trade.

THE DISPERSAL OF FOOD PRODUCTION

The question of the spread of agriculture and animal husbandry beyond the zones of initial domestication is just as important as the process of domestication itself. In addressing this issue, a variety of factors must be studied. It is necessary to differentiate between the expansion of agricultural communities into zones where they previously had not been found and the adoption of the techniques of agriculture and animal husbandry by communities that had previously practised only foraging. Both types of agricultural dispersals took place at various times around the world.

A number of different factors need to be taken into account in studying agricultural dispersals. One is the organization of early farming communities and why they might be expected to expand into new ecological zones. Another factor is the environmental conditions that prevailed at the moment when domestic plants and animals became available to local foraging populations and whether these encouraged or retarded the adoption of food production. Finally, it is necessary to understand the nature of the foraging populations that inhabited the area prior to the appearance of cultivation and animal husbandry.

Agricultural dispersal by colonization of wide areas was apparently rare in prehistory, but it can be documented for certain regions with some level of confidence. For instance, on the loess soils of central Europe, an area hitherto sparsely settled

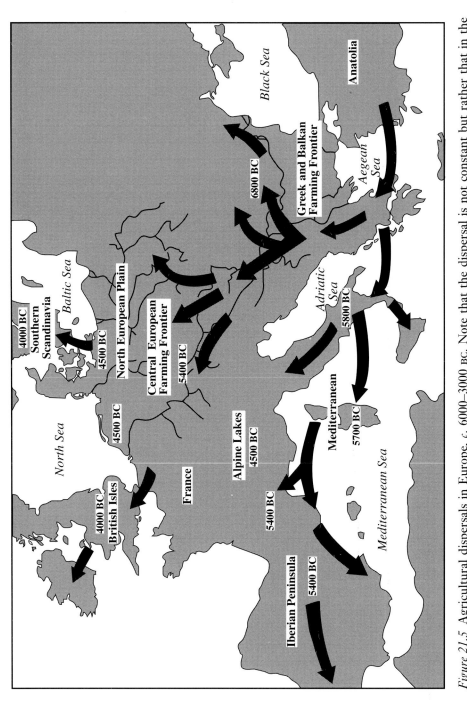

Figure 21.5 Agricultural dispersals in Europe, *c.* 6000–3000 BC. Note that the dispersal is not constant but rather that in the Balkans and in central Europe there were periods during which the frontier did not advance steadily. Reproduced with permission of *American Scientist*.

by foraging peoples, communities of the Linear Pottery culture settled between 6000 and 5000 BC (Barker 1985; Bogucki 1988, 1996; Bogucki and Grygiel 1993; Hodder 1992; Price *et al.* 1995). Sharp contrasts in house form, chipped-stone tool types, and settlement location between earlier foragers and the Linear Pottery culture, and its fully developed pottery technology, suggest that this does indeed represent the spread of agriculture through the dispersal of people (Fig. 21.5). Similarly, the Austronesian-speaking colonization of Polynesia between *c.* 1600 and 500 BC brought with it a dispersal of cultigens and domestic animals (pig, dog and fowl), along with a variety of 'stowaways', including lizards, rodents, molluscs and weeds (Kirch 1983).

A more frequent occurrence in prehistory was the adoption of agriculture and animal husbandry by peoples who had previously engaged in foraging – what Minnis (1985) calls 'primary crop acquisition'. Indeed, outside of the rare instances of colonization, the adoption of agriculture by foragers has been the dominant mode of agricultural dispersals over the last ten millennia. As Minnis (1985: 337) points out, however, the adoption of cultigens by foragers has received comparatively little attention alongside cases of pristine domestication. Yet 'primary crop acquisition' was crucial to the eventual success of agriculture as a food production system and often involves processes that are quite interesting in their own right.

In the south-western United States, foragers began to cultivate maize shortly before 1000 BC, according to the best available evidence (Wills 1988: 149), clearly deriving the domesticated plants from Mesoamerican sources further south. Early maize was a subtropical plant not well suited to the Sonoran desert, and its adoption by the mobile foragers of this region did not at first result in a radical transformation of society. 'The initial introduction of domesticated plants in the Southwest was a monumental non-event with little *immediate* impact on native human populations' (Minnis 1985: 310). It was not until much later, in the first millennium AD, that the inhabitants of many parts of the south-western United States came to depend on maize as their primary food source. Wills (1988) has advanced the hypothesis that the initial adoption of maize was an effort by foragers to alter their pattern of seasonal movement in order to spend more time in rich upland zones to monitor and exploit the wild resources there. In other words, in Wills's view, the introduction of agriculture to this region was to sustain and enhance a foraging system.

A similar situation existed in north-central Europe, in northern Germany and Poland, Denmark, and the Netherlands, shortly before 4000 BC (Bogucki 1996). Domestic plants and animals had been present just to the south in the areas colonized by the Linear Pottery culture for at least a millennium, yet they were not immediately adopted by the foraging populations of the northern European lowlands. These foraging populations, particularly in coastal regions of Denmark, Germany, and the Netherlands, exploited a rich environment with abundant terrestrial and marine resources (Price and Gebauer 1992). Several hypotheses have been offered to explain why the foragers in various parts of north-central Europe adopted agriculture, including imbalances between populations and resources caused by environmental change (for example: Larsson 1986; Rowley-Conwy 1985) and competition for prestige necessitating surplus production (Jennbert 1985). Price *et al.* (1995: 125) note that in southern Scandinavia there seems to be no evidence of population pressure or climatic change directly involved in the adoption of domesticates, which suggests that social competition and demand may have been the primary factors.

A common theme in studies of 'primary crop acquisition' is that the mere *availability* of domesticated plants and animals did not lead immediately to their adoption by foraging populations (Zvelebil and Rowley-Conwy 1984). In both of the cases mentioned above as well as elsewhere, for example in southern Africa (Hitchcock and Ebert 1984), the presence of neighbouring populations practising agriculture did not demonstrate the 'superiority' of food production. Instead, there is normally a significant time lag between the moment a population becomes aware of food production and the eventual integration of domesticated plants and animals into its own subsistence economy. The challenge for archaeologists, then, is to understand *why* foraging populations choose to practise food production, but the answer to this question, as was the case with 'pristine domestication', is often elusive.

AGRICULTURAL COMMITMENT

The adoption of domesticated plants and animals was not the end of the transition to fully agricultural societies. Welch (1991), paralleling Bronson's (1977) comparison of 'cultivators' and 'farmers', has made the crucial distinction between, on the one hand, the initial use of domesticates, integrated into an economy similar in other respects to the preceding one based on foraging, and on the other, the *commitment* to agriculture reflected in the full linkage of human behaviour – economic, social, even ritual – with the maintenance of the agro-ecosystem and its production of reliable harvests. The commitment to agriculture represents the final step in the transition from one set of premises on which society is organized to another. In the Levant, for instance, the domestication process itself, and the onset of cultivation, appears to have taken place relatively rapidly (Bar-Yosef and Belfer-Cohen 1992). On the other hand, the commitment to agriculture, with the establishment of communities that were specifically adapted to the maintenance of an agro-ecosystem, seems to have taken place more slowly over 2,000 years (Byrd 1992). By contrast, in the south-western United States, after a long period of practising mixed horticulture (gardening, hunting and collecting), communities rapidly made the transition to sedentary life structured around sustainable agriculture (Welch 1991).

Considerable archaeological research has been dedicated to the documentation of the initial appearance of cultigens and domestic animals, while much less has been devoted to the shift to committed agriculture. Yet the eventual dependence on agriculture is not simply the inevitable result of the initial use of domestic plants and animals. It is the product of a further set of choices, decisions and responses which resulted in fundamental organizational changes in society (Hodder 1990; Whittle 1996). In both regions of 'pristine domestication' and of 'primary crop acquisition', most prehistoric populations eventually crossed the threshold of commitment to agriculture. The discussion below focuses on some of the issues that faced societies which have crossed this threshold.

SEDENTISM AND OPTIONS

A significant correlate of the transition to an agricultural economy is sedentism. According to Kent (1989: 2), sedentism is the opposite of nomadism along a continuum of mobility. In other words, if nomadism represents the movement of a group on a landscape, sedentism is the lack of such mobility. Of course, no human group or community is entirely sedentary, just as none is absolutely nomadic. All fall between the two extremes on this continuum, although for classification purposes they can be characterized as one or the other depending on which state of mobility or non-mobility is most prevalent. Although it is not possible to say that there is a causal relationship between agriculture and sedentism (Rindos 1984: 173), it is clear that agriculture can *change* patterns of mobility and residence.

The transition to agriculture, specifically by the establishment of fixed locations where crops grow, forces a group to reconcile its patterns of mobility with the demands of the agricultural system. Rindos (1984: 176) terms this reconciliation *agrilocality*, as it represents a dynamic interaction between human locational strategies and the demands of a new agricultural system. It would be wrong to say that agriculture is incompatible with mobility or that sedentism is restricted to agriculturalists. Indeed there are many known groups who are not completely sedentary who grow crops. In Massachusetts in the seventeenth century, for example, the Wampanoag tribe maintained winter inland settlements and summer coastal settlements, where crops were raised (Williams [1643]1973: for a critical review, see Bragdon 1996). In the Amazon drainage, a number of horticultural groups could be categorized as semi-sedentary, the best known being perhaps the Siriono of Bolivia (Holmberg 1969). Some Kalahari hunter-gatherers combine food production and a nomadic way of life (Hitchcock and Ebert 1984). None the less, the fact that agriculture represents an investment of effort and time, however minimal, in a fixed location, causes a society that incorporates some measure of mobility into its residential pattern to confront the question of whether it can continue its nomadic mobility patterns to the degree hitherto practised.

For nomadic societies, mobility provides a variety of options for adjusting conflicts and imbalances: in scheduling, in resource availability, in population, in social transactions. Increasing sedentism, or lack of mobility, implies that the options afforded by mobility would also decrease. Alternative structures would need to be developed to resolve the same imbalances. In large measure, the social and economic consequences of the transition to agriculture revolve around the decreasing options afforded by mobility and the elaboration of alternative structures for addressing conflict and imbalances: storage, exchange, social structure, ritual, warfare.

Sedentism also represents a shift in the human approach to territoriality and time (Carlstein 1982). It also permits the accumulation of material possessions and enhances conditions for population growth. These factors, however, open the door to further challenges posed by increasing complexity in social and economic structures, which Johnson (1982) has called 'scalar stress'. One solution would be to invoke the remnants of the mobility option, as settlements fission and relocate. Another would be to elaborate extramural ways of addressing imbalances, such as trade and warfare.

LABOUR

Among small-scale agriculturalists in the world today, land, labour and capital form the elements of the productive system, and their control is the basis for access to status, power and wealth. Early agricultural societies are generally considered to be 'pre-capitalist' in the sense that they did not have the conditions under which productive assets constituted capital and there was not a category of people who earned their living solely from the accumulation and exchange of such assets. Thus, land and labour are usually considered to be the critical factors in determining the productivity of agricultural systems such as those which would have been found in the first several millennia following the transition to agriculture. Today, in most parts of the world, ability to acquire land is viewed as the primary limiting factor on subsistence production, yet for most early agricultural societies it is likely that arable land was relatively abundant in absolute terms. Although optimal habitats might have soon been thoroughly settled, adequate amounts of arable land on lesser-quality soils or in otherwise suboptimal habitats would have been available. Instead of land, labour supply was probably the major limitation on early agricultural production (Bogucki 1988).

There are periods in the agricultural cycle, such as land clearance, planting, weeding and harvesting, which require considerable amounts of labour, but over relatively short periods of time. Such periods are typically referred to as 'labour bottlenecks' (Jaeger 1986: 7; Richards 1985: 68). The agricultural community must balance its labour requirements for these bottlenecks against its ability to support this workforce over the remainder of the agricultural year. Generally, a compromise results which constrains the overall productivity of the subsistence system, perhaps in terms of the amount of land it can bring under cultivation or the degree to which fields can be weeded. Labour, then, is a very inelastic resource, which limits the ability of an agricultural community to produce both for its own survival and for accumulation and exchange.

Along with sedentism, the transformation of the mobilization and control of labour was an important structural change that accompanied a commitment to agriculture. Societies which were still largely based on foraging with some cultivation would not have needed to make many adjustments to accommodate labour bottlenecks. Once a society was primarily dependent on agriculture and animal husbandry, however, the size and structure of the labour pool would have been a primary determinant of agricultural productivity. It is possible, then, to see limitations on labour, particularly at the bottleneck times, as a factor in the eventual development of innovations which permit human energy to be invested in agriculture in other ways to increase the productivity of a parcel of land (see, for

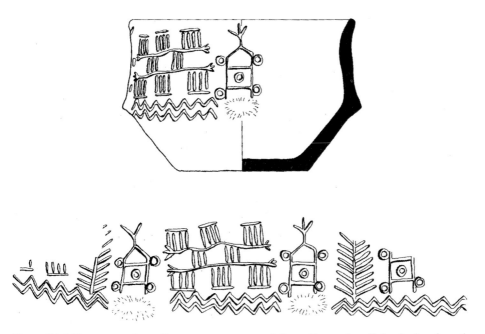

Figure 21.6 Representation of a wagon on a vessel from Bronocice, Poland, dated to the fourth millennium BC, indicating an early use of animal traction for cartage. Source: Milisauskas and Kruk 1982.

example, Bogucki 1993). Such innovations would include animal traction for ploughing and cartage (Fig. 21.6), irrigation and raised fields, and manuring. The management of livestock and the digging of irrigation ditches clearly involve human labour, but these can be done mostly at times other than those of the labour bottlenecks that constrain the productivity of agriculture.

HAZARDS, RISKS AND UNCERTAINTY

Agriculturalists must constantly make decisions, the consequences of which they must predict, on the basis of available information, experience and intuition. In this process, the farmer must make some assessment of the range of potential outcomes. Economists and ecologists have recently taken an interest in the fact that farming decisions are not made on the basis of complete certainty. Instead, agricultural decision-makers must incorporate some consideration of the unknown, the random, and the unpredictable into their behaviour, which in turn determines how they respond to their environment. An ideal world of full information and complete certainty bears little resemblance to the conditions under which human groups operate. Instead, we must recognize that prehistoric societies did not have complete information about their environment or ways to predict random environmental hazards.

The environment of early agricultural groups had considerable potential for hazards and stress. Hewitt (1983) has pointed out that the removal of domesticated plants from their original habitats increased their vulnerability to hazards. The subsistence system of agricultural peoples is based on an artificial association of plants and animals that can be maintained only through human intervention. As such, it is inherently unstable and prone to fluctuations of environmental conditions – rainfall, sunlight, insects, diseases – and changes in the ability of human groups to invest the labour required to maintain fields and livestock (Fig. 21.7). We cannot simply assume that these variables can be eliminated from consideration and still hope to develop models that accurately explain the archaeological record.

Economists and ecologists identify two important conditions under which decisions can be made: risk and uncertainty. This distinction was first made by the economist Frank Knight in 1921, but since then there has been little consensus about the dividing line between risk and uncertainty, or whether the two concepts can be separated at all. Knight differentiated between *risk*, in which probabilities could be assigned to a range of known outcomes, and *uncertainty*, in which an absence of information or predictive data made the range of outcomes unknowable. Some economic anthropologists have argued that this distinction is useful in dealing with small-scale agrarian societies. Cancian, for instance, noted that there are differences between how farmers take account of known environmental variation

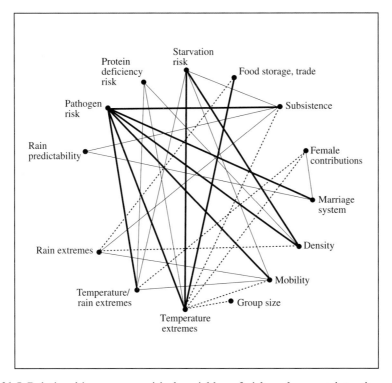

Figure 21.7 Relationships among critical variables of risk and uncertainty. According to Low's analysis, heavy lines indicate at least one relationship of $p < 0.001$ or more than one relationship of $p \leq 0.01$; light lines indicate at least one relationship of $p \leq 0.01$, or more than one of $p \leq 0.05$; dotted lines indicate at least one relationship of $p \leq 0.05$. Source: E. Cashdan, redrawn by D. Miles-Williams.

such as rainfall in their decision-making and how they deal with the unknown results of new technology (Cancian 1980). Others have maintained that this distinction is artificial, for 'probabilities of future events are never "known" with complete certainty' (Berry 1980: 325).

Social scientists recognize several components of risk (Merkhofer 1987). First, there must be a source of risk, a *hazard*. Second, there must be a process by which people and their property are *exposed* to the hazard. Third, there must be a process by which the exposure produces adverse results. The *perception* of the risk by individuals and groups involves a further process that incorporates an evaluation that the severity or inequity of the adverse results is sufficient to be of concern. This final process of risk perception is generally subjective, but none the less constitutes a probability judgement about the frequency or likelihood of an unpleasant event.

How do farmers reduce risk? One way is to subdivide and thus multiply the number of units (fields or crop varieties, for example) exposed to hazards. Rather than have one large field on a single soil type, farmers can have a number of small fields on a variety of soil types. The trade-off for this is a loss of efficiency in travel and scheduling, but if the probability of environmental hazard is judged sufficiently high, such a cost might be acceptable. Another diversification strategy is to grow a variety of different crops that respond differently to climatic variation (see, for example, Halstead and Jones 1989). Minnis (1996: 62–64) points out that the use of low-preference foods, or 'famine foods', which are neglected in times of plenty, constitute yet another form of diversification. Storage can also be viewed as a response to risk (Bettinger 1991). Finally, the establishment of reciprocal exchange relationships with other individuals and households can be viewed as a form of insurance which spreads the exposure to hazard over a number of units (Cashdan 1985).

The position taken here is that the distinction between risk and uncertainty can provide an important insight into different patterns of prehistoric behaviour. Calavan (1984), for instance, points out that farmers, in making production choices, operate differently under these two conditions. Farmers producing a long-established crop with a familiar and traditional technology will obtain yields that will vary from year to year but within predictable limits. Based on their observations of environmental conditions, they can allocate subjective, but reasonably accurate, probabilities to these yields, and base their investment of labour and time accordingly. In such a circumstance, farmers operate under conditions of risk. On the other hand, farmers who are trying a new technology or a new crop, or who are colonizing new environmental zones, will find themselves in a situation where the yields cannot be predicted with confidence. While such innovation can pay off richly if the guess is correct, it can also be catastrophic if the farmer guesses wrong in allocating his resources. In this situation, the farmer operates under conditions of uncertainty. Such uncertainty can be turned into risk through experience and learning, although this may take several generations for knowledge of the range of possible outcomes to accumulate.

The question of innovation is another important dimension of early agriculture. Studies of subsistence farmers today show that they are avid experimenters (Richards 1985), and there is no reason to believe that prehistoric farmers were not equally prone to experimentation. Innovation is closely linked with risk and uncertainty (Cancian 1979; van der Leeuw 1989), particularly in situations where there is pressure from external sources on the agricultural economy to increase production. When does the need to increase production offset the risks involved in new and untried methods? This brings us to yet another critical issue in the study of small-scale subsistence agriculture – that of *intensification*.

INTENSIFICATION

Intensification can have a variety of meanings and connotations for different researchers, and it is important to be explicit about what the term actually means. A broad definition is offered by Brookfield (1972: 31), who defines it as 'the addition of inputs up to the economic margin', the margin where the application of further inputs will not increase total productivity. The inputs can take a variety of forms. Anthropologists have tended to concentrate on raw labour inputs and 'skills' as easily quantifiable and indexed dimensions of intensification, but Brookfield emphasized that there are many other components to consider, including organization of labour and structure of land use (1972: 32).

A somewhat narrower concept of intensification has been used by other anthropologists and economists who have studied agricultural societies (for example: Boserup 1965; Conklin 1961). Their definition of intensification is focused on the length of the fallow period, the time in which fields lie unplanted, with the degree of intensification inversely correlated with the length of the fallow. While narrower in scope, such a definition of intensification is related to that proposed by Brookfield in that a shorter fallow period usually demands an increase in labour and related inputs per plot.

Most archaeologists who employ the concept of intensification come to it via the so-called 'Boserup hypothesis', which links intensification to population growth. Boserup argued that agriculture will be intensified, by shortening of fallow length and the introduction of the plough and irrigation, as population increases. Since settlement sizes and distribution are believed by many archaeologists to be reliable proxy indicators of population increase, the causal relationship between population growth and intensification is attractive. We have already discussed how the Boserup model was extended to form the basis for some of the prevalent 'push' models for the origin of agriculture, and it also forms the theoretical rationale for many attempts to explain changes in early agricultural societies as well.

The expression of intensification only in terms of fallow length and as strictly related to population growth is but a limited version of a much broader process that can touch society in many other ways. For instance, the dispersal of settlements to minimize travel time to and from fields and the integration of animal traction into the household economy can be viewed as intensification strategies, even though they do not involve the direct input of labour into agricultural work. Bogucki (1988, 1993) has argued that both of these were employed in the fourth millennium BC in Europe to intensify the agricultural system. If this is the case, then there are clear implications for the social and economic relationships implicated in a change in settlement pattern and the investment in assets such as draught animals. Moreover, an equally plausible trigger for agricultural intensification is constituted by changes in social relationships that make demands on the subsistence system for greater production of materials to be used in social transactions (Bender 1978; Nassaney 1987).

Intensification is not a unilinear process, and there are examples known from the ethnographic record of shifts from more to less intense levels of land use, referred to as 'deintensification' (Guillet 1987) or 'disintensification' (Brookfield 1972). While in many cases these examples can be correlated with population shifts, their existence suggests that intensification is dependent on a number of factors besides raw population size or its rate of change. One interesting issue is the relationship between intensification and agricultural risk. For example, Nichols (1987) has argued that the emergence of intensive irrigation agriculture in the Basin of Mexico was a response to the risks posed by annual variation in water supply. In her model, intensification occurs before there is an imbalance between population and resources. The implication of this model is that if the source of risk were to dissipate (which would be unlikely with populations, unless they moved away), then there is at least the theoretical possibility that the process of intensification could be arrested or even reversed.

FORAGERS AND FARMERS

The adoption of agriculture around the world was not instantaneous, of course, or even inevitable. Food-producing populations have often lived in proximity to human groups for whom farming and herding had little importance. Moreover, the adoption of agriculture is not a one-way street, and it is possible for groups to decide to give up sedentary farming life if conditions allow them to do so. Even among populations that were fully committed to agriculture, such as those of medieval and early modern Europe, gathered foods played an important role in the diet.

Ingold (1984: 5) has noted that anthropologists have the tendency to remove people from the category of foragers if they have any attributes of agriculture or pastoralism. There are really, however, four basic categories of human groups in terms of subsistence systems: (1) those who subsist on uncultivated plants and wild fauna – foragers; (2) those who have a mixed subsistence economy, based partly on domestic and partly on wild resources: these can be subdivided further into two sub-categories, (2a) foragers who farm (yet still closer to category 1), and (2b) farmers who hunt (yet still closer to category 3); (3) those who gain no significant subsistence from uncultivated plants or wild fauna – agriculturalists and pastoralists. In general, anthropologists have tended to view the universe of human subsistence economies as a binary set: those in category 1 and those in category 3. The root of the problem may be that the colonization of Africa, the Americas, Australia, and the Pacific in the eighteenth and nineteenth centuries essentially 'froze' many societies as either foragers or food producers depending on their circumstances at the time of European contact. The point of this frozen moment was then assumed to be fixed on the unilinear scale of progress from hunting and gathering to farming and stock-herding. Early anthropological studies that were based on short-term contact tended to reinforce this viewpoint. Yet all does not seem to be so simple. Long-term studies of a number of groups reveal fluctuations between foraging and farming with an annual or even longer periodicity.

There is a prevailing belief among anthropologists that once a society heads down the road to agriculture it cannot return. In general, it is widely believed that once population growth occurs as a result of the 'improved' food supply brought about by food production, the society comes to depend more and more on its crops (for example, Cassidy 1980). Actually, there is little evidence to suggest that population growth is an automatic effect of the adoption of agriculture, and it appears that even among agricultural societies there are mechanisms that restrain population growth and fertility (see, for example, Englebrecht 1987 for a discussion of this among the Iroquois). It is entirely possible for societies at this boundary between foraging and farming to slide back and forth from one strategy to another, following one for a few years, then reverting to the other, and back again. For instance, the Agta in the Philippines, long thought to be prototypical hunter-gatherers (Peterson 1978a, 1978b), actually are opportunists who make use of the subsistence strategy that best suits the conditions of the moment (Griffin 1984).

These conditions can be determined both by the natural environment and by the sort of interactions that a group is having with agricultural neighbours at any given moment. In studying the dispersal of agriculture beyond areas of 'pristine' domestication, archaeologists have begun to draw on comparative ethnological studies of forager–farmer interaction and to propose models for such interaction in prehistory (for example: Bogucki 1995; Gregg 1988). Often these involve the exchange of hunted or collected resources from the foragers for cultivated products of farmers, although the potential of forager populations for providing agricultural labour cannot be underestimated. The study of such forager–farmer interactions holds great promise for the understanding of the spread of food production, particularly in cases where foragers adopted domesticated plants and animals from nearby farming populations.

CONCLUSION

The establishment of sedentary agricultural communities in both the Old World and the New World laid the foundation for subsequent changes in human society. It is important to realize, however, that despite the rise of urbanism and state societies in some regions, rural agrarian communities have continued in a way of life that had its roots millennia earlier. Farmers continue to make decisions about how to allocate land and labour under conditions of risk and uncertainty. Agrarian societies respond to needs and challenges by intensifying their production. Although a tractor can be substituted for oxen, and cultigens can be selected and improved, farmers seek the same opportunities and work under the same basic constraints today as did their counterparts millennia ago.

The two most significant changes in agriculture in the last several millennia have been the emergence of cash-cropping, in which choices are determined by market concerns rather than nutritional needs, and the global dimensions of agriculture. A potato farmer in Poland today worries about the productivity of an Andean domesticate, while the plains of the central United States are covered by fields of wheat first domesticated in the Levant 10,000 years ago. Pigs in Iowa, descended from animals first domesticated in Anatolia in the seventh millennium BC, are fattened on maize, domesticated in highland Mexico. Considered in this light, the origins and, just as importantly, the dispersal of food production as a successful economic strategy have truly shaped human existence for the last ten millennia.

REFERENCES

Bar-Yosef, O. and Belfer-Cohen, A. (1992) 'From foraging to farming in the Mediterranean Levant', in A. B. Gebauer and T. D. Price (eds) *Transitions to Agriculture in Prehistory*, Madison: Prehistory Press: 21–48.

Barker, G. (1985) *Prehistoric Farming in Europe*, Cambridge: Cambridge University Press.

Bender, B. (1978) 'Hunter-gatherer to farmer: a social perspective', *World Archaeology* 10: 204–22.

Berry, S. (1980) 'Decision making and policy making in rural development', in P. Barlett (ed.) *Agricultural Decision Making. Anthropological Contributions to Rural Development*, New York: Academic Press: 321–36.

Bettinger, R. (1991) *Hunter-Gatherers. Archaeological and Evolutionary Theory*, New York and London: Plenum Press.

Binford, L. (1968) 'Post-Pleistocene adaptations', in S. Binford and L. Binford (eds) *New Perspectives in Archaeology*, Chicago: Aldine: 313–41.

Bogucki, P. (1988) *Forest Farmers and Stockherders. Early Agriculture and its Consequences in North-Central Europe*, Cambridge: Cambridge University Press.

Bogucki, P. (1993) 'Animal traction and household economies in neolithic Europe', *Antiquity* 67: 492–503.

Bogucki, P. (1995) 'Prelude to agriculture in north-central Europe', in D. V. Campana (ed.) *Before Farming: the Role of Plants and Animals in Early Societies*, MASCA Research Papers in Science and Archaeology, Volume 12 Supplement, Philadelphia: University Museum: 105–16.

Bogucki, P. (1996) 'The spread of early farming in Europe', *American Scientist* 84: 242–53.

Bogucki, P. and Grygiel, R. (1993) 'The first farmers of central Europe', *Journal of Field Archaeology*, 20 (3): 399–426.

Boserup, E. (1965) *The Conditions of Agricultural Growth*, Chicago: Aldine.

Bragdon, K. (1996) *Native People of Southern New England 1500–1650*, Norman: University of Oklahoma Press.

Braidwood, R. (1960) 'The agricultural revolution', *Scientific American* 203: 130–48.

Bronson, B. (1977) 'The earliest farming: demography as a cause and consequence', in C. Reed (ed.) *The Origins of Agriculture*, The Hague: Mouton: 23–48.

Brookfield, H. C. (1972) 'Intensification and disintensification in Pacific agriculture. A theoretical approach', *Pacific Viewpoint* 13: 30–48.

Byrd, B. (1992) 'The dispersal of food production across the Levant', in A. B. Gebauer and T. D. Price (eds) *Transitions to Agriculture in Prehistory*, Madison: Prehistory Press: 49–61.

Calavan, M. M. (1984) 'Prospects for a probabilistic reinterpretation of Chayanovian theory: an exploratory discussion', in E. P. Durrenberger (ed.) *Chayanov, Peasants, and Economic Anthropology*, Orlando: Academic Press: 51–69.

Cancian, F. (1979) *The Innovator's Situation. Upper Middle Class Conservatism in Agricultural Communities*, Stanford: Stanford University Press.

Cancian, F. (1980) 'Risk and uncertainty in agricultural decision making', in P. Barlett (ed.) *Agricultural Decision Making. Anthropological Contributions to Rural Development*, Orlando: Academic Press: 161–76.

Carlstein, T. (1982) *Time Resources, Society, and Ecology. On the Capacity for Human Interaction in Space and Time. Volume I: Preindustrial Societies*, London: George Allen and Unwin.

Cashdan, E. (1985) 'Coping with risk: reciprocity among the Basarwa of northern Botswana', *Man* 20: 454–74.

Cassidy, C. M. (1980) 'Nutrition and health in agriculturalists and hunter-gatherers: a case study of two prehistoric populations', in N. Jerome, R. Kandel and G. Pelto (eds) *Nutritional Anthropology. Contemporary Approaches to Diet and Culture*, Pleasantville, N.Y.: Redgrave Publishing Company: 117–45.

Childe, V. G. (1928) *The Most Ancient East*, London: Routledge and Kegan Paul.

Clutton-Brock, J. (ed.) (1989) *The Walking Larder. Patterns of Domestication, Pastoralism, and Predation*, London: Unwin Hyman.

Cohen, M. (1977) *The Food Crisis in Prehistory*, New Haven: Yale University Press.

Conklin, H. (1961) 'The study of shifting cultivation', *Current Anthropology* 2: 27–61.

Crabtree, P. J. (1993) 'Early animal domestication in the Near East and Europe', in M. Schiffer (ed.) *Advances in Archaeological Method and Theory 5*, Tucson: University of Arizona Press: 201–45.

Englebrecht, W. (1987) 'Factors maintaining low population density among the prehistoric New York Iroquois', *American Antiquity* 52: 13–27.

Flannery, K. V. (1968) 'Archaeological systems theory and early Mesoamerica', in B. Meggers (ed.) *Anthropological Archaeology in the Americas*, Washington, DC: Anthropological Society of Washington: 67–87.

Flannery, K. V. (1969) 'Origins and ecological effects of early domestication in Iran and the Near East', in P. Ucko and G. Dimbleby (eds) *The Domestication and Exploitation of Plants and Animals*, London: Duckworth: 73–100.

Flannery, K. V. (1973) 'The origins of agriculture', *Annual Review of Anthropology* 2: 271–310.

Flannery, K. V. (1986) *Guila Naquitz. Archaic Foraging and Early Agriculture in Oaxaca, Mexico*, Orlando: Academic Press.

Ford, R. I. (1985) 'The processes of plant food production in prehistoric North America', in R. I. Ford (ed.) *Prehistoric Food Production in North America*, Ann Arbor: Museum of Anthropology, University of Michigan: 1–18.

Fritz, G. J. (1994) 'Are the first American farmers getting younger?', *Current Anthropology* 35: 305–9.

Gebauer, A. B. and Price, T. D. (eds) (1992) *Transitions to Agriculture in Prehistory*, Madison: Prehistory Press.

Gregg, S. (1988) *Foragers and Farmers. Population Interaction and Agricultural Expansion in Prehistoric Europe*, Chicago: University of Chicago Press.

Griffin, P. B. (1984) 'Forager resource and land use in the humid tropics: the Agta of Northeastern Luzon, the Philippines', in C. Schrire (ed.) *Past and Present in Hunter Gatherer Studies*, Orlando: Academic Press: 95–121.

Guillet, D. (1987) 'Agricultural intensification and deintensification in Lari, Colca Valley, southern Peru', *Research in Economic Anthropology* 8: 201–24.

Halstead, P. and Jones, G. (1989) 'Agrarian ecology in the Greek Islands: time stress, scale, and risk', *Journal of Hellenic Studies* 109: 41–53.

Harlan, J. (1971) 'Agricultural origins: centers and non-centers', *Science* 174: 468–74.

Harlan, J. (1995) *The Living Fields. Our Agricultural Heritage*, Cambridge: Cambridge University Press.

Harris, D. R. (1989) 'An evolutionary continuum of people–plant interaction', in D. R. Harris and G. C. Hillman (eds) *Foraging and Farming. The Evolution of Plant Exploitation*, London: Unwin Hyman: 11–26.

Harris, D. R. and Hillman, G. C. (eds) (1989) *Foraging and Farming. The Evolution of Plant Exploitation*, London: Unwin Hyman.

Hassan, F. (1977) 'The dynamics of agricultural origins in Palestine: a theoretical model', in C. A. Reed (ed.) *The Origins of Agriculture*, The Hague: Mouton: 589–609.

Hayden, B. (1992) 'Models of domestication', in A. B. Gebauer and T. D. Price (eds) *Transitions to Agriculture in Prehistory*, Madison: Prehistory Press: 11–19.

Henry, D. (1989) *From Foraging to Agriculture. The Levant at the End of the Ice Age*, Philadelphia: University of Pennsylvania Press.

Hewitt, K. (1983) 'Interpreting the role of hazards in agriculture', in K. Hewitt (ed.) *Interpretations of Calamity from the Viewpoint of Human Ecology*, Boston: Allen and Unwin: 123–39.

Hitchcock, R. K. and Ebert, J. I. (1984) 'Foraging and food production among Kalahari hunter/gatherers', in J. D. Clark and S. Brandt (eds) *From Hunters to Farmers. The Causes and Consequences of Food Production in Africa*, Berkeley: University of California Press: 328–48.

Hodder, I. (1990) *The Domestication of Europe*, Oxford: Basil Blackwell.

Hole, F. (1984) 'A reassessment of the Neolithic Revolution', *Paleorient* 10: 49–60.

Holmberg, A. (1969) *Nomads of the Long Bow. The Siriono of Eastern Bolivia*, Garden City, N.Y.: Natural History Press.

Ingold, T. (1984) 'Time, social relationships, and the exploitation of animals: anthropological reflections on prehistory', in J. Clutton-Brock and C. Grigson (eds) *Animals and Archaeology: 3. Early Herders and their Flocks*, Oxford: British Archaeological Reports, International Series 202: 3–12.

Jaeger, W. K. (1986) *Agricultural Mechanization. The Economics of Animal Draft Power in West Africa*, Boulder: Westview.

Jennbert, K. (1985) 'Neolithisation – a Scanian perspective', *Journal of Danish Archaeology* 4: 196–97.

Johnson, G. (1982) 'Organizational structure and scalar stress', in C. Renfrew, M. J. Rowlands and B. Segraves (eds) *Theory and Explanation in Archaeology*, New York: Academic Press: 389–421.

Kent, S. (1989) 'Cross-cultural perceptions of farmers as hunters and the value of meat', in S. Kent (ed.) *Farmers as Hunters. The Implications of Sedentism*, Cambridge: Cambridge University Press: 1–17.

Kirch, P. V. (1983) 'Man's role in modifying tropical and subtropical Polynesian ecosystems', *Archaeology in Oceania* 18: 26–31.

Knight, F. H. (1921) *Risk, Uncertainty and Profit*, Boston: Houghton Mifflin Company.

Larsson, M. (1986) 'Neolithization in Scania – a Funnel Beaker perspective', *Journal of Danish Archaeology* 5: 244–47.

Low, B. S. (1990) 'Human responses to environmental extremeness and uncertainty: a cross-cultural perspective', in E. Cashdan (ed.) *Risk and Uncertainty in Tribal and Peasant Economies*, Boulder: Westview Press: 229–55.

McCorriston, J. and Hole, F. (1991) 'The ecology of seasonal stress and the origins of agriculture in the Near East', *American Anthropologist* 93: 46–69.

Meadow, R. (1984) 'Animal domestication in the Middle East: a view from the eastern margin', in J. Clutton-Brock and C. Grigson (eds) *Animals and Archaeology: 3. Early Herders and their Flocks*, Oxford, British Archaeological Reports, International Series 202: 309–37.

Meadow, R. (1989) 'Osteological evidence for the process of animal domestication', in J. Clutton-Brock (ed.) *The Walking Larder. Patterns of Domestication, Pastoralism, and Predation*, London: Unwin Hyman: 80–96.

Merkhofer, M. (1987) *Decision Science and Social Risk Management*, Dordrecht: D. Reidel.

Milisauskas, S. and Kruk, J. (1982) 'Die Wagendarstellung auf einem Trichterbecher aus Bronocice in Polen', *Archäologisches Korrespondenzblatt* 12: 141–44.

Minnis, P. (1985) 'Domesticating people and plants in the Greater Southwest', in R. Ford (ed.) *Prehistoric Food Production in North America*, Ann Arbor: Museum of Anthropology, University of Michigan, Anthropological Papers 75: 309–39.

Minnis, P. (1996) 'Notes on economic uncertainty and human behavior in the prehistoric North American Southwest', in J. A. Tainter and B. B. Tainter (eds) *Evolving Complexity and Environmental Risk in the Prehistoric Southwest*, Reading: Addison-Wesley Publishing Company: 57–78.

Moore, A. M. T. (1982) 'Agricultural origins in the Near East: a model for the 1980s', *World Archaeology* 14: 224–36.

Moore, A. M. T. (1989) 'The transition from foraging to farming in Southwest Asia: present problems and future directions', in D. R. Harris and G. C. Hillman (eds) *Foraging and Farming. The Evolution of Plant Exploitation*, London: Unwin Hyman: 620–31.

Nassaney, M. (1987) 'On the causes and consequences of subsistence intensification in the Mississippi alluvial valley', in W. F. Keegan (ed.) *Emergent Horticultural Economies of the Eastern Woodlands*, Occasional Papers No. 7, Carbondale: Center for Archaeological Investigations, Southern Illinois University: 129–51.

Nichols, D. (1987) 'Risk and agricultural intensification during the Formative period in the northern Basin of Mexico', *American Anthropologist* 89: 596–616.

Peterson, J. T. (1978a) *The Ecology of Social Boundaries*, Urbana: University of Illinois Press.

Peterson, J. T. (1978b) 'Hunter-gatherer/farmer exchange', *American Anthropologist* 80: 335–51.

Price, T. D. and Feinman, G. N. (1993) *Images of the Past*, Mountain View: Mayfield Publishing Company.

Price, T. D. and Gebauer, A. B. (1992) 'The final frontier: foragers to farmers in southern Scandinavia', in A. B. Gebauer and T. D. Price (eds) *Transitions to Agriculture in Prehistory*, Madison: Prehistory Press: 97–116.

Price, T. D. and Gebauer, A. B. (eds) (1995) *Last Hunters, First Farmers. New Perspectives on the Prehistoric Transition to Agriculture*, Santa Fe: School of American Research Press.

Price, T. D., Gebauer, A. B. and Keeley, L. H. (1995) 'The spread of farming into Europe north of the Alps', in T. D. Price and A. B. Gebauer (eds) *Last Hunters, First Farmers. New Perspectives on the Prehistoric Transition to Agriculture*, Santa Fe: School of American Research Press: 95–126.

Richards, P. (1985) *Indigenous Agricultural Revolution. Ecology and Food Production in West Africa*, London: Hutchinson/Boulder: Westview.

Rindos, D. (1984) *The Origins of Agriculture. An Evolutionary Perspective*, Orlando: Academic Press.

Rowley-Conwy, P. (1985) 'The origin of agriculture in Denmark: a review of some theories', *Journal of Danish Archaeology* 4: 188–95.

Runnels, C. and van Andel, Tj. (1988) 'Trade and the origins of agriculture in the Eastern Mediterranean', *Journal of Mediterranean Archaeology* 1: 83–109.

Smith, B. D. (1989) 'Origin of agriculture in eastern North America', *Science* 246: 1566–71.

Smith, B. D. (ed.) (1992) *Rivers of Change. Essays on Early Agriculture in Eastern North America*, Washington, DC: Smithsonian Institution Press.

Smith, B. D. (1995) *The Emergence of Agriculture*, New York: Scientific American Library.

Smith, P. E. L. and Young, T. C. (1972) 'The evolution of early agriculture and culture in Greater Mesopotamia: a trial model', in B. Spooner (ed.) *Population Growth: Anthropological Implications*, Cambridge: MIT Press: 1–59.

Stark, B. (1986) 'Origins of food production in the New World', in D. Meltzer, D. Dowler and J. Sabloff (eds) *American Archaeology Past and Future*, Washington, DC and London: Smithsonian Institution Press: 277–321.

Tainter, J. A. and Tainter, B. B. (eds) (1996) *Evolving Complexity and Environmental Risk in the Prehistoric Southwest*, Reading, Mass.: Addison-Wesley Publishing Company.

van der Leeuw, S. (1989) 'Risk, perception, innovation', in S. van der Leeuw and R. Torrence (eds) *What's New? A Closer Look at the Process of Innovation*, London: Unwin Hyman: 300–29.

Watson, P. J. and Cowan, W. (eds) (1992) *Origins of Agriculture: An International Perspective*, Washington, DC: Smithsonian Institution Press.

Welch, J. R. (1991) 'From horticulture to agriculture in the late prehistory of the Grasshopper region, Arizona', in P. H. Beckett (ed.) *Proceedings of the Fifth Biannual Mogollon Conference*, Las Cruces: Coas Publishing and Research: 75–92.

Whittle, A. (1996) *Europe in the Neolithic: the Creation of New Worlds*, Cambridge: Cambridge University Press.

Williams, R. ([1643]1973) *A Key to the Language of America*, Detroit: Wayne State University (new edition by John J. Teunisson and Evelyn J. Hintz).

Wills, W. H. (1988) 'Early agriculture and sedentism in the American Southwest: evidence and interpretations', *Journal of World Prehistory* 2: 445–88.

Zohary, D. and Hopf, M. (1993) *Domestication of Plants in the Old World. The Origin and*

Spread of Cultivated Plants in West Asia, Europe, and the Nile Valley (2nd edition), Oxford: Clarendon Press.

Zvelebil, M. and Rowley-Conwy, P. (1984) 'The transition to farming in northern Europe: a hunter-gatherer perspective', *Norwegian Archaeological Review* 17 (2): 104–28.

SELECT BIBLIOGRAPHY

The last decade has seen a proliferation of books which discuss the transition from foraging to farming and early agricultural societies. This is probably the ultimate result of the concentration of archaeological field research on this problem in the 1970s and 1980s. For comprehensive overviews of the botanical and zoological basis for early domestication, the basic sources remain Harris and Hillman (1989) and Zohary and Hopf (1993) for plants, and Clutton-Brock (1989) for animals. Harlan's *The Living Fields* (1995) is a memoir of a remarkable botanical career which includes reflections on the current status of the study of agricultural origins. Archaeological anthologies of articles discussing the transition to agriculture include Watson and Cowan (1992), Gebauer and Price (1992) and Price and Gebauer (1995). A highly readable, single-author treatment of agricultural origins is Smith's *The Emergence of Agriculture* (1995). Stark's 1986 article is a classic discussion of the models used to explain agricultural origins and remains widely cited a decade later. Regional studies of early agricultural societies are fairly numerous and include Smith (1992) for the eastern United States, Wills (1988) for the south-western United States, and Bogucki (1988) and Barker (1985) for Europe. An up-to-date synthesis of agricultural origins in Mesoamerica has yet to appear. Discussions of issues such as labour, risk, and uncertainty in early agricultural societies are relatively rare, but examples include Bogucki (1988), Wills (1988), and papers in Tainter and Tainter (1996).

22

THE DEVELOPMENT OF RANK SOCIETIES

Stephen J. Shennan

INTRODUCTION

The idea of the 'development of rank societies' is a problematical and ambiguous one, which the position of this chapter in the *Encyclopedia* highlights: the two previous chapters are defined in terms of types of subsistence economy, while the subsequent one is concerned with a specific form of socio-political organization, the state, which only occurred in the context of certain productive agricultural economies. Rank societies, in so far as the term is meaningful (see below), can be and have been argued to exist in the context of hunter-gatherer economies, of early agriculturalists, and of societies with agricultural modes of existence which lasted for thousands of years.

This chapter will review the concept of rank society and the way it was introduced into archaeological discussion. Various criticisms of the concept, its application, and its archaeological uses will then be examined. Next, a series of case studies of 'rank societies' from different parts of the world will be presented. Finally, some rather different approaches will be suggested which in various respects both build on and depart from the original concept of rank society.

THE CONCEPT OF RANK SOCIETY

The idea of '*rank society*' (Fried 1967) derived from the renewed concern with social evolution which developed in American anthropology in the 1950s and 1960s following the earlier pioneering works of Julian Steward (1955) and Leslie White (1959). These latter authors were reacting against the ethnographic particularism of the Boasian school, itself opposed to the nineteenth-century evolutionism of such authors as Morgan, Tylor and Engels (see Chapters 2 and 12). White proposed a theory of general evolution in terms of which progress could be traced in human societies through time, based on their increasing capacity for energy capture from the environment, which culminated in the emergence of industrial societies. However, energy capture cannot easily be measured, especially for societies which existed in the past, and it was proposed that a suitable proxy measure for its study in the past and the present would be a society's investment in social structure, defined in terms of social differentiation (Sahlins and Service 1960). Societies can be differentiated vertically, in terms of hierarchical levels, and also horizontally, in terms of the division of labour. The categorization of societies in terms of their degree of social differentiation was the basis of the enormously influential evolutionary scheme produced by Service (1962). His categories, from simplest to most complex, were band, tribe, chiefdom and state, with the implication of a general evolutionary progression from one to the next (Fig. 12.2). As we will see, his tribe and chiefdom categories correspond broadly to the idea of 'rank society'.

This latter category was introduced by Fried in reaction to Service and differs in certain important respects. First, Fried's concern was not with social *differentiation* but with mechanisms of social *integration* – how societies were held together. He, too, proposed a fourfold categorization with evolutionary implications: egalitarian society, rank society, stratified society, and the state. He specifically eschewed Service's 'tribe' category, since he argued that tribes as units were the result of the impact of colonial conquest on groups whose membership and inter-connections had previously been much more fluid. In this chapter we are concerned with Service's 'tribe' and 'chiefdom' categories and with Fried's 'rank society' and, to a lesser extent, 'stratified society'.

Service (1962) saw his tribal level as more complex than the band, in that tribes possessed new forms of integration and were internally more diverse. However, the two were seen as similar in that they were egalitarian and did not have distinct organizations of political control or economic or religious specialization. Indeed, the basic residential units of tribal society were seen as alike – largely self-sufficient economically and with a great deal of autonomy; in fact, still characterized by what Durkheim (1933) called *mechanical solidarity* – the relatively limited solidarity arising from the fact that people in similar situations tend to have similar interests.

In this and many other respects, tribes contrasted with chiefdoms in Service's scheme, the latter defined as 'redistributional societies with a central agency of coordination' (Service 1962: 144). The basis of the chiefdom was ecological, in that it was argued that chiefly territories were ecologically diverse so that different parts were suitable for producing different crops. In order for the whole population to acquire an adequate supply of the various resources, it was necessary for resources from each of the zones to go to the central agency, the chief, and then be redistributed to those areas which lacked that particular resource. Chiefdoms were thus characterized by *organic solidarity*, involving specialization and the mutual dependence of unlike parts, and the chiefs were the managers of the system. In terms of Service's scheme, the great contrast, and in effect the great transition in human history, was that between bands and tribes on the one hand and chiefdoms and states on the other, because it involved the loss of local autonomy.

In Fried's scheme the category of 'simple egalitarian societies' corresponded to Service's 'bands', whilst 'rank societies', the next step up from egalitarian societies, were those 'in which positions of valued status are somehow limited, so that not all those of sufficient talent to occupy such statuses actually achieve them' (1967: 109); in other words, apart from bands, no societies are egalitarian. Rank societies were conceived to have a number of specific characteristics. They tended to have larger and denser populations and were usually agriculturally based. There was little in the way of specialized craftsmanship, and age and sex were the bases of the division of labour. Of particular importance in these societies was the emergence of formal descent principles, defined in terms of kinship relations and affecting people's rights to resources. Genealogy became important and the potential existed (and was frequently realized) for a hierarchical arrangement of kin to develop in terms, for example, of genealogical proximity to a particular ancestor. Rank societies, in Fried's scheme, are characterized by an ideology of kinship, whereas egalitarian or band societies have an ideology of co-residence.

In the economic sphere, the major process of integration was redistribution, as with Service's chiefdom category, but conceived on a smaller scale in that there could be village redistributors, one of whose key roles was the giving of feasts through which prestige was acquired. Such feast-giving depended on mobilizing the resources of the community and involved the redistributor in encouraging local production for such purposes. There were, however, few effective sanctions to maintain the authority of such leaders. On the one hand, it depended on success in feasting and other communal activities; on the other, it was associated with ritual leadership and the usually pre-eminent position of the leader in the kinship system as the living person nearest to the ancestors, in turn connected with the gods. However, Fried concluded, the power of groups or individuals of higher rank was distinctly limited, in that local communities were economically autonomous: the differences between egalitarian and rank societies were slight, since the new institutions impinged in only a minor way on everyday life. It was only at the 'stratified society' stage that economic dependence of the general population on the élite arose, associated with a differential distribution of the basic resources to sustain life, and for Fried this was a transitional stage on the way to the state. However, within his scheme there was potential for varying degrees of ranking within the same broad social blueprint, without the radical disjuncture present in Service's scheme, which contrasted bands and tribes with chiefdoms and states. Fried's view on this matter is paralleled by that of Sahlins (1968), whose study of what he called *tribal societies* suggested that these covered a range with chiefdoms at one end and segmentary tribes at the other, and that particular societies could oscillate through time between more and less ranked states.

RANK SOCIETIES AND CHIEFDOMS IN ARCHAEOLOGY

These neo-evolutionary ideas were introduced to archaeology in the late 1960s and early 1970s as part of the emergence of the 'New Archaeology' (see Chapter 2). Archaeology was rejecting its normative and culture-historical past in favour of new goals, and in particular an anthropological orientation towards the study of past societies. There were very few models available for such studies, especially those not concerned with early states and civilizations, for which, in any event, written sources of some sort were often available. Conventional history was largely concerned with the analysis of particular sequences of events over short periods, while the majority of anthropology was devoted to the examination of societies in the present. Neither was appropriate as a basis for social archaeology, whereas the neo-evolutionary framework of Service, Sahlins and Fried provided exactly what was felt to be wanted: a broad-scale view of human societies within an evolutionary framework. The fact that the framework was largely based on the comparative study of present or recently existing societies was an asset, because it offered an account of the functional principles of those societies to which archaeological evidence could be related. For those areas of social and economic life where archaeological evidence was unavailable, the detail could be filled in by a straightforward inferential process, because within a given stage there were relatively fixed patterns of social and economic relations: for example, if settlement pattern studies pointed to the existence of a centre in a region in a particular period, then redistribution could be assumed to be the mode of exchange. Inferences about past societies, especially prehistoric ones, had previously been regarded as beyond the grasp of archaeologists using archaeological evidence alone, but now a set of ideas was available which made them possible. Two types of archaeological project were particularly appropriate for realizing the new aims: settlement pattern studies based on archaeological survey, which could identify centres and their dependent sites; and cemetery analyses, since the differences between graves in terms of their monumentality or the quality of their grave-goods could apparently provide direct information on the relative social ranking of their occupants.

Two studies may be mentioned here as characteristic. Renfrew (1973) examined the distribution and scale of neolithic (*c.* 4000–2000 BC) monuments in the Wessex area of southern England and argued that the development of a series of chiefdoms could be traced over the course of this period, with the monuments, which represented large investments of labour, representing the chiefly centres. In another study Peebles (1971) analysed the burials from Moundville and surrounding sites belonging to the Mississippian of the south-eastern United States (*c*. AD 1000–1500) and showed that there were marked differentials between them. In particular, the richest and most distinctive grave-goods were restricted to the Moundville ceremonial centre itself and to specific locations within it, where they made up about 5 per cent of the population in the Moundville II phase (Peebles 1987). On the basis of this and other evidence, he postulated that Moundville was an élite centre, dominating the surrounding area.

As we shall see below (pp. 879–85, 891–94), where they are presented at greater length, both these studies have in many respects stood the test of time, but the neo-evolutionary ideas which provided the background for them have been much criticized and it is to these criticisms that we must now turn.

CRITIQUE OF THE CONCEPTS OF 'CHIEFDOM' AND 'RANK SOCIETY'

One of the first issues to be subject to critical examination was the role of the chief or leader as redistributor. Earle (1977) examined the historic organization of Hawaii, where chiefdoms existed and where there was a great deal of ecological diversity. He showed that chiefs did not play the role of redistributor, despite the apparently ideal circumstances. On the contrary, local communities ensured their own subsistence by various means and the chiefs levied tribute from them to finance their own activities. The role of the chief, not merely as a redistributor but as a beneficial manager ensuring the evolutionary advance of his community, was called into question. The same argument was made on general grounds from a Marxist perspective (e.g. Gilman 1981): far from being beneficial, chiefs were exploiters of their societies, exercising their desire for power in circumstances where local populations could not escape them, for example where people were tied to their land as a result of such major investments in subsistence resources as irrigated or cleared fields.

Today, definitions of the term 'chiefdom' are more generalized. Earle (1997) defines a chiefdom as:

> a regional polity with institutional governance and some social stratification organizing a population of a few thousand to tens of thousands of people. Chiefdoms are intermediate-level polities, bridging the evolutionary gap between small, village-based polities and large, bureaucratic states . . . Characteristically the organization at this scale requires political hierarchy or an overlapping series of hierarchies for coordination and decision-making; the advantages gained by a few within such a hierarchy result in a measure of social stratification.

> (Earle 1997: 14)

874

Other definitions take a rather different perspective. Feinman (1991: 230) follows Wright in seeing them as forms of organization in which social control activities are 'externally specialized vis-a-vis other activities, but not internally specialized in terms of different aspects of the control process' (Wright 1984: 52). In other words, there will be 'a supra-household decision-making structure or relatively permanent positions of leadership, but not the marked internal differentiation of such structures' (Feinman 1991: 230).

Whereas Earle still sees the chiefdom as a useful, meaningful, and relevant category for characterizing societies, the proponents of Wright's view see it as referring solely to a political form and not to a type of society, since societies possessing this form of political organization can be in other respects enormously diverse (Feinman 1991: 230). From this perspective the term 'chiefdom' may be a useful generalized label but offers little in the way of analytical usefulness (Drennan and Uribe 1987). In short, while there is still general agreement that the term usefully refers to societies which are not states but show some degree of centralized organization, it goes little further than that.

The same may be said for the term 'rank society', which has likewise been largely drained of its specific content and in particular has been subjected to detailed criticism by Khazanov (1985). As he points out, where leadership is present, which is more or less universally, 'there always exist formal or informal rules and selective criteria, regulating access to leadership and thus restricting the number of leading positions . . . The principle of limitation of leading positions is inseparable from the very essence of leadership and its functions' (1985: 83), even in egalitarian societies. Indeed, one could take Fried's characterization of a rank society as 'one in which positions of valued status are somehow limited so that not all those of sufficient talent to occupy such statuses actually achieve them' (1967: 109), and turn it around. In societies where statuses are achieved, such as the Big Man societies of Papua New Guinea, which Fried and others regard as rank societies, the process of social competition is such that there are indeed as many positions of valued status as persons capable of filling them (Khazanov 1985: 85). If one takes Fried's criteria seriously, Khazanov concludes (1985: 89), 'essentially, a limited number of societies, mostly the Polynesian ones, may be referred to as ranked on the basis of the criteria and characteristics suggested by Fried'. In fact, this is precisely because Fried's rank society is an attempt to universalize a local Polynesian phenomenon, the conical clan, 'a descent group in which all subgroups (lineages) and members are ranked by criteria of genealogical priority or proximity to the common ancestor' (Khazanov 1985: 90).

In short, if we wish to continue using and working with the concept of rank society, we have to use it in a generalized way as simply indicating societies in which there are status and power differentials but social stratification is not marked and the state form of organization is not present. This is clearly pretty vague, and indeed even more so than the chiefdom, which at least has the notion of a centre. In particular, the question arises whether, in these terms, there have ever been any societies which were not rank societies.

THE POSITION OF RANK SOCIETIES AND CHIEFDOMS IN EVOLUTIONARY SEQUENCES

In what we may call the traditional neo-evolutionary view, these societies had precursors in the band (Service) and egalitarian society (Fried) categories. The basis for these categories were such hunter-gatherer groups as the Shoshone of the Great Basin in the western deserts of North America and the !Kung/San groups of southern Africa. The latter provided the classical model of what an original hunter-gatherer band should look like, with their small-scale egalitarian form of organization. Indeed, in neo-evolutionary terms, if the San hadn't existed it would have been necessary to invent them, because the evolutionary scheme, like its nineteenth-century predecessors, presupposed an initial undifferentiated form of organization out of which more complex forms could then develop. It now turns out, however, that the San were in a sense invented, at least as representatives of some original pre-Fall state of human society. Work has shown that they have a complex history of interaction with neighbouring groups, including episodes of pastoralist activity (see, for example: Kent 1993; Shott 1992). More generally, it has become clear that the hunter-gatherer societies available for study by ethnographers, and which have provided the basis for archaeological models, are largely marginal remnants pushed into harsh and remote corners of the world; there is no reason to believe that they provide valid models for the hunter-gatherers of the past. This belief has been strengthened by the increasing archaeological evidence for 'complex hunter-gatherers' (Brown and Price 1985), who do not appear to fit the standard egalitarian band model (see the final case study, pp. 902–3).

The basis for believing that many hunter-gatherers, as opposed to a few exceptional groups like those on the north-west coast of North America, were indeed non-egalitarian has been clarified by an important discussion on the difference between *delayed-return* and *immediate-return* systems of subsistence among hunter-gatherers (Woodburn 1980). In immediate-return systems, food is consumed by members of a group as soon as it is obtained, on a day-to-day basis. Delayed-return systems involve investment in such facilities as traps or fish weirs, or the need for storage, often associated with seasonal climates. Although they involve the use of wild resources, in the fact that returns are delayed such systems are comparable to agricultural ones, where crops need to be grown and animals reared. There is an initial investment which is only repaid later; thus groups practising such systems will have a greater commitment to staying together. The contrast, then, is not between hunting/gathering and agriculture, but between immediate and delayed return. Delayed-return systems involve defining rights and obligations between categories of people; inequality between households in terms of power, wealth and status is often present (Brunton 1989). In any event, as Ingold has pointed out, the number of cases of immediate-return egalitarian societies 'is so few, and their existence so hedged round by special circumstances, that doubts must inevitably arise as to the significance of these societies as constituting the supposed baseline of social evolution' (Ingold 1983: 554, quoted in Brunton 1989).

If we accept this line of argument, we may suggest that human societies have always been characterized by varying degrees of inequality and social differentiation (*contra* Erdal and Whiten 1994). The problem then becomes not one of explaining the origin of rank societies, but accounting for their many and varied forms in different places over the course of human history.

However, though we can cast doubt on the idea that human societies evolved from some primeval egalitarianism, we can raise similar concerns about the extent to which, at the other end of the scale, chiefdoms must be precursors of states, as the standard neo-evolutionary schemes imply. Within the context of such schemes, 'something must precede states that is not even crypto-egalitarian, yet is not exactly state-like, and it requires a name' (Yoffee 1993) – hence the chiefdom. However, some time ago Sanders and Webster (1978) argued that chiefdoms were an alternative to state development and were typical of subsistence environments of low risk and low diversity. In a similar vein, it has recently been argued for the specific case of Mesopotamia that early states developed not out of chiefdoms but as a result of the emergence of socially differentiated households (Maisels 1987; Yoffee 1993). The basis of the argument is that chiefdoms and states are structurally incompatible with one another, since the former are organized in terms of kinship and lineages, while the key point about the Mesopotamian city-states was that their forms of organization subverted kinship links.

We are left with an enormously diverse range of societies which were not states and were not egalitarian, many of which seem to have remained in this situation for thousands of years – or rather, when specific societies disappeared, they were replaced by others with similar forms of life and organization. Within these societies, we may distinguish those characterized by some degree of centralization from those which were not, but we should not think of the distinction as a major qualitative break, nor should we imagine that all centralized societies conformed to our idea of the chiefdom (see pp. 871–72), although some undoubtedly did.

EXPLANATIONS OF CHANGE IN RANK SOCIETIES

Most studies of change in rank societies have been concerned with how they emerged from egalitarianism or developed into states, a perspective we have already criticized. Although a great variety of explanations emphasizing different factors have been employed in the explanation of change, especially change in the direction of 'more complex' forms of society, undoubtedly the most important group has been social circumscription models (Carneiro 1970). Societies are constrained to change their way of life and form of organization as a result of the appearance of new pressures, whether internally generated or from outside, which they cannot escape. By far the most important cause cited for the growth of circumscription has been population pressure, whether in the form of the expansion of neighbouring groups, leading to competition for resources and ultimately warfare, or internally generated population growth leading to subsistence degeneration and the emergence of new managerial requirements if society is to survive. These have been seen by their proponents as universal models, relevant to increased ranking at one end of the scale and the emergence of the state at the other (Johnson and Earle 1987).

Although population pressure may be a relevant factor in certain circumstances, it is increasingly clear that relationships between this and other factors are complex and variable, especially within the range of societies being considered in this chapter. In an ethnographically based study of some non-state American societies, Feinman and Neitzel (1984: 77–78) found that total population, population of the largest settlement, number of status markers, number of functions of leaders, and number of administrative levels failed to form the closely related group of traits that one might have anticipated for the chiefdom category, nor could they find an association between their status, leadership and administrative variables for this group of non-state societies.

Feinman and Neitzel's dataset has been reanalysed by Upham (1987) to investigate further aspects of the relationship between population and social organization in non-state societies. Of particular interest is his examination of population thresholds. At a global level there are clearly relationships between the population sizes and densities of societies and aspects of their organization: when one is contrasting small hunter-gatherer groups with modern urban societies this is hardly surprising. Much more interesting is the population scale at which organizational distinctions appear to be relevant. Such aspects of hierarchy and complex organization as the control of storage, the presence of special burials, the use of forms of obeisance, the existence of special food types, and the presence of a number of administrative levels in the society, all had a statistically higher probability of occurrence in societies with total regional populations larger than c. 10,500. In fact, the threshold varied for different attributes: for special burials it was 9,200, while for special food and control of storage it was 14,000. It is thus apparent that it is only at a relatively large scale that issues of population size become relevant. Furthermore, the results say nothing about the role of population size in the appearance of these phenomena: they merely indicate that societies with populations above the threshold are more likely to possess those attributes.

A great variety of other factors has also been advanced in studies of the development of ranking and inequality and some of them will be seen in the case studies below. However, it is clear from the earlier part of this chapter that explaining the development of ranking, complexity, or stratification is not, as such, the issue. Primeval egalitarianism cannot be assumed as the default state of human society, nor population as the motor which drove it away from that state. What we have is an enormous range of variation which cannot be placed straightforwardly in an evolutionary line even if that were desirable.

CASE STUDIES OF THE EMERGENCE OF CHIEFDOMS

The vast majority of the concrete work which has been carried out subscribes to some version of the evolutionary perspective. Nevertheless, much of it is extremely interesting in its demonstration of what may be achieved using archaeological evidence. Its strength, however, lies in its documentation of archaeological sequences, rather than in the explanations offered for them. Three case studies are presented and discussed below.

Neolithic and bronze age Wessex

In 1973 Renfrew postulated the evolution of chiefdoms in Wessex during the Neolithic, on the basis of the labour investment in monuments: he suggested that the chiefdoms continued into the Bronze Age but became different in nature since they were now evidenced by burial mounds with rich grave-goods (Renfrew 1973, 1974). His ideas have been developed and to some extent modified, especially by Bradley (1984, 1991). The account which follows is based particularly on Earle (1991).

During the period 4000–3000 BC, settlements were distinctly ephemeral and the major demands on labour were made by funerary monuments – long mounds (Bradley 1991). These monuments, present from the beginning of the sequence, already point to at least some symbolic differentiation among the population, in that the number of human remains found in the burials is too small to account for the whole of the local population – it seems likely that successive phases of the burial ritual were increasingly selective (Bradley 1991: 50). In other words, even at the beginning of the sequence we are dealing with societies where symbolic distinctions were already in existence between different elements of the local population.

879

During the course of this period, towards *c.* 3500 BC a series of 8–10 'causewayed enclosures' were also constructed in Wessex. These are characterized by 1–3 concentric ditches and banks enclosing areas of 1.5–7.7 ha. A number of activities seem to have gone on at these sites, including feasting, exchange, and the exposure of the dead; they may have been used for seasonal aggregations (Bradley 1991: 50). Both the funerary monuments and the enclosures were apparently constructed in segments, possibly by different work parties, and this may reflect the participation of separate communities in their construction. The function of the causewayed enclosures seems to have changed through time: some became residential and defensive in nature and there is evidence that some of these were attacked and destroyed. Bradley (1991: 50) draws attention to the marginal position of the enclosures in relation to settled areas and to the fact that they were often built in woodland to argue that they are unlikely to have been the centres of social territories, but Earle takes the two-tiered settlement pattern implied by at least the later phases of the enclosures as evidence for a political arrangement of simple chiefdoms. On the basis of the distribution of the enclosures and the long barrow funerary monuments, Earle postulates the existence of four distinct polities believed to represent chiefdoms, made up of local groups which worked together to construct larger monuments, together with a number of smaller less centralized groups.

In the subsequent later neolithic phase (3000–2200 BC), settlements continue to be ephemeral although later neolithic lithic scatters are denser and more extensive than earlier periods, perhaps suggesting reduced mobility, and the Wessex landscape comes to be dominated by a different kind of monument: the henges. These are circular banked enclosures with a ditch typically inside the bank, varying very considerably in size (0.1–12.5 ha) as well as in elaboration. Like the causewayed enclosures which preceded them, the larger ones required enormous numbers of man-hours for their construction, but Bradley (1991: 53) suggests that this was now organized on a different and more centralized basis, as there is no longer any indication of the 'segmentary' construction seen in the causewayed enclosures. The largest henges are postulated to have been the centres of individual polities (Fig. 22.1), with the smaller ones serving more local populations.

Although the henges continued to be used and modified for a considerable period of time, from around 2200 BC round burial mounds began to be constructed, eventually over 8,000 altogether. These are often complex monuments used for a series of burials and enlarged over time, but they are much smaller in scale than the henges and could have been constructed by much smaller-scale groups. What distinguishes at least some of them is the deposition of grave-goods, such as copper, gold and amber items, which must have been obtained by long-distance exchange, a phenomenon which had begun in the Later Neolithic. The small scale of the burial mounds might be taken as an indicator of a change to a more localized form of

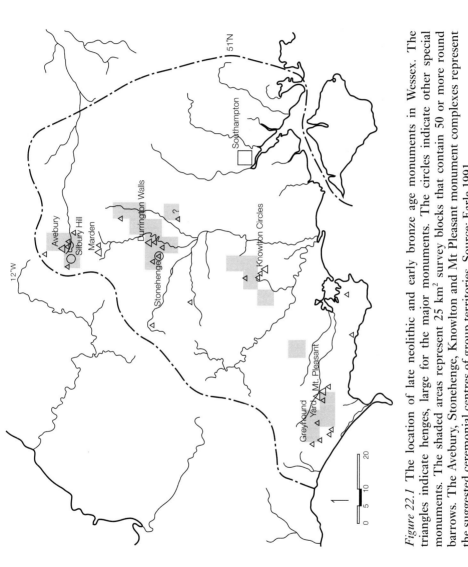

Figure 22.1 The location of late neolithic and early bronze age monuments in Wessex. The triangles indicate henges, large for the major monuments. The circles indicate other special monuments. The shaded areas represent 25 km² survey blocks that contain 50 or more round barrows. The Avebury, Stonehenge, Knowlton and Mt Pleasant monument complexes represent the suggested ceremonial centres of group territories. Source: Earle 1991.

organization; however, although they are widely scattered across the landscape, the barrows are concentrated around the four pre-existing major henge monuments (Figs 22.1, 22.2), and the fact that most of the more exotic grave-goods also tend to be in burials within the major concentrations suggests that the region continued to be divided into four major political units centred in the area of the monuments.

Around 1400 BC this long-lasting pattern changed. Whereas previously settlements had been ephemeral and difficult to detect archaeologically, the Wessex landscape now came to be characterized by new large-scale field systems and associated small settlement enclosures, indicating the first appearance of mixed arable subsistence farming. As Earle says (1991: 93), the overall impression is that, in contrast with the preceding periods, the landscape was divided into many small political units. The subsequent Early Iron Age was characterized by the appearance of hill-forts, defended enclosures often with multiple banks and ditches, but the distances separating even the larger ones are small, averaging *c.* 6.5 km, emphasizing this small-scale pattern. Earle (1991: 94) suggests that the chiefdoms of the Early Bronze Age had fragmented and that political units remained small because their foundation was now the control of subsistence resources, seen in the field systems and centralized storage facilities, whereas previously it had been based on the control of people and wealth.

Suggesting explanations for the pattern of change observed is very problematical. The earlier neolithic causewayed enclosures may have been the centres at which local groups who recognized themselves as in some way part of a single larger entity came together for occasional ceremonies. What is not at all clear is how this system came to be transformed into that characterized by the henges. In this case there are much stronger grounds than for the earlier neolithic monuments to think in terms of a regionally centralized form of organization focused on people with a distinctive social status and special powers. It is noteworthy that, although one can apparently detect the same four regional units as in the Earlier Neolithic, the 'centres' are now more central and in a better position to have the kind of role they are supposed to have in centralized organizations. Furthermore, as Earle (1991: 96) says, the major henge monuments with their enormous external banks and internal ditches may well represent sacred spaces for ceremonies, involving the separation of the officiants from the rest of the population. Their legitimacy was supported by their identification with universal cosmological forces, exemplified by the celestial orientation of some of the monuments, contrasting with the emphasis on ancestors in the Earlier Neolithic. However, rather than suggesting that the monuments and their rituals simply legitimized the power of an élite group, it is at least as plausible to suggest that it was the process of building the monuments and being associated with the rituals within them which actually created the central power and the polity around it, as a newly imagined community perhaps based on a longer-standing feeling of common identity (Kertzer 1988).

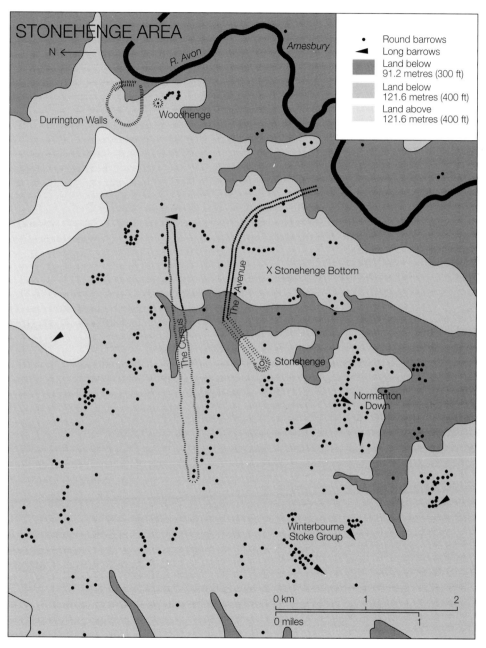

Figure 22.2 The Stonehenge area and its monuments. Source: D. V. Clarke (1985) *Symbols of Power*, Edinburgh: HMSO.

The extent of that power initially and the spheres in which it was operative are more or less impossible to assess, although clearly it involved enough control for the labour to be organized for the construction of the monuments in what may have been a process of competitive emulation between different groups. Bloch (1977) has sketched out the kind of process which may be relevant to the ensuing institutionalization of power by its holders:

> They do this by creating an office of which they are the legitimate holders, but which has reality beyond them. This is done by gradual ritualization of the power-holder's communication with the rest of the world and especially his inferiors. As this ritualization process proceeds, communication loses the appearance of a creation on the part of the speaker and appears like repeats of set roles specified by the office which appears to hold him. Reality is thus reversed and the creation of the power-holder appears to create him.
>
> (Bloch 1977: 330–31)

However, neither the power-holders themselves nor the rest of the population can completely see through this situation: both subscribe to some degree to the values being promulgated. The process is one of 'negotiation' in day-to-day and year-to-year practice. One relevant analogy may be with aspects of the caste system, in which high ritual status is associated with greater power and influence, but not necessarily wealth, and in which part of the political process in the contesting of caste positions and rights centres on such issues as what clothes people are entitled to wear (Kertzer 1988: 110–13). Such processes, of course, will be centred on the symbolic resources existing at the time in that particular place.

In other parts of Britain henges were less important, and during the period of henge construction there is increasing evidence of long-distance exchange and the deposition of burials with exotic goods. From *c*. 2200 BC onwards these connections come to be extended to the European mainland. In Wessex, however, these developments were slow to penetrate, although when they eventually did the burials of the region represent a concentration of exotic materials not matched elsewhere in Britain. This is no doubt a reflection of the special nature of the local hierarchies, who on the one hand may have been able to call on greater wealth, for example in the form of animals, from surrounding populations, and on the other may have exchanged esoteric knowledge for foreign valuables (cf. Harrison 1993).

The end of this system may have come about because of the strain it imposed on the landscape. Although there is little evidence of agricultural intensification during the Early Bronze Age, it is clear that there was an expansion of the settled area onto marginal soils, which came under pressure just as the long-occupied areas started showing signs of soil erosion (Bradley 1991: 55). The consequent decline in available resources, which may have coincided with or been the cause of loss of control of long-distance exchanges, led to the decline of the system. As we have seen, it was replaced by one in which political units were much smaller in scale, subsistence was centred on fixed mixed agriculture, and social organization was based on the control of the resources for this, including the ownership of arable land.

Polynesia

It was the ethnography of Polynesia which provided much of the basis for the construction of the neo-evolutionary typologies discussed above. However, in recent years there have been enormous advances in the archaeology of Polynesia which have led to the construction of an overarching model of diachronic change in Polynesian society (Kirch 1984).

At the time of European contact, different parts of Polynesia had widely divergent forms of society. Kirch has developed a phylogenetic model of Polynesia, in which the colonization of the Pacific is associated with a branching evolution of social forms from an original common ancestral form which he calls Ancient Polynesian Society. The origins of this lie in the so-called Lapita cultural complex, which had spread eastwards to the Fiji–Tonga–Samoa area by *c*. 1500 BC. Its reconstruction is based on both archaeology and linguistics. Central to this original social form was the conical clan (see p. 875), in which rank was determined on the basis of proximity to a founding ancestor. The ranking system and associated kinship terminology made an important distinction between senior and junior individuals, although initially there were no elaborate material or behavioural distinctions associated with rank differentials. These societies had as their titular heads hereditary chiefs, belonging to the senior line of the conical clan, who formed a critical link in the chain from the gods to the earth and thus occupied the central role in rituals of production. This role was of key importance in the subsequent development of Polynesian societies. In Kirch's model these basic structural elements were carried with them by all the colonizing groups as they moved out into the Pacific, and the key to understanding what went on is the interaction between the structural elements which the people brought with them and the conditions on the new islands which they colonized. However, more recently it has been argued that Kirch did not give sufficient attention to the role of continued interaction between islands, subsequent to their initial colonization (Terrell *et al.* 1997).

In all the islands which were successfully colonized, population grew rapidly, leading to densely settled societies in which competition for land and other resources was pervasive. The high level of resource exploitation had a serious impact on local ecosystems. The result was the development of intensive forms of production, including irrigation. However, a further factor leading to intensification was the demands of the chiefs on their populations; the development of such mechanisms as irrigation systems provided them with a further source of control. Warfare also played an important role in the transformations which Ancient

Polynesian Society underwent, and not solely because of local demographic or ecological conditions: it was both a means of preserving the divine power and status of chiefs and an opportunity for rivals to usurp that status and achieve positions to which they were not entitled on hereditary grounds. Indeed, in some places the basis of political power underwent a transformation from one based on descent to one based on the ability to apply coercive force, with repercussions for economic organization as well as religion.

One Polynesian trajectory is represented by Easter Island, which was reached in the first half of the first millennium AD. The initial colonists brought with them the concept of *ahu* or temple, which was then locally developed. By AD 1000 many such monuments, including the famous statues, were being constructed (Fig. 22.3). It is generally agreed that the *ahus* were constructed and used by ancestor-based kin groups. Examination of the stone quarries suggests the activity of many groups working independently of one another. Subsistence was based on intensive dry-field agriculture, but fishing was also important. During this period a developed form of the Ancestral Polynesian lineage system characterized the island, in which the direct descendants of the original founding chief had high rank and provided a paramount chief whose power was more ritual than secular.

However, it appears that by *c.* AD 1300 Easter Island was chronically over-populated and environmental degradation was setting in as a consequence. The result was endemic warfare and social disintegration. Stronger groups seized the land and enslaved the populations of weaker ones. Archaeologically, the developments are indicated by the appearance of huge numbers of flaked obsidian spear-heads, the end of *ahu* construction, and the deliberate destruction of the *ahu* and their statues; and by settlement pattern changes, especially the occupation of defensible caves. Power was taken over by warriors and the warring groups organized themselves into two loose opposing coalitions. This was the state of Easter Island when it was first discovered by Europeans.

In this case, then, there was no trend towards increasing hierarchization or organizational complexity, but rather one towards devolution and destruction: population increase and pressure on resources do not always call forth the organizational innovations which were believed to be associated with them in the traditional evolutionary models.

A rather different pattern is visible in the Marquesas Islands (Kirch 1991). Archaeological evidence suggests that population remained fairly low until *c.* AD 1100, when a population upswing began, seen in greatly increased numbers of sites and the appearance of new forms of site, including fortifications. By AD 1400 population had outstripped resources. Resource degradation can be clearly seen in the archaeological record, including the erosion of arable land and the depletion of wild foods, including the extinction of a number of bird species, leading to an intensification of breadfruit cultivation and increased pig husbandry and pit storage, whilst human flesh may also have become a significant part of the diet. There were also changes in monumental architecture and settlement patterns, including large-scale labour investment in the *tohua* ceremonial centres, and domestic architecture became more elaborate and a basis for prestige distinctions. After AD 1400 there was a rapid increase in the number of *me'ae* temple structures. In the historic period these were inhabited by powerful ritual specialists, again a development of an original Ancestral Polynesian concept, and the increase in the number of *me'ae* structures may be an index of their growth in power and prestige. At the same time there was a general population shift indicative of pervasive warfare: whereas earlier the people had lived in small hamlets scattered along the coast, during the population increase phase between AD 1100 and 1400 and afterwards the population moved to the inland valleys, to situations which were more readily defensible and which were often further strengthened by means of fortifications.

These changes were not, in Kirch's model, *determined* by the ecological degradation and population increase which occurred. Rather, these were forces affecting the evolution of the Polynesian socio-political organization of the islands' inhabitants. In this case the pressures made it possible for rivals to usurp the position and roles of the traditional chiefs, rather than enabling the latter to strengthen their power. Shaman priests, who achieved rather than inherited their position, were able to use ecological crises to suggest that the traditional chief's inherited sacred power was no longer effective (Kirch 1991: 141), while competition for resources enabled warriors to achieve greater secular power (Fig. 22.4).

These trends developed still further in the subsequent Classic period after AD 1400, leading to the situation found at first European contact. Production and storage increased, and because the storage facilities were controlled by the élites, they were increasingly used for their own purposes. Prestige rivalry and competition increased at two levels: inter-tribal competition for scarce resources; and within-group competition between the traditional chiefs, shaman priests, and warriors for control over the group's resources.

Unlike some of the other Polynesian islands, such as Hawaii, the societies of the Marquesas did not approach early states in their complexity or population. Rather, despite their similar social, economic, and cultural starting points, the process of competition tended to destroy its own conditions of existence through social violence and the destruction of the means of production (Kirch 1991: 143). Here again, 'the evolution of chiefship did not proceed towards increased and encompassing hierarchy' (Kirch 1991: 143).

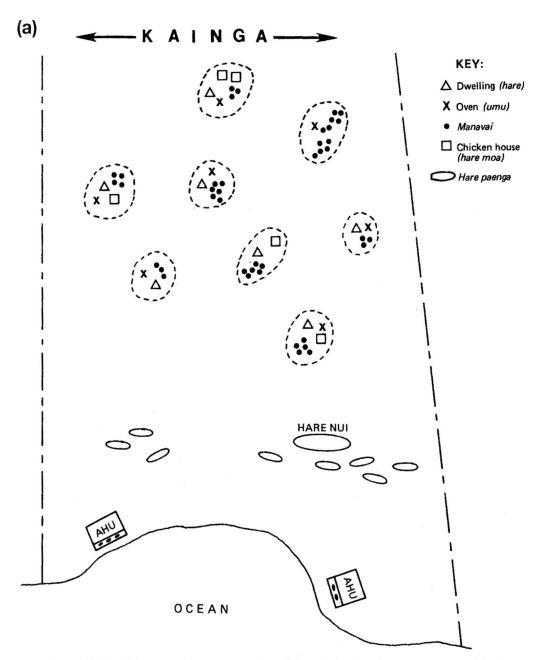

Figure 22.3 (a) Diagrammatic representation of Easter Island settlement patterns, with *ahu* (temples) and residences of high-ranking households near the coast, dispersed commoner households inland. (b) Plan and elevation of a typical Easter Island *ahu* or temple. Source: Kirch 1984, figs 91 and 90.

(b)

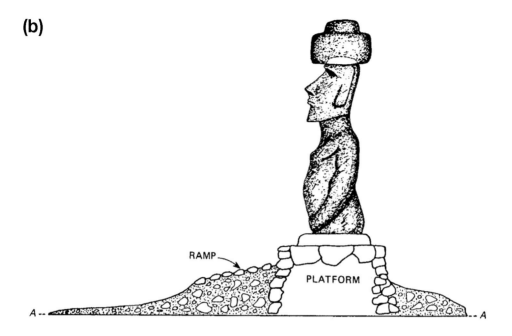

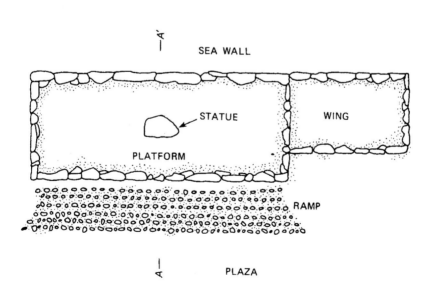

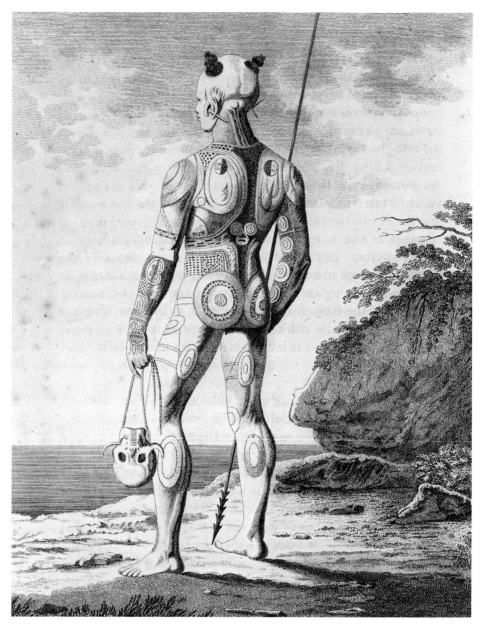

Figure 22.4 A Marquesan warrior with trophy skull, as sketched during the voyage of Krusenstern in 1803. Source: Bishop Museum, Hawaii.

Moundville and the Mississippian

Unlike the Polynesian examples, where we have evidence from linguistics, genealogies, and ethnohistory as well as archaeology, our knowledge of the chiefdoms of the south-eastern United States *c.* AD 900–1500 is based entirely on archaeological evidence. This case study focuses on the site of Moundville and its region in the Black Warrior Valley in Alabama (Peebles 1987; Steponaitis 1991; Fig. 22.5).

At the beginning of the sequence, *c.* AD 900, there is a settlement pattern of small villages with estimated populations of 50–100 people, as well as much smaller, possibly seasonal, occupation sites. Despite variation in village sizes, there is no evidence for any social differentiation between them, in that no sites are known to possess mounds or elaborate burials. Steponaitis (1991: 97) postulates a situation characterized by autonomous villages and a relatively egalitarian society. Around AD 1050 there were major changes in this pattern. Single mounds were built at four of

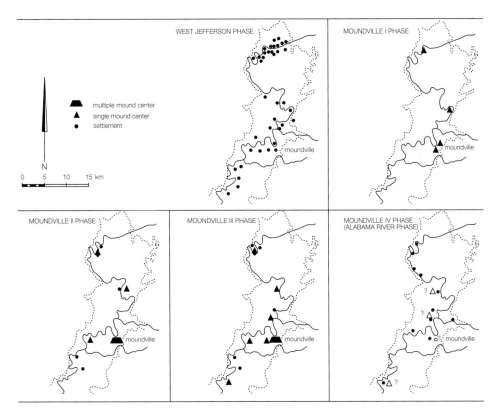

Figure 22.5 Major settlements in the Black Warrior river valley AD 900–1600. Source: Peebles 1987.

891

the previous villages and some of these had nearby cemeteries which included elaborate burials containing exotic grave-goods. Mound construction coincided with a change in settlement pattern, in which the previously relatively nucleated population spread out across the landscape; the mound sites are assumed to have been centres for the dispersed population. At this point there appears to have been no difference between Moundville and any of the other centres in terms of their social or political standing. However, the area around it seems to have had an unusually high population density, despite the fact that it had no obvious advantages in terms of subsistence resources.

When Moundville became the dominant political centre around AD 1200–1250, a very extensive ceremonial area was laid out and an extensive programme of mound construction begun which lasted until *c.* AD 1500. Other centres continued to exist but orientated towards supporting Moundville. The centres with the largest mounds are those furthest from Moundville, where more labour was available for local use and Moundville's control was weaker. Development as a ceremonial centre led to a drop in the local population at Moundville. Presumably residence there became more exclusive and was restricted to members of the local élite and their retainers. It has been argued that this group was supported by tribute, seen, for example, in the differential distribution of deer body parts in élite versus non-élite rubbish deposits (Steponaitis 1991: 200). But although the population *living* at Moundville decreased, it is clear that it was a burial centre for a much wider area, a point which clearly emphasizes its ritual role. Differentiation in the burials suggests very marked social distinctions, with a small group of burials, about 5 per cent of the population, accompanied by very elaborate grave-goods and interred in or near the mounds. These individuals also seem to have had a superior diet and health, including a lesser likelihood of injuries.

Around AD 1500 the polity centred on Moundville began to collapse: there were fewer burials, whilst burial and further mound-building began at outlying centres. Shortly afterwards all the centres, including Moundville, fell out of use, the population once more became aggregated into large villages, indications of social differentiation except in terms of age disappeared from the burials, and the health of the population deteriorated. A century later the area had been largely abandoned (Steponaitis 1991: 202–3).

Subsistence developments may have been some sort of precondition for this dramatic pattern of rise and collapse. Around AD 900 subsistence was based on a mixture of wild and cultivated resources and maize represented less than one per cent of the diet, but around AD 1000 there was a rapid increase in maize production, which came to represent half the diet. Craft activity also changed over the period: between AD 900 and 1050 the manufacture of shell beads occurred in every village, whereas after that date it declined and the manufacture of items from exotic materials was largely restricted to the local centres. Indeed, after *c.* AD 1250 it was largely restricted to Moundville itself, an indication that it was most probably being carried out by attached specialists (Brumfiel and Earle 1987) dependent on the local paramount chief and carefully controlled for social/political reasons.

Apart from its use as evidence for the pattern of political centralization, the settlement pattern can also provide a basis for inferences about the prevalence of warfare, on the assumption that settlement nucleation represents a response to warfare that is intense and/or unpredictable. This would suggest that conflict was frequent in the period AD 900–1050, lessened during the *floruit* of the Moundville centre, but rose again as the latter declined, an argument supported by the distribution of skeletal evidence for injuries. The evidence for long-distance trade also shows a pattern related to the emergence and decline of Moundville: a jump in the import of marine shell beads and greenstone apparently occurred *c.* AD 1000 and foreign materials continued to increase until *c.* AD 1200, when Moundville became the paramount centre; the succeeding period saw the highest frequencies of exotic materials in burials, until a drastic decline *c.* AD 1500, some time before the collapse of political centralization, at a time when there are no signs of decline in production and consumption of locally made goods.

It seems clear that there is some kind of relationship between all these different developments; it is its nature that is the issue. The argument that has been advanced in the past – that centralization arose as a means of organizing production to avoid large-scale crop failure – does not seem to work, since it has been demonstrated that the risk of such failure was virtually non-existent (Scarry 1986, cited in Steponaitis 1991). Steponaitis integrates a number of lines of evidence. The early, relatively egalitarian, phase of the sequence was a time of conflict and competition, during which the production of such craft items as beads and beaded clothing greatly increased. These may well have served as exchange items in social transactions associated with the gaining of prestige. At the same time, the developments in the subsistence economy led to a system which was capable of producing much greater amounts of surplus than previously, and thus of providing the basis for new political developments. The positive feedback between prestige competition and increased production led to growing social differentiation in which the emergent élite were eventually able to 'symbolically split themselves off from the commoners by placing their residences atop mounds' (Steponaitis 1991: 214). These mounds were most probably regarded as sacred – indeed, they had forerunners in the region which had been used to delimit areas used in funerary rituals; thus the new élite was in effect appropriating this symbol as an aspect of legitimation. The centralization of regional burial may be seen as part of this same phenomenon.

During the Moundville I phase, *c.* AD 1050–1250, when there were four regional centres, the manufacture of socially valued goods was increasingly restricted to these centres, at the same time as the acquisition of exotic goods through long-distance exchange also increased. By the end of this phase, regional political activity was characterized by a 'prestige goods economy' in which the acquisition of exotic goods both demonstrated the power of the élite and enabled them to control their followers through limited redistribution of the less important items (Peebles 1987; Steponaitis 1991: 214). As a result of such processes, Moundville itself emerged as a paramount centre, for reasons probably connected with its greater population. This was not because of a pressure on resources leading to a requirement for greater management; rather, a larger population meant a greater aggregate production, of which a portion could be diverted to the newly emergent élite 'in return for' their ritual services and their limited distribution of exotic goods.

The centralized system remained in existence for c. 300 years before the collapse which has been described above. Steponaitis (1991: 216) is sceptical of the view that its demise was associated with the arrival of Europeans, noting that the decline seems to have begun before the earliest European incursions. The latter may have merely contributed to a process which was already underway as a result of such factors as the severing of long-distance exchange routes, which may have arisen from declining success in warfare with neighbouring groups, and declining surpluses. Once Moundville lost its dominance, competition developed within the region, especially for hunting territories. The result was warfare, a decline in the health of the population, and eventually a decline in the population itself.

ALTERNATIVE CONCEPTUALIZATIONS

The three case studies described in the preceding section may all be considered classic archaeological examples of the development of rank societies/chiefdoms, in that we see the emergence of social-political units which are in some way regionally centralized, with clear evidence of social hierarchies. All of them confirm the arguments outlined earlier about the role of population pressure. In two of the cases – Wessex and Moundville – there is no suggestion of such pressure. In the case where it is evident, the two Polynesian examples, the result is the appearance of what we may call, if we wish to make a value judgement, social pathologies, endemic warfare, and collapse, not the emergence of new managerial capacities. On the other hand, large regional populations, so long as they do not lead to pressure, may well be an enabling factor or precondition for the development of such centralized polities. However, there is no sense in which any of these societies could be seen as going on to become states in some inexorable evolutionary process. The Moundville system collapsed after 300 years, again leading to warfare. Wessex is perhaps more unusual in that there is quite good evidence that the same pattern of polities remained in existence for c. 1,500 years, from the beginning of the Neolithic to the end of the Early Bronze Age. Here too, however, the evidence suggests that when pressure on resources did finally develop, the system collapsed.

Moreover these studies, important and interesting though they are, in many respects do not challenge some of the basic assumptions of the neo-evolutionary school, in that all involve increased centralization of organization (and thus increased complexity in terms of the standard definitions), and movement towards more hierarchical social relations, or even stratification in Fried's sense. Broadly speaking, in other words, none of them challenges the view that there is really only a single important dimension in terms of which social change can and should be studied. But even if one accepts that this is true of the cases just presented, and it is certainly arguable in the case of Wessex, it does not mean that this is so universally. Furthermore, again in at least the Wessex example, explanations for the emergence of the phenomena described are distinctly lacking, perhaps as a result of an inadequate conceptualization of what needs explaining.

There are other schemes available which divide up social reality in rather different kinds of ways, or disentangle some of the strands in social patterns which have usually been bundled together. For example Flanagan (1989), in discussing hierarchy in simple 'egalitarian' societies, distinguishes between:

1 Social stratification, referring to the dominance of entire communities which endow all their members, irrespective of age and sex, with prerogatives and privileges over all other members of the dominated communities.
2 Hierarchy, implying the existence of inequalities between persons.
3 Complexity, usually referring to organizational arrangements, especially the number of administrative levels and the differentiation between the units which the administration manages.
4 Egalitarian ideologies, which are 'equality of opportunity' ideologies: societies espousing these may have enormous inequalities in both material resources and access to power, attributed to the differential abilities of the people concerned.
5 Egalitarian practices, or equal-outcome systems, where measures are taken to override and negate any differences which might emerge.
6 An autonomy dimension, distinguishing between situations in which individuals have high degrees of autonomy from those where it is low; this may relate to the extent to which monopolies of various kinds can be created within societies.

Flanagan further suggests that there are no egalitarian societies, but that there may be egalitarian contexts or situations. Even societies which in many respects are rigidly hierarchical may contain such situations, while so-called egalitarian systems may contain insidious hierarchies. He, like others such as Trigger (1990), suggests that the interesting question may not be how hierarchical societies arose, but how it is that some societies have had extensively egalitarian situations which have been strongly maintained. Some of the complexities in characterizing hierarchy and inequality which Flanagan explicates concern gender, which in many societies is a key idiom of domination/subordination.

THE ARCHAEOLOGY OF GENDER IN RANK SOCIETIES

Two examples are described here to illustrate the likely complexity of gender relations in rank societies.

The first concerns the importance of gender relations in the preparation and consumption of food discerned by Hastorf (1991) in the archaeological evidence associated with the incorporation of an Andean chiefdom into the Inca empire, taking into account local ethnographic and historical information about female roles in food preparation. Examination at settlement sites of the spatial distribution of botanical remains, especially those of maize, suggests that, as the region lost its autonomy, there was increased circumscription of day-to-day female activities within the household, seen in the more restricted distributions of botanical remains of crop- and food-processing. At the same time, the quantity of maize processed increases, suggesting increased female processing labour for the preparation of a crop which historical data indicate was largely consumed by males.

The argument is expanded through the use of skeletal evidence from the two phases. Isotope analysis of male and female skeletons indicates that in the earlier phase their diet parallels the local production data, including a small amount of maize, and that there were no differences in this respect between males and females. Inasmuch as historical evidence suggests that maize was mainly consumed in the form of beer used in ritual/political gatherings, this suggests that both genders participated equally in ritual events, provisioned by female labour. In the subsequent Inca phase, however, the diets of 50 per cent of the male individuals whose skeletons were examined included a greater proportion of maize than females. The women were processing larger quantities of maize than before, but it was being consumed largely by men, who also appear now to have been consuming more meat than women. We know from other sources that incorporation in the Inca empire would have meant participation in gatherings and obligatory workforces for which meat and maize beer would have been provided. The isotope data suggest that it was largely males who participated in these activities. Women did not join in non-domestic political consumption and their position outside the household as well as inside became increasingly restricted. Here we see a large-scale political change having a significant effect on gender relations and their construction.

Whilst Hastorf's study has the advantage of relevant historical and ethnographic information for a period not long after that with which the study is concerned, my second example illustrates how it is also possible to carry out such investigations when only archaeological information is available, the case study being the Late Neolithic of south-central Europe *c.* 3500–2500 BC, particularly the 'lake village' sites of the Alpine area (Petrequin and Petrequin 1988). In the Jura region of eastern France these lake sites were reoccupied *c.* 3100 BC after a gap of some 300 years. In the material assemblage from the sites one finds a new emphasis on bows and arrows, stone hammer-axes, flint daggers and various kinds of ornaments. Arrowheads are found not only in larger numbers but also in a greater variety of types, many derived from southern France. Since hunting was beginning to decrease in practical importance at this time, the attention devoted to the arrowheads is better seen as an indication of a new symbolic significance for the bow which, together with the hammer-axe and the dagger, came to be one of the defining features of a new male status. This argument is supported by Petrequin and Petrequin (1988) on a variety of grounds. Most of the imported items which are found, such as the daggers, are male-associated. Bifacially retouched flint sidescrapers, on the other hand, may have been a woman's tool and these were usually made of local flint. More generally in fact, exotic materials and aesthetic considerations played a decreasing role in those items of equipment which stayed in the house, while exotic materials obtained by exchange were sought out for male weapons and tools. As men invested increasing amounts of energy in the competition for prestige items, they simplified the manufacture of domestic tools of stone, bone and antler, a process which contributed further to the devaluation of the domestic realm with which women were associated.

An analysis of contemporary rock art from an adjacent area of northern Italy points in a similar direction (Robb 1994). Weapon symbolism is linked to males. In hunting scenes weapons are used by males, while on stelae associated with burials, halberds, axes and particularly daggers are consistently used to distinguish males from females. Furthermore, although we know from bone assemblages that a variety of different animals were hunted, the only one commonly represented in art is the deer, and in particular the stag with its antlers; if the gender of hunters is represented, it is male, distinguished by a phallus. Images of ploughing show a similar situation – male oxen are indicated by their horns and the people using the ploughs are frequently identified as male. It is very plausibly suggested by Robb that the various representations have a common pattern to do with the expression of male gender: daggers, male hunters, male ploughmen, oxen and stags: 'scenes using these ideologically-highlighted symbols emphasize the maleness of both subject and object. The male vitality of the animal, symbolized visually through horns and antlers, implies the male strength of the hunter killing it or the ploughman controlling it' (Robb 1994: 34).

These representations would have contributed to an ideology of male power in which the male–female distinction was a hierarchical one and women were excluded from at least the public power structure. The dagger was the key icon in representing this and it was this role which was the source of its public use, rather than its 'prestige' as such, although it was male status items which were made of exotic prestigious materials. On this view, the distinctions defined through prestige competition were not those between élite and commoner but between male and female; although prestige goods circulated, there was little formal hierarchy, political or economic: 'distinctions among males were probably due to differential realization of an ideal to which all males had access; they were competing for parity . . . while excluding females' (Robb 1994: 37). This male-orientated ideology valorized male activities at the expense of female ones, and was based on values centred on hunting, violence and the importance of exchange activities for obtaining exotic materials; the domestic domain was symbolically devalued. While men and women were symbolically unequal, males were symbolically equal, although no doubt varying in their prestige according to their role in local kin groups and their success in prestige-creating activities. On the basis of this model, the key social dynamic in late neolithic south-central Europe was not concerned with the development of ranking as such, but with the definition of male–female symbolic distinctions and thus a restructuring of gender relations, although competition between males may have led to rank/prestige differentials of a different nature from those which existed earlier (see Shennan 1993). The point is, however, that without the focus on gender relations the whole process would be completely misunderstood.

INDIVIDUALS, INTENTIONS AND RANKING

The approaches to the study of ranking which developed in the 1970s emphasized the notion of *system*. Broadly speaking, individual societies were conceived as systems, made up of sub-systems such as social organization, subsistence, ideology, and exchange. Changes arose from the interaction between the sub-systems. So, for example, subsistence intensification might be conceived as producing social change in the direction of increased ranking. The problem is that all these sub-systems are abstractions which do not have any reality: what exist in the world are people with intentions, resources, and perceived constraints. One of the features of 'post-processual' archaeology was an insistence on refocusing attention on individuals and their intentions and contexts, but this insistence did not go far enough: it did not recognize the possibility of micro-scale interactions between such individuals having unpredicted and unpredictable effects in terms of the larger-scale patterns to which they give rise. Such interactions lead back to the idea of systems, not now in terms of abstract variables, but modelling groups of interacting individuals and seeing what larger patterns emerge from their interactions. Such a framework also tends to have the effect of playing down the significance of ranking as such – it is something which may emerge from a particular system of changing interactions. Some of these issues are well illustrated in the study described below of cooperation and 'sequential hierarchy' in the south-west United States.

Between AD 900 and 1300, centres appeared in this region which included elaborate architecture, large-scale ritual, other structures such as the 'roads' of the Chaco Canyon area, indications of long-distance exchange contacts, craft specialization, and considerable variation in the elaboration of burials. Some have seen these features as evidence of developed social stratification (in Flanagan's (1989) sense, see p. 895) and the existence of élites, while others have argued that they could have been produced by egalitarian societies of the kinds known from the recent ethnography of the region. Johnson (1989) has reviewed the evidence and argued for a distinctly limited degree of inequality and an organizational pattern which has a number of levels but is essentially non-hierarchical in nature.

The amount of surplus available to these communities was small because of the marginal nature of agriculture in the region. However, if social stratification existed, one would expect élites to have the benefit of what there was in terms of better access to food. At Chacoan centres such as Pueblo Alto, there appears to have been more animal bone than expected in relation to its size, which might be taken as evidence of élite consumption. On the other hand, skeletons from burials with elaborate grave-goods at these centres suffered subsistence stress sufficient to generate skeletal pathologies, and the large quantities of animal bone are better seen as a reflection of consumption by large numbers of periodic visitors to the centres.

As far as the concentration of large amounts of labour in the monumental architecture is concerned, Johnson argues that the construction of residential room blocks was not a particularly labour-intensive activity and that the same was true of the construction of ceremonial 'kivas'. Furthermore, the number of kivas at sites seems to be directly proportional to community size, implying a relatively low degree of centralization of ritual activity. Finally, although there is a considerable amount of variation between burials, Johnson notes that the most elaborate ones were almost invariably adults, and that there is little evidence of status differences ascribed at birth through kin group membership. In addition, most 'rich' burials only contained one type of trade good, when in fact a variety of items obtained by long-distance exchange was available. The conclusion again is that this is a pointer against social stratification.

Johnson accounts for the existence of social variability, population aggregation, labour coordination, and exchange in terms of the idea of 'sequential hierarchy' (Johnson 1982), seen as a solution to the problems of achieving cooperation in human groups, since it is well established that cooperation tends to break down when groups become too large. In the face of such cooperation problems there are three possibilities: the group can split; a non-consensual hierarchy can be imposed; or a consensual 'sequential hierarchy' can be developed:

> in the sequential solution, basal organizational units are aggregated into larger (and thus fewer) entities among which consensus can be obtained more easily. Lower order units are subject to minimal potential coercion by higher order organizational entities because the former retain the fission option characteristic of egalitarian [entities] that can be applied if higher order consensus is locally unsatisfactory.
>
> (Johnson 1989: 379)

899

On this view, the small kivas or ceremonial rooms found on small sites represent a level above the household where cooperation problems were resolved in a sanctified context. The larger special structures at large sites then represent one or more levels of sequential hierarchy above the 'household cluster' level. The larger sites were in fact multiples of these household clusters, which represented the 'social modules' from which they were built up, and a constant ratio of roughly one kiva to 4–6 units was maintained. In the Chacoan settlements a three-level settlement hierarchy can be seen, reflecting different scale aggregations of such modules and their need for the sacred legitimation of cooperation at different scales. The basic household units, however, were essentially autonomous, potentially mobile, and able to disperse, an option which was exercised at intervals: 'social complexity' of the Chacoan type was something which appeared and disappeared at intervals in the south-west.

Chaco itself seems to have had storage facilities on an exceptionally large scale, given that the resident population on the basis of the number of rooms and kivas was relatively small. However, as we have noted already, the fact that individuals in elaborate burials seem to have suffered dietary stress suggests that the local population did not gain any special benefit from these storage facilities. Johnson suggests that participants in the Chacoan system could have made use of these stored reserves in times of difficulty, which would justify their contribution to their maintenance. However, the system was fragile, in that the reserves were not great on a regional *per capita* basis, so that the emergence of continued subsistence problems, for example as a result of climatic change, would rapidly have exhausted them and made them impossible to replenish. At this point there would have been few advantages in joining the system, and withdrawal by only a small proportion of participants would have led to the collapse which actually occurred.

A wider explanatory framework for these phenomena has recently been developed by Kohler and van West (1996) from a similar basis in the self-interest of individual households. They begin by showing that pooling of food is most likely to develop in circumstances of high mean productivity, high variability in productivity from year to year, and great spatial differences in productivity. This contrasts with the standard models of risk and its implications which have been used in archaeology, since these presuppose great variability in space/time but *low* mean productivity – in other words, where there appears to be most need for sharing. However, analysis of production functions produces the apparently counter-intuitive conclusion that sharing is not actually in the best interests of the individual households when little food is available, since greater utility is obtained, on average, by not sharing. In such circumstances, sharing will be likely to break down if it is present, and if it is not present it is unlikely to develop.

Kohler and van West obtained palaeo-productivity estimates for a 1,500 km^2 region in south-west Colorado, covering the period AD 900–1300, taking into account soil depth and estimates of soil moisture derived from palaeoenvironmental studies. These were used to define periods of high and low average production. Measures of spatial and temporal variability were also calculated. Aspects of the archaeological record believed to be relevant as evidence for food sharing included community growth and aggregation, the existence of great kiva ritual structures, and the presence of reservoirs. The breakdown of sharing was taken to be evident in the dissolution of aggregated sites. In general terms, the patterning in the archaeological record follows that predicted by the model, in that aggregation episodes are associated with periods when expected cooperation is high; this is the case, for example, with the appearance of the so-called Chacoan system, involving the development of a ritually based regional centre with spectacular architecture. The break up of this system and the final abandonment of the region both occur in periods when defection from sharing arrangements is the advantageous thing to do from the point of view of household self-interest. Evidence for cannibalism also occurs in periods when abandonment of sharing is predicted. However, the pattern is complicated by indications of high levels of cooperative behaviour at times when population is high. This is the opposite of what is anticipated by the model, since higher population would be expected to lead to lower levels of food per household. It appears that, while defection into an open landscape at times of low production was easy when population was low, this changed as population increased because alternative resources to defect to were no longer available. When the region was abandoned towards AD 1300, climatic factors were cutting productivity – and thus the utility of sharing – at the same time that the increasingly full landscape was removing the option of defecting.

From this study it emerges that a model of behaviour based entirely on the self-interest of the participants generates patterns in the settlement of the region which correspond closely to those actually found, in terms of the aggregation and dispersal of settlement. This appears to be in marked contrast to ethnographically known patterns of social organization in the south-west, which place great emphasis on the group at the expense of the individual. However, there is also a contrast in settlement processes: while the period from AD 900 to 1300 was characterized by the cyclical patterns we have seen, since that time aggregated village settlement in areas actually occupied has been uninterrupted. The reason for this, Kohler and van West suggest, is the emergence of new sharing rules emphasizing village level activities, combined with new sanctions against defection. In the societies which then emerged, egalitarianism and an emphasis on group values represented an active commitment, not an absence of evolution (cf. Trigger 1990). As we have seen already, the move towards centralized hierarchy represents only one possible trend in social change: other patterns are possible, including trends towards an asserted equality of outcome. To call such changes 'devolution' would be to subscribe to the progressive metaphor which this chapter has been at pains to criticize.

HOUSEHOLDS AND RESOURCE CONTROL ON THE CANADIAN NORTHWEST PLATEAU

A recent study by Hayden (1997) of the social and economic organization of pre-historic foragers on the Canadian Northwest Plateau brings together many of the points which have been made earlier in this chapter, showing how archaeological data can be used to reconstruct patterns of behaviour and organization in different spheres of prehistoric life and thus not only provide descriptions of prehistoric social differentiation but suggest how this differentiation relates to the control of resources.

The starting point of the study is an analysis of the spatial patterning in the archaeological residues within the larger structures excavated at the Keatley Creek site near the Fraser River. The structures were circular housepits around 10 metres in diameter containing a series of hearths forming a ring around the wall. Each hearth was associated with a range of debris consistent with domestic rather than specialized functions, suggesting that the hearths represented a series of domestic groups. However, there were differences in the patterns between the eastern and western halves of the housepits: for example, all the large hearths were in the western half of the houses and the large storage pits were associated with them, even though both halves seem to have been occupied by domestic groups rather than used for different activities – there was archaeological evidence of bedding material along the walls of both sides of the house, and anthropogenic soil chemical patterns were also the same. Hayden concluded that the pattern existed because the large houses were occupied by high status domestic groups in one half and lower status groups in the other.

The question then arose as to why these residential groups had come into existence and why some groups seemed to be richer and more powerful than others. An analysis of the salmon remains which were the subsistence staple revealed that residents of smaller and poorer housepits consumed only pink salmon, which are the easiest species to catch but the least desirable of those available, whereas residents of larger houses were the exclusive consumers of larger sockeye and chinook salmon, varieties that keep further away from the shore and can thus only be caught from rocks jutting out into the river or from specially constructed fishing platforms. In recent times such sites were largely owned by specific families and Hayden infers from the bone distribution that only the residents of the larger houses had access to the best fishing locations. He concludes that the main reason for the formation of the large residential groups was control of the most productive fishing sites which, on the evidence of ethnographically recorded trade in dried salmon, would also be the most lucrative. Élite members of the house groups would have had the rights to the production sites and poorer families without such rights would have attached themselves to them for the benefits they would receive in providing a source of labour, although how much choice they would have had in the matter is another issue. The resources and labour that élite members of such groups controlled are indicated by the presence of prestige burials including such items as trade shells and whalebone from the coast.

Scientific analyses of stone debitage from the large housepits showed that each was associated with a distinctive combination of lithic materials. This not only confirmed that each group associated with a large housepit represented a distinct economic entity, but also suggested that each group had exclusive access to the resources of a different mountain area containing the specific lithic resources used (and no doubt other resources as well on the basis of what is known ethnographic-ally). In addition, the fact that the same distinctive types of materials are found in the earliest levels of the housepit middens as in the latest indicates a continuity of inherited rights to territory and resources associated with particular housepit groups lasting in some cases for over a thousand years. It also suggests that the large housepits were in the possession of the same residential group for extremely long periods:

> the persistence of the largest and most successful of these residential corporate groups as discrete, identifiable entities for over 1000 years is a remarkable testimony to the powerful effect that control over lucrative economic resources can exert over the social structure of [what Hayden calls] transegalitarian communities, whether complex hunter-gatherers or agriculturalists.
>
> (Hayden 1997: 259)

CONCLUSION

A number of points have emerged from this consideration of rank societies and chiefdoms and the social processes which are characteristic of them as evidenced in the anthropological and archaeological record. In the first place, the terms have lost the specific meaning content which they had on their introduction to archaeology, because that content has been subject to detailed and justified critique. The terms remain as very useful generalized labels for a valid but very wide-ranging field of anthropological and archaeological investigation. It is not satisfactory to see these societies as an intervening stage in an evolutionary progression from the band to the state: the reality and validity of the supposed preceding stage are open to consider-able doubt, and development into states is not the characteristic fate of chiefdoms – their disappearance and/or the emergence of endemic warfare are far more likely outcomes.

The relationship between various aspects of population size and density and political organization is enormously complex and varied. In addition to the examples described above, Netting (1990: 56) has pointed out that in some regions chiefdoms with territorially defined political and landholding groups are found in areas of low population density and extensive resources, while areas with high densities are characterized by non-centralized descent-based lineage systems. This merely emphasizes Johnson's (1982) point, and indeed Gilman's (1981) Marxist view, that cooperation problems, if they occur, can be solved by sequential hierarchies at least as well as by forms of organization based on major power differentials and extensive institutionalized inequalities. In short, what the neo-evolutionary approach saw as a tightly correlated set of economic and social attributes all co-varying through time together, can now be seen as largely independent of one another, albeit contingently related in particular circumstances. It is this realization, among others, which has led to the new interest by archaeologists studying these societies in analytical and typological schemes which include a variety of different distinctions and operate at a more detailed level. At the same time, the new work in the anthropology and archaeology of gender has demonstrated that this is a key dimension in terms of the structuring of society and therefore the trajectories of change which societies follow.

In terms of this multidimensional perspective, it seems rather dubious to privilege the emergence of centralized hierarchies and stratified class-based systems above all other topics as subjects of investigation in connection with the sorts of societies described in this chapter – the tendency to do this is simply a reflection of our preoccupation with the 'rise of civilization' as the only subject of interest to archaeology once modern humans had emerged and agriculture had appeared. However, if we are to continue the investigation of these subjects in the context of rank societies, there are clearly a number of requirements. First, it is important to take into account the various distinctions made by Flanagan (1989) described earlier. Second, we must investigate the circumstances in which 'sequential hierarchies' arise as distinct from conventional ones, and the ways in which the former may change into the latter (Aldenderfer 1993). It may well be that ritual and symbolic distinctions have a key role here: as we have seen, it appears that Polynesia developed in a 'conventional' hierarchical direction at least partly because a set of original symbolic categories channelled subsequent developments. Such symbolic distinctions will also have an impact on the form taken by resistance to hierarchy and inequality. In effect, many of the studies of the past twenty-five years have accepted the propaganda of élites that all social power emanates from them. Next, analysis of competing interests in a changing symbolic environment must have a theoretical foundation at the level of the individuals in whose daily lives those interests were at stake. Finally, Hayden's case study shows us that, by working at a detailed level of analysis, it is possible to use archaeological data to draw conclusions about the organization of rank societies which are not contained in their premises and which can surprise us with their novelty and their implications.

REFERENCES

Aldenderfer, M. (1993) 'Ritual, hierarchy and change in foraging societies', *Journal of Anthropological Archaeology* 12: 1–40.

Bloch, M. (1977) 'The disconnection between power and rank as a process: an outline of the development of kingdoms in Central Madagascar', *Archives Européenes de Sociologie* 18: 107–148.

Bradley, R. (1984) *The Social Foundations of Prehistoric Britain: Themes and Variations in the Archaeology of Power*, London: Longman.

Bradley, R. (1991) 'The pattern of change in British prehistory', in T. K. Earle (ed.) *Chiefdoms: Power, Economy and Ideology*, Cambridge: Cambridge University Press: 44–70.

Brown, J. and Price, T. D. (eds) (1985) *Prehistoric Hunter-Gatherers: The Emergence of Cultural Complexity*, Orlando: Academic Press.

Brumfiel, E. and Earle, T. K. (1987) 'Specialisation, exchange and complex societies: an introduction', in E. Brumfiel and T. K. Earle (eds) *Specialisation, Exchange and Complex Societies*, Cambridge: Cambridge University Press: 1–9.

Brunton, R. (1989) 'The cultural instability of egalitarian societies', *Man* (n.s.) 24: 673–81.

Carneiro, R. (1970) 'A theory of the origin of the state', *Science* 169: 733–38

Drennan, R. and Uribe, C. (1987) 'Introduction', in R. Drennan and C. Uribe (eds) *Chiefdoms in the Americas*, Lanham, Md: University Press of America: vii–xii.

Durkheim, E. (1933) *The Division of Labour in Society*, Glencoe, Ill.: Free Press.

Earle, T. K. (1977) 'A reappraisal of redistribution: complex Hawaiian chiefdoms', in T. K. Earle and J. E. Ericson (eds) *Exchange Systems in Prehistory*, New York: Academic Press: 213–32.

Earle, T. K. (1991) 'Property rights and the evolution of chiefdoms', in T. K. Earle (ed.) *Chiefdoms: Power, Economy and Ideology*, Cambridge: Cambridge University Press: 71–99.

Earle, T. K. (1997) *How Chiefs Come to Power*, Stanford: Stanford University Press.

Erdal, D. and Whiten, A. (1994) 'On human egalitarianism: an evolutionary product of Machiavellian status escalation', *Current Anthropology* 35: 175–85.

Feinman, G. (1991) 'Demography, surplus and inequality: early political formations in highland Mesoamerica', in T. K. Earle (ed.) *Chiefdoms: Power, Economy and Ideology*, Cambridge: Cambridge University Press: 229–62.

Feinman, G. and Neitzel, J. (1984) 'Too many types: an overview of sedentary pre-state societies in the Americas', in M. Schiffer (ed.) *Advances in Archaeological Method and Theory*, Vol. 7, New York: Academic Press: 39–102.

Flanagan, L. (1989) 'Hierarchy in simple "egalitarian" societies', *Annual Review of Anthropology* 18: 245–66.

Fried, M. (1967) *The Evolution of Political Society*, New York: Random House.

Gilman, A. (1981) 'The development of social stratification in bronze age Europe', *Current Anthropology* 22: 1–24.

Harrison, S. (1993) 'The commerce of cultures in Melanesia', *Man* (n.s.) 28: 139–58.

Hastorf, C. (1991) 'Gender, space and food in prehistory', in J. Gero and M. Conkey (eds) *Engendering Archaeology: Women and Prehistory*, Oxford: Basil Blackwell: 132–59.

Hayden, B. (1997) 'Observations on the prehistoric social and economic structure of the North American Plateau', *World Archaeology* 29: 242–61.

Ingold, T. (1983) 'The significance of storage in hunting societies', *Man* (n.s.) 18: 553–71.

Johnson, A. and Earle, T. K. (1987) *The Evolution of Human Societies: From Foraging Group to Agrarian State*, Stanford: Stanford University Press.

Johnson, G. A. (1982) 'Organisational structure and scalar stress', in C. Renfrew, M. J. Rowlands and B. A. Segraves (eds) *Theory and Explanation in Archaeology: the Southampton Conference*, New York: Academic Press: 389–421.

Johnson, G. A. (1989) 'Dynamics of Southwestern prehistory: far outside – looking in', in L. S. Cordell and G. J. Gumerman (eds) *Dynamics of Southwest Prehistory*, Washington, DC: Smithsonian Institution: 371–89.

Kent, S. (1993) 'Sharing in an egalitarian Kalahari community', *Man* (n.s.) 28: 479–514.

Kertzer, D. (1988) *Ritual, Politics and Power*, New Haven: Yale University Press.

Khazanov, A. (1985) 'Rank society or rank societies: processes, stages and types of evolution', in H. J. M. Claessen, P. van der Velde and M. Estellie Smith (eds) *Development and Decline: the Evolution of Sociopolitical Organisation*, Massachusetts: Bergin and Harvey Publishers: 82–96.

Kirch, P. V. (1984) *The Evolution of the Polynesian Chiefdoms*, Cambridge: Cambridge University Press.

Kirch, P. V. (1991) 'Chiefship and competitive involution: the Marquesas Islands of eastern Polynesia', in T. K. Earle (ed.) *Chiefdoms: Power, Economy and Ideology*, Cambridge: Cambridge University Press: 119–45.

Kohler, T. and van West, C. (1996) 'The calculus of self-interest in the development of cooperation: sociopolitical development and risk among the northern Anasazi', in J. A. Tainter and B. Bagley-Tainter (eds) *Evolving Complexity and Environment: Trade in the Prehistoric Southwest*, Reading, Mass.: Addison-Wesley: 169–96.

Maisels, C. K. (1987) 'Models of social evolution: trajectories from the neolithic to the state', *Man* (n.s.) 22: 331–59.

Netting, R. (1990) 'Population, permanent agriculture, and politics: unpacking the evolutionary portmanteau', in S. Upham (ed.) *The Evolution of Political Systems: Sociopolitics in Small-scale Sedentary Societies*, Cambridge: Cambridge University Press: 21–61.

Peebles, C. S. (1971) 'Moundville and surrounding sites: some structural considerations of mortuary practices II', in J. A. Brown (ed.) *Approaches to the Social Dimensions of Mortuary Practices*, Society for American Archaeology Memoir 25: 68–91.

Peebles, C. S. (1987) 'Moundville from AD 100 to 1500 as seen from AD 1840 to 1895', in R. D. Drennan and C. A. Uribe (eds) *Chiefdoms in the Americas*, Lanham, Md.: University Press of America: 21–41.

Petrequin, A. and Petrequin, P. (1988) *Le Néolithique des Lacs*, Paris: Errance.

Renfrew, C. (1973) 'Monuments, mobilisation and social organisation in neolithic Wessex', in C. Renfrew (ed.) *The Explanation of Culture Change*, London: Duckworth: 539–58.

Renfrew, C. (1974) 'Beyond a subsistence economy: the evolution of social organization in prehistoric Europe', in C. B. Moore (ed.) *Reconstructing Complex Societies: An Archaeological Colloquium*, Chicago: Supplement to the Bulletin of the American Schools of Oriental Research 20: 69–95.

Robb, J. (1994) 'Gender contradictions, moral coalitions, and inequality in prehistoric Italy', *Journal of European Archaeology* 2 (1): 20–49.

Sahlins, M. (1968) *Tribesmen*, Engelwood Cliffs, N.J.: Prentice-Hall.

Sahlins, M. and Service, E. R. (1960) *Evolution and Culture*, Ann Arbor: University of Michigan Press.

Sanders, W. and Webster, D. (1978) 'Unilinealism, multilinealism, and the evolution of complex societies', in C. L. Redman, M. J. Berman, E. V. Curtin, W. T. Langhorne Jr.,

N. M. Versaggi and J. C. Wanser (eds) *Social Archaeology: Beyond Subsistence and Dating*, New York: Academic Press: 249–302.

Scarry, M. C. (1986) 'Change in Plant Procurement and Production during the Emergence of the Moundville Chiefdom', Ann Arbor: University of Michigan, Department of Anthropology Ph.D. dissertation.

Service, E. R. (1962) *Primitive Social Organisation: An Evolutionary Perspective*, New York: Random House.

Shennan, S. J. (1993) 'Settlement and society in central Europe 3500–1500 BC', *Journal of World Prehistory* 7: 121–62.

Shott, M. (1992) 'On recent trends in the anthropology of foragers: Kalahari revisionism and its archaeological implications', *Man* (n.s.) 27: 843–71.

Steponaitis, V. (1991) 'Contrasting patterns of Mississippian development', in T. K. Earle (ed.) *Chiefdoms: Power, Economy and Ideology*, Cambridge: Cambridge University Press: 193–228.

Steward, J. (1955) *Theory of Culture Change*, Urbana: University of Illinois Press.

Terrell, J., Hunt, T. L. and Gosden, C. (1997) 'The dimensions of social life in the Pacific: human diversity and the myth of the primitive isolate', *Current Anthropology* 38: 155–96.

Trigger, B. (1990) 'Maintaining economic equality in opposition to complexity: an Iroquoian case study', in S. Upham (ed.) *The Evolution of Political Systems: Sociopolitics in Small-scale Sedentary Societies*, Cambridge: Cambridge University Press: 119–45.

Upham, S. (1987) 'A theoretical consideration of middle range societies', in R. Drennan and C. Uribe (eds) *Chiefdoms in the Americas*, Lanham, Md.: University Press of America: 345–68.

White, L. (1959) *The Evolution of Culture*, New York: McGraw-Hill.

Woodburn, J. (1980) 'Hunters and gatherers today and reconstruction of the past', in E. Gellner (ed.) *Soviet and Western Anthropology*, London: Duckworth: 95–117.

Wright, H. T. (1984) 'Prestate political formations', in T. K. Earle (ed.) *On the Evolution of Complex Societies: Essays in Honor of Harry Hoijer*, Malibu: Undena Publications: 41–77.

Yoffee, N. (1993) 'Too many chiefs? (or, Safe texts for the 90s)', in N. Yoffee and A. Sherratt (eds) *Archaeological Theory: Who Sets the Agenda?*, Cambridge: Cambridge University Press: 60–78.

SELECT BIBLIOGRAPHY

The best source for following up the archaeological study of the sorts of society described in this chapter is Earle (1997), which adopts a comparative approach to the study of the ideology, economics, and politics of chiefly societies by comparing developments in Europe, the Pacific and South America. Earle's edited book *Chiefdoms: Power, Economy and Ideology* (1991) is also a very useful collection of case studies, while Kirch (1984) explores the range of social variations on the rank society theme which emerged as a result of the Polynesian colonization of the Pacific in the contexts of particular islands and their resources. In fact, most archaeological studies of prehistoric agricultural societies which were not states, all over the world, fall under the rubric of this chapter, while the papers in Brown and Price (1985) make the point emphasized in this chapter that agricultural subsistence was not a prerequisite. It seems that rank societies, like the bourgeoisie in more recent times, were always rising!

23

URBANIZATION AND STATE FORMATION

Simon Stoddart

INTRODUCTION

This chapter covers the development and maintenance of state-organized society in the pre-industrial era, concentrating on the earliest forms which took place some five millennia ago. In the writings of most social theorists (including archaeologists), this transformation is considered the most radical development since the transition to agriculture. Agriculture was generally a necessary precursor, since it provided the potential surplus production, once politically orchestrated, to maintain power over people and materials (see Chapter 21).

State formation has brought both the potential for well-being and opportunities for exploitation and disadvantage. Approaches to the question tend to emphasize beneficence or exploitation. For the first time in human development, many major achievements were possible, whether measured materially as expenditures of energy or conceptually in the form of new ideologies. The rate of innovation following the formation of the first state was much greater than before. Yet many of these early states were based on the mobilization of manpower where a few individuals managed to deprive the majority of the full benefits of the extracted surplus.

Only archaeology has the ability to examine the full chronological development of cities and states. Archaeological evidence – material culture – can be employed to register long-term change, appreciate spatial organization and penetrate periods before the development of informative literacy. Other disciplines are dependent on a type of literacy which itself remained in the hands of a few and then, as an informative source, only developed relatively late in the sequence of cities and states. The formation of cities and states is embedded in long political and economic sequences where textual data provide clarification of only discrete, limited zones in time and space. Archaeology, even though itself plagued with sampling problems, covers a much wider range of contexts.

It can perhaps even be argued that this long-term perspective provides a scenario of long-term trends which has implications for the world today. However, it needs to be stressed that, although there is archaeological evidence (material culture) of the modern world, the present chapter concentrates on the pre-industrial, pre-capitalist, versions of city and state and thus analyses constructs which have differences in character from the modern. One major difference is that of scale. Industrial scale of population is dependent on an industrial scale of communication which has only been developed in the last two centuries (Chapter 29). In particular, transport provided severe, but not insuperable, problems for the sustenance of large populations in pre-industrial periods (Fletcher 1995).

The two processes, urbanization and state formation, are too frequently employed as interchangeable in describing this radical change. It is correct that in most cases they are strongly interrelated, but, in fact, they refer to two different measures of socio-political development. The city is generally defined as a dense nucleated population. The state is generally defined as a hierarchical organization (both politically and administratively) set up to control large populations which may, or may not, be densely nucleated. Thus urbanization generally requires state formation for its successful long-term implementation. As a consequence, states can occur without cities, but cities tend to be highly unstable without states. At the most extreme, urbanism can be envisaged as merely subsidiary to state formation (Adams 1972). Ultimately, even this issue can be confused and clouded by differing definitions. Early settlements, such as seventh- to sixth-millennium BC Çatal Hüyük in Anatolia, have been claimed to be towns, although never envisaged as states. The 'oppida' of first-millennium BC central Europe are further examples of low density urbanism on the definitional boundary (Collis 1984).

The definition of the city and the state is clearly key to the resolution of their origins. Is there a clear break between the pre-state/city and the state/city? How does this translate into rates of change? Which characteristics should be stressed – the quantitative, more positivistic components such as scale, or the qualitative, more humanistic, components such as ideology?

DEFINITIONS

As Wheatley (1972: 601) has suggested, the term 'urbanism' changes character like a wild mythical animal. It is very difficult to define in terms that are acceptable across cultures and time. Consequently, many definitions of urbanism have been devised which vary in their specificity and degree of overlap, ranging between approaches based on dynamism, way of life, economics and demography.

A very common view of the city is that of an ideal type based on models derived from the classical world (Rykwert 1988). Ancient historians, in the tradition of Fustel de Coulanges (1883), tend to deal with rationalization of the city, not how it was actually built, as would be revealed by archaeology. Great emphasis is laid on the ideological component, starting with the foundation rites of the city. For instance, heroes are often cited as necessary founders of cities, under the guidance of divine inspiration. Less emphasis is laid on the material component, which took a less ordered or ideological form in many cities, except at major phases of reconstruction.

At the most general level there is a distinction of urban from non-urban which Wheatley (1972: 602–5) defines as an *ideal type* definition. Such a distinction is found in many other cultures and reflects the organization of categories into paired opposites as recognized by structuralists. These definitions are, though, by their very nature difficult to transfer between different contexts. At a more theoretical level, Redfield was responsible for defining a pre-urban *folk* society from urban and peasant society. He also went further by attempting to distil the nature of urban societies from examples as disparate as the Mayan and Roman (Redfield 1968). His major contribution was to attempt to understand the nature of the rural and the urban which he successively understood as a dichotomy and then as a continuum.

One of the most dominant schools of urban study in archaeology has attempted to define relevant traits (Wheatley 1972: 608–13). Childe in his seminal paper of 1950 selected ten indices based on Mesopotamian urbanism: the concentration of a relatively large number of people in a restricted area; craft specialization; the political appropriation of an economic surplus; monumental public architecture; developed social stratification; writing; exact and predictive sciences; naturalistic art; foreign trade; and group membership beyond kinship. In common with many descriptive approaches, this definition was very static and failed to examine the dynamic process of urbanism. Furthermore, even the static elements have proved to be inexact, since Childe, in spite of his Australian upbringing, was very much restricted to his European cultural origins, aided and abetted by his philological and classical training. The more recent global research of archaeology has shown that writing was not always used in cities (see p. 937) and that monuments were constructed by pre-urban societies.

A further major branch of urban studies has defined the city as a centre of power or dominance (Wheatley 1972: 613–20). An influential, although controversial, geographical theory of this type was developed by Sjoberg (1960). In his account, the élite of pre-industrial cities were located close to the monumental architecture and the positions of power at the centre of the city. Other variation was, to his mind, less significant: in particular, he suggested that pre-industrial cities had little functional segregation (and correspondingly much overlap between workplace and residence) except with respect to the location of power. This generalization does not stand up to the range of archaeological evidence (McIntosh and McIntosh 1993).

Many archaeological studies of urbanism and state organization share the general interest in power and have borrowed heavily from spatial geography. These have developed models for the most efficient implementation of power from the urban centre over a dependent territory (see pp. 928–31) and compared them with archaeological reality. In this approach the function of the city is very important. The city secures resources (food, manpower and raw materials) from its territory and concentrates a range of specialist activities (administration, craft production, religion and trade regulation) in a city to work those resources efficiently. Within this definition, it is more easy to fit the distinction of city from town: the town is simply a smaller settlement under the political control of a major city.

The simplest approach to urbanism has been based on population size (Wheatley 1972: 620–21). For the modern geographer armed with census returns, the advantages of easy quantification are obvious. A figure of 5,000 inhabitants can provide the easy, quantifiable, threshold. For the archaeologist, the approach has still proved attractive, although the problems are more complex. Population sizes have to be estimated from the size of settlements. Many archaeologists have rejected the simplicity of this type of definition and suggested that urbanism must be examined in a broader context (Alexander 1972: 844).

A major problem with the concept of the town or city is the high degree of variation that it conceals. At an empirical level, major differences can be seen in the centres classified as urban in the archaeological world. Locally and internally perceived criteria vary greatly between cultural contexts. The Muslim city required a *jami* (mosque), *hammam* (public bath) and a *suq* (permanent market). Mayan cities were almost certainly defined by their ritual centres. The Moche city of Chan Chan in South America appears to have been principally connected with élite administration. The same degree of variation can be detected in the considerable range of density of population in urban centres (Fletcher 1995).

Origins of the term 'state'

The use of the state construct is by no means as new as that of other stages employed in neo-evolutionary theory, because it is a term borrowed from classical Antiquity. There exists a long tradition of use and an equally rich connotation of meaning by researchers of many and varied intellectual backgrounds (Engels [1884]1985; Finley 1963; Oppenheimer 1923). Many of these works are rooted in the classical or, at least European, political tradition. The fathers of political theory and sociology have, in turn, given their own gloss on the concept of the state. Marx emphasized the unequal control over the means of production. Weber emphasized central authority. The challenge for the archaeologist is that his or her laboratory is not simply a micro-region of historical heritage, such as Europe, but a much wider global setting. The archaeologist must not be bound by one particular cultural trajectory. In this respect the work of Lewis Henry Morgan was an important breakthrough by bringing anthropology into play and developing a sense of different stages of human development (Morgan 1877) which had a global range (see Chapter 12).

A revival of interest in the term 'state' took place in the United States under the influence of the neo-evolutionists in the 1960s (Service 1962; Fried 1967), inspired by the method, if not the full terminology, of Julian Steward (1949). The aim was to provide a cross-cultural framework for the new global level of research in the post-war period. Much prior research had been directed towards the study of alternative, but vaguer, constructs such as civilization and urbanism, which are ultimately culturally specific. The term 'civilization' suffers from too great a generality. The term 'urbanism' is too specific to a given cultural context. For example, it would be strange to exclude ancient Egypt, the Maya or some early African societies from the study of ancient complex society simply because they did not have urbanism in a western form, although none would deny them the status of a state. Equally, the term 'civilization' has been too widely employed (particularly in the French language) to allow a rigorous definition.

The term 'state' has a much wider acceptance than other neo-evolutionary constructs. It has a more acceptable coherence and cross-cultural application. As Tainter puts it, 'most anthropologists . . . feel comfortable with the term' (Tainter 1988: 28). However, this very acceptance may be, according to some scholars (Gledhill 1988; Kohl 1987), because the state is part of our own culture and may consequently have provided a too rigid view of the past determined by the present. This view appears extreme to many, but does stress the need for caution in the use of the very terms with which we feel most comfortable.

THE HISTORY OF RESEARCH INTO STATE TRANSFORMATION

Historical trends can be noted in the development of theories for the development of the state. Many theories, until recently, assumed that a general theory of the origin of the state could be discovered. The first theories tended to emphasize the 'prime mover'; that is, a single principal cause of state formation. A number of archaeological studies in the 1970s were directed towards studying the validity of these prime movers, generally with negative results (Wright and Johnson 1975). By contrast, many theories have emphasized the multi-variant and the systemic. These theories may be considered less elegant because of their decreased simplicity, but potentially they cope better with the complexity of the evidence. They have in turn produced critiques particularly from Marxist-derived accounts, which sometimes share an evolutionary framework, but which criticize the positive attitude towards a beneficent, stable state. Some of the more influential approaches have laid stress on the power of social formations (Friedman and Rowlands 1977) rather than the simply materialistic.

Theories of the late 1980s and 1990s have sometimes moved away from general explanations, usually under the influence of Giddens (1984). The results are often pluralistic and relativistic, allowing a major role for historical contingency and the role of the actor. The emphasis on the actor is visible in many of the current schools of thought about state formation (Lewis 1981; Roscoe 1988). The most successful applications of the role of the actor in concrete case studies have, though, come from a background – the Midwest of the United States – which has generally professed the power of process. For example, the work of Kus in the study of Madagascar gives an active role to the individual (1989).

One alternative is a more synthetic approach which would give some role for the actor within the constraints of the wider processes of society. As Price (1993) points out, these constraints operate at different levels: the immediate present (registered by the individual) and the long-term systemic (not necessarily appreciated by the individual). An evolutionary approach still retains a profound influence on many explanations of social change and as such is the subject of much criticism (Shanks and Tilley 1987).

A cynical view notes that the early generalizing theories were heavily dependent on the primary research area of the scholar involved and generalized to cover other regions before the full development of archaeological research. Irrigation theories were developed in Mesopotamia where mobilization of manpower for such works was a preoccupation of early literacy and material evidence. Circumscription theories were developed in Peru, arguably the most geographically constrained location of early state formation. As archaeological research progressed, it has become apparent that the historical rules of one area cannot be strictly applied to another.

The state defined

In a definition of the state it is essential to go beyond a mere list of traits, or the definition will have the same weaknesses as some definitions of urbanism. In spite of this, it is worth beginning by listing some of the commonly stated characteristics, if not traits, of the state (Tainter 1988: 29): 'territorial organization, differentiation by class and occupation rather than by kinship, monopoly of force, authority to mobilize resources and personnel, and legal jurisdiction'. Roscoe (1993: 113) has defined three analytically separate dimensions: political centralization (the concentration of power in the hands of the few); socio-economic differentiation (occupational specialization); and social stratification (the differentiation of status).

By contrast, the Mediterranean classical tradition, prioritized by its perceived great influence on the European politics, has emphasized the Greek definition of the state: 'a genuine political community to which men belonged by free choice as equal citizens and in which they shared a common life and a communal responsibility' (Finley 1963: 38; Fig. 23.1). Unfortunately, not only is this a difficult definition to unearth archaeologically but, when unearthed, the surviving evidence is more likely to disprove than confirm the classicist's definition. Archaeology is likely to stress the disparity of wealth and power (including extensive slave ownership and low literacy), thus weakening the very definition itself. However, the Greek polis does provide an example of a small-scale state which fits uneasily within the definitions that have emphasized scale and centralization.

Definitions tend to emphasize the positive or negative attributes of the state (Cohen 1978; Haas 1982; Hayden and Gargett 1990; Service 1975; Tainter 1988). On the one hand, there are theorists who emphasize the great positive achievements of the state in providing a management of people and information, serving the needs of society. The needs serviced by society may include irrigation (Wittfogel 1957), redistribution (Sahlins 1963), exchange (Sanders and Price 1968) and information (Wright 1977). Definitions such as those of Wright (1977: 383), which emphasize centralized decision-making accompanied by external and internal specialization, can be subsumed under this type of definition. The theoretical work of Johnson (1978) on horizontal and vertical specialization also links into this. As the scale of a society increases, so do the stresses within egalitarian society in controlling the individuals involved. Institutions have to be developed which efficiently control the interrelationships of individuals in an increasingly complex human environment. However, there are examples, such as the Greek polis, which developed state institutions without the stress of scale.

On the other hand there are those who emphasize exploitation and manipulation of people and information. An important approach within the study of negative attributes is to see the state as based on conflict. This has been an important part of, but not exclusive to, the Marxist approach to the state. Fried (1960: 729; 1967: 225) envisages the state as coterminous with stratification, or rather with the resolution of conflicts that are the consequences of stratification. The emphasis of Webster (1975) on the role of warfare in acquiring wealth is consistent with this more negative approach.

In reality, it is clear that both negative and positive elements occur in all states in varying measures. A simple conflict model, whilst providing the dynamic for the formation of the state, fails to consider adequately its maintenance and functioning. Stability is achieved through a combination of incentive and coercion. A model such as that presented by Service (1975: 167) aims to achieve this compromise:

Figure 23.1 The Acropolis of Athens. Photograph: S. Stoddart.

'bureaucratic governance by legal force'. Flannery (1972) also defines the state as an entity that combines government and force. A unifying theme of most current approaches is that of power and its counterpart, domination: the means of imposing and implementing effective power over others (Cherry 1987; Giddens 1979, 1984). The central question is how power came to be exercised and how it was maintained

915

once in existence. A primary debate is about the relative emphasis on the material (economic) or on the social, cultural, and symbolic in the exercise of power.

Some traditions in the study of early state formation have also considered the state to be a too all-embracing term. Early distinctions defined dichotomies: the unitary and segmentary state (Southall 1956). More recent scholars (Claessen and Skalnik 1978) have divided early states into separate categories of increasing complexity: inchoate, typical early, and transitional early. Another distinction sometimes made is between primary and secondary state formation. Primary states are those which developed independently of any other (Mesopotamia, Egypt, China, Indus valley, Mexico and Peru). Secondary states are those of later date which can be considered to have been in some way affected by early developments. The leading question is whether these sub-categories share more similarities than dissimilarities.

THEORIES OF STATE FORMATION

The prime mover

The most famous prime mover, irrigation, is in fact the most culturally specific. Wittfogel (1957) considered water to be an essential, politically manipulable, resource. The creation of the state was inextricably linked to control of water by state authorities. However, subsequent research has shown that, where irrigation was important, it only developed on sufficient scale to require centralized authority once the state had formed. Furthermore, work outside the Mesopotamian area has demonstrated that large-scale irrigation is only required in certain ecological contexts and cannot be considered a general mechanism.

Population pressure has been singled out as another alternative prime mover (Sanders and Price 1968). This prime mover has the advantage of being a potential general mechanism for all social change, yet its very generality causes problems in explaining the lack of immediacy of state formation in all regions following agriculture. Alternatively, if there are cultural or natural mechanisms restraining population growth, then additional reasons need to be found to explain the release of population pressure. In reality, population pressure is often a response to other local factors which provide constraints.

Other potential prime movers suffer from similar problems. They are too difficult to isolate, are too specific to particular case studies, or are too general to society at all levels of complexity. Warfare has frequently been cited, but conflict has a much longer history than that of the state. Moreover, the periods of most intense conflict often follow the state rather than precede it. Nevertheless, conflict as an extension of competition remains an important factor in the development of states

916

and is currently being reinvestigated as an important constituent of state formation (Marcus 1992a). The internalized warfare of class conflict is another suggested mechanism, but again its claimed generality can only with difficulty be applied exclusively to the period of state formation.

Trade is frequently advanced as one of the most important prime movers. For some it is considered the most likely activity to favour innovation, including state formation (Renfrew 1972: 440). For others, it is an essential factor in maintaining integration (Friedman and Rowlands 1977: 270). However, in the opinion of many this can be taken too far and should not replace a proper understanding of social change (Renfrew 1972: 441). Much recent work has examined the relationship between state-organized and non-state-organized societies, leading in time to state formation amongst the latter. However, trade cannot operate in isolation. The trade must have its impact on a society already in some way prepared for change, but may provide the appropriate conditions. This type of approach has been much favoured in the study of relations between the Mediterranean and central Europe. Wells envisages entrepreneurs in first-millennium BC central Europe taking advantage of the opportunities for trade to accumulate wealth and political power (Wells 1984). In this case the consequent centralization was short-lived and the state apparatus never fully developed until just before the Roman conquest.

The systems approach

Systems theory was introduced into archaeology from engineering via anthropology (Rappaport 1971) in order to avoid the simplistic explanations of the prime mover. This approach envisaged humanity as a system and involved the breaking down of that system into defined component parts. The interrelationship of these component parts was also specified and considered to balance each other under normal conditions, leading to a stable operation of society. The difficulty occurred in trying to explain imbalance or change in the whole system.

The classic theoretical attempt to explain change is that of Flannery (1972; Fig. 23.2). He measured social complexity in terms of *segregation* (the amount of internal differentiation and specialization of sub-systems) and *centralization* (the degree of linkage between the various sub-systems and the highest-order controls in society). Change in these two processes represented state formation. He claimed universality for the processes and the mechanisms by which they took place. Yet he allowed local specificity for the socio-environmental stresses (in many cases the prime movers, population growth, social circumscription, warfare, irrigation, trade, and so on) which selected for the mechanisms.

In total, he envisaged a hierarchical system subject to change by transforming mechanisms. The hierarchical system was composed of higher-order control

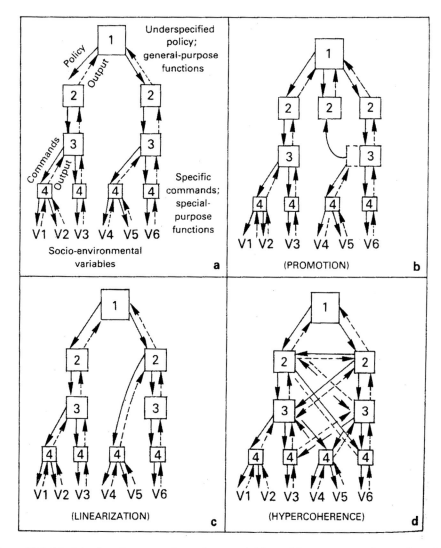

Figure 23.2 Models for the operation of control hierarchies; see text for explanation. Source: Flannery 1972.

engaged in general-purpose functions and lower-order control engaged in special-purpose functions. Two prominent mechanisms were identified, following Rappaport. The first, *promotion*, led to the move of a specific lower-order specialized institution to a generalized higher-order position. For instance, an informal headman might be promoted to a more permanent position. The second, *lineariza-tion*, led to the direct control of lower-order functions from the upper parts of the hierarchy. For instance, local irrigation might become directly administered from the centre. These mechanisms can lead to instability and stress, *usurpation* and *meddling*, respectively, which in turn may promote further change. On the other hand, too many interconnections may lead to *hypercoherence* and collapse of the whole system. The complete breakdown of local autonomy leads to too great a reliance on conditions in other parts of the state.

Flannery made this abstract model more understandable by an illustration from the recent ethnohistory of Mesoamerica. The rotating office for financial sponsorship of the local fiesta was subverted by a great family with the aid of the church, presumably under certain socio-environmental conditions (or stresses). In Flannery's judgement, a levelling mechanism was turned into a debt-creating mechanism. A lower-order specialist institution was promoted to a higher-order institution. Debt was manipulated by the great family and exchanged for control of land. The great family thus assumed control of the vast majority of land in the village. However, the whole process was cut short by the Mexican revolution at an even higher level, which led to the redistribution of land. This fruitful source of data has also been used by other authors (Hayden and Gargett 1990).

In summary, Flannery suggests that in certain socio-environmental conditions of stress, lower-order controls may prove insufficient and are subverted (through promotion or linearization) by higher-order controls. The cost of administration (processing information) is increased, as this process is repeated many times. *Centralization* and *segregation* increase, and at a certain threshold the state comes into existence.

One of the few elaborate archaeological attempts to use systems theory for the study of state formation (although classified as minor states or principalities) is that of Renfrew (1972). Renfrew envisaged the emergence of Aegean civilization from the third millennium BC 'in terms of positive interactions between the various subsystems' (Renfrew 1972: 476). In the specific instance of the Aegean, Renfrew defined (1972: 480–85) a redistributive system for subsistence commodities and the development of metallurgy and maritime trade as the key factors in the emergence of civilization and of stratified society, without considering any one component a prior event. Change in one sub-system stimulated change in another, which in turn stimulated change in the first. Production of new commodities led to new trade, which in turn stimulated new production. Indeed, Renfrew would argue that the different sub-systems would have to work in unison to achieve urbanization or civilization (1972: 503).

The systems approach assumes stability of the system and subservience of the social actors. The approach has, therefore, been criticized principally on the grounds that some condition external to the system has to be devised to explain change (Shanks and Tilley 1987: 138–43). These may be the socio-cultural stresses of Flannery or trade for Renfrew (1972).

Marxist approaches

In the modern pluralistic world it is increasingly difficult to isolate a purely Marxist approach. Many theories contain elements of class struggle, unequal access to resources, or competing interest groups, without earning a purely Marxist label. Early Marxist accounts tended to be determined by materialist concerns and productive forces. More recent approaches emphasize social or ideological relations. One influential approach, that of Friedman and Rowlands (1977), has been defined by the authors as 'epigenetic'. A general model is outlined which has different outcomes according to particular regional conditions; the framework is thus a multilinear evolutionary trajectory. The approach lays stress on an evolutionary methodology derived from Marxist analysis. Primacy is given to the socially determined set of productive relations. This contrasts with the emphasis given by some other Marxists to ideology on the one hand or productive forces on the other.

Under these circumstances, there are different forms of state determined by their social relations. The Asiatic, or conical clan, state, found in early stages, is characterized by the fact that noble lineages are defined by their kinship position to the royal line (Friedman and Rowlands 1977: 216ff.). The state remains an enlarged version of the tribe and, therefore, cannot achieve the scale of later oriental despotic empires. Stronger political forces are required to retain the cohesion of larger units. The development of prestige-good systems was seen as a considerable step in this direction (Friedman and Rowlands 1977: 225ff.). This in turn leads to the expansion of the trading system and the organization of territorial and city-states (1977: 232).

PREREQUISITES OF STATE FORMATION

Three powerful prerequisites are frequently defined as necessary for the development of states. First, there has to be a context of intensification of subsistence generally achieved through agriculture. Agriculture (including some types of pastoralism (Genito 1994)) provides a potential for producing a surplus which can be transferred away from the producers of subsistence. Second, there has to be what is frequently termed circumscription. This has been defined to describe the constraints of geography, society or resources (Carneiro 1970, 1988; Fig. 23.3). The society moving towards the state level of organization has to be subject to some form of constraint, making the constituent population unable to find some less-arduous solution. State formation has many material and less tangible costs which would not be taken on unless the position was circumscribed. Third, except in cases of extreme coercion, social formations need to be present which are receptive of state formation. Many early societies had checks and balances which prevented the

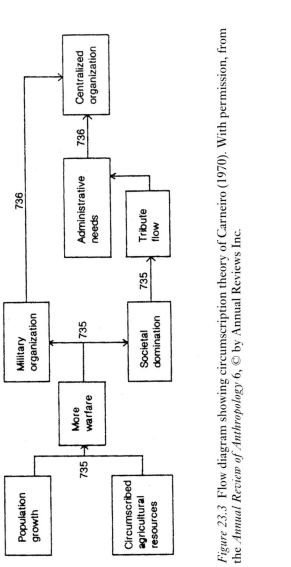

Figure 23.3 Flow diagram showing circumscription theory of Carneiro (1970). With permission, from the *Annual Review of Anthropology* 6, © by Annual Reviews Inc.

assumption of excessive power by sub-groups of society. Taking account of this third factor also acknowledges the importance of the local history of a particular area, reducing the impact of some theories based on simple cross-cultural generalization.

The importance of intensification of subsistence is twofold. First, agriculture realizes the potential for a surplus of produce, releasing certain sections of society for other specialized roles. Resources (measured in time and manpower) can be reallocated from subsistence production to political control. Second, intensification frequently has implications for investment which reinforce sedentary behaviour and can require protection (Gilman 1981). Intensification can involve the implementation of vulnerable, labour-intensive operations such as terracing, irrigation networks, and cultivation of slow-growing crops such as trees which take much time to nurture but which are quick to destroy if not protected by a regional authority.

Circumscription reinforces the conditions set by the intensification of production. In some cases this may take a geographical form. The dry valleys of coastal Peru, the location of the earliest states in South America, were sharply defined by high mountains. The island of Hawaii had a sharp maritime boundary (although it required an outside catalyst to produce a unified state). Carneiro (1970, 1988) also emphasizes two further factors of population and warfare. In other cases it may take a social form; in this there is no physical circumscription, but the local society has developed in such a way as to provide a cultural circumscription. The competitive emulation described by peer-polity interaction took place in a landscape of competing political centres (Renfrew and Cherry 1986) and thus provided a powerful force of circumscription. Relocation in these circumstances of circumscription has severe costs (Roscoe 1993: 116) and, therefore, the move towards state formation becomes more acceptable to all in society as the less costly of alternatives.

The crucial phase of state formation may not be the implementation of the state itself but the development of important social changes prior to state formation (see Chapter 22). For many this is the more significant threshold (Hayden and Gargett 1990; Sahlins 1963; Wright 1984). Accumulation of wealth by Big Men, associated with competitive feasting, ritual display, and gift giving, can be seen in many regions of the world with emerging socio-economic differentiation (Hayden and Gargett 1990: 7). This is also true of a number of archaeological contexts just prior to state formation, such as the Orientalizing period in the first-millennium BC Mediterranean. The crucial threshold is the level to which this differential accumulation of wealth was tolerated. The usual response is that it was tolerated in time of crisis. Ethnographic studies of the cargo system in Mesoamerica suggest that self-interest continues to operate in time of crisis and that individual advancement is available to those with energy, motivation, and skill (Hayden and Gargett 1990: 7).

An illustration of a parallel type of development can be seen in Mesopotamia, although it is dangerous to construct general theories out of mere anecdotes.

Political power rested, from an early stage, in the hands of the king (*lugal*). This figure may have become institutionalized out of a temporary role as head of an assembly set up on an *ad hoc* basis in moments of crisis (Jacobsen 1957). By preserving and enhancing temporary powers, the king may have consolidated his position in a pattern reminiscent of some of the Mesopotamian myths of the God Ninurta. He built on influence inherited from his father through his role as leader in war and administrator of justice. He then punished by death or severe penalties those who opposed his rule. The Mesopotamian epic tales centred on human heroes have an even more coercive feel. Cities are destroyed and water from canals is diverted towards the victors, recalling the tensions over the control of water in this region up to the present day. In these circumstances, administration became increasingly an extension of the king's household and thus under centralized political control.

Population pressure, population density, settlement nucleation and hierarchy

Social and cultural anthropologists have had considerable debate about the relationship between population size, density, and the degree of political development. Fortes and Evans-Pritchard, in a work originally published in 1940, suggested that a large population, a high degree of political centralization, and great density, were not necessarily related (Fortes and Evans-Pritchard [1940]1975: 7–8). Other, more extensive, cross-cultural studies by Carneiro (1967) have claimed to show a relationship between population size and the complexity of social organization. Stevenson (1968) reacted against the synchronic studies undertaken by the British social anthropologists (Fortes and Evans-Pritchard [1940]1975) and took an explicitly historical and evolutionary approach. By extending the time depth he claimed to demonstrate the interrelationship of population density and state formation. Against this Cordy (1986), working on evidence from the island societies of the Pacific, has claimed to show a negative correlation between social stratification (not necessarily coterminous with the state) and population density. All these accounts have relied heavily on ethnographic or ethnohistoric data. Only archaeology can effectively study the timing of the relationship, although the close interlinkage of density, nucleation, and population pressure makes them very difficult to separate with archaeological chronologies.

One of the claimed achievements of archaeological research has been to show that population could be at a plateau or in decline at the time of state formation (Wright 1986; Wright and Johnson 1975), although this has since been disputed by Carneiro (1988). This possible exclusion of the role of high population pressure at the time of state formation does not exclude its part in the creation of pre-state, but nevertheless differentiated, social formations.

Alternatively, if population levels are generally low at the time of state formation, there is the possibility that labour shortage may be an important factor. In other words, it might not be pressure of too many people, but the stress of a lack of manpower to maintain the status quo which pressured those in political control. Under these conditions, the development of the institutionalized means to retain the available manpower could have been crucial and this might be most readily achieved by fostering nucleation and the state necessary to maintain it.

The change in population distribution at the time of state formation was frequently an increase in localized densities, otherwise defined as nucleation. One of the most extreme examples of this nucleation process is one of the earliest in its local region: Teotihuacán in the Valley of Mexico. The city was founded in 100 BC and grew to cover 20 square kilometres by AD 500, occupied by an estimated population of 125,000. This appears to have been an explicit political process, since the main avenues of the city were extended in preparation for an influx of population and the local countryside was drained of people by what must have been enforced or at least constrained immigration.

A more normal range of examples of this process can be seen in societies as widely separated as those from the Valley of Oaxaca (Mexico) and pre-Roman central Italy. In the Valley of Oaxaca, two cycles of population growth and nucleation took place up to and just beyond state formation: first around San José Mogote and then at the time of state formation around Monte Albán (Blanton *et al.* 1981: 58–75; Fig. 23.4). Intensive field survey of the Oaxaca valley has shown the complexity of population distribution over time in different parts of this tripartite region (Feinman *et al.* 1985). In these cycles, nucleation appears to precede rural colonization, registered by decrease in the primacy index (Kowalewski *et al.* 1989: 510). In the first phase (between 700 and 500 BC), the valley had an estimated population of 2,500–5,000 housed in some eighty-five communities, controlled from about three centres. Between 500 and 300 BC, the whole valley was united under the control of a new foundation at Monte Albán, drawing political support from the three sectors of the valley (Marcus 1992a: 399–401). This was the phase of greatest territorial control. A crucial debate is over the motivation of this nucleated state formation: iconographic evidence (see p. 939) suggests that the unification was not entirely voluntary. The growing nucleation continued long after the foundation of the state, while the exent of territorial control decreased (Marcus 1992a: 400).

A similar sequence appears to have taken place in central Italy at the time of state formation between the first and second millennia BC. Population growth is detectable in the last centuries of the first millennium BC, succeeded by a possible drop in population levels and considerable nucleation in the ninth century BC. As at Monte Albán, the nucleation was the population base on which state formation was founded, but not clearly preceded by social ranking. As in the Valley of Oaxaca,

Figure 23.4 Monte Albán. Photograph: S. Stoddart.

it was also the basis for subsequent rural colonization, in this case in the seventh century BC, again registered by a decrease in the degree of primacy, but unlike the Valley of Oaxaca it entailed a strengthening of territorial control, in competition with closely placed, equally ranked centres, undergoing similar processes of nucleation and colonization.

Nucleation, however, appears to be but one route towards state formation. There is strong evidence from some regions of the world, less well-known archaeologically, that nucleation was not a necessary accompaniment of state formation. In some cases such as the Greek polis, nucleation was small scale. In other cases, the state based on a dispersed population was generally much more unstable (Genito 1994; Moses and Halkovic 1985: 19–25). The nomads of the Asiatic steppes, the Maya in Mesoamerica, the Shang and the western Chou in China, Zimbabwe in central Africa and Angkor in Indo-China are examples of radically different distributions of population, suggesting considerably different mechanisms of state control, communications, and processes of formation. There is considerable current debate over the degree of centralization of groups such as the Maya (Fox *et al.* 1996).

925

Interaction

Interaction, in various levels of intensity, has always been an important constituent of theories of state formation. At the one extreme there are the mythical charters of the early states themselves, which give a simple picture of an exotic hero transforming society or of the arrival of society fully formed from some distant source. In some studies of state formation (central Italy, for example), such sources have been accepted literally until very recently. In others, diffusionism has been closely linked to trade. Even after the rejection of these extreme accounts, involving external interaction, interaction is still given a strong role in recent theories of 'peer-polity' interaction and 'core–periphery' relations.

Peer-polity interaction was established by its authors as a general theory of internal interaction affecting all forms of cultural organization, but has been most widely applied to complex societies (Renfrew 1982; Renfrew and Cherry 1986). The theory is based, at least in part, on the empirical generalization that states do not generally arise in isolation but in groups. The components of these groups are, it is claimed, competitive equals. It is the very process of competition and emulation between equal polities under conditions of intensification that leads to the growth of complexity and, at a later stage of development, to the formation of control hierarchies.

This approach has been explored in a number of different societies, but generally represents a simplification. Competition does not necessarily lead to precise emulation either of cultural practice or physical size. In some cases, the reverse can take place. To cite a few examples of this, Athens, in the mid-first millennium BC, employed writing extensively, whereas Sparta differentiated itself from its rivals by a public denial of literacy. In the Valley of Mexico, Teotihuacán was an unrivalled master of its region and considerably larger than any contemporary rival centre in Mesoamerica. In central Italy, approximately twelve city-states in the mid-first millennium BC competed with each other but varied considerably in size and cultural practice. Nevertheless, some types of state formation are much stimulated by the presence of rival communities developing at the same time.

Others have pointed out both practical and more theoretical difficulties (Cherry 1982). A major practical problem is establishing the independence of individual polities. Unless there are written sources, it is difficult to establish the political ranking or, conversely, the political rivalry of contemporary centres. However, in many cases of incipient state formation, the presence of incipient naturalistic iconography, early (even if politicized) literacy, and hints from later sources, have allowed the independence of centres to be established: examples include central Italy in the first millennium BC and the Maya lowlands in the first millennium AD. An associated theoretical problem is that the peer-polity interaction only explains change once the peer polities are in existence. How did the rival centres come into existence? As repeated elsewhere in this chapter, and as discussed in Chapter 21, it is the appearance of pre-state social ranking that is perhaps the most difficult transition to explain: state formation is merely the culmination of process. The theory also has difficulty in explaining the timing and rate of change. State formation is frequently rapid. This rapidity may be inherent in competitive emulation, or it may simply be the only way that the stresses of an imposition of manifest inequality can be tolerated. Finally, the archaeological chronologies available do not always achieve the level of precision necessary to assess the contemporaneity of the emulation proposed by the model. Few archaeological chronologies approach the refinement of a generation, the time period over which some of the most rapid changes may have taken place.

The most current external interaction model is that of core–periphery (Champion 1989; Rowlands *et al.* 1987). This is a theoretical model borrowed from studies of the interconnectedness of world development since the sixteenth century (Wallerstein 1974). This analysis contrasts the consumers of the core/centre with the producers of the periphery constrained to meet the economic and political demands of the core/centre. Many archaeologists have ignored a further contrast made by Wallerstein (1974: 348) between subsistence-based autonomous early empires, the subject of their investigations, and the Modern World Economy, based on the efficient location of production, which was the subject of Wallerstein's investigations. In other words, a model is drawn from its original application to a modern world economy and applied by archaeologists to a political economy that its original authors considered inappropriate! The approach has been extensively criticized as a eurocentric rationalization of the pre-modern world, imposing utilitarian principles where other value systems, particularly in connection with luxuries, may have been more appropriate. At its worst, it is diffusionism by a different name.

In spite of this basic difficulty, many archaeologists have applied the basic differentiation between core and periphery to many cases of secondary state formation (Champion 1989; Rowlands *et al.* 1987). The effects of the expanding Roman empire have been studied in this framework in Britain and Gaul (Haselgrove 1982, 1987). In the period before incorporation in the empire, there was frequently a phase of state formation in the buffer area between core and periphery. The phase was generally short-lived since it was truncated by incorporation in the empire, but its earlier development appears to have been inextricably related to interaction with the same empire that was later to destroy it.

CRITICAL CHARACTERISTICS OF THE STATE

Those who study state-organized societies, in spite of disagreements in detail, have isolated a number of dimensions which appear to be shared by all states. First, state-organized societies organize space in a strikingly different way from other forms of society. This organization of space forms the setting or context for all other characteristics of the state. Second, all states share highly developed levels of social stratification, economic specialization and politicized administration. Third, these elements are inextricably linked with a changed ideology. Finally, one of the frequent, but not necessary, changes in technology is related to changed ideology in the development of precise systems of measurement and communication, including most prominently writing.

Organization of space

In one sense it is self-evident to state that space or the landscape provides the essential setting of all other characteristics of the state, but less self-evidently this is a transformed setting. It was increasingly a cultural and political landscape which replaced the predominantly physical landscape that had provided the setting for other types of social formation. Many definitions of the state emphasize their 'territorial integrity' (Tainter 1988: 27). Pre-state societies imprinted cultural categories on the physical landscape (Bradley 1993), but state societies brought the cultural landscape to a much more dominant position. The landscape is thus a very sensitive measure of political complexity, with a high rate of survival in the archaeological record.

In the zones as diverse in time and space as Mesopotamia and Etruria, cities were organized with respect to each other, creating their own political space rather than responding to the environment. The Uruk political environment was characterized by a series of competitive cores in fierce competition with each other and surrounded in turn by unoccupied buffer zones beyond (Algaze 1993: 115). The Etruscan city was surrounded by centrifugal zones of activity which had a political origin: funerary commemorative space, dependent agricultural space, subordinate settlements, and ritual boundaries (temples and emporia) (Fig. 23.5). In many states the organization of space was profoundly ideological. This ideological expression is most clearly seen in imperial states such as China and that of the Inca, where the capital formed the central focus of the known world beyond.

Some of the most effective advances in the state formation have been developed in the study of spatial organization and its relationship to the organization of power (Cherry 1987). This has taken two forms: the undertaking of large-scale field surveys of many of the key areas of the world where state formation has taken place, and the implementation of appropriate analytical techniques.

The success of field surveys is dependent on dry, open, conditions and an extensive regional method. This has been achieved most effectively in the Valleys of

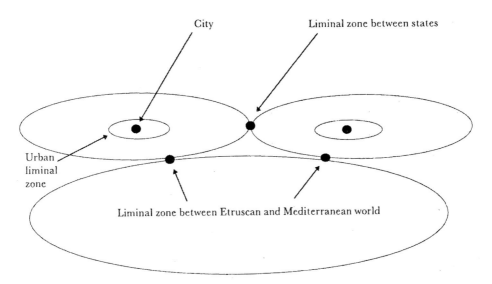

Figure 23.5 Ritualized boundaries around Etruscan city-states. Source: Accordia Research Centre, University of London.

Mexico (Parsons *et al.* 1982; Sanders *et al.* 1979) and Oaxaca (Kowalewski *et al.* 1989) in Mesoamerica, some of the coastal valleys of Peru (Wilson 1983), and in Mesopotamia (Adams 1981). All these regions are primary centres of state formation with good conditions for recovery. Furthermore, complete coverage was attempted, allowing the perception of the contrasting processes of nucleation of population and evacuation or desertion of space. Field surveys have been attempted in Greece (Bintliff and Snodgrass 1988) and Italy (Potter 1979), but recovery conditions have proved to be much more complex, although a very necessary complement to traditional studies of cemeteries and major settlements.

One major area of research is mapping the territorial extent of state power (Cherry 1987: 152–59). These techniques have traditionally involved the use of historic or ethnohistoric sources, or employed other assumptions to match political boundaries and natural catchments. More recently, the techniques of spatial geography have been brought to bear. The simplest is the concept of the Thiessen polygon. This requires the simple, and equal, division of territory between centres. A weighting derived from the size of individual centres can also be added. A more dynamic approach is that of XTENT, which enables a developing landscape to be mimicked (Renfrew and Level 1979). The XTENT of territory is a mathematical expression determined principally by the size of the centre, but with other components which can be varied to extend the territory. These variations can mimic the full range of political development, from a virtually empty political territory through to a packed and competitive landscape.

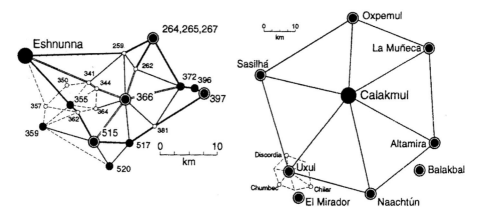

Figure 23.6 Comparative spatial characteristics of states. Reproduced with permission of J. Marcus and K. Flannery.

Once the territory has been mapped by whatever means, the hierarchy within that territory can be examined. Much of the work is heavily influenced by economic geography (Hodges 1987; Smith 1976a, 1976b), as a development of the work of Christaller (Fig. 23.6). In more strictly archaeological work, the simplest approach is to examine the quantity of sites of each size class (Fig. 23.7). This can establish a sense of the hierarchy of sites in any given area. A different approach is to arrange the sites in order of rank size. In modern studies of cities, the curves produced by such orders of rank size have been assumed to show different types of settlement system. The addition of archaeological evidence appears to show a typical development over the period of state formation from a convex curve through an intermediate stage of primacy of a number of principal nucleated centres towards a straight or lognormal distribution. These sequences have been explored very effectively in the earliest cases of state formation (Wright 1986) and in a number of cases of *secondary* state formation such as bronze age Levant (Falconer 1993) and iron age Etruria (Guidi 1985).

A critical problem remains. The scale of necessary spatial analysis is often beyond the range of a single survey: for example, the total territory covered by some Mesoamerican states (not empires) approached 100,000 square kilometres. Fluctuations of population density and political control must also be perceived at a broad scale (Marcus 1992a). In this sense, state formation in one region is related to the opportunities provided by state decline or collapse in another. In Mesoamerica, states seemed to have been formed as part of a competition between rival centres, where one centre became more successful than its neighbours and rapidly reached its greatest territorial extent by incorporation early in its trajectory. Subsequently, the mature state grew at its centre, whilst declining in territorial control at its periphery; investment shifted from expansion to centralization. Later, a peripheral

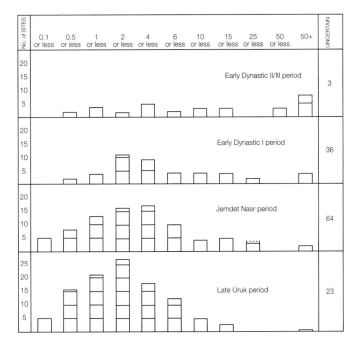

Figure 23.7 Site sizes in the Uruk countryside. Source: Adams and Nissen 1972.

area very often set up its own trajectory of expansion, or at least with allies managed to weaken the original successful centre.

The understanding of this type of development requires detailed survey in central and peripheral areas. Furthermore, these central and peripheral areas shifted through time as, for example, Teotihuacán at the centre was replaced by Tula, the latter originally on the periphery and one of a number of roughly equal centres. After a period of expansion, Tula itself was replaced by Azcapotzalco, again one of a number of rivals for power. Finally, Tenochtitlan surfaced from a number of rival centres and founded a state that became the well-known Atzec empire (Marcus 1992a: 399). State formation here, therefore, was not aligned and synchronous, but composed of shifts of spatial focus which will require generations of archaeologists to unravel. A similar pattern is repeated in the Maya lowlands (Marcus 1992a: 406–8). Early states, particularly perhaps those in the New World with greater transport logistics (without the horse, for example), lacked the long-term spatial cohesion and effective control of their declared territories. In Italy, the relationship between the Latins and the Etruscans was not dissimilar: the Etruscans were the dominant political force in central Italy until the sixth century BC, until the hitherto peripheral town of Rome became dominant and toppled the neighbouring Etruscan polities.

931

Social stratification

Social stratification stands at the core of many definitions of the state (Fried 1967; Krader 1978). There are few early states which lack clear evidence (in terms of settlement structure and funerary remains) of distinctions in access to wealth between members of society. The major exception to this rule is the early civilization based in the Indus and Ghaggar-Hakra (Sarasvati) river systems in the third millennium BC (Kenoyer 1991). The cities lack clear internal differentiation along social lines and lack the evidence for prominent cemeteries so visible in other case studies. The ideology in this case was such that any differentiation in wealth and power was strictly controlled and sublimated. Miller (1985) has defined this society as authoritarian, but not ranked, providing an important contrast with many definitions of states.

Highly visible funerary remains were nevertheless the rule at the formative and transitional stages of state formation. Some societies, in particular, were pre-occupied with the rituals of death and provide excellent studies of the sudden differentiation of access to wealth and power. The most notable case is that of ancient Egypt, where state unification was accompanied by a dramatic change in tomb construction (Kemp 1989: 53–63). Whereas the predynastic tombs at Nagada and Hierakonpolis were modest constructions, tombs of the First Dynasty (early third millennium BC) suddenly combined monumental scale and distinctive architectural symbolism, with the niched and decorated façade of the tomb becoming a symbol of power. The step pyramid at Sakkara (*c.* 2695 BC) represented a further elaboration of burial monumentality, providing an appropriate setting for the pageantry surrounding the king; the true pyramids, constructed from the Fourth Dynasty onwards, reflected the increasing deification of the king (Fig. 23.8). Etruscan burials in central Italy reflect the same transitions on a lesser scale: the most prominent burials are precisely at the moment of state formation in the early seventh century BC.

Mortuary rites are thus a particularly prominent part of the display strategies of some early states. The most extreme example is elaborated through a linkage to coercion in the case of China. Whole retinues were interred with the dead ruler. China is a particularly fruitful case study since the process of state formation was based on the success of competing conical clans, each searching to make material expression of their power. The excavations at Erh-li-t'ou in early Shang China have begun to elucidate this process (Chang 1980). An earthen palace platform measuring 108 by 100 metres was placed at the centre of the settlement within a separate compound. Nearby are a number of burials, many clearly victims of socially embedded religious ceremonies, providing the ultimate distinction of social stratification: power over life and death. Recent discoveries in Mesoamerica suggest a similar powerful display. The dedication of the temple of the Feathered Serpent at

Figure 23.8 Egyptian pyramids. Photograph: S. Stoddart.

Teotihuacán contained the sacrifice of about 200 bound – and therefore captive – male warriors (Cabrera Castro *et al.* 1991).

Economic specialization

Division of the economy into specialist sectors is generally agreed to be an important constituent of state-organized society, even if the articulation of that specialization within complex society is more controversial and the importance of its role varies from society to society (Brumfiel and Earle 1987). In some models of specialization, the political intervention of the rulers is crucial to development. In many such cases, monopolies of production were established to control not only the necessities of life (such as subsistence products), but also the luxuries which became exclusively linked to political power.

State specialization in subsistence production can be a very effective support of the maintenance of political control which, when present, is strongly linked to the development of an effective administration (see pp. 934–35). Large aggregations of individuals in states and cities require feeding for survival, and specialization is one strategy for its effective implementation. Even so, many states developed without a

933

major specialization in the sector of subsistence production (Brumfiel and Earle 1987: 6–7); the problem was reduced if manpower was plentifully available.

Mesopotamia provides one of the clearest cases where specialization of subsistence production was developed (Galvin 1987; Zeder 1991). At a basic level, significant proportions of the population became involved in non-subsistence production, leaving livestock production as a segregated, specialized section of the economy. According to Galvin (1987), by 2100 BC specialization of livestock production was beginning to be established. Special livestock collection points, fattening establishments, and legal codes were developed. In a more detailed analysis of Banesh in levels as early as 3300 BC, Zeder (1991) claims to have found specialized systems of meat distribution among the élite. Through time, more complex and indirect processing systems appear to have been developed to channel animal products from the herds to the consumers.

State specialization in luxury production can be a very effective means for validating control. Specialization of luxury production was much more uniformly present in early state societies, but élites were not always successful in establishing monopoly positions (Brumfiel 1987). The Aztec and Inca states reserved certain materials for the use of the ruler. Cloth was particularly subject to these restrictions in upland South America (Earle 1987). One of the most striking studies of specialized craft production has been undertaken as part of the mapping project of the site of Teotihuacán in the Valley of Mexico (Millon 1981). Clear differentiation of obsidian and ceramic production zones as well as merchant quarters can be detected within the confines of this city of 20 square kilometres. Craft specialization is also prominent in the case of the Harappan civilization (Kenoyer 1991), providing one of the rare signs of differentiation in this society. Similar studies have also been undertaken at Doganella in Etruscan central Italy, exploring the internal economic differentiation of an important gateway settlement between two states (Perkins and Walker 1990).

Administration

A central element of any state was its administration; indeed this role is linked to many theories of state formation, particularly where administrative data are abundant (Wright 1969, 1977, 1978). The bureaucratic apparatus for the supply of food, the control of personnel, and the regulation of information, were essential for long-term stability and may have provided the motivation for the creation of the state.

The most influential studies of the administration within an early state have been based on the archives of early Mesopotamia. These place the temple at the centre of the urban community, buffering the effects of changing economic and political conditions. The temple was in a position to collect and distribute surpluses of produce. The temple also had an independence, based on wealth collected from gifts and offerings, its landed estates, and access to labour. A major subject of debate is the relative degree of involvement of the temple in the administration of the state (Postgate 1972). In Early Dynastic times (the early third millennium BC), the role was probably considerable, but reduced with the arrival of secular authority. It has now been conclusively shown that by 2500 BC the temple only owned a minority of the land, with the majority in the hands of the ruling family, palace administrators and priests (Diakonoff 1972).

Studies of the varying types of archives give a good impression of the interconnecting levels of administration. Foster (1982) has identified three types of archives in Sargonic Mesopotamia: family/private, household, and great household. The family archives are largely composed of round tablets, with varied handwriting covering local legal transactions of land and sale/purchase of goods, involving few individuals. Household archives have a principal administrator specializing in a principal subject important in the local area, such as agriculture (land management and food distribution). Draft copies appear to precede polished copies prepared for more central administration. Great household archives have a greater diversity of subjects (agriculture, industry, military) and complexity of filing. Political rulers appear as principal administrators or points of reference. Interlinkage between these levels provided the essence of administration.

Another well-researched classic case of the administration of what is generally considered a state-organized society is that of Minoan Crete. The tablets principally derive from three categories (Renfrew 1972: 296–97): receipts of goods, disbursements of goods, and inventories. Payments out include rations for personnel and ritual gifts. Payments in include assessments of tribute. At the very least there is evidence here of the central control of information about subsistence products arriving at and leaving the palaces. This information, when combined with the level of nucleation, the local agricultural capacity, and the evidence of storage, strongly suggests that the central administration in the palaces was collecting a surplus to support a population too large to be supplied from local fields.

Ideology

A very important aspect of the maintenance of states is the definition, measurement, and control of commodities, both material and immaterial. Ideological requirements are shared by all complex societies, but the state needs a much more effective strategy commensurate with the greater differentiation of wealth and political power.

State-organized societies developed forms of standardized measurement as part of their mechanism of control: weights, volume, the law, and time. Calendars appear for the first time. Economical use of time became important and was marked as a resource in itself, under rigorous control. It also reinforced the preference towards nucleation of population which reduced the costs of distance. The control of time is thus a fundamental segment of state ideology, which was particularly emphasized beyond the boundary of directly experienced physiological time: the unexperienced time of the distant past. In state-organized societies the control of the content of the past allows the claim of continuity to be made when, in fact, major social and political changes had undoubtedly taken place. A new view of the past was created, but the novelty was disguised. In many societies, writing in the hands of the state authorities was employed to facilitate this process.

Ethnographic accounts allow exploration of this process. Those of the Asante state allow a fairly detailed appraisal. Control of time was highly visible. Any evidence for a separate origin of the constituent units of the state was consciously controlled, with 'the government politically undermining every monument, which records the distinct origins of their subjects' (Bowdich 1819: 228). A taboo on the discussion of clan origins persisted until the time of the later ethnographer, Rattray (1929: 65): 'one dares not discuss the origin of another'. In the place of the individual origins of the constituent parts, new forms of history were put in its place. At one level, the state was reported as merely the enlargement of an ancient relationship between housefather and family (Rattray 1929: 105). The state's version of origins seems to have misled even the same respected ethnographer in a convincing demonstration of the power of this state's ideology: 'every germ of the more advanced system of government with which we have to deal already existed in this little family democracy' (Rattray 1929: 403).

At another level, the historically imprecise ancestors of the non-élite were contrasted with the official ancestors of the state itself. All the sources, ancient and modern, refer to Osei Tuku (the Asantehene) and Okomfo Anokye (his priest) as the creators of all precedent, structural and ideological. This position was also given a point of reference in material culture that emphasized the 'enlargement of the ancient relationship between housefather and family'. The Golden Stool was the extrapolation of an image that pervaded the whole of Asante life to the highest of hierarchical levels. Each individual, however humble his office, had a stool that mimicked the highest ideal of the state. By this technique, the state could claim that it was no more than a logical culmination of preceding existence, even if, in fact, it represented enormous innovation.

Archaic Greece provides a wealth of similar evidence of respect for the past through the cult activities at the tombs of the earlier bronze age dead. These have been collectively classified as hero cults (Whitley 1988), although it may be too simple to see these as part of a wider pattern of ancestor respect linked to early states. The important emphasis is on the right of burial within a demarcated cemetery earned as a member of the citizen body of the state. In ancient Meso-potamia, some research into the past by the rulers of states almost has an archaeo-logical dimension to it (Schnapp 1993; and see Chapter 1). Narbonides was very conscious that he followed a long line of rulers and examined the material culture of the past – stelae, clay tablets – to allow the proper restoration of a lost cult (Reiner 1985). This gave his rule in the present the necessary legitimacy.

Writing and literacy

Writing, the material counterpart of language, is not a prerequisite of state organ-ization in spite of the emphasis given to it by Gordon Childe (1950), or indeed dependent on state formation for its development (Marcus 1992b: 32). It is rather a technology adopted by some states for practical and ideological purposes. A number of state-organized societies, notably the Yoruba and the three major civilizations of Peru (the Moche, the Chimu and the Inca), employed no writing system. Others, such as those based on Teotihuacán and Sparta, made minimal use of it, in spite of, or perhaps because of, its prominence in neighbouring societies.

The development of scripts is no longer seen as simple progression from pictures to signs, to syllables and then to the supreme achievement of the alphabet (Whitehouse and Wilkins 1986: 130–31). Formalization, a necessary ingredient of a usable writing system, took place at a very early stage. An examination of New World writing systems shows the heterogeneity of writing, the combination of pictographic, logographic/ideographic and phonetic elements in the choice of component parts. Writing developed in the late fourth millennium BC in both Egypt and Mesopotamia, where good preservation of papyri and clay tablets respectively has allowed detailed study to be made of the strikingly different uses of literacy in these two early societies. Writing only developed in Mesoamerica from c. 700–400 BC.

The treatment of literacy has varied in its emphasis on its technological effects (Goody 1968) and its social implications (Street 1984). As a technology, writing stores information and allows transfer of that information over large distances independently of individual personalities. The implications of writing depend heavily on the social context where it is employed. Wherever it is used it can be very effectively exercised for display and propaganda even for those unable to penetrate its meaning.

Literacy was highly restricted before the advent of the printing press. In most early states, the political élite saw to it that literacy remained their closely guarded monopoly. The restricted access to literacy was aided by the complexity of the scripts of early states, which required extensive training to allow competent use: the Mayan and Egyptian writing systems, for example, employed 700–1,000 signs. Access to literacy was not, though, simply a matter of technical proficiency. The more simple alphabetic script may have enabled, but never led to, extensive literacy (Harris 1989; Stoddart and Whitley 1988), until the state-developed systems of mass education of the modern era.

Many studies of state formation and writing have stressed the bureaucratic concerns of scribes and priests. In Mesopotamia, the painstaking records were made to record movement of commodities and were thus essentially economic. The Mesopotamian temple is the institution where the earliest collections of written documents have been found. They comprise two types: lexical texts or reference works and administrative documents. The lexical texts supported the unilateral nature of this type of literacy, the primary aim of which was to service the large estates as recorded in the administrative documents (Postgate 1984). This was an internalized administrative system, allowing transport of information through time rather than space. The Mesopotamian system was, though, greatly extended in the succeeding centuries (Postgate 1984): the new roles included many aspects of law, particularly land transactions, business records, letters, and literary texts. Literate administration was even transacted at the household level, suggesting a quite considerable distribution of literacy (Foster 1982).

The Mesopotamian use of writing does, however, appear to be exceptional and uses in other early states depended greatly on the social and political context. In China, the early use of writing was strongly connected to social identification rather than to the economy. Kinship was the key to early Chinese society and this is reflected in writing itself (Chang 1980: 247–48). A similar pattern is visible in the early use of writing in Etruria, where writing was initially restricted to an élite engaged in ritualistic gift exchange (Cristofani 1975; Stoddart and Whitley 1988). The situation was not even straightforward in the early Greek states: writing was sometimes associated with barbarians and one state, Sparta, wielded immense political power without visibly adopting the literacy of its neighbours (Thomas 1992: 130–31).

Public display of literacy appears to be a unifying theme of many early states, often linking the figurative to the literate. The fifth-century BC state of Athens took great care to display tribute lists. The early Cretan city-states displayed their laws (Stoddart and Whitley 1988). Literacy was public and monumental. In many cases, it was linked to public rituals where the act of writing was as important as the content (Beard 1985).

The most evident use of writing as political display can be seen in the Mesoamerican and Egyptian state-organized societies (Marcus 1992b; Fig. 23.9). The visual effect of symmetry and balance was as important as the content. In Mesoamerican cases, myth, history and propaganda were combined in the annotated images of the political élite. The concept of time was radically different to the linearity which we employ today. Historical events were woven into cycles of natural phenomena which had the predictability so much required by the political élite.

938

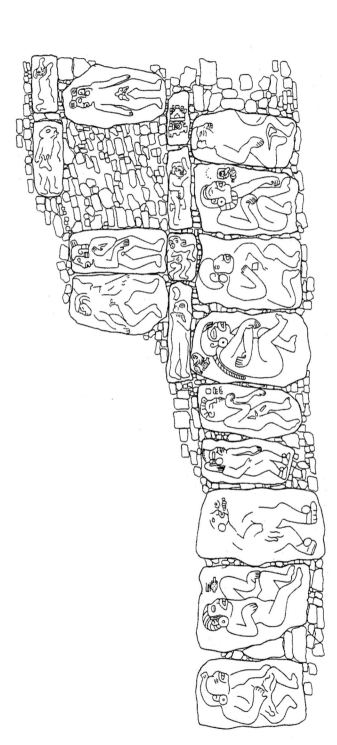

Figure 23.9. Stone sculptures at Monte Albán. The lowest row of victims features individuals whose hieroglyphic names could be read by persons standing close to the gallery; all those individuals face to the viewer's right. The second row shows corpses in a horizontal position. The third row shows victims facing to the viewer's left; the fourth row again shows horizontal corpses. Source: Marcus 1992b.

Truth was defined with reference to the political present. As Marcus (1992b: 15–16) explains, this covered a wide field: the identification of vanquished individuals and places and the resulting limits of political territory; the nodal points of genealogy (ancestors, birth, marriage and titles); and damage, obliteration of rivals and reworking of time to cover the gaps. In Mesoamerica, the most prominent example of rewriting history is that of the Mexica in the reign of Itzcoatl (c. AD 1428–40), who as founders of the Aztec state required a more substantial past. Similar strategies were employed in ancient Egypt. The most famous, if indeed exceptional, case here is that of Amenhotep, who started deliberate political action against the priests of Amun and set in train a series of fluctuating political processes over the period c. 1450–1300 BC. Amenhotep changed his name to Akhenaten and moved his capital to Akhetaten from Thebes. His successor was Tutankhaten, better known as Tutankhamun because he reversed the process to protect his political position. Their successors attempted to erase these political aberrations from history. At each stage, inscriptions were remodelled to reflect the political present.

Visual display was often the counterpart of coercion, although completely absent from the material culture of some state-organized societies such as those of the Indus. An extreme expression of the interlinkage of writing, iconography, and coercion is the prisoner staircase at Tamarindito, one of a number of Maya sites, where bound, almost naked, prisoners form the steps, crushed by the victorious élite. An even more emphatic monument was set up at Monte Albán in the Valley of Oaxaca between 500 and 400 BC at the transition to state formation. This monument provides a display of some 300 naked corpses (Fig. 23.9), with mutilated bodies arranged in awkward positions and the most eminent identified by name. A later building on the same site appears to record fifty localities or landmarks on the boundaries of conquered territory to a limit of 50–150 kilometres from the central place (Marcus 1992b: 394–400). Other Mesoamerican maps do not necessarily show accurate measurement, but the political map as the state wished it to be conceived. Political dependency was the key information.

Many of the monumental inscriptions fall within the class of vertical propaganda, devised by the élite for viewing by the majority. These were displayed in prominent positions and had to be impressive visually since literacy would not have been widely available. Some were coercive as described above. Others simply provided the authority of codified law and other public statements. In other cases the propaganda had a more private audience of the élite itself and can be classified as horizontal propaganda. This type of propaganda was employed in Mesoamerica, for instance at the Maya site of Palenque: in the Temple of the Inscriptions, the depiction of the dead ruler's fictive genealogy in iconographic form could only have been seen by an élite few. The same is particularly true of the paintings of Etruscan tombs, to which only a restricted group belonging to the élite family would have gained access.

The balance between public and private propaganda reflected the type of political structure of the individual state. In Mesoamerica, the Aztec emphasized the public monuments, whereas the Mixtec concentrated on relatively private codices. The Zapotec and the Maya combined both techniques. In Archaic Crete, the only form of literacy that has survived was inscribed as public law codes. In Athens, a much wider use of literacy has been preserved.

Coercion

The ultimate sanction of any state was the implementation of force. It is very easy to interpret visible fortifications and panoplies of military hardware in élite graves as the operation of this final sanction. In reality, such material culture may be more a sign of the vertical propaganda already discussed.

The use of force is perhaps better conceived as a failure of other means to achieve the same ends: the control of the large populations by relatively few. Undoubtedly, coercion was more frequently threatened than activated, but certain cultural traditions of state organization resorted to such methods more frequently: Mesoamerican and Chinese societies certainly give an impression that violent warfare was a frequently employed method of control of large populations.

Generally, however, coercion is more often a product of major transitions: formation and collapse (Chapter 25). If coercion was used repeatedly, the state would simply have ceased to exist, since over the extensive territory controlled by a state it would have been impractical to use it simultaneously. The energies of the state would have been too much distracted from other activities. In some societies, such as Mesoamerica, where coercion does appear to have been extensively used, early states appear to have fragmented at their margins because of the impossibility of bringing coercion to bear at the geographical limits of physical power.

CONCLUSION

State organization brings advantages and disadvantages. The study of the collapse of states and empires is covered in Chapter 25, but it is worth pointing out here that states and empires close to collapse often expose more readily their mechanisms for maintenance, shifting the balance from advantage to disadvantage. One only has to read the moving accounts of Ethiopia in the last days of Haile Selassie to see the increasingly ineffective and visible mechanisms for the maintenance of a state: in particular, attempts by the state to secure information and respond to it with increasingly weak coercion. These mechanisms would have remained concealed if all was well.

Many authors have pointed out the disadvantages of civilization even when functioning effectively. The primary area of disadvantage is that of exploitation. The organizers of many early states made successful attempts to extract labour from the majority. Many of the characteristics of states described above derive directly or indirectly from this basic characteristic. There are many consequences. One prominent area is that of the well-being of the population, which can be calibrated by the simple measure of physical health. Increased population density has provided fertile ground for the development of diseases which differentially affected those at a material disadvantage; an infectious disease such as tuberculosis benefited greatly from the development of urbanism and the differentiation presented by the state apparatus (Blakely and Mathews 1986).

The presence of the state is, therefore, a dynamic balance between the imposition of taxes (in the broadest sense) and the benefits of services and security. The limit of tolerance, if that formula went awry, varied between different societies. Many early states were under pressure to expand and extract more from the majority, producing tensions between the rulers and the ruled. For the majority of the population, this would have disturbed the stable equation of advantage and disadvantage. Thus in most early states, long-term trajectories were in the minority, since there were always potential tensions leading towards decline and collapse.

In the final analysis, state formation is no more than the climax of a longer process where social inequality is held more firmly in place. Some of the formative phases prior to state formation have already been explored in the two previous chapters. It is the development of the effective institutions of control and coercion, not just in the urban centre but in the whole landscape, seeking to provide more stable and resolute political power, that lies at the heart of the state. In reality, this control was never absolute and states exhibit varying control over space and through time. Considerable wealth differentiation may seem a very efficient implementation of power in the short term but may present a less stable political trajectory in the long term. This is perhaps the simple lesson that the knowledge of long-term trends from archaeology can provide for certain parts of the modern world.

REFERENCES

Adams, R. M. (1972) 'Patterns of urbanization in Early Southern Mesopotamia', in P. J. Ucko, R. Tringham and G. W. Dimbleby (eds) *Man, Settlement and Urbanism*, London: Duckworth: 735–49.

Adams, R. M. (1981) *Heartland of Cities*, Chicago: Chicago University Press.

Adams, R. M. and Nissen, H. J. (1972) *The Uruk Countryside. The Natural Setting of Urban Societies*, Chicago: University of Chicago Press.

Alexander, J. (1972) 'The beginnings of urban life in Europe', in P. J. Ucko, R. Tringham and G. W. Dimbleby (eds) *Man, Settlement and Urbanism*, London: Duckworth: 843–50.

Algaze, G. (1993) *The Uruk World System. The Dynamics of Expansion of Early Meso-potamian Civilization*, Chicago: University of Chicago Press.

Beard, M. (1985) 'Writing and ritual. A study of diversity and expansion in the Arval Acta', *Papers of the British School at Rome* 53: 114–62.

Bietti-Sestieri, A. M. (1992) *The Iron Age Community of Osteria dell'Osa. A Study of Socio-political Development in Central Tyrrhenian Italy*, Cambridge: Cambridge University Press.

Bintliff, J. L. and Snodgrass, A. M. (1988) 'Off-site pottery distributions: a regional and inter-regional perspective', *Current Anthropology* 29: 506–12.

Blakely, R. L. and Mathews, D. S. (1986) 'What price civilization? Tuberculosis, for one', in M. Richardson and M. C. Webb (eds) *The Burden of Being Civilized. An Anthropological Perspective on the Discontents of Civilization*, London: University of Georgia Press: 11–23.

Blanton, R. E., Kowalewski, S. A., Feinman, G. and Appel, J. (1981) *Ancient Mesoamerica. A Comparison of Change in Three Regions*, Cambridge: Cambridge University Press.

Bowdich, T. E. (1819) *Mission from Cape Coast Castle to Ashantee*, London: Murray.

Bradley, R. (1993) *Altering the Earth: the Origins of Monuments in Britain and Continental Europe*, Edinburgh: Society of Antiquaries of Scotland.

Brumfiel, E. M. (1987) 'Élite and utilitarian crafts in the Aztec state', in E. M. Brumfiel and T. K. Earle (eds) *Specialization, Exchange, and Complex Societies*, Cambridge: Cambridge University Press: 102–18.

Brumfiel, E. M. and Earle, T. K. (1987) 'Specialization, exchange, and complex societies: an introduction', in E. M. Brumfiel and T. K. Earle (eds) *Specialization, Exchange, and Complex Societies*, Cambridge: Cambridge University Press: 1–9.

Cabrera Castro, R., Sugiyam, S. and Cowgill, G. L. (1991) 'The templo de Quetzalcoatl project at Teotihuacán: a preliminary report', *Ancient Mesoamerica* 2: 77–92.

Carneiro, R. L. (1967) 'On the relationship between size of population and complexity of social organization', *Southwestern Journal of Anthropology* 23: 234–43.

Carneiro, R. L. (1970) 'A theory of the origin of the state', *Science* 169: 733–38.

Carneiro, R. L. (1988) 'The circumscription theory: challenge and response', *American Behavioural Scientist* 31: 497–511.

Champion, T. C. (ed.) (1989) *Centre and Periphery. Comparative Studies in Archaeology*, London: Allen and Unwin.

Chang, K. (1980) *The Archaeology of Ancient China*, New Haven and London: Yale University Press.

Cherry, J. (1982) 'Polities and palaces: some problems in Minoan state formation', in C. Renfrew and J. Cherry (eds) *Peer Polity Interaction and Socio-political Change*, Cambridge: Cambridge University Press: 19–45.

Cherry, J. F. (1987) 'Power in space: archaeological and geographical studies of the state', in J. Wagstaff (ed.) *Landscape and Culture. Geographical and Archaeological Perspectives*, Oxford, Blackwell: 146–72.

Childe, V. G. (1950) 'The urban revolution', *Town Planning Review* 21: 3–17.

Claessen, J. M. and Skalnik, P. (1978) *The Early State*, The Hague: Mouton.

Cohen, R. (1978) 'Introduction', in R. Cohen and E. Service (eds) *Origins of the State: the Anthropology of Political Evolution*, Philadelphia: Institute for the Study of Human Issues: 1–20.

Collis, J. (1984) *Oppida. Earliest Towns North of the Alps*, Sheffield: Department of Prehistory and Archaeology, University of Sheffield.

Cordy, R. (1986) 'Relationships between the extent of social stratification and population in Micronesian polities at European contact', *American Anthropologist* 88: 136–42.

Cristofani, M. (1975) 'Il dono in Etruria arcaica', *Parola del Passato* 30: 132–52.

Diakonoff, I. M. (1972) 'Socio-economic classes in Babylonia and the Babylonian concept of social stratification', in D. O. Edzard (ed.) *Gesellschaftsklassen in Alten Zweistromland und in dem angenzenden Gebieten*, Munich: XIII Rencontre Assyriologie Internationale: 41–52.

Earle, T. K. (1987) 'Specialization and the production of wealth: Hawaiian chiefdoms and the Inka empire', in E. M. Brumfiel and T. K. Earle (eds) *Specialization, Exchange, and Complex Societies*, Cambridge: Cambridge University Press: 64–75.

Engels, F. ([1884]1985) *The Origin of the Family, Private Property and the State*, Harmondsworth: Penguin.

Falconer, S. E. (1993) 'The development and decline of bronze age civilization in the southern Levant: a re-assessment of urbanism and ruralism', in C. Mathers and S. Stoddart (eds) *Development and Decline in the Mediterranean Bronze Age*, Sheffield: Sheffield University, Sheffield Archaeological Monographs 8: 305–33.

Feinman, G. M., Kowalewski, S. A., Finsten, L., Blanton, R. and Nicholas, L. (1985) 'Long-term demographic change: a perspective from the valley of Oaxaca, Mexico', *Journal of Field Archaeology* 12 (3): 333–62.

Finley, M. I. (1963) *The Ancient Greeks*, New York: Viking Press.

Flannery, K. V. (1972) 'The cultural evolution of civilizations', *Annual Review of Ecology and Systematics* 3: 399–426.

Fletcher, R. (1995) *The Limits of Settlement Growth*, Cambridge: Cambridge University Press.

Fortes, M. and Evans-Pritchard, E. E. ([1940]1975) 'Introduction', in M. Fortes and E. E. Evans-Pritchard (eds) *African Political Systems*, Oxford: Oxford University Press: 1–23.

Foster, B. R. (1982) 'Archives and record-keeping in Sargonic Mesopotamia', *Zeitschrift für Assyriologie* 72 (1): 1–27.

Fox, J. W., Cook, G. W., Chase, A. F. and Chase, D. Z. (1996) 'The Maya state: centralized or segmentary? Questions of political and economic integration', *Current Anthropology* 37 (5): 795–801.

Fried, M. (1960) 'On the evolution of social stratification and the state', in S. Diamond (ed.) *Culture in History*, New York: Columbia University Press: 713–31.

Fried, M. (1967) *The Evolution of Political Society*, New York: Random House.

Friedman, J. and Rowlands, M. J. (1977) 'Notes towards an epigenetic model of the evolution of civilization', in J. Friedman and M. J. Rowlands (eds) *The Evolution of Social Systems*, London: Duckworth: 201–76.

Fustel de Coulanges, N. D. (1883) *La cité antique: étude sur le culte, le droit les institutions de la Grece et de Rome*, Paris: la Hatchette.

Galvin, K. F. (1987) 'Forms of finance and forms of production: the evolution of specialized livestock production in the ancient Near East', in E. M. Brumfiel and T. K. Earle (eds) *Specialization, Exchange, and Complex Societies*, Cambridge: Cambridge University Press: 119–29.

Genito, B. (1994) *The Archaeology of the Steppes. Methods and Strategies*, Papers from the International Symposium in Naples, 9–12 September 1992 (Series Minor 44), Naples: Istituto Universitario Orientale.

Giddens, A. (1979) *Central Problems in Social Theory*, London: Macmillan.

Giddens, A. (1984) *The Constitution of Society*, Cambridge: Polity Press.

Gilman, A. (1981) 'The development of social stratification in bronze age Europe', *Current Anthropology* 22: 1–23.

Gledhill, J. (1988) 'Introduction. The comparative analysis of social and political transitions', in J. Gledhill, B. Bender and T. Larsen (eds) *State and Society*, London: Unwin and Hyman: 3–21.

Goody, J. (ed.) (1968) *Literacy in Traditional Societies*, Cambridge: Cambridge University Press.

Guidi, A. (1985) 'An application of the rank size rule to protohistoric settlements in the middle Tyrrhenian area', in C. A. T. Malone and S. K. F. Stoddart (eds) *Papers in Italian Archaeology IV. Vol. 3. Patterns in Protohistory*, Oxford: British Archaeological Reports, International series 245: 217–42.

Haas, J. (1982) *The Evolution of the Prehistoric State*, New York: Columbia University Press.

Harris, W. V. (1989) *Ancient Literacy*, Cambridge: Harvard University Press.

Haselgrove, C. (1982) 'Wealth, prestige and power: the dynamics of political centralization in south-east England', in C. Renfrew and S. Shennan (eds) *Ranking, Resource and Exchange*, Cambridge: Cambridge University Press: 79–88.

Haselgrove, C. (1987) 'Culture process on the periphery: Belgic Gaul and Rome during the late Republic and early Empire', in M. Rowlands, M. Larsen and K. Kristiansen (eds) *Centre and Periphery in the Ancient World*, Cambridge: Cambridge University Press: 104–24.

Hayden, B. and Gargett, R. (1990) 'Big man, big heart? A Mesoamerican view of the emergence of complex society', *Ancient Mesoamerica* 1: 3–20.

Hodges, R. (1987) 'Spatial models, anthropology and archaeology', in M. Wagstaff (ed.) *Landscape and Culture. Geographical and Archaeological Perspectives*, Oxford: Blackwell: 118–33.

Jacobsen, T. (1957) 'Early political development in Mesopotamia', *Zeitschrift für Assyriologie* 18 (52): 91–140.

Johnson, G. (1978) 'Information sources and the development of decision making organizations', in C. Redman, M. J. Berman, E. V. Curtin, W. T. Langhorne, N. M. Vesaggi and J. C. Wanser (eds) *Social Archaeology: Beyond Subsistence and Dating*, New York: Academic Press: 87–112.

Kemp, B. (1989) *Ancient Egypt: Anatomy of a Civilization*, London: Routledge.

Kenoyer, J. M. (1991) 'The Indus valley tradition of Pakistan and Western India', *Journal of World Prehistory* 5 (4): 331–85.

Kohl, P. L. (1987) 'State formation: useful concept or idée fixe?', in T. C. Patterson and C. W. Gailey (eds) *Power Relations and State Formation*, Washington, DC: American Anthropological Association: 27–34.

Kowalewski, S. A., Feinman, G. A., Finsten, L., Blanton, R. and Nicholas, L. M. (1989) *Monte Alban's Hinterland, Part II. Prehispanic Settlement Patterns in Tlacolula, Etla, and Ocotlan, the Valley of Oaxaca, Mexico*, Ann Arbor: University of Michigan, Memoirs of the Museum of Anthropology 23.

Krader, L. (1978) 'The origin of the state among the nomads of Asia', in H. J. M. Claessen and P. Skalnik (eds) *The Early State*, The Hague: Mouton: 93–107.

Kus, S. (1989) 'Sensuous human activity and the state: towards an archaeology of bread and circuses', in D. Miller, C. Tilley and M. Rowlands (eds) *Domination and Resistance*, Cambridge: Cambridge University Press: 140–54.

Lewis, H. S. (1981) 'Warfare and the origin of the state: another formulation', in J. M. Claessen and P. Skalnik (eds) *The Study of the State*, The Hague: Mouton: 201–21.

McIntosh, S. K. and McIntosh, R. J. (1993) 'Cities without citadels: understanding urban origins along the middle Niger', in T. Shaw, P. Sinclair, B. Andah and A. Okpoko (eds) *The Archaeology of Africa. Food, Metal and Towns*, London: Routledge: 622–41.

Marcus, J. (1992a) 'Political fluctuations in Mesoamerica', *National Geographic Research and Exploration* 8 (4): 392–411.

Marcus, J. (1992b) *Mesoamerican Writing Systems. Propaganda, Myth and History in Four Ancient Civilizations*, Princeton: Princeton University Press.

Marcus, J. and Flannery, K. (1996) *Zapotec Civilization. How Urban Society Evolved in Mexico's Oaxaca Valley*, London: Thames and Hudson.

Miller, D. (1985) 'Ideology and the Harrappan civilization', *Journal of Anthropological Archaeology* 4 (1): 34–71.

Millon, R. (1981) 'Teotihuacán: city, state and civilization', in J. Sabloff (ed.) *Supplement to the Handbook of Middle American Indians*, Austin, University of Texas Press: 198–243.

Morgan, L. (1877) *Ancient Society*, London: Macmillan.

Morris, I. (1987) *Burial and Ancient Society. The Rise of the Greek City State*, Cambridge: Cambridge University Press.

Moses, L. and Halcovic, J. (1985) *Introduction to Mongolian History and Culture*, Uralic and Altaic Series 149, Bloomington, Ind.: Research Institute for Inner Asian Studies, Indiana University.

Oppenheimer, F. (1923) *The State: its History and Development Viewed Sociologically*, London: George Allen.

Parsons, J. R., Brumfiel, E., Parsons, M. and Wilson, D. J. (1982) *Prehispanic Settlement Patterns in the Southern Valley of Mexico. The Chalco–Xochimilco Region*, Ann Arbor: University of Michigan, Memoirs of the Museum of Anthropology 14.

Perkins, P. and Walker, L. (1990) 'Survey of an Etruscan city at Doganella, in the Albegna valley', *Papers of the British School at Rome* 58: 1–143.

Postgate, J. N. (1984) 'Cuneiform catalysis: the first information revolution', *Archaeological Review from Cambridge* 3 (2): 4–18.

Postgate, N. (1972) 'The role of the temple in the Mesopotamian secular community', in P. J. Ucko, R. Tringham and G. W. Dimbleby (eds) *Man, Settlement and Urbanism*, London: Duckworth: 811–25.

Potter, T. W. (1979) *The Changing Landscape of South Etruria*, London: Elek

Price, B. J. (1993) 'Comment on Roscoe, P.B. 1993. Practice and political centralization. A new approach to political evolution', *Current Anthropology* 34 (2): 130–31.

Rappaport, R. A. (1971) 'The sacred in human evolution', *Annual Review of Ecology and Systematics* 2: 23–44.

Rattray, R. S. (1929) *Ashanti Law and the Constitution*, Oxford: Clarendon.

Redfield, R. (1968) *The Primitive World and its Transformations*, Harmondsworth: Penguin Books.

Redman, C. L. (1978) *The Rise of Civilization: from Early Farmers to Urban Society in the Ancient Near East*, San Francisco: W. H. Freeman.

Reiner, E. (1985) *Your Thwarts in Pieces, your Mooring Rope Cut. Poetry from Babylonia and Assyria*, Ann Arbor: University of Michigan Press.

Renfrew, A. C. (1972) *The Emergence of Civilization: the Cyclades and the Aegean in the Third Millennium BC*, London: Methuen.

Renfrew, A. C. (1982) 'Socio-economic change in ranked societies', in C. Renfrew and S. Shennan (eds) *Ranking, Resource and Exchange. Aspects of the Archaeology of Early European Society*, Cambridge: Cambridge University Press: 1–8.

Renfrew, A. C. and Cherry, J. F. (eds) (1986) *Peer Polity Interaction and Socio-political Change*, Cambridge: Cambridge University Press.

Renfrew, A. C. and Level, E. V. (1979) 'Exploring dominance: predicting polities from centres', in C. Renfrew and K. C. Cooke (eds) *Transformations. Mathematical Approaches to Culture Change*, New York: Academic Press: 145–67.

Riva, C. and Stoddart, S. (1996) 'Ritual landscapes in Archaic Etruria', in J. B. Wilkins (ed.) *Approaches to the Study of Ritual. Italy and the Ancient Mediterranean*, Accordia Specialist Studies on the Mediterranean 2, London: Accordia Research Centre: 91–109.

Roscoe, P. B. (1988) 'From big-men to the state: a processual approach to circumscription theory', *American Behavioral Scientist* 31: 472–83.

Roscoe, P. B. (1993) 'Practice and political centralization. A new approach to political evolution', *Current Anthropology* 34 (2): 111–40.

Rowlands, M., Larsen, M. and Kristiansen, K. (eds) (1987) *Centre and Periphery in the Ancient World*, Cambridge: Cambridge University Press.

Rykwert, J. (1988) *The Idea of a Town. The Anthropology of Urban Form in Rome, Italy and the Ancient World*, Cambridge, Mass.: MIT Press.

Sahlins, M. (1963) 'Poor man, rich man, big man, chief', *Comparative Studies in Society and History* 5: 285–303.

Sanders, W. and Price, B. (1968) *Mesoamerica*, New York: Random House.

Sanders, W. T., Parsons, J. R. and Santley, R. (1979) *The Basin of Mexico: the Cultural Ecology of a Civilization*, New York: Academic Press.

Schnapp, A. (1993) *La Conquête du Passé. Aux Origines de l'Archéologie*, Paris: Éditions Carré.

Service, E. (1962) *Primitive Social Organization*, New York: Random House.

Service, E. (1975) *Origins of the State and Civilization*, New York: Random House.

Shanks, M. and Tilley, C. (1987) *Social Theory and Archaeology*, Cambridge: Polity Press.

Sjoberg, G. (1960) *The Pre-Industrial City*, New York: The Free Press.

Smith, C. A. (1976a) 'Regional economic systems: linking geographical models and socio-economic problems', in C. A. Smith (ed.) *Regional Analysis. Volume 1. Economic Systems*, New York: Academic Press: 3–63.

Smith, C. A. (1976b) 'Exchange systems and the spatial distributions of élites', in C. A. Smith (ed.) *Regional Analysis. Volume 2. Social Systems*, New York: Academic Press: 309–74.

Southall, A. W. (1956) *Alur Society: a Study in Process and Types of Domination*, Cambridge: Heffer.

Spivey, N. and Stoddart, S. (1990) *Etruscan Italy*, London: Batsford.

Stevenson, R. F. (1968) *Population and Political Systems in Tropical Africa*, New York: Columbia University Press.

Steward, J. (1949) 'Cultural causality and law: a trial formulation of the development of early civilizations', *American Anthropologist* 51: 1–27.

Stoddart, S. K. F. and Whitley, J. (1988) 'The social context of literacy in Archaic Greece and Etruria', *Antiquity* 62 (237): 761–72.

Street, B. (1984) *Literacy in Theory and Practice*, Cambridge: Cambridge University Press.

Tainter, J. A. (1988) *The Collapse of Complex Societies*, Cambridge: Cambridge University Press.

Thomas, R. (1992) *Literacy and Orality in Ancient Greece*, Cambridge: Cambridge University Press.

Wallerstein, I. (1974) *The Modern World-System: Capitalist Agriculture and the Origins of the European World-Economy in the Sixteenth Century*, New York: Academic Press.

Webster, D. (1975) 'Warfare and the evolution of the state: a reconciliation', *American Antiquity* 40: 464–70.

Wells, P. (1984) *Farms, Villages and Cities: Commerce and Urban Origins in Late Prehistoric Europe*, Ithaca, N.Y.: Cornell University Press.

Wheatley, P. (1972) 'The concept of urbanism', in P. J. Ucko, R. Tringham and G. W. Dimbleby (eds) *Man, Settlement and Urbanism*, London: Duckworth: 601–37.

Whitehouse, R. and Wilkins, J. (1986) *The Making of Civilization. History Discovered through Archaeology*, London: Collins.

Whitley, J. (1988) 'Early states and hero-cults: a reappraisal', *Journal of Hellenic Studies* 108: 173–82.

Wilson, D. J. (1983) 'The origins and development of complex pre-hispanic society in the Lower Santa Valley, Peru: implications for theories of state origins', *Journal of Anthropological Archaeology* 2: 209–76.

Wittfogel, K. (1957) *Oriental Despotism*, New Haven: Yale University Press.

Wright, H. T. (1969) *The Administration of Rural Production in an Early Mesopotamian Town*, Ann Arbor: University of Michigan, Anthropological Papers of the Museum of Anthropology.

Wright, H. T. (1977) 'Recent research on the origin of the state', *Annual Reviews in Anthropology* 6: 379–97.

Wright, H. T. (1978) 'Toward an explanation of the origin of the state', in R. Cohen and E. R. Service (eds) *Origins of the State: the Anthropology of Political Evolution*, Philadelphia: Institute for the Study of Human Issues: 49–68.

Wright, H. T. (1984) 'Pre-state political formations', in T. Earle (ed.) *On the Evolution of Complex Societies: Essays in Honor of Henrey Hoijer*, Los Angeles: Undena Press: 41–77.

Wright, H. T. (1986) 'The evolution of civilizations', in D. Meltzer, D. D. Fowler, and J. A. Sabloff (eds) *American Archaeology, Past and Future: a Celebration of the Society for American Archaeology, 1935–1985*, Washington, DC: Society of American Archaeology: 323–65.

Wright, H. T. and Johnson, G. A. (1975) 'Population, exchange and early state formation in south-western Iran', *American Anthropologist* 77: 267–89.

Zeder, M. A. (1991) *Feeding Cities. Specialized Animal Economy in the Ancient Near East*, London and Washington, DC: Smithsonian Institution Press.

SELECT BIBLIOGRAPHY

The 1970s provided a number of abstract accounts of state formation, attempting all-embracing cross-cultural explanations of the rise of complexity. One of the seminal approaches is that of Flannery (1972), employing systems theory. A further influential branch is that of Wright (1977, 1978), who aimed to dissect changing variables and causes of state formation. A contrasting Marxist approach was contributed by Friedman and Rowlands (1977). In the 1980s and 1990s, often after regional research projects generated by general theory, explanations of local and regional sequences have become more prominent, although many of the best of these are visibly aware of the importance of comparison. Blanton *et al.* (1981) provide an overview of Mesoamerican state formation, but recent works, particularly from the Maya area, show that much debate over the interpretation of evidence still remains (Fox *et al.* 1996; Marcus 1992b). Kemp (1989) provides an important account of Egypt which goes beyond the hieroglyphic detail. For Mesopotamia, Redman (1978) still provides an effective balance between archaeology and textual information, and Adams (1981) gives an excellent account of the spatial dynamics. Work in the Indus valley has seen many recent advances and these are summarized in Kenoyer (1991). Work in China is more difficult to assess and the successive editions of Chang remain one of the best sources (1980). Wright (1986) has written an excellent overview of all the evidence then available to allow a comparison of the major early states. The different cultural and developmental characteristics of Greek state formation are covered by Morris (1987), whereas similar coverage of the central Italian evidence is more difficult to achieve without knowledge of the Italian language, although Bietti Sestieri (1992) and Spivey and Stoddart (1990) make a contribution.

24

THE DEVELOPMENT OF EMPIRES

Stephen L. Dyson

BACKGROUND AND DEFINITIONS

The conquest and subjection of other social and political groups has been a process in human history ever since the appearance of *Homo sapiens*. Most of those conquests have been savage, but transitory. The concept of empire implies a systematic, long-term organization of that conquest. This organization developed around a series of institutions that allowed the initial domination to turn into stable control based on a whole variety of exploitations. Among these were systems of military control such as forts and garrisons, the extraction of economic resources in the form of tribute and taxation, trade dominated by the imperial power, the purposeful spread of the political, social and economic institutions of the imperial society into the conquered areas, and systematic efforts to acculturate at least members of the conquered élite into the dominant society.

The history of empires has been mainly studied through written documents, both official and unofficial, and, in the case of more recent empires, through oral history and contemporary accounts. This documentary approach reflects the tendency of historians to base their research on the written word; but the perspective on any form of imperialism derived from written documents is often a limited one: written texts largely reflect the views and bias of the ruling social and political élite within the dominant power. Written accounts illuminate only parts of the imperial process. They emphasize military and administrative developments over long-term social and cultural change. The world of the governor-general is represented more than that of the conquered warrior, the slave, or even the lower class members of the imperial society. This élite view of history is no longer acceptable at a time when scholars seek to understand the 'forgotten' in history and look at the history of imperialism through the post-colonial perspective of the colonized rather than the colonizer (Tiffin and Lawson 1994; Woolf 1992). Other historical sources need to be found, which will provide information on these other individuals and groups which are under-reported or unreported in the traditional histories.

Archaeology has a key role to play in this search for a fuller history of empire. Archaeology deals in physical monuments, and many imperial governments have been great builders. The Great Wall of China, Hadrian's Wall in Britain, the Roman roads found all over western Europe and the Mediterranean, and Inca roads in Peru, substantiate this connection between empire and engineering. However, the political and economic impact of empires is also represented by more humble objects, be they a Staffordshire plate in a British frontier fort on the Great Lakes or a piece of Roman silver in the grave of a German prince. Archaeologists today use in their reconstructions of past societies the full range of surviving objects, including such humble items as cooking pots and chewed animal bones. Such artefacts sometimes provide the only information that we have on groups like slaves and peasants, who played an important, if oppressed, role in the imperial process.

The archaeology of empires, like all branches of historical studies, has changed dramatically over the last one hundred years. For a long time the research of such archaeologists centred on military questions. They excavated forts, located battlefields and combined forces with document-based historians to reconstruct the advance of empires and the campaigns of famous generals like Julius Caesar and the first-century AD Roman governor of Britain Agricola (Hanson 1987; Le Gall 1990; Pinon 1991). The archaeological study of the Roman empire can trace many of its roots back to nineteenth-century research in military archaeology carried out in France by the emperor Napoleon III on the battlefields of Julius Caesar, along the Roman Rhine frontier in Germany and on Hadrian's Wall in Britain (Birley 1961; Pinon 1991; Schleiermacher 1961).

Changing scholarly and social values and a different concept of colonialism and imperialism have moved both historical and archaeological studies beyond a focus on the administrative acts of proconsuls and the developmental history of forts, roads and marching camps. The study of empire has become more holistic, considering the full range of impacts, political, social, economic, intellectual, ecological, and biological that the imperial process had on the conquering as well as the conquered (Cooper and Stoler 1997; Crosby 1975, 1986; Greenblatt 1991). More emphasis has been placed on considering all the different aspects of imperialism from conquest to trade and ecological change. Many historians of imperialism, influenced by the views of Immanuel Wallerstein on the development of early modern empires (Wallerstein 1974), emphasize the unequal development that took place between the imperial core and its provincial peripheries and the high level of social and especially economic dependency which that created. Others have argued that Wallerstein's theories exaggerate this dependency and underestimate the ability of the conquered to resist and adjust to imperial exploitation (Stern 1988; Williams 1992). Archaeology, with its ability to represent those outside of the written record, can contribute significantly to this debate. However, this means that the archaeology of empire must also be an archaeology of trade, of rural development, of ecology, of disease, and of slavery.

An archaeological approach is theoretically applicable to any past imperial system. However, most archaeological research has been centred on a limited number of well-known empires. Rome has received special attention. Imperial systems associated with other ancient Mediterranean civilizations such as Mesopotamia, Egypt, Greece, and Phoenicia, have also been the objects of considerable research. In the New World, the empires of Mesoamerica and South America, especially of the Aztecs and Incas, have been extensively studied (Conrad and Demarest 1984; Hyslop 1984; Smith and Berdan 1992). Much less archaeological work has been done on other imperial systems, such as those of China and Islam.

Historical archaeology has become an important field of study in North America since the 1950s, and historical archaeologists there have centred much of their research on the colonial and post-colonial eras of the sixteenth century to the mid-nineteenth (see Chapter 28). This has meant the development of an archaeology of early modern European imperialism. For a long time this research was almost totally concentrated on eastern North America and was concerned mainly with the results of British imperialism. More recently, this archaeology of European empires has been extended not only to Spanish, French, and Dutch colonialism in North America, but also to other parts of the imperial network in places like Australia and South Africa (Schrire 1988). Since these early modern imperial systems had worldwide impacts, the need is to develop a global archaeology to study the material remains of this colonial process and evaluate their material impact on different cultures (Falk 1991).

This chapter will apply such a holistic approach to the archaeology of empires. It will consider military archaeology, but also the archaeology of acculturation, trade, rural change, and slavery. Most examples will be drawn from the better investigated imperial systems of Rome and the Americas. It does not claim to be comprehensive, but aims to provide an overview and indicate some promising areas for future archaeological research.

THE ARCHAEOLOGY OF IMPERIAL INSTITUTIONS

Empires are often best remembered by the structures and monuments that they left behind. These can range from Hadrian's Wall in the north of England to the railroad stations of the British Raj in India (Davies 1987). They represent efforts by the imperial power to impose military and political control, improve trade and communications, and acculturate the conquered to the conqueror by symbolic manipulation and the radical restructuring of the belief structures of the natives.

Military archaeology

Military archaeology has been central to the archaeological investigation of empires and has contributed in important ways to the origins of the discipline. Antiquarian studies on Hadrian's Wall in Britain began in the sixteenth century, reaching their height in the eighteenth and nineteenth centuries (Birley 1961). In the later nineteenth century frontier archaeology, especially in Germany and Austria, became more scientific. This research was designated *Limesstudien* from the Roman name for border or frontier. German and Austrian scholars undertook a long-term programme of archaeological research on the Roman frontier forts along the Rhine and the Danube (Fig. 24.1). In the systematic manner of the epoch, great effort was devoted to the identification and mapping of the forts, towns, roads, and walls that were part of the Roman border defence system, the careful excavation of military sites, and the study of their material culture. A strong interest in connecting the archaeological discoveries with historical events known from the ancient writers led to an emphasis on the precise dating of the occupation phases of sites through pottery and coins (Schleiermacher 1961). Many of the sites investigated had long been known through their striking visible remains. Others had been discovered by accident through farming activities, building construction or through the patient on-the-ground investigations of generations of antiquaries.

The development of aerial photography provided an important new tool for frontier research. Archaeological photographs made visible the plans of sites, which had left little or no trace above ground. New information on roads, camps, and field systems became especially abundant. Much of the pioneering research was done by O. G. S. Crawford between the world wars, flying over the grassy, open countryside of much of southern England, a landscape that proved especially suitable for this type of research (Crawford 1928). These investigations expanded dramatically after the Second World War, stimulated in part by the thousands of air photographs taken during the war (Bradford 1957). It has proved especially useful for the investigation of inaccessible Roman frontier zones in areas like North Africa (Baradez 1949) and the Middle East (Kennedy and Riley 1990). It has also allowed the development of an overview of frontier systems that is not possible even with the best ground research conditions. In countries like Great Britain and France, aerial photography has continued to produce abundant new information on certain types of military sites such as turf- and wood-built forts and marching camps that were occupied for only a brief period of time and left little or no surface remains (Welfare and Swan 1995).

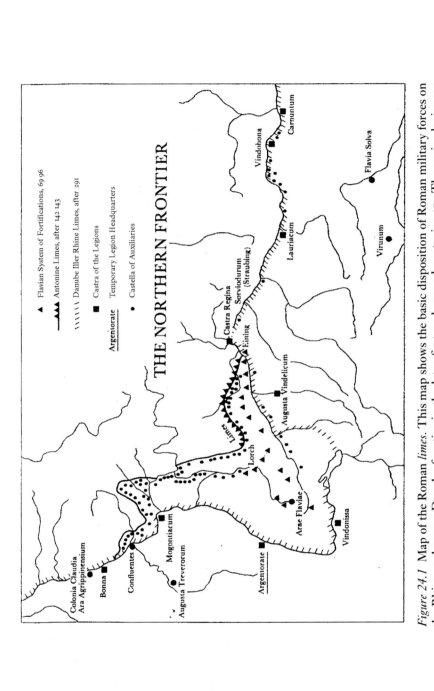

Figure 24.1 Map of the Roman *limes*. This map shows the basic disposition of Roman military forces on the Rhine and upper Danube frontier in the later first and second centuries AD. The major legionary bases were connected by a line of small unit, auxiliary forts. Source: H. Schutz (1985) *The Romans in Central Europe* (New Haven and London: Yale University Press).

Air research always has to be coordinated with ground survey and excavation. Seldom can sites like Roman camps be dated solely on the basis of their plans: information on occupation history must be obtained through the collection of surface material like pottery and through excavation. These newly discovered and dated sites, which range from the short-term marching camps regularly built by the Roman army, through forts in wood and turf designed for intermediate-term occupation, to permanent stone facilities, can then be related to military campaigns known from the ancient Roman historians. Much of this research in Northern Britain and Scotland has concentrated on the reconstruction of campaigns, such as those of the Roman general Agricola during the AD 80s (Hanson 1987) and the Roman emperor Septimius Severus in the early third century AD (Breeze 1993). A well-preserved and studied example of this type of temporary fort was the legionary camp at Inchtuthil in Scotland erected during the Agricolan campaigns and abandoned shortly thereafter (Fig. 24.2).

Many of the Roman garrison camps were occupied for long periods of time, and developed into complex military–civilian societies. The soldiers not only drilled and fought, but also worshipped their own gods, raised food, produced manufactured goods like tiles and pottery, founded families, and enjoyed the non-military aspects of life.

The complex realities of military life on the British frontier have recently been illustrated by the discovery of written documents at Vindolanda, a fort near Hadrian's Wall. The damp, oxygen-free soil at the fort site preserved objects in wood and leather that normally do not survive from the Roman period. Among the unusual finds at Vindolanda were letters and official documents written on thin sheets of wood. They ranged from muster rolls of the army unit stationed at Vindolanda in the late first century AD to an invitation to a birthday party from one garrison commander's wife to another. They tell much about the often-gritty realities of garrison life and society in north Britain under the Roman empire that would not be found in other sources (Birley 1987; Bowman 1994).

Around many of the forts small civilian communities or *vici* developed (Fig. 24.3). Their shops, taverns, and brothels serviced many of the needs of the military. Their populations were swelled by the legal and extra-legal families of soldiers and by retired veterans. Most of these villages did not survive the life of the garrison. Others became important Roman and post-Roman cities: Cologne in Germany and York in England are good examples of this process (Ottaway 1993; Woolf 1981). This social and economic aspect of garrison and civilian life, as illustrated by the remains found in the communities outside the fort walls, has received increasing archaeological attention. It not only provides insight into the civil side of soldiers' lives, but also documents their interactions with local native communities (Whittaker 1994).

The interaction of Roman soldier and civilian was even more complex when a

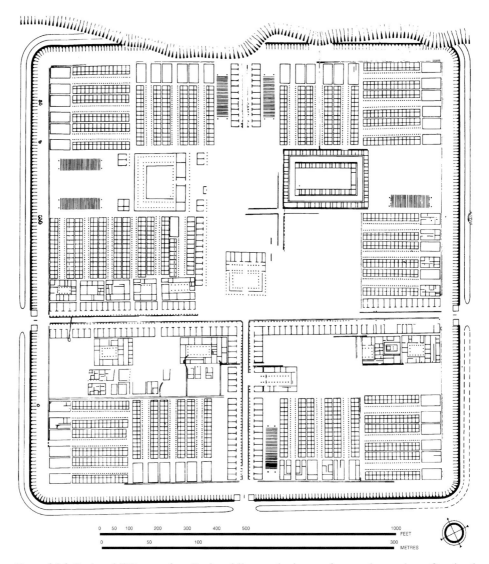

Figure 24.2 Inchtuthil Roman fort. Inchtuthil was a legionary fortress in southern Scotland that was occupied briefly in the later years of the first century AD. Aerial photography and careful excavation allowed reconstruction of the plan of the fort with headquarters building, barracks, workshops and storage facilities. Source: Breeze 1993.

military garrison was imposed on an already existing community. This was the case at Dura Europos on the upper Euphrates river. Excavations there during the 1920s and 1930s revealed a city that was first Greek, then Persian and finally a Roman garrison town. In the AD 250s it was besieged by the neighbouring Persians and

956

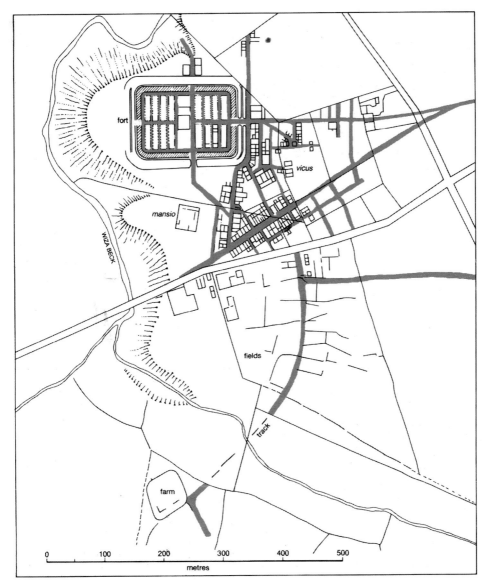

Figure 24.3 Old Carlisle, northern England: fort, *vicus* and farmstead. Source: Jones and Mattingly 1993.

either captured or abandoned. The burial of part of the residential area by siege works, the rapid abandonment after the capture of the city, and the dry desert climate, combined to preserve not only military artefacts and written records, but also a range of archaeological indications of an ethnically complex civilian and

957

military community. This complexity was illustrated by the discovery of a temple of the Persian god Mithras, a Jewish synagogue and a Christian chapel in one neighbourhood behind the wall (Hopkins 1979; Perkins 1973).

Archaeological research on colonial military sites has not been limited to the Roman empire. On the upper Nile in modern Sudan, a series of forts dating to the period of the Middle Kingdom pharaohs (*c.* 2000 BC) were initially seen as instruments of frontier control and protection of Egyptian traders moving up and down the Nile. The original excavators interpreted these as outposts of the Egyptian empire, manned by Egyptian officials who at times adopted certain aspects of the local culture including human sacrifice. Current interpretation sees them initially at least as isolated Egyptian trading outposts in what was one of the earliest complex African political organizations (Connah 1988: 35–40). The Great Wall of China, built in the third century BC, is the greatest and possibly the most famous archaeological monument known from any civilization, although it has received relatively little systematic archaeological research (Waldron 1990: 4–6, 17, 21). Medieval castles, many of which were built to consolidate expanding spheres of control, be they on the Welsh and Scottish borders of Britain, or the crusader regions of Palestine, have increasingly attracted archaeological interest (Brown 1980; Fig. 26.1).

Much of the archaeology at North American colonial sites has been military archaeology. The British, French, Spanish and Dutch all built forts to protect their often small and threatened territories (Fig. 28.9). Initially such research concentrated on the location of seventeenth- and eighteenth-century fort sites known from historical accounts and on the use of archaeological investigations to aid in their physical reconstruction as historical tourist centres. Excavation concentrated on the recovery of ground plans and of military artefacts. As has been the case with Roman frontier archaeology, however, a growing interest in social and economic history has led to a concentration of research on the illumination of daily life aspects of garrison life. This has been much of the focus for the excavations at the eighteenth-century French and British fort at Michilimackinac in northern Michigan (Peterson 1964; Stone 1974; Fig. 24.4). Finds of items like Chinese porcelain illustrate the complexity of life on the North American frontier, where rough, whiskey-drinking fur traders intermingled with British officers who drank their tea out of porcelain tea cups. A similar blend of European sophistication and frontier roughness characterized other frontier outposts, such as those of the French in northern Maine (Faulkner 1992).

Imperialism has not been limited to Rome and early modern Europe and the Americas. The Aztecs and the Incas of the New World developed impressive imperial systems. The Incas, especially, developed physical instruments of control and exploitation such as roads, forts and supply depots, which allowed them to control extensive territories in rough, mountainous terrain. They also undertook terracing and canalization schemes which allowed them to enhance the productivity

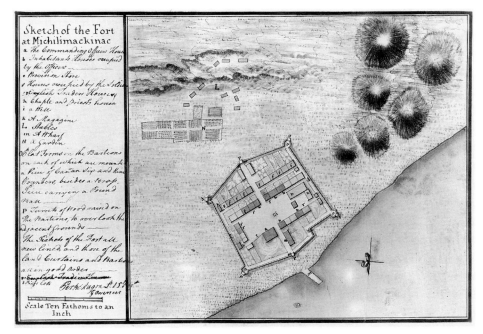

Figure 24.4 This 1766 plan of Fort Michilimackinac shows the fort shortly after the British seized it from the French. Located at the Straits of Mackinac between Lake Michigan and Lake Huron, the fort played an important part in the eighteenth-century European struggle to control the upper Great Lakes. Source: Stone 1974, fig. 4. Reproduced with permission of the William L. Clements Library, University of Michigan.

of conquered lands. These have become the object of systematic research by archaeologists using the same combination of document analysis, air photography, survey and excavation as has been employed at Roman sites.

Walls, forts, and garrisons could hold conquered territory and defend it from external forces. However, the long-term success of most empires depended on the ability of the ruling élite to create institutions, both physical and cultural, which would facilitate the integration of the conquered peoples into the larger imperial system. Towns and religious centres have been used extensively for this purpose.

Cities and towns

Newly founded cities have been major instruments of imperial administrators from Greek and Roman Antiquity to the British and French empires of the nineteenth century. Cities not only promoted economic growth and social change, but also provided locales where natives could learn imperial ways. Greek colonies ful-filled this role when the Greeks were extending their control of territory in the

959

Mediterranean. During the eighth, seventh and sixth centuries BC, these new foundations were established by the dozen on locations from Spain on the west to the Black Sea on the east (Boardman 1980). While the Greek mother cities exercised very limited direct political control over the colonial territories, they nevertheless represented a very dynamic ethnic, cultural, and economic imperialism. Greek language and culture spread to the new areas, and the indigenous populations often faced the choice of accommodation or extinction.

The temples that the Greek colonists erected to their gods are today the most visible monuments at such sites as Paestum in southern Italy and Agrigento and Selinus in Sicily. They have long been known to archaeologists. More recent archaeological research, however, has illustrated the complex planning processes that involved a grid-like layout of both the city centres and the surrounding countryside (Greco 1992). Air photographs taken at sites like ancient Metaponton in southern Italy have revealed a grid pattern of fields extending far into the countryside, marking the plots of land assigned to the settler farmers, much as it was done in the Midwest of the United States. Excavations have produced abundant evidence for the farmhouses, shrines, and cemeteries of these early Greek rural settlers.

Archaeology has also illustrated the complex interaction that these Greek colonists had with the native populations. Like historians of the American frontier, Greek archaeologists long considered these natives as expendable elements in the process of the advance of civilization, but changing judgements about imperialism have produced a growing interest in how the indigenous societies reacted to Greek colonization. Sicily and southern Italy (known as Magna Graecia in Antiquity) both provide good evidence for this process of interaction between Greeks and natives: it is reflected not only by the presence of Greek goods in indigenous burials, but also by a complex blend of native and Greek elements in habitation sites and shrines (Greco 1992; Holloway 1991). As will be seen elsewhere in the colonial process, archaeology is increasingly demonstrating that imperialism produced a complex interaction between two dynamic societies, rather than the inevitable replacement of an inferior by a superior social and economic order. This was especially true in an area like southern France, where the Greeks controlled only a small coastal hinterland but traded extensively with the Celtic groups in the interior. The dynamics of this trade produced major internal changes within Celtic society, which continued until the Roman conquest (Wells 1980, 1984).

The successors of Alexander the Great in the later fourth and third centuries BC were also great founders of cities which were to be used as instruments of imperialism. The Hellenistic Middle East was dotted with cities bearing names like Alexandria, Antioch and Seleucia, testaments to the urbanistic activities of the Hellenistic kings (Rostovtzeff 1941). However, these centres played a rather different role from the early Greek colonies. The new cities were located in newly established empires that were much more tightly administered than the domains of the original Greek colonies. They were generally founded in densely populated areas with ancient and distinguished, but non-Greek, civilizations. Some of the recently conquered territories had long-standing urban traditions; others, such as Egypt, did not. The new cities served partly as centres of power, but also as foci of Hellenization. Many of these urban ventures were short-lived. At other places such as Dura Europos, archaeological research has demonstrated how the new Greek foundation gradually evolved into a typical Mesopotamian city. Other centres like Antioch in Syria and Alexandria in Egypt grew to become the largest cities in the Hellenistic and Roman world.

The Greeks were not the only colonizers in the early Mediterranean. Beginning shortly after 1000 BC, traders from Phoenicia moved westward, founding small trading colonies to serve their commercial needs. These tended to be small centres, located on offshore islands or on easily defended protected peninsulas. Motya in Sicily and Tharros in Sardinia are good examples of these. Initially, these Phoenician settlements lived in good symbiotic relationships with the indigenous groups. Later, Carthage, the most successful of these Phoenician colonies, established its own empire based on more aggressive conquest and exploitation of local mineral and agricultural resources. At its height in the sixth, fifth and fourth centuries BC, Carthage controlled considerable territories in Spain, Sicily, North Africa, and Sardinia. Phoenician cities expanded under Carthaginian rule. In Sardinia, there is even evidence for systematic frontier fortification (Barreca 1986; Sherratt and Sherratt 1993).

The Etruscans, whose civilization dominated central Italy contemporary with the Greek colonies of Magna Graecia, also used colonies as an instrument of political and economic expansion: this is particularly well illustrated by the excavated site of Etruscan Marzabotto near Bologna, with its grid of streets and well-ordered houses (Spivey and Stoddart 1990; Fig. 24.5). It was designed to expand Etruscan influences and trading contacts across the Apennine mountains into the upper Po valley.

The Romans drew inspiration from the colonizing activities of the Greeks, the Hellenistic kings, and their neighbours, the Etruscans. During the fourth, third, and second centuries BC, as part of the process of consolidating their Italian empire, they founded colonies which recalled the Greek colonies in that they were intended as economically self-sustaining urban–rural garrison centres. However, the Romans maintained much tighter control over their colonies than the Greeks ever did and, in fact, used them as models of Romanization for the local natives (Salmon 1970).

The well-excavated Roman site of Cosa located in Tuscany some one hundred miles north of Rome provides a good illustration of this (F. Brown 1980). It was founded in 273 BC as a fortified garrison centre. The streets within the walls were laid out at regular intervals and the countryside around the city was divided into plots, which were distributed to the colonists. As the colonists prospered, they

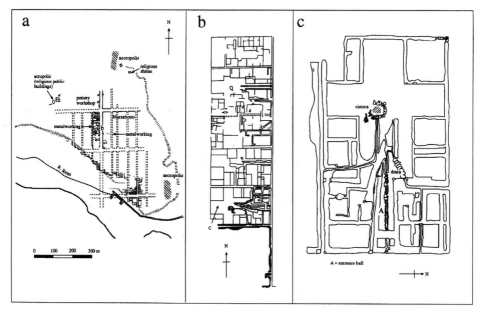

Figure 24.5 The fifth-century BC Etruscan city of Marzabotto, showing (a) its overall struc-
ture, (b) the ground-plan of one of the *insulae*, and (c) one of the houses within this *insula*.
(After Barker and Rasmussen 1993: 172.) Source: A. Pekins, *The Art of Dura-Europos*
(Oxford: OUP, 1973).

added temples and a forum with shops and public meeting places, including a
basilica and a local senate house. These civic and religious buildings were modelled
on similar structures in Rome and remind us of the role that colonies played in
spreading Roman values throughout the empire.

The Romans founded new planned cities like Cosa throughout their empire.
They were especially important in the area of modern western Europe, where there
had not been a tradition of urban development. Some of these colonies replaced
military camps, abandoned as the frontier advanced. Others replaced native centres.
In some cases, the Romans forced the natives to abandon their hill-forts and settle in
new, lowland locations which could be more easily controlled. In other instances,
the transition from hill-fort to Roman town was a gradual one, stimulated by the
development of greater local security and changes in transportation systems and
social and economic life (Burnham and Wacher 1990; Wells 1984).

In all instances, the new settlements served as foci for Romanization. Some, like
Cosa, had a limited period of usefulness and prosperity and then slid into decline.
However, the success of many of these experiments is shown by the fact that great
European cities such as London, Paris and Cologne have developed over Roman
urban centres. One of the most active areas of archaeology since the Second World
War has centred on the investigation of the Roman remains of cities like London

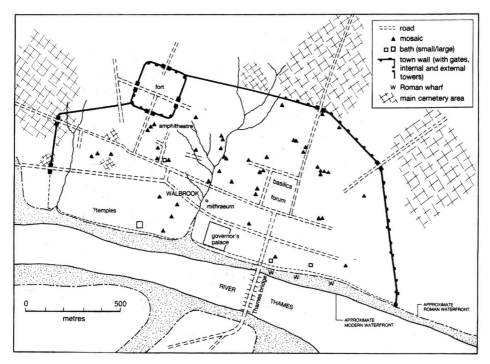

Figure 24.6 Roman London. Source: Jones and Mattingly 1993.

and Cologne (Carver 1987: 22–39; Fig. 24.6). This was necessitated by the destruction caused by the war and the massive rebuilding that followed. Archaeologists have been able to reconstruct the evolution of Roman cities like London in England and Amiens in France from their foundation to the late Roman period and even into the early Middle Ages (Marsden 1986; Massy 1979).

Colonial foundations with a military and acculturative function were not limited to the Mediterranean empires. The Han emperors of China used such settlements to consolidate their hold on Korea (Pai 1992). Modern European imperialists drew inspiration from the Romans in their use of city foundations as an instrument of colonial control and acculturation (Wright 1991). The Spanish led the way, establishing dozens of cities in North and South America (Kubler 1985: 88–110). In some instances like St Augustine, these were totally new foundations; in other cases, as with Mexico City, they represented the reuse of Native American urban centres. The more successful foundations like Mexico City remain flourishing urban centres and, as is the case with London and Paris, only limited archaeological research can be undertaken there today. As has happened with Roman colonies, the less successful Spanish foundations offer the best archaeological possibilities.

This is the case with St Augustine in Florida, which was founded in 1565, and

963

where the modern city has not overwhelmed the colonial centre, making extensive archaeological research possible (Deagan 1991). The research at St Augustine has combined architectural archaeology, useful to the development of the city as a tourist site, with social archaeology, which aimed at reconstructing the complex mix of Spanish and native elements that went into the early city. For instance, analysis of excavated ceramics has shown the presence of tablewares that were mainly imported from Spain, but food processing wares that were local. This provides insights into gender distinctions in the community, where Spanish men were incorporating native women into their households (Deagan 1991; McEwan 1991a, 1992–3).

The Dutch and the English were also great founders of towns and cities in the New World. Again successful centres like Boston and New York have buried and largely destroyed their own past. However, luck and archaeological skill occasionally produce evidence of colonial or early post-colonial settlement in such places as Philadelphia or New York (Cotter *et al.* 1993). One of the most dramatic recent finds in New York was that of an early African-American cemetery, discovered largely intact in the midst of the heavily developed financial district (Harrington 1993).

Again, cities with a more limited period of prosperity and later decline serve the archaeologist better. This has been the case with colonial Williamsburg, which was for a brief period in the eighteenth century the capital of Virginia and one of the most important centres in British North America. The capital of Virginia moved to Richmond shortly after the American Revolution, and Williamsburg became a sleepy southern town. The decision to make Williamsburg into a major reconstructed historical tourist centre, combined with generous support from the Rockefeller family, has led to large-scale archaeological research (Kopper 1986). Excavation was used first to assist in the restoration of the historical structures and in their accurate refurnishing. This assisted in the accurate reconstruction of structures like the Governor's Palace, of which only foundations survived. More recent archaeological research has focused on the reconstruction of a broader picture of daily life and society in the colonial city (Noel Hume 1968; and see Chapter 28).

Religious structures

Religion has long been a force closely associated with the imperial process, and it is no accident that temples are today the most striking ruins at many Greek colonial sites, especially those in Sicily and southern Italy. They reflect not only the wealth of the new settlements, but also the role that religion played in enhancing community cohesion in a strange and hostile land. Anglican churches and French cathedrals in India and Tunisia recall a similar interconnection between religion and the colonial experience.

Religion was also used as a force to integrate the conquered into the world of the conquerer. The Romans employed first their own traditional cults (like that of Jupiter) and later newly created religious institutions (like the worship of the emperor) to rally the colonial élites of the new empire to the Roman cause (Fishwick 1987). Temples to the emperors were established in new urban centres, and more Romanized members of the native aristocracy were made into priests of this cult. Remains of the large temple dedicated to the Emperor Claudius have been excavated at Colchester in Britain, the first capital of the province that he conquered and organized (Lewis 1966: 61–64).

With the creation of the early modern Christian empires, this use of religion as an instrument of acculturation was joined with a desire to save souls. Preachers generally arrived with the soldiers and the administrators. In the Americas both Protestant English and Catholic French and Spanish engaged in mission activities, but it was the Spanish whose missions were most successful and who created physical as well as social and spiritual forms that survive and provide evidence for the archaeologists. The Spanish missions in Florida, the American Southwest and California were formed for the purpose of spiritual conversion, but they also served as instruments for social and economic change. In areas like California, the indigenous populations, who had been largely hunter-gatherers, were forced to settle in the vicinity of missions, adopt their lifestyle, and adapt their productive activities to European ways. Missions were intended not only as places of worship but also as productive centres that would turn the Native Americans into European-style peasants (McEwan 1991b; Thomas 1988).

Few of the Spanish missions are active today. Some, like the Jesuit missions of Paraguay, are now picturesque ruins that have been little studied (Blanch 1982). Others, such as those of California, Florida, and the American Southwest, have become the objects of increasing archaeological and documentary research (Chapter 28; Fig, 28.10). Starting as exercises in architectural archaeology (again often to aid in the restoration of the missions as historical sites), this research has turned more to a consideration of the way that the mission community, whose population was generally overwhelmingly Native American, integrated European and native values. The material culture often reflects this complex blending of Spanish with native ways. Imported pottery, beads, and building techniques appear. However, important categories of archaeological material like ceramics remain overwhelmingly native (Farnsworth 1992; McEwan 1991b).

TRADE

Trade has been intimately connected with the development of empire throughout history. Traders often preceded military forces, providing intelligence and at times softening the native societies for conquest. Archaeology provides important evidence for this economic imperialism, well beyond the area of political control. Roman pottery and coins have been found in wide areas of Europe that the Romans never conquered (Wells 1992; Wheeler 1954). Much of this trade was in the hands of individual entrepreneurs and even native middlemen. In other instances formal outposts or enclaves were established that provided continuity and security to the external traders. Such mercantile colonies or emporia are known from a number of contexts: among the earliest were Assyrian trading centres established in what is now eastern Turkey. Both objects and written texts showed Assyrian traders living in enclaves in close association with the native élite (Lloyd 1989: 26–27, 35–38).

The impact of this advance guard of imperialism was complex and often devastating, especially in modern times. In North America, the most immediate impact was biological, with the spread of previously unknown diseases that devastated the indigenous populations and facilitated European settlement and conquest. However, the disruptive impact of this early trans-frontier trade was also cultural, as studies of institutions like the fur trade have shown. Competition to control sources of furs and access to the colonial trading centres led to fierce indigenous rivalries similar to those that changed Celtic Europe. Some of these processes can be reconstructed only through the colonial written records. However, archaeological research has increasingly focused on contact sites, settlements inhabited by indigenous groups during the early stages of imperial contact. There, the relation between European and indigenous material culture can be employed to analyse continuity and change in native life (Fitzhugh 1985).

In the development of empires, the traders have often led the way in turning the conquered areas into sources of raw materials and markets for finished goods. This is what is called a core–periphery relationship, in which the colonial zones supply raw materials to sustain the core industrial production units. (Wallerstein 1974). This model of colonial development was developed to explain aspects of the early modern colonial experience, but it has a certain relevance for earlier periods as well (Rowlands et al. 1987; Santley and Alexander 1992), though it has to be used with caution in dealing with the early modern and especially with the pre-modern colonial world. In the latter case, the ability of the imperial groups to project power was much more limited. The example of the Greeks and Celtic Europe has already been cited. Greek painted pottery, wine jars and bronze drinking vessels have been found on sites scattered from the Black Sea to the Paris basin. While the Greeks had some military superiority and some advantages in production methods and distribution networks, both sides in the trading process worked as relative equals, meeting mutual economic and social needs.

With the development of the Roman empire the power balance changed to a certain degree. The Romans developed a large politically stable empire, which lasted for centuries. They created a complex currency, with units in gold, silver and bronze that facilitated trading at all levels of society. They also had the ability to produce consumer goods in large quantities. Cheap, attractive products like ceramic lamps, decorated pottery and glass vessels made their way into most households in the provinces and were carried in large numbers beyond the imperial frontiers. Roman decorated ceramics show up in native sites from northern Scotland to India (Fig. 24.7).

Archaeologists have researched many aspects of this economic imperialism within the Roman world and beyond (Greene 1986). The most brutal economic burden placed on the provinces was the mining for precious metals and quarrying for

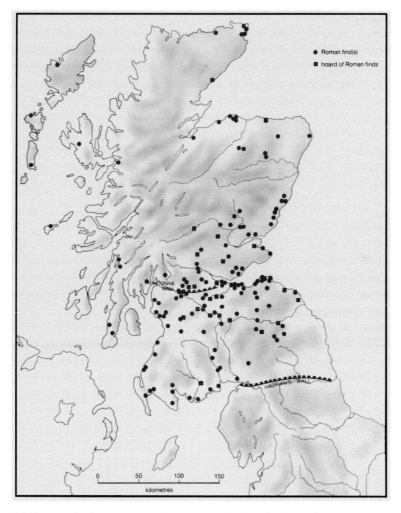

Figure 24.7 Roman finds from non-Roman sites in Scotland in the second century AD. Source: Jones and Mattingly 1993.

967

building stones. Some Roman mining sites in Spain and Britain have been investigated archaeologically (Davies 1935; Keay 1988). The circulation of metals such as lead (a by-product of silver mining) has been reconstructed through finds of stamped metal ingots. Most of the stones used by the Romans in their buildings and their sculptural decoration came from quarries outside of Italy. Their mining, shipping and finishing became complex economic activities. Systematic research on quarries and quarrying is just beginning, with special emphasis on sites in Egypt and North Africa. Underwater archaeology, through the discovery of wrecked ships loaded with building stone and statuary, has provided important information on the movement of stone and stone products during the Roman period.

Roman production facilities, especially for ceramics, have been identified and studied. Numerous kiln sites have been excavated. Scientific analysis (see Chapter 9) has provided precise information on which pots came from which kilns, allowing the reconstruction of the circulation of goods (Peacock 1982). The Roman economy was a pre-industrial one, where transport costs were high and investment in capital equipment limited (Duncan-Jones 1982, 1990). However, the relocation of the heavy, complicated, production machinery characteristic of modern industry was generally not a problem. If basic raw materials like clay were available, craftsmen like potters with their tools and moulds could move to new locations, build kilns and soon be in business. This meant that manufacturers could move their production centres closer to major markets. These movements can be reconstructed for the red glazed pottery known as *terra sigillata* or Arretine, which was in common use during the first, second and third centuries AD. The first *terra sigillata* potteries were located at Arezzo in Tuscany, but by the early imperial period most had moved, first to southern and then to central France. This allowed them to supply more efficiently not only the rich provinces of Gaul and Britain, but also the large armies located on the Rhine. By the second century AD these *terra sigillata* production centres were challenged and then replaced in the Mediterranean by the massive output of glazed pottery in North Africa. This simpler, red-orange glazed pottery remained the dominant luxury pottery in the Mediterranean until the end of the Roman empire (Hayes 1972).

More utilitarian ceramic objects have also proved useful to the archaeologist in reconstructing the Roman economy. During Antiquity, bulk goods like wine, olive oil, and even grain were generally shipped in large ceramic containers known as amphorae. The shape of the amphorae used varied from place to place and over time. The dates of production and places of origins can thus be determined from those variations in shape. Massive quantities of amphorae were discarded after the agricultural products had arrived at their destination. At Rome there is an artificial hill called Monte Testaccio formed from the sherds of thousands of broken Roman amphorae. Statistical study of amphora remains at sites like Monte Testaccio allows the reconstruction of shifting trade patterns in essential items like wine and olive oil

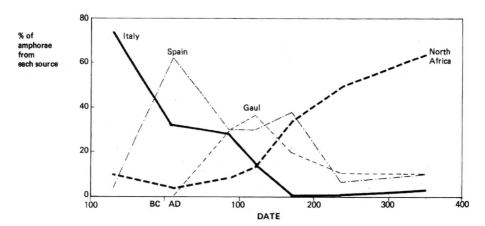

Figure 24.8 Changing frequencies of amphorae at Rome's port of Ostia. (After Greene 1986: 15.) Source: K. Greene, with permission of the Audio Visual Centre, University of Newcastle.

and can be related to the rise and fall of agricultural economies in Roman Italy, Spain, and North Africa (Carandini 1989; Fig. 24.8).

This land-based research has been complemented in recent years by underwater archaeology (Bass 1966, Muckelroy 1980). Since the Second World War, divers using aqualungs have identified hundreds of wrecks in the Mediterranean and elsewhere, many of which date to the Roman period. Very recently, submarines have begun to be used to recover ancient deep-water wrecks. The cargoes preserved on such wrecks, which range from wine and olive oil amphorae to stone coffins and columns, provide information on the complex and changing economic relationships between Rome and her provinces.

Such underwater discoveries have not been limited to the Roman period. In the Mediterranean, for example, bronze age, Greek, and Islamic wrecks have all been excavated. Elsewhere, among the most interesting recent discoveries have been Chinese wrecks off the Philippines, which illustrate the range and power of that commercial empire. The coasts of North America are dotted with submerged vessels of Spanish, French, and British origins.

The early modern colonial empires were started in the pre-industrial era, though in a period when trade and mercantile activity were rapidly expanding (see Chapter 28). Each national empire had a very different attitude towards commercial activity. For the Spaniards, empire was to be used for the extraction of precious metals, and then for settlement: the natives were first looted and then forced to supply the labour for the mines that produced the gold and other precious metals and then for the agricultural estates. This was often an élite settler empire, where transplanted Iberians became an increasingly important force both in the towns and in the countryside. A major aim of the settlers was to produce agricultural wealth through cheap native labour. There was a low level of industrial production and commercial development. The middle class was small and markers for local goods limited. This is reflected in the limited Iberian material culture found at Spanish-American archaeological sites. Imported pottery and glass were present in some quantities, especially in the towns, although less than at Anglo-American sites (Deagan 1991).

Very different was the French imperial system established in North America during the seventeenth and eighteenth centuries (Walthall 1991). It was an empire based on limited political and military control, religious conversion, and on the development of complex trading networks centred on the acquisition of furs. French agents, both secular and religious, traversed large areas of north-eastern and north-central North America, exchanging European goods for animal furs and other forest products, cementing political alliances with the Native Americans against the British and other imperial powers, and spreading the Roman Catholic faith. They established a relatively limited number of small military and civic centres on the borders of the vast territory that was theoretically their domain.

Many of these French settlements were short lived. Some were abandoned or destroyed by indigenous groups. Others were replaced or overwhelmed by the more complex and successful British settlements. French colonial material culture in North America was relatively also limited in quantity and variety. They included practical trade objects such as guns and iron pots. Others consisted of decorations for clothing, and luxury utensils used for eating and drinking. Some of these objects reflected the desire of the Frenchmen to maintain their sense of European civilization and status on the frontier. Distinctive trade goods such as the Jesuit rings distributed by the missionaries do allow the French presence to be documented at native sites (Walthall 1991). However, the fact that the trade was often in perishable items like furs and that the French, like the Spanish, did not develop a large consumer goods industry, means that archaeology cannot provide a full picture of the extent and the complexity of the French imperial effort in North America.

With the British, the relation between trade and empire for the first time reached a complexity that equalled and then surpassed that of Rome. The British not only traded, but they also produced: in fact, the Industrial Revolution was beginning as the British empire was being established (see Chapter 29). Much of this new industrial production took the form of durable goods like ceramics which are well preserved at archaeological sites. The great potteries founded by Josiah Wedgwood and other ceramic manufacturers in the Staffordshire area of Britain during the eighteenth century manufactured a great range of attractive and relatively inexpensive pottery vessels that were well suited to the taste and purses of a growing middle class in both England and the colonies. Decorative styles were changed rapidly to stimulate the market and this allows these wares to provide precise dates for archaeological sites. The creamwares and pearlwares of the English Midlands allowed England to dominate the international ceramics markets. Like the Roman *terra sigillata* eighteen centuries before, these new ceramics became indicators of the spread of British influence, both within her empire and beyond. They appeared on the shores of West Africa, in South Africa, and in Australia. Chris Gosden in Chapter 12 describes a remarkable example of this phenomenon: Port Essington near Darwin in northern Australia, a short-lived outpost in the nineteenth century (Fig. 12.6), where the inhabitants were at the extreme end of a trade system that brought British goods first to Sydney and eventually to them another 4,000 kilometres away on the other side of the continent (Allen 1973).

CHANGES IN THE LAND

Before the nineteenth century all societies were basically agricultural. Acquisition of land and the wealth that could come from agricultural and pastoral production were major incentives for imperialism. This meant that the creation of any empire was bound to produce major reorganizations in the countryside of the conquered and colonized territories. Production was often intensified to provide food for the new cities and garrisons. New crops and animals were introduced. This was especially evident in the Americas, where there was no tradition of large domestic animals. Increased farming and grazing produced ecological changes like deforestation and erosion. Historians and archaeologists are just beginning to realize the full impact of this part of the imperial and colonial process (Cronon 1983).

These rural settlement changes affected people as well as land. Scattered rural populations were concentrated in village communities to facilitate political control and the collection of taxes. Great estates or plantations were established dominated by a new rural élite and often staffed by either slaves or dependent peasant labour. However, these rural changes brought about by the creation of empires have not received the attention they deserve. Historians, both past and present, have tended to be urbano-centred in their research and have shown limited understanding of and concern for the countryside. This has been especially true for societies like ancient Greece or Rome, where the written sources say little about country life and other records are sparse. This means that it is left to the archaeologists to provide much of the basic evidence for life and change in the countryside during the past.

For archaeologists, the rural history and archaeology of empire have long centred on the study of the major estates which dominated rural life in the new colonial empires: investigations have focused on the great villas of the Roman provinces, the haciendas of New Spain, and the plantations of colonial Virginia and South Africa (Burke 1978; Deetz 1993; Kelso and Most 1990; Markell *et al.* 1995; Percival 1976). Several reasons explain this emphasis. Such establishments were major reorganizing forces in the new imperial countryside. They linked city and countryside and provided insight into the lives of the élite, the slaves and the peasants. They offered a better possibility of finding objects of value and beauty: they were centres of wealth and display, so impressive and interesting physical remains and many fragments of decoration survive.

Early interest in the villas of Roman provinces like Britain centred on the recovery of mosaics, and a number of treasures of Roman silver plate have come from villa sites. Relatively well-preserved remains encouraged the excavation of villas, many of which in Britain, France, Germany, and Spain have become important tourist centres (Percival 1976). Fishbourne in southern England, a villa probably built in the first century AD for a Romano-British client king, is an excellent example of this phenomenon (Cunliffe 1971).

Historical archaeologists in the United States turned early to the excavations of plantations in the American South. The purpose of many of these excavations was to provide information for the restoration of buildings, their accurate furnishing and the reconstruction of daily life (Noel Hume 1963, 1974, 1982; and see Chapter 28 and Fig. 28.6). These plantations had strong nostalgic associations for many Americans, and they have become prime tourist centres. Displays tended to feature the artefacts and lifestyle of the élite, with little said about the slave and peasant labour which made such displays of conspicuous consumption possible.

Changing social values have produced changes in rural historical and archaeological research. Estate archaeology in recent years has no longer concentrated just on the lives of the rural élite. Both plantation excavations in North America and villa excavations in the Roman provinces have expanded their horizons, studying not only grand architecture and luxury items like fancy pottery and glass but also the houses of slaves and peasants, facilities involved in rural production like olive and wine presses, and even items like seeds and animal bones, which provide information on differences in diet and eating habits among the various classes in rural society (Adams and Boling 1989; Ferguson 1991; and see Chapter 14). Villas and plantations are investigated as total social and economic units, and all of their components are of interest to the archaeologist (Fig. 24.9).

Archaeologists are also attempting to reconstruct the larger rural settlement context in which these estates existed, which included other major establishments, smaller farms and homesteads, field systems and the landscape itself (see Chapter 13). The reconstruction of these broad patterns requires the use of a range of archaeological techniques besides excavation, two of the most useful of which have been aerial photography and surface survey. The use of air photography in Roman military archaeology has already been discussed. Roman villa sites show up as clearly in the air photographs as do the Roman camps. Aerial surveys of certain regions like the Somme valley of France and the south-east of Britain have revealed a density of rural sites not previously expected (Agache 1978).

Again, as is the case with military sites, the villas discovered through air photographs cannot usually be dated solely on the basis of the plans. It is necessary to

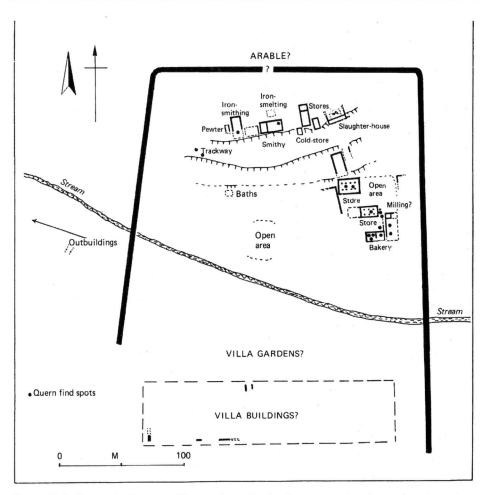

Figure 24.9 Gatcombe Roman villa, southern England, an example of a modern investigation of the working part of a Roman villa. Source: Greene 1986, with permission of the Audio Visual Centre, University of Newcastle.

visit the sites, search for surface material, and even to conduct excavations. Surface survey is also needed to investigate large sections of countryside, searching for sites that are not known either from their standing remains or from techniques like air photographs. Survey emphasizes field-walking and the collection of artefacts like pottery fragments and tiles which have been revealed by frost, ploughing or other human or natural actions. While this method usually provides only limited information about dates of occupation and general size for any one site, it does allow the investigation of a total landscape area, the discovery of a large number of sites, and the use of that information to develop large-scale reconstructions of rural settlement history (Barker and Lloyd 1991).

973

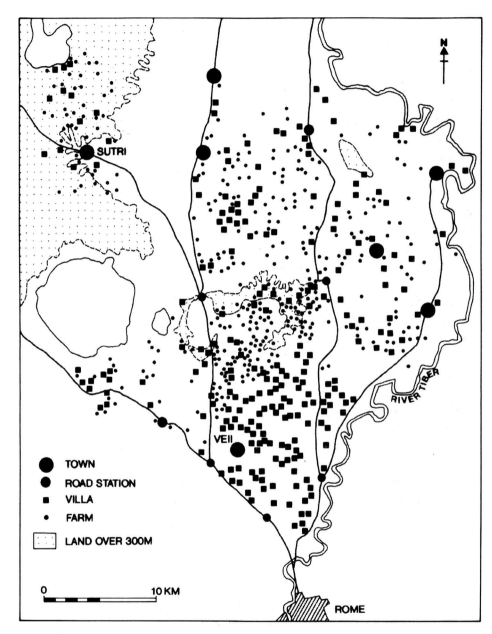

Figure 24.10 The Roman landscape of South Etruria *c.* AD 100, revealed by systematic field survey. Source: Barker 1995.

Intensive surface survey of this type was pioneered by British archaeologists in the countryside around Rome shortly after the Second World War (Potter 1979; Fig. 24.10). Changes in that countryside including building construction and the introduction of mechanical agriculture with its deeper ploughing resulted in the discovery of hundreds of previously unknown sites. It also led to their rapid destruction, lending a certain urgency to survey research. Survey work was shown to be an effective and relatively inexpensive way not only of mapping large numbers of sites, but also of reconstructing the changing organization and use of a landscape over long periods of time. For archaeologists of empire, it meant that one could understand the structure of an area before conquest, document the effect of conquest, and also document the limits of imperial transformations. For instance, in Roman Britain distribution maps show that the development of the villa system was largely confined to the south-east sections of the province and in other areas, probably pre-Roman, systems of agricultural production dominated (Fig. 24.11).

Contemporaneous with the British rural research near Rome, Gordon Willey of Harvard University was undertaking very similar survey-settlement investigations in the Viru valley of Peru (Willey 1953). His aim, too, was to study changes in rural settlement and land organization over time and to document the relation of that valley's settlement history to the rise and fall of large imperial systems in Peru.

Combinations of air and ground survey research have now been undertaken in many sections of Europe and the Mediterranean, and in Mesoamerica and South America (Barker and Lloyd 1991; Parsons 1982). In north-eastern France, the dramatic increase of villas has been linked to the need to supply the Roman frontier armies with grain (Agache 1978). In North Africa, survey research has documented the way that incorporation of the countryside into the larger Roman economic system led to the spread of farmsteads engaged in specialized types of agricultural activities like olive oil production (Barker and Reynolds 1985 – and see the case study described in Chapter 14; Hitchner 1990). In the central valley of Mexico, the ebb and flow of centralized political power and outside imperial control are reflected in the centralization and decentralization of rural life (Sanders *et al.* 1979; Parsons 1982).

Rural archaeologists studying the impact of empire have been researching ways that political and economic changes produced by the creation of empires impacted not only on settlement form and distribution, but also on the organization and use of the land itself. Aerial photographs have been especially useful in providing information on such large-scale changes in land use. An example of this is the identification of Roman land organizational patterns. The Romans, as part of rural reorganization after conquest, undertook a process of division known as centuria-tion (Dilke 1971). Land that had been seized from conquered peoples was sur-veyed, divided into regular plots, the boundaries marked, and units allotted to the new settlers. The process recalls the system of land division used in many parts of

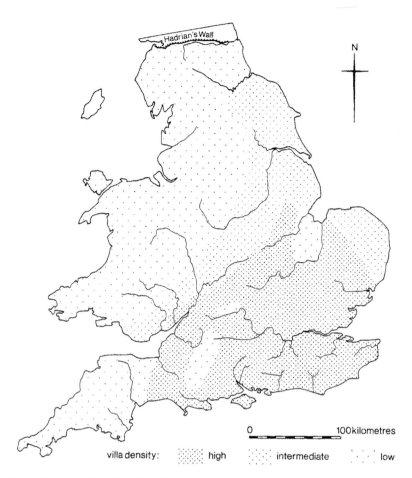

Figure 24.11 Romano–British villa distribution. This map shows the relative density of known Roman villa sites in Britain. The heaviest densities were in the south-east of Britain, where the agricultural land was best and the process of Romanization started earliest. Source: Hingley 1989, fig. 68.

the mid-western United States as the American empire spread westward. High-level air photographs, many of them taken during the bombing runs of the Second World War, have revealed many traces of these Roman centuriation grids surviving in the modern field systems of Europe and the Mediterranean (Bradford 1957). Italy has provided the most abundant evidence, but centuriation grids are now known from France, Spain, North Africa and other sections of the Roman world. Nor was the Roman empire the first colonial system associated with such radical reorganizations of the countryside: aerial photographs have also shown similar large reorganization schemes in southern Italy associated with Greek colonies like Metaponto.

SLAVERY

Imperial advance has often been associated with slavery and the slave trade. Individuals and whole groups were enslaved, and slave labour has played a major role in most imperial systems. The empires of Rome and early modern Europe provide well-documented examples of the relation between slavery and empire. Much of the rural labour in both Roman Italy and the provinces and in the post-conquest Americas was provided by slaves. In the Roman empire the slaves came first from conquest and then increasingly from trade with groups beyond the borders of the empire (Bradley 1987). In the Americas, the enslavement of the indigenous population was soon replaced by the importation of captives from Africa. Historical research on slavery in any society is inherently biased by the fact that most written information comes from the masters and reflects their views of the slaves and slave society. The slaves themselves have only a limited voice in that written testimony. Here the archaeologists have an important role to play. While it is true that most slaves had only a few material goods, they could and did use what they had in ways that reflected their own lifestyles and expressed their own cultural values (Ferguson 1991).

Research on the plantations of the American South and the West Indies has proved especially fruitful for an understanding of the complex relationship between the culture of the dominant group and that of the oppressed (Handler and Lange 1978; Singleton 1985; and see Chapter 28). Written documents and estate maps provide information on the location of slave quarters, which can then be excavated (Higman 1988). Sites like Monticello, the home of Thomas Jefferson, have yielded considerable information on slave life. Information comes from finds ranging from cabin plans to slave-made ceramics to animal bone fragments. Combinations of studies in materials like ceramics and animal bones allow not only the identification of the meats eaten by the slaves but also the reconstruction of complex eating rituals which served to distinguish the ways of the slaves from those of the masters (Crader 1990; Ferguson 1991: 31–37; Kelso 1986). Heated debates have arisen about the relation of this material evidence to large questions of the treatment and condition of slaves on *antebellum* plantations.

Roman archaeologists have also become increasingly interested in research on rural slavery, reflecting a growing intellectual and ideological debate among Romanists about the nature and impact of slavery in Roman society (Bradley 1987; Finley 1980). Villa excavators in particular have tried to identify slave quarters and highlight slave activities. The best example of this type of research has been the Italian excavations at the Roman villa at Sette Finestre in Tuscany (Carandini *et al.* 1985; Fig. 24.12). However, Roman archaeologists face special research problems, which make the reconstruction of slave activities very difficult. They do not have the type of detailed written documentation about individual estates that North American

977

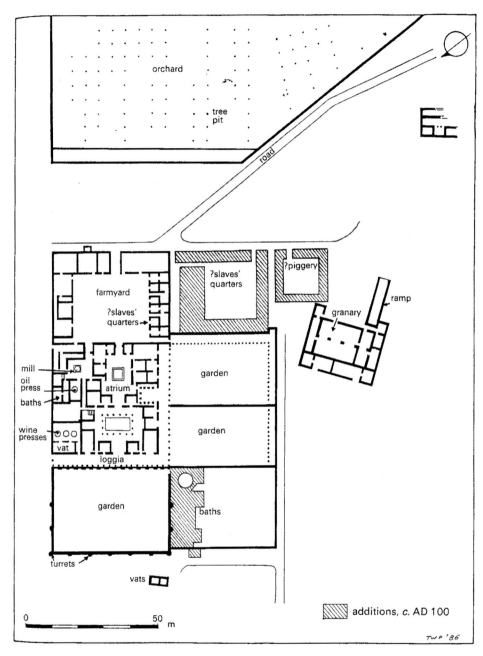

Figure 24.12 The Roman villa at Sette Finestre near Cosa in southern Tuscany represents the best excavated example of an élite rural residence of the late Republic and early Empire. It included not only elegant living quarters, but also work areas and probably slave quarters. Source: T. Potter (1987) *Roman Italy*, London: British Museum Press.

978

historical archaeologists possess. This makes the identification of features like slave quarters rather more problematic. There is also the danger that an emphasis on slavery may lead both archaeologists and historians to underestimate the complexity of the social and economic make-up of the countryside, and underplay the role of free and freed farmers in agricultural production (Dyson 1992). This concern applies to both the Roman and the *antebellum* North American world.

ASSIMILATION AND RESISTANCE

Influenced by the imperialistic values of the nineteenth century, archaeologists of empire have long tended to stress the overwhelming success of various colonial ventures. This has been especially true of the Roman empire, where the remains both in the towns and in the countryside suggested that the imperial system had triumphed and that those natives who had not perished had been turned into good Romans. A historical scenario was reconstructed in which the indigenous élites abandoned their farmsteads and hill-forts, moved into villas and town houses, learned Latin, and adopted Roman ways. In the colonial Americas, the processes were seen as both more simple and more complex. The Anglo-America frontier areas of North America saw either the extermination or the marginalization of the native population, and the creation of a new society. For much of Spanish America, the situation was different, since the Native American population was too numerous to exterminate totally. However, the native civilization and the élite that maintained it were destroyed and the surviving natives marginalized. Study of their culture became the task of anthropologists and folklorists and not of historians of empire and archaeologists specializing in high culture.

The conquered natives had not been totally forgotten. European nationalism of the nineteenth century first focused archaeological interest on questions of resistance to Roman expansion. Sites like Numantia in Spain, Alesia in France, and the Teutoberger Forest in Germany, which were associated with local Celtic and German resistance to the advance of Rome, have long been objects of research. The nineteenth-century French emperor Napoleon III sponsored excavations at Alesia, the site associated with the doomed stand of Vercingetorix and his Gauls against the army of Julius Caesar (Le Gall 1990). German antiquarians and archaeologists have long been engaged in a search for the location of the battle site in the Teutoberger Forest where the German forces under Arminius destroyed the three legions of the Roman general Varus in AD 9. In the late nineteenth century a massive monument to Arminius was erected at one of the presumed sites of the battle. Very recently German archaeologists seem to have definitely located the site of the battle at another location nearby, a claim apparently confirmed by the discovery of Roman military artefacts there (Dornberg 1992).

Decolonization and the growing interest of groups like Native Americans and Afro-Americans in asserting their own cultural continuity and identity have led both historians and archaeologists to reassess their views about the relation between colonialism and the survival of native social and cultural values (Deagan 1991; Mattingly 1997; Simmons 1986; Webster and Cooper 1996). Archaeologists have focused special attention on two areas of research. One is the countryside, where more unacculturated natives might be expected to survive. This research was modelled on the example of Latin America, where native languages and thinly veiled native ways survive in many rural areas (Farnsworth 1992). In the Roman empire, fieldwork has turned from the investigation of those symbols of successful Romanization, the villas, to the search for survivals of pre-Roman settlements and rural ways of life. Increasing evidence for such survivals is emerging. In Britain, for instance, archaeologists have increasingly stressed the geographical limitations of the villa culture: in areas like the Midlands, few villas were built and native rural community organization and lifeways seem to have persisted (Hingley 1989). In rural Sardinia, one of the oldest provinces in the Roman empire, many of the pre-Roman towered sites called *nuraghi* continued to be inhabited throughout the Roman period and few villas or rural towns were built (Dyson and Rowland 1992). Such research is still in its early stages, but it is clear that a new version which stresses the limitations of Romanization in the countryside will emerge.

Another fruitful area of research has focused on the study of symbolic systems, as they are reflected in areas like religion. Here the researches of the field archaeologist merge with those of the art-historical archaeologist (Henig and King 1986; Salomon 1987). Contemporary advertising and the use of symbols for political control have made scholars more aware of the importance of the use of symbolic control in the past. Archaeologists who have until recently been concerned with social and economic studies are now paying more attention to the role of past symbolic systems. Important studies of the relation between political symbolism and imperial power have been done for empires as diverse as the Mayas (Marcus 1976) and the Rome of Augustus (Zanker 1988). Clearly complex imperial systems like to control political symbolism, from the statues of emperors in Roman provincial towns to statues of Queen Victoria in British India.

Religion provides a more complex example of conflict and compromise between colonial control and native resistance (Webster 1997). Both ancient Romans and early modern Spaniards used religion as an instrument of domination. The Romans only suppressed those elements of the native religions that provided a focus for resistance to their rule. This explains their violence against the Celtic Druids (Piggott 1975). It is clear that they encouraged the natives to adapt Roman religious ways: the major religious centres, especially in the towns, bear witness to their success (Henig and King 1986). However, in both the names of gods and the iconography of religious activities, the study of less official and more rural religion shows a much more complex interaction of Roman and native culture with a high level of native survival: Celtic deities not only retain their own names, but are depicted in ways that bear little resemblance to the high culture art values of Rome (Webster 1997).

The Spanish were much more rigorous in their reinforcement of religious conformity: native religious sites and institutions were destroyed and forceable conversion dominated (Stern 1982, 1987). A Roman Catholic religious hierarchy complete with an Inquisition was established throughout Spanish America. Native artists and artisans were trained in the European manner. Yet the anthropologists who study religious ritual or the art historians who study iconography, especially in the rural areas of modern Mesoamerica, rapidly note the degree to which there is continuity from the pre-Roman Catholic past (Stern 1982, 1987).

Since imperial history has largely been written by those closely associated with the imperial powers, there has been even less emphasis on successful resistance to imperial expansion. For internal political reasons, the Germans have taken great pride in their repulse of Rome. Other, more recent, examples exist: one of the most interesting is the long successful resistance by the natives of Madagascar to various European colonial efforts.

CONCLUSION

It was noted at the beginning of this chapter that a contemporary archaeology of empire has to reflect a very complex historical view of the imperial process. No longer can it be just a military or colonial élite archaeology: it has to reflect the relation between imperialism and trade, the way that empire reorganized social, productive, and symbolic systems, and the ability of the natives to resist and survive imperial advance. Some areas of research like military archaeology have a long history, whereas archaeological research in areas like slavery and resistance is just beginning. A gender-orientated archaeology of empire hardly exists.

The archaeology of empire offers not only challenges but also opportunities to the discipline as a whole. It provides a range of stimulating challenges. The complex intersection of written records and diverse material cultures sharpens interpretive skills. The wide commonality of imperial processes across time and space provides an opportunity for the archaeologist to move beyond specific cultural areas and adopt a more holistic view of the imperial process. The new archaeology of empire, with its concern with all actors in the imperial process, requires the development of both new research techniques and new paradigms of interpretation. Methods as diverse as field survey and botanical and faunal analysis have already demonstrated their worth in recreating the history of ordinary people caught up in the imperial process. More complex may be the determination of the questions to be asked. The archaeologists have long tended to come from the élite, male, ranks of the old imperial societies: a re-thought archaeology of empire is going to have to involve all groups and genders that were caught up in the imperial process.

REFERENCES

Adams, W. H. and Boling, S. J. (1989) 'Status and ceramics for planters and their slaves on three Georgia coastal plantations', *Historical Archaeology* 23 (1): 69–96.

Agache, R. (1978) *La Somme Pre-romaine et Romaine*, Paris.

Allasan-Jones, L. (1989) *Women in Roman Britain*, London: British Museum Press.

Allen, J. (1973) 'The archaeology of nineteenth century British imperialism: an Australian case study', *World Archaeology* 5 (1): 44–51.

Baatz, D. (1993) *Der römische Limes*, Berlin: Mann Verlag.

Baradez, J. (1949) *Fossatum Africae*, Paris: Arts et Métiers.

Barker, G. (1995) *A Mediterranean Valley*, London: Leicester University Press.

Barker, G. and Lloyd, J. (eds) (1991) *Roman Landscapes: Archaeological Survey in the Mediterranean Area*, Archaeological Monographs 1, London: British School at Rome.

Barker, G. and Rasmussen, T. (1998) *The Etruscans*, Oxford: Blackwell.

Barker, G. and Reynolds, J. (eds) (1985) *Cyrenaica in Antiquity*, Oxford: British Archaeological Reports, International Series 236.

Barreca, F. (1986) *La Civiltà Fenico-Punica in Sardegna*, Sassari: Carlo Delfino.

Bass, G. (1966) *Archaeology under Water*, Harmondsworth: Penguin.

Birley, E. (1961) *Research on Hadrian's Wall*, Kendal: Titus Wilson and Son.

Birley, R. (1987) *Vindolanda: A Roman Frontier Post on Hadrian's Wall*, London: Thames and Hudson.

Blanch, J. M. (1982) *Lost Cities of Paraguay*, Chicago: Loyola University Press.

Boardman, J. (1980) *The Greeks Overseas*, Harmondsworth: Penguin.

Bowman, A. K. (1994) *Life and Letters on the Roman Frontier*, London: British Museum Press.

Bradford, J. (1957) *Ancient Landscapes*, London: Bell.

Bradley, K. (1987) *Slaves and Masters in the Roman Empire*, Oxford: Oxford University Press.

Breeze, D. J. (1993) *The Northern Frontier of Roman Britain*, London: Batsford.

Breeze, D. J. and Dobson, B. (1976) *Hadrian's Wall*, London: Allen Lane.

Brown, F. (1980) *Cosa: The Making of a Roman Town*, Ann Arbor: University of Michigan Press.

Brown, R. A. (1980) *Castles: A History and Guide*, New York: Greenwich House.

Burke, J. (1978) *Life in the Villa in Roman Britain*, London: Batsford.

Burnham, B. and Wacher, J. (1990) *The Small Towns of Roman Britain*, London: Batsford.

Carandini, A. (ed.) (1985) *Settefinestre: Una Villa Schiavista nell' Etruria Meridionale*, Modena: Pannini.

Carandini, A. (1989) 'Italian wine and African oil: commerce in a world empire', in K. Randsborg (ed.) *The Birth of Europe: Archaeology and Social Development in the First Millennium AD*, Rome: L'Erma di Bretschneider: 16–24.

Carver, M. O. H. (1987) *Underneath English Towns*, London: Batsford.

Cathcart King, D. J. (1991) *The Castle in England and Wales*, London: Routledge.

Chevalier, F. (1963) *Land and Society in Colonial Mexico: The Great Hacienda*, Berkeley and Los Angeles: University of California Press.

Connah, G. (1986) *African Civilizations: Precolonial Cities and States in Tropical Africa: An Archaeological Perspective*, Cambridge: Cambridge University Press.

Connah, G. (1988) *The Archaeology of Australia's History*, Cambridge: Cambridge University Press.

Conrad, G. W. and Demarest, A. A. (1984) *Religion and Empire: The Dynamics of Aztec and Inca Expansion*, Cambridge: Cambridge University Press.

Cooper, F. and Stoler, A. L. (1997) *Tensions of Empire*, Berkeley: University of California Press.

Cotter, J., Roberts, D. and Parrington, M. (1993) *The Buried Past, An Archaeological History of Philadelphia*, Philadelphia: University of Pennsylvania Press.

Crader, D. (1990) 'Slave diet at Monticello', *American Antiquity* 55: 690–717.

Crawford, O. G. S. (1928) *Wessex from the Air*, Oxford: Clarendon.

Cronon, W. (1983) *Changes in the Land*, New York: Hill and Wang.

Crosby, A. W. (1975) *The Columbian Exchange*, Westport, Conn.: Greenwich Press.

Crosby, A. W. (1986) *Ecological Imperialism*, Cambridge: Cambridge University Press.

Cunliffe, B. (1971) *Fishbourne: A Roman Palace and its Garden*, Baltimore, Md.: Johns Hopkins University Press.

Davies, O. (1935) *Roman Mines in Europe*, Oxford: Oxford University Press.

Davies, P. (1987) *Splendours of the Raj*, Harmondsworth: Penguin.

Deagan, K. (1991) *America's Ancient City: Spanish St Augustine, 1564–1763*, New York: Garland.

Decorse, C. R. (1992) 'Culture contact, continuity and change on the Gold Coast AD 1400–1990', *African Archaeological Review* 10: 163–96.

Deetz, J. (1993) *Flower Dew Hundred: The Archaeology of a Virginia Plantation 1619–1864*, Charlottesville: University of Virginia Press.

Dilke, O. A. W. (1971) *The Roman Land Surveyors*, New York: Barnes and Noble.

Dornberg, J. (1992) 'Battle of the Teutoberg Forest', *Archaeology* 45 (3): 26–33.

Duncan-Jones, R. (1982) *The Economy of the Roman Empire*, Cambridge: Cambridge University Press.

Duncan-Jones, R. (1990) *Structure and Scale in the Roman Economy*, Cambridge: Cambridge University Press.

Dyson, S. L. (1985) *The Creation of the Roman Frontier*, Princeton: Princeton University Press.

Dyson, S. L. (1992) 'Age, sex and states: the view from the Roman Rotary Club', *Echos du Monde Classique / Classical Views* 36: 369–85.

Dyson, S. L. and Rowland, R. J. (1992) 'Survey and settlement reconstruction in west-central Sardinia', *American Journal of Archaeology* 96: 203–24.

Ewen, C. (1990) *The Archaeology of Spanish Colonialism and the Caribbean*, Tucson: The Society for Historical Archaeology.

Falk, L. (ed.) (1991) *Historical Archaeology in Global Perspective*, Washington, DC: Smithsonian Institution Press.

Farnsworth, P. (1992) 'Missions, Indians and cultural continuities', *Historical Archaeology* 26: 22–36.

Farrington, I. A. (1992) 'The characterization of the provinces of the Inka heartland', *World Archaeology* 23: 368–85.

Faulkner, A. (1992) 'Gentility on the frontier of Acadia 1635–1740: an archaeological perspective', in P. Benes (ed.) *New England/New France 1600–1850*, Boston, Mass.: Boston University: 82–100.

Ferguson, L. (1991) 'Struggling with pots in colonial South Carolina', in R. H. McGuire and R. Paynter (eds) *The Archaeology of Unequality*, Oxford Blackwell: 28–39.

Ferguson, L. (1992) *Uncommon Ground: Archaeology and Early African America, 1650–1800*, Washington, DC: Smithsonian Institution Press.

Finley, M. I. (1980) *Ancient Slavery and Modern Ideology*, Harmondsworth: Penguin.

Fishwick, D. (1987) *The Imperial Cult in the Latin West*, Leiden: Brill.

Fitzhugh, W. (1985) *Cultures in Context*, Washington, DC: Smithsonian Institution Press.

Fogel, R. and Engerman, S. (1974) *Time on the Cross: The Economics of American Negro Slavery*, Boston: Little Brown.

Goddio, F. (1988) *Discovery and Archaeological Excavation of a 16th century Trading Vessel in the Philippines*, Lausanne: World Wide First Press.

Greco, E. (1992) *Archeologia della Magna Grecia*, Rome-Bari: Laterza.

Greenblatt, S. (1991) *Marvelous Possessions*, Chicago: University of Chicago Press.

Greene, K. (1986) *The Archaeology of the Roman Economy*, London: Batsford.

Handler, J. and Lange, F. (1978) *Plantation Slavery in Barbados: An Archaeological and Historical Investigation*, Cambridge, Mass.: Harvard University Press.

Hanson, W. S. (1987) *Agricola and the Conquest of the North*, London: Batsford.

Harrington, S. (1993) 'Bones and bureaucrats', *Archaeology* 46: 28–38.

Hayes, J. W. (1972) *Late Roman Pottery*, London: British School at Rome.

Henig, M. and King, A. (1986) *Pagan Gods and Shrines of the Roman Empire*, Oxford: Oxford Archaeology Monographs.

Higman, B. W. (1988) *Jamaica Surveyed: Plantation Maps and Plans of the Eighteenth and Nineteenth Centuries*, Kingston: Institute of Jamaica.

Hingley, R. (1989) *Rural Settlement in Roman Britain*, London: Seaby.

Hitchner, B. (1990) 'The Kasserine Survey – 1987', *Antiquités Africaines* 26: 231–59.

Holloway, R. R. (1991) *The Archaeology of Ancient Sicily*, London: Routledge.

Hopkins, C. (1979) *The Discovery of Dura Europos*, New Haven: Yale University Press.

Hyslop, J. (1984) *The Inka Road System*, Orlando: Academic Press.

Hyslop, J. (1990) *Inka Settlement Planning*, Austin: University of Texas Press.

Isaac, B. (1990) *The Limits of Empire*, Oxford: Clarendon Press.

Jones, B. and Mattingly, D. (1993) *An Atlas of Roman Britain*, Oxford: Blackwell.

Jones, M. J. (1987) 'The Roman period', in J. Schofield and R. Leech (eds) *Urban Archaeology in Britain*, London: Council for British Archaeology: 27–45.

Keay, S. (1988) *Roman Spain*, London: British Museum Press.

Kelso, W. (1984) *Kingsmill Plantation 1619–1800*, Orlando: Academic.

Kelso, W. (1986) 'Mulberry Row: slave life at Thomas Jefferson's Monticello', *Archaeology* 39 (5): 28–35.

Kelso, W. and Most, R. (1990) *Earth Patterns: Essays in Landscape Archaeology*, Charlottesville: University of Virginia Press.

Kennedy, D. and Riley, D. N. (1990) *Rome's Desert Frontier from the Air*, Austin: University of Texas Press.

King, A. (1990) *Roman Gaul and Germany*, London: British Museum Press.

Kopper, P. (1986) *Colonial Williamsburg*, New York: Abrams.

Kubler, G. (1985) *Studies in Ancient American and European Art*, New Haven, Conn.: Yale University Press.

Le Gall, J. (1990) *Alesia, Archéologie et Histoire*, Paris: Editions Errance.

Lewis, M. J. T. (1966) *Temples in Roman Britain*, Cambridge: Cambridge University Press.

Lloyd, S. (1989) *Ancient Turkey*, Berkeley: University of California Press.

McEwan, B. (1991a) 'The archaeology of women in the Spanish New World', *Historical Archaeology* 25 (4): 33–41.

McEwan, B. (1991b) 'San Luis de Talimoli: the archaeology of Spanish–Indian relations at a Florida mission', *Historical Archaeology* 25 (3): 36–60.

McEwan, B. (1992–3) 'The role of ceramics in Spain and Spanish America during the 16th century', *Historical Archaeology* 26: 92–108.

Marcus, J. (1976) *Emblem and State in the Classic Maya Lowlands*, Washington, DC: Dumbarton Oaks.

Markell, A., Hall, M. and Schrire, C. (1995) 'The historical archaeology of Vergelegen, an early farmstead at the Cape of Good Hope', *Historical Archaeology* 20: 10–34.

Marsden, P. (1986) *Roman London*, London: Thames and Hudson.

Massy, J.-C. (1979) *Amiens Gallo-Romain*, Heilly: Printex.

Mattingly, D. (ed.) (1977) 'Dialogues in Roman imperialism', *Journal of Roman Archaeology* (Michigan), Supplementary Series 23.

Millett, M. (1990) *The Romanization of Britain*, Cambridge: Cambridge University Press.

Muckelroy, K. (ed.) (1980) *Archaeology under Water: An Atlas of the World's Submerged Sites*, New York: McGraw-Hill.

Noel Hume, I. (1963) *Here Lies Virginia*, New York: Knopf.

Noel Hume, I. (1969) *Historical Archaeology*, New York: Knopf.

Noel Hume, I. (1974) *Digging for Carter's Grove*, New York: Knopf.

Noel Hume, I. (1982) *Martin's Hundred*, New York: Knopf.

Ottaway, P. (1993) *Roman York*, London: Thames and Hudson.

Pai, H. I. (1992) 'Culture contact and culture change: the Korean peninsula and its relation with the Han dynasty commandery of Lelang', *World Archaeology* 23: 306–17.

Parker Pearson, M. (1997) 'Close encounters of the worst kind: Malagasy resistance and colonial disasters in Southern Madagascar', *World Archaeology* 28: 393–417.

Parson, J. R. (1982) *Prehispanic Settlement Patterns in the Southern Valley of Mexico: The Chalico/Xochimilco Region*, Ann Arbor: Museum of Anthropology.

Peacock, D. P. S. (1982) *Pottery in the Roman World*, London: Longman.

Peacock, D. P. S. and Williams, D. F. (1986) *Amphorae and the Roman Economy*, London: Longman.

Percival, J. (1976) *The Roman Villa*, Berkeley: University of California Press.

Perkins, A. (1973) *The Art of Dura Europos*, Oxford: Oxford University Press.

Peterson, E. (1964) *Gentlemen on the Frontier*, Mackinac Island, Mich.: Mackinac Island State Park Commission.

Piggott, S. (1975) *The Druids*, London: Thames and Hudson.

Pinon, P. (1991) *La Gaule Retrouve*, Paris: Gallimard.

Potter, T. W. (1979) *The Changing Landscape of South Etruria*, London: Paul Elek.

Reitz, E. J. (1992) 'The Spanish colonial experience and domestic animals', *Historical Archaeology* 26: 84–91.

Rostovtzeff, M. (1941) *The Social and Economic History of the Hellenistic World*, Oxford: Clarendon Press.

Rowlands, M., Larsen, M. and Kristiansen, K. (1987) *Centre and Periphery in the Ancient World*, Cambridge: Cambridge University Press.

Salmon, E. T. (1970) *Roman Colonization under the Republic*, Ithaca: Cornell University Press.

Salomon, F. (1987) 'Ancestor cults and resistance to the state in Arequipa, ca. 1748–54' in S. Stern (ed.) *Resistance, Rebellion and Consciousness in the Andean Peasant World, 18th to 20th Centuries*, Wisconsin: University of Wisconsin Press: 148–65.

Sanders, W. T., Parsons, J. R. and Santley, R. S. (1979) *The Basin of Mexico*, New York: Academic Press.

Santley, R. S. and Alexander, R. T. (1992) 'The political economy of core–periphery systems', in E. M. Schortman and P. A. Urban (eds) *Resources, Power and Interregional Interaction*, New York: Plenum: 23–50.

Schaedel, R. (1992) 'The archaeology of the Spanish Colonial experience in South America', *Antiquity* 66: 217–42.

Schleiermacher, W. (1961) *Der römische Limes in Deutschland*, Berlin: Mann.

Schrire, C. (1988) 'The historical archaeology of the impact of colonialism in 17th century South Africa', *Antiquity* 62: 214–25.

Scott, E. M. (1991) 'A feminist approach to historical archaeology: eighteenth century fur trader society at Michilimackinac', *Historical Archaeology* 24 (4): 42–53.

Sheridan, T. E. (1992) 'The limits of power: the political ecology of the Spanish Empire in the Greater Southwest', *Antiquity* 66: 153–71.

Sherratt, S. and Sherratt, A. (1993) 'The growth of the Mediterranean economy in the first millennium BC', *World Archaeology* 24: 361–78.

Simmons, W. S. (1986) *Spirit of the New England Tribes*, Hanover, N.H.: University Press of New England.

Singleton, T. (ed.) (1985) *The Archaeology of Slavery and Plantation Life*, New York: Academic Press.

Smith, M. E. and Berdan, F. F. (1992) 'Archaeology and the Aztec Empire', *World Archaeology* 23: 353–67.

Spivey, N. and Stoddart, S. (1990) *Etruscan Italy*, London: Batsford.

Stern, S. (1982) *Peru's Indian Peoples and the Challenge of Spanish Conquest*, Madison, Wisc.: University of Wisconsin Press.

Stern, S. (ed.) (1987) *Resistance, Rebellion and Consciousness in the Andean Peasant World, 18th–20th Centuries*, Madison, Wis.: University of Wisconsin Press.

Stern, S. (1988) 'Feudalism, capitalism and world systems in the perspective of Latin America and the Caribbean', *American Historical Review* 93: 829–73.

Stocking, G. (ed.) (1991) *Colonial Situations*, Madison, Wis.: University of Wisconsin Press.

Stone, L. M. (1974) *Fort Michilimackinac 1715–1781*, East Lansing: Michigan State University.

Taylor, C. (1975) 'Roman settlements in the Nene valley: the impact of recent archaeology', in P. J. Fowler (ed.) *Recent Work in Rural Archaeology*, Totowa, N.J.: Rowan and Littlefield.

Thomas, D. H. (1988) 'Saints and soldiers at Santa Catalina: Hispanic designs for colonial America and the recovery of meaning', in M. Leone and P. P. Potter Jnr (eds) *Historical Archaeology*, Washington, DC: Smithsonian Institution Press: 111–23.

Thompson, M. W. (1991) *The Rise of the Castle*, Cambridge: Cambridge University Press.

Tiffin, C. and Lawson, A. (1994) *De-scribing Empire*, London/New York: Routledge.

Verano, J. W. and Ubelaker, D. (eds) (1992) *Disease and Demography in the Americas*, Washington, DC.: Smithsonian Institution Press.

Waldron, A. (1990) *The Great Wall of China: From History to Myth*, Cambridge: Cambridge University Press.

Wallerstein, I. (1974) *The Modern World System: Capitalist Agriculture and the Origins of European World-Economy in the Sixteenth Century*, New York: Academic Press.

Walthall, J. A. (1991) *French Colonial Archaeology*, Urbana and Chicago: University of Illinois Press.

Webster, J. (1995) 'Translation and subjection: *intepretatio* and the Celtic gods', in J. D. Hill and C. Cumberpatch (eds) *Different Iron Ages: Studies on the Iron Age in Temporate Europe*, Oxford: British Archaeological Reports, International Series 602: 170–83.

Webster, J. (1997) 'Necessary comparisons: a post-colonial approach to religious syncretism in the Roman provinces', *World Archaeology* 28: 50–64.

Webster, J. and Cooper, N. (eds) (1996) *Roman Imperialism: Post-Colonial Perspectives*, Leicester: Leicester Archaeological Monographs 3.

Welfare, H. and Swan, V. (1995) *Roman Camps in England*, London: Royal Commission on the Historical Monuments of England.

Wells, P. (1980) *Culture Contact and Culture Change*, Cambridge: Cambridge University Press.

Wells, P. (1984) *Farms, Villages and Cities*, Ithaca, N.Y.: Cornell University Press.

Wells, P. (1992) 'Tradition, identity and change beyond the Roman frontier', in E. M. Schortman and P. A. Urban (eds) *Resources, Power and Interregional Interaction*, New York: Plenum: 175–92.

Wheeler, R. E. M. (1954) *Rome Beyond the Imperial Frontiers*, London: Bell.

Whittaker, C. (1994) *Frontiers of the Roman Empire*, Baltimore, Md.: Johns Hopkins University Press.

Willey, G. (1953) *Prehistoric Settlement Patterns in the Viru Valley, Peru*, Washington, DC: Bureau of American Ethnology, Bulletin 155.

Williams, J. S. (1992) 'The archaeology of underdevelopment and the military frontier of north New Spain', *Historical Archaeology* 26: 7–21.

Woolf, G. (1981) *Das Römische-Germanische Köln*, Köln: Bachem Verlag.

Woolf, G. (1990) 'World systems analysis and the Roman empire', *Journal of Roman Archaeology* 3: 44–58.

Woolf, G. (1992) 'Imperialism, empire and the integration of the Roman economy', *World Archaeology* 23: 283–93.

Wright, G. (1991) *The Politics of Design in French Colonial Urbanism*, Chicago: University of Chicago Press.

Zanker, P. (1988) *The Power of Images in the Age of Augustus*, Ann Arbor: University of Michigan Press.

SELECT BIBLIOGRAPHY

The literature on the Roman Empire is vast. The archaeology has to be studied on a regional basis. Good recent studies of parts of the western empire include Keay (1988) and King (1990). For an effort to see the archaeology of modern colonialism in a world-wide context, see Falk (1991), and for the archaeology of North American plantation life and slavery, see Singleton (1985) and Ferguson (1992).

25

POST-COLLAPSE SOCIETIES

Joseph A. Tainter

INTRODUCTION

If there is a historical generalization that is widely considered true, it is that human societies tend to become larger and more complex, but a corollary equally true is that complex societies often collapse. Collapses are a paradox: they are common enough to warrant systematic study, yet are usually seen as an aberration of social evolution.

Complex societies have been collapsing nearly as long as they have existed, yet this process and its aftermath are poorly understood. This stems in part from a paucity of material remains of post-collapse societies, but the bigger obstacle is our intellectual prejudice. There is genuine bias against so-called 'Dark Ages', a bias instilled by a pejorative label, and by texts that portray such periods as times of disorder, poverty, and unrelieved bleakness. Even scholars who study post-collapse societies are vulnerable to this prejudice, as in the following characterizations of the Greek Dark Ages.

> From the point of view of material culture, the Greek Dark Ages have little to offer or excite . . . One has . . . the feeling of depressed isolation . . . At first sight, the overall impression of Athens in the Dark Ages is not a very exciting one.
>
> (Desborough 1972: 12, 77, 157)

> Apart from pottery, the archaeological evidence for the next two or three centuries [after the Mycenaean collapse] is very thin and unrevealing in any positive sense . . . [A] uniform dullness sets in everywhere . . .
>
> (Finley 1981: 65, 70)

Post-collapse societies are to many scholars an annoying interlude, their study a chore necessary to understand the renaissance that follows. One problem is the paucity of material remains, but there are also conceptual reasons for this bias: post-collapse societies violate both the nineteenth-century belief in unilineal 'progress', and the twentieth-century assumption that societies evolve inexorably to greater complexity. Moreover, when a complex society collapses it may take with it those trappings of complexity that form the popular image of a civilization: great traditions of art, architecture, and literature. Most people believe that great complexity (that is, civilization) is a desirable condition of human affairs. Civilization is commonly seen as the ultimate accomplishment of the human species, and industrial civilization as the culmination of history. Adopting such a view, which most of us assimilate when young, collapse seems a catastrophe.

In contrast, this chapter argues that complexity is rare in human history. It is a costly mode of organization that must be constantly maintained. Collapse is in fact normal and expectable in the evolution of complexity. As a recurrent phenomenon, post-collapse societies must be included in historical studies. While each post-collapse society has its own characteristics, many show recurrent patterns. These patterns mean that many aspects of post-collapse societies should be amenable to generalization and explanation.

DEFINITIONS

The concept of complexity is straightforward and potentially quantifiable: complexity refers to the size of a society, the number of its parts and their distinctiveness, the variety of specialized roles, the number of distinct social personalities, and the number and effectiveness of mechanisms for integrating these into a functioning whole. Increasing any of these factors increases the complexity of a society (Tainter 1988: 23, 1996: 4–7). Thus hunter-gatherer societies are composed of no more than a few dozen social personalities, whereas modern European censuses recognize 10,000 to 20,000 distinct occupations, and industrial societies may overall embody more than a million different social personalities (McGuire 1983: 115). As another example, ethnographers documented among the native peoples of western North America some 3,000 to 6,000 cultural elements, including technology, ideology, and social relations, yet when US military forces landed at Casablanca in the Second World War, they brought with them more than 500,000 artefact types (Steward 1955: 81), and a corresponding logistical service.

Collapse too is a straightforward concept, and pertains also to quantifiable social dimensions: *collapse is a rapid, significant, loss of an established level of socio-political complexity* (Tainter 1988: 4). Collapse is fundamentally a matter of the socio-political sphere. It may and frequently does have consequences in such areas as art, architecture, and literature but, contrary to widespread belief, these are not its essence. It is incorrect to speak of a civilization collapsing, though this is commonly done. A civilization (that is, a great tradition of art, architecture, and literature) is the cultural system of a complex society (Tainter 1988: 41). What is called civilization is an epiphenomenon or product of complexity. Great traditions of art, architecture, and literature emerge to serve social and economic classes, and social and economic purposes, that exist only in complex societies. Civilization emerges with socio-political complexity, exists because of it, and disappears when complexity disappears. Civilizations do not collapse; specific political structures do.

The only societies that can collapse are ones that have existed at a level of complexity, or have been evolving towards higher complexity, for more than a few generations. The demise of a short-lived entity such as the Carolingian empire is not a collapse, merely an unsuccessful attempt at empire building. A collapse, moreover, must be quick, taking no more than a few decades, and it must entail a substantial loss of socio-political structure. Cases of prolonged weakness and territorial loss, such as the Byzantine and Ottoman empires, are not examples of collapse (Tainter 1988: 4). Figure 25.1 shows a clear collapse, the rapid abandonment of major Mayan political centres at the end of the Late Classic period.

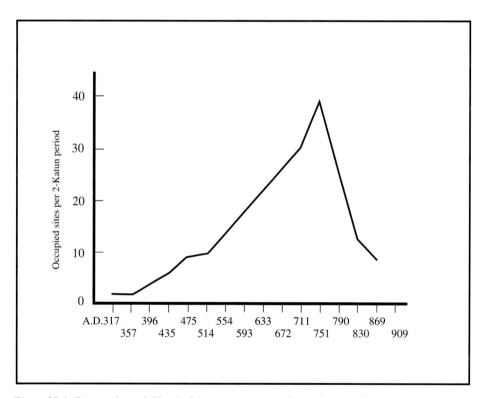

Figure 25.1 Occupation of Classic Maya centres; one *katun* is approximately twenty years. Adapted from Erickson 1975: 40. Source: J. Tainter. Redrawn by D. Miles-Williams.

While it is common to think of collapse as something that afflicts only states and empires, in fact any kind of society can collapse, even fairly simple ones. Societies vary along a continuous scale, and any society can increase or decrease in complexity along the progression of this scale. Collapse is relative to the complexity of the society. Mid-range societies, such as the prehistoric Chacoans of what is now the south-western United States, or even foragers like the Ik of northern Uganda, have been known to collapse (Tainter 1988: 4–5, 14–15, 17–18). This discussion will not concentrate on such examples, but it is important to understand that collapse is a universal process that can affect virtually any society.

THE COSTS OF COMPLEXITY

The citizens of modern industrial states are taught that their societies are the normal form of human organization. In fact we are an anomaly. Throughout several million years of human existence, the common political unit was the small, autonomous community, making decisions and acting independently, and largely self-sufficient. Carneiro estimates that such communities were the dominant political form for 99.8 per cent of our history (1978: 219). Truly complex societies, those organized as hierarchical, centralized states, have emerged only within the last 6,000 years or so. Complex societies are thus historically rare, and statistically are an unusual form of organization. In this sense post-collapse societies are not aberrations, but represent a return to the usual condition of low cultural complexity.

A matter typically overlooked in the study of cultural evolution is that complexity costs: more complex societies are more expensive to maintain than simpler ones, and require greater support levels per capita (Tainter 1988: 91–92). In a society that is more complex there are more groups and social roles; there are more networks among individuals and groups; there are more controls, both horizontal and hierarchical; more information is processed; there is more centralization of information; and there are more specialists who are not engaged directly in producing resources (Johnson 1978, 1982; McGuire 1983; Tainter 1988: 91). Correspondingly, while a simple cultural system activated primarily by human energy requires only about one-twentieth horsepower per capita per year (White 1949: 369, 1959: 41–42), industrial societies depend on hundreds to thousands of horsepower per capita per year. Not only can complex societies utilize more energy, they require it. In the days before fossil fuels and industrial technologies, the higher cost of supporting a more complex society typically meant that people worked harder.

The costs of complexity do much to explain why it is rare. At one point most archaeologists and historians assumed that human societies have a latent tendency towards complexity, that it is the inevitable result of surplus food, leisure time, and human creativity. Some scholars still believe this scenario, and it is widespread among the public. In fact, the costs of becoming more complex have always restrained growth in complexity. Peasants particularly bear the cost of supporting complex institutions, through taxation or direct requisitioning of their labour. Participating in a complex society is a benefit/cost equation. While peasants may lack the option not to participate, their participation is not irrational. When supporting complex institutions becomes too high in cost or too low in benefits, peasants have historically responded with degrees of resistance ranging from apathy to rebellion (Eisenstadt 1963: 209; Wolf 1969).

Two points emerge from this. First, since complexity is costly and may be resisted by the support population, it must emerge under conditions of compelling need or perceived benefit. Scholars have identified a number of factors that contribute to the emergence of complex institutions: (1) the need to mobilize labour for public works, such as irrigation (Wittfogel 1957); (2) the need to centralize and process information (Johnson 1978; Wright 1969); (3) the need to manage internal and external economies (Isbell 1978; Raish 1992; Rathje 1971); (4) the need to regulate conflict within a society (Childe 1951: 181–82; Fried 1967); (5) the need to organize for military operations (Carneiro 1970; Webster 1975); or (6) cumulative and interactive effects among these factors (Renfrew 1972: 27). Complexity, in other words, is a problem-solving strategy.

Second, complexity must constantly be maintained. Complex societies are, as Simon has labelled them, 'nearly decomposable systems' (1965: 70). They are built up of political units (villages, cities, ethnic groups, smaller states) that were at one time independent, and could become so again. To the extent that these 'building blocks' of complexity retain the potential for independent action, the administrators of a complex society must work continuously to assure their allegiance. Recent developments in the former USSR illustrate this point as forcefully as any historical example.

Membership in a complex polity can be maintained through coercion, or by incorporation as full members of the dominant system. Both courses have been employed. Often the incorporation of smaller political units into an overarching system, such as an empire, involves coercion initially followed by incorporation. The classic example is the Roman empire. In AD 212 the emperor Caracalla extended Roman citizenship to all free inhabitants of the empire. In the later empire provincials from such places as North Africa, Thrace, Syria, and Illyria aspired to, and regularly achieved, the highest office, and even Germans and Huns wielded power.

Coercion is an expensive and ineffective strategy, and must eventually be replaced by legitimacy, the belief that rule is proper and valid. This requires not only ideology and manipulation of symbols, but real returns of goods and services to the populace (Easton 1965). Both coercion and legitimacy require leaders continuously to amass resources, and to expend these to maintain the political order. Should they fail to do so, the society will 'decompose' to the 'building blocks' out of which it was created.

BENEFITS AND COSTS IN THE EVOLUTION OF COMPLEXITY

Complexity is clearly an investment, in which costs are assumed and benefits obtained. As with any economic activity, the efficiency of investing in complexity must be gauged by weighing the costs against the benefits.

To the extent that they have the information to do so, human populations will usually seek a rational return on expenditures of labour and other resources: that is, they will attempt to keep costs at an acceptable level, while obtaining a desired return of goods and services. Thus people initially use sources of food, energy, and raw materials that meet their needs at a reasonable level of effort. When such resources are no longer sufficient, people turn to secondary sources: foods, energy, and raw materials that are costlier to acquire, extract, process, and distribute, while perhaps yielding no higher returns (Asch *et al*. 1972; Boserup 1965; Clark and Haswell 1966; Wilkinson 1973). This yields the situation that economists refer to as the 'point of diminishing returns', where the cost of an investment rises but the return fails to grow proportionately.

Investment in complex social and political institutions follows the same pattern. In the growth of complexity, less costly social features are logically adopted before more costly ones. For example, part-time leaders have preceded those employed full-time. Generalized administration has given way to specialized. Whereas at one time many administrative functions may be fulfilled by a single individual, it is common in human societies to respond to problems by appointing specialized administrators, and by engaging more of the population in administrative tasks.

Organizational developments, moreover, tend to be cumulative. Complex social features are rarely dropped. In any complex organization there seems always to be more information to process. It is rare for the number of specialists to decline. Social welfare and political legitimization are unending requirements. Military forces typically do not get simpler or less costly. The compensation of élites usually moves upward. Complex societies create ever more public monuments, each requiring maintenance. The lesson is that when there is growth of complexity it tends to be exponential, always increasing by a proportion of an already inflated size.

As more parts are added to any system, the possible interactions among them increase factorially. Complex systems generate more complexity simply by being diversified. For example, in contemporary societies taxes are established and regulations are issued. Lobbyists seek loopholes, and administrators try to close these. There unfolds a potentially unending spiral of loophole discovery and closure, in which complexity and costs grow (Olson 1982: 69–73). The administrators of any complex system must set aside resources – not only to solve the real problems the society faces but also to solve the problems created by their own existence, and by overall societal complexity (Tainter 1988: 115–16).

The growth of socio-political complexity also yields benefits, such as producing and managing resources, internal order and external defence, processing information, and public works. As low-cost solutions to societal needs are adopted first, the benefit/cost ratio for investment in complexity may at first increase favourably. The Romans, for example, in the course of their expansion, engaged subject Italian peoples to assist them in their military campaigns, and later employed the wealth of conquered nations to finance further expansion (Jones 1974: 114–15). As the empire reached its maximum extent, costs were minimized by creating a buffer of client states as Rome's first line of defence (Luttwak 1976). It was a strategy of empire-building that yielded high returns for minimal Roman expenditures.

Yet while a society's first investments in growing complexity may be rational and productive, that is a state of affairs which cannot last. As the least-costly organizational solutions are exhausted, requirements for further growth in complexity elicit more costly responses. As the cost of organizational solutions grows, the point is reached where greater investments do not yield a proportionate return. This is the point of diminishing returns to complexity. The benefits per unit of investment in complexity start to drop. Constant or increasing investments yield static or decreasing returns.

Stresses and challenges are inevitable, and no society can avoid adjusting continuously to its circumstances. As stresses arise, new organizational solutions must often be adopted, which involve increasing costs and diminishing returns. What economists would call the marginal return on investment in complexity (that is, the return per extra unit of investment) starts to decline. This may be so slight at first that it is hardly noticed. Ultimately marginal returns decline with accelerated force, and the decline becomes evident. At this point a complex society starts to become vulnerable to collapse.

Two general problems make a society vulnerable to collapse at this point. First, as the marginal return on investment in complexity declines, the society becomes economically weakened. As the society invests more heavily in a strategy with proportionately less return, excess productive capacity and financial reserves may be allocated to current operations. When major stresses arise there is little or no reserve for countering them. If the challenge is surmounted, the society may be so weakened economically that it is vulnerable to the next crisis. Thus older, established societies sometimes succumb to problems that they might have overcome when their return on investment in complexity was growing. Rome, for instance, was able to withstand major military disasters at the start of the Second Punic War

(218–201 BC), and still went on to ultimate victory, yet in AD 378 a much larger, wealthier, and more powerful Roman empire was badly weakened at the Battle of Adrianople by losses that were comparatively less severe.

Second, diminishing returns make complexity an unattractive strategy. As costs rise and there is less return to the local level, the 'building blocks' of a complex system (villages, cities, ethnic groups, small states) perceive that independence would be more advantageous. They may passively or actively resist, or overtly attempt to break away. In the later Roman Empire local insurrections lasted for decades; many citizens offered no resistance to the German invaders, while others actively welcomed the intruders (Tainter 1988: 118–23, 195–96, 1994: 1248). Gunderson suggests that for many late Roman provincials 'the net value of local autonomy exceeded that of membership in the Empire' (1976: 61).

Complex societies faced with external threats, or internal dissension, or both, have often yielded to the temptation to expand territorially, producing an economic windfall of agricultural produce and peasant populations, but new provinces and their populations must be controlled, administered, garrisoned, and defended. Subject populations become citizens, and so less suitable for exploitation. The subsidy obtained from a conquest is highest initially, due to plunder, but then declines as occupation and administrative costs rise, and as provincials gain political rights and benefits. Rome, for a one-time infusion of wealth from each conquered province, had to undertake administrative and military responsibilities that lasted centuries. Ultimately the marginal return on being an empire starts to drop, whereupon the society is back to its previous predicament. Territorial expansion provides only a temporary respite from diminishing returns to complexity. What it does ensure is that collapse, when it finally occurs, affects a wider territory and a larger population in a more devastating manner than would otherwise have been the case (Tainter 1988: 124–26).

A recent survey disclosed nearly two dozen cases of collapse, known historically or archaeologically or both, ranging from the very simplest societies, such as the Ik of Uganda, to the great empires of the ancient world (Tainter 1988: 5–18). Given that small to mid-range societies are prone to collapse, and rarely developed writing, there must have been dozens or hundreds of collapses that have not been discerned archaeologically, though gradually these are being recognized (for example, Mathers and Stoddart 1994). In the remainder of this chapter I focus on twelve well-documented post-collapse societies, though as post-collapse societies cannot be understood without knowing the contexts from which they developed, each case study will cover both pre- and post-collapse characteristics.

THE ROMAN EMPIRE AND POST-ROMAN EUROPE

The Roman empire reached its logical extent with the conquest of the Mediterranean basin. During the sailing months, the Mediterranean provided efficient transport and rapid communication, both vital to maintaining the empire. Julius Caesar's conquest of central and northern Gaul (58–51 BC) was not a logical extension of the Mediterranean conquests, but the Romans appreciated it none the less: Gauls had often been a threat. Later conquests, of Britain by Claudius (AD 41–54) and of Dacia by Trajan (98–117), may not have paid for themselves, for these were poor frontier provinces at a great distance from the capital (Hammond 1946: 75–76). The Romans held Britain and Dacia through recurrent crises, but abandoned them when they proved indefensible. Trajan's conquests in Assyria and Mesopotamia (AD 115) were wisely relinquished by his successor, Hadrian (117–38).

Despite fiscal difficulties, resulting in a progressive debasement of the silver coinage (by increasing the proportion of copper), the early empire was peaceful and successful. Significant stresses appeared in the reign of Marcus Aurelius (161–80), when a devastating plague coincided with serious Germanic incursions. The empire's first life-threatening challenges came in the third century AD, and particularly in the half century from 235 to 284. This was a time of unparalleled crisis, during which the empire nearly came to an end. There were frequent barbarian incursions and foreign conflicts, punctuated by civil wars. Many provinces were devastated. The army and bureaucracy grew. The government's response produced financial distress and higher taxes, great debasement of the currency, and unparalleled inflation. The average reign during this period was only a few months. In a fifty-year period there were at least twenty-seven recognized emperors, and so many usurpers that the number of emperors and pretenders averages out to one per year for half a century.

The situation was rescued for a time by reforming emperors, beginning with Gallienus (253–68) and Aurelian (270–75), though the major work was done by Diocletian (284–305) and Constantine (306–37). The solution was larger government, greater power, and higher complexity. The empire that was redesigned under Diocletian and Constantine was larger, more complex, and more highly organized. It commanded military forces more than double the previous size. It taxed more heavily, conscripted citizens' labour, and regulated lives and occupations. The empire became a coercive organization that intruded into and subdued individual interests for one paramount goal: the survival of the state.

As the Roman empire became more complex, it naturally became more costly. Each citizen, each guild, and each locality was expected to produce what the empire needed. Taxes were raised to the point where they threatened the capital resources of taxpayers. Diocletian's tax was a flat rate levied on the land and on the number of residents. It did not accommodate variations in the quality of land or fluctuations in yield. The land tax had to be paid whether a parcel was cultivated or not. If a farmer could not be found, an uncultivated parcel was assigned to other landowners, to all local landowners, or to municipalities for payment of taxes. Even if a crop was poor, the tax had to be paid, whether or not enough was left for the farmer and his family. People who couldn't meet their taxes were jailed, sold their children into slavery, or abandoned their homes and fields. Yet the state always had a back-up, extending tax obligations to widows or children, even to dowries.

Under such circumstances marginal land went out of production, as too often it could not yield enough for taxes and a surplus. The population of the empire had been declining for some time under the pressures of plagues and wars. The former population could not be re-established, as conditions were most unfavourable for the formation of large families. Acute shortages of agricultural labour resulted in imperial legislation tying farmers to the soil. As smallholders could not pay their taxes or their debts, they abandoned their farms and fled to large landowners. Tied by law to large estates, effectively they became serfs, and the forerunners of the feudal structure of the Middle Ages (Chapter 27). None the less, many late Roman peasants found rent-paying more attractive than tax-paying, and both peasants and landlords chose feudal social relations rather than a state-centred society (Wickham 1984: 17–18).

It was not only the countryside that suffered. In Gaul the cities of the later empire shrank, sometimes to the size of earlier villages. Vienne, for example, declined from 200 to about 20 hectares, Lyon from about 160 to 20, and Autun from about 200 to 10 hectares (Hodgett 1972: 36; Randsborg 1991: 91).

The Roman government's response to crisis was to increase its size, complexity, and costliness, but this was undertaken only to maintain the *status quo*. No new lands were conquered and no major booty was won. Costs rose precipitously, benefits at best remained level or even declined, and the return on maintaining the Roman empire plummeted. By the fifth century AD the Roman empire survived by consuming its capital resources: producing lands and peasant population. The decreased wealth and manpower of the western empire contributed to the military successes of the invaders. Military disasters in turn weakened finances, as productive provinces were plundered or stripped away. A downward spiral began, and ultimately the shrunken state was unable to pay its German mercenaries, who demanded one-third of the land of Italy in lieu of payment. This being refused, they revolted, elected as their king a commander named Odovacer, and deposed the last emperor of the west, Romulus Augustulus, in AD 476. A small section of northern Gaul remained under Roman administration for another ten years, until annexed by the Franks. Its leader, Syagrius, was styled the 'Roman King of Soissons' – that is, just another petty chieftain (Barker 1924: 425; Brown 1971; Duncan-Jones 1974; Finley 1973; Frank 1940; Gibbon 1776–88; Gunderson 1976; Hammond 1946; Heichelheim 1970; Jones 1964, 1974; Levy 1967; Luttwak 1976;

MacMullen 1976; Mazzarino 1966; Rostovtzeff 1926; Russell 1958; Tainter 1988: 128–48, 1994).

Most of the western provinces had been lost to Roman control before 476, and were divided among the Germanic invaders. In Gaul at least the process was not significantly resisted. Wickham argues that in the fifth century many landowners preferred the Germanic successor states to the financial structure and taxes of the Roman state (1984: 16). Some Gallic towns (or what was left of them) actually invited the invaders to occupy territory. In 378 Balkan miners went over to the Visigoths *en masse*. '[By] the fifth century', concludes R. M. Adams, 'men were ready to abandon civilization itself in order to escape the fearful load of taxes' (1983: 47).

The invaders appropriated up to one-half of the lands they occupied. Since the later empire had lost population, and formerly cultivated lands were abandoned, this caused less impact than one might expect. The appropriated lands were in some cases owned by the Roman state, and in others were parts of privately held estates. In many instances, though, Roman landowners were evicted altogether, and among the landowning class there was hardship. Some Roman landowners adapted wisely to the new realities, changing their names to Germanic forms, and even commanding German armies (Wickham 1984: 30).

The cultural traditions that survived the Roman collapse were those supportable by land ownership. The Merovingian dynasty of Gaul (AD 428–751) still taxed land, and people still complained, but the levy was much reduced. Late Roman taxes had taken from one-fourth to one-third of gross yields, and thus from one-half to two-thirds of what was left after paying rent. Now taxes were reduced to perhaps under 10 per cent, and taxation no longer dominated the economy. The legitimacy of taxation declined, as its main purpose was to enrich the Merovingian kings. Taxes declined primarily because there was less to spend money on. The main expense of the Roman empire had been the army. That cost was now virtually gone since Frankish warriors provided their own equipment and sustained themselves from their estates. When troubles arose, troops were raised locally: the standing force was very small.

The king's expenses were limited to maintaining his court and giving donations to leading men and the churches. These expenses were covered by revenues from the royal domains. Court officials had no salaries, but received the revenues of certain estates. When the king and his officials travelled, private persons were obliged to furnish food, lodging, and transport. Initially some Roman imposts were kept, such as customs dues. By Carolingian times (beginning AD 751) all that was left of the land tax was an assortment of fragments with regional names, whose origins were lost to memory (Pfister 1913; Vinogradoff 1913; Wickham 1984).

In the later sixth century AD, Gregory of Tours used the term 'Senator' for any major Gallo-Roman landowner – the original meaning of the term had been forgotten, although the Roman Senate survived until about 600. Hierarchies were simplified and authority greatly reduced. Merovingian society had definite gradations, but initially no hereditary nobility. Aristocrats were those who owned great estates. Offices were valued because they conveyed land. Aristocrats were not bound to the state by abstract concepts of obligation or duty. The king distributed land to obligate leading men to himself, expecting military service in return (Pfister 1913; Wickham 1981, 1984).

There was no remedy against autocratic rule but revolt or assassination, and Pfister has described the Merovingian government as 'a despotism tempered by assassination' (1913: 135). Still, royal authority was limited by the tribal social relations from which it had sprung. At the conquest of Soissons (AD 486), Clovis tried to save a precious chalice for the church. He appropriated it as an extra share of loot, whereupon a common soldier, so as not to allow the king an extra privilege, chopped the chalice in two. Clovis, realizing that the soldier's comrades would feel similarly, took no immediate action; at the next review, though, he cut the man's skull in two (Vinogradoff 1913: 640).

In the late Merovingian period an annual spring assembly was held, which by the Carolingian era was the most important part of government. The assembly was an army, a council, a legal tribunal, and a source of revenue. The assembly decided the king's recommendation whether to go to war. Those summoned to the assembly brought gifts of money and food, which became the state's principal source of revenue (Pfister 1913: 135, 140). Feudalism continued to develop at the opposite end of the social hierarchy. Troubled times in the seventh century kept poor freemen on protracted military duty. Once again patron–client relations developed, as poor freeholders commended themselves and their land to large proprietors, both lay and clerical, in exchange for the right of occupancy. The number of smallholdings declined while estates grew (Pfister 1913: 151–52; Vinogradoff 1913: 649).

From the mid-fourth century few monumental buildings were erected in Gaul other than churches. Decaying masonry buildings were patched up, or demolished and replaced in timber. Many ancient monuments were destroyed in the invasions and those remaining were typically mined for building materials. Towns took on a country-like atmosphere: they were sparsely populated and had much cultivated land within their walls. The only substantial buildings were churches, and many 'towns' consisted of little other than monasteries. The Roman roads still converged on such places, so they retained their names and in some cases a small measure of centrality. While there is evidence for industry within the former cities, they had become primarily administrative and ecclesiastical centres, where bishops tried to carry on a semblance of Roman tradition. After 600 there is little archaeological evidence for continuity of towns, and a strong case can be made for discontinuity. In the Carolingian period, while settlements grew and came to resemble villages, the major locations were monasteries, royal centres, and trade emporia (Hodges and

Whitehouse 1983: 83–86; Pfister 1913: 155; Randsborg 1991: 20, 69; Wickham 1984: 27).

Both the Merovingians of Gaul and the Lombards of Italy initially minted only gold coins. These were supplemented by a Merovingian silver coin introduced in the 670s and 680s, but silver was not reintroduced to Italy until the Carolingian period. This must indicate growing commerce and a need for smaller-unit currency. Yet silver coins were still too valuable for peasants. Money was available but not widely employed: it would have served as a standard of comparison rather than a medium of exchange, although peasants could have sold their produce for coins to pay rents. Landowners, who participated in urban markets, would have used coins in a more recognizably commercial manner (Hodges and Whitehouse 1983: 93–94; Wickham 1981: 113).

In Italy, although the western Roman empire was gone, there was initially no collapse. The late imperial administration was continued under Odovacer (AD 476–93), and the Ostrogothic king Theodoric (490–526) and his successors. The latter had at his command all the cultural resources of late Roman society and used them effectively. His palace at Ravenna dwarfed that built by Charlemagne at Aachen nearly 300 years later. The power of the state over the Italian economy was not broken until the wars of 535 to 605. Lombard Italy, like Merovingian Gaul, was supported by settlement on the land. The land tax disappeared. Landowning became the source of power, and the state depended on the consent of powerful landowners. In the seventh century the army was transformed into a landowning aristocracy, in both Lombard and Byzantine Italy.

By AD 700 each zone of Italy had its own customs and idiosyncracies in social hierarchy, legal formulae, and weights and measures. By 900 Italy was a complex ethnic mosaic. The bulk of the population was Roman (themselves, by late Antiquity, a complex ethnic mixture), but there were also Lombards, Franks, Alemans, some Burgundians and Bavarians, and Byzantine Greeks. The Lombards themselves numbered about 200,000 persons, only 5–8 per cent of the population in their territory. Not surprisingly, the Lombards lost their language by 700. The Ostrogoths are heard of little more after the Byzantine conquest.

Urban settlement never disappeared from Italy, but it was seriously impaired by the weakening and collapse of the empire. The fortunes of Rome are illustrative. From the first century BC until AD 367 it was an enormous city, holding a million people. Then in less than a century, by 452, it had declined to about 400,000, and in the next few centuries it dwindled to a few tens of thousands, standing at perhaps 30,000 in the tenth century. Where Rome had once been fed from Egypt, North Africa, and Sicily, its needs could now be met by farms within a few kilometres. The ancient monuments were converted into fortresses or mined for building materials, and the forum reverted to swamp.

To the north of Rome, settlement patterns in the *Ager Faliscus* testify to the insecurity of the times: the number of open country settlements dropped and, particularly in the last quarter of the first millennium AD, many hilltop villages were founded (Fig. 25.2). The latter continue to dominate the Italian landscape. As in Gaul there was sometimes farming within city walls. Large, state-organized projects came to an end, so that the drainage systems of the Po and Arno valleys were allowed to decay (Burns 1984; Hodges and Whitehouse 1983; Randsborg 1991; Wickham 1984).

Post-Roman Europe is the era for which the term 'Dark Age' was coined. While literacy had never been widespread even in classical times, certainly after the Roman collapse even fewer people could read and write. The paucity of original literature is striking. Gregory of Tours was almost the only historian of the sixth century, and he could not understand much of what was happening to his world. After him there is nothing of real history, merely some scraps attributed to a chronicler named Fredegar. The sole poet of the era was Fortunatus. After them

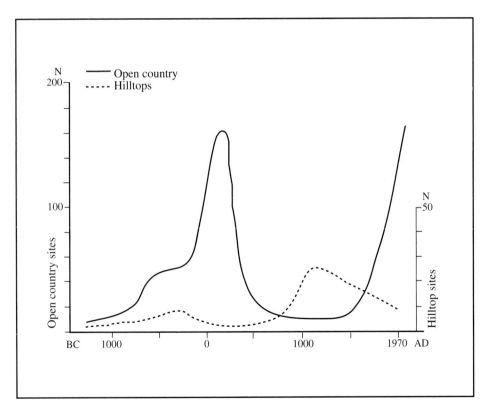

Figure 25.2 Changing settlement patterns in the *Ager Faliscus*, north of Rome in central Italy; note the shift to hilltop settlement in the second half of the first millennium AD. Adapted from Potter 1976: 214 as modified by Randsborg 1991: 71. Source: J. Tainter. Redrawn by D. Miles-Williams.

there is only a monotonous series of lives of saints, most of which read alike (Pfister 1913: 156–57).

The picture may seem bleak indeed: decaying monuments and public works, cities given over to cultivation, political simplification, disintegration, illiteracy, and depopulation. Yet there were developments that are significant for understanding the process and aftermath of collapse. The Germanic states that succeeded Roman rule were more successful at resisting further invasions (for example of Huns and Arabs) than had been the later empire. Theodoric was the most successful ruler of Italy since Valentinian (364–75), yet he held it with an army of only 25,000 to 30,000 and gave peace and prosperity. While some Romans disliked his Ostrogothic mannerisms, most approved of his rule. If there are fewer monuments to marvel at today, it is because buildings were economical and appropriate to the scale of the society. If Gallic and Italian aristocrats were less wealthy than their late Roman counterparts, peasants farmed better land and enjoyed higher productivity to their labour (Burns 1984; Carr 1992: 208; Hodges and Whitehouse 1983: 106; Weber 1976: 389; Wickham 1981: 21, 1984: 30). Such developments are among the paradoxes of collapse.

CHINA: THE WESTERN AND EASTERN CHOU

The collapse of the Western Chou dynasty (771 BC) marked the end of Chinese unity and the beginning of protracted fragmentation. The period of the Eastern Chou dynasty (770–256 BC) was a post-collapse phase, for the complex governmental apparatus and territorial unity of the Western Chou were gone. It represents, though, one extreme of the collapse process, for the independent polities which succeeded the Western Chou were well-integrated states. They were certainly more complex than the states of post-Roman Europe. The drop in complexity at the end of the Western Chou was much less than after the fall of the western Roman empire (Hsu and Linduff 1988).

The Chou were preceded by the Shang (c. 1766–1122 BC), China's first historical dynasty. The Shang are poorly known from isolated bronzes, so-called 'oracle bones', and unreliable writings of later times, though fortunately they are beginning to be better known archaeologically. The Shang ran a well-integrated empire, and were capable of impressive labour organization. Around 1500 BC their city of Cheng-chou was surrounded by walls of pounded earth 28 kilometres long. These walls contain 870,000 cubic metres of earth, and would have taken 13 million working days to complete – four years' work for a force of 10,000 labourers.

To overcome this powerful state the Chou, then a small peripheral people in the west of China, gradually encircled the Shang, or forged encircling alliances. Chou foot-soldiers had body armour and bronze swords that gave superiority over Shang forces. At the climactic battle of Mu-yeh, the Shang forces were drawn into rough terrain, where their advantage in chariots was negated, and where the clumsy formations of the Shang infantry worked to their disadvantage. The Chou could not hold China with their small forces, and to maintain their rule they developed two strategies. The first was to rule through a feudal hierarchy, with power devolving on regional leaders. This proved ultimately to be part of their undoing, and laid the structure for China's eventual fragmentation.

The second strategy was sacred legitimization, which was to have a lasting effect. Shang religious practices had been pantheistic and shamanistic. The Chou asserted stronger sacred legitimization: they claimed to have the 'Mandate of Heaven', a charter from *T'ien* (roughly 'the solemnity of the dome of the sky') to rule in the interests of the people. This was a brilliant manoeuvre which influenced much subsequent Chinese history: when a Chinese dynasty would grow corrupt, or fail to serve the needs of the people, rivals would claim that the Mandate of Heaven had devolved on them. This provided a legitimate basis for challenging established authority.

The Western Chou campaigned to expand their empire to the east and south, achieving some success and establishing an eastern administrative centre at Loyang. They also fought frequently with northern nomadic peoples, yet within a few centuries their power started to decline. The royal house began to lose authority as early as the tenth century BC, and by the ninth century their expansion may have stopped, weakened by the wars with the nomads and by the burden of sustaining large defensive forces. Chou expansion in the south was challenged by rebellion. In their waning years the Western Chou faced a number of concurrent problems: drought and famine, perhaps earthquakes, injustice and incompetent administration, encroachment of nomads, loss of population, vagrancy, and general disintegration of the social order. An excerpt from the contemporary poem *Shao-min* seems to express the multitudinous problems of the times.

Compassionate Heaven is arrayed in anger
Heaven is indeed sending down rain,
Afflicting us with famine,
So that the people are all wandering fugitives;
In the settled regions and on the border all is desolation.
Heaven sends down its web of crime;
Devouring insects weary and confuse men's minds,
Ignorant, oppressive, negligent,
Breeders of confusion, utterly perverse;
These are the men employed to tranquilize our country.
A pool becomes dry;
Is it not because no water comes to it from its banks?
A spring becomes dry,
Is it because no water rises in it from itself?

Great is the injury (all about),
So that my anxious sorrow is increased:
Will not calamity light on my person?
Formerly when the former Kings received their mandates,
There were such ministers as the Duke of Shao,
Who would in a day enlarge the kingdom a hundred *li*.
Now it is contracted in a day a hundred *li*.
Oh! Alas!
Among the men of the present day,
Are there not still some with the old virtue?

(Hsu and Linduff 1988: 283–84)

Finally an allied force of several northern Jung groups invaded the district of the capital city, Hao. In 771 BC the last Western Chou ruler, King Yu, was killed and the city sacked.

The Western Chou conquests had increased the importance of the eastern administrative centre, Loyang. After the disaster the capital was moved here, and the Eastern Chou dynasty established (770–256 BC). Chinese unity, however, effectively collapsed with the Western Chou. Regional leaders owed nominal allegiance, but the Eastern Chou were powerless figureheads. Subsequent Chou rulers were kept primarily to perform sacrifices legitimately. Real power shifted to the vassal states.

The post-collapse phase is conventionally divided into the Spring and Autumn (770–464 BC) and Warring States (463–222) periods. After the fall of the Western Chou there was a period of social upheavals: power was usurped by lords and ministers who arranged complex, shifting alliances, and strong states subjugated weaker ones as the powerful became more so. A later Chinese saying asserted that 'during the Spring and Autumn period, no wars were righteous' (Xueqin 1985: 7).

The most important states of the Spring and Autumn period were Lu, Ch'i, Chin, Ch'in, Ch'u, Sung, Zheng, Wu, and Yue (Fig. 25.3). The so-called Hua Xia states, in the central Chinese plains, were distinguished from the peripheral states, Ch'u, Wu, Yue, and Ch'in, which were regarded as barbarians. The latter group had the great competitive advantage of almost unlimited ability to expand at the expense of the tribal groups surrounding China. The Ch'in in particular honed their military capabilities in battles with the nomads on China's western and northwestern frontiers. In 678 BC an alliance was formed of the central states, with Ch'i paramount, for protection against the southern state of Ch'u. During the Spring and Autumn period Ch'u absorbed forty to fifty other states. Competitors were attempting to do likewise. The Ch'in moved their capital frequently, generally towards the east, as their conquests led in this direction.

This era of disintegration and conflict is paradoxically China's 'classical' period, when some of the most renowned developments in philosophy, literature, science and technology were produced. In philosophy the 'Hundred Schools' contended.

1004

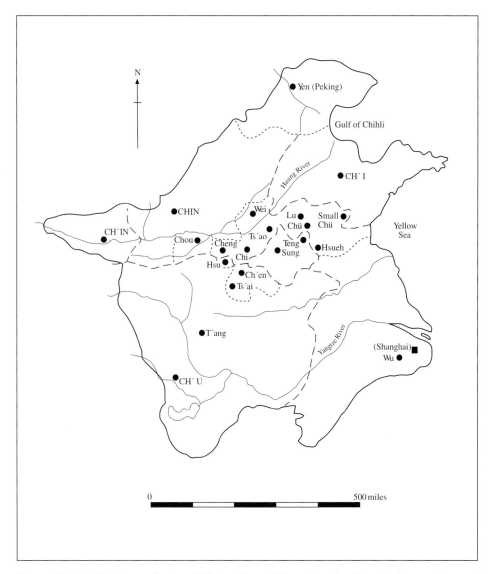

Figure 25.3 Political boundaries of China about 560 BC; heavier lines indicate spheres of influence. Adapted from Hsu 1965: xii. Source: J. Tainter. Redrawn by D. Miles-Williams.

The most lasting contributions came from Confucius (*c.* 551–479 BC), who promulgated a rational administrative system, and Mo Tzu (*c.* 480–390 BC), who articulated the view that rulers were stewards for the people, and that natural catastrophes revealed loss of the Mandate of Heaven. These writers were products of a post-collapse era, when unity, peace, order, and good government were wistfully recalled. The period also witnessed technical developments in craftsmanship and methods of production: the animal–drawn plough made its appearance, more land was brought under irrigation, market places multiplied, money came into wider use, iron technology spread, and the crossbow was introduced.

In the period from 770 to 221 BC there were only seventeen years that were entirely free of hostility. Warfare underwent a competitive spiral – in the seventh and sixth centuries BC battles rarely involved more than 10,000 men, but by the third century BC that figure had increased tenfold. Tactics changed accordingly: aristocrats armed with bows and riding in chariots gave way to massed infantry conscripts armed with spears and swords, and supported by horse archers. Chronic problems of supply and command affected the political structure, and helped bring about autocratic states run by bureaucracies. With larger armies and competent civil services, wars became longer, less numerous, and more decisive.

As this process neared its culmination, states became fewer but larger. In 403 BC there were fourteen states, of which the most powerful were Ch'in, Ch'u, Ch'i, Yeh, Han, Chau, and Wei. In 293 BC the Ch'in crushed the armies of Han and Wei. In 280 they defeated the state of Chau. In 249 the Ch'in took the Eastern Chou, and the dynasty ceased to exist. Finally, between 246 and 221 BC, Prince Cheng of Ch'in destroyed the remaining states and created an empire of 50 million persons (Creel 1953, 1970; Hirth 1923; Hsu and Linduff 1988; Hucker 1975; Levenson and Schurman 1969; Needham 1965; Parker 1988; Xueqin 1985).

OLD KINGDOM EGYPT AND THE FIRST INTERMEDIATE PERIOD

Old Kingdom Egypt (2686–2181 BC) was a centralized state headed by a king with qualified supernatural authority. The government was run by a highly organized, literate bureaucracy. Initially the government had substantial income from crown lands and mobilized large labour forces. It virtually monopolized some essential materials and imported luxuries. The government undertook to increase productive capabilities, expand the frontiers, and maintain supernatural relations. Over time, however, the Old Kingdom experienced some of the problems encountered later by the Western Chou. The provinces showed strong feudal characteristics. The political authority of the king declined as the power of provincial rulers and the wealth of the administrative nobility rose. Royal finances were weakened as Crown lands were divided. Monuments were built at royal expense and tax-exempt funerary endowments established. Phiops II, the last ruler of the Sixth Dynasty, built a splendid tomb in the face of sharply declining royal power.

In 2181 BC the Sixth Dynasty ended and the Old Kingdom collapsed: national unity was disrupted, several independent and semi-independent statelets emerged, and there were many rulers and generally short reigns. The period is sometimes referred to as the Egyptian Dark Age. The collapse generated a pessimistic literature, which reveals a breakdown of order and disregard for law. There were conflicts between districts and foreign incursions into the Nile delta. Anarchy and revolutions led to looting, killing, and plundering of royal tombs. Royal women were clothed in rags and officials suffered insults. Foreign trade dropped. Peasants carried shields as they tilled their fields. There were recurrent famines and life expectancy declined.

With the Eleventh Dynasty, beginning in 2131 BC, the Middle Kingdom was established, and order and unity began to be restored, though it was not until about 1870 BC that local and regional independence were totally suppressed, and Egypt fully reunited (Bell 1971; O'Connor 1974; Smith 1971).

MESOPOTAMIA

There were two periods in Mesopotamian history when powerful regimes attempted to maximize agricultural production, which in Mesopotamia means extending the scope and intensity of irrigation. These were the Third Dynasty of Ur (*c.* 2100–2000 BC), and the late Sassanian (AD 236–637) and early Islamic (post-637) periods.

The Third Dynasty of Ur and its aftermath

The Third Dynasty of Ur expanded the irrigation system, encouraged growth of population and settlement, and established a vast bureaucracy to collect taxes and tribute. Excessive irrigation in this region leads to good short-term harvests and to temporary increases in prosperity, security, and stability. Yet this strategy contains the germ of its own demise: after a few seasons of overirrigating, saline groundwaters rise and erode or destroy agricultural productivity. The result seems regularly to be destabilization of the political system.

Local populations were probably more secure at this time, but the complex superstructure took a high toll in labour. It was a system that could not be sustained. A few centuries earlier, in the Early Dynastic period (*c.* 2900–2350 BC), average crop yields had been about 2,030 litres per hectare, but under the Third Dynasty of Ur they declined to 1,134 litres. At the same time seeding rates had climbed sharply: Ur III farmers needed an average of 55.1 litres per hectare, more than twice the previous rate. The Third Dynasty of Ur was clearly pursuing an economic strategy of diminishing returns.

Badly salinized lands go out of production almost indefinitely, which intensifies pressures on the remaining fields. The Third Dynasty of Ur persisted through five kings and then collapsed. The consequences were catastrophic. By 1700 BC yields had declined to about 718 litres per hectare. More than one-fourth of the fields in production yielded on average only 370 litres per hectare. Labour demands were inelastic, so for equivalent effort farmers took in harvests less than one-fourth the size of those 800 years earlier. Soon there was extensive abandonment of southern Babylonia. Within a millennium or so of the end of the Third Dynasty of Ur, there was a 40 per cent reduction in the number of settlements and a 77 per cent reduction in settled area (R. McC. Adams 1978, 1981).

The collapse of the Abbasid Caliphate

Beginning in the last few centuries BC and continuing into the Islamic period, there was an irregular but generally sustained increase in the scale and integration of the agricultural regime. By the Sassanian and early Islamic periods, city-building, population density, and other manifestations of complexity had reached their highest levels. Population increased fivefold in the last few centuries BC and the first few centuries AD. There was a 900 per cent increase in the number of urban sites. These trends continued through the Sassanian period, when population densities came to exceed significantly those of the Third Dynasty of Ur. At its height, the area of settlement was 61 per cent greater than in Ur III.

The fullest development of Sassanian urbanism and agriculture came in the early to mid-sixth century AD. Under Khosrau I (AD 531–79) the dynasty reached its height, but his policies were reminiscent of those of the later Roman empire. The needs of the state took precedence over the ability to pay. Taxes were no longer remitted for crop failure. Because the tax was fixed whatever the yield, peasants were forced to cultivate intensively. State income rose sharply under Khosrau II (590–628). Much of this production may have been needed for the perpetual wars with the Byzantines. Their final war ended in a Byzantine victory, but left both powers so weakened that they were easily defeated by the new Islamic forces. The Byzantines managed to keep about half their empire, but the Sassanian dynasty was completely destroyed. The year 637 begins the Islamic period in Mesopotamia.

Under the Abbasids (beginning AD 750), taxation became abusive: tax assessments increased in every category, and 50 per cent of a harvest was owed under the caliph Mahdi (775–85), with many supplemental payments. Sometimes taxes were demanded before a harvest, even before the next year's harvest. On this unstable base the Islamic rulers built a new imperial structure. Under the Abbasids there was unprecedented urban growth: Baghdad grew to five times the size of tenth-century Constantinople, and thirteen times the size of the Sassanian capital Ctesiphon. Yet the state did not always fulfil its irrigation responsibilities. As the irrigation system grew in size and complexity, maintenance that had once been within the capacity of local communities was no longer so. Local communities came to depend on the imperial superstructure, which in turn became increasingly unstable.

Peasants had no margins of reserve, and revolts were inevitable. Civil war and rebellion meant that the hierarchy could not manage the irrigation system. Mesopotamia experienced an unprecedented collapse. In the period from AD 788 to 915 revenues dropped from 479,550,000 to 217,500,000 dirhems. The Sawad region, at the centre of the empire, had supplied 50 per cent of the government's revenues, but this dropped within a few decades to 10 per cent, mostly between the years 845 and 915. In many strategic and formerly prosperous areas there were revenue losses of 90 per cent within a lifetime. The perimeter of state control drew inward, which diminished any chance to resolve the agricultural problems. By the early tenth century, irrigation weirs were listed only in the vicinity of Baghdad.

In portions of Mesopotamia the occupied area had shrunk by about 94 per cent by the eleventh century. Population dropped to the lowest level in five millennia. Urban life in 10,000 square kilometres of the Mesopotamian heartland was eliminated for centuries (R. McC. Adams 1978, 1981; Waines 1977; Yoffee 1988). Robert McC. Adams has eloquently described the aftermath of this collapse:

> Much of the central floodplain of the ancient Euphrates now lies beyond the frontiers of cultivation, a region of empty desolation. Tangled dunes, long disused canal levees, and the rubble-strewn mounds of former settlement contribute only low, featureless relief. Vegetation is sparse, and in many areas it is almost wholly absent. Rough, wind-eroded land surfaces and periodically flooded depressions form an irregular patchwork in all directions, discouraging any but the most committed traveler. To suggest the immediate impact of human life there is only a rare tent . . . Yet at one time here lay the core, the heartland, the oldest urban, literate civilization in the world.
>
> (R. McC. Adams 1981: xvii)

THE HITTITE EMPIRE AND ITS AFTERMATH

The Hittites are a poorly known people of Anatolia. Their political history begins about 1792 BC with the conquests of Anitta. The building of the Hittite empire was an uncertain affair, and over the succeeding centuries their fortunes rose and fell. Periods of conquest and expansion were cancelled by episodes of defence and disintegration. During these times Hittite armies were defeated, provinces were lost, and little-known tribes called the Kaska raided and burned Hittite cities. At the lowest point the Hittite capital, Khattusha, fell to the Kaska.

The Hittite position was restored by their great ruler Shuppiluliumash, who came to the throne c. 1380 BC. During this and successive reigns the empire was established firmly in Anatolia and Syria. The Hittites successfully challenged Egypt for domination of Syria, concluding a treaty with Ramesses in 1284 BC. In the early thirteenth century BC the Hittites and Egypt were the premier powers in the region.

The Hittite empire included most of Anatolia, Syria, and Cyprus. Yet with the exception of Egypt they encountered troubles in nearly all directions, including the Assyrians to the south-east, the Kaska to the east, and little-known peoples in western Asia Minor and Cyprus. Their written records decline towards the end of the thirteenth century BC, then finally cease.

With the collapse of the Hittite empire there were major but little understood catastrophes across the region. Excavated sites in Anatolia and Syria are consistently found to have burned about this time. In the central Anatolian plateau life was disrupted for a century or more after 1204 BC. There were no urban settlements. While the archaeological record of this time could no doubt reveal further details, at present it seems that the area was thinly populated or used by nomads. As in Mesopotamia, there was a major demographic decline corresponding to the political collapse (Akurgal 1962; Barnett 1975; Goetze 1975a, 1975b, 1975c; Gurney 1973a, 1973b; Hogarth 1926).

MYCENAEAN, DARK AGE AND GEOMETRIC GREECE

Mycenaean society can be distinguished archaeologically by about 1650 BC. It was characterized throughout central Greece by a high level of homogeneity in art, architecture, and political organization. The region was divided among a number of independent polities, each centred on a fortified palace/citadel complex, and headed by a single ruler. Mycenaean palaces served as political and economic centres, and much of the Linear B writing (an early form of Greek script) was devoted to accounting. Mycenaean administration was particularly complex. All classes of persons had strictly allotted roles. All raw materials and manufactured goods, people, and animals were meticulously scrutinized and recorded. Mycenaean art and architecture are widely admired. The palaces had frescoes and bathrooms. Artisans produced carved gemstones, metalwork, pottery, inlay, and items of ivory, glass, and faience. Roads and aqueducts were built, and Mycenaean wares were traded about the Mediterranean.

Around 1200 BC troubles began. Most of the palaces were destroyed. In the following century there were unstable conditions, repeated destructions of political centres, and population movement. Fortifications were built across the Isthmus of Corinth and elsewhere. At the citadels of Mycenae, Tiryns and Athens wells were cut at great labour through solid rock. Uniform Mycenaean pottery gave way to local styles. Metalwork became simpler. There is no further trace of the craft workers and artisans. Trade declined sharply. Writing disappeared from Greece for at least 450 years. The number of settlements declined precipitously (Fig. 25.4). While there seems to have been some movement of people to less troubled areas, there was still a 75–90 per cent population decline. Even areas that escaped

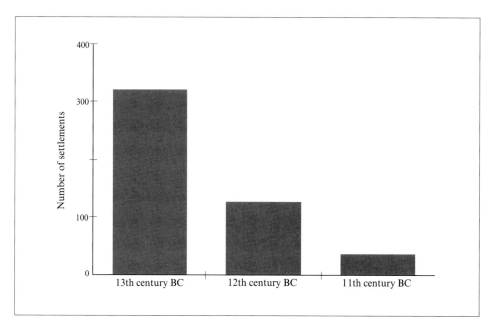

Figure 25.4 Declining numbers of Mycenaean settlements, thirteenth through eleventh centuries BC. Data from Snodgrass 1971: 354. Source: J. Tainter. Redrawn by D. Miles-Williams.

devastation, such as Athens, ultimately experienced political collapse. In the twelfth century, when Mycenaean society still existed in an attenuated form, communities were small and independent. There were few stonemasons or craft workers, and insufficient personnel to fortify settlements. There seems to have been no building in stone. At Tiryns a cemetery overlay the Mycenaean settlement. Some archaeologists have the impression that there was little conflict. After the initial round of catastrophes there was a period of stability and rebuilding, but by 1050 BC what was left of Mycenaean society was everywhere gone.

The post-collapse period is difficult to characterize. The archaeological record recovered to date consists predominantly of burials (Fig. 25.5), from which have come a fair number of pottery vessels and some scraps of metal. Not surprisingly, archaeologists who study this period tend to concentrate on the development of tomb types and pottery styles. In the Protogeometric period of pottery style (*c.* 1050–900 BC), there appears still to have been a substantial settlement at Athens. This settlement is evidenced, however, by only a few pottery sherds from the Acropolis, and by pits, wells, and burials in the area of the later Agora.

At the time when one major synthesis was written in 1972, over the whole of Greece and the Aegean there were fewer than thirty sites of this period on which settlement evidence had been recognized (Desborough 1972: 261). This evidence is mainly pottery. Only about a dozen sites have yielded actual features of settlement such as structural remains. Hardly a single temple can be shown archaeologically to have been built in the ninth century BC. The impression is of a population that was comparatively low, with only a few, mostly small, settlements. The peaceful conditions probably reflect the low population, lack of personnel for combat, or inability to conduct campaigns. Political organization changed from centralized monarchies served by literate bureaucracies to small units dominated by aristocrats and their families. The Mycenaean royal citadels were used as communal refuges. Burial data suggest that dark-age society was socially stratified, with an aristocratic class and great emphasis on adult ranking.

The Dark Age technically ends with the adoption of Phoenician-derived alphabets around 750 BC. Even in this there is evidence for continued isolation and local development. Early Greek alphabets have much in common, but also exhibit peculiarities, suggesting that each is an individual adaptation of Phoenician (Betancourt 1976; Chadwick 1976; Coldstream 1977; Desborough 1972, 1975; Finley 1981; Hooker 1976; Morris 1987; Mylonas 1966; Snodgrass 1971, 1980; Stubbings 1975a, 1975b; Taylour 1964).

Archaeologists of the Greek Dark Age must cultivate precious inferences from

Figure 25.5 Sub-Mycenaean cist graves at Athens. German Archaeological Institute at Athens, Neg. Nr. Ker. 2324: reproduced by kind permission of the German Archaeological Institute at Athens.

a flimsy record. Some scholars see an increase, shortly before 850 BC, of sea communications within the Aegean, and of exchanges with the Near East. The cities involved in these exchanges experienced an increase in material prosperity. Yet, not unusually for dark-age archaeology, 'the most substantial evidence of this progress comes from well over a dozen graves at Athens and Lefkandi' (Coldstream 1977: 55).

THE CLASSIC MAYA COLLAPSE AND THE POSTCLASSIC PETEN

The Lowland Classic Maya have long been puzzling. They were one of the few early complex societies that did not develop in semi-arid conditions. The Maya are also, as Netting put it, 'a people whose greatest mystery is their abrupt departure from the stage of world history' (1977: 299).

The Maya of the southern Lowlands underwent a rapid, dramatic, and justly famous collapse between about AD 790 and 890 (Fig. 25.1). It will be useful to refer to the Mayan chronology, which Willey (1982) gives as follows:

Middle Preclassic	1000–400 BC
Late Preclassic	400–50 BC
Protoclassic	50 BC–AD 250
Early Classic	AD 250–550
Hiatus	AD 550–600
Late Classic	AD 600–800
Terminal Classic	AD 800–1000
Postclassic	post-AD 1000

Not all authors make the distinction between Terminal Classic and Postclassic, and in this discussion the important contrast is between the Late Classic and the subsequent post-collapse occupations.

The evolution of Maya political organization may be traced to the Late Preclassic and Early Classic. The tropical rainforest of the southern Lowlands had been extensively cleared and planted by this time. Intensive agricultural systems and hydraulic engineering efforts were underway. Major fortifications have been dated to the Early Classic. Formal public architecture and social differentiation are in evidence by the Middle and Late Preclassic. In the Late Preclassic there was an administrative hierarchy of two or three levels. Public architecture became truly monumental, and the site of Tikal emerged as a major centre.

Throughout the Classic era these patterns intensified. There was continued growth in population, agricultural development, socio-political complexity, architectural elaboration, and conflict. Classic monuments and art styles reached their maximum extent in the sixth century. Major centres emerged which may have been regional capitals. The hierarchy of places developed at least four levels, and secondary centres were arranged around regional capitals in hexagonal lattices.

These trends culminated in the Late Classic. Between AD 652 and 751 there was remarkable homogeneity across the southern Lowlands in the style and iconography of monuments. A standardized lunar calendar, the most accurate of its time, was adopted throughout the region within a ten-year period. Major Mayan sites, once thought to have been vacant ceremonial centres, are now known to have been cities. Tikal held a population of perhaps 49,000, with defensive earthworks and moats up to 9.5 kilometres to a side. (Ancient Sumerian cities, by comparison, may have held about as many people.)

At its height the Lowlands population averaged about 200 persons per square kilometre, which made it one of the most densely populated areas for a non-industrial society. Late Classic populations were approaching an upper limit, for population peaked, in various localities, between the sixth and ninth centuries AD. Complexity, and its costly manifestations, did not stop growing when population did. An expanded building programme had to be supported by a static population, many of whom appear from their skeletal remains to have been in poor health. At Altar de Sacrificios the size and extent of formal architecture, number of stelae (dated stone monuments), and amounts of elaborate pottery reached a peak between AD 613 and 771. At the sites of Yaxchilan and Bonampak, the greatest quantities of sculptural art preceded the end of monumental construction by a brief interval. The greatest building period at Tikal was between 692 and 751. Across the southern Lowlands as a whole, 60 per cent of all dated monuments were built in a period of sixty-nine years, between 687 and 756.

Power decentralized during the collapse. New centres proliferated along the peripheries of the central southern Lowlands (the area known as the Peten). Even as construction ceased at major centres, many smaller sites erected monuments for the first time. Between 830 and 909, 65 per cent of monuments were built at minor centres. Of the centres that erected monuments at this time, more than 40 per cent did so for the first time. In many cases this was the only monument that such sites dedicated before they, too, collapsed.

As Figure 25.1 shows, the collapse was rapid: in 790, nineteen centres erected dated monuments; in 810, twelve did so; in 830 there were three. AD 889 is the date of the last certain stela with full calendrical inscriptions. There is no evidence for construction at Tikal after 830. With the collapse, many aspects of complexity were lost: administrative and residential structures, building and maintaining temples, stela carving, manufacture of luxury items, and Classic calendrical and writing systems. The élite class for which these things were created ceased to exist. The most startling aspect of the collapse is an enormous loss of population: estimates range from a decline of a million in a century, to a loss of 2.5 million over seventy-five years. Either scenario indicates a demographic disaster.

Unlike most cases discussed so far, careful excavation at Tikal has revealed much about the post-collapse occupation. It is called the Eznab occupation, and is dated *c.* 830 to 900. The Eznab occupation was by a materially impoverished population of 1,000 to 2,000, who tried to carry on a semblance of Classic ceremonialism. They lived in the great structures, and deposited their refuse in courtyards, down stairways, even within rooms. Deteriorated Classic structures were not rebuilt. Eznab constructions were small and rudimentary, and their pottery compares unfavourably with the perfection of Classic ceramics. The Eznab people buried their dead in the same places as Classic élites, but their graves are minimally equipped. Tombs and caches of the earlier era were looted. The Eznab occupants tried to imitate Classic ceremonialism, but clearly had lost the correct knowledge. As many as 40 per cent of Tikal stelae were reset at this time, but by Classic standards it was done improperly. The reset stelae consistently wound up in the wrong places, or even upside down. Similar patterns are seen in the behaviour of the post-collapse occupants of other major centres: Uaxactun, San José, Palenque, and Piedras Negras. Among the rural Maya of Barton Ramie, post-collapse construction was minimal even though there continued to be extensive occupation.

While the Classic Maya collapse in the southern Lowlands was 'the most devastating demographic and cultural disjuncture prehistoric Mesoamerica ever experienced' (Freidel 1985: 293), it was not the end of Maya civilization. The northern Maya Lowlands were not affected by the southern collapse. The Puuc sites here show a Terminal Classic occupation in no way diminished from former times. In the central Peten itself there was much continuity of occupation, though there was a decline of some magnitude in the number of structures occupied from the Late Classic, and much reuse of earlier structures. Most notably, there were densely settled communities situated on naturally defensible landforms: islands and isthmuses. The Peten, though, was no longer the centre of the Mayan world: the evolution of complexity had shifted to the northern periphery (R. E. W. Adams 1973a, 1973b, 1977, 1981; Andrews and Sabloff 1986; Cowgill 1979; Culbert 1973, 1974, 1977, 1988; Erickson 1975; Freidel 1979, 1981, 1985; Hammond 1977, 1982; Haviland 1967, 1969, 1970; Marcus 1976, 1983c; Matheny 1978; Netting 1977; Rands 1973; D. S. Rice 1976, 1986; P. M. Rice 1986; Sanders 1962; Saul 1972, 1973; Tainter 1988: 152–78; Thomas 1981; Webster 1976, 1977; Willey 1973, 1977a, 1977b, 1982; Willey and Shimkin 1973; Wiseman 1978).

TEOTIHUACÁN AND THE VALLEY OF MEXICO

Teotihuacán was the largest native city in the New World (and in AD 600 the sixth largest in the world), with a population of roughly 125,000. Its central feature, the Street of the Dead, holds over 2 kilometres of monuments. There are more than seventy-five temples, including the pyramids of the Sun and the Moon. The former is the largest structure in pre-Columbian America, being 64 metres high, measuring 210 metres along each axis and holding an estimated 1 million cubic metres of material. At the south end of this street was an élite residential structure, the Ciudadela, with twin palaces. The city contained more than 2,000 residential compounds, and hundreds of craft workshops specializing in obsidian, pottery, jade, onyx, and shell. There were hundreds of painted murals. Networks of drains carried off rainwater.

Teotihuacán exerted compelling influence throughout Mesoamerica. Its leaders could mobilize labour at unprecedented levels. The population and resources of the Valley of Mexico and beyond were thoroughly reorganized. Exotic materials were imported from locations up to hundreds of kilometres distant. Tens of thousands of people were relocated to Teotihuacán and its vicinity. For 600 years or more, 85–90 per cent of the population of the eastern and northern Valley of Mexico lived in or near the city.

In Teotihuacán's later phase, military themes became prominent in art. The flow of some goods into the city was reduced. Around AD 700 Teotihuacán abruptly collapsed. The political and ceremonial centre of the city, the Street of the Dead and its monuments, was systematically burned, an act which in Mesoamerica signified defeat and subjugation. Within fifty years the population dropped to no more than a fourth of its peak level. This remnant population sealed off doorways, and partitioned large rooms into smaller ones. In its emptiness, post-collapse Teotihuacán must have resembled medieval Rome. Population declined also in the rural areas of the Basin of Mexico, from perhaps 250,000 to around 175,000.

A period of political fragmentation followed. Despite its relative decline, Teotihuacán remained a major city. Power diffused outward, though, and autonomous regional centres emerged. Often these were in defensible locations, such as hilltops, in what had been politically marginal zones. Central Mexico was divided into several competing political and economic systems. These were organized for warfare, which apparently was recurrent, and which influenced the development of social, political, and economic systems. As in Warring States China, polities grew through conquest; some of the new powers were Xochicalco, Teotenango, Cacaxtla, Cholula, and El Tajin. Local styles developed in ceramics, architecture, iconography, and other cultural elements (Diehl 1989; Diehl and Berlo 1989; Hirth 1989; Mastache and Cobean 1989; Millon 1981; Sanders et al. 1979).

One of the competing centres, Xochicalco, was built on a hilltop, with defensive architecture. Among its public buildings is a structure known as the Pyramid of the Plumed Serpent. It contains carved panels that illustrate the inter-polity competition and conquest that characterized the region after Teotihuacán's collapse. Some of this sculpture portrays repeated elements which may be pictographic (Fig. 25.6). Each group of elements shows a seated figure whose mouth is open, signifying

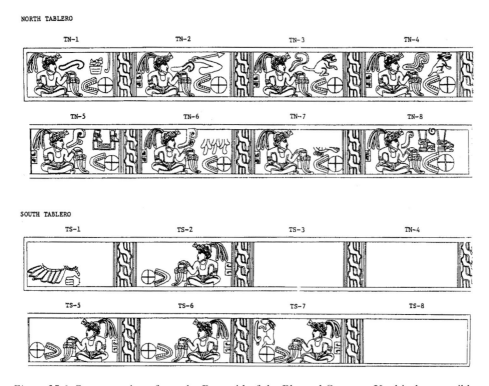

Figure 25.6 Stone carvings from the Pyramid of the Plumed Serpent, Xochicalco, possibly listing subject places. Reproduced from Hirth 1989: 74, with permission. Source: Dumbarton Oaks 1989.

speech. In front of each seated figure is an open jaw, devouring a four-part circle. Above each circle is a non-repeating iconographic element. Research suggests that the last were toponyms, depicting specific places. If so, then each panel portrays the themes of warrior, conquest, and tribute, and the whole scheme may list the places once subject to Xochicalco (Hirth 1989: 73–74).

MONTE ALBÁN AND THE VALLEY OF OAXACA

Monte Albán, in the Oaxaca Valley south of the Basin of Mexico, was a political centre roughly coeval with Teotihuacán. The city and its walls were built on a mountain-top, a large section of which was levelled to build a community and an arena of public architecture. The city contained pyramids, temples, ballcourts, stelae, and frescoes. There was craft production in obsidian, shell, and other commodities. Monte Albán was the political centre of Oaxaca, and experienced its major growth between AD 600 and 700.

Its collapse came at roughly the same time as that of Teotihuacán. This coincidence has led some archaeologists to suggest that the hierarchy at Monte Albán was supported by the Oaxacans as a response to the threat from the imperial power to the north. When this threat ended, so also did the need for Monte Albán to be a political centre (Blanton 1978: 103). The collapse came after a period of rapid regional population growth, but with it the population of the city itself dropped from about 30,000 persons to 4,000–8,000; its role as a major administrative centre was over by AD 700.

After the collapse of Monte Albán, new centres emerged which apparently controlled sectors of the valley. Some of these had been occupied before, but as secondary or tertiary centres; now they, and Monte Albán itself, emerged as petty, autonomous states. At some point in the Monte Albán IV period (*c*. 600–950) there was a major settlement reorganization. During Monte Albán III (*c*. 400–600) occupation was well distributed throughout the Valley of Oaxaca, though sparse in the south-east quadrant (Fig. 25.7a), but in Monte Albán IV there was significant reduction in the north-west part of the valley, with concentration of the remaining population around fortified hilltops in the south-east (Fig. 25.7b).

Monte Albán no longer held a near-monopoly on writing. At its height Monte Albán had used writing to convey militaristic themes. These themes were carved on large stones which were placed in public buildings, and meant to be seen from a distance. Now the Zapotec hieroglyphic writing system spread to the new valley-floor centres, and it was employed in a different manner. A new type of stone monument was created that Marcus calls the 'genealogical register' (1983a: 191). These are small and were meant to be read close in. They were placed in tombs or élite residences, and deal with such matters as ancestry, birth, ritual events, and marriages of Zapotec lords and nobility. In a political environment of decentralized competition, these monuments legitimized claims to rulership and recorded marriage alliances with heads of other polities.

The succeeding period, Monte Albán V (*c*. 950–1530), and coeval periods elsewhere, were a time of 'Balkanization' (Marcus and Flannery 1983: 217). There were many small, hostile states. Codices (native documents) and ethnohistoric records describe frequent military conflicts, interrupted by tenuous truces brought about through royal marriages or military alliances. Yet this was also a period of regional cultural similarities. Ceramic complexes were widely distributed. Terms for state offices were widespread, and in some cases the same term was used in different languages. Officers of competing armies shared a common technology. It was a time of convergent evolution, as the Aztecs, Mixtecs, Cuitecs, and Zapotecs, in continual contact and conflict, emulated each other at an accelerated rate (Blanton 1978, 1983; Blanton and Kowalewski 1981; Kowalewski 1983; Marcus 1983a, 1983b, 1989; Marcus and Flannery 1983; Paddock 1983).

a

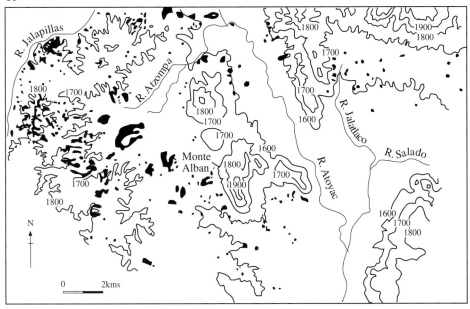

b

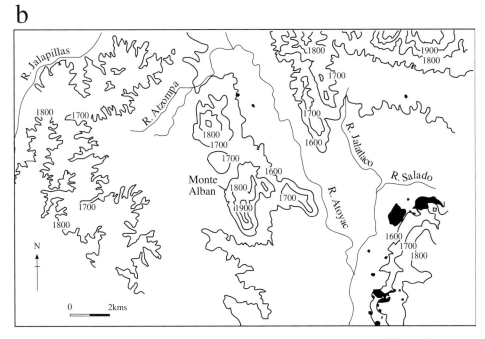

Figure 25.7 Settlements in the Valley of Oaxaca during (a) the Monte Albán IIIb period (*c.* AD 400–600) and (b) the Monte Albán IV Period (*c.* AD 600–900). Figures redrawn from Kowalewski, 'Monte Albán IIIb-IV settlement patterns in the Valley of Oaxaca', in K. V. Flannery and J. Marcus (eds), *The Cloud People: Divergent Evolution of the Zapotec and Mixtec Civilizations* (NY: Academic Press, 1983). Adapted from Kowalewski 1983: 188–89 by D. Miles-Williams.

HUARI, TIWANAKU, AND THE POST-COLLAPSE ANDES

The Huari and Tiwanaku polities are discussed together, since they seem to have been closely related and to have followed similar patterns of development and collapse.

Between 200 BC and AD 700, Peruvian societies developed extensive irrigation systems and agricultural terracing, in conjunction with a growing population. Cities were built which were the capitals of regional states. They shared a heritage of technology and common ideology, but were divided by local art styles, separate governments, and competition for land and food. Out of this competitive background two empires emerged: Huari in the north and Tiwanaku in the south. Huari is the better known.

The Huari empire dominated almost the entire central Andes and much of the adjacent coastal lowlands. The empire imposed economic, social, and cultural changes on the areas it dominated. Major urban centres were established in each valley. Buildings in the Huari architectural style seem to have been administrative structures, storehouses, or barracks. Goods and information were exchanged across the central Andes on an unprecedented scale. Huari-derived ceramic styles (themselves influenced by Tiwanaku wares) appeared in many regions. As these wares spread, local styles became less important.

The extent of a contemporary Tiwanaku empire is less clear. Recent work has shown that much of the high-altitude Lake Titicaca Basin (3,800 metres above sea level), where the city of Tiwanaku is located, was transformed under central management into an artificial agricultural landscape. There were massive public reclamation and construction projects, which required large, coordinated labour forces. The basin contains at least 190 square kilometres of raised agricultural fields. Tiwanaku itself may have held between 20,000 and 40,000 persons, and below it there were smaller cities and tertiary settlements.

Both states collapsed c. AD 1000–1100. In the Lake Titicaca Basin the Tiwanaku collapse brought political decentralization and simplification. The fall of Huari had widespread consequences. All cities of the southern highlands were abandoned and their populations returned to the countryside. The north Peruvian coast was apparently depopulated. Regional stylistic traditions emerged again, as did local and regional political organizations. As with the collapses of Rome, the Western Chou, Teotihuacán, and Monte Albán, the fall of Huari brought an era of smaller, contending states (Graffam 1992; Kolata 1986, 1991; Lanning 1967; Lumbreras 1974; Willey 1971).

SYNTHESIS: POST-COLLAPSE SOCIETIES

Of the cases examined, only post-Roman Europe offers a reasonably coherent picture of a post-collapse period, yet specialists in this area find their data frustrating and inadequate. The other cases yield a little information on some topics, less on most. Yet with this survey, and previous work by Renfrew (1979: 482–85) and Tainter (1988: 18–20), it is possible to begin to synthesize a composite picture of the process and aftermath of collapse.

Population

Whether as cause, consequence, or both, depopulation frequently accompanies collapse. Not only do urban populations decline, so also do the support populations of the countryside. Many settlements are concurrently abandoned. The levels of population and settlement may revert to those of centuries or even millennia before.

Population decline is clear in the collapses of Rome, the Third Dynasty of Ur, the Abbasid Caliphate, the Hittite empire, Mycenaean Greece, the southern Lowland Maya, Teotihuacán, and portions of the Huari empire. If life expectancy declined in the Egyptian First Intermediate Period, then population should have dropped as well. Exceptions include the Valley of Oaxaca, where Blanton sees regional population increase at the time of Monte Albán's collapse (1983: 186), and the Lake Titicaca Basin, where a substantial population continued after Tiwanaku (Graffam 1992: 887).

In several cases population seems to have stopped growing, or even declined, some time prior to collapse. Two well-known examples are the Roman empire and the southern Lowland Maya. Apparently the late rulers of the Western Chou had reason to fear that the population they administered had shrunk. Two different and somewhat contradictory forces may be at work here. Levelling or decline of population prior to a collapse seems due at least partly to the stresses on rural populations of supporting a complex hierarchy. In the case of the Roman empire the population could not recover from plagues and wars because high taxes precluded supporting large families. Taxation levels under the Abbasid Caliphate were higher still. The Mayan peasantry are known to have been highly stressed. Yet the population crashes that accompanied many collapses (Ur III, the Abbasids, the Hittites, the Mycenaeans, the Maya, and Teotihuacán) indicate also that hierarchical, centralized management was required to support large populations. Thus while complexity is needed to support dense populations, it is so costly that in non-industrial economies it can do so for only limited periods.

Perceptions of collapse

As societies become vulnerable to collapse there are no doubt great differences of opinion of what is wrong, or whether anything is wrong at all. In late Rome, pagans blamed Christians for the troubles, and conversely. Yet there are notable convergences in how peoples of different times and places have perceived impending collapse. China at the end of the Western Chou produced a remarkable literature on the many disturbances unfolding simultaneously (Hsu and Linduff 1988: 280–87). One poem related the natural catastrophes of the times.

> At the conjunction (of the sun and the moon) in the tenth month
> On the first day of the moon which was Hsin-Mao
> The Sun was eclipsed,
> A thing of very evil omen,
> Then the moon became small,
> And now the sun became small.
> Henceforth the lower people,
> Will be in a very deplorable case.
> [. . .]
> Grandly flashes the lightning of the thunder;
> There is a want of rest, a want of good.
> The streams all bubble up and overflow.
> The crags on the hill-tops fall down.
> High banks become valleys;
> Deep valleys become hills.
> Alas for the men of this time!
> Why does (the King) not stop these things?
>
> (Hsu and Linduff 1988: 281)

Compare this to the tone of the following tract by Cyprian, written during Rome's crisis of the third century AD:

> [The] age is now senile . . . the World itself . . . testifies to its own decline by giving manifold concrete evidences of the process of decay. There is a diminution in the winter rains that give nourishment to the seeds in the earth, and in the summer heats that ripen the harvests. The springs have less freshness and the autumns less fecundity. The mountains, disembowelled and worn out, yield a lower output of marble; the mines, exhausted, furnish a smaller stock of the precious metals: the veins are impoverished, and they shrink daily. There is a decrease and deficiency of farmers in the field, of sailors on the sea, of soldiers in the barracks, of honesty in the marketplace, of justice in court, of concord in friendship, of skill in technique, of strictness in morals . . . Anything that is near its end, and is verging towards its decline and fall is bound to dwindle . . . This is the sentence that has been passed upon the World . . . this loss of strength and loss of stature must end, at last, in annihilation.
>
> (quoted in Toynbee 1962, IV: 8)

The collapse of the Old Kingdom is mirrored similarly in a pessimistic Egyptian literature (Smith 1971: 200).

Disruption of the social order

Immediately following a collapse there may be a time when the social order is disrupted, or even a period of lawlessness. The Egyptian First Intermediate Period provides a good example, though the widespread destruction at the end of the Mycenaean period suggests similar troubles. The government of Visigothic Spain was unable to suppress brigandage (Carr 1992: 151–52). It is difficult to see how the population crash of the Maya collapse could have occurred without civil disorder. In China, after the collapse of the Western Chou, there were usurpations by subordinate officials, and even alliances between the rulers of some states and the ministers of others. A Chinese poet of the time wrote that 'the people desire disorder' (Creel 1970: 431).

Hierarchy and political order

Simplification of the political hierarchy is almost by definition an attribute of collapse. Sometimes the highest-ranking position, associated with overarching territorial control, disappears entirely or is changed in its meaning. Where it is retained, as with the Eastern Chou or the Egyptian First Intermediate Period, it may signify only a powerless figurehead.

Below the position of highest rank the status hierarchy will, depending on the extent of the collapse, undergo further simplification. In Europe the late Roman hierarchy and bureaucracy rapidly disappeared as local administration became the basis of society. In Gaul of the sixth century the term 'Senator' underwent a change of meaning, from designating a political class to an economic one. The Mycenaean bureaucracy disappeared entirely. At the opposite extreme, following the Western Chou collapse, political hierarchies may have become more differentiated, as states grew larger and tried to resolve the logistical bottlenecks of large-scale warfare.

The Mycenaean and Roman collapses, although occurring among very different societies, provide parallel examples of political simplification. In each case the supreme title dropped from use, and what had been secondary or tertiary positions were promoted by default. Among the Mycenaeans the paramount had been accorded the title *wanax*, with a subordinate labelled *basileos* (pa_2-si-re-u in Linear B). In post-Mycenaean times the *wanax* no longer existed, and *basileos* became the supreme title (Morris 1987: 172; Snodgrass 1971: 387).

In the Roman empire the supreme title *Augustus* was accorded only to the ruler of the Roman state. In the immediate post-collapse period only the eastern Roman Emperor held this title; the élites of the west were designated *rex* (king), *dux* (duke), or *comes* (count). *Rex* was a title the late Romans had awarded to tribal chieftains. *Dux* and *comes* were Roman administrative titles, which in the Middle Ages were transformed to designate semi-autonomous rulers of small- to moderate-sized territories.

Societal simplification

Not only is the hierarchy simplified in post-collapse societies, in many cases the society as a whole recognizes fewer distinctions among people. The driving force is economic and political change. As the political hierarchy simplifies or disappears, there is less demand for craft workers or artisans. As local self-sufficiency increases, there is less need for economic specialists and centralized production. As states become smaller, there is more potential for conflicts, making trade dangerous, and with more boundaries there are more barriers to trade. The result is that specialization decreases, except as it is necessary at the local level and can be sustained at that level.

While societal simplification may seem intuitively clear, it is not well documented. Few ancient historians were concerned with social processes among those of low to moderate rank, and until recently few archaeologists were either. Still there are supporting instances, and more will no doubt be documented. Mycenaean archaeologists, for example, have concluded that craft workers and artisans disappeared with the Mycenaean collapse. Certainly their work seems no longer to have been produced. In Merovingian Gaul there were still cloth, pottery, and jewellery industries, but these were much reduced from Roman times, and served only the aristocracy and the church. Trade was dominated by persons from the eastern Mediterranean. The period produced only one poet and one major historian (Pfister 1913: 155–57). Visigothic Spain, on the other hand, differentiated more sharply among slaves, clients, tenants, and freedmen (Carr 1992: 146).

Built environment

With reversion to local self-sufficiency, the main institutions to continue are those supportable by local resources. There is an end to monumental construction, and to publicly supported art, at the earlier scale. Characteristically in urban centres there is little new construction, and that which is attempted may be much less substantial, or may concentrate on adapting existing buildings: great rooms are subdivided, flimsy façades are built, and public space is converted to private. People may reside in upper-storey rooms as lower ones disintegrate, and when a building starts to collapse, the occupants move to another. At best the former monuments are just allowed to deteriorate, at worst they are mined as easy sources of building materials. This post-collapse use of architecture is well illustrated at Rome, in Mayan sites, and at Teotihuacán. In both town and country of post-Roman Britain, rooms in élite houses were converted to grain-drying kilns (Davis 1982: 21–23) and many sites were abandoned altogether (Higham 1992: 115).

Were the Dark Ages really dark?

It is easy to apply the term 'dark age' to post-collapse societies, but the term is ambiguous and should be used with care. It refers to the declines in literacy, writing, and communication that often result from collapse. Yet until recent times literacy and travel were the preserves of select groups of élites, merchants, and military officers. Even in the ancient classical world, most people were illiterate, and the major foci of interaction were always neighbourhood and community. Some history texts give an impression of medieval peasants as poor, tired, huddled masses, yearning to read. Actually, peasants typically did not read Thucydides or Tacitus, or other such literature, either before or after the fall of Rome. In Europe and elsewhere, a Dark Age means the transition from a situation where only a minority can read and write, to one where a smaller minority can do so. Dark Ages, for most people, were only slightly less luminous than preceding periods.

There is also the matter of the Mesoamerican Highlands. Here, after the collapses of Teotihuacán and Monte Albán, writing actually spread (Marcus 1989: 205–6). Collapse fostered the spread of writing as new centres and élites broadcast their political messages. The lesson is that writing may have different functions in different cultural contexts. The purpose of writing must be known to understand its development after collapse.

Return on investment in complexity

Societies that collapse are often considered to have 'failed', but such a view is both unfortunate and misplaced. Under a situation of diminishing returns to complexity, collapse is not a failure but may be the most appropriate response (Tainter 1988: 197–98). If a society collapses from economic weakness induced by diminishing returns to complexity, then collapse yields both a reduction in the costs of complexity and an increase in the return on social investment. There is both less cost to supporting social institutions and a higher return per unit of cost. The result is a more efficient society in which, if the hierarchy produces fewer goods and services, those that it does produce represent a better investment. This is a paradox of collapse: a process that we regard as the worst fate that can befall a society may actually bring economic and administrative gains. What may be a catastrophe to élites and administrators need not be to most people.

Post-Roman Europe illustrates this point. The smaller kingdoms that succeeded Roman rule in the west were, as noted, more successful at resisting invasions (for example, of Huns and Arabs) than had been the late empire. They did so at lower administrative and military costs. Peasants enjoyed lower taxes and better productivity in the post-Roman period. The prosperity of North Africa actually rose under the Vandals, but declined under Justinian's reconquest (AD 533), when imperial taxes were reimposed (Hodges and Whitehouse 1983: 28).

Yet little of history is uncomplicated. In the cases of the Mycenaeans and the Maya, the dramatic loss of population can hardly mean that collapse was a net benefit to most people. Carr concludes that Spanish peasants were marginally better off under Roman than Visigothic rule, in part because of population decline (1992). Even still, those who survived these collapses will have found themselves less burdened by bureaucracies and state obligations, and able to realize a greater return to their endeavours.

Territorial and political fragmentation

The breakdown of political centralization means that petty states emerge in the previously unified territory. One of these may be the former capital itself. Typically these contend for domination, and the result is a long period of conflict. This was the outcome in China of the Spring and Autumn and Warring States periods, in post-Roman Europe, in the Mesoamerican Highlands, and in the Andes after the fall of Huari and Tiwanaku. Under conditions of conflict, settlements are often relocated to defensible locations, as in Highland Mesoamerica, the Peten Lakes, the *Ager Faliscus* north of Rome, and some settlements of post-Mycenaean Greece and Crete. The latter may be exceptional, since Greece at this time seems to have been peaceful, due perhaps to low population and lack of military personnel and organization.

Evolution of complexity after collapse

Where complex societies are surrounded by less-complex neighbours, the evolution of complexity after collapse often shifts to what had been politically peripheral areas, and new peoples rise to prominence. Two famous examples are the development of complexity among the peoples of the Arabian peninsula, and somewhat later of northern Europe, after the decline of Roman power. Another case is the growth of the Puuc cities of northern Yucatan after the collapse of the southern Lowland Maya (Andrews and Sabloff 1986). In Highland Mesoamerica, following the collapse of Teotihuacán, new powers emerged in what had been politically marginal zones: Xochicalco, Teotenango, Cacaxtla, Cholula, and El Tajin (Diehl and Berlo 1989; Mastache and Cobean 1989). After the Western Chou, power shifted to the peripheries, and ultimately to the Ch'in of the far west.

Lower complexity and other post-collapse characteristics persist for various times, as the following examples illustrate:

Chou China: from the collapse of the Western Chou (771 BC) to the reunification by the Ch'in (221 BC): 550 years.

Egypt: from the collapse of the Old Kingdom (2181 BC) to reunification (1870 BC): 311 years.

Hittites: from the collapse of the Hittite empire (late thirteenth century BC) to the emergence of the Phrygians (ninth century BC): *c.* 300 years.

Mycenaeans: from the final disappearance of Mycenaean society (*c.* 1050 BC) to the end of the Greek Dark Age: 400 years.

Rome: in Italy, from the wars of the sixth century AD to the full emergence of the Italian Renaissance in the fourteenth century: *c.* 800 years (longer periods elapsed in other parts of western Europe).

Huari: from the collapse of the Huari empire (conservatively *c.* AD 1100) to the expansion of the Inca: *c.* 300 years.

Maya: after the collapse of the southern Lowland Maya (*c.* AD 800), native populations never did re-establish a similar level of complexity in the Peten.

Regional differentiation

With decline of centralization and of trade, local idiosyncrasies often take the place of regional uniformity. This is evident in the realm of material culture, where widespread pottery styles are replaced by local wares. Thus following the Mycenaean, Huari, and Tiwanaku collapses, regional ceramic uniformity gave way to styles developed in, and peculiar to, individual localities. Linguistic diversification is another consequence of collapse and regional differentiation: the most famous case is the growth of the Romance languages from Latin, but something similar seems to have happened with the Maya collapse (Fig. 25.8). In the Postclassic period new languages formed in the Mayan area at an unprecedented rate (Dahlin *et al.* 1987), a pattern which is even more impressive when one recalls the depopulation of the collapse. Each new Postclassic language was spoken by comparatively few people.

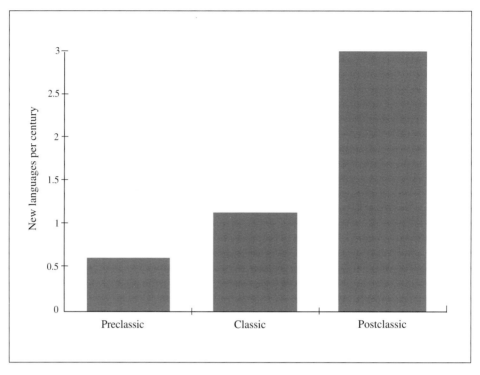

Figure 25.8 Increasing linguistic divergence in the Maya Postclassic following the Classic Maya collapse. (Data from Dahlin *et al.* 1987: 369.) Source: J. Tainter. Redrawn by D. Miles-Williams.

Post-collapse mythology

Often the fall of early states and empires comes later to represent a paradise lost, a golden age of good government, wise rule, harmony, and peace, when all was right with the world. This is evident in the writings of Gibbon (1776–88) on the Roman empire of the second century AD, of the 'Hundred Schools' on the Western Chou (Creel 1970; Fairbank *et al.* 1973; Needham 1965), and of Nehru (1959) on the Mauryan empire of India (*c.* 300–100 BC). The following characterization of several early Chou kings was inscribed on a bronze vessel during the middle Western Chou period (between 927 and 908 BC), and exemplifies similar idealization:

> In antiquity, King Wen reigned. God bestowed upon him virtues which allowed him to possess a multitude of states between Heaven and Earth. The powerful King Wu campaigned in four directions, took over the Yin (Shang) people, and quelled troubles with (nomadic) Ti and the I peoples (on the east coast). The wise, sage King Ch'eng was assisted by strong helpers and consolidated the Chou. The virtuous King K'ang was the one who divided the territory (by enfeoffing feudal lords). The broad-minded King Chao campaigned southward in the region of Ch'u-Ching. The brilliant King Mu developed a

1028

model to educate the current Son of Heaven in the ways of the old Chou kings Wen and Wu. A Son of Heaven who enjoyed long life and good health, who served the deities well, who glorified the previous kings and royal ancestors, who brought good harvest and made people of all places come to pay their respects was the model.

(Hsu and Linduff 1988: 115)

Myths of a former paradise are simultaneously an attempt to comprehend current conditions, and a philosophy of how a civil society should be led. The stories of lost golden ages explain much of the persistent interest in collapse.

In the latter half of the eighth century BC the Greeks became increasingly aware of a vanished 'heroic' age (what we call the Mycenaean period). Sagas like the Iliad and the Odyssey were developed, hero-cults emerged, votive offerings were left at Mycenaean tombs, and some attempted to emulate 'heroic' funerals. Heroic-age themes appeared in art, especially pottery (Coldstream 1977: 341–56), much as Renaissance art was to be influenced by classical themes. Yet as Snodgrass points out, 'one of the greatest attractions of a Heroic Age is the impracticality of any return to it' (1980: 18).

POST-COLLAPSE ARCHAEOLOGY

The extent to which post-collapse archaeology relies on burials is striking. Human interments are commonly the primary data for historical periods lasting up to several centuries. This is the case in post-Mycenaean Greece, Merovingian Gaul, Anglo-Saxon England, Lombard Italy, the post-Roman Balkans, and even China of the Eastern Chou period. Much of what we know of these post-collapse societies comes from a very small number of graves. This situation is emphasized when compared against, for example, Roman archaeology, which relies very little on mortuary remains. It is clear, moreover, that the disproportionate emphasis on mortuary data comes only partially from a propensity to excavate graves (though in China there is great emphasis on élite tombs): it reflects to a large degree what has been available to excavate.

Archaeologists who study these periods are not averse to excavating settlements, but they are able to locate surprisingly few. Writing of the early Slavic occupation of the Balkans (c. AD 600–900), Evans has succinctly stated the empirical problem:

If there is one certainty in the archaeology of the period it is that the individuals that were buried in the cemeteries must have lived somewhere. There must have been settlements, presumably close to the burial grounds, as demonstrated at Ždrijac, where the cemetery lies close to a town that is known to have been occupied through at least part of the cemetery's usage. Yet in spite of the likelihood of individuals living in the vicinity of the cemeteries before their burials, there are very few indications of the settlements, and no properly excavated settlement in the Dalmatian area. This absence is one of the severest lacunae in the archaeological record for the period.

(Evans 1989: 108)

This statement could apply equally well to many parts of post-Roman Europe, and to other post-collapse societies.

While this is deplorable from the perspective of representative data, it does reflect the nature of post-collapse societies. Simpler societies produce a more ephemeral archaeological record. They erect fewer substantial buildings and make less elaborate artefacts. Their archaeological record is weakly structured (that is, not characterized by salient features or strong statistical patterns), and in some cases is difficult to detect at all. In Italy no monumental buildings were constructed anew in over 500 years, between the sixth-century churches at Ravenna and the eleventh-century cathedral at Pisa. Late Roman buildings and fortifications were used whenever possible, and new construction was often in timber (see, for example, Higham 1992: 104). For post-Mycenaean Greece the number of excavated buildings is statistically negligible. British archaeologists are very familiar with the problem of finding Anglo-Saxon occupational remains.

Yet recent work has demonstrated that much more can be done. Research on late Roman/early medieval Italy (Hodges 1993, 1995; Hodges and Wickham 1995; Potter 1979), the Peten of Guatemala (D. S. Rice 1986; P. M. Rice 1986), the Mesoamerican Highlands (Diehl 1989), the Guadalquivir Valley of Spain (Ponsich, cited in Carr 1992), and the West Heslerton Anglo-Saxon settlement (Powlesland 1987) is showing that detailed information on post-collapse societies can be developed. Two complementary approaches should be adopted widely in post-collapse archaeology. The first is systematic regional surveys employing the best chronological controls. Such surveys must cover large areas and be thorough, so that virtually all locatable remains are found. The second is careful excavation of post-collapse occupation levels, which may be disturbed upper levels, as at Wroxeter (P. Barker 1979). These approaches will require more intensive research than has been customary in many areas, but are necessary unless post-collapse societies are to remain dark. Complex societies leave archaeological remains that are impossible to avoid, whereas the study of disintegrated societies requires fine-grained research at nearly a microscopic level.

Post-collapse societies are a logical and regular product of social evolution. As a recurrent social form they are fully amenable to comparative analysis, generalization, and explanation. Post-collapse societies can no longer be treated as a tedious interlude between more interesting periods. They represent, in fact, a return to the normal human organization of low complexity, and as such reflect more accurately the human experience than do the rare, complex societies to which so many scholars are drawn. While it may be that social evolution tends in general towards greater complexity, periodic simplification is to be expected as well, and is worth our best efforts to understand.

ACKNOWLEDGEMENTS

My thanks go to Bonnie Bagley Tainter for technical editing of this chapter and to J. Scott Wood for advice on Anglo-Saxon archaeology.

REFERENCES

Adams, R. E. W. (1973a) 'The collapse of Maya Civilization: a review of previous theories', in T. P. Culbert (ed.) *The Classic Maya Collapse*, Albuquerque: University of New Mexico Press: 21–34.

Adams, R. E. W. (1973b) 'Maya collapse: transformation and termination in the ceramic sequence at Altar de Sacrificios', in T. P. Culbert (ed.) *The Classic Maya Collapse*, Albuquerque: University of New Mexico Press: 133–63.

Adams, R. E. W. (1977) *Prehistoric Mesoamerica*, Boston: Little, Brown.

Adams, R. E. W. (1981) 'Settlement patterns of the central Yucatan and southern Campeche regions', in W. Ashmore (ed.) *Lowland Maya Settlement Patterns*, Albuquerque: University of New Mexico Press: 211–57.

Adams, R. M. (1983) *Decadent Societies*, San Francisco: North Point.

Adams, R. McC. (1978) 'Strategies of maximization, stability, and resilience in Meso-potamian society, settlement, and agriculture', *Proceedings of the American Philosophical Society* 122: 329–35.

Adams, R. McC. (1981) *Heartland of Cities*, Chicago: Aldine.

Akurgal, E. (1962) *The Art of the Hittites* (translated by Constance McNab), New York: Harry N. Abrams.

Andrews, E. W. V and Sabloff, J. A. (1986) 'Classic to Postclassic: a summary discussion', in J. A. Sabloff and E. W. Andrews V (eds) *Late Lowland Maya Civilization: Classic to Postclassic*, Albuquerque: University of New Mexico Press: 433–56.

Asch, N. B., Ford, R. I. and Asch, D. L. (1972) 'Paleoethnobotany of the Koster site: the Archaic horizons', in *Illinois State Museum Reports of Investigations* 24, *Illinois Valley Archaeological Program, Research Papers* 6.

Barker, E. (1924) 'Italy and the West, 410–476', in H. M. Gwatkin and J. P. Whitney (eds) *The Cambridge Medieval History, Volume 1, The Christian Roman Empire and the Foundation of the Teutonic Order* (2nd edition), Cambridge: Cambridge University Press: 392–431.

Barker, P. A. (1979) 'The latest occupation of the site of the baths basilica at Wroxeter', in P. J. Casey (ed.) *The End of Roman Britain*, Oxford: British Archaeological Reports, British Series 71: 175–81.

Barnett, R. D. (1975) 'Phrygia and the peoples of Anatolia in the Iron Age', in I. E. S. Edwards, C. J. Gadd, N. G. L. Hammond and E. Sollberger (eds) *The Cambridge Ancient History II (2)* (3rd edition), Cambridge: Cambridge University Press: 417–42.

Bell, B. (1971) 'The dark ages in ancient history: 1. The first dark age in Egypt', *American Journal of Archaeology* 75: 1–26.

Betancourt, P. P. (1976) 'The end of the Greek Bronze Age', *Antiquity* 50: 40–47.

Blanton, R. E. (1978) *Monte Albán: Settlement Patterns at the Ancient Zapotec Capital*, New York: Academic Press.

Blanton, R. E. (1983) 'The urban decline at Monte Albán', in K. V. Flannery and J. Marcus (eds) *The Cloud People: Divergent Evolution of the Zapotec and Mixtec Civilizations*, New York: Academic Press: 186.

Blanton, R. E. and Kowalewski, S. A. (1981) 'Monte Albán and after in the Valley of Oaxaca', in J. A. Sabloff (ed.) *Supplement to the Handbook of Middle American Indians, Volume I: Archaeology*, Austin: University of Texas Press: 94–116.

Boak, A. E. R. (1955) *Manpower Shortage and the Fall of the Roman Empire in the West*, Ann Arbor: University of Michigan Press.

Boserup, E. (1965) *The Conditions of Agricultural Growth: the Economics of Agrarian Change Under Population Pressure*, Chicago: Aldine.

Brown, P. (1971) *The World of Late Antiquity*, London: Thames and Hudson.

Burns, T. (1984) *A History of the Ostrogoths*, Bloomington: Indiana University Press.

Carneiro, R. L. (1970) 'A theory of the origin of the state', *Science* 169: 733–38.

Carneiro, R. L. (1978) 'Political expansion as an expression of the principle of competitive exclusion', in R. Cohen and E. R. Service (eds) *Origins of the State: the Anthropology of Political Evolution*, Philadelphia: Institute for the Study of Human Issues: 203–23.

Carr, K. E. (1992) 'Did Roman Government Matter? The Standard of Living in the Guadalquivir Valley, A.D. 300–700', Ann Arbor, University of Michigan: Ph.D. dissertation (University Microfilms).

Chadwick, J. (1976) *The Mycenaean World*, Cambridge: Cambridge University Press.

Childe, V. G. (1951) *Man Makes Himself*, New York: Mentor.

Clark, C. and Haswell, M. (1966) *The Economics of Subsistence Agriculture*, London: Macmillan.

Coldstream, J. N. (1977) *Geometric Greece*, London: Ernest Benn.

Cowgill, G. L. (1979) 'Teotihuacán, internal militaristic competition, and the fall of the Classic Maya', in N. Hammond and G. R. Willey (eds) *Maya Archaeology and Ethnohistory*, Austin: University of Texas Press: 51–62.

Creel, H. G. (1953) *Chinese Thought from Confucius to Mao Tse-Tung*, Chicago: University of Chicago Press.

Creel, H. G. (1970) *The Origins of Statecraft in China, Volume I: the Western Chou Empire*, Chicago: Aldine.

Culbert, T. P. (1973) 'The Mayan downfall at Tikal', in T. P. Culbert (ed.) *The Classic Maya Collapse*, Albuquerque: University of New Mexico Press: 63–92.

Culbert, T. P. (1974) *The Lost Civilization: the Story of the Classic Maya*, New York: Harper and Row.

Culbert, T. P. (1977) 'Maya development and collapse: an economic perspective', in N. Hammond (ed.) *Social Process in Maya Prehistory: Studies in Honour of Sir Eric Thompson*, London: Academic Press: 509–30.

Culbert, T. P. (1988) 'The collapse of Classic Maya Civilization', in N. Yoffee and G. L. Cowgill (eds) *The Collapse of Ancient States and Civilizations*, Tucson: University of Arizona Press: 69–101.

Dahlin, B. H., Quizar, R. and Dahlin, A. (1987) 'Linguistic divergence and the collapse of Preclassic civilization in southern Mesoamerica', *American Antiquity* 52: 367–82.

Davis, K. R. (1982) *Britons and Saxons: The Chiltern Region 400–700*, Chichester: Phillimore.

Desborough, V. R. (1972) *The Greek Dark Ages*, London: Ernest Benn.

Desborough, V. R. (1975) 'The end of Mycenaean Civilization and the dark ages: (a) the archaeological background', in I. E. S. Edwards, C. J. Gadd, N. G. L. Hammond and

E. Sollberger (eds) *The Cambridge Ancient History II (2)* (3rd edition), Cambridge: Cambridge University Press: 658–77.

Diehl, R. A. (1989) 'A shadow of its former self: Teotihuacán during the Coyotlatelco period', in R. A. Diehl and J. A. Berlo (eds) *Mesoamerica After the Fall of Teotihuacán, A.D. 700–900*, Washington, DC: Dumbarton Oaks: 9–18.

Diehl, R. A. and Berlo, J. C. (1989) 'Introduction', in R. A. Diehl and J. A. Berlo (eds) *Mesoamerica After the Fall of Teotihuacán, A.D. 700–900*, Washington, DC: Dumbarton Oaks: 1–8.

Duncan-Jones, R. (1974) *The Economy of the Roman Empire: Quantitative Studies*, Cambridge: Cambridge University Press.

Easton, D. (1965) *A Framework for Political Analysis*, Englewood Cliffs, N.J.: Prentice-Hall.

Eisenstadt, S. N. (1963) *The Political Systems of Empires*, Glencoe, Ill.: Free Press.

Erickson, E. E. (1975) 'Growth functions and culture history: a perspective on Classic Maya cultural development', *Behavior Science Research* 10: 37–61.

Evans, H. M. A. (1989) *The Early Mediaeval Archaeology of Croatia*, Oxford: British Archaeological Reports, International Series 539.

Fairbank, J. K., Reischauer, E. O. and Craig, A. M. (1973) *East Asia: Tradition and Transformation*, Boston: Houghton Mifflin.

Finley, M. I. (1973) *The Ancient Economy*, Berkeley and Los Angeles: University of California Press.

Finley, M. I. (1981) *Early Greece: the Bronze and Archaic Ages* (2nd edition), London: Chatto and Windus.

Frank, T. (1940) *An Economic Survey of Ancient Rome, Volume V: Rome and Italy of the Empire*, Baltimore, Md.: Johns Hopkins Press.

Freidel, D. A. (1979) 'Culture areas and interaction spheres: contrasting approaches to the emergence of civilization in the Maya Lowlands', *American Antiquity* 44: 36–54.

Freidel, D. A. (1981) 'The political economics of residential dispersion among the Lowland Maya', in W. Ashmore (ed.) *Lowland Maya Settlement Patterns*, Albuquerque: University of New Mexico Press: 371–82.

Freidel, D. A. (1985) 'New light on the dark age: a summary of major themes', in A. F. Chase and P. M. Rice (eds) *The Lowland Maya Postclassic*, Austin: University of Texas Press: 285–309.

Fried, M. H. (1967) *The Evolution of Political Society, an Essay in Political Anthropology*, New York: Random House.

Gibbon, E. (1776–88) *The Decline and Fall of the Roman Empire*, New York: Modern Library.

Goetze, A. (1975a) 'The struggle for the domination of Syria (1400–1300 B.C.)', in I. E. S. Edwards, C. J. Gadd, N. G. L. Hammond and E. Sollberger (eds) *The Cambridge Ancient History II (2)* (3rd edition), Cambridge: Cambridge University Press: 1–20.

Goetze, A. (1975b) 'Anatolia from Shuppiluliumash to the Egyptian war of Muwatallish', in I. E. S. Edwards, C. J. Gadd, N. G. L. Hammond and E. Sollberger (eds) *The Cambridge Ancient History II (2)* (3rd edition), Cambridge: Cambridge University Press: 117–29.

Goetze, A. (1975c) 'The Hittites and Syria (1300–1200 B.C.)', in I. E. S. Edwards, C. J. Gadd, N. G. L. Hammond and E. Sollberger (eds) *The Cambridge Ancient History II (2)* (3rd edition), Cambridge: Cambridge University Press: 252–73.

Graffam, G. (1992) 'Beyond state collapse: rural history, raised fields, and pastoralism in the South Andes', *American Anthropologist* 94: 882–904.

Gunderson, G. (1976) 'Economic change and the demise of the Roman Empire', *Explorations in Economic History* 13: 43–68.

Gurney, O. R. (1973a) 'Anatolia, c. 1750–1600 B.C.', in I. E. S. Edwards, C. J. Gadd, N. G. L. Hammond and E. Sollberger (eds) *The Cambridge Ancient History II (1)* (3rd edition), Cambridge: Cambridge University Press: 228–55.

Gurney, O. R. (1973b) 'Anatolia, c. 1600–1380 B.C.', in I. E. S. Edwards, C. J. Gadd, N. G. L. Hammond and E. Sollberger (eds) *The Cambridge Ancient History II (1)* (3rd edition), Cambridge: Cambridge University Press: 659–85.

Hammond, M. (1946) 'Economic stagnation in the early Roman Empire', *Journal of Economic History*, Supplement 6: 63–90.

Hammond, N. (1977) 'Ex oriente lux: a view from Belize', in R. E. W. Adams (ed.) *The Origins of Maya Civilization*, Albuquerque: University of New Mexico Press: 45–76.

Hammond, N. (1982) *Ancient Maya Civilization*, New Brunswick: Rutgers University Press.

Haviland, W. A. (1967) 'Stature at Tikal, Guatemala: implications for Classic Maya demography and social organization', *American Antiquity* 32: 316–25.

Haviland, W. A. (1969) 'A new population estimate for Tikal, Guatemala', *American Antiquity* 34: 429–33.

Haviland, W. A. (1970) 'Tikal, Guatemala, and Mesoamerican urbanism', *World Archaeology* 2: 186–97.

Heichelheim, F. M. (1970) *An Ancient Economic History, Volume III* (translated by Joyce Stevens), Leyden: A. W. Sijthoff.

Higham, N. (1992) *Rome, Britain and the Anglo-Saxons*, London: Seaby.

Hirth, F. (1923) *The Ancient History of China to the End of the Chou Dynasty*, New York: Columbia University Press.

Hirth, K. G. (1989) 'Militarism and social organization at Xochicalco, Morelos', in R. A. Diehl and J. A. Berlo (eds) *Mesoamerica After the Fall of Teotihuacán, A.D. 700–900*, Washington, DC: Dumbarton Oaks: 69–81.

Hodges, R. (1982) *Dark Age Economics: the Origins of Towns and Trade A.D. 600–1000*, London: Duckworth.

Hodges, R. A. (ed.) (1993) *San Vincenzo al Volturno*, London: British School at Rome, Archaeological Monographs 7.

Hodges, R. A. (ed.) (1995) *San Vincenzo al Volturno*, London: British School at Rome, Archaeological Monographs 9.

Hodges, R. A. and Whitehouse, D. (1983) *Mohammed, Charlemagne and the Origins of Europe*, Ithaca, N.Y.: Cornell University Press.

Hodges, R. A. and Wickham, C. (1995) 'The evolution of hilltop villages', in G. Barker, *A Mediterranean Valley: Landscape Archaeology and* Annales *History in the Biferno Valley*, London: Leicester University Press: 254–85.

Hodgett, G. A. J. (1972) *A Social and Economic History of Medieval Europe*, London: Methuen.

Hogarth, D. G. (1926) 'The Hittites of Asia Minor', in J. B. Bury, S. A. Cook and F. E. Adcock (eds) *The Cambridge Ancient History II*, New York: Macmillan: 252–74.

Hooker, J. T. (1976) *Mycenaean Greece*, London: Routledge and Kegan Paul.

Hsu, C.-Y. (1965) *Ancient China in Transition: An Analysis of Social Mobility, 722–222 B.C.*, Stanford: Stanford University Press.

Hsu, C.-Y. and Linduff, K. M. (1988) *Western Chou Civilization*, New Haven and London: Yale University Press.

Hucker, C. O. (1975) *China's Imperial Past*, Stanford: Stanford University Press.

Isbell, W. H. (1978) 'Environmental perturbations and the origin of the Andean state', in C. L. Redman, M. J. Berman, E. V. Curtin, W. T. Langhorne Jr, N. M. Versaggi and J. C. Wanser (eds) *Social Archaeology: Beyond Subsistence and Dating*, New York: Academic Press: 303–13.

Johnson, G. J. (1978) 'Information sources and the development of decision-making organizations', in C. L. Redman, M. J. Berman, E. V. Curtin, W. T. Langhorne Jr, N. M. Versaggi and J. C. Wanser (eds) *Social Archaeology: Beyond Subsistence and Dating*, New York: Academic Press: 87–112.

Johnson, G. J. (1982) 'Organization structure and scalar stress', in C. Renfrew, M. J. Rowlands and B. A. Segraves (eds) *Theory and Explanation in Archaeology: the Southampton Conference*, New York: Academic Press: 389–421.

Jones, A. H. M. (1964) *The Later Roman Empire, 284–602: a Social, Economic and Administrative Survey*, Norman: University of Oklahoma Press.

Jones, A. H. M. (1974) *The Roman Economy: Studies in Ancient Economic and Administrative History*, Oxford: Basil Blackwell.

Kolata, A. L. (1986) 'The agricultural foundations of the Tiwanaku state: a view from the heartland', *American Antiquity* 51: 748–62.

Kolata, A. L. (1991) 'The technology and organization of agricultural production in the Tiwanaku state', *Latin American Antiquity* 2: 99–125.

Kowalewski, S. (1983) 'Monte Albán IIIb–IV settlement patterns in the Valley of Oaxaca', in K. V. Flannery and J. Marcus (eds) *The Cloud People: Divergent Evolution of the Zapotec and Mixtec Civilizations*, New York: Academic Press: 188–90.

Lanning, E. P. (1967) *Peru Before the Incas*, Englewood Cliffs, N.J.: Prentice-Hall.

Levenson, J. R. and Schurman, F. (1969) *China: an Interpretive History*, Berkeley and Los Angeles: University of California Press.

Levy, J.-P. (1967) *The Economic Life of the Ancient World* (translated by J. G. Biram), Chicago: University of Chicago Press.

Lumbreras, L. G. (1974) *The Peoples and Cultures of Ancient Peru* (translated by B. J. Meggers), Washington, DC: Smithsonian Institute Press.

Luttwak, E. N. (1976) *The Grand Strategy of the Roman Empire: From the First Century A.D. to the Third*, Baltimore, Md.: Johns Hopkins University Press.

McGuire, R. H. (1983) 'Breaking down cultural complexity: inequality and heterogeneity', in M. B. Schiffer (ed.) *Advances in Archaeological Method and Theory* 6, New York: Academic Press: 91–142.

MacMullen, R. (1976) *Roman Government's Response to Crisis, A.D. 235–337*, New Haven and London: Yale University Press.

Marcus, J. (1976) *Emblem and State in the Classic Maya Lowlands: an Epigraphic Approach to Territorial Organization*, Washington, DC: Dumbarton Oaks.

Marcus, J. (1983a) 'Changing patterns of stone monuments after the fall of Monte Albán, A.D. 600–900', in K. V. Flannery and J. Marcus (eds) *The Cloud People: Divergent Evolution of the Zapotec and Mixtec Civilizations*, New York: Academic Press: 191–97.

Marcus, J. (1983b) 'A synthesis of the cultural evolution of the Zapotec and Mixtec', in K. V. Flannery and J. Marcus (eds) *The Cloud People: Divergent Evolution of the Zapotec and Mixtec Civilizations*, New York: Academic Press: 355–60.

Marcus, J. (1983c) 'Lowland Maya archaeology at the crossroads', *American Antiquity* 48: 454–88.

Marcus, J. (1989) 'From centralized systems to city-states: possible models for the

Epiclassic', in R. A. Diehl and J. A. Berlo (eds) *Mesoamerica After the Fall of Teotihuacán, A.D. 700–900*, Washington, DC: Dumbarton Oaks: 201–8.

Marcus, J. and Flannery, K. V. (1983) 'An introduction to the Late Postclassic', in K. V. Flannery and J. Marcus (eds) *The Cloud People: Divergent Evolution of the Zapotec and Mixtec Civilizations*, New York: Academic Press: 217–26.

Mastache, A. G. and Cobean, R. H. (1989) 'The Coyotlatelco culture and the origins of the Toltec state', in R. A. Diehl and J. A. Berlo (eds) *Mesoamerica After the Fall of Teotihuacán, A.D. 700–900*, Washington, DC: Dumbarton Oaks: 49–67.

Matheny, R. T. (1978) 'Northern Maya Lowland water-control systems', in P. D. Harrison and B. L. Turner (eds) *Pre-Hispanic Maya Agriculture*, Albuquerque: University of New Mexico Press: 185–210

Mathers, C. and Stoddart, S. (eds) (1994) *Development and Decline in the Mediterranean Bronze Age*, Sheffield Archaeological Monographs 8, Sheffield: J. R. Collis.

Mazzarino, S. (1966) *The End of the Ancient World* (translated by G. Holmes), London: Faber and Faber.

Millon, R. (1981) 'Teotihuacán: city, state, and civilization', in J. A. Sabloff (ed.) *Supplement to the Handbook of Middle American Indians, Volume I: Archaeology*, Austin: University of Texas Press: 198–243.

Morris, I. (1987) *Burial and Ancient Society: the Rise of the Greek City-State*, Cambridge: Cambridge University Press.

Mylonas, G. E. (1966) *Mycenae and the Mycenaean Age*, Princeton: Princeton University Press.

Needham, J. (1965) *Science and Civilization in China, Volume 1: Introductory Orientation*, Cambridge: Cambridge University Press.

Nehru, J. (1959) *The Discovery of India*, New York: Doubleday.

Netting, R. M. (1977) 'Maya subsistence: mythologies, analogies, possibilities', in R. E. W. Adams (ed.) *The Origins of Maya Civilization*, Albuquerque: University of New Mexico Press: 299–333.

O'Connor, D. (1974) 'Political systems and archaeological data in Egypt: 2600–1780 B.C.', *World Archaeology* 6: 15–38.

Olson, M. (1982) *The Rise and Decline of Nations*, New Haven, Conn.: Yale University Press.

Paddock, J. (1983) 'Some thoughts on the decline of Monte Albán', in K. V. Flannery and J. Marcus (eds) *The Cloud People: Divergent Evolution of the Zapotec and Mixtec Civilizations*, New York: Academic Press: 186–88.

Parker, G. (1988) *The Military Revolution: Military Innovation and the Rise of the West, 1500–1800*, Cambridge: Cambridge University Press.

Pfister, C. (1913) 'Gaul under the Merovingian Franks', in H. M. Gwatkin and J. P. Whitney (eds) *The Cambridge Medieval History, Volume II, The Rise of the Saracens and the Foundation of the Western Empire*, Cambridge: Cambridge University Press: 132–58.

Potter, T. W. (1976) 'Valleys and settlement: some new evidence', *World Archaeology* 8: 207–19.

Potter, T. W. (1979) *The Changing Landscape of South Etruria*, London, Elek.

Powlesland, D. (1987) *The Heslerton Anglo Saxon Settlement*, York: North Yorkshire County Council.

Raish, C. (1992) *Domestic Animals and Stability in Pre-State Farming Societies*, Oxford: British Archaeological Reports, International Series 579.

Rands, R. L. (1973) 'The Classic Maya collapse: Usumacinta zone and the northwestern periphery', in T. P. Culbert (ed.) *The Classic Maya Collapse*, Albuquerque: University of New Mexico Press: 165–205.

Randsborg, K. (1991) *The First Millennium AD in Europe and the Mediterranean: an Archaeological Essay*, Cambridge: Cambridge University Press.

Rathje, W. L. (1971) 'The origin and development of Lowland Classic Maya Civilization', *American Antiquity* 36: 275–85.

Renfrew, C. (1972) *The Emergence of Civilization: the Cyclades and the Aegean in the Third Millennium B.C.*, London: Methuen.

Renfrew, C. (1979) 'Systems collapse as social transformation: catastrophe and anastrophe in early state societies', in C. Renfrew and K. L. Cooke (eds) *Transformations: Mathematical Approaches to Culture Change*, New York: Academic Press: 481–506.

Rice, D. S. (1976) 'Middle Preclassic Maya settlement in the central Maya Lowlands', *Journal of Field Archaeology* 3: 425–45.

Rice, D. S. (1986) 'The Peten Postclassic: a settlement perspective', in J. A. Sabloff and E. W. Andrews V (eds) *Late Lowland Maya Civilization: Classic to Postclassic*, Albuquerque: University of New Mexico Press: 301–44.

Rice, P. M. (1986) 'The Peten Postclassic: perspectives from the central Peten lakes', in J. A. Sabloff and E. W. Andrews V (eds) *Late Lowland Maya Civilization: Classic to Postclassic*, Albuquerque: University of New Mexico Press: 251–99.

Rostovtzeff, M. (1926) *The Social and Economic History of the Roman Empire*, Oxford: Oxford University Press.

Russell, J. C. (1958) 'Late ancient and medieval population', *Transactions of the American Philosophical Society* 48 (3).

Sanders, W. T. (1962) 'Cultural ecology of the Maya Lowlands, Part I', *Estudios de Cultura Maya* 2: 79–121.

Sanders, W. T., Parsons, J. R. and Santley, R. S. (1979) *The Basin of Mexico: Ecological Processes in the Evolution of a Civilization*, New York: Academic Press.

Saul, F. P. (1972) 'The human skeletal remains of Altar de Sacrificios: an osteobiographic analysis', *Papers of the Peabody Museum of Archaeology and Ethnology*, Harvard University 63 (2).

Saul, F. P. (1973) 'Disease in the Maya area: the Pre-Columbian evidence', in T. P. Culbert (ed.) *The Classic Maya Collapse*, Albuquerque: University of New Mexico Press: 301–24.

Simon, H. (1965) 'The architecture of complexity', *General Systems* 10: 63–76.

Smith, W. S. (1971) 'The Old Kingdom in Egypt and the beginning of the First Intermediate Period', in I. E. S. Edwards, C. J. Gadd and N. G. L. Hammond (eds) *The Cambridge Ancient History I (2)* (3rd edition), Cambridge: Cambridge University Press: 145–207.

Snodgrass, A. M. (1971) *The Dark Age of Greece*, Edinburgh: Edinburgh University Press.

Snodgrass, A. M. (1980) *Archaic Greece: the Age of Experiment*, London: J. M. Dent and Sons.

Steward, J. H. (1955) *Theory of Culture Change*, Urbana: University of Illinois Press.

Stubbings, F. H. (1975a) 'The expansion of the Mycenaean civilization', in I. E. S. Edwards, C. J. Gadd, N. G. L. Hammond and E. Sollberger (eds) *The Cambridge Ancient History II (2)* (3rd edition), Cambridge: Cambridge University Press: 165–87.

Stubbings, F. H. (1975b) 'The recession of Mycenaean civilization', in I. E. S. Edwards, C. J. Gadd, N. G. L. Hammond and E. Sollberger (eds) *The Cambridge Ancient History II (2)* (3rd edition), Cambridge: Cambridge University Press: 338–53.

Tainter, J. A. (1988) *The Collapse of Complex Societies*, Cambridge: Cambridge University Press.

Tainter, J. A. (1994) 'La fine dell'amministrazione centrale: il collaso dell'Impero Romano in Occidente', in J. Guilaine and S. Settis (eds) *Storia d'Europa, Volume Secondo: Preistoria e Antichità*, Turin: Einaudi: 1207–55.

Tainter, J. A. (1996) 'Introduction: prehistoric societies as evolving complex systems', in J. A. Tainter and B. B. Tainter (eds) *Evolving Complexity and Environmental Risk in the Prehistoric Southwest*, Reading, Mass.: Addison Wesley (Santa Fe Institute, Studies in the Sciences of Complexity, *Proceedings* Volume XXIV: 1–23).

Taylour, W. (1964) *The Mycenaeans*, New York: Praeger.

Thomas, P. M. Jr (1981) *Prehistoric Maya Settlement Patterns at Becan, Campeche, Mexico*, Middle American Research Institute Publication 45.

Toynbee, A. J. (1962) *A Study of History* (12 volumes), Oxford: Oxford University Press.

Vinogradoff, Paul (1913) 'Foundations of society (origins of feudalism)', in H. M. Gwatkin and J. P. Whitney (eds) *The Cambridge Medieval History, Volume II, The Rise of the Saracens and the Foundation of the Western Empire*, Cambridge: Cambridge University Press: 630–54.

Waines, D. (1977) 'The third century internal crisis of the Abbasids', *Journal of the Economic and Social History of the Orient* 20: 282–306.

Weber, M. (1976) *The Agrarian Sociology of Ancient Civilizations* (translated by R. I. Frank), London: NLB.

Webster, D. (1975) 'Warfare and the evolution of the state: a reconsideration', *American Antiquity* 40: 464–70.

Webster, D. (1976) *Defensive Earthworks at Becan, Campeche, Mexico*, Middle American Research Institute Publication 44.

Webster, D. (1977) 'Warfare and the evolution of Maya Civilization', in R. E. W. Adams (ed.) *The Origins of Maya Civilization*, Albuquerque: University of New Mexico Press: 335–72.

White, L. A. (1949) *The Science of Culture*, New York: Farrar, Straus and Giroux.

White, L. A. (1959) *The Evolution of Culture*, New York: McGraw-Hill.

Wickham, C. (1981) *Early Medieval Italy: Central Power and Local Society 400–1000*, London: Macmillan.

Wickham, C. (1984) 'The other transition: from the ancient world to feudalism', *Past and Present* 103: 3–36.

Wilkinson, R. G. (1973) *Poverty and Progress: an Ecological Model of Economic Development*, London: Methuen.

Willey, G. R. (1971) *An Introduction to American Archaeology, Volume 2: South America*, Englewood Cliffs, N.J.: Prentice-Hall.

Willey, G. R. (1973) 'Certain aspects of the Late Classic to Postclassic periods in the Belize Valley', in T. P. Culbert (ed.) *The Classic Maya Collapse*, Albuquerque: University of New Mexico Press: 93–106.

Willey, G. R. (1977a) 'The rise of Classic Maya Civilization: a Pasion Valley perspective', in R. E. W. Adams (ed.) *The Origins of Maya Civilization*, Albuquerque: University of New Mexico Press: 133–57.

Willey, G. R. (1977b) 'The rise of Maya Civilization: a summary view', in R. E. W. Adams (ed.) *The Origins of Maya Civilization*, Albuquerque: University of New Mexico Press: 383–423.

Willey, G. R. (1982) 'Maya archaeology', *Science* 215: 260–67.

Willey, G. R. and Shimkin, D. B. (1973) 'The Maya collapse: a summary view', in T. P. Culbert (ed.) *The Classic Maya Collapse*, Albuquerque: University of New Mexico Press: 457–501.

Wiseman, F. W. (1978) 'Agricultural and historical ecology of the Maya Lowlands', in P. D. Harrison and B. L. Turner II (eds) *Pre-Hispanic Maya Agriculture*, Albuquerque: University of New Mexico Press: 35–61.

Wittfogel, K. (1957) *Oriental Despotism: a Comparative Study of Total Power*, New Haven, Conn.: Yale University Press.

Wolf, E. R. (1969) *Peasant Wars of the Twentieth Century*, New York: Harper and Row.

Wright, H. T. (1969) *The Administration of Rural Production in an Early Mesopotamian Town*, Ann Arbor: Museum of Anthropology, University of Michigan Anthropological Papers 38.

Xueqin, L. (1985) *Eastern Zhou and Qin Civilizations* (translated by K. C. Chang), New Haven and London: Yale University Press.

Yoffee, N. (1988) 'The collapse of ancient Mesopotamian states and civilization', in N. Yoffee and G. L. Cowgill (eds) *The Collapse of Ancient States and Civilizations*, Tucson: University of Arizona Press: 44–68.

SELECT BIBLIOGRAPHY

Two recent books synthesize current thinking on collapse and provide guidance to earlier literature: *The Collapse of Ancient States and Civilizations* (Tucson: University of Arizona Press, 1988) is a compendium of papers edited by N. Yoffee and G. Cowgill, and *The Collapse of Complex Societies* (1988) by J. A. Tainter gives further details of the theoretical perspective of this chapter, and of the Roman and Mayan collapses.

The outline of late Roman and early medieval history can be found in *The Cambridge Medieval History*, and see also Jones (1964); the potential of medieval archaeology is well illustrated by Hodges and Whitehouse (1983) and Randsborg (1991). Early Chinese history is covered by Creel (1970), and Chou archaeology by Hsu and Linduff (1988) and Xueqin (1985). For the archaeology and history of Mesopotamia see R. McC. Adams (1981) and Yoffee (1988). Post-Mycenaean archaeology is synthesized by Snodgrass (1971, 1980), Desborough (1972) and Coldstream (1977), whilst Morris (1987) interprets the development of the Greek city-state. For the Maya, Culbert (1973) is a fundamental source, whilst recent research on the Postclassic is reported in A. F. Chase and P. M. Rice (eds) *The Lowland Maya Postclassic* (Austin: University of Texas Press, 1985) and J. A. Sabloff and E. W. Andrews V (eds) *Late Lowland Maya Civilization* (Albuquerque: University of New Mexico Press, 1986). Sanders *et al.* (1979) synthesize extensive regional surveys into a comprehensive model of long-term cultural evolution in Highland Mesoamerica, K. V. Flannery and J. Marcus (eds) *The Cloud People* (New York: Academic Press, 1983) describe the prehistory of the southern highlands, and both areas are covered in R. A. Diehl and J. A. Berlo (eds) *Mesoamerica After the Fall of Teotihuacán* (Washington, DC: Dumbarton Oaks, 1989) which concerns the post-collapse period AD 700–900.

26

EUROPE IN THE MIDDLE AGES

Neil Christie

DATES AND DEFINITIONS

The term 'Middle Ages' is a cumbersome one, bracketing the thousand-year expanse between the end of classical Antiquity and the Renaissance. It embraces the 'Dark Ages', the rise of feudalism, the Crusades, the Black Death and the introduction of gunpowder. It sees castles and monasteries rise and fall, trade and manufacture re-blossom, and closes with the meeting of the Old and New Worlds. However, despite extensive survivals of military and ecclesiastical architecture and culture, medieval Europe is generally viewed as a grubby successor to classical Rome both socially and physically, marked by a slow recovery of lost culture, restored (at least in the eyes and minds of Renaissance scholars) only from the late fifteenth century.

Yet it is nowhere easy to define when the Middle Ages commence. It is too sweeping a term to insert immediately after Rome's fall, since Rome's influence lingered long into the 'Dark Ages', mutated but still evident. In the eastern Mediterranean and the Near East, Constantinople (Istanbul) was Rome's direct heir and survived with many reversals full into the thirteenth century and the pillaging of the Fourth Crusade and then beyond that until 1453; and whilst the Arab expansion of the seventh and eighth centuries had certainly forced a military mutation upon Constantinople, her political and religious importance saw no curtailment and thus no traumatic break with which we can define a transition from antique to medieval (Holmes 1988). As in the whole development of human society, change is, or at least was, slow and rarely perceptible to contemporaries, and transitions are largely modern inventions (Braudel 1992). Even in instances of martial conquest, the political name may have changed but the basic social fabric persisted and only slowly mutated into new forms.

Thus for the medieval world, divisions such as 'early', 'low', 'high' or 'late' are our own crude historical conveniences, broadly partitioning up the wide time period of *c*. AD 600–1500, but with an astonishingly wide variation in the way the terms are applied throughout Europe. To some the terms 'Late Antiquity', 'Dark Ages', 'early Byzantine' and 'early Middle Ages' are all one and the same, an archaeological and historical blur, but all demarcating a breakdown in the transmission of the written word. The 'Middle Ages' are in fact an invention of the Renaissance, its contemporaries rejecting the immediate past and seeking instead to resurrect the learning of the more refined classical world. Yet while there is a blur at the start of this 'medieval' period, its end is equally indistinct: in terms of urban living, for instance, the standards and range of amenities of a typical early imperial Roman town were not matched in most of Europe until the nineteenth century; and the ordinary peasant farmer will not have identified any major material change with the passing of the late Middle Ages. Indeed, the Renaissance itself meant no cessation to the wars between kingdoms and empires, nor to religious turmoils: rather it marks a phase when art, architecture, and words take over centre stage and form a new focus for modern historical debate.

ARCHAEOLOGY AND HISTORY

For Europe, discussion of these medieval centuries is still largely dominated by politics, people, dates and places – all elaborations of the vast array of documentary sources that emerge after *c*. AD 1000. A redistribution of literacy in the wake of a rebirth of political, social, religious and economic vitality resulted in the progressively escalating need for more extensive means and levels of recording, in the form of land charters and grants, sales documents, wills, theological treatises, trade pacts and so on, to be set alongside re-disseminated and even forged ancient texts. This wealth of detail – almost exclusive to the Old World, but more than matched in the decadently stable Chinese realm – has since Renaissance times in Europe been variously processed and repackaged, synthesized and expanded, and is reflected in the evolving nature of the modern historian (Cantor 1991). The ceaseless investigation of these medieval texts, constantly enhanced through the discovery of lost or overlooked archive material, until recently allowed little time or space for what were considered subsidiary academic cousins: *art and architectural history*, so long tied to the study of religious or élite secular structures; *economic history*, applied primarily to modern and early modern periods; *historical geography*, tied tightly to documentary premises; and *archaeology*, viewed chiefly as a means by which castles and other high-brow establishments could be further analysed in order to provide occasional illustrative back-up to the rich pageant of social historical evolution.

As disciplines have evolved, so scholars have been made aware of the opportunities and needs for cross-fertilization beyond the scope of mere academic support (see, for example, the approach by Rackham 1986). In the case of archaeology, the advancement of theoretical frameworks and in particular the growing union with anthropology, allows for a more exacting range of questions to be asked of its own field and of modes of investigation and interpretation. Such reassessments have enabled archaeology to 'intrude' more capably and more scientifically into the sphere of medieval history. The range of questions archaeology is employed against can rarely be coherently met by historical documents: literacy may have spread but it still remained in the domain of the élite and rooted in the intellectual concepts of property, society and wealth (Champion 1990). Archaeology of course begins at the grass-roots, the foundations and physical manifestations of all medieval societies: tools, houses, dress, diets, rubbish and burials. Analyses of these help identify and interpret social hierarchies and gender contexts, settlement evolution, economic change, environmental relationships and technological skills. Documents may now and then allow a vivid picture to emerge of the *actions* of everyday life, as witnessed in the detailed confessions of the inhabitants of the hamlet of Montaillou near the Pyrenees in the mid-thirteenth century (Le Roy Ladurie 1980; compare also Origo 1986), but the *mechanics* and *make-up* of this medieval lifestyle are improperly understood without the integration of information derived from excavation.

Yet archaeology's intrusions into the Middle Ages are still rather tentative: in Europe and beyond, university lectureships in medieval and post-medieval/industrial archaeology are rare at best, few Masters courses exist in medieval studies, and there is limited back-up in terms of academic journals. In Mediterranean countries like Spain, medieval studies remain very much the preserve of the historian, although the development of systematic urban excavation and the adoption of multi-period field surveys is everywhere forcing changes, pushing history and archaeology together. The discipline of medieval archaeology is thus expanding rapidly, as was demonstrated in the huge attendance of the Medieval Europe conferences held in York, England, and in Brugge, Belgium, in 1992 and 1997 respectively. Potential study in so many quarters is, however, still at a very preliminary stage: for instance, more is known of Roman than medieval material culture and ceramic type-series still require to be formulated for much of the medieval world; land and sea transport remains obscure; and precious little is known of the physical characteristics of Deserted Medieval Villages (DMVs), a common phenomenon in Britain but one not properly recognized elsewhere in Europe. Documents survive to frame archaeological investigations but insufficient excavation means that scholars remain ill-informed of village and house morphologies, structural histories, local and extra-local industrial and commercial industries, and economies.

Medieval archaeology may be looking beyond the castles to the villages and from manors to field systems, but progress remains slow: even at the DMV of Wharram Percy in the Yorkshire Wolds in north England, where research has been going on since 1948 (with excavation proper from 1952), only about 7 per cent of the overall site has been systematically sampled (Beresford and Hurst 1990: 131). The Wharram Research Project itself fully illustrates the changing face of medieval archaeology in Britain, with the goals of the project constantly being expanded as new techniques of sampling and analysis evolve. Similarly, one can note the change-over in title of the Deserted Medieval Village Research Group – a body formed in the time of the first Wharram Percy investigations – in 1971 to the Medieval Village Research Group and its subsequent merger in 1986 with the Moated Sites Research Group (founded in 1972) to form the Medieval Settlement Research Group, whose constitution seeks to promote wide-ranging 'interdisciplinary involvement in the collection, analysis and dissemination of data relating to the history, geography and archaeology of medieval rural settlement'.

The theoretical aims of medieval archaeology, as with the discipline of archaeology as a whole, have been under close scrutiny (Austin 1990; Moreland 1991), with critical self-reassessment of the discipline's utilization and range of data and its relationship with textual tools. Post-processualist approaches seek clearer perceptions into past material expressions – whether archaeological, artefactual, documentary or architectural – to allow for more defined images of past landscapes, settings and mentalities: 'meaning in these [historical] periods was conveyed through the complex interaction of these alternative forms of discourse, and to concentrate on one – whether it be the written or the "artefactual" – to the exclusion of the others is to diminish our understanding of the complexity and richness of the past and its inhabitants' (Moreland 1991: 25). To meet these new demands, excavations and surveys draw on ever wider specialist and scientific input to provide more comprehensive databanks. The overturning of previous conceptions of the early medieval rural and urban landscape, the beginnings of closer analysis of medieval, post-medieval and early modern settlement forms and of socio-economic mechanics, and the raising of gender debates, all reflect the expanding aims of the new breed of medieval archaeologists. The revised discipline is still somewhat in its infancy, however, and is still not met with universal approval or pursuit. In Germany, for instance, a strongly positivist approach remains to the fore in medieval archaeology, with these scholars seeking primarily to combine more systematically with other related sources, whilst constantly working within a historical framework. Fehring (1991: 235) argues that medieval archaeology 'is to be understood today as an historical science. Its concern, like that of all historical disciplines, is to investigate "past reality", history'. The results, to some degree, are the same, with a new eagerness evident to reveal the medieval world and all its material workings. Ideas, as in any healthy discipline, however, are constantly in flux, and accordingly much more change is to be expected from medieval archaeology in the next decades.

THE EVOLUTION OF MEDIEVAL SOCIETY AND THE STRUCTURES OF THE FEUDAL ÉLITE

The term 'feudal' has long been synonymous with 'medieval', designating the strict localization of power in the hands of lords and castellans, overseeing the lives and labours of dependent peasants. Too often viewed merely as an invented relationship of the period post-AD 1000, revised documentary analyses and historical archaeology have revealed the roots of feudalism in the immediate post-Roman period, as central powers degenerated and potentates seized the reins of local power, based on town or fortress, and with the local populations readily turning to foci of strength in times of insecurity. However, the formalization of feudalism is indeed a 'medieval' invention of the period *c*. AD 1000, created by the signing of bonds of dependence and made evident to us by the emergence of textual data (Bartlett 1993; Reynolds 1994). Ties of loyalty between king and lord/noble consolidated through grants of lands and of jurisdictional rights were extended downwards between lord and vassal. Vassals held lordly lands as fiefs – not always through a uniform manner of adoption but with a variety of origins and levels of obligations – and were required in consequence to render military service to the lord, to pay taxes, to attend court and to place themselves under the lord's legal protection.

The extension of such feudal authority went hand-in-hand with the building of castles, with the right to fortify once the prerogative of the king but in time watered down to become a seigneurial privilege. Castles provided protection, authority and status in the landscape and acted as physical reminders to dependent vassals and serfs. The castles tended to emerge less in times of war or threat, but rather came to proliferate in the stable eleventh century, a period when economic structures were again expanding, population levels rising and rural exploitation increasing. Consolidation of power in the form of castles and acts of patronage all required revenue and this came through tighter control of land and human resources, through the creation of a legal servitude of peasants, often fostered by means of the formal foundation of new villages (Bois 1992; Whitton 1988: 118–30). Monasteries too were forced to participate in this feudalization of the landscape, yet maintained a clearer conscience through offering a less rigid mode of lordship to farmers and communities settled on their lands – indeed the survival of many monastic archives detailing landed possessions and grants of land has provided invaluable databanks for analysing the evolution of the countryside through archaeological field survey (Wickham 1987).

These structural changes are the elements that are best visible in the archaeological record of medieval Europe: the rise of castles and villages, the clearance of new lands, urban growth, and church and monastic patronage. The image throughout is one of general economic buoyancy, but one that is not easily tied into the documented pattern of social remodelling. Rather, a high level of continuity in the urban and rural landscape can be identified, suggesting in many cases that 'feudal' structures such as castles and villages have a much longer and more involved origin than that suggested by the textual sources. In Italy, for example, the process of castle formation (termed *incastellamento* in Italian) and of settlement nucleation (termed *accentramento*) can be traced in some instances back into the ninth and tenth centuries, if not earlier (papers in Noyé 1988: 411–535; Wickham 1987). Here, of course, definitions inevitably become problematic: how far do these earlier fortified and upland sites relate to direct state control, how far to feudal-style nobility and how far to locally initiated refuge? Should castles be defined solely as the developed stone-built edifices of the period post-1000? What structural elements are in fact required to define a castle?

The problem is geographical too: in continental Europe, excavations have begun to clarify the roots of the castle-building tradition, extending it far back to the period of the break-up of Roman rule, the fragmentation of society and economy, the related decay of open rural and urban settlement patterns, and the subsequent emergence of semi-independent rural lordships which were in part attempts to maintain a semblance of the past order (Fehring 1991: 89–108). In Britain, by contrast, the castle is seen as a fully fledged Norman introduction, strategically installed within and over Saxon fortress towns or *burhs* (themselves an attempt at centralized defence) or as new foci in the countryside. Here, then, a changeover is apparent, offering a ready guide to the consequences of the extension of feudal society. Elsewhere, as in eastern Europe, castles develop within Slavic, Bohemian, Magyar and other young kingdoms as central places for the wielding of royal power and as trading nodes. Here, castle growth appears as an elaboration of former hill-forts, but with the creation of palaces, churches and stone walls as a western or even a Byzantine borrowing, a response to the transmission of ideas from commercial exchange and from military conflict (Gerevich 1990).

Inevitably, however, the castle remains emblematic of the medieval European landscape, a symbol of state and élite power. Stone built and imposing, castles have long been viewed as the domain of architectural historians, providing a powerful physical image of a militarized society, and at the same time allowing, through structural analysis, detailed reconstructions of defensive evolution. Yet, as such, they have long remained distinct as items of study from the towns and communities they dominated: more tangible and thereby more valued. As discussed below, however, they are part of a bigger, more complex, human landscape which only now is being adequately scrutinized and appreciated.

In Britain, a spate of castle excavations, such as at Castle Acre, Hen Domen and

Portchester, has done much to extend our understanding of the range of castle types and to analyse the internal everyday workings of these sites through discussion of internal buildings and of the associated material artefacts (Kenyon 1990; McNeill 1991). The principal contribution of these modern archaeological investigations has been the recognition of timber precursors to defences, towers and halls, often part of a long sequence of timber construction. Indeed, many motte-and-bailey and ring-work sites never developed into stone castles and so excavation alone will provide information regarding form and chronology. Overall, studies have shown that for Europe as a whole no single, simple, sequence of castle building can be reconstructed: differing political, military, territorial, economic and geological contexts mean that data gained from one excavated site need not correlate tidily with another (Kenyon 1990: 3–38).

There are of course general conformities in plan, as in the arrangement of mottes, keeps, barbicans and baileys, but the transition from timber to stone, the provision of outer defences, and the location of domestic structures follow no neat pattern. The recent excavations at Hen Domen in Powys, Wales, have, for example, discerned a complex arrangement and evolution of the domestic buildings within the bailey, comprising halls, kitchens, houses, barns, cisterns and chapel, all constructed in timber and undergoing frequent rebuildings into the thirteenth century (Higham and Barker 1992; Fig. 26.1). The relative clutter of buildings is surprising, but may be reflective of a high military profile to the site and thus denotes the quartering of soldiery within the castle confines. Elsewhere such fighting men were an impermanent feature – retainers would otherwise have only been called upon by the lord when required – and would have lived outside the main walls. But whilst the densely packed interior of Hen Domen need not be typical, air photography of castle earthworks, standing remains, and limited excavation do point at least to a significant scatter of domestic buildings inside the castle baileys, designed to serve the lord's seat and table: as such, this greatly modifies the usual artistic reconstructions of castles, which tend to leave the bailey all but empty (on domestic structures see Kenyon 1990: 97–180).

Clearly, also, defence was not always the overriding factor in the layout of these castles, even if mottes, gates and moats indicate that security was an essential ingredient. Status played as important a role, as denoted in the mere control of labour, and the use of imposing architecture set on a height overlooking the dependent urban or rural population. It was further manifested from the mid-twelfth century in the translation from timber to stone, an act requiring much time and effort but resulting in the greater permanency of the site. Status needs should also be identified in the desire to 'upgrade' residences to castle-style standards: hence at Castle Acre in Norfolk, excavations have shown how the first stone buildings on the site, dating from the eleventh century, comprised a two-storey mansion with ditch and bank surround; later on, in the 1140s, the ditch and bank were

Figure 26.1 Hen Domen, Powys: reconstruction drawing of the timber housing and defences of *c.* AD 1150 excavated in the castle bailey; note the presumed single-storey height of the buildings and the presence of rooms butting up to the inner face of the circuit. Source: Higham and Barker 1992.

modified to create a motte and the house was remodelled in two stages as a smaller but taller keep through a doubling of the wall thickness in the northern half of the old manor. Although this remodelling can be set to a time of political and military unrest, building work may have covered many years and this probably left the site open to attack in that time – if an attack was even expected. As a result it may not denote a militarizing of the site, merely a cosmetic upgrade. In fact, after 1200 the keep appears to have fallen out of use and the lower ward or bailey instead came into prominence.

Of similar interest is the sequence at Lydford in Devon, where the square tower was long viewed as a rare example of a stone keep set on a motte. However, excavations showed a first phase free-standing tower of late twelfth-century date set some distance away from the original eleventh-century Norman ring-work, which was subsequently part-demolished; a 5-metre high motte was then created around the tower base before new walls were constructed to create the extant keep structure (Kenyon 1990: 43–44, 49–51; Saunders 1980). Despite its layout, documents record this not as a castle but as a prison. In effect, 'the creation of a motte and miniature bailey was perhaps a deliberate anachronistic conceit intended to give visual confirmation of the title Lydford Castle while at the same time manifesting the power and authority of the Earl of Cornwall' (Saunders 1980: 162). Lesser nobility were also keen to exhibit status through structures, and a common feature in the landscape are manors and low motte-and-bailey-type sites, where the defences appear nominal at best (Aberg 1978; Cherry 1986).

For Britain, artificial hills and, later on, rings of stone defences provided the key elements to castle formats. In continental Europe greater topographical diversity meant a more prominent utilization of natural hills, heights and promontories as the seats of fortifications, dominating rivers, roads, passes or harbours. Formats are accordingly more varied, dependent on natural contours; often, medieval castles are found to overlie much earlier installations, whether late bronze age or iron age hill-forts or early medieval refuges, and regularly reuse elements of their defensive cordons. In Italy, many of the sites documented as castles from the tenth and eleventh centuries have been shown through excavation to possess timber antecedents, an uncertain mixture of refuge and fortress, difficult to date precisely because of the poverty and paucity of early medieval material culture. A good example of this occurs at Montarrenti (Fig. 26.2) not far from Siena in central Italy, where excavations between 1985 and 1988 uncovered most of the interior space of a medieval castle-cum-village and in so doing revealed traces of a wooden palisade and of post-built houses which stratigraphically predated the tenth century. Radio-carbon dates of grain deposits relating to the first stone phase at the site pointed to a restructuring in c. AD 950–1000, while a single radio-carbon date for the initial phase with timber buildings was calculated to the late eighth century (Francovich and Hodges 1989). Montarrenti is in fact not documented before 1156

Figure 26.2 Montarrenti, central Italy: a typical case of medieval upland movement and defence dating from the tenth or eleventh century, where excavation has revealed that wooden dwellings and defences preceded the visible stone buildings. Photograph: G. Barker.

and yet the excavations have shown a vibrant community well established by 1100 and with a peak of prosperity coming in the thirteenth century. Prominent structural elements were the tower houses on the summit of the hill denoting the lordly zone, though these can have been only petty nobility; below these a tidy village fanned out along the contours of the hilltop, with various stone-built houses set into the bedrock slopes. Finds from these structures, which appear to have housed both humans and animals, with animal byres forming the lower storeys, suggest an economically healthy community, receiving some of the seigneurial prosperity.

PEOPLE AND THE LANDSCAPE:
THE ARCHAEOLOGY OF MEDIEVAL VILLAGES

The example of Montarrenti serves to show how a recent goal of medieval archaeology has been to break free of the architectural scrutiny of the élite, and instead to analyse the relationship between castle and community, by seeking in the character of the excavated structures something of the minds of the medieval inhabitants.

While the castles may show changes in their fabric to reflect power and wealth, the houses and material culture of the associated villagers provide far more tangible data regarding how the rest of society functioned. Indeed, it is often the case that the villages persist long after the decline of the castle structures, with many of these medieval sites only undergoing a decline and a shift in location from hill to plain in the present century, generally because of the simple desire of the inhabitants to be closer to the amenities of modern life. Thus examination of hilltop sites in the Mediterranean is starting to yield essential information regarding medieval human mechanics: notably the resilience of the medieval and post-medieval rural population in terms of economy, architecture and basic lifestyle (again, in general, see Braudel 1992).

Villages need not congregate on hilltops. Natural topography dictates the location and human choice moulds the character of the actual settlements. The plains of Mongolia, Hungary and Britain are dominated by open villages established, for the most part, in the course of the early Middle Ages. Many persist as villages today of course, or have expanded into towns and thus largely shroud their rural origins. In other regions, the medieval centuries marked a notable growth of population and of rural settlement, checked viciously by economic decay, plague and climatic change from the thirteenth and fourteenth centuries. Remnants of this rural recession occur as earthworks, buried features in the landscape, marking abandoned farm and village structures. Identification of these earthworks is not new, but detailed archaeological research is a modern phenomenon, still offering only patchy coverage. Such study is reasonably advanced in Britain, however, where over 3,000 earthwork sites of presumed medieval date have been recognized through field survey, mapwork and air photography. Here it has been clearly demonstrated how landscape archaeology can offer new dimensions to old themes by looking beneath the humps and bumps of these lost or shrunken villages and manors. Integrated studies allow for the examination not just of the buildings but also of field boundaries, ridge and furrow, fishponds and mills, presenting thereby an image of the settlement in its fullest context (Aston 1985).

Most prominent in this regard has of course been the long-running project at Wharram Percy in Yorkshire: here, around the village the surrounding system of earthwork boundaries and fields has been scrutinized, revealing elements dating back to Saxon, Roman and even prehistoric times, indicating thereby an unexpected sequence of almost continuous land-use (Beresford and Hurst 1990). The project has discerned a planned late Saxon village comprising two regular rows of timber-built houses set in enclosures, gravitating around manors and church and fronting onto a central thoroughfare (Fig. 26.3). Documents record two early lords as the major landowners, the Percys and the Chamberlains; but after 1250 the Percys alone presided over the village. Excavations have analysed the building history of the Percys' manor house and have also revealed that of the ejected

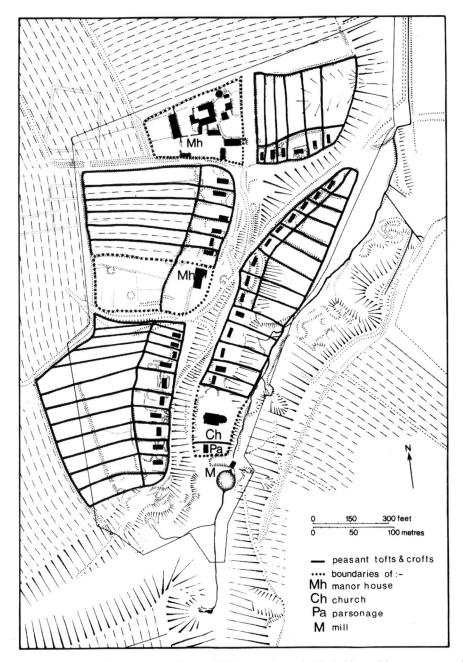

Figure 26.3 Plan of the deserted village of Wharram Percy in Yorkshire, with reconstructed toft (farmyard and dwelling) and croft (paddock) and manor property arrangements. Illustration by Peter Dunn. © Wharram Research Project. Source: Beresford and Hurst 1990.

Chamberlains, demolished in the mid-thirteenth century with the ground subsequently given over to peasant houses, thus blotting out the traces of the rival manor. The architectural pretensions of each family as identified by archaeology in both manors and church had otherwise gone unrecorded by the written sources.

Meanwhile, excavation of peasant 'tofts' (farmyards and dwellings) and 'crofts' (paddocks) has illuminated the changing character of rural domestic architecture and offers a useful comparison with urban housing. In towns, so far, a distinction between social classes is hard to identify in terms of building types before the fifteenth century, after which date building in brick or stone begins to become fairly commonplace. At Wharram, the transition from timber to stone and timber falls largely in the thirteenth century, although the changeover was presumably very much dependent on individuals' finances. Even in regions where stone was in ready supply, timber seems to have long remained in vogue, thus highlighting the resilience of traditional vernacular architecture (Clarke 1984: 35–40; Granville 1997, ch. 5). (For continental forms, see Chapelot and Fossier 1985; Fehring 1991: 148–71; on 'house' and 'farm' interpretation, see Austin and Thomas 1990: 53–64.)

In the countryside three basic house types can be identified: at the bottom end of the market lay the labourer's cot or cottage, a small single- or double-roomed building; higher up the scale, and typical of many villages like Wharram Percy, comes the more prosperous peasant's long-house combining both human and animal space; the wealthiest peasant's accommodation comprised a farm with detached byre and barns, structures which in some instances overlie earlier long-houses, suggestive of improved financial status to earlier middle-range peasants. In the case of the long-houses, the animal presence, whilst undoubtedly offering warmth and a ready supply of milk (and flies!), appears to have also necessitated a notable state of cleanliness, in stark contrast with urban-dwelling (see below pp. 1055–56). Manure and rubbish was stored outside and then scattered onto the fields, with only a few small items left inside the house confines for future archaeological benefit.

Studies at Wharram also highlighted the shifting nature of the rural settlement, with almost regular shifting of position of houses within their enclosures: dating such movement is not easy, but a thirty-year lifespan is suggested for the timber buildings, with subsequent rebuilding seen as the better alternative to major on-the-spot repairs; only with the adoption of stone footings and stone superstructures does the mobility come to a halt here. Thus well-preserved earthwork plans at many villages may denote only the final seat of the houses; earlier arrangements may differ quite markedly in terms of the house alignments, although enclosures seem overall more fixed.

Yet it is still fairly true to say that our understanding of the morphology and of the actual units of medieval rural life still remains vague at best – villages, manors, farmsteads are such a common feature of the landscape that while field archaeology has done much to identify and locate these sites and structures, excavation has still barely scratched the surface. Furthermore, the work at Wharram Percy has shown that no straightforward format to house forms and evolution can be expected, but that considerable variability exists and that each village and each phase within a village must be scrutinized carefully (Aston *et al.* 1989; Taylor 1992).

Various surveys of the scale and range of that of Wharram Percy have been undertaken to fill out this rather sparse image. Such regional surveys in Britain include that conducted around Royston Grange in the Derbyshire Peak District, sampling sites and features relating to all periods, and with an emphasis on analysing the living landscape and assessing the level of continuity and/or discontinuity, notably in terms of field boundaries and rural house forms (Hodges 1991). Evolving field survey analysis has greatly contributed to the debate regarding medieval field systems, as for instance in reconstructing manuring patterns around villages on the basis of artefact scatters. Field walls, ridge and furrow, and trackways were all integral elements of the medieval countryside: all of these provide clues regarding land management, animal husbandry and property demarcation, as well as agricultural practices (Astill and Grant 1992). Just as towns are improperly understood without setting them into a broader economic context, so village and farm life cannot be divorced from their local contexts. This concept of panoramic scrutiny is slowly infiltrating Mediterranean surveys too: a like explosion of data can be promised from these (Mannoni *et al.* 1988; Noyé 1988).

The end of Wharram Percy as a village came in the late fifteenth century, a result of a change in ownership, with the village's new patrons pursuing the fashionable switch from the old arable farming practices to sheep rearing and pasturage – all to the obvious cost of the peasants. This trend had lasting effects elsewhere across many parts of the landscape. Various of the 3,000 Deserted Medieval Villages identified in Britain are linked with this new trend, and many others with the devastating effects of the Black Death, the plague that ravaged Europe in the mid-fourteenth century and periodically thereafter (Hawkins 1990; Platt 1996; Ziegler 1969). However, despite the documentation that allows for local and regional sequences to be built up in terms of village decay, no uniform sequence can be claimed. Enforced removal of villagers to make way for sheep could occur from the twelfth century onwards and yet is only easiest recognized from the fifteenth century; economic expansion in the twelfth century saw many marginal lands settled by farms and villages, but thirteenth-century economic recession, in part caused by the Little Ice Age climatic deterioration, ended this expansion and began a rural decline accelerated drastically by the Black Death. Yet many affected villages clearly survived to endure still today, shrunken but alive, often with a church or chapel standing isolated amongst earthworks – symbolic of the resilience of both the farmer and the Church (Aston 1985: 53–81).

MEDIEVAL TOWNS: STRUCTURES AND RELATIONSHIPS

Serfs, peasants, pilgrims and lords did not of course live in total isolation. There was still, as in the classical world, an important relationship between the country-side and the towns: the castle builders generally kept roots in the towns; towns acted as key markets and exchange points for manufactured goods; pilgrims came from towns to the monasteries; the clergy of the monasteries liaised with the urban clergy; and the countryside still fed the towns. Rural archaeology cannot in effect be divorced from urban archaeology: the results from one have essential bearing on the other. Yet systematic urban archaeology remains a fairly novel discipline. Town excavations until the 1960s tended to be virtual treasure hunts, ploughing down to find solid Roman levels with suitably impressive buildings, mosaics and material culture. Medieval contexts were truly an overburden important only for the level of destruction they had wrought on the antique phases. Obviously there has been much redirecting of archaeological thought to the degree that most urban studies now are designed to record equally modern, industrial, medieval and earlier layers to provide complete images of urban transformation. (Fig. 26.4). Consequently a

Figure 26.4 Bonner's Lane, Leicester: excavation within the urban context, demonstrating the damage caused by Victorian cellaring and medieval and later pitting and cutting. The post holes here belong to a fifth- or sixth-century Saxon building. Photograph: N. Finn, University of Leicester Archaeological Services.

mass of data is becoming available for study, constantly requiring the integration of archive research – in medieval and later urban studies the close working relationship of a variety of disciplines is essential (Barley 1977; Carver 1987; Platt 1976; Schofield and Vince 1994).

Urban excavations now seek far more to understand the structures and lives of the ordinary town-dwellers, to identify elements of survival from Roman to medieval, and from medieval to modern times (Carver 1993; Christie and Loseby 1996; Ottaway 1992). The level of such work is increasing all the time but results are still in their infancy and the non-documentary urban world remains rather shadowy. For Britain and Ireland, the Viking impact on urban growth has of course been revealed by the large-scale excavations at both York and Dublin, highlighting the role of commercial regeneration in stimulating the birth/rebirth of these centres (Edwards 1990: 179–88; Hodges and Hobley 1988). For York, excavations in the Coppergate between 1976 and 1981 yielded remarkable vestiges of the Anglo-Scandinavian period settlement (AD 850–1066), preserved chiefly due to damp ground conditions and limited later intrusions into these deposits. Here a series of tenements was identified running back some 25 metres from the street frontage, with wicker fences as property boundaries. The actual buildings of the early tenth-century town were constructed of upright posts and timbers with wattle between; later in the century these were replaced by houses of post and plank construction. Internally the buildings featured central clay hearths lined with tile set into a beaten earth floor. These were the houses of craftsmen engaged in various activities, notably metalworking, the debris and tools from which were scattered about, with products including dress fittings, weapons and knives. Even if these should properly be called mere cottage industries, these craftsmen were technically highly skilled, producing fine blades, some pattern-welded, designed for long use. Besides metalwork, wooden cups and bowls were being made, bone and antler carving was practised, plus textile working, all perhaps indicative of family industries geared to supplying an expanding urban market. The place-names of York give further clues as to the commercial din of the Anglo-Scandinavian centre, with the '-gate' names deriving from the Old Norse word *gata* meaning street: hence Coppergate, signifying the Street of Wood-turners (not coppersmiths), Jubbergate (Market Street), Skeldergate (Street of the Shieldmakers) and Fishergate (Hall 1984; Ottaway 1992: 146–55).

Despite these varied practical and technical skills, housekeeping did not seem to have figured highly on the lists of domestic priorities for the inhabitants of Anglo-Scandinavian York. The Coppergate excavations found abundant evidence for piles of waste food, bones and other refuse cluttering up backyards, which the house-owners clearly allowed to decompose close to cess pits and wells; human faeces, suitably infested with parasitic worms, were even found on yard surfaces and on some house floors. Interestingly, only a few of these fine medieval sights and smells are on offer to visitors to the Jorvik Centre established over the Coppergate site which recreates this bustling part of the tenth-century township. Noticeably, after 975, the Anglo-Scandinavian Coppergate tenements seem to have been cleared of metalworkers, either in a move to counteract the fire risk or perhaps because of noise pollution, although the level of squalor was not alleviated, and so was presumably seen as acceptable.

Later medieval towns may not have differed much in terms of smell and activity, but there are signs from the thirteenth and fourteenth centuries of greater urban hygiene, seen through the provision of town-tips, the cleaning of roads, and the use of earth-closets; at the same time many industrial activities such as potting and metalworking were sited outside of the towns, although actual trade remained rooted to specific urban quarters. Personal standards obviously varied too and town-dwellers undoubtedly must have often kept a clean house. Indeed, it is the case that the archaeologist is often faced with the debris of households relating to their abandonment phase, when their sites would have swiftly been choked up with the neighbourhood's rubbish – thus it should not always be assumed that medieval townsfolk lived side-by-side with the leftovers of their meals (Carver 1987: 96–100; Platt 1976: 69–72; Schofield and Vince 1994: 99–123; on household goods and dress, see Crowfoot et al. 1992; Egan 1996; on housing forms see Grenville 1997, chapter 6).

Where food waste is suitably stratified, it provides valuable data on diet, as well as on the supply of meat, butchery methods, and animal husbandry (Clark 1989; Grant 1992). As is to be expected, studies indicate that the rich were able to dine on choice cuts supplemented by wild animals, while the poorer townsfolk stuck to sheep and pig. Whilst bones are a common find in both urban and rural contexts, archaeobotanical remains are generally quite restricted and prevent a clear assessment as yet of the range and quantity of non-meat products on offer. Here documentary and artistic sources must be combined with the archaeological evidence of bread ovens, ceramics, amphorae, ridge and furrow, granaries, and so on, to create a more balanced image of medieval diet (Clark et al. 1989; Broberg and Svensson 1987; Schofield and Vince 1994: 189–203). Thus while the range of meat types is a good enough indicator of the ties between town and country and the healthy provisioning of urban markets, archaeology has much untapped potential for the investigation of medieval food and diet (see Chapter 14).

It is possible to argue that Scandinavian trading input of the level recognized at York stimulated rapid urban growth elsewhere in eastern England, and was matched by commercial expansion in late Saxon towns like London and Winchester. Identification of this economic vitality helps explain the early prosperity of Norman rule in England and the swift diffusion of Norman architectural forms. Indeed, in Britain, as across much of Europe, the eleventh century marks a remarkable regeneration of town life, back towards the population levels reached under Rome. The image may be surprising, perhaps, given the relative political disunity within the various kingdoms, empires or caliphates of Europe, North Africa and the East. Urban communes in Italy, for example, appear to have been in near constant conflict under the direction of various noble families, yet these struggles seem to have little impaired the towns' ability for architectural embellishment and innovation. The rise of feudalism may have placed local territorial power in the hands of lords, but although these expressed some of their power in castle building or in moated manors, most of the nobility remained largely town-dwellers, contesting primacy through feud, patronage and even tower-building (Waley 1988). Much like the old Roman aristocracy, the medieval élite possessed country retreats yet always felt the need to exhibit their wealth in an urban context.

New towns in previously non-urbanized northern and eastern Europe appear from excavations to have generally evolved as *Burgstädte*, around fortified royal or noble seats which acted as magnets to traders and craftsmen and the like, many of foreign extraction. Hand-in-hand with this was the Christianization of these kingdoms, with new clergy drawn to the courts and using their influence to reinforce their missionary activities (Brachmann and Herrmann 1991). Here again, the vital role of trade has been highlighted as the prime prompter of urbanization, although generally under the direction of the élite (Hasselmo 1992 for Sweden; Yeoman 1994: 53–71 for Scottish towns or burghs; and see Chapter 16). In many cases the documentary sources suggest that actual, that is written, urban status was only achieved or granted from the twelfth to fourteenth centuries, and yet archaeology has demonstrated fully functioning market settlements with roads and churches in constant evolution from the eleventh century.

In the case of Prague, for example, the foundation of the royal castle belongs to the ninth century as the central place of the emergent Bohemian state. It rapidly attracted a myriad of small dependent village settlements filled with clergy, foreign merchants, craftsmen and farmers and these expanded slowly as suburban style agglomerations or *vici*. Only in the 1230s was much of this sprawl collectively walled and granted the status of town with legal rights, creating the Stare Mesto ('Greater Town'); soon after, a new planned township, the Mala Strana ('Lesser Town') was created on the opposite side of the river through clearing away old housing and roads. Finally, the fourteenth century saw unabated expansion of extramural suburbs, in time leading to the creation of a third urban zone, the New Town, also walled, lying to the south of the Old Town (Hüml 1989). Closely comparable is the rise of royal castles and trading centres at Obuda, Buda and Pest on either side of the Danube in Hungary to form medieval Budapest, and of other western Magyar towns like Szekesfehervar and Esztergom (Gerevich 1990).

The development of the Burgstädte therefore resembles the transition from pre-Roman *oppida* to Roman *civitates*, with a cumulative formalization of the largely commercial suburban quarters. To a large degree the growth of these medieval towns was paralleled by the decline in royal power from the thirteenth century on, though their central place role was generally maintained. The problem is merely one of definition: many *vici* were clearly urban equivalents well before the thirteenth century but the royalty withheld formal granting of an urban charter to these. Without the documentation archaeologists would have little hesitation in viewing the presence of markets, churches, public buildings and roads as indicative of urban status. In many of these regions, the fourteenth and fifteenth centuries are characterized by the extension of the urban form: the creation of royal towns and Burgstädte had generally dictated wider agricultural exploitation and the prosperity of many of the villages thus encouraged brought about the creation of late medieval market centres. Such quasi-urban units are well attested in regions like east-central Hungary and Scandinavia (Broberg 1992; Kubinyi 1990), though as yet they have received little archaeological attention.

Urban populations suffered most from the effects of the Black Death of the late 1340s: the rather primitive character of urban living, revealed at York and adequately described in documentary sources contemporary with the plague (by such as the Italian Boccaccio in his *Decameron*), allowed the pestilence to take a decisive hold and to carry off vast numbers of the population. Mass graves outside of a few towns, as at the Royal Mint site in London, give suitable visual confirmation of the written images, although the full impact of the plague is not easy to trace otherwise archaeologically within the towns (Hawkins 1990; Platt 1996). There is a clear tail-off in building activity in and after this period, and even beforehand too, suggesting that the plague seriously aggravated an already ailing medieval world. Unlike settlement in the countryside, however, the urban fabric was by then so well established that the devastations of the Black Death could in no way cancel out town life. Urban populations had long suffered from plague, food shortages and fire – and all would continue to do so, even after the late Middle Ages.

PIETY AND POWER IN MEDIEVAL RELIGION

The rise of the feudal élite created notable changes also in the religious sphere. In the post-Roman or Dark Age world, religion had become central to the organization and control of both state and society, as witnessed in the secular authority exercised by the Pope in Rome and in the extensive landed wealth of abbeys such as Farfa, San Vincenzo and Monte Cassino in central Italy (Hodges 1993; 1995: 138–75). After AD 1000, however, seigneurial powers prompted a redistribution of territorial control, though this did not force the Church into a secondary role, since Christianity formed an essential ingredient of daily life and its structures remained the principal focus of patronage. The strength of the Church is nowhere better illustrated than in the rapid spread of monasticism, prompted first by the revitalization of Benedictine monasticism at Cluny in the early tenth century and then by the subsequent emergence of various assorted daughter and breakaway rules such as the Cistercians and Augustinians, all of which contributed to the blossoming of Romanesque architecture (Chadwick and Evans 1987: 52–74; Lawrence 1984). Building activity is attested across most of Europe, creating new village and town churches or creating sizeable rebuilds of older edifices. Scale is everywhere impressive, contrasting powerfully with the lacklustre and tiny early medieval churches. Belltowers, portals, murals and sculpture are common survivors of these medieval centuries.

The most striking feature of medieval religion – bar the multinational crusades against eastern infidels and the inquisitional uprooting of heresies – is indeed the growth of monasticism. Monastic fervour is duly attested in the extension across Europe of grandiose and lesser structures, each stamping a powerful mark on both the urban and rural landscape. Church power was now scattered amongst a whole number of monastic units to which the local nobility all contributed. The castle-building élite frequently sought to register their piety through founding monastic seats and donating rich offspring. For France alone, it has been estimated that between AD 1098 and 1600 up to 400 Cistercian houses were founded; for England more than a thousand monasteries of all sizes and denominations are known before the dissolution of 1536–40. The towering naves and broad chapter houses certainly reflect the popularity of the medieval monastic ideal and its architectural and financial vitality. Inbred greed and state jealousies, however, combined with internal reform movements, eventually brought monastic power to a close, to be replaced by mendicants and friars, free from architectural expressions. Various abbeys of course still survive in mutated form, but only their dimensions fully reveal the strength of the medieval monastic world (Coppack 1990; Greene 1992).

Elements at least of the church and cloisters of many of these monasteries remain visible today to give a ready image of the central portion of the monastic plan; these buildings have long been the focus of architectural and archaeological interest (Fig. 26.5). Extant remains allow for some determination of the general structural sequence, whether in terms of basic plan or of architectural competence, but excavation helps to reveal more closely the chronological and physical evolution of these sites and has recently begun to extend investigations to cover the whole area of the monastic precinct and beyond, to study elements such as mills, tileries and granges, structures which at best are merely listed in inventories. Details of water management, storage facilities and industrial production are now forthcoming for monasteries like Norton Priory in Cheshire or Rievaulx Abbey in North Yorkshire (Fig. 26.6), highlighting the highly self-sufficient character of these establishments (Coppack 1990: 100–28; Greene 1992: 109–58). These were not all inward-looking, however, for they did produce an industrial surplus and duly assisted in the secular

Figure 26.5 Air photograph of West Dereham Abbey, Norfolk: this provides a clear indication of the extent of both the claustral complex and the monastic precinct. Traces are evident of various of the outer structures and in particular the gate and roadway leading to the church. Photograph: D. Edwards reproduced with permission of the Norfolk Museums Service Air Photographic Unit.

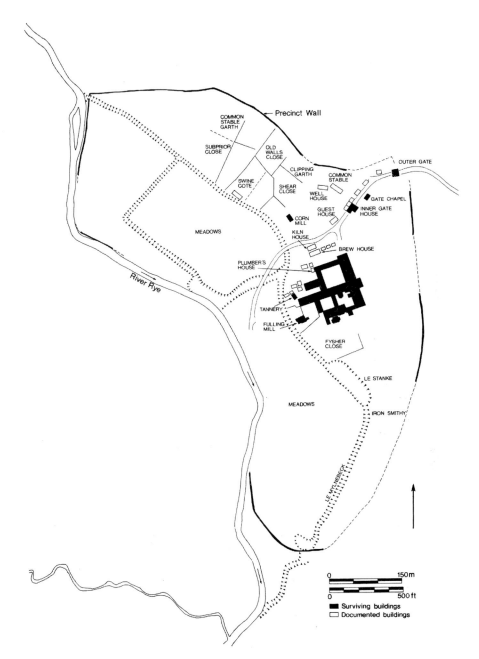

Figure 26.6 Plan of Rievaulx Abbey, identifying structures beyond the claustral confines, as interpreted from sixteenth-century documentation, earthwork analysis and air photographs. © English Heritage. Source: Coppack 1990.

economy. Landscape archaeology meanwhile shows the varied impact monasteries had with time on the countryside: whole village communities could be ejected to make way for monastic granges and sheep farms; yet elsewhere monastic growth created a need for wider rural exploitation to feed the monks and lay brothers and so meant the formation of new villages. Monasteries were also foci for fairs and markets and these in some cases became established settlements, in effect urbanizing the monastery, as in the case of Shrewsbury (Greene 1992: 173–77).

Other unsuspected features may emerge from the excavation of these and other religious sites: for example in France and Italy many monasteries have been shown to overlie Roman villas, suggestive of continuity of activity, an early Christian precursor, or at least a survival of the villa ruins and their availability for reuse or quarrying (Hodges 1995: 131–37; Percival 1981: 183–99). In the case of parish churches in Britain or early Slavic churches in eastern Europe, excavation alone may reveal primary timber-built cult edifices, with their successive phases of enlargement, rebuilding in stone and embellishment. Church archaeology is indeed becoming an important component of settlement research; churches are in many ways a mirror to their dependent settlements and, as stone-built structures, are often our sole extant architectural guide to the medieval years. By and large, there-fore, settlement vitality is reflected in the fabric of the church, in its decoration and in the tombs that surround or lie within it (Morris 1989; Rodwell 1989). A number of cemeteries have accordingly also seen excavation: even if medieval burials lack the array of informative grave-goods typical of so many 'Dark Age' cultures such as the Franks and Vikings, and are often conspicuous for their plainness, none the less the growing skills of archaeological science and palaeopathological study are begin-ning to provide fascinating new data regarding medieval monastic as well as urban and rural populations through analysis of diet and disease. The detailed skeletal analysis undertaken for the medieval cemeteries in York at St Helen-on-the-Walls, Fishergate, and in particular Jewbury (Fig. 26.7) are examples of this valuable new direction of research (Dawes and Magilton 1980; Lilley *et al.* 1994; Stroud and Kemp 1993). This, combined with the renewed use of tombstones and grave-markers from the later Middle Ages, furthermore allows for preliminary compari-son of the diets of different social groupings. Now at last it may be possible to see how well monks, merchants and ordinary consumers looked after their stomachs.

TECHNOLOGY, TRADE AND TRANSPORT IN THE MIDDLE AGES

Monasteries were, in the Middle Ages, important production centres and, as noted above (p. 1059), accordingly attracted fairs for distribution or exchange of their manufactures with the secular world. Manufactures require technology, and money for this largely came from lordly patronage, though it would be dangerous to

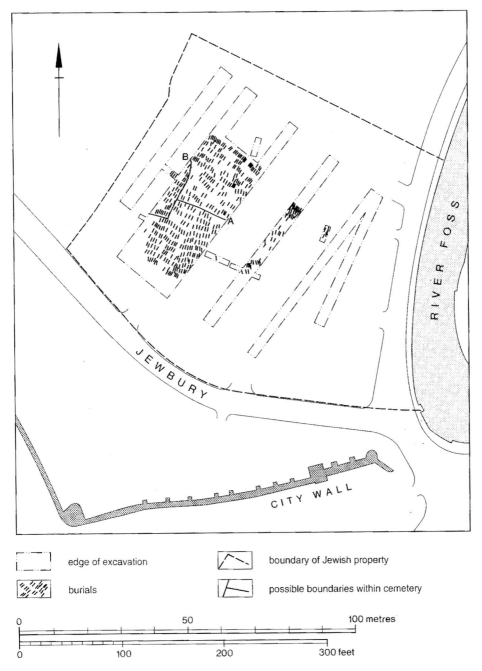

Figure 26.7 Location and layout of the later twelfth- and thirteenth-century Jewish cemetery at Jewbury, York; the plan shows the documented boundaries of Jewish property and possible boundaries (marked A and B) within the graveyard itself. © The York Archaeological Trust for Excavation and Research Ltd. Source: Lilley *et al.* 1994.

overstress this relationship. Indeed, many elements of medieval technology – windmills, dams, metalworking, glazing – have too often been viewed as inventions which produced dramatic social changes across Europe (White 1962). Partly this belief stems simply from the greater availability of written documents after AD 1100 recording fully for the first time new social structures, whether gentry with manors and mills or knights with spurs, and partly this belief is due to a lack of adequate archaeological scrutiny. Many aspects of medieval technology can now instead be shown to have clear antique roots, generally Roman, and these by and large appear to have persisted, if at a reduced level of availability, through the 'Dark Ages'. Social evolution may have been the spur for revival or rather expansion of this technology: wider trading activity created trading emporia, each requiring greater economic supply mechanisms; that is, more land needed to be ploughed. Elements of the 'new' technology may appear to have been the preserve of the élite (for instance, with mills far better attested alongside manor sites than elsewhere), but this seems more to represent an artificial bias in the sources, both historical and archaeological. As excavations expand to explore more rural sites, technology gains a more even distribution across the human landscape.

It is the case that monastic archives relating to the lands of abbeys such as Farfa and San Vincenzo in central Italy or secular documents such as the Domesday Book of 1086 readily attest the widespread use of watermills and windmills in the early and full medieval landscape of Europe. In the case of Domesday, over 6,000 mills are noted in England, but this must certainly imply that mill construction was an ancient survival rather than, as has too often been assumed, a Norman introduction (Crossley 1981; Holt 1988). These devices gave a degree of productive stability to the farms and villages, and expansion of these settlements in turn signals the effectiveness of farming created by such mills. The massed ranks of windmills in the Don Quixote country of central Spain are picturesque symbols of former rolling fields of grain, with produce largely destined for the blossoming urban centres (Fig. 26.8). Their fate has varied: in some parts of Spain many have been revamped as tourist attractions, whereas in others only earthen platforms survive; the situation is the same in Greece, in particular on its islands. Careful manipulation of water resources is shown also in the presence of fishponds in the rural and monastic landscape, demonstrating a desire for variety in diet, or at least an availability of fish for religious festivals. Again here a survival of or readaptation from antique models is argued, if little investigated (Aston 1988; Grant 1992; Greene 1992: 124–28).

In terms of pottery and metalworking, production had resumed the industrial levels and complexities of the Roman era by the thirteenth century, with the proliferation of kilns and furnaces readily testifying to the wide demand for these material goods in both urban and rural contexts (Crossley 1981; McCarthy and Brooks 1988). The emphasis appears to have been, as under Rome, on 'on-site'

Figure 26.8 The Don Quixote windmills at Campo de Criptana, central Spain; now white-washed and semi-functional for tourist appeal, the location, height, and narrow windows of these windmills may betray a former defensive role. Photograph: N. Christie.

production in the immediate environs of clay and ore sources. Smaller-scale premises persisted within the towns, but here there was now clear appreciation of the fire risks; less hazardous operations like fulling, dying and cloth-making, meanwhile, remained fully accommodated within the urban and suburban environment. Archaeology allows for full recognition of the structural processes of these varied crafts, otherwise only cursorily described in contemporary documents (Schofield and Vince 1994: 98–127). Hence for potteries, the distribution of the puddling pits, drying sheds and dump sites has come under study, whilst working kilns have been reproduced to help assess the technology involved. For the thirteenth-century village of Lyveden in Northamptonshire, excavations of a group of potting tenements revealed that the potters were not full-time in their profession but rather had periodic bouts of agricultural work, baking, or smithing; in one phase one kiln was used by two potters, each identified by their respective waster dumps. All stages of pottery production occurred within the same tenement, although none of these activities were static, since the site of the kiln and the storage points shifted fairly frequently even within one workshop (McCarthy and Brooks 1988: 74–76).

Potters seem to have kept pace with fashion also, as in the adoption of glaze in the firing process, for both decoration and functional sealing. Close study of the waster heaps from fifteenth- to seventeenth-century kiln sites in Halifax, however, have revealed something of the human cost of this pace of change: whereas early discarded glazed material was of good quality with consistent forms, a progressive deterioration could be witnessed, to the degree that misfirings and poor vessel forms became frequent. It is argued that the use of raw lead in the glazing process effectively curtailed a potter's working life to around fifteen years maximum (Moorhouse 1986: 29). Notable also is the fact that experimental firings have shown that failed pots would have been a common feature of medieval pottery production and that inadequate preparation of the clay for firing might have resulted in exploding pots. With lead poisoning and terracotta bombs abounding, it is understandable why potters tended to break off for an agricultural season and for potteries to be shifted outside of towns.

A blossoming of local and regional manufacturing denotes a blossoming of production and trade on a much wider setting. The Middle Ages mark an expanding of horizons, recreating a semblance, though not a unified semblance, of the Roman imperial trading economy. The rise of the powerful Pisan and Venetian trading empires is one principal event signalling the regeneration of Mediterranean and east–west trade in the eleventh and twelfth centuries, as reflected in new ship technology, developing trade manufactures, the transmission of ideas, and of course the wanderlust of the Crusaders, who made their special contribution to stimulation of art and architecture by their despoliation and dispersal of various treasures of Constantinople (Holmes 1988: 223–34; Lewis and Runyan 1990: 64–78). The Italian trading despots were based on amazingly small city units, with little or no agricultural back-up, most apparent in the hemmed-in port of Amalfi and the watery wastes around Venice. It was chiefly this lack which led ultimately to their decline, as greater land-based units took also to the sea and challenged Italian dominance: Spanish, Portuguese, French and Dutch boats and manpower opened the seas up again to all and sundry and of course led in time to such an intensity of trading rivalry that required the discovery of new worlds and new markets (Braudel 1992: 214–24, 430–58).

The rapid development in recent decades of underwater archaeology has provided numerous opportunities to extend our knowledge of the form and workings of these vessels, whether traders or men-of-war. These include the eleventh-century Serçe Limani ship, located off the south-western coast of Turkey, and nicknamed the 'Glass wreck' because of its cargo of over three tons of waste glass plus eighty complete, saleable products. Finds from this ostensibly Arab wreck highlight the vital role of the merchant in the Mediterranean economy in this politically turbulent era: whilst the glass was of Islamic manufacture and the anchor had an Arabic inscription, there were also Byzantine coins and lamps, plus amphorae and net weights inscribed with Greek graffiti and Christian symbols. The ship perhaps was carrying Greek-speaking passengers and was certainly carrying goods drawn from Byzantine-held ports. The crew meanwhile were equipped with swords, lances and javelins, showing that cross-cultural trade needed to be defended (Throckmorton 1987: 88–96). The mobility of such cargoes is notable: the Torre Civica, adjoining the cathedral at Pavia in central-north Italy, before its collapse in 1989, was decorated with twenty-nine glazed bowls or *bacini* datable to the first half of the eleventh century, all Islamic manufactures, and mainly deriving from Fatimid Egypt and Tunisia. Many Italian centres like Pisa, Noli (Fig. 26.9) and Pomposa brightened their brick-built religious architecture with these brightly coloured vessels, unworried by their non-Christian origin (Blake and Aguzzi 1990); and in Sicily, Norman fusion with Arabs and pre-existing Greek cultures fashioned stunning examples of art and architecture.

The early medieval centuries have been shown to have marked the transition to frame-first boat construction from the slower, if longer-lasting, shell-first boat types of classical Antiquity. A virtual industrialization of ship-building developed, with concomitant advances in ship design, such as in the adoption of stern rudders

Figure 26.9 The Romanesque (eleventh-century) church of San Paragorio, Noli, on the Italian riviera, overlying a part-excavated Byzantine (sixth century) and early medieval complex; the top of the apse displays a number of imported Islamic *bacini*. The eleventh century marked a major rebuilding and expansion of many church and monastic sites across Italy and Europe. Photograph: N. Christie.

and triple-masted rigs by the fourteenth and fifteenth centuries. For some time boats remained relatively small in size: on the Atlantic shores the cog emerged as an established boat type, with high forward and aft ends and a flat base, enabling it still to be drawn up on land; here the width generally exceeded the length, giving the cog a sturdy, box-like image (Fig. 26.10). From the cog developed ever-larger vessels, most notably the carrack, which rapidly gained supremacy in the Mediterranean, providing heavy duty trading vessels of capacities up to 1,000 tons, carrying salt, grain and timber; Christopher Columbus's flagship in 1492, the *Santa Maria*, was a small carrack. A western rival was the caravel, a multiple-masted ship of likely Islamic design, successfully employed by the Portuguese in the fifteenth century in the Atlantic and as far afield as western Africa; Columbus also employed two such caravels in his journey west. The vitality of this far-flung trade is duly reflected in the creation of warfleets, militarized versions of the cogs and carracks, replacing the traditional galleys of the old Italian republics: excavated remains plus contemporary depictions on seals and in paintings reveal deep-draught boats, with crenellated towers or castleworks erected over both stern and stem and with fighting tops at the masthead (Hutchinson 1995; Lewis and Runyan 1985; Throckmorton 1987: 134–47). By the mid-sixteenth century huge vessels such as the *Mary Rose* acted as

Figure 26.10 A seal from Winchelsea, England. © The National Maritime Museum, Greenwich, London.

flagships to these powerful fleets: the *Mary Rose* herself was equipped with an assortment of guns ranged from gunports in her hull, some set fatally close to the waterline. Despite the ever-increasing numbers of guns, archers remained useful elements on board these vessels, as shown by the *Mary Rose*'s stock of 250 longbows and 4,000 arrows. The new artilleries played vital roles in the capture of Muslim Granada in 1492 and even earlier in the Ottoman capture of Constantinople in 1453, but served more to create a political and maritime technological stalemate between West and East in the Mediterranean. The stalemate did more than anything to stimulate the drive outward in search of the New Worlds.

The introduction and development of gunpowder and artillery on the land had equally far-reaching consequences. To counteract the employment of these new vehicles of war, the castle architects in the fourteenth and fifteenth centuries responded by angling circuit and tower walls, by building in brick, and by providing broad platformed bastions for mounting artillery upon. However, the relative lack of manoeuvrability of these defensive measures meant that the days of the 'military' castle were numbered – indeed, castles were well in decline as fortifications from the fourteenth century, reflecting the fact that warfare tended to be pursued more in open battle than in the siege and defence of strongholds (Thompson 1987: 32–42, 112–16). None the less, urban fortifications persisted and evolved in continental Europe, with the elaborate 4-kilometre long, early sixteenth-century defences at Lucca in Italy amongst the most stunning survivals of new-wave heavily bastioned and moated anti-artillery compounds. Such 'Italian style' defences, as instigated by Machiavelli in 1526, dictated urban fortifications into the late seventeenth century (Parker 1995: 106–17). This trend did not totally negate the need for independent military fortifications: many harbours or ports could be well defended by the provision of powerfully munitioned blocktowers or the like – the twin harbours at Cartagena on the south-eastern coast of Spain are defended by five such fortlets. But more significantly this transition marked another end: a decline in the patronage of and role of rural castles and a concomitant shrinkage in the associated villages. Many upland villages persisted, dwindling only slowly as settlers budded off to found new villages or select open farmsteads. The decline was slow but constant, creating a dismembering and defeudalization of the old medieval landscape (Fig. 26.11).

CONCLUSION

The Middle Ages in Europe terminated with neither a traumatic collapse nor a conquest of states, nor even with an economic explosion: trade, technology and settlement had been on an upward curve since *c.* AD 1000 and these maintained themselves beyond the thirteenth- and fourteenth-century crises to stand

Figure 26.11 Kirby Muxloe castle/fortified manor in north-west Leicestershire: dating to *c*. 1480, this unfinished residence, built for Lord Hastings, marks the transition from defensive stronghold to aristocratic retreat and status marker, with moat and battlements denoting the persistence of threats – represented also in Lord Hastings' own beheading! Photograph: N. Christie.

reinforced by the end of the fifteenth century. The powerful stimulus of trade in the early medieval period had laid the foundations for this regeneration, but much time was needed to recall the far-flung net and quality of Rome. None the less, vitality is everywhere reflected in medieval society, religion and economy in all their material manifestations, whether castles, churches, or rubbish pits. Yet it is true to say that these manifestations of the medieval past are only now being properly subjected to archaeological scrutiny, and thereby have only just begun to embellish and elaborate upon the documentary image that has for so long held sway. Human and animal debris are generating many words, words largely omitted from the records of the medieval élite. The forthcoming dialogue between archaeology and history will be vital in reinterpreting the structures and fabric of the medieval world.

REFERENCES

Aberg, F. (ed.) (1978) *Medieval Moated Sites*, Research Report 17, London: Council for British Archaeology.

Astill, G. and Grant, A. (eds) (1992) *The Countryside of Medieval England*, Oxford: Basil Blackwell.

Aston, M. (1985) *Interpreting the Landscape. Landscape Archaeology in Local Studies*, London: Batsford.

Aston, M. (ed.) (1988) *Medieval Fish, Fisheries and Fishponds in England*, Oxford: British Archaeological Reports, British Series 182.

Aston, M., Austin, D. and Dyer, C. (eds) (1989) *The Rural Settlements of Medieval England*, Oxford: Basil Blackwell.

Austin, D. (1990) 'The "proper study" of medieval archaeology', in D. Austin and L. Alcock (eds) *From the Baltic to the Black Sea. Studies in Medieval Archaeology*, London: Unwin Hyman, One World Archaeology 18: 9–42.

Austin, D. and Alcock, L. (eds) (1990) *From the Baltic to the Black Sea. Studies in Medieval Archaeology*, London: Unwin Hyman, One World Archaeology 18.

Austin, D. and Thomas, J. (1990) 'The "proper study" of medieval archaeology: a case study', in D. Austin and L. Alcock (eds) *From the Baltic to the Black Sea. Studies in Medieval Archaeology*, London: Unwin Hyman, One World Archaeology 18: 43–78.

Barker, G. and Grant, A. (eds) (1991) 'Ancient and modern pastoralism in central Italy: an interdisciplinary study in the Cicolano mountains', *Papers of the British School at Rome* 59: 15–88.

Barley, M. W. (ed.) (1977) *European Towns: Their Early History and Archaeology*. London: Academic Press for the Council for British Archaeology.

Bartlett, R. (1993) *The Making of Europe. Conquest, Colonization and Cultural Change, 950–1350*, London and New York: Book Club Associates.

Beresford, M. and Hurst, J. (1990) *Wharram Percy Deserted Medieval Village*, London: Batsford/English Heritage.

Blake, H. and Aguzzi, F. (1990) 'Eleventh century Islamic pottery at Pavia, north Italy: the Torre Civica *bacini*', *Accordia Research Papers*, 1: 95–152.

Bois, G. (1992) *The Transformation of the Year One Thousand. The Village of Lournand from Antiquity to Feudalism*, Manchester: Manchester University Press.

Brachmann, H. and Herrmann, J. (eds) (1991) *Frühgeschichte der europaischen Stadt. Voraussetzungen und Grundlagen*, Berlin.

Braudel, F. (1992) *The Mediterranean and the Mediterranean World in the Age of Philip II*, London and New York: Book Club Associates (translated from 2nd revised edition 1966).

Broberg, B. (1992) 'The late medieval towns of Sweden – an important research resource', in L. Ersgard, M. Holmstrom and K. Lamm (eds) *Rescue and Research. Reflections of Society in Sweden, 700–1700 AD*, Stockholm: Riksantikvarieambetet: 56–77.

Broberg, A. and Svensson, K. (1987) *Urban and Rural Consumption Patterns in Eastern Central Sweden, A.D. 1000–1700. Theoretical Approaches to Artefacts, Settlement and Society*, Oxford: British Archaeological Reports, International Series 366.

Butlin, R. A. (1933) *Historical Geography Through the Gates of Space and Time*, London and New York: Edward Arnold.

Cantor, N. F. (1991) *Inventing the Middle Ages. The Lives, Works and Ideas of the Great Medievalists of the Twentieth Century*, New York: W. Morrow.

Carver, M. O. H. (1987) *Underneath English Towns*, London: Batsford.

Carver, M. O. H. (1993) *Arguments in Stone. Archaeological Research and the European Town in the First Millennium*, Oxford: Oxbow, Oxbow Monograph 29.

Chadwick, H. and Evans, G. (1987) *Atlas of the Christian Church*, London: Macmillan.

Champion, T. C. (1990) 'Medieval archaeology and the tyranny of the historical record', in D. Austin and L. Alcock (eds) *From the Baltic to the Black Sea. Studies in Medieval Archaeology*, London: Unwin Hyman, One World Archaeology 18: 79–95.

Chapelot, J. and Fossier, R. (1985) *The Village and House in the Middle Ages*, London: Batsford.

Cherry, J. (1986) 'Technology, towns, castles and churches, A.D. 1100–1600', in I. Longworth and J. Cherry (eds) *Archaeology in Britain since 1945*, London: British Museum: 161–96.

Christie, N. and Loseby, S. (eds) (1996) *Towns in Transition. Urban Evolution in Late Antiquity and the Early Middle Ages*, London: Scolar Press.

Clark, G. (1989) 'Animals and animal products in medieval Italy: a discussion of archaeological and historical methodology', *Papers of the British School at Rome* 57: 152–71.

Clark, G., Costantini, L., Finetti, A., Giorgi, J., Jones, A., Reese, D., Sutherland, S. and Whitehouse, D. (1989) 'The food refuse of an affluent urban household in the late fourteenth century: faunal and botanical remains from the Palazzo Vitelleschi, Tarquinia (Viterbo)', *Papers of the British School at Rome* 57: 200–321.

Clarke, H. (1984) *The Archaeology of Medieval England*, London: British Museum.

Coppack, G. (1990) *Abbeys and Priories*, London: Batsford/English Heritage.

Crossley, D. (ed.) (1981) *Medieval Industry*, Research Report 40, London: Council for British Archaeology.

Crowfoot, E., Pritchard, F. and Staniland, K. (1992) *Textiles and Clothing, c. 1150–c. 1450*, London: HMSO, Medieval Finds from Excavations in London 4.

Dawes, J. and Magilton, J. (1980) *The Cemetery of St. Helen-on-the-Walls, Aldwark*, York: York Archaeological Trust, The Archaeology of York, The Medieval Cemeteries, vol. 12, and London: Council for British Archaeology.

Dodgshon, R. and Butlin, R. (eds) (1990) *An Historical Geography of England and Wales*, London: Academic Press.

Edwards, N. (1990) *The Archaeology of Early Medieval Ireland*, London: Batsford.

Egan, G. (1996) *The Medieval Household: Daily Living, c. 1150–c. 1450*, Medieval Finds from Excavations in London 6, London: HMSO.

Ersgard, L., Holmstrom, M. and Lamm, K. (eds) (1992) *Rescue and Research. Reflections of Society in Sweden, 700–1700 AD*, Stockholm: Riksantikvarieambetet.

Fehring, G. P. (1991) *The Archaeology of Medieval Germany. An Introduction* (translated by R. Samson), London: Routledge.

Francovich, R. (ed.) (1987) *Archeologia e Storia del Medioevo Italiano*, Rome: Nuova Italia Scientifica.

Francovich, R. and Hodges, R. (1989) 'Archeologia e storia del villaggio fortificato di Montarrenti (SI): Un caso o un modello?', *Archeologia Medievale* 16: 15–38.

Gerevich, L. (1990) 'The rise of Hungarian towns along the Danube', in L. Gerevich (ed.) *Towns in Medieval Hungary*, Budapest: Akademiai Kiado: 26–50.

Gerevich, L. (ed.) (1990) *Towns in Medieval Hungary*, Budapest: Akademiai Kiado.

Grant, A. (1992) 'Animal resources', in G. Astill and A. Grant (eds) *The Countryside of Medieval England*, Oxford: Basil Blackwell: 149–87.

Greene, J. P. (1989) *Norton Priory: The Archaeology of a Medieval Religious House*, Cambridge : Cambridge University Press.

Greene, J. P. (1992) *Medieval Monasteries*, London: Leicester University Press.

Grenville, J. (1997) *Medieval Housing*, London: Leicester University Press.

Hall, R. (1984) *The Viking Dig*, London: Bodley Head.

Hasselmo, M. (1992) 'From early medieval central-places to high medieval towns – Urbanisation in Sweden from the end of the 10th century to *c.* 1200', in L. Ersgard, M. Holmstrom and K. Lamm (eds) *Rescue and Research. Reflections of Society in Sweden, 700–1700 AD*, Stockholm: Riksantikvarieambetet: 32–55.

Hawkins, D. (1990) 'Black Death cemeteries of 1348', *Antiquity* 64: 637–42.

Higham, R. and Barker, P. (1992) *Timber Castles*, London: Batsford.

Hodges, R. (1991) *Wall-to-Wall History. The Story of Roystone Grange*, London: Duckworth.

Hodges, R. (ed.) (1993) *San Vincenzo al Volturno 1*, London: British School at Rome, Archaeological Monographs 7.

Hodges, R. (ed.) (1995) *San Vincenzo al Volturno 2*, London: British School at Rome, Archaeological Monographs 9.

Hodges, R. and Hobley, B. (eds) (1988) *The Rebirth of Towns in the West, AD 700–1050*, London: Council for British Archaeology, Research Report 68.

Holmes, G. (ed.) (1988) *The Oxford Illustrated History of Medieval Europe*, Oxford: Oxford University Press.

Holt, R. (1988) *The Mills of Medieval England*, Oxford: Basil Blackwell.

Hoskins, W. G. ([1955]1977) *The Making of the English Landscape*, London: Hodder and Stoughton.

Hüml, V. (1989) 'Research in Prague – a historical and archaeological view of the development of Prague from the 9th century to the middle of the 14th century', in D. Austin and L. Alcock (eds) *From the Baltic to the Black Sea. Studies in Medieval Archaeology*, London: Unwin Hyman, One World Archaeology 18: 267–84.

Hurst, J. (1986) 'The medieval countryside', in I. Longworth and J. Cherry (eds) *Archaeology in Britain since 1945*, London: British Museum: 197–236.

Hutchinson, G. (1995) *Medieval Ships and Shipping*, London: Leicester University Press.

Kenyon, J. R. (1990) *Medieval Fortifications*, London: Leicester University Press.

Kubinyi, A. (1990) 'Urbanisation in the east-central part of medieval Hungary', in L. Gerevich (ed.) *Towns in Medieval Hungary*, Budapest: Akademiai Kiado: 103–49.

Lawrence, C. (1984) *Medieval Monasticism. Forms of Religious Life in Western Europe in the Middle Ages*, London: Longman.

Le Goff, J. (1988) *Medieval Civilization, 400–1500*, Oxford: Basil Blackwell.

Le Roy Ladurie, E. (1980) *Montaillou. Cathars and Catholics in a French Village, 1294–1324*, Harmondsworth: Penguin.

Lewis, A. R. and Runyan, T. J. (1985) *European Naval and Maritime History, 300–1500*, Bloomington: Indiana University Press.

Lilley, J., Stroud, G., Brothwell, D. and Williamson, M. (1994) *The Jewish Burial Ground at Jewbury*, York: York Archaeological Trust, The Archaeology of York, The Medieval Cemeteries, vol. 12, and London: Council for British Archaeology.

Longworth, I. and Cherry, J. (eds) (1986) *Archaeology in Britain since 1945*, London: British Museum.

McCarthy, M. and Brooks, C. (1988) *Medieval Pottery in Britain, 700–1600*, London: Leicester University Press.

McKitterick, R. (ed.) (1996) *The New Cambridge Medieval History. Volume 2: c. 700–c. 900*, London: Cambridge University Press.

McNeill, T. (1991) *Castles*, London: Batsford/English Heritage.

Mannoni, T., Cabona, D. and Ferrando, I. (1988) 'Archeologia globale del territorio. Metodi e risultati di una nuova strategia della ricerca in Liguria', in G. Noyé (ed.) *Structures de l'Habitat et Occupation du Sol dans le Pays Méditerranéens*, Rome: École Française de Rome, Collections de l'École Française de Rome 105: 43–58.

Moorhouse, S. (1986) 'A note on the terminology of pottery making sites', *Medieval Ceramics* 11: 25–30.

Moreland, J. (1991) 'Method and theory in medieval archaeology in the 1990s', *Archeologia Medievale* 18: 7–42.

Morgan, D. (1986) *The Mongols*, Oxford: Basil Blackwell.

Morris, R. (1989) *Churches in the Landscape*, London: Dent.

Noyé, G. (ed.) (1988) *Structures de l'Habitat et Occupation du Sol dans le Pays Méditerranéens: les Méthodes et l'Apport de l'Archéologie Extensive*, Rome: École Française de Rome, Collections de l'École Française de Rome 105.

Origo, I. (1963) *The Merchant of Prato*, Harmondsworth: Penguin.

Ottaway, P. (1992) *Archaeology in British Towns. From the Emperor Claudius to the Black Death*, London: Routledge.

Parker, G. (ed.) (1995) *The Cambridge Illustrated History of Warfare*, Cambridge: Cambridge University Press.

Percival, J. (1981) *The Roman Villa*, London: Batsford.

Pirenne, H. (1925) *Medieval Cities. Their Origins and the Revival of Trade*, Princeton: Princeton University Press.

Platt, C. (1976) *The English Medieval Town*, London: Secker and Warburg.

Platt, C. (1978) *Medieval England*, London: Routledge.

Platt, C. (1984) *Medieval Britain from the Air*, London: George Philip.

Platt, C. (1996) *King Death: The Black Death and its Aftermath in Late Medieval England*, London: University College London Press.

Rackham, O. (1986) *The History of the Countryside*, London: Dent.

Reynolds, S. (1994) *Fiefs and Vassals. The Medieval Evidence Reinterpreted*, Oxford: Oxford University Press.

Riley-Smith, J. (1991) *The Atlas of the Crusades*, London: Times Books.

Ritchie, A. (1993) *Viking Scotland*, London: Historic Scotland/Batsford.

Rodwell, W. (1989) *Church Archaeology*, London: Batsford/English Heritage.

Rosener, W. (1992) *Peasants in the Middle Ages*, Cambridge: Polity Press.

Saul, N. (ed.) (1997) *The Oxford Illustrated History of Medieval England*, Oxford: Oxford University Press.

Saunders, A. (1980) 'Lydford Castle, Devon', *Medieval Archaeology* 24: 123–86.

Schofield, J. and Vince, A. (1994) *Medieval Towns*, London: Leicester University Press.

Stroud, G. and Kemp, R. (1993) *Cemeteries of St. Andrew, Fishergate*, York: York Archaeological Trust, The Archaeology of York, The Medieval Cemeteries, vol. 12, and London: Council for British Archaeology.

Taylor, C. C. (1992) 'Medieval rural settlement: changing perceptions', *Landscape History* 14: 5–17.

Thompson, M. (1987) *The Decline of the Castle*, Cambridge: Cambridge University Press.

Throckmorton, P. (ed.) (1987) *History from the Sea. Shipwrecks and Archaeology*, London: Mitchell Beazley.

Unger, R. (1980) *The Ship in the Medieval Economy*, London: Croom Helm.

Waley, D. (1988) *The Italian City-Republics* (3rd edition), London: Longman.

White, L. (1962) *Medieval Technology and Social Change*, Oxford: Oxford University Press.

Whitton, D. (1988) 'The society of northern Europe in the High Middle Ages, 900–1200', in G. Holmes (ed.) *The Oxford Illustrated History of Medieval Europe*, Oxford: Oxford University Press: 115–74.

Wickham, C. (1987) 'Castelli ed incastellamento nell'Italia centrale: la problematica storica', in R. Francovich (ed.) *Archeologia e Storia del Medioevo Italiano*, Rome: Nuova Italia Scientifica: 83–96.

Yeoman, P. (1994) *Medieval Scotland*, London: Historic Scotland/Batsford.

Ziegler, P. ([1969]1996) *The Black Death*, London: Penguin.

SELECT BIBLIOGRAPHY

A mere taster of the range of historical documentation available from the tenth century AD is offered by P. Geary (ed.), *Readings in Medieval History* (Ontario: Broadview, 1989). A bibliographical lead-in to the medieval world is offered by E. Crosby, C. Bishko and R. Kellogg, *Medieval Studies. A Bibliographical Guide* (New York and London: Garland, 1983), though its 'Archaeology' section (pp. 953–59) is noticeably minimal and out of date. Of recent historical surveys, that by Holmes (1988) is well-illustrated, and it makes some use of data from archaeological excavations; Le Goff (1988) offers a full overview; and key summaries are now offered in Vol. II (950–1250) and Vol. III (1250–1520) of the *Cambridge Illustrated History of the Middle Ages* edited by R. Fossier (Cambridge: Cambridge University Press, 1996, 1997). Austin and Alcock (1990) provide up-to-date discussions on the nature of medieval archaeology and a series of summary papers addressing questions of state formation, and urban and rural development, chiefly in the regions of central and eastern Europe, but with relevance for much of Europe. Clarke (1984) offers an ideal introduction to the broader themes of medieval archaeology in both town and country and it is useful to compare this with Fehring (1991) on Germany, where the emphasis is strongly on the early medieval centuries and the study of graves and castles; Saul (1997) provides a more recent survey of medieval England. A useful summary for medieval Scandinavia is provided by Ersgard *et al.* (1992). For medieval villages in England, Beresford and Hurst (1990) illuminate the range of material data to be derived from detailed archaeological study of a single rural site. The *Annual Reports* of the Medieval Settlement Research Group provide valuable summaries on current surveys and excavations throughout Britain and abroad. Detailed reports on excavations of sites, cemeteries and churches, on small finds and other aspects of medieval material culture are published in many specialist academic journals, including *Medieval Archaeology* (Britain), *Archéologie Medievale* (France), and *Archeologia Medievale* (Italy). A much wider range of journals exists, such as *Early Medieval Europe*, *Journal of Medieval History*, and *Past and Present*, for studies on medieval history and art history. For Britain, bodies such as English Heritage and Historic Scotland are publishing a series of excellent and wide-ranging site-, period- or theme-oriented studies (for example, Coppack 1990 and Yeoman 1994) which provide well-illustrated introductions; it is hoped that other European countries will aim for similar well-researched but accessible treatments of their medieval archaeology.

27

ARCHAEOLOGY AND ISLAM

Alastair Northedge

INTRODUCTION

The Middle East in medieval times is normally connected with Islam, which appeared from the time of the first revelation of the Qur'an to the Prophet Muhammad about AD 610 at Mecca in Arabia (Fig. 27.1). In addition to his qualities as a prophet, Muhammad was also a political leader, and created a community of believers, which by the time of his death in 632 stretched in a network of tribal alliances across the Arabian Peninsula. The subsequent early rulers of the Islamic state were called *khalifa* (in Arabic) or caliph (in English), successor or deputy, but more often Prince of Believers (*Amir al-Mu'minin*). Under the first four caliphs, the energies of the united tribesmen were diverted into raiding Syria and Iraq, respectively under the control of the Byzantium and the Sassanian Iranian dynasty (226–637 in Iran and Iraq). The unexpected success by hitherto despised tribesmen in defeating two of the major world powers of the time caused the collapse of the Sassanian empire, and the permanent amputation of the rich Near Eastern and North African provinces of the Byzantine empire. Lack of serious resistance permitted the Muslim armies in the west to reach Spain by 711, and Samarqand and the Indus valley by about the same time. Nevertheless, the natural limits of military expansion brought a halt, with the defeat of a raid at Poitiers in central France in 732, and a battle against the Chinese at Talas (present-day Dzhambul in Kazakhstan) in 751.

The state was initially Arab; the Umayyad family of Meccan origin settled in Syria and provided the first dynasty of caliphs (AD 661–750), governing a vast population of unbelievers. Under the succeeding Abbasid caliphs in Iraq (750–1258), the frontiers of the Islamic world stabilized, and increasing numbers

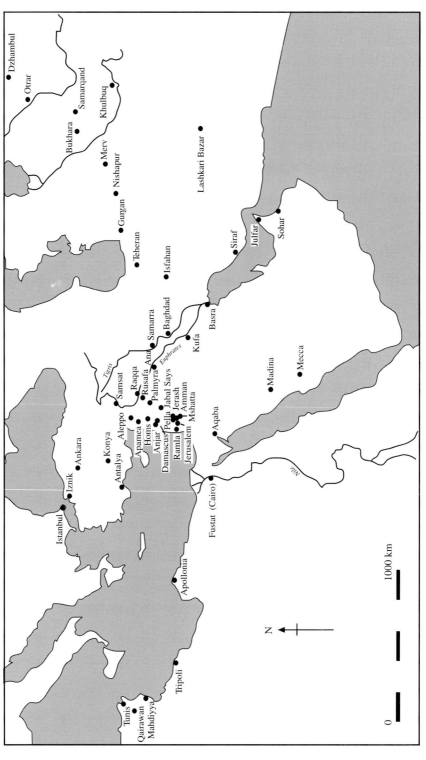

Figure 27.1 Map of Middle East and adjacent region, showing the principal sites mentioned in the chapter. Source: A. Northedge. Redrawn by D. Miles-Williams.

converted to Islam (Bulliet 1979). These two caliphal dynasties, and their imitators, the Umayyads in Spain (AD 756–1010) and the Fatimids in North Africa and Egypt (AD 907–1171), bear some resemblance to the empires of Late Antiquity. However, although the Muslim world has always retained a sense of unified identity since then, the vast areas under Islamic control led inevitably to political fragmentation, notably as a result of the decline of the Abbasid caliphate in the middle of the tenth century.

Out of the decay of empire and the decentralization of power was born the brilliant civilization of medieval Islam – the Saljuqs and their successors in Iran and Anatolia (eleventh–thirteenth centuries), the Ayyubids and Mamluks in Syria and Egypt (AD 1171–1260, 1260–1517), and further dynasties in North Africa, Yemen, Afghanistan and India. Although Arabic became the lingua franca of the Semitic Near East, partly because of its primordial role in the Qur'an, the Arab ethnic component of the population ceased to play an important role in politics, and was replaced by Iranians, and later Turks, who were introduced from the central Asian steppes as slave soldiers, and then arrived in tribal groups. Turks peopled the governments of the Muslim world from the Saljuqs until the early twentieth century. One effect was a new expansion of the frontiers of Islam. Turkish nomads flooded into Byzantine Anatolia after the battle of Manzikert in 1071, and it was a small group of Turkish *ghazis* or frontier fighters facing Byzantium, who created the Ottoman empire in the fourteenth century by invading the Balkans, reaching the gates of Vienna in 1529 and 1683, and finally seizing Constantinople in 1453. The Ghaznavid Turks invaded India in the eleventh century, and their successors up to the Moguls (1526–1858) islamized north-west India and Bengal to the extent that those areas now form the basis of Pakistan and Bangladesh.

The striking economic and cultural success of a society without centralized power – and thus permanent political conflict – received a setback from the Black Death in the fourteenth century but more from the peculiar geographical exposure of the Middle East to great conquerors: the meteoric passage of Alexander the Great through the region was repeated by the Mongols under Genghis Khan (1219–21) and the Il-Khans (1258–1335), by Timur (1370–1405), and finally by Nadir Shah (1736–47). Islam ceased to spread by conquest, but by contacts with neighbouring peoples, such as the Golden Horde in the now Russian Steppe, or the Uighurs in Sinkiang. Particularly trade played an important role – it was by that that Islam spread to Java, Sumatra and Borneo in the sixteenth century (Colless 1969), along the East African coast (Chittick and Rotberg 1975; Horton 1986), and by trans-Saharan trade to West Africa.

Although the Middle East experienced no renaissance of European type (for classical philosophy and scientific knowledge had never been lost, only rejected as unnecessary in the face of divine revelation), the re-emergence of centralized states occurred at about the same time as in Europe. The administration of the Ottoman empire was reformed during the later fifteenth and sixteenth centuries, Safavid Iran was forced to follow, and Mogul India kept pace. It was only from the end of the seventeenth century onwards that the Islamic world ceased to rival the West, although it is now experiencing a revival.

THE ROLE OF ARCHAEOLOGICAL EVIDENCE

The study of the history of the pre-modern Islamic world has until recently been largely conducted through the medium of texts. The principal skill of orientalists lay in the decipherment and interpretation of Arabic, Persian and Turkish texts. Until the end of the 1960s even the analytical tools used by western historians were little known. Study of the archaeological remains of the Islamic world dates back to the end of the nineteenth century: it was an inevitable concomitant of the discoveries of early archaeologists in the Holy Land and elsewhere in the Middle East. However, they often lacked the dating tools to distinguish Islamic from earlier remains, a problem which still exists for the period before the introduction of polychrome glazed pottery in the ninth century. For example, a controversy continued for nearly a century, from its initial discovery in the 1840s, over the identification of the Umayyad desert castle of Mshatta in Jordan (Creswell 1969: 622–41). Worse, although some good work was done in the earlier part of this century, notably by the German archaeologist Ernst Herzfeld, by the French historian Jean Sauvaget and his archaeological compatriot Daniel Schlumberger, and by the English architectural historian K. A. C. Creswell, from the 1960s onwards the study of Islamic material remains has tended to be dominated by a group of art historians who even today are unskilled in the interpretation of the primary material which is the daily bread and butter of archaeologists, and who often pose only a narrow range of questions on the artistic development of Islam. The discovery of the possibilities of archaeology for giving a new viewpoint on the history of the Islamic world is a very recent development, starting not more than twenty years ago, and the organization of the basic tools of analysis, notably the pottery typologies, is still underway. At the time of writing, a useful dialogue is beginning to take place between Islamic historians, that is, textual specialists, who have not been aware of the different kind of questions that archaeology is capable of answering, and Islamic archaeologists, who have not had time to look beyond the primary material with which they have been dealing and who often only have limited access to the textual sources, which are voluminous but mostly not translated.

The theoretical arguments for the advantages and disadvantages of archaeological material compared with texts for explaining the past have been well-rehearsed: archaeology does not suffer from the prejudices and ideological biases of chronicle authors, although the material is often more difficult to interpret than a text. It is well-adapted to explaining long-term economic and social evolution, but not so good at illuminating particular events, although many archaeologists would like that to be the case. At present the usefulness of archaeological evidence for explaining the evolution of Islamic society declines from early Islamic times onwards, as the quantity of surviving texts increases. Under the caliphs, archaeological evidence is vital for explaining the development of society and economy in the face of obscure and partial textual accounts; under the Ottomans it does not at present have much to add, by comparison with the quantities of data still to be deciphered from the central government archives in Istanbul, and the local archives of the *Shari'a* law courts, both of which go back at least four centuries.

THE HUMAN AND PHYSICAL ENVIRONMENT

The Middle East has always been a multi-cultural area. Within the eastern Roman empire, the Jews were the only major religious community to survive the three centuries of intense and rather intolerant Christianity between the Edict of Constantine and the Muslim conquests. At the same time, however, Christianity was also dominant, though not unrivalled, in areas outside the imperial frontier – in Ethiopia, some parts of Arabia, Iraq (but not Iran), Armenia, and Georgia. Islam was in practice much more easy-going, in spite of its current image of fanaticism. The first Muslims aimed to live from taxes on the other communities – the three religious groups which were declared protected communities ('People of the Book'): the Christians, the Jews and the Zoroastrians (the last by concession of equivalence). Logically, this implied permitting their continued existence, and indeed discouraging conversion. Although discouragement was only briefly applied, and financial exploitation only lasted two centuries, the recognition could not be revoked. Christian and Jewish communities, if they were willing to accept a second-class status, and were able to outlast periodic bouts of bigotry from their Muslim neighbours, were generally tolerated. The recently published excavation of the great basilica of the Holy Cross at Rusafa in Syria illustrates the continuation of the pilgrimage to this desert site until the time of the Mongol invasions *c.* 1260 (Ulbert 1986).

The Middle East is a particular type of environment, lying as it does in the desert belt of the northern hemisphere. While most of the mountain chains and the Mediterranean coast receive rainfall adequate for cultivation, the remainder of the region is dependent on water originating from outside the area (for example the Nile), or from the well-watered mountains. The irrigation methods used before modern mechanical devices were variable, ranging from simple flooding, and canals fed by animal- or human-driven lifting machines, to diversion of floods in the wadis (Yemen), long surface canals derived from the Tigris and the Euphrates (Iraq), and underground channels (*qanat*, *foggara* and other terms) derived from raised water-tables in the mountains of Iran and elsewhere (see Chapter 14). This means that the environment in which humans live in the Middle East is more their own artificial creation than elsewhere, and it is relatively fragile: the best example is the south of Iraq, where a natural desert was turned into the home of one of the world's great civilizations in ancient Mesopotamia by irrigation from its two rivers (Adams 1965), but whose agriculture has today largely been ruined by a variety of natural and man-made disasters, including salinization and river-bed movement, the exact role of each of which stills remains controversial. But it is also true that the limited areas which could be turned into cultivable land by irrigation, together with the mountain and coastal areas where non-irrigated agriculture is possible, are intermixed in a patchwork with areas of desert.

The desert remained until modern times the domain of nomadic animal breeding, mainly camels, horses, sheep and goats. The settled states feared and disliked the desert and the bedouin (and their Iranian, Turkish and Berber equivalents), but always had to deal with the desert dwellers, and could often be toppled by them. While we may consider too simplistic the cyclic theory of history propounded in the fourteenth century by Ibn Khaldun, whereby a young and vigorous nomadic group conquers the settled land from a decadent dynasty, in its turn to become wealthy and decadent and replaced by yet another group, a surprisingly large number of Middle Eastern empires had tribal origins, both under Islam and long before. Islam itself came out of this milieu: although its leadership was of urban origin in Mecca, and its armies were manned by Yemenis, Omanis, Hijazis, and Syrian Arabs, all of whom were mainly cultivators, 'desert and sown' in Arabia are so closely intermixed that members of the same clan may be nomadic herders or sedentary peasants. The unifying factor is the tribal organization, which subsequently came to have a much more important role under Islam than before.

When Islam spread beyond its home region of the Middle East, it encountered new environments. The Muslim Arabs regarded the southern shore of the Mediterranean, with its dry Mediterranean vegetation and hinterland of desert, as not very different from the Middle East: Spain resembled Syria to the Muslims. However, Islam spread further than those environments which even remotely resembled the Middle East. In the steppes of Central Asia, the dense inhabited plains of northern India, the jungles of Indonesia and the desiccated lands of sub-Saharan Africa, it became a global civilization, where religion and its cultural baggage became the sole unifying factor.

THE ARCHAEOLOGY OF CONQUEST

The tribal origins of the Islamic state are clear: the Umayyad caliphate (661–750), conquering all before it from Spain to the Chinese frontier, was essentially supported by the Arab tribesmen. In its metropolitan province of Syria – in the larger sense of the modern countries of the Levant – it has been compared with the barbarian kingdoms of the west: a tribal aristocracy dominating a Roman provincial population, the principal difference being the existence of an ideology – Islam (Crone 1980). The written sources on Umayyad Syria are particularly poor, the early Arab chroniclers being mainly from Iraq and the east, and the Byzantine sources are fragmentary. Archaeology therefore plays a particularly large role in explaining the characteristics of this short period of rapid change, but the resemblance of the material – both the traces of building activity and evidence for pottery and other production – to their late Roman/Byzantine equivalents makes it difficult for archaeologists to reach a consensus. The Romanists see the continuation of the empire, and the Islamicists see a new beginning, in the same material. For example, the octagonal Dome of the Rock in Jerusalem (AD 691–92) is regarded by many Byzantinists as a perfect case of a palaeo-Christian *martyrium*, disregarding its differences in function and decoration from Christian architecture (Creswell 1969: 65–131; Fig. 27.2). These differences, relatively slight at first sight, are in fact important because they document a cultural revolution taking place slowly over two centuries. The archaeological remains of this period are also very rich. The Umayyad aristocracy loved decorated architecture, and the subsequent poverty of Syria during the ninth, tenth and eleventh centuries has left the remains on the surface.

Recent archaeological work in the Middle East has concentrated on those Roman cities which were abandoned under Islam. The location of the major cities changed very quickly after the conquest, partly because of the closure of the Mediterranean to international trade during the seventh century, but also because of the orientation of the Muslim world towards the Middle East rather than the Mediterranean. We know relatively little about Amman (Philadelphia) in Jordan (Northedge 1993), Damascus or Homs (Emesa) in Syria, or Tripoli in Libya, because those cities continue to be important today, whereas we have considerable knowledge of Jerash (Kraeling 1938; Zayadine 1986, 1989) or Pella in Jordan (McNicoll *et al.* 1982; Smith 1973, 1989; Walmsley 1988), Apamea in Syria (Balty 1981, 1984), or Apollonia in Cyrenaica, cities equally important in the late Roman period, because those cities disappeared from the map at an early stage, and with relatively little change after the conquest. The evidence of the excavations at Jerash and Pella, or Baisan on the West Bank (Tsafrir and Foerster 1994), has shown considerable continued small-scale construction and many finds under the Umayyads, but little monumental construction and no large mosques. This picture reflects the accounts in the historical sources of heavy taxation, and probably demonstrates that these cities

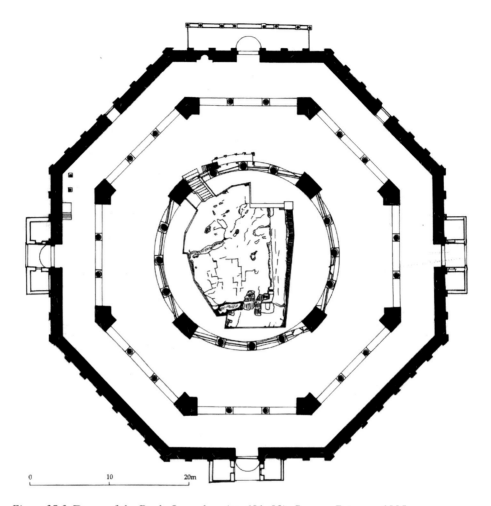

Figure 27.2 Dome of the Rock, Jerusalem (AD 691–92). Source: Petersen 1995.

remained largely non-Muslim until their abandonment. The preferred Muslim centres of settlement such as Amman and Damascus received large mosques at an early date (Fig. 27.3). Theoretical reconstructions, with some support from excavation, illustrate the narrowing of broad colonnaded streets into irregular market alleys, and have been taken as proof of deterioration from the Roman to a medieval mentality that was not interested in town planning (Hourani and Stern 1970; Kennedy 1985). One can, however, look at the question differently, and ask whether the organized town plans of the Hellenistic and Roman periods were not the exception, and the medieval city plans not simply a return to the pre-Hellenistic plans of the Iron Age.

The impact of the tribal aristocracy on Syria was very visible. The caliph 'Abd

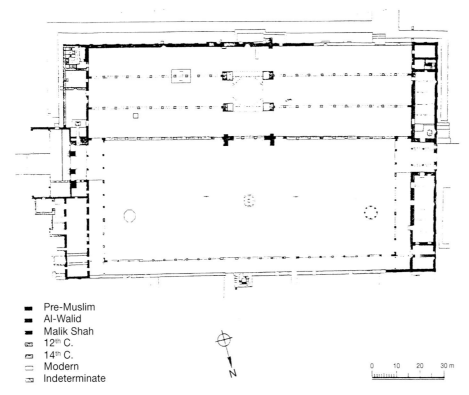

Pre-Muslim
Al-Walid
Malik Shah
12ᵗʰ C.
14ᵗʰ C.
Modern
Indeterminate

Figure 27.3 Plan of Umayyad mosque of Damascus (AD 706–14). Source: Creswell 1969.

al–Malik (685–705) introduced a programme of monumental religious architecture, beginning with the Dome of the Rock in Jerusalem (Fig. 27.2), which may have been intended as an Umayyad sanctuary based on Arabian sanctuaries such as at Mecca and elsewhere in the pre-Islamic period. At any rate it proved to be the sole building of its type, for Mecca came to be considered a unique symbol of God's intervention on earth (Creswell 1969: 65–131; Hawting 1986: 59–61). His successors continued the construction of monumental mosques, such as al–Aqsa in Jerusalem and the Umayyad mosque of Damascus (Fig. 27.3). These mosques varied in size from single chambers with a *mihrab* (the niche indicating the direction of Mecca), found in towns with small Muslim populations, such as at 'Ana in Iraq (Northedge *et al.* 1988: 17–19) and Jerash in Jordan, and in the princely settlements, to courtyard mosques of about 2,000 square metres in towns of greater significance to the Umayyads, such as Amman in Jordan (Northedge 1993) or Rusafa in Syria (Sack 1996), and finally to the courtyard mosques of the great cities, 10–15,000 square metres in size, such as in Damascus and Harran in Syria, Madina in Arabia, and Kufa or Wasit in Iraq (Creswell 1969, 1989).

The presence of the tribal aristocracy was also marked by a series of new constructions on the desert edge and other traditional Arab settlement areas. Some come under the heading of the 'Umayyad Desert Castles'. In their most developed form, these were complexes of a quasi-feudal nature, composed of a square lightly fortified residence, an audience hall with bath, a small mosque, a series of houses of different sizes, together with storehouses and other buildings (Gaube 1979; Sauvaget 1967). The most perfectly preserved plan is Jabal Sais, located in the bowl of an extinct volcano in the Syrian desert 105 kilometres from Damascus (Sauvaget 1939), while the most grandiose was the residence of Caliph Hisham (AD 724–43) outside the walls of Rusafa in Syria (the plan of which is regrettably not yet published): four square castles and about thirty other buildings, with a garden pavilion recently excavated. The hierarchy of the plans suggests the attachment of a considerable number of followers to the lord in question – who was not necessarily the caliph, or even a member of the Umayyad clan, in spite of the superficial tendency today to attribute everything to the caliph – and this hierarchy reflects well the importance of clientage to a tribe (*walâ'*) during the Umayyad period. The square castles themselves are subdivided into independent apartments called Syrian *bayts* (Arabic for room, apartment, or small house) by Creswell, suggesting a familial structure of the entourage. The same hierarchy of plan is visible in the fortified orthogonally planned urban settlements of the period, such as at 'Anjar in Lebanon, where the same elements as in the desert castle complexes are present, but in a form which resembles a planned Roman city (Northedge 1994; Fig. 27.4).

According to the historical sources, the Arab tribal armies in Syria were settled in existing cities, and the only new foundation was Ramla in present-day Israel, founded by the Caliph Sulaiman (*c.* 715); regrettably little is known about its archaeology, as Ramla is still a substantially sized town. Outside of Syria, the Muslims settled in new cities, effectively tribal garrison cities, which were generic-ally called *amsâr* (singular: *misr*), though use of this term in the texts is rather vague, and it is often used to mean simply a major city. The first two *amsâr* were Kufa and Basra in Iraq (*c.* 637); the organization of their tribal allotments around the mosque and governor's palace is well known from textual descriptions, but owing to later occupation the particular characteristics remain little known from the archaeo-logical point of view, although the governor's palace at Kufa (*Dâr al-Imâra*) has been excavated (Creswell 1969: 46–64). Only at Fustat in Egypt, later replaced by Cairo, has a short section of the seventh-century plan been revealed in the recent French excavations at Istabl Antar – two narrow alleys with little booths and irregular houses (Gayraud 1991).

However, in general it is true to say that, outside the Fertile Crescent and Egypt, the archaeological traces of the transitional period are not very easy to see: the large investments made in architecture in Syria, and the new cities of Iraq and Egypt, at least leave easily visible traces. The principal obstacle is the pottery typology, the

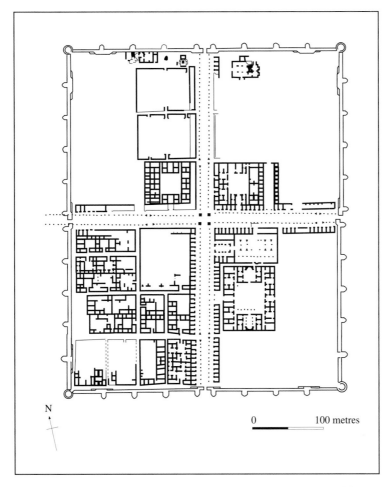

Figure 27.4 Plan of 'Anjar, Lebanon (AD 714–15). Source: Petersen 1995 (redrawn by D. Miles-Williams with additions).

main source of dating evidence in the Middle East for building remains which are not monumental architecture. The principal late Roman fine wares in the Mediterranean ceased to be manufactured at the end of the seventh century, but the first easily recognizable Islamic types with polychrome glaze date to two centuries later (Northedge 1997). As a result, many archaeologists have failed to detect eighth- and ninth-century remains, if they are not obviously new settlements such as Qairawan, the *misr* founded in Tunisia in the late seventh century and known for its ninth-century mosque. In the recent excavations at the sixth-century Byzantine fortress at Haïdra in Tunisia, the existence of transitional occupation was only recognized because settlement continued into the polychrome glaze period. The difficulty of identifying new changes until well into the ninth century suggests that, for many people, life changed slowly and that there was relatively little economic activity, but it is also very likely that new work may well alter this picture in the future.

THE CREATION OF THE NEW CULTURE

In 750 the Umayyad regime was overturned by the Abbasid revolution, a genuine revolution caused by the stresses of rapid societal change. The Umayyads were accused of being irreligious, the truth of which is evident in the luxurious decoration of their palaces, such as Khirbat al-Mafjar at Jericho, where excavations revealed large quantities of mosaics and stucco decoration, including sculptures, a richness of decoration far surpassing their late Roman equivalents (Hamilton 1959). Underlying this was the crumbling away of the tribal state, with the increasing conversion of non-Arabs to Islam – there were scarcely any anti-Islamic revolts – and the economic dominance of Iraq over Syria. The Abbasid caliphate, established in Iraq from 750 to 1258, was in fact, at least initially, a late version of an ancient Mesopotamian empire, and an urban civilization, building on the bases of Kufa and Basra. We have little trace of early Baghdad, founded by al-Mansur in 762, as it lies under the modern city, but it was much written about and described (Lassner 1970). Its reflection survives in the residence of Caliph Harun al-Rashid (786–809) at Raqqa in Syria, a walled city built in 772 with the mud-brick and *pisé* palaces of Rashid scattered outside the walls (Creswell 1940: 39–48; Heusch and Meinecke 1985, 1989), and in the second temporary capital of the Abbasids at Samarra' on the Tigris to the north of Baghdad (836–92).

At Samarra' (Fig. 27.5) the Abbasids spread their brick and *pisé* palaces, and the military cantonments of their Iranian and Turkish army, out over 57 square kilometres of steppe only reoccupied in the last few years, around several former small towns, of which Samarra' itself developed into a city (Creswell 1940: *passim*; *Encyclopaedia of Islam* 1960–: s.v. Samarra'; Rogers 1970). The massive amount of data about military installations, Abbasid housing and living conditions, and industrial structures, has only begun to be analysed, in spite of eighty years of excavations. The Abbasid army was quartered at the capital, not on the frontier, and the cantonments are composed of grids of streets of small courtyard houses, dominated by the palace of the general (Northedge 1994). Evidence of hunting in game reserves, and horse-racing on courses 10.5 kilometres long, is also well-preserved (Northedge 1990).

The wealth of the Abbasid state, depicted by the remains of Raqqa and Samarra', was based on the land tax (Arabic: *kharaj*) – contrary to the conclusion of Hodges and Whitehouse (1983) – and the main contributor was Iraq. Under the late Sassanians in the sixth century the irrigation system was reorganized, and reached a

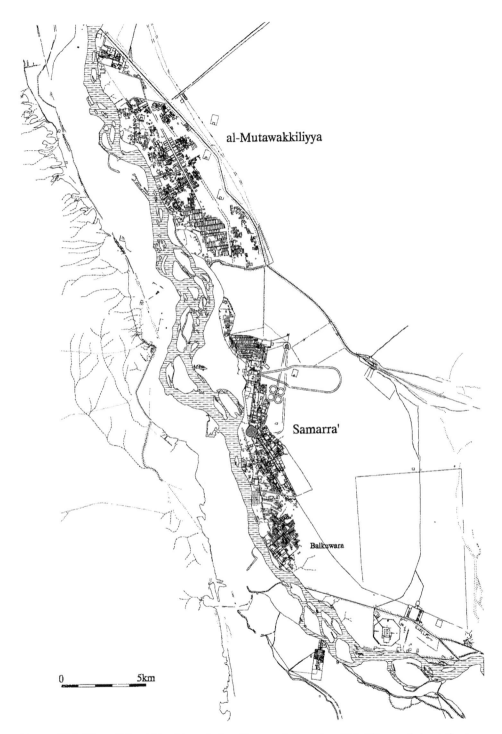

al-Mutawakkiliyya

Samarra'

Balkuwara

0   5km

Figure 27.5 Plan of the Abbasid capital at Samarra', Iraq (AD 836–92); north is at the top.
Source: Samarra' Archaeological Survey.

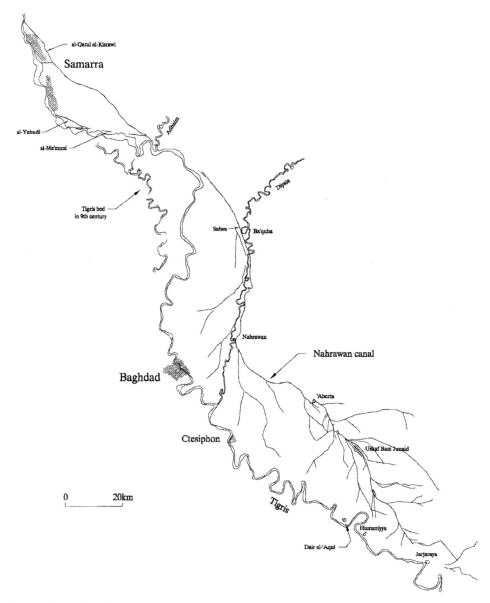

Figure 27.6 Map of Nahrawan canal system, Iraq; north is at the top. Source: Adams 1965, redrawn with permission of the Samarra' Archaeological Survey.

high degree of efficiency. Robert Adams, in his classic archaeological surveys of southern Iraq, revealed dense areas of village settlement around branch canals (Adams 1965, 1981; Fig. 27.6). Regrettably, no adequate excavation has yet taken place of sample villages; the village site of Tell Abu Sarifa in southern Iraq has been excavated, but only for its archaeological sequence (Adams 1970). The character of life in the Jewish villages can be deduced from the Babylonian Talmud and other texts (Oppenheimer 1983). The surveys have shown that the system continued to develop until the early tenth century: Adams gave the ninth century for the date of large-scale contraction, but this date now has to be corrected to the tenth century, based on newer pottery dating, and corresponds to a point when the chronicles lament the dissolution of the Abbasid administration.

The collapse of the Iraqi economy, which did not recover until the twentieth century, is a central motif of Islamic history, for economic and political power passed from Iraq to Iran and Egypt. The reasons for the failure to rebuild the Iraqi system, destroyed in a relatively brief period of weakness, have proved a subject of controversy: was the land becoming uncultivable owing to salinization provoked by the flood of new irrigation water, as proposed by Adams, or was it that the fragmented medieval states which succeeded to political power were incapable of the effort to rebuild and administer a system of which the longest canal was 225 kilometres? At any rate, the most agriculturally successful regions in the Middle East subsequently were those that depended on short canals, easily repaired at a local level, such as in Iran and Egypt.

The most visibly successful economic phenomenon, from the late eighth century onwards, was trade and commercial investment. While the Arabs and ethnically related peoples had a long tradition of trade, being situated on the land bridge between the Indian Ocean and the Mediterranean, and the western end of the Silk Road, the initial impetus may have been given by the fact that the taxation system, which weighed heavily on peasants, scarcely touched merchants in the early days of Islam. Other factors also played a role: the importation of silkworm eggs to Byzantium in the sixth century – the revelation of a Chinese commercial secret – put an end to the Silk Road, and land transport from China. Arab seafarers penetrated further than their Sassanian predecessors, and established a colony at Canton from the middle of the eighth century (Sauvaget 1948). At this time new developments in Chinese ceramic technology, the invention of stoneware, porcelain and polychrome glazes, provided attractive products worth exporting which are easily visible in the archaeological record (Rougeulle 1991). The relative ease of long-distance transport for fragile objects across the Indian Ocean displaced the land route, and concentrated in the early period on the Gulf. The excavations at Siraf, an entrepôt situated in inhospitable terrain on the Iranian coast, directed by David Whitehouse between 1968 and 1974, have well illustrated the wealth of this trade, even in circumstances of political conflict (Whitehouse 1970, 1980). However, virtually every other port excavated on the Red Sea, the Gulf, and the Indian Ocean has revealed a similar story, for example Aqaba in Jordan (Whitcomb 1988), Sohar in Oman (Costa and Wilkinson 1987; Kervran 1984), and Julfar in the Emirates (Hansman 1985; Hardy-Guilbert 1991). With the decline of Iraq, the western terminus became the

Red Sea, and activity continued to develop until the penetration of European shipping into the Indian Ocean at the beginning of the sixteenth century.

Chaudhuri (1985), working on the seventeenth-century records of the East India Company, showed that, although the initial investment in ship and cargo was high, and there was a certain danger of loss of the ship, the profit realized on safe return was enormous. In the ninth century at least, profits were invested in local development, partly visible in the archaeological record, such as extensive copper mining in Oman (Costa and Wilkinson 1987), and steatite vessel production in the Saudi desert, far from the Yemeni origins of the type. But in the end, decline in internal security probably ended these initiatives, although Weisgerber (1980) suggests that exhaustion of potential fuel for smelting terminated copper production. At the same time, cross-Saharan routes were developed for importation of gold from West Africa, and coin hoards of ninth-century dirhams in Scandinavia demonstrate Viking trade along the Volga with the Middle East (Hodges and Whitehouse 1983).

The model of the Abbasid caliphate and its world was fundamental to the future of Islamic civilization. Its administrative systems, its architecture, and even its pottery, were imitated both in the east and the west – for example by the successor caliphates of the Fatimids in Tunisia and later in Egypt (909–1171), and the Umayyads of Spain (758–1010). In both these cases, the monumental architectural pattern of the Abbasids was followed: fine mosques in the city – al-Azhar in Cairo and the mosque of Cordoba – and an administrative city outside – Mahdiyya (916) and Sabra-Mansuriyya (947) in Tunisia, al-Qahira outside Fustat in Egypt (969), and Madinat al-Zahra' outside Cordoba in Spain (936). In the west, the minor architectural details were derived more from the Roman tradition: mosques were adorned with square buttresses, wall mosaics of glass *tesserae* as at Cordoba, and horseshoe arches invented in Syria. In the east, in Iraq, Iran and central Asia, the Samarran tradition of architecture, with round buttresses, decorations in carved stucco and brick, continued until the twelfth century. Central Asian palaces, such as at Khulbuq in Tajikistan and Lashkari Bazar (Fig. 27.7) in Afghanistan (Schlumberger 1978; Sourdel-Thomine 1978), both eleventh century, are directly derived from Samarra'.

THE MEDIEVAL WORLD

The collapse of the Abbasid caliphate in the second quarter of the tenth century led to the 'medievalization' of the Middle East, although the dynasty itself survived until the Mongol capture of Baghdad in 1258. The centralized bureaucracy of the caliphate, however theoretical its effectiveness may have been across the vast distances from Tunisia to India, was replaced by an ever-changing mosaic of states founded largely by military or tribal leaders with only rudimentary administration.

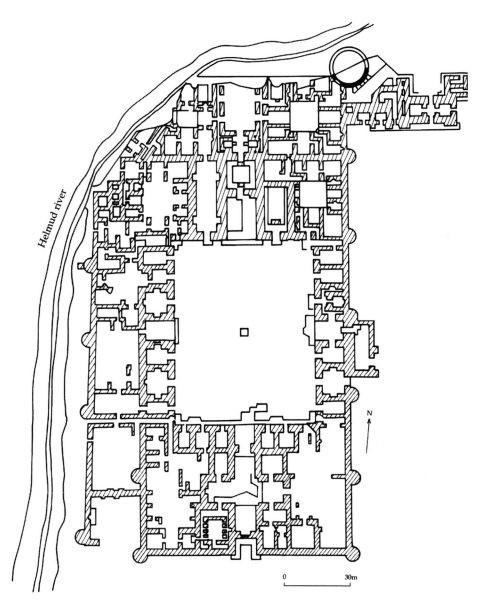

Figure 27.7 The South Palace, Lashkari Bazar, Afghanistan (AD 998–1030). Source: Petersen 1995.

In the course of the financial failure of the caliphate, an informal feudalism was introduced, the *iqta'*. To pay the army, tax collection rights over a region were offered to military leaders in return for providing an agreed number of soldiers; although the rights were in principal limited, in practice they were not, for officials

1093

were excluded. Nevertheless, the *iqta'* did not lead to the kind of formal relationships of lord, knight and peasant typical of European feudalism.

These relatively ephemeral dynasties lacked legitimacy, which was vested in the caliph, and the caliph did not control the mosque, which was in the hands of the '*ulama*', the religious scholars. The '*ulama*' were drawn largely from the ranks of the urban notables, often merchants. As a result, city and village became autonomous entities within the Muslim commonwealth, little – and usually only negatively – influenced by governments and their armies. It was for this reason that economic prosperity was possible in the absence of political stability. In particular, when an alliance was made between urban and rural institutions and the ruler, such as under the Saljuqs in Iran (1038–1157), a highly successful synthesis could take place, with great economic development, a period which was only terminated by the Mongol invasions (1219–58). It is unfortunate that, with the exception of Spain (for example: Bazzana *et al.* 1988), very little planned archaeological research has taken place on the evolution of urban and rural society in the medieval period.

Medieval urban settlement

A substantial number of excavations has brought to light urban data for the medieval period (eleventh–fourteenth centuries), but it is mostly fragmentary, for two reasons. In the case of the major medieval cities of Islam, the city is still occupied, and one can only reconstruct the medieval pattern under the overlay of later changes. For example, studies of this type have been made of Damascus (Sack 1989) and Aleppo (Sauvaget 1941). In the case of abandoned cities, only the two cases of Qsar es-Seghir in Morocco (Redman 1986; Figs 4.9, 16.7), and the port of Siraf in Iran mentioned earlier have been pursued with adequate persistence, resources and an overall vision; and not much of the latter excavation has been published in final form (Whitehouse 1970, 1980). The excavation of Aqaba in Jordan has also had considerable success in revealing an early medieval small port (Whitcomb 1988). Otherwise, greater or lesser areas of many cities have been cleared, only revealing parts of streets and houses without relationship to urban structure. In Iran, excavations have been published of Gurgan (Kiani 1983) and Nishapur (Wilkinson 1986); in Kazakhstan, Otrar (Baipakov 1992); in Syria, the citadel of Hama, Balis-Meskene and Mayadine; in Turkey, Samsat (Redford 1995); in Egypt, Fustat and the port of Qusair al-Qadim on the Red Sea (Whitcomb and Johnson 1978, 1982). Nevertheless, these excavations have normally brought to light rich finds, in particular large quantities of evidence for the evolution of ceramic production.

The essential problem is that urban structure was evidently different in medieval Islam from medieval Europe. The urban studies of surviving later Islamic cities, such as those of Damascus and Aleppo mentioned above, and studies based on textual evidence (such as Lapidus 1967), show this clearly. The stereotypical physical model of the Islamic city, with its narrow alleys leading to the bazaar and the mosque, which was an oasis of peace at the heart of a densely inhabited city without open spaces (von Grunebaum 1961), is hardly likely to have been true of all Islamic cities during the millennium and a half of the religion's existence, and across the vast distances from Spain to India. Only archaeology can really answer this question, but it has not yet done so.

One question is that of fortification (Creswell 1952; *Encyclopaedia of Islam* 1960–: s.v. Sur [City Fortification]). Earlier Islamic cities were either not fortified, such as Baghdad, Samarra' and Fustat (Cairo) in the eighth and ninth centuries, or they followed the traditions of late Roman urban fortification, with regularly spaced projecting towers and no citadel. A citadel does not seem to have been built in Damascus until the eleventh century. It was the Crusades and their military technical developments that led to the construction of massive new citadels in Cairo, Damascus and Aleppo (Fig. 27.8) at the end of the twelfth and beginning of the

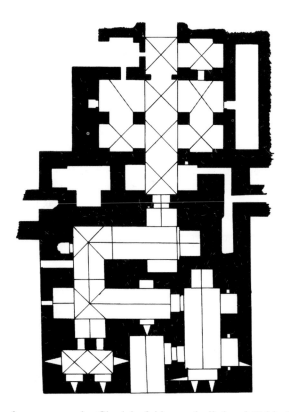

Figure 27.8 Plan of gateway to the Citadel of Aleppo, built by al-Zahir Ghazi in 1209–10.
Source: Petersen 1995.

thirteenth centuries. Politics also played a role: it was at this point that sultans came to live in urban citadels. In later Islamic cities, citadels of considerable dimensions were built to accommodate palatial residences of the rulers, as for example in 1321 at Tughluqabad outside Delhi in India (Shokoohy and Shokoohy 1994; Fig. 27.9), or the eighteenth-century Arg at Bukhara in Uzbekistan. Urban fortifications were also later dominated by massive bastions, such as the thirteenth-century round tower at the entrance to the harbour at Antalya in Turkey. However, Islamic fortifications, although they installed loopholes for cannons, did not develop a new defensive architecture to adapt to the possibilities of firearms, as occurred in Europe.

Considerable evidence of urban domestic architecture has now been recovered from excavation, to the extent that it would now be possible to write a history of the Muslim house from Roman times to the present day. There is a considerable literature on the architecture and functioning of the house in the Middle East, written mainly by architects (for example: Warren and Fethi 1982), but this is based principally on surviving houses not more than a century or two old. The interesting but

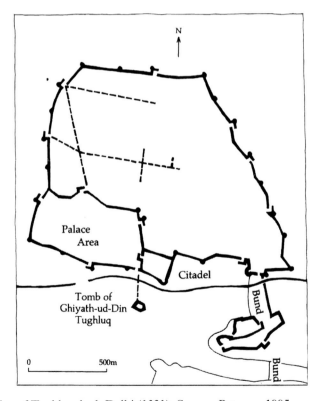

Figure 27.9 Plan of Tughluqabad, Delhi (1321). Source: Petersen 1995.

static vision of this literature can now be filled out by excavation results to reveal a significant chronological evolution. All the early Islamic houses that have been found are based on the courtyard plan inherited from Antiquity – the eastern Roman empire and the Near Eastern tradition. Even in the eighth century there are some rare cases where it is possible to distinguish a house inhabited by Muslims rather than by Christians – for example a house at the Amman Citadel destroyed with its contents in the earthquake of 747 and excavated by Harding (1951), or the early houses of Fustat (Gayraud 1991). The desert castles of the Umayyad period are characterized by the subdivision of their accommodation into separate apartments, suggesting the complexities of the extended family, and this type of subdivision was carried over into larger town houses, for example at 'Anjar in Lebanon (715) (Fig. 27.4), or Samarra' in Iraq (836–92). The specialized room functions found in larger Roman houses disappeared, and were replaced by a simple structure of reception rooms, multiple side rooms, kitchens and store-rooms. It is evident that what are called reception rooms were in fact the living rooms of the house, at least for the men. The form of the reception room in the Middle East became increasingly that of the *iwan*, a hall open on one side to the courtyard, first used in Parthian Mesopotamia in the second century AD. The *iwan* is common in the eastern Islamic world, and in Syria and Egypt, but did not spread to the western Mediterranean. The limitations on space in cities did not permit the complicated plans to be found at Samarra'. The smaller houses of the ninth century have one, two or four *iwans* and a number of side-rooms on a courtyard, as at Siraf in Iran (ninth–tenth centuries), or the levels of the same period at Fustat in Egypt (Fig. 27.10). This type of plan is carried over into thirteenth-century Syria, for example at Mayadine, or the Ayyubid palace in the Citadel of Aleppo. From the eleventh–twelfth centuries onwards, but not before, the installation of stone or brick benches intended to be laid with carpets for sitting on has been commonly observed. Nevertheless, in the smaller houses, there is no trace of the separation of the sexes, such as in a harem – the strict segregation of women was limited to the upper classes.

The picture is much brighter for urban monumental architecture, mainly religious, where this has been preserved within the matrix of later cities. Mosques, *madrasas* (theological schools), and mausolea from the medieval period have been widely preserved (Hillenbrand 1994). On the other hand not many of the palaces and large houses of the political élite have survived, apart from the houses of the Mamluks in Cairo. The political élite being transitory, it was not necessary to preserve the houses of vanished princes. The mosques, *madrasas* and mausolea served an ongoing function in the urban society. While the mosque obviously served as the focal point of the city's or quarter's prayer, the salaries of the *imam* (prayer leader) and muezzin being paid from the state budget or a *waqf* (religious endowment), the institution of the *madrasa*, having appeared in early form probably in the tenth century, has continued to evolve until today, mainly for the training of

Figure 27.10 Medieval house plan of the pre-Mongol period, Merv, Turkmenistan (twelfth–thirteenth centuries). Source: Petersen 1995.

the personnel who served in the religious institutions. Large numbers of mausolea have survived, either because they were situated outside of the city, and their ruins have been preserved, or because they were situated in the cities and continued to be maintained, being included in the endowment of mosque–*madrasa* complexes, or because they served as the focus of saint veneration. Although this religious architecture served a function within the society, much of it has the names of emirs and sultans on it, to the extent that one recent book has described Islamic art as essentially a royal art (Brend 1991). In part it was the political élite that had access to sufficient capital funds (Lapidus 1967: 195–210), but also in an autocratic society it was not always wise for others to be ostentatious.

Trade and production

Several sections of medieval bazaars have been identified in excavation, such as at Siraf in Iran, and at Palmyra in Syria, but it is not possible to conclude much more at present than the simple observation that they were composed of small booths aligned on both sides of a street. In the state-built palace complexes, there is clear evidence of formal market construction composed of long lines of shops along an avenue, as found at Samarra' in al-Mutawakkiliyya (861) and Balkuwara (*c.* 854), and at Lashkari Bazar in Afghanistan (built 998–1030). Allen hypothesizes that a courtyard building attached to the market at Lashkari Bazar may have been intended for the market supervisor, the *muhtasib* (Allen 1990). These formal markets were probably intended for provisioning the army, as individual soldiers would have been responsible for feeding themselves.

The architectural evidence of the traditional Islamic trading system – the urban *khan* which served as an entrepôt for the arrival of a caravan's merchandise, and the caravanserai which served as a stopping point along the traditional high-roads of the Middle East – is rather late in date. Although admonitions to princes to provide halting places in the desert can be found in texts as early as the beginning of Islam, the earliest buildings one can identify as having been constructed as caravanserais may be as late as the eleventh century. The first great wave of caravanserai construction took place in Anatolia under the Saljuqs in the first half of the thirteenth century, and thenceforth the provision for the trains of donkeys and camels that criss-crossed the Middle East became more and more elaborate up to the nineteenth century. Earlier than this time, it may be that accommodation was provided in forts along the road, such as at Örnek to the east of Dzhambul in Kazakhstan (Northedge and Rousset 1995). Surviving urban khans go back to the fourteenth century in Cairo, but it is highly probable that earlier courtyard structures identified in archaeological work served similar functions of storage and exchange.

In comparison to the extensive lists in texts and archives of products traded, the archaeological evidence from excavation remains fragmentary for the moment. Although considerable success has been achieved in identifying products from the Indian subcontinent on ancient Near Eastern sites, such as cloves, a similar level of work for the Islamic period is only just beginning. An interesting comparison for the importation of woods has been carried out on the materials excavated at the port of Qusair al-Qadim on the Red Sea coast of Egypt; in the Roman period many of the wood types were typical of India, whereas in the Islamic period all the types could be accounted for from the Nile valley (Hiebert 1991). Without doubt this difference is an indicator of the activity of one port, for the texts indicate the importance of woods, notably teak, as imports from the Indian subcontinent in Islamic times.

The most extensive work in the domain of trade and production has been done on pottery. Pottery plays a much larger role in excavation finds in the Middle East than in some other parts of the world, because of its quantity and state of preservation even in adverse environmental conditions. Although relatively few kiln-sites have been excavated, more extensive work has been done on the geographical and chronological distribution of excavation finds. It is evident that near the beginning of the Islamic period, probably in the early ninth century, a revolution occurred in the production of finewares, which led to the replacement of the classical tradition of glossy finishes, and the Mesopotamian tradition of monochrome glazes, by poly-chrome glazed earthenwares (Northedge 1997). There is no doubt that the technical advances made in China a century earlier in the invention of stoneware, porcelain and T'ang three-colour earthenwares (*san-tsai*) – products imported to the Middle East (Rougeulle 1991) – stimulated Middle Eastern potters to new ideas, which then spread rapidly. The new ideas included decorative techniques not thought of in China, particularly metallic lustre painting. Nevertheless over the centuries the new advances which emerged from China, such as blue and white porcelain from the fourteenth century onwards, continued to dominate Muslim taste; for example, fifteenth-century finewares are frequently imitations of blue and white or celadon. In the twelfth century, or possibly a little earlier, a new stonepaste body, of silica with a small admixture of white clay and glaze, was invented to simulate the undiscovered secret of porcelain, and this fabric was used on finewares until modern times.

While Islamic pottery was much exported to East Africa and elsewhere in the Indian Ocean from the ninth century onwards (Horton 1986), the Chinese seem not to have been interested in pottery from the Middle East; however, they did appreciate Islamic glass, which has been found in a number of tombs, and temple treasuries. Although the quantity of Islamic glazed wares found on European medieval sites is not large, the technical superiority of Islamic pottery was appreciated by medieval Europeans, as can be seen in the *bacini*, Islamic glazed bowls which were used to decorate the exterior of two eleventh-century churches in Pisa, and the invitations to *mudéjar* potters living in Valencia in Spain after the *Reconquista* to work in France (Amigues 1992). The interesting point to note is that the technical advances in ceramics made by the Chinese were already having a world-wide effect, if indirect, long before the arrival of European explorers in the Indian Ocean in the sixteenth century.

It is equally interesting to note that excavation has shown that the increasing sophistication in fineware production, concentrated in a few specialist centres, was accompanied by a decline in unglazed commonwares. From the thirteenth century onwards, in the regions of the Arab Middle East, commonwares in rural areas are often handmade, roughly potted, and painted with elaborate primitive designs. A cognate process took place in North Africa, where the modern traditional pottery of Tunisia, Algeria and Morocco reflects a similar evolution, and probably also appeared not earlier than the thirteenth century. It remains controversial why this happened, but it probably reflects the economic relationship between village and city.

Rural settlement and agriculture

Study of the evidence for the evolution of rural society in medieval times has been limited. Many archaeologists have observed that occupation of the land in Islamic times was slighter in terms of numbers of sites than in the Roman or equivalent periods. For example, the UNESCO Libyan Valleys Survey in the region south of Tripoli found many fewer Islamic sites than Roman (Sjöström 1993). Large areas of Iraq surveyed by Adams had no Islamic occupation (Adams 1965, 1981). On the other hand in Syria there are more thirteenth-century sites than Roman ones in some survey areas (Bartl 1994; Northedge 1981).

Watson suggested that importation of new crop types from the Far East may have reduced the land area necessary for cultivation (Watson 1983). The truth is certainly more complex. Nomadic animal-breeding was more important than before. Farmers may have adapted better to the possibilities of the land, and given up the cultivation of steep slopes which were exposed to erosion. Minor environmental changes made different areas more productive. The most important factor, however, was probably security. Agglomeration of settlement into hilltop villages typical of medieval Italy was not possible in the Middle East, apart from in mountain areas. Security was in the fortified town, and the areas which could be cultivated around it. Nevertheless, in the only detailed study of the character of rural settlement made so far, at Khirbat Faris on the Kerak plateau in Jordan, Johns (1994) has concluded that the evidence shows a continuum of occupation in the area from Roman times to the present.

CONCLUSION

This brief survey points to the usefulness of archaeology as a source for the history of Islam. The archaeology of Islam is not the archaeology of a religion, but rather of a single world culture in the same way as Roman archaeology. However, Islam is a much more diffuse culture combining many different geographical regions in a single civilization. Over most of its spread, though not all, it took with it the cultural baggage of its Middle Eastern origins: the architecture, the patterns of living, and the styles of art. It is for this reason that it is possible to compare the fortress-palace of Tughluqabad outside Delhi in India (1321) with the Alhambra at Granada in Spain, developed over several phases in the same century. In the east, it was mainly of Iranian inspiration, though the Iranians themselves drew heavily on ancient Mesopotamia. In the Mediterranean it was principally Syro-Egyptian. The role of archaeology in Islam, as everywhere in historical archaeology, is to explore the alternative visions of the past that material evidence offers, and to fill out the aspects of that past that authors of the time were unable to see, or thought too familiar to explain.

REFERENCES

Adams, R. M. (1965) *Land Behind Baghdad*, Chicago: University of Chicago Press.

Adams, R. M. (1970) 'Tell Abu Sarifa, a Sassanian-Islamic ceramic sequence from southern Iraq', *Ars Orientalis* 8: 87–119.

Adams, R. M. (1981) *Heartland of Cities*, Chicago: University of Chicago Press.

Allen, T. A. (1990) 'Notes on Bust (continued)', *Iran* 28: 23–30.

Amigues, F. (1992) 'Potiers mudéjares et chrétiens de la région de Valence', *Archéologie Islamique* 3: 129–68.

Baipakov, K. (1992) 'Les fouilles de la ville d'Otrar', *Archéologie Islamique* 3: 87–110.

Balty, J. Ch. (1981) *Guide d'Apamée*, Paris: Boccard.

Balty, J. (ed.) (1984) *Colloque Apamée de Syrie, Bilan de Recherches Archéologiques 1973–79*, Paris: Boccard.

Bartl, K. (1994) *Frühislamische Besiedlung im Balîh-Tal/Nordsyrien*, Berlin: Dietrich Reimer Verlag, Berliner Beiträge zum Vorderen Orient 15.

Bazzana, A., Cressier, P. and Guichard, P. (1988) *Les Châteaux Ruraux d'al-Andalus. Histoire et Archéologie des Husun du Sud-Est de l'Espagne*, Madrid: Casa de Velázquez.

Brend, B. (1991) *Islamic Art*, London: British Museum Press.

Bulliet, R. W. (1979) *Conversion to Islam in the Medieval Period*, Cambridge, Mass.: Harvard University Press.

Chaudhuri, K. N. (1985) *Trade and Civilisation in the Indian Ocean*, Cambridge: Cambridge University Press.

Chittick, H. N. and Rotberg, R. I. (eds) (1975) *East Africa and the Orient*, New York: Africana Publishing Co.

Colless, B. E. (1969) 'Persian merchants and missionaries in medieval Malaya', *Journal of the Malaysian Branch of the Royal Asiatic Society* 42: 10–47.

Costa, P. M. and Wilkinson, T. J. (1987) 'The hinterland of Sohar; archaeological surveys and excavations within the region of an Omani seafaring city', *Journal of Oman Studies* 9.

Creswell, K. A. C. (1940) *Early Muslim Architecture* (volume II, 1st edition), Oxford: Oxford University Press.

Creswell, K. A. C. (1952) 'Fortification in Islam before AD 1250', *Proceedings of the British Academy* 38: 89–125.

Creswell, K. A. C. (1969) *Early Muslim Architecture* (volume I, 2nd edition), Oxford: Oxford University Press.

Creswell, K. A. C. (1989) *A Short Account of Early Muslim Architecture* (revised and supplemented by J. W. Allan), Aldershot: Scolar Press.

Crone, P. (1980) *Slaves on Horses*, Cambridge: Cambridge University Press.

Encyclopaedia of Islam (1960–), Leiden: Brill (new edition).

Gaube, H. (1979) 'Die syrischen Wüstenschlösser. Einige wirtschaftliche und politische Gesichstpunkte zu ihrer Entstehung', *Zeitschrift des Deutschen Palästina-Vereins* 95: 182–209.

Gayraud, R.-P. (1991) 'Istabl Antar (Fostat) 1987–1989. Rapport des fouilles', *Annales Islamologiques* 25: 57–87.

Golvin, L. (1974–78) *Essai sur l'Architecture Religieuse Musulmane*, Paris: Editions Klincksieck (3 volumes).

Hamilton, R. W. (1959) *Khirbat al Mafjar: an Arabian Mansion in the Jordan Valley*, Oxford: Clarendon Press.

Hansman, J. (1985) *Julfar, An Arabian Port. Its Settlement and Far Eastern Ceramic Trade from the 14th to the 18th Centuries*, London: Royal Asiatic Society Prize Publication Fund 22.

Harding, G. L. (1951) 'Excavations on the Citadel, Amman', *Annual of the Department of Antiquities of Jordan* 1: 7–16.

Hardy-Guilbert, C. (1991) 'Julfar, cité portuaire du golfe arabo-persique à la période islamique', *Archéologie Islamique* 2: 161–203.

Hawting, G. R. (1986) *The First Dynasty of Islam*, London and Sydney: Croom Helm.

Heusch, J.-Chr. and Meinecke, M. (1985) 'Grabungen im 'abbasidischen Palastareal von ar-Raqqa/ar-Rafiqa 1982–3', *Damaszener Mitteilungen* 2: 85–106.

Heusch, J.-Chr. and Meinecke, M. (1989) *Die Residenz des Harun al-Raschid in Raqqa*, Damascus: Deutsches Archäologisches Institut.

Hiebert, F. (1991) 'Commercial organization of the Egyptian port of Quseir al-Qadim: evidence from the analysis of the wood objects', *Archéologie Islamique* 2: 127–60.

Hillenbrand, R. (1994) *Islamic Architecture. Form, Function and Meaning*, Edinburgh: Edinburgh University Press.

Hodges, R. and Whitehouse, D. (1983) *Mohammed, Charlemagne and the Origins of Europe*, London: Duckworth.

Horton, M. (1986) 'Asiatic colonisation of the East African coast: the Manda evidence', *Journal of the Royal Asiatic Society* 2: 202–13.

Hourani, A. and Stern, S. M. (eds) (1970) *The Islamic City*, Oxford: Bruno Cassirer.

Hourani, G. (1951) *Arab Seafaring in the Indian Ocean in Ancient and Early Medieval Times*, Princeton: Princeton University Press.

Ibn Khaldun (1958) *al-Muqaddima*, (tr. F. Rosenthal, *The Muqaddimah*), New York: Pantheon.

Johns, J. (1994) 'The Longue Durée: state and settlement strategies in southern Trans-jordan across the Islamic centuries', in E. L. Rogan and T. Tell (eds) *Village, Steppe and State: The Social Origins of Modern Jordan*, London and New York: British Academic Press: 1–31.

Kennedy, H. (1985) 'From Polis to Madina: urban change in Late Antique and Early Islamic Syria', *Past and Present* 106: 3–27.

Kennedy, H. (1986) *The Prophet and the Age of the Caliphates*, London and New York: Longman.

Kervran, M. (1984) 'A la recherche de Suhâr: état de la question', in R. Boucharlat and J.-F. Salles (eds) *Arabie Orientale, Mésopotamie et Iran Méridional de l'Age du Fer au Début de la Période Islamique*, Paris: Recherches sur les Civilisations: 285–98.

Kiani, M. Y. (1983) *The Islamic City of Gurgan, Archäologische Mitteilungen aus Iran Erganzungsband 11*, Berlin: Dietrich Reimer Verlag.

Kraeling, C. H. (ed.) (1938) *Gerasa, City of the Decapolis*, New Haven: American Schools of Oriental Research.

Lapidus, I. M. (1967) *Muslim Cities in the Later Middle Ages*, Cambridge, Mass.: Harvard University Press.

Lassner, J. (1970) *The Topography of Baghdad in the Early Middle Ages*, Detroit: Wayne State University Press.

McNicoll, A. *et al.* (1982) *Pella in Jordan 1: Report of the Joint Sydney University–Wooster College Ohio Excavations 1979–81*, Canberra: Australian National Gallery.

Northedge, A. (1981) 'Selected Late Roman and Islamic coarse wares', in J. Matthers (ed.)

The River Qoueiq, Northern Syria, and its Catchment, Oxford: British Archaeological Reports, International Series 98: 459–71.

Northedge, A. (1990) 'The racecourses at Samarra'', *Bulletin of the School of Oriental and African Studies* 53: 31–60.

Northedge, A. (1993) *Studies on Roman and Islamic 'Amman*, Vol. 1, *History, Site and Architecture*, Oxford: British Academy Monographs in Archaeology No. 3.

Northedge, A. (1994) 'Archaeology and new urban settlement in Early Islamic Syria and Iraq', in G. R. D. King and A. Cameron (eds) *Studies in Late Antiquity and Early Islam II, Settlement Patterns in the Byzantine and Early Islamic Near East*, Princeton: Darwin Press: 231–65.

Northedge, A. (1997) 'Les origines de la céramique à glaçure polychrome dans le monde islamique', in G. Demians D'Archimbaud (ed.) *La céramique médiévale en Méditerranée, Actes du VIe Congrès de l'AIECM2*, Aix-en-Provence: Narration Editions: 213–24.

Northedge, A. and Rousset, M.-O. (1995) 'Örnek, étape de la Route de la Soie', *Archéologie Islamique* 5: 97–122.

Northedge, A., Bamber, A. and Roaf, M. (1988) *Excavations at Ana*, Warminster: Aris and Philips, Iraq Archaeological Reports 1.

Oppenheimer, A. (1983) *Babylonia Judaica in the Talmudic Period*, Wiesbaden: L. Reichert, Tübinger Atlas des Vorderen Orients, Beiheft B47.

Petersen, A. (1995) *Dictionary of Islamic Architecture*, London: Routledge.

Redford, S. (1995) 'Medieval ceramics from Samsat, Turkey', *Archéologie Islamique* 5: 54–80.

Redman, C. L. (1986) *Qsar es-Seghir: an Archaeological View of Medieval Life*, Orlando, Fla.: Academic Press.

Rogers, J. M. (1970) 'Samarra, a study in medieval town-planning', in A. Hourani and S. M. Stern (eds) *The Islamic City*, Oxford: Bruno Cassirer: 119–55.

Rougeulle, A. (1991) 'Les importations de céramiques chinoises dans le golfe arabo-persique (VIIIe–XIe siècles)', *Archéologie Islamique* 2: 5–46.

Sack, D. (1989) *Damaskus: Entwicklung und Struktur einer orientalisch-islamischen Stadt I*, Mainz am Rhein: Verlag Philipp von Zabern, Damaszener Forschungen.

Sack, D. (1996) *Resafa IV: Die Grosse Moschee von Resafa-Rusafat Hisham*, Mainz am Rhein: Verlag Philipp von Zabern.

Sauvaget, J. (1939) 'Les Ruines Omeyyades du Djebel Seis', *Syria* 20: 239–56.

Sauvaget, J. (1941) *Alep. Essai sur le Développement d'une Grande Ville Syrienne, des Origines au Milieu du XIXe Siècle*, Paris: Geuthner, Bibliothèque Archéologique et Historique 36.

Sauvaget, J. (1948) *Relation de la Chine et de l'Inde*, Paris: Les Belles Lettres.

Sauvaget, J. (1967) 'Chateaux Umayyades de Syrie', *Revue des Études Islamiques* 35: 1–52.

Schlumberger, D. (1978) *Lashkari Bazar, une Résidence Royale Ghaznévide et Ghoride, t. 1A, l'Architecture*, Paris: Boccard.

Shokoohy, M. and Shokoohy, N. H. (1994) 'Tughluqabad: the earliest surviving town of the Delhi Sultanate', *Bulletin of the School of Oriental and African Studies* 57: 516–50.

Sjöström, I. (1993) *Tripolitania in Transition: Late Roman to Early Islamic Settlement*, Aldershot: Avebury.

Smith, R. H. (1973) *Pella of the Decapolis*, Wooster, O.: College of Wooster.

Smith, R. H. (1989) *Pella of the Decapolis* (Vol. 2), Wooster, O.: College of Wooster.

Sourdel-Thomine, J. (1978) *Lashkari Bazar, une Résidence Royale Ghaznévide et Ghoride, t. 1B, le Décor Non-Figuratif et les Inscriptions*, Paris: Boccard.

Tsafrir, Y. and Foerster, G. (1994) 'From Scythopolis to Baisan – changing concepts of urbanism', in G. R. D. King and A. Cameron (eds) *Studies in Late Antiquity and Early Islam II. Settlement Patterns in the Byzantine and Early Islamic Near East*, Princeton: Darwin Press: 95–116.

Ulbert, T. (1986) *Resafa II: Die Basilika des Heiligen Kreuzes in Resafa-Sergiupolis*, Mainz am Rhein: Verlag Philipp von Zabern.

von Grunebaum, G. E. (1961) 'The structure of the Muslim town', in G. E. von Grunebaum, *Islam: Essays on the Nature and Growth of a Cultural Tradition*, Menasha, Wis.: American Anthropological Association: 141–58.

Walmsley, A. (1988) 'Pella/Fihl after the Islamic conquest (AD 635–c. 900): a convergence of literary and archaeological evidence', *Mediterranean Archaeology* 1: 142–59.

Warren, J. and Fethi, I. (1982) *Traditional Houses in Baghdad*, Horsham: Coach House Publishing.

Watson, A. M. (1983) *Agricultural Innovation in the Early Islamic World: the Diffusion of Crops and Farming Techniques 700–1100*, Cambridge: Cambridge University Press.

Weisgerber, G. (1980) 'Patterns of early Islamic metallurgy in Oman', *Proceedings of the Seminar for Arabian Studies* 10: 115–26.

Whitcomb, D. (1988) *Aqaba, 'Port of Palestine on the China Sea'*, Amman: Al Kutba Publishers.

Whitcomb, D. (1990) 'Archaeology of the Abbasid period: the example of Jordan', *Archéologie Islamique* 1: 75–85.

Whitcomb, D. and Johnson, J. H. (1978) *Quseir al-Qadim 1978: Preliminary Report*, Cairo: American Research Center in Egypt.

Whitcomb, D. and Johnson, J. H. (1982) *Quseir al-Qadim 1980*, Malibu: Undena Press.

Whitehouse, D. (1970) 'Siraf: a medieval port on the Persian coast', *World Archaeology* 2: 141–58.

Whitehouse, D. (1980) *Siraf III, The Congregational Mosque and Other Mosques from the 9th to the 12th Centuries*, London: British Institute of Persian Studies.

Wilkinson, C. K. (1986) *Nishapur: Some Early Islamic Buildings and their Decoration*, New York: Metropolitan Museum of Art.

Zayadine, F. (ed.) (1986) *Jerash Archaeological Project 1981–1983* (Vol. I), Amman: Department of Antiquities.

Zayadine, F. (ed.) (1989) *Jerash Archaeological Project: 1984–8* (Vol. II), Paris: Institut Français de l'Archéologie du Proche-Orient 18.

SELECT BIBLIOGRAPHY

At the time of writing there are no worthwhile general studies of the archaeology of the Islamic world, or even interpretative studies of particular periods. It is particularly important to have an understanding of the history of the Islamic world: the *Cambridge History of Islam* provides a brief introduction, and the Longman *History of the Near East* series, edited by P. M. Holt, provides sufficient detail for archaeologists. Kennedy (1986) is the best introduction to the early period. For Iran, the *Cambridge History of Iran* is detailed and useful. For Islamic architecture, the most comprehensive starting point is Hillenbrand (1994). For the mosque, a particular but comprehensive approach can be found in Golvin (1974–78). Adams (1965, 1981) provides a classic discussion of long-term patterns of rural settlement and irrigation in Mesopotamia as reconstructed from air photography that includes Islamic settlement, and there are useful papers on settlement issues in G. R. D. King and A. Cameron (eds) *Studies in Late Antiquity and Early Islam II. Settlement Patterns in the Byzantine and Early Islamic Near East* (Princeton: Darwin Press, 1994). Redman (1986) describes the detailed excavation of an Islamic city, and other site-based studies include Hansman (1985) on Julfar, Kiani (1983) on Gurgan, McNicoll *et al.* (1982) on Pella, Northedge (1993) on 'Amman, Sourdel-Thomine (1978) on Lashkari Bazar, Whitcomb (1988) on Aqaba, and Wilkinson (1986) on Nishapur.

28

ARCHAEOLOGY OF THE MODERN STATE: EUROPEAN COLONIALISM

James A. Delle, Mark P. Leone and Paul R. Mullins

The historical archaeology of the modern state examines the various ways material culture is used by the state to generate and reproduce power over its essential creation, the individual. This intellectual enterprise analyses both the construction of the individual as a social unit and the ways power is mediated through the material relationships that exist between the modern state and this defined individual. The construction and reproduction of the individual within the state involves the interplay of two social mechanisms. First is the built environment which enables the state to command its subjects (defined as 'citizens' by the late eighteenth century). Second is a distinct social context which defines how that physical environment is experienced and successfully reproduced. This chapter examines a series of built environments, dating mainly from European colonial contexts, which illustrate how colonial and national states materially and socially reproduced their authority over the individual, whether as a subject or citizen. It is not our purpose here to offer a hegemonic definition either of historical archaeology or of the modern state. It is, rather, our goal to define a problem within the scholarly literature of historical archaeology, thereby unifying much otherwise scattered work done by archaeologists who conduct research on the modern era. We will thus not present an exhaustive survey of the canon of historical archaeology, but rather will examine a coherent research problem through which a set of objects and subjects will be seen more clearly. A further aim of ours is to show how archaeological knowledge can inform us on the creation and perpetuation of the state and its institutions.

Our definition of the relationship between the state and the individual is derived from the work of Michel Foucault and James Deetz. Our arguments build upon Deetz's use of the concept of individualism and on Foucault's definition of panopticism and his dismantling of the lengthy philosophical tradition by which individualism is defined. As anthropological archaeologists, we bring two additional aims to Deetz's and Foucault's projects. The first is to expand the traditional definition of historical archaeology. We believe it is profitably understood as the archaeology of the modern state, its institutions and political economy. This enterprise therefore entails an analysis of the mechanisms of surveillance and the social definition of the individual. We hope to demonstrate that state mechanisms operate in common ways regardless of whether they were employed by the Spanish, French, Dutch, British or North American state authorities.

MECHANISMS OF SURVEILLANCE: THE PANOPTICON, THE BAROQUE, AND SURVEILLANCE INSTITUTIONS

Modern states use a variety of mechanisms through which centralized authority is created and reproduced. For the purpose of this chapter, we will consider two such mechanisms whose logic of control was based on surveillance, and which left distinctive imprints in the archaeological record. The first of these is actually the later phenomenon: the panopticon and the related ideal of panopticism. We will then consider the antecedent to panopticism, the baroque architectural order, as a type of surveillance mechanism crucial to understanding the material manifestations of the authority of colonial states in North America and beyond.

We begin our discussion of surveillance mechanisms with the concept of panopticism. In the late eighteenth century, Jeremy Bentham theorized and designed a building he called the panopticon. In Bentham's ideal panopticon, one centrally positioned person could watch everyone held in an institution's care or custody. Panoptic buildings have several characteristics crucial to the creation and maintenance of state power. At the periphery of Bentham's idealized panopticon was a circular row of cells oriented towards the centre of a circular or octagonal building. Each cell had two windows or sets of windows, one set orientated towards the centre of the building, the other facing outwards. At the centre of the building was situated a separate tower or platform with windows facing towards the row of cells. From the tower a supervisor could see into every cell in the complex, with the cells' outer windows backlighting each individual occupant (Foucault 1979). The ceiling of the central part of the building was open, or featured skylights, lighting the interior of the structure (Fig. 28.1). The panopticon makes greatest sense when viewed from within. The panopticon inverted the dungeon's imprisoning principles of darkness and solitary enclosure by using light and constant visibility to confine the individual in each cell. While the guardian in the central tower could see into every backlit cell, the occupants could not see anyone except their watcher. Each inmate, patient, student, or worker in a panoptic complex was thus impressed

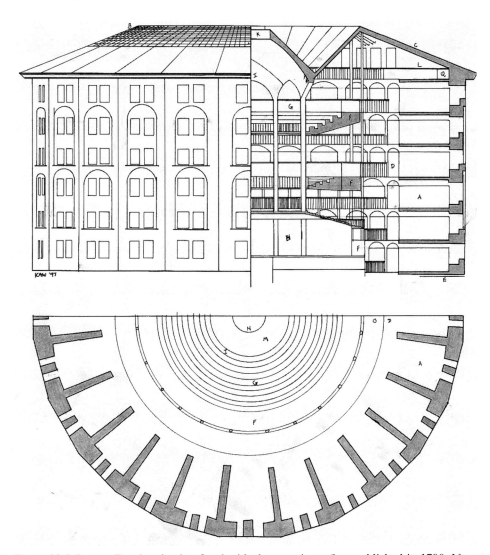

Figure 28.1 Jeremy Bentham's plan for the ideal panopticon, first published in 1790. Note the orientation of the cells towards the central tower, the backlighting provided by the pairs of windows in each cell, the circular shape of the building, and the huge skylight, all elements underscoring the importance of the watcher's gaze. Source: P. Kaw.

with a 'conscious and permanent visibility'. Escape plots between prisoners, contagion spread among the sick, and the threat of violence among the insane were to be eliminated by the separation of the masses into individual spaces characterized by a solitude dominated by the tower's visual omnipresence which reminded each occupant that s/he could be observed at any moment (Foucault 1979).

In North America, the panopticon was widely used throughout the early nineteenth century for a number of purposes; numerous panopticon forms were developed to fit specific surveillance contexts. Some examples of these buildings still exist, while others exist only in the archaeological record. The most obvious panoptic form is the prison (Fig. 28.2). More subtle examples include octagonal buildings, national libraries such as the Parliamentary Library in Ottawa and the reading room in the United States Library of Congress, and university libraries. Grade schools, hospitals, and some churches used the panopticon as a model (Fig. 28.3). When the panoptic principle is illuminated in each of these apparently dissimilar contexts, it becomes evident that surveillance of people's behaviour was employed on a very wide scale by institutions controlled by, or inherent in, the state.

Foucault's analysis of surveillance institutions elaborated on Bentham's model. By philosophically placing himself in the mind of the observed, Foucault was able to portray the observed as capable of imagining the process through which s/he was being watched. Bentham's placement of a tower at the centre of the panopticon

Figure 28.2 Illinois State Penitentiary: several key elements of panoptic surveillance are visible, including the central guard tower, backlit cells and polygonal skylight. Courtesy: Illinois Department of Corrections.

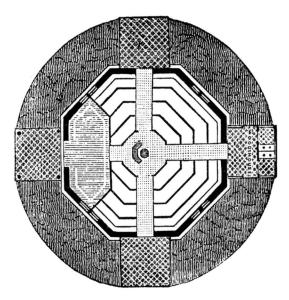

Figure 28.3 Plan of rustic octagonal schoolhouse, designed so that panopticism could be used to control the behaviour of young scholars (the dark circular area represents an exterior pavement). Here, scholars' chairs could be swivelled to face the schoolmaster at his central desk or the blank wall. Either way, the pupil would be subject to the teacher's gaze. Reproduced by permission of the publisher from J. and R. McClintock (eds), *Henry Barnard's School Architecture* (New York: Teachers College Press, © 1970 Teachers College, Columbia University. All rights reserved), Figure 12, p. 137.

provided a platform from which such a watcher could operate. Foucault realized that power over inmates was not exercised so much from the tower, but from the impact the tower had on the mind of the person who imagined s/he could be viewed from it. Foucault recognized the psychological process whereby the watched became inured to an imagined discipline which produced the kind of behaviour desired by the watcher. Once Foucault made this connection, he quickly saw that there needed to be no consistent gaze from the centre, only the suspicion of one. Such observation sustained from within is the key to the panoptic discipline which was employed simultaneously as state- and self-scrutiny, or what Foucault called surveillance (Foucault 1980). Foucault defined critical surveillance phenomena of panopticism 'gaze' and 'interiorization' (Foucault 1980: 155). Gaze, or observing social agents in order to normalize or control their behaviour, was nothing new to the eighteenth century. Indeed, monumental baroque architecture always contained some element for observing society (Foucault 1979: 216). However, the interiorization of the panopticon's gaze, to be observed not simply by something external but by the self, was a quite new form of surveillance of the individual in which subjects became their own disciplinarians.

Foucault's greatest insight into modern disciplinary principles stemmed from his analysis of panoptic architecture. Foucault argued that Bentham's panoptic prison was evidence of an eighteenth-century shift in built forms, from architecture which commanded authority through visibility to built spaces which addressed 'problems of population, health and the urban question' (Foucault 1980: 148). Examples of such built spaces include prisons, hospitals, schools, sanitariums, and the urban street plans which linked such institutions. During the eighteenth and nineteenth centuries, many of these institutions throughout the world copied or adapted the panoptic principles which Bentham outlined. Often they did so by modifying earlier baroque architecture which was also built to solidify state authority by calling the individual's attention to it.

The immediate antecedent to panopticism was the baroque order. Expressed through a style of architecture, interior decoration and exterior urban and rural landscaping, the baroque order is a combination of political theory and created physical environment. Baroque theory attempted to address the issue of how to sustain a public hierarchy within the state when there was a conflict between the actual existence of many centres of wealth, but a desire for one centre of power. At the core of baroque theory was a tension within the state's attempt to create uniform loyalty in a world which featured many actual sources and centres of power. From this tension emerged a discourse centred on the individual as subject to the state. The ideal mechanism of the baroque state was the dual acceptance by subjects of personal liberty and submission to a central authority, whose place at the head of the social order was, to both the state and the subject, self-evident. By the late eighteenth century, the baroque theory of society had become ineffective. Baroque states had failed to maintain the loyalty and discipline they required of their subjects. In the closing decades of the eighteenth century the baroque was succeeded in some places by its own creation: a panoptic view of the state with a particular definition of the individual as citizen.

We agree with the now nearly standard definition of historical archaeology as the study of the material culture of European colonial expansion, a phenomenon we believe was integral to the development of the modern state (Deetz 1977, 1991). Because colonialism is, in essence, a discourse of power, we are concerned with the institutions through which power was negotiated by the colonizing state. Colonialism is a process which assumes the expansion and maintenance of state control over subjected areas and peoples. This process therefore produced a panoply of both baroque and panoptic manifestations which ranged in form from missionary compounds, forts, plantations, frontier schools, mining machinery, haciendas and ranches, and factory clock towers. Many of these built environments incorporated a tower – bell tower, clock tower, watch tower, anthracite breaker (Fig. 28.4) – from which a person could see panoptically and which could be seen from many directions around. These institutions are normally described as functionally distinct, yet

Figure 28.4 A late nineteenth-century anthracite coal breaker from Pennsylvania: from the upper stories of this building, mine supervisors could observe activities occurring in the yard, the railroad loading area, and in the nearby town. © Pendor Natural Color, Dartonsville, PA, USA.

each possesses the possibility of watching and inculcating among the population the capacity to imagine that each individual is constantly being observed. It is this internal observation that is the consistent panoptic effect in the republican state of all these otherwise disparate institutions.

HISTORICAL ARCHAEOLOGY IN THE CHESAPEAKE REGION

The Chesapeake Bay region, as thoroughly excavated as any region in colonial North America, offers a useful archaeological illustration of both baroque and panoptic mechanisms of state power. Historical archaeologists of the Chesapeake have established the relationships between buildings in topographic space, and have established reliable chronologies among them and their planned landscapes – landscapes often marginalized, abandoned, or built over during the later evolution of the modern state. Out of the material recovered from the numerous excavations conducted in the Chesapeake, we can examine how urban plans, everyday ceramic tableware, and formal gardens can reveal key transformations in the relationship between material culture and state authority.

1113

Material forms which simultaneously commanded and observed people were included in numerous seventeenth-century North American settlements. In the Chesapeake, examples include the church tower at Jamestown, Virginia, the 1676 statehouse in St Mary's City, Maryland, the 1660s baroque town plan of St Mary's, and the 1694 baroque plan of Annapolis, Maryland (Miller 1988; Shackel 1994). All are examples of material forms built to command people's attention. These architectural examples were associated with the effort to manifest church and state authority. Without the weight of other forms of surveillance, these towers and cityscapes were essentially restraining mechanisms which could not alone create the effect of interiorization. Their 'gaze' tended to act only on the level of the social group, like the ancient amphitheatre; that is, they did not really monitor individuals, rather they watched the entire undifferentiated social body. Perhaps more importantly, their gaze was part of a broad range of practices which patrolled society through physical violence and harsh socio-economic penalties. Consequently, Jamestown's church tower and Annapolis's statehouse reminded people they were being monitored and regulated by a powerful institution, but there remained numerous spaces in which to hide effectively from this gaze.

The urban plans of St Mary's City and Annapolis, both cities located in Maryland, provide a suggestive indication of the shift from a generalized state observation to interiorized individual discipline. St Mary's City became Maryland's capital in 1634. The predominantly Catholic settlement remained the state capital until 1694, when it was moved to Annapolis in the wake of the Glorious Revolution. The capital city was a small settlement; historians have generally, though wrongly, assumed that it was an unplanned colonial frontier town. In contrast, Annapolis was intentionally designed by Maryland's second royal governor using typical baroque planning principles. The baroque urban plans of European cities used institutions of symbolic significance in positions which were emphasized visually through geometric approaches (e.g., long streets) and positioning (e.g., high points). In Annapolis, the church and statehouse were seated within two neighbouring circles on the town's highest points, with streets radiating out from the circles (Fig. 28.5). These two seats of power were visible from everywhere in Annapolis, much as they were in contemporaneous baroque European cities (Shackel 1993, 1994).

Despite their apparent differences, the two Maryland cities were both planned to enable surveillance. Extensive archaeological investigations at St Mary's City indicate that key elements of the city's layout were taken from baroque urban design principles (Miller 1988; Shackel 1993). In an apparent contrast to baroque European cities, St Mary's had only a few dozen buildings prior to the 1660s. During this era, the town's centre featured four wooden structures: two taverns, a lawyer's home and office, and a building that doubled as a government meeting place and inn. In addition to these wooden buildings, the St Mary's town centre had four

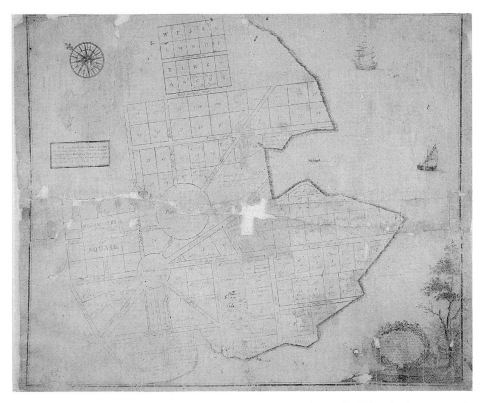

Figure 28.5 The 1718 Stoddert survey of Annapolis, as redrawn in 1743; the baroque order is apparent in the layout of the city. Reproduced with permission of Maryland State Archives.

brick structures. Two of those, the chapel and statehouse, were exactly a half-mile apart, with each structure 1,400 feet from the town centre. The other two brick buildings, a prison and a Jesuit school, were an equal distance from the statehouse and chapel respectively, roughly 800 feet. Consequently, the early capital was laid out on two symmetrical triangles extending from the town centre, with a symbolic-ally significant brick structure at each corner and principal roads leading to these corners (Miller 1988: 65–66; Shackel 1994). It is unlikely that this landscape alone produced enough conscious apprehension that people interiorized surveillance to become their own disciplinarians. The long-term impact of the city plan remains enigmatic as the city was abandoned as Maryland's capital soon after its initial layout. The plan never was linked with surveillance forms related to eighteenth-century transformations in, for instance, class dynamics (Isaac 1982) or discourses on individuality (Shackel 1993).

The construction of church towers or street plans could not alone produce the type of interiorization that Foucault recognized in late eighteenth-century Europe.

Foucault argued that such an internalization of personal control required a dense network of mechanisms that conditioned both the social whole and the individual existing within that whole. While urban plans and clock towers like those in St Mary's City monitored the social body, eighteenth-century institutions developed mechanisms like school training and personal etiquette to discipline quotidian behaviour. It is the distinction between societal and individual surveillance that characterizes the difference between baroque and panoptic disciplinary mechanisms.

Even so, St Mary's is suggestive of the directions that individual surveillance would take into the eighteenth century. In addition to the hallmarks of colonial authority, the plan's symbolically important points included a prison, a Jesuit school, and a cluster of public taverns. While the church, state, and prison are primarily repressive institutions, the school is typical of institutions which would come to regulate society from within rather than from above (Foucault 1980: 39). For Foucault, the shift from the infliction of repressive penalties to the willing self-discipline of individuals was critical to understanding the exercise of power in the eighteenth century and beyond. We suspect that such a transition to the self-disciplined individual had already begun at St Mary's.

Annapolis's 1694 city plan was larger and somewhat more complex than the plan for St Mary's, but it too was based on principles which used perspective and topography to stress symbolically important points. In Annapolis, church and state circles were built beside each other, integrating their interests and blurring distinctions between political authority and religion. In Annapolis's plan, the state was projected as a union of those two forms. At St Mary's, church and state were spatially alienated at the furthest reaches of the plan, despite their symbolically significant positions. Perhaps a more critical difference between the two plans was the position of the school and prison, two modern surveillance institutions which ultimately depended upon the definition of individual citizenship. While the St Mary's plan accorded significant, separate positions to the school and prison, the Annapolis plan subordinated both to the state by placing them along a street like a house or a business. Prisons and schools were certainly as important to the development of discipline in Annapolis as they were in St Mary's, yet their unobtrusiveness in the Annapolis cityscape may have made their disciplining power seem less repressive.

The emergence of surveillance institutions certainly promoted the technologies of individualism, yet the seemingly organic and even innocuous appearance of jails, schools, and asylums was dependent upon changes in everyday material culture: domestic architecture and standardized tablewares are the sort of objects which projected surveillance technologies into everyday life, thus acting as mechanisms through which discipline was internalized by individuals. For example, historical archaeologists of the Chesapeake have recently shown how portable material culture, particularly ceramics, played a part in the construction of individualism, and thus can be interpreted as a form of surveillance mechanism. At the turn of the eighteenth century, the American colonial gentry began conspicuously to consume material goods, a phenomenon which distinguished them as the dominant class. Conspicuous consumption was part of an elaborate set of mutually dependent material and social discourses which separated the élite from the lower classes and situated their power in a presumed natural order (Leone 1988). Explicit behavioural rules defined personal interaction, dining, and material presentation (Shackel 1993). For example, élite tables were set with an elaborate material assemblage, including forks and knives, individual ceramic dishes intended for particular functions, and certain types of food. All these items were associated with specific rules. Deetz was the first archaeologist to explore these relationships, which had not been noticed by many other scholars, principally historians (Deetz 1977). Following Deetz's work, it became possible to understand why ordinary colonial farmers used globes and maps, or a telescope, sextant and a clock, to explain the world and divide it into orderly units. Historical archaeologists have been the first to notice these many connections and to tie them to prevailing notions of individualism (Leone 1988).

There are two components to the logic that connects tableware, tea ware, furniture, room patterns, disposal patterns, gravestone decoration, landscapes, and scientific and musical instruments to the concept of individualism. The first, and the one emphasized by Deetz, considers that the forms of all these things change when people see themselves as separate from all others, as potentially equal, or having histories, futures, and rights (Deetz 1977). Each individual sees himself or herself as a distinct individual when items like these become equal, contain separate functions, are segregated, stress achievement, or are used to illustrate control over natural principles. Second, in use, these objects produce people who believe they are separate, have special knowledge, are meritorious, and deserve a place in a natural order, but who are in fact rule-abiding and thus, from the perspective of the state, profoundly interchangeable.

The ambiguity produced by individualism can be appreciated through an analysis of eighteenth-century Chesapeake landscapes. Mid-eighteenth-century architecture was one mechanism used to distinguish the gentry while promoting social deference to the gentry's 'natural' right to rule society, and did so through the use of the idea of individualism. This may be nowhere more evident than in the architecture of élite gardens (Kryder-Reid 1994; Leone 1984, 1988). For example, in the 1760s, the Annapolitan lawyer William Paca built a Georgian home at the top of a 'pleasure garden' (Leone 1984, 1988). Paca, who would later sign the Declaration of Independence and become a prominent constitutional lawyer, was one of a series of Chesapeake gentry who built such formal gardens during the late eighteenth century. The gardens were characterized by rolling topography (i.e., flat terraces alternating with sloping falls) and carefully manicured spaces which distort optical perception within the garden. The gardens contain shrubs, trees, some exotic plants, ponds and fountains arranged in geometric forms reflecting the symmetry of Georgian architecture. The expression of distances and the relative size of objects in the garden is distorted visually by the effect of the topography, prominent features (e.g., gazebos, houses, vegetation), and shades of green in the vegetation which manipulate the impact of lines of sight on a visitor. Although the style itself was originally most popular in England beginning a century earlier, a series of such gardens was built in eastern Maryland, including a dozen in Annapolis alone (Leone and Shackel 1990). Hundreds of gardens were built in the Chesapeake during this period; hundreds more were built throughout the British North American colonies.

Formal gardens created two fundamental ideological effects. First, they ordered nature in a specific way, and, second, they constructed a distinct past for that nature. The ordering of nature included systematic observation done in the garden, enabling the gardener to predict natural growth cycles. This ability to deploy precedent, control optical relations, and display that comprehension in the garden created a social space which displayed a class's ability to order time and nature. Second, the gentry hoped that members of other classes would see the garden as a metaphor linking their owners to a postulated right to rule others. Gardens linked a tangible understanding of natural law to the enaction of that law in everyday social relations. Gardens were thus a material mechanism to legitimize class relations because they were intended to promote underclass deference to gentry decision-making grounded in natural law. They were one of many efforts to project class authority onto nature itself and further the notion that the gentry possessed a specialized knowledge which was necessary to administer society. Such means of social control required the attention of the individual subject; since the master's view was returned, the double looking found within baroque and early modern institutions offers a prelude to classic panopticism.

DISCIPLINE AND PLANTATION SLAVERY

The political economy of the Chesapeake, as was the case in much of eighteenth-century North America, was driven by plantation production. During this time plantations were worked by slaves, managed by overseers who were sometimes slaves themselves, and owned by people who ranged from the phenomenally wealthy to those who were slightly less than wealthy. The larger plantations were run by a regime of terror, violence, and overwork. These were exploitative colonial institutions, based on the crudest abuse of human beings. Most eighteenth-century plantations employed baroque principles embodied in both architecture and landscape on the one hand, and in a quest for absolute hierarchy on the other.

We have dealt so far with baroque settings in which the members of all classes were nominally considered to be free. In these settings there were slaves from place to place and from time to time, but we have not argued that they were included in the designs of baroque planning. We therefore cannot definitively demonstrate the effects this ostentatious kind of rule had on enslaved populations. We can, however, suggest how both baroque and modified panoptic principles were installed in the material culture of slave-based plantation agriculture. In doing so, we must deal both with violence and with a kind of explicit surveillance that itself could lead to acts of violence. Plantations do not incorporate panoptic surveillance in the truest sense, which presupposes either common citizenship or common values, but they do demonstrate how the architecture of baroque hierarchy and the deliberately focused gaze of surveillance institutions acted as a modified form of panoptic discipline.

The intentions and effects of treating a large segment of society neither as individuals nor citizens are nowhere better expressed than on agricultural plantations. The design and management of plantations were largely baroque, even into the nineteenth century, but, we argue, came to include some of the surveillance disciplines of panopticism. For our purposes, we follow Orser's definition of 'plantations' as economic institutions which exist primarily to increase the wealth of the plantation owner or owners through agricultural production. The plantation is further defined by its distinctive power relations between owners, defined as planters, and its primary producers, who may either be wage labourers or slaves. The social relations between the two groups are best understood in terms of class relations, often reproduced by a socially created racial hierarchy, through which the planters extracted surplus through the exploitation of the labour power of the workers. Defining the relations between the two groups are the dialectics of discipline and resistance: the planters attempt to create a disciplined workforce while the workers resist the inequity promoted by those disciplined social relations (Epperson 1990, forthcoming; Orser 1988a, 1988b, 1988c).

Discipline among plantation slaves was in part created through the public spectacle of corporal punishment, a means of discipline which the later panoptic ideal hoped to replace (Foucault 1979). Slaves were required to perform specific tasks at specific times; both work and social routines were imposed upon them. If an individual failed to keep the specified regimes, s/he could be the victim of physical torture. In the case of West Indian sugar plantations, that punishment could come in the form of flogging, being held in 'bedstocks' (i.e., literally with the feet held in a stock at the end of a bed), or having an iron mask or collar secured over the head or neck to prevent drunkenness or geophagy ('dirt eating'), a disorder brought on by malnutrition.

Crippling punishment was a crucial form of plantation discipline regulated by the state but dispensed by local planters. As colonial plantations were an integral part of pre-industrial European states, the state regulated the type and severity of punishment to be meted out to slaves (Epperson 1990: 29; Tomich 1990: 242). Despite attempts at state regulation, the individual planters and their agents exerted great control over disciplining their own labour force. For example, Matthew Lewis, a Jamaican planter who knew both Coleridge and Goethe, reported in his published journal that he implemented a code of laws upon one of his plantations which included a registry of punishment (Lewis [1834]1929: 195). A passage in Lewis's journal underscores the relation of punishment to the work expected by the plantation labourer. During one of Lewis's absences, several injuries against the plantation were committed. In the first, a slave referred to as Hazard stole sugar from a second slave named Frank who had previously stolen the sugar from the plantation boiling-house. The resolution of this conflict came when 'Frank broke Hazard's head, which in my opinion settled the matter so properly, that I declined spoiling it by any interference of my own' (Lewis [1834]1929: 315). Lewis reports that no action was taken against Frank despite the fact that he had both stolen sugar from the plantation and apparently killed another slave. In a second incident, which Lewis refers to as being 'more serious', a slave named Toby refused to load sugar cane onto a cart. Lewis reports that as a result the sugar processing for that day had stopped. Of the two incidences the latter was considered to be more serious, as the action taken by Toby threatened the labouring discipline of the plantation, and in Lewis's words 'amounted to an act of downright rebellion' (Lewis [1834]1929: 316).

The punishment dealt to Toby demonstrates how the planters attempted to internalize discipline among the plantation workforce. During the Easter holiday, a time during which the slaves were allowed to celebrate with salt-fish, rum, and sugar dispensed by Lewis, Toby was confined in a small room within earshot of the raucous festivities. Upon his release the following Monday, other slaves began to 'censure his folly . . . advising him to humble himself and to beg [Lewis's] pardon' (Lewis [1834]1929: 316). Upon being humiliated by his fellow workers, Toby returned to work. Thus, at least according to Lewis's account, the individual, in this case Toby, experienced a humiliation by breaking the social code of the plantation as defined by the planters. The scorn that Toby faced, reinforced by his ostracism from society during his confinement, was a mechanism through which Lewis hoped Toby would become a self-regulating, disciplined worker. This is a fundamentally different kind of discipline from inflicted violence.

The plantation was a distinct type of surveillance institution in which planters attempted to supervise ('oversee') completely the lives of the workers. There was considerable variation in the disciplinary strategies adopted by planters, depending on the intensity of cultivation and the labour requirements demanded by specific plantation crops. For example, historical archaeology has informed our knowledge of material and social relations on seventeenth- and eighteenth-century tobacco plantations near the Chesapeake Bay (e.g., Carson *et al.* 1981; Deetz 1977, 1988; Epperson 1990; Hudgins 1990; Kelso 1984, 1986; Klingelhofer 1987; McKee 1987; Neiman 1978; Noël Hume 1982; Pogue 1988a, 1988b; Reinhart 1984; Upton 1985, 1986, 1990). The historical importance of tobacco plantations is reflected in the simple reality that four of the first five United States presidents were tobacco planters (Carson *et al.* 1981; Menard *et al.* 1988: 185). Historical archaeology has played a significant role in interpreting seventeenth-century Chesapeake plantations, primarily because few of the wooden buildings that characterized Chesapeake architecture remain standing for traditional architectural analysis. Seventeenth-century buildings in the Chesapeake were generally of impermanent, earthfast timber construction; no more than six such structures remain standing (Carson *et al.* 1981).

To be effective over a large population, however, not all forms of plantation discipline could be physically coercive; many strategies relied on panoptic surveillance. The most evident material expressions of such strategies on tobacco plantations are the relationships between the landscapes of the planters and the landscapes of the slaves (Upton 1988). Chesapeake tobacco plantations were generally isolated and self-contained communities which Dell Upton has likened to a village, with the planter's house serving as the centre of power. As a centre of administrative and economic power, the planter's house was both physically and socially elevated above other buildings and was physically separated from the surrounding countryside by systems of terraces and fences. Plantation houses were intentionally constructed to dominate the landscape. Philip Fithian, a tutor employed at Nomini Hall, reported in his journal that the plantation house could be seen from a distance of six miles. By the late eighteenth century, plantation houses like Thomas Jefferson's Monticello were constructed to command an enormous view of the landscape, to both see and be seen (Upton 1988). The effect of such a spatial division was that both slaves and masters shared an attitude about the possession of space (Upton 1988: 367). This afforded some measure of spatial proprietary rights to the slave. For instance, Upton reports that Fithian was obliged to pay a forfeit to several slaves for trespass. Yet such a shared consciousness, if it did indeed exist, reified the work discipline of the plantation because the space that planters and slaves acknowledged as the domain of the slaves included the work spaces: bakeries, blacksmith shops, fields, and so on (Upton 1988: 367). This spatial division of the plantation created a disciplined labour force out of enslaved people by internalizing and naturalizing the social and racial hierarchies embedded in plantation production.

By the middle of the nineteenth century, the cotton plantation had replaced the tobacco plantation in relative economic importance in North America. The importance of the cotton plantation has not been lost on historical archaeologists, who have studied both pre-emancipation and post-emancipation plantations (e.g.,

Adams and Smith 1985; Ascher and Fairbanks 1971; Fairbanks 1974; Moore 1985; Orser 1988a, 1991; Orser and Nekola 1985; Otto 1977, 1984; Reitz *et al.* 1985; Singleton 1985a, 1988). The archaeology of cotton plantations in the American South can be divided along a common line drawn in United States history, the *antebellum* and *postbellum* periods (i.e., before and after the American Civil War). This historical division is significant, for both the relations of production in the American South and the power of the United States federal government *vis-à-vis* the individual states changed dramatically with the defeat of the Confederate States of America and the concomitant abolition of slavery in the United States. Taken together, two influential works of historical archaeology, Otto (1984) and Orser (1988a), can shed light on how our interpretations of surveillance mechanisms defined social relations on *antebellum* and *postbellum* cotton plantations.

Otto excavated an *antebellum* cotton plantation, Cannon's Point, which is located on one of the barrier islands off the Georgia coast. Otto infers that, taken collectively, plantations which existed along the stretch of the coast between South Carolina and northern Florida constituted 'a distinctive environmental zone, cash crop region, and cultural area of the Old South' (Otto 1984: 9). According to Otto, because this 'cultural area' was distinguished by labour-intensive large-scale rice and cotton planting, only the larger plantations were economically successful. Otto builds this argument by examining and comparing the houses and middens of slaves, an overseer, and the planter at Cannon's Point, offering a site-specific study of a stratified society which he considers a microcosm of the *antebellum* cotton plantation south. The plantation's material division of space defined the relationship between Otto's three status groups (i.e., planter–overseer–slave). The planter's domain, which Otto defines as the 'administrative and technical nucleus' of the plantation, consisted of the planter's house, kitchen, cotton houses, and store houses (Otto 1984: 13–14). According to Otto, the family who owned the plantation, the Coupers, were considered to be 'conspicuous consumers' by their planter peers (Otto 1984: 127); that is, they expressed their power and status through the purchase and display of material culture. The house in which the family lived was 'a massive 2 1/2-story frame structure' with as many as ten rooms and as much as '1786 square feet of living space, excluding stairways, basement, and loft' (Otto 1984: 132).

The domestic space over which the planter exerted direct control included a detached kitchen, which was separated from the great house by approximately 20 metres. While the distance between the structures can be partially explained by the desire of the planter to remove the smells and sounds of cooking from the immediate living space and to limit the danger of fire to the great house, this can also be seen as the intentional distancing of a work space dominated by slaves from those they served, underscoring the social distance between the cook and her staff and the planter, his family and guests. The cotton gin houses in which the crop was prepared and stored for export were within 30 metres of the great house. The proximity of this industrial space to the planter's domain allowed the planter direct surveillance of the crop as it was prepared for export down the river which fronted the house (Otto 1984).

Otto suggests that surveillance technologies were used by the planters to create a status hierarchy among the slaves. Drivers responsible for assigning daily tasks had the power to punish their fellow slaves and carried the symbol of their disciplinary authority, a short whip with a heavy handle. During the excavation of Cannon's Point, one of the eight slave houses examined differed from the others by being set on brick piers rather than on sills lying on the ground. It had a plank rather than a dirt floor, and the cabin was somewhat larger than the other cabins on the plantation. Otto suggests that this dwelling may have housed the drivers and their families. If Otto's suggestion is correct, then this house would be a visible material representation of the extended disciplinary power required to run a slave-based plantation (Otto 1984).

It was the ultimate responsibility of the overseer to establish and maintain discipline over the enslaved labour force; similar surveillance mechanisms were thus used to mediate the relationship between these men and the enslaved population. For example, Otto reports that the overseer's house at Cannon's Point was situated approximately half-way between two groups of four slave cabins. The size and form of the overseer's house more closely resembled the great house than the slave quarters – not surprising considering that William Couper, one of the sons of the planter John Couper, served as overseer for a time at Cannon's Point. Otto reports that the overseer's house at Cannon's Point had exterior dimensions of 34 by 36 feet, and the interior was divided into four rooms each measuring 12 by 15 feet, plus a central hall, providing about 790 square feet of living space (Otto 1984: 99). While not nearly as massive as the great house, the one and a half storey overseer's house would have stood in stark and imposing contrast to the small slave cabins which would have housed as many as ten people. The symbolic expression of power and authority vested in the overseer and displayed to the field slaves provided everyday reminders that they were under someone else's authority (Otto 1984).

In contrast to Cannon's Point, which was abandoned before the Civil War, Millwood Plantation, located along the border between South Carolina and Georgia, operated during both the *antebellum* and *postbellum* periods (Orser 1988a). The planter-owner of Millwood plantation was James Edward Calhoun, a well-connected member of the southern élite. As early as 1833, Calhoun began the system of plantation tenancy which would become the dominant regime at the plantation after the Civil War (Orser 1988a). The defeat of the Confederacy forced planter élites like Calhoun to reorganize their system of production and élite/labourer relations. According to Orser, although the planters were confused and frightened about their future after the war, there was general resolve not to transfer plantation ownership to the emancipated slaves. As a result, several strategies of labour extraction were established, including farm wage-labour and systems of time and crop sharing. During the years following the war, the South Carolina élite created new systems of discipline at both the state level, through the establishment of a so-called 'Black Code', and on the level of the individual plantations. The Black Code, established in 1865, legally restricted the movements and labour of black workers and their families. Individual planters entered into contracts with labourers which sought to construct a labour discipline that would be beneficial to the planter (Orser 1988a, 1991). Two classes of tenancy resulted: renting and share-cropping. A legal distinction was made between renters and sharecroppers vis-à-vis the crop they produced, with renters considered legal owners of their crops and sharecroppers merely cultivators of a landlord's crops (Orser 1991).

The restructuring of labour resulted in the restructuring of plantation settlement space, which has been discovered archaeologically (Fig. 28.6). Unlike *antebellum* plantation settlements which put a premium on both physical violence and the direct surveillance of the labourers, *postbellum* plantation settlements tended to

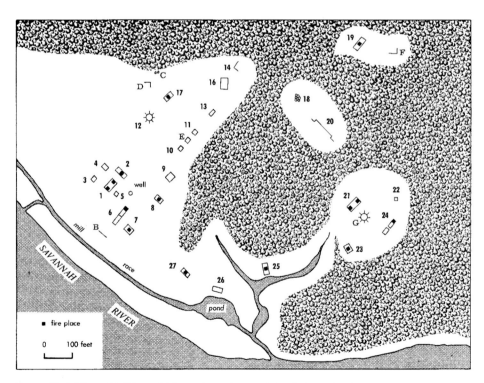

Figure 28.6 Plan of Millwood Plantation: the spatial relationships between the great house (1), overseer's house (8), and the slave houses (10, 11 and E) were designed to reinforce the social hierarchy of the *antebellum* South. Illustration by Charles E. Orser.

be dispersed. Each farmer, whether renter or sharecropper, lived with his or her family near the fields which they worked. Significantly, Orser suggests that where sharecroppers made up the bulk of the plantation tenants, the settlement form would resemble *antebellum* spaces more closely, with the barns, sheds and other outbuildings located near the planter's central home. This provided the planter-landlord with the capability of supervising the sharecroppers directly. When a farmer wanted to use a mule or a plough, s/he would be forced to approach the planter's house under the direct observation of the landlord. Likewise, by locating the barns within sight of the house, the landlord could maintain direct surveillance over the harvested crop. Renters were the objects of relatively less surveillance because the landlords had less direct interest in the renters' crop (Orser 1988a).

Sugar plantations have been thoroughly examined by historical archaeologists, especially in the Caribbean (e.g., Armstrong 1985, 1990; Craton 1978; Craton and Walvin 1970; Delle 1989, 1994; France 1984; Handler 1979; Handler and Lange 1978; Higman 1974; Lange and Handler 1985; Pulsipher and Goodwin 1982b). In addition, scholars recently have turned their attention to maroon (escaped slaves) villages in sugar-producing areas (e.g., Agorsah 1990; Orser 1992, 1993, 1996). A consideration of sugar plantations is crucial to our purposes here, for of the several cash crops raised on slave-based plantations, sugar demanded the most highly disciplined labour force.

The majority of labourers on sugar plantations were forced to toil in unsafe conditions under strict surveillance. On some plantations, surveillance did not end with the work day but was extended into the domestic world of the slaves. For example, the first of two slave villages at the Seville Estate in St Ann's Parish, Jamaica were located immediately behind and up slope from the planter's great house, allowing the planter increased visibility during daylight hours and when the moon was bright. At this same plantation, a separate building, the overseer's house, was located in front of the great house, commanding a view of both the industrial complex and sugar-cane fields. A single person standing on the veranda of this structure could supervise all the workings of the plantation. Notably, several small cannons from its period of operation still exist in front of the overseer's house. Permanently aimed towards the cane fields, the cannon symbolized the power exerted by the planter and his overseers over the lives of the labourers. The over-seer's complex would in turn have been visible from the cane fields and the sugar works, creating and maintaining the surveillance required to enforce and internalize the self-discipline of the enslaved workforce (Armstrong forthcoming).

The centre of industrial life on a sugar plantation was the sugar mill/boiling house complex (Delle 1989, 1994; Pulsipher and Goodwin 1982a, 1982b; Tomich 1990). It was in this series of structures that cane was reduced into exportable form. The planters were concerned with the close supervision of labour during this crucial processing phase. Schwartz (1985: 142–49) reports that on plantations in Brazil, managers and foremen kept constant supervision over labour during each stage of the sugar-making process. Genuine terror was used by these overseers to maintain industrial discipline and an alert labour force. Schwartz (1985: 143) notes that it was common to keep a small axe near the mill machinery to amputate any limbs that were inadvertently caught in the machinery. The sight of such a hasty amputation would have underscored the importance of maintaining concentration on the tasks at hand. The boiling house and mill structures were often the most physically imposing structures on a plantation (Delle 1994; Pulsipher and Goodwin 1982b). Given the intense surveillance inside the structures and their imposing forms, these buildings were a significant part of the plantation's disciplinary reproduction.

This brief analysis does not cover all New World plantation systems that have been studied by historical archaeologists. For example, there is a wealth of literature on rice plantations (e.g., Ferguson 1991, 1992; Lewis 1984, 1985; Singleton 1992), and some work has been done on indigo plantations (e.g., Friedlander 1985; Wheaton and Garrow 1985) and more recently on coffee plantations (Delle 1996, 1998; Joseph et al. 1987). There has also been a recent trend to take a more critical approach to the discipline of plantation archaeology (e.g., Epperson 1990; Ferguson 1992; Orser 1988b, 1988c, 1989; Potter 1990, 1991; Singleton 1990).

SURVEILLANCE IN INDUSTRIAL LANDSCAPES

During the course of the first half of the nineteenth century the economic base of the northeastern United States shifted from agriculture to industry, a shift that involved the transformation of a rural agricultural peasantry into a disciplined industrial labour force. This social transition was drastic as it involved the redefinition of the relationship between workers and both time and space. The regimen of the factory demanded a disciplined workforce which would arrive to work at a specific time, operate machinery for as long as possible, and then return the next day to do the same repetitive tasks. This routine was radically different from the seasonal cycle of agricultural work and demanded that people work indoors in what amounted to very unsafe and unhealthy conditions. In order to discipline the workforce to operate in such an environment, new landscapes of surveillance were intentionally created by the factory owners. Historical archaeologists have studied several of these industrial landscapes (e.g., Beaudry 1989; Beaudry and Mrozowski 1987a, 1987b, 1988, 1989; Beaudry et al. 1991; Candee 1985; Gross 1988; Kulik 1988; Langhorne 1976; McGuire 1991; Miller and Pacey 1985; Mrozowski 1987, 1991; Nassaney and Abel 1993; Orr 1977; Paynter 1988; Sande 1977; Starbuck 1983; Wurst 1991), but we shall concentrate on two case studies examined by historical archaeologists: Lowell, Massachusetts, a planned industrial urban centre (Mrozowski 1991; Mrozowski *et al.* 1996) and Harper's Ferry, Virginia, the seat of one of the first United States government firearms manufactories, or armouries (Shackel 1996).

Lowell presents an interesting case because of the amount of historical archaeology that has been completed there over the years (e.g., Beaudry 1989; Beaudry *et al.* 1991; Beaudry and Mrozowski 1987a, 1987b, 1989; Mrozowski *et al.* 1996). The historical significance of Lowell lies in the deliberate spatial organization of the city, designed and implemented by a group of founding capitalists to maximize the efficiency and profitability of industry. That city plan was based on the principles of surveillance to ensure an industrial discipline among the working class and to secure profits for the capitalist class.

Mrozowski reports that the design of the city was intended to function as a system of moral policing (Mrozowski 1991: 90). The mill, workers' housing and overseer's and mill agent's housing were built in close proximity to each other in such a way that the overseer could supervise both the working and private lives of the labourers with the intention of creating a disciplined workforce. The manufacturing corporations owned, controlled, and supervised both work and domestic space. Such control served to unite the conception of work and home, reinforcing a sense of discipline in the workers.

The latter were housed in a series of large, multi-storeyed boarding houses. At the Boott Mill complex, eight blocks of such boarding houses were constructed. Each block was flanked at either end by a tenement meant to house a mill agent and his family. These supervisory employees could thus maintain surveillance over two blocks of boarding houses at a time, and thus a worker could be supervised from either or both of two perspectives at any given moment (Beaudry 1989: 23). An additional layer of surveillance existed in the placement of the mill agent's house. The rear of this duplex house was oriented to command a view of the overseer's housing; the supervisors were thus supervised. This house was raised above the tenements and boarding houses on an artificial terrace, providing a material symbol of the industrial social hierarchy (Beaudry 1989: 23) and a visible reminder of industrial discipline.

Beaudry and Mrozowski suggest that the domestic interiors of the boarding houses were often the only areas over which workers exercised control (Beaudry and Mrozowski 1988: 5), as these were the only areas which could not be seen by the industrial supervisors. However, in early nineteenth-century Lowell, the mills employed boarding-house keepers who were responsible for feeding the tenants, cleaning the house, and maintaining 'order and discipline, and for upholding morality within the boardinghouse' (Beaudry and Mrozowski 1988: 6). Clearly, the industrialists who designed Lowell had every intention of supervising the domestic as well as the work environments of the employees with the hope of creating and maintaining an industrial order that would ensure profit maximization.

This social control was extended into the domestic lives of the mill employees through a series of regulations. Employees were required to attend Sunday worship and refrain from alcohol consumption. All workers were required to live in the mill-owned boarding houses unless they secured special permission from the company. The boarders were not allowed to entertain guests after ten o'clock at night (Bond 1989: 24). Bond reports that individuals who failed to keep to this social discipline were often fired or expelled from the boarding houses. From her interpretation of the documentary evidence of the Boott Mills, Bond suggests that alcohol consumption and inebriation were among the most serious offences against the discipline of production. She suggests that the corporation would inter-pret drunkenness as the breakdown of self-control, which would threaten the 'industrial work ethic', which we believe can be equated with industrial discipline. Bond examined thirty-three letters written by Boott Mills paymaster James G. Marshall to keepers, overseers and mill workers: of these, sixteen complained of workers' drinking (Bond 1989: 29). The surveillance and regulation of behaviour was clearly an important component in the creation of industrial discipline at Lowell.

Similar processes were at work within the industrial landscape of Harper's Ferry, an industrial city situated at the confluence of the Potomac and Shenandoah Rivers, in what is today the state of West Virginia (Shackel 1996; see also Shackel and Winter 1994 and Shackel and Larson forthcoming). In the middle of the nineteenth century, the organic landscape of this small city was intentionally reconfigured, Shackel argues, as part of a larger project to increase the efficiency of arms produc-tion. A key element within this project was the transformation of armoury workers from skilled artisans to semi-skilled machine tenders. In the effort to accomplish this radical transformation in the relations of production, armoury supervisors, beginning in about 1840, instituted a number of reforms, including regular work hours, the introduction of a time clock and bell, the surveillance of visitors to the factory, and, notably for archaeologists, the reconfiguration of the factory complex layout and the street grid for the city. Shackel argues that the construction of standardized factory buildings and the imposition of a geometric city plan were part of a strategy intended to increase the ability of armoury managers to supervise the workers, as well as to break down the traditional craft-based nature of arms manufacture (Shackel 1996).

REFORM AND INCARCERATION AS SELF-DISCIPLINE

In the late eighteenth century, prisons and asylums began to re-conceive their central mission as one of rehabilitation, rather than simple incarceration. The Walnut Street Prison in Philadelphia is one example of such an institution in the early stage of this transition which has been examined archaeologically (Fig. 28.7). The city built the prison in 1775 to replace its public gaol. The new prison eventually became partly like Bentham's panoptic jail: when originally constructed, it was a baroque Georgian building, but with a renovation executed in 1797, a workshop building was added to the complex. The new two-storey workshop building was a five-sided structure, resembling an unfinished octagon. The prison's adoption of panoptic workspaces, together with its reform strategy, reflects panoptic philosophy: inmates learned a trade as part of a programmme intended to reform them and return them to society as productive and rehabilitated citizens. The prison also adopted solitary confinement as a punishment for its worst offenders, in the hope of isolating them from bad influences. This adoption of panoptic principles resulted in a decrease in the Walnut Street prison's rate of recidivism, but the building gradually fell into disrepair, was replaced by the Eastern State Penitentiary, and was eventually torn down in 1835 (Cotter *et al.* 1992: 175; Cotter *et al.* 1988; Upton 1992).

In the United States, the panoptic reform concept was probably most systematically followed at the Eastern State Penitentiary (Fig. 28.8), which was designed in 1821 and remained a working prison until 1970. The 10-acre granite fortress had a central observation tower with seven rows of cellblocks radiating from it like spokes, contained within four massive walls with corner turrets which wholly concealed the outside. The rows contained as many as 250 cells which could not be individually monitored from the central tower, as they would be in a true panopticon; the prison adapted Bentham's notion of constant surveillance by attempting to make each individual his or her own confiner. Upon entry to the prison, inmates were hooded and placed in one of the solitary cells, ostensibly never to be seen by another prisoner. They were trained in crafts and received a Bible and regular visits from Quakers, all of which were intended to turn the prisoner to a more useful calling upon their release. The complex was the state of the art in its time and was one of the largest and costliest buildings in the United States – Charles Dickens even listed it, along with Niagara Falls, as one of the two sites he most wanted to see on his 1842 tour of America! When he arrived at Eastern State, Dickens quickly comprehended that the prison's reform principles relied upon prisoners' eventual consent to the mores of their captors: to re-enter society, inmates had to discipline themselves to the values of their keepers and eliminate all of the signs of their criminality.

Both baroque and panoptic modes of discipline were used to restrain and rehabilitate other individuals defined by the state as aberrant or as dangerous to society's order, including criminals, prostitutes, and those defined as insane. The best example of an insane asylum known to archaeologists is the now reconstructed public hospital for the insane in Williamsburg, Virginia. This institution first opened in 1773, and eventually developed a rehabilitation philosophy similar to that

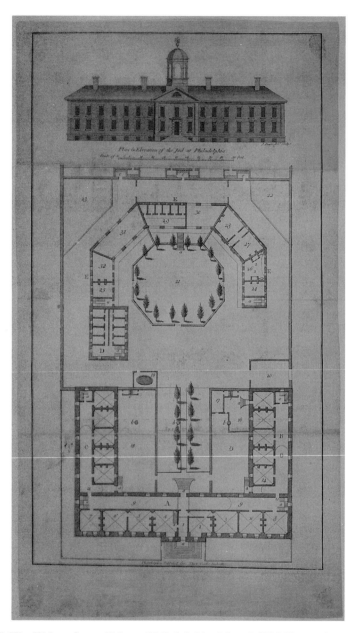

Figure 28.7 The Walnut Street Prison, Philadelphia: (above) 1798 illustration and plan and (opposite) 1970s excavation of the part of the prison workshop, as seen from an adjacent building. Source: Historical Society of Pennsylvania (plan) and Cotter *et al.* 1988 (photograph).

Figure 28.7 (continued)

espoused at the Walnut Street prison, and used music, games, and dancing in attempts to cure the insane. The public hospital did not originally attempt to reform or rehabilitate its inmates; solitary restraint of patients was commonly used into the nineteenth century. A 1796 visitor to Williamsburg commented that the hospital was 'a fine building; but in it the unfortunate maniacs are rather abandoned to their wretched state than subjected to any treatment which might tend to their recovery' (Dain 1971: 26–27). The hospital experimented with new scientific modes of caregiving based on observation, plans to return citizens to conventional, productive life, and other panoptic practices. The hospital officially began to organize patient interaction and activities in the 1840s, making it appear to be a panoptic organ of the state.

The mechanisms of social reform were extended in the attempt to control what was considered sexual deviance. Archaeologists know the material expression of this element of social control through the Magdalen Society of Philadelphia, which operated between 1800 and 1850. The excavations conducted and analysed by Lu Ann De Cunzo (1995) have shown that this organization for reforming prostitutes provided workshops and a store for selling goods made by its inmates. The primary purpose of this institution was to teach prostitutes how to return to respectable society by becoming members of the industrializing workforce. De Cunzo has recognized the relationship between such reform institutions, and other forms of social control:

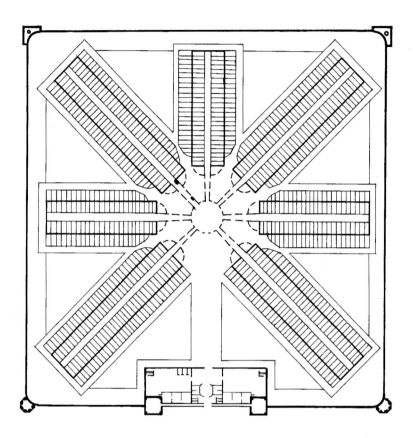

Figure 28.8 (above) Plan of the Eastern State Penitentiary, built in the early nineteenth century, and (opposite) that of the reference area of the Cecil H. Green Library at Stanford University, built in the late twentieth century: note the similarity of design, the emphasis on control of space, and the adaptation of panoptic principles. Sources: Eastern State Penitentiary: P. Kaw and P. D. Leighton; Stanford Library: D. C. Weber, *Planning Academic and Research Library Buildings*, 2nd edn (Chicago and London: American Library Association, 1986).

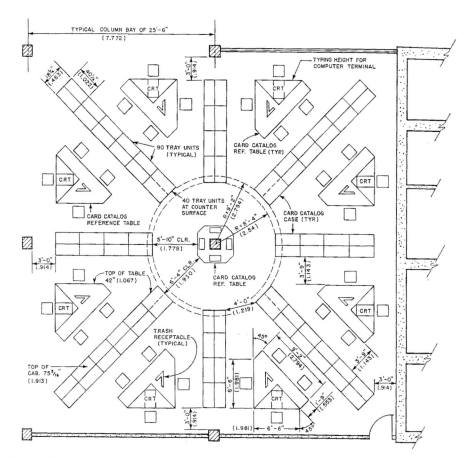

Figure 28.8 (continued)

the early 19th century prison and asylum shared with the cloister, school, military regiment, family home, boarding house, almshouse, hospital, and ... workshop ... [the] commonalities ... of the new discipline of the modern world and [functioned] as mechanisms of a pervasive, insinuating, naturalizing power.

(De Cunzo 1995: 34)

Having concentrated thus far on how disciplinary mechanisms were used by the British colonial state in eastern North America, and by its successor the United States, we shall now consider briefly how such mechanisms were manifested in other colonial contexts, taking as examples the Dutch colonial state that developed in South Africa, the Spanish and later American states that developed in the North American Southwest, and the colonial expansion of the United States into the North American West, and the role consumerism has played in creating a population of individual, disciplined consumer-citizens in the United States.

1133

SURVEILLANCE INSTITUTIONS IN DUTCH SOUTH AFRICA

Historical archaeology in South Africa is relatively new and was founded and is now widely practised in the area around the Cape of Good Hope and Cape Town. The Cape was settled in the mid-seventeenth century by the Dutch as a station for resupplying ships on their way to the East Indies. In the course of the seventeenth and eighteenth centuries, the Dutch, Germans, and French established plantations throughout the interior of southern Africa beyond Cape Town (Hall 1992; Schrire 1991, 1992, 1996; Schrire and Merwick 1991). The colonizing process disrupted indigenous lifeways whenever native people came into contact with Europeans. The colonizing process was taken over by the British later in the eighteenth century and affected all of what is now the Republic of South Africa, parts of Namibia, Botswana, and Zimbabwe, as well as areas farther into the interior.

As part of the material expression of their colonizing process, the Dutch built a star-shaped fort near the shore of what was to become Cape Town. Although it has been modified several times, including a heightening by the British, this structure, known as the Castle, still stands and has been carefully excavated and restored (Fig. 28.9). Over the years, several archaeologists have worked on the Castle and its environs. The Castle is a standard planned military enclosure, similar to those seen all over the colonial world from the seventeenth century on. From without, the fortress in its final form is tall and imposing and can be seen from all directions. It is clearly an object of view and is meant to be the centre of attention. Regardless of how the surrounding landscape was planned, the fort was deliberately situated to be viewed from the water and land. It was thus in the way of everyone in the environment. Like baroque planning in general, it represented the power of the state by capturing each individual's attention. While force guaranteed rule in the Cape, central placement guaranteed attention on a daily basis.

Although little scholarly attention has been paid to the interior of such forts, recent archaeological investigations have provided indispensable information. The Castle at Cape Town has a double row of two-storey buildings which were placed back to back and which were situated on the fort's longest axis. This acts to cut the interior of the fort in half. In front of each row of buildings was a large courtyard into which all openings went. These parade grounds were viewing spaces and acted to keep all passers-by under surveillance. This would have included indigenous Africans, slaves, civilians, soldiers, officers and even the élite of the Dutch East India Company. The Castle has to be thought of as a prison, in so far as it contained slaves. But its disciplinary powers enhanced the hierarchy of the Dutch East India Company because all its inhabitants were on view at predictable times throughout the day. Since there is no citizenry in the republican sense involved in the Cape area, it would not be appropriate to call the Castle a true panopticon. This structure

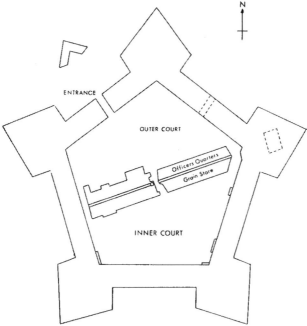

Figure 28.9 Star-shaped forts, like Fort Ticonderoga in New York (above), and (below) the Castle at Cape Town in South Africa, used a rudimentary form of panopticism to monitor activities both inside and outside the fortress walls. Fort Ticonderoga photograph reproduced with permission of *Fort Ticonderoga Museum*. The Castle at the Cape of Good Hope plan reprinted with permission from A. Yentsch and M. Beaudry (eds), *The Art and Mystery of Historical Archaeology: Essays in Honor of James Deetz*, Florida: CRC Press, 1992. Copyright © CRC Press, Boca Raton, Florida.

was, however, designed for surveillance and to discipline and subordinate individual subjects (Hall 1992).

The plantations of the Cape, usually referred to as farms, are historically the most important feature of Dutch settlement. These very large private holdings produced wine, wheat, and cattle. The plantations were centrally planned and their regularity can be seen both in surviving plans and the material remains of the surviving farms. The great houses typically have the famous Dutch gable which adds height and calls attention through baroque elaboration. The houses were frequently surrounded by walls and gardens, and the corners of the property were frequently marked by mills, barns, pigeon houses, and slave quarters. All of these structures could be built in the baroque style, which featured gables, cupolas, domes, barrel vaults, mission-like belfries, and similar architectural devices intended to impress the eye. All of these structures were designed and laid out according to a fairly standard plan and were combined with topography and other buildings so as to call attention to a hierarchically organized central authority (Hall 1992). All served to discipline individuals in colonial South Africa.

RELIGION, STATE POWER AND THE AMERICAN SOUTHWEST

During their colonization of South Africa, the Dutch introduced a severe form of Calvinism: Reformed Dutch Protestantism. The association of this variation of Puritanism with baroque architecture in South Africa seems anomalous until the architectural style is associated with planned landscapes and street plans, as well as with the public buildings in and along them. Baroque architecture and landscape planning used the laws of perspective to focus the human eye. Through the baroque built environment, authority governed by commanding the vision of the individual. Europe's colonizing nations used these techniques and definitions as they developed their imperial churches and missions, plantations, shipping institutions, administrative centres, forts, prisons and hospitals.

The use of hierarchical institutions built in baroque style appear to characterize power already achieved. However, archaeological chronologies show that such building episodes were much more likely used to centralize authority at times when it was weak or marginal. This can be seen in the material manifestations of colonialism in the North American Southwest. In the Southwest we not only see an attempt to build state authority from scratch, but we also see the use of baroque architecture to achieve it. In the Southwest the baroque order developed into a fully panoptic form, coupling religious zealousness to a developing sense of nationalism which governed baroque and panoptic expressions.

During their colonization of the Southwest, the Spanish built several sets of missions. Once a chain of at least two dozen missions went through what is now the

Mexican state of Sonora into southern Arizona. Tucson's well-known San Xavier del Bac is the most visible survivor of this mission chain (Fig. 28.10). These institutions were built in the later eighteenth century and represent an attempt to colonize Native Americans in the hope of transforming them into agricultural workers. Mission chains were used throughout the northern Mexican frontier, including what is now the American Southwest and California (Cheek 1974; Farnsworth 1986; Farnsworth and Williams 1992a, 1992b; Hoover 1992).

Mission establishments were used as colonizing instruments by the Spanish in Mexico from the beginning of the Conquest in the 1520s. Virtually all the architecture of these churches is baroque, which range from the relatively undecorated to those which are quite elaborate. San Xavier is typically baroque, featuring two front towers with octagonal tops and a central dome. It towers over a relatively small Indian village today but can be seen from miles away; it is a central point in a familiar landscape. The towers are pierced with eight openings, one on each side,

Figure 28.10 Mission San Xavier del Bac: the white towers of the mission compound literally rise out of the desert floor, dominating the viewscape of the small village which surrounds the mission. Photograph: Ansel Adams. © 1997 by the Trustees of the Ansel Adams Publishing Rights Trust. All rights reserved.

and, while they were not intended as viewing platforms, it is quite possible to imagine the view from them. That view would be in all directions through the entire southern part of the Tucson valley. The mission buildings in this chain and in many of the others have been criticized frequently as wasteful expressions of wealth. It is apparent that these churches are far more substantial and more highly decorated than some would judge necessary. These larger and more decorated churches usually succeeded simpler ones as the archaeology of San Xavier mission has shown. The purpose of these baroque architectural elaborations was to impress local Native Americans. Since the Southwest experienced a series of bloody and effective native rebellions against the Spanish, and because the missions existed to create cheap labour bases for Spanish enterprises, the political environment was never stable. Thus, baroque architecture on a grand scale accompanied political weakness (Arthur *et al.* 1975; Cheek 1974; Olson 1985).

The place of the pulpit and the place of the towers indicates an early understanding of panoptic techniques. Since these were preaching churches, the pulpit's view and shadow reached into the middle of the congregation, just as the towers' view and shadows reached into the middle of the village. The viewing platforms command attention and returned it, bringing in the westernizing and disciplining arm of the state via the established church. Religion was to teach 'salvation' by adherence to rules which touched all aspects of life.

Spanish missions have been excavated widely in the United States by historical archaeologists (e.g., Barbolla-Roland 1983; Costello 1991, 1992; Costello and Walker 1987; Deagan 1983; Deetz 1968; Farnsworth 1985, 1987, 1992; Hoover and Costello 1985; McEwan 1992, 1993; Saunders 1996; Thomas 1993; Williams 1992). Little historical archaeology has been done on them in Latin America, which is unfortunate since the colonial documentation there is extensive (Cohen-Williams 1992; Fournier-Garcia and Miranda-Flores 1992; Gasco 1992; Joseph and Bryne 1992; Myers *et al.* 1992; Reitz 1992; Skowronek 1992). On the other hand, Spanish missions in what is now the United States are rarely if ever compared to Protestant missions in similar frontier areas, or even to utopian compounds such as those constructed by the Shakers or those built by the early Mormons (Leone 1973; Savulis 1992). The all-seeing eye which stems from the panoptic quality of these sets of buildings is largely unrecorded. No comparison between such institutions has been completed, largely because no theoretical model has yet been available through which such a comparison could be attempted.

With an appropriate model, we can begin to address the socio-political issues characteristic of colonial areas which change hands and identities, but not the structure of governance. The Southwest was absorbed by the United States following a war of conquest in the 1840s; a new building style arrived with the new government. Traditionally, south-western history is segregated chronologically into four periods: prehistoric, Spanish, Mexican, and American, the latter referring to the period of United States hegemony in the region. Each of these is treated in popular and scholarly writing as a horizon. Under this schema, the United States presence in the Southwest appears short and unarticulated to any local past group. This is essentially misleading as the appropriation of the Southwest by the United States was in many ways simply an extension of the programme of European colonization begun by Coronado in the 1540s. The extent and continuity of European colonization in this region can be revealed through an analysis of the building called Old Main, the building which was built as the initial structure for the University of Arizona in Tucson in the late 1880s.

San Xavier del Bac and Old Main are structurally the same despite the different state authorities under which they were built, and despite their superficially different functions. Old Main is a cruciform building with towers at the ends of each of its four arms. The towers have louvred openings in their peaks and the building in turn is placed in a circle at the chief intersections of the campus. It thus sees in all directions. The building is situated in the middle of a planned landscape where, originally, it could be seen from any direction. Today it is in the middle of a developed landscape whose centre it still dominates.

The church and the school, San Xavier and Old Main, are baroque and panoptic buildings, respectively creating centralizing power where little or none existed before the structures were built. Their interiors are characterized by corridors and rooms where visibility is at a premium. The church and school were both colonizing institutions, and both used the interiorization of surveillance to create believers and citizens, one hierarchical, the other democratic. Rote learning, lectures, rituals of cleanliness, recitations, and supervised daily living routines characterize their functions. Analysing these structures through the logic of state power allows us to unify the Spanish and the US periods in the Southwest. This region has experienced a long-term European colonizing presence. The conventional interpretation of the region, which depicts a short-term US presence featuring American ideals of independence and freedom triumphing over superstition, is patently misleading, as can be seen when one uses anthropological archaeology to focus on colonialism, as opposed to trivializing historical detail.

Old Main was built in the 1880s and is more than a manifestation of baroque planning. It builds upon the self-disciplining attitudes taught at San Xavier in order to create a fully panoptic environment. In it, students were taught and watched by teachers and they learned to teach and watch themselves in a way that was more effective because it was free and voluntary. Thus the all-seeing eye of the panopticon could be more effective because it was done in the name of public education and rational advancement. Any discipline involved was clearly for one's own good. Old Main has not been archaeologically investigated in the conventional sense, but one can clearly see that lines of sight inside and outside the building, the position of windows, doors, rows, desks, and hallways should be recorded. Old Main's interior and exterior landscapes are of equal importance to the ceramics and glass assemblages a historical archaeologist would normally analyse.

IDEOLOGY, THE INDIVIDUAL, AND THE AMERICAN WEST

Although the great majority of American historical archaeology has been conducted on the eastern seaboard, there is a rich and growing literature on the historical archaeology of the nineteenth-century American West (e.g., Adams 1976; Evans 1980; Hardesty 1986, 1988, 1994; Henry 1987; Pastron and Hattori 1990; Praetzellis and Praetzellis 1989, 1992; Purser 1991, 1992; Riordan and Adams 1985; Staski 1993; Szuter 1991; Zeier 1986). The conquest of the American West – that is, the territory lying between the Mississippi River and the Pacific Ocean – has played a crucial part in defining the American imagination, character, and the ideology of the 'rugged individual' (Athearn 1986; Truettner 1991). In many ways, the birth and proliferation of many archetypal western myths – the lone cowboy riding the range, the hermit mountain man, the solitary fur trapper – can be seen as simultaneously *resulting* from the fragmentation of American society from communities to individuals and *creating* an ideology which reifies the central importance of the individual. This ideology contends that just as the United States succeeded in conquering the continent by itself, so too will strong and dedicated individuals – the cowboy, mountain man, or trapper – succeed in bettering their own lives. Those who do not succeed must likewise be to blame for their own failure; the ideology of the individual lays responsibility for the very existence of institutionalized systems of inequality on those who suffer most from them.

As it involved the conquest of people and territory, the western expansion of the United States should be seen as a colonial process. As was the case in other colonial contexts, in the American West surveillance technologies were used to divide society into a series of nominally independent and disciplined individuals; these mechanisms are retrievable archaeologically. While such negotiation can be seen to have occurred in many contexts – for example, through the proliferation of consumer culture (Henry 1987; McDougall 1990) or the negotiation of gender relations in brothels (e.g., Costello 1998; Spude 1998) – the two contexts most thoroughly known are mining camps and Chinese American sites.

Donald Hardesty has been studying the historical archaeology of mining camps in the West, particularly Nevada, for over a decade (e.g., Hardesty 1986, 1988, 1994). His analysis does much to disprove the myth that the social structure of frontier mining towns in the American West was based on an ideology of personal freedom and social egalitarianism. Quite on the contrary; mining, as it was practised in the nineteenth-century American West, was an activity that required strict labour discipline. Social and spatial segregation is evident in the archaeological records of even small, temporary mining camps like Gold Bar, Nevada, which employed fewer than a hundred people for less than a decade. Hardesty notes that there are several types of houses identifiable archaeologically: family houses which included, minimally, an adult male and an adult female; boarding houses which sheltered as many as sixty miners; and superintendents' bungalows, which at Gold Bar apparently housed a single supervisor (Hardesty 1988). As was the case in both eastern industrial and southern plantation contexts, the domestic and work lives of the miners were controlled through panoptic supervision. Mining camps were often located downhill from the mine shifts and associated mills. From the industrial structures, miners could be seen on their way to work and in their domestic settings. The presence of the superintendent's bungalow among the houses and tents of the miners would be a constant reminder that they were under the surveillance of their employers. While inexpensive to build, boarding houses would serve to contain the miners in an easily controlled and supervised area; the camp superintendent could keep a watchful eye on the bodies housed therein. Most importantly, the looming shadows of the mills, furnaces, and mine headframes would remind the miners of their position as the dependent, individual, watched employees of a mining company.

For over two decades, historical archaeologists have identified the presence of Chinese immigrants on archaeological sites based on the recovery of high percentages of Chinese porcelains and the presence of opium-smoking paraphernalia (Etter 1980; Evans 1980; Sando and Fenton 1993; Stenger 1993; Wylie and Fike 1993). The presence both of large numbers of Chinese labourers and opium pipes can be seen as the consequence of British colonial expansion in the Far East. The forced introduction of opium into the Chinese economy following the Opium Wars of the mid-nineteenth century resulted in the widespread use of opium among Chinese men, filling the coastal Chinese urban centres with populations of relatively impoverished mobile, unattached men, many of whom hoped to travel to the United States, make their fortune, and return to China. The population that did emigrate to the United States was primarily young and male; in 1870 only 8.5 per cent of the Chinese population in the United States were female (Greenwood 1993).

At first glance the use of opium might seem to run counter to the state's desire to create a disciplined, individualized workforce. However, the use of opium created a dependency on the purchase of the drug, and thus to wage labour in order to afford its purchase; it has been estimated that between 15 and 50 per cent of Chinese labourers' wages went on opium (Wylie and Fike 1993). Furthermore it has been suggested that the use of the drug may have enhanced the work performance of labourers in railroad camps and mines (Wylie and Fyke 1993). The experience of the Chinese immigrants in the nineteenth century was marked not only by the negotiation of consumer and wage-earner identities but also by new expressions of gender and racial identities. As so few women emigrated to the United States in the nineteenth century, and, as it has been argued, the ratio of European women to men in urban centres was relatively small, Chinese men found employment in what might otherwise be female spheres: as launderers, cooks, or domestic servants for wealthy Euro-Americans in the cities, and for labour gangs in the country. The Chinese were also racially segregated into 'Chinatowns'; while it is certain that Chinese emigrants found some measure of comfort living and working in close proximity both to relatives and to fellow Chinese, such segregation facilitated the surveillance and control over the Chinese by the Euro-Americans. As the state did not want to incorporate the Chinese as citizens, and indeed since many Chinese hoped to return to China once they had earned their fortune, surveillance was of a somewhat different nature. The Chinese simultaneously were defined as individual, disciplined wage-earners and consumers, and were segregated out from the citizenry. Where they refused to accept these conditions they were likely to meet with violence, as was the case with the Douglas Bar massacre of 1885, in which thirty-two independent Chinese miners were killed by eight Idaho cowboys (Sisson 1993).

CONSUMER DISCIPLINE AND THE IDEOLOGY OF INDIVIDUAL IDENTITY

Surveillance mechanisms were structured by more-or-less complementary discourses of inequality, such as racial and gender ideologies. These discourses took myriad material forms whose success was dependent upon individuals' capacity to accept systemic and even personal inequality as appropriate to their identity. Many of these inequalities were played out in the consumer culture which developed in America between the 1870s and 1930s. In the final quarter of the nineteenth century American consumer space's rapid expansion was fuelled by a flood of new commodities, novel marketing venues, and innovative marketing and advertising strategies. Beyond these objective material mechanisms, consumer space moved ever-closer to the heart of American identity because Americans internalized a distinct consumer discipline. It was a discipline in which consumption – and the fiction of impending universal affluence – was more critical to individual identity than any other totalizing discourse (e.g., religion, nationalism, ethnicity, etc.). Marketers explicitly promised an affluence which inevitably would reach the masses, and mail order 'wish books', credit sales, and densely stocked sales spaces implicitly emphasized the vast abundance of objects available to all American consumers. This mass vision of material abundance was entertained by many Americans who were willing to ignore or endure their present material and social subordination. At the same time, many Americans tacitly were considered unsuited to an even share of this universal abundance: African-Americans, for instance, were considered racially incompatible with the white consumer ideal, and most European immigrants and women were extended circumscribed privileges in consumer space.

Venues such as department stores disciplined consumers to a distinct form of genteel social behaviour and encouraged a somewhat paradoxical embrace of individual material desire (Campbell 1987). Through their strategic abundance of vast quantities of commodities arranged by form and style, the proximity of shoppers to goods, and the powerful displays of pane glass display windows, department stores radically changed the material desire once stifled in modestly stocked general stores. The disciplined genteel shopper absorbed tacit codes for how to imagine the possibilities of seemingly innocuous mass-produced goods; for department stores, this day-dreaming dimension of consumption was critical because it produced consumers who tolerated or ignored inequality in lieu of the profound possibilities of consumer goods. Department stores aspired to fuel a hedonism in which consumers were driven not by functional need but instead by the capacity of an object to negotiate, evade, or symbolically reconfigure contradictions in their lives. Whether objects actually can mediate social contradiction is at best questionable, but consumer spaces thrived on their capacity to produce a self-monitoring consumer who at least entertained the notion that commodities could recast everyday repression.

The contradictions in affluence ideology were constantly being masked and negotiated in department stores. Plate glass window displays, for example, were introduced in American stores in the 1870s and were a staple element of all urban department stores by 1910 (Leach 1993: 61–63). Mid-nineteenth-century shoppers were instructed that it was indiscreet to stare at goods or handle commodities which the consumer did not intend to purchase. In 1860, for example, etiquette writer Florence Hartley (1860: 112–13) observed that 'A lady who desires to pay strict attention to etiquette, will not stop to gaze in at the shop windows. If she is alone, it looks as if she were waiting for someone else; and if she is not alone, she is victimizing someone else, to satisfy her curiosity.' An 1869 guide succinctly dictated 'Do not enter a store unless you have some errand' (Shields 1869: 92).

However, such puritanical counsel stood on unstable ground by the 1890s, when spectacular window displays arranged objects in settings which encouraged active day-dreaming. Indeed, some stores hired people to stand in front of windows and encourage the assembly of crowds (Leach 1993: 61). Displays arranged objects in settings which ambiguously suggested their symbolism in domestic space, what English traveller Katherine Busbey (1910: 158) called 'glass-enclosed rooms' which 'resemble the various exhibits in the Eden Musee'. Such displays hoped to muddle the distinction between fantasy and reality, encouraging consumers to envision the fantastic possibilities of material goods. These displays were made particularly magnetic by bright lights, rich decorative backgrounds, and an army of mannequins which gave the displays a certain theatricality whose implied subject was the consumer staring into the tableau.

Window displays created the suggestion of intimacy between object and consumer, apparently leaving only the immaterial glass itself between consumer and commodity. At once they stimulated desire but deferred it. Yet the implication that display windows democratized desire, if not consumption, was an illusion. Department stores overwhelmingly were located in élite downtown shopping districts rarely frequented by marginalized consumers, and in some cases such stores barred African-Americans from entry. Other stores arrested 'undesirable' window shoppers: in 1908, a young man pondering a women's underwear display in Spokane, Washington was escorted to jail after his refusal to leave, and in 1915 a crowd of African-Americans window shopping in Washington, DC were arrested on the wishes of apprehensive anti-Black marketers (Leach 1993: 66; Mullins in press). Stores in the American South often placed numbers by goods being sold in the window so that African-Americans could request a good by number (Mullins in press). Such a marketing strategy secured the spending of African-Americans but denied them the privilege of shopping a store's full stock.

Inside department stores, consumer discipline faced a persistent flood of challenges. Perhaps the most interesting reflection of gender ideology and the contradictions of affluence was the phenomenon of middle-class women shoplifters. During the late nineteenth century and the early twentieth, department stores were plagued by a rash of shoplifting by 'respectable' genteel women (Abelson 1989). Rather than scattered irrationality by disconnected shoppers, Elaine Abelson (1989) observes that shoplifting was a pervasive social negotiation of class and gender inequalities which converged in consumer space.

The department store floors which witnessed such shoplifting were spectacular shows of an enormous range of splendidly displayed goods. Unlike rarely pilfered general stores or public markets, department stores were intense spaces in which crowds gathered in mass affirmation of material desire. Yet for some shoppers rational consumer restraint, the ambiguity of genuine 'need', and the constraints of class and domestic subjectivity harboured profound contradictions. Most shoplifting women were homemakers, with no economic independence and little power over their lives, who were driven by no universal impetus. Their transgression of consumer discipline and the domestic ideal threatened mainstream morality by illuminating the incongruities of rational desire and femininity. Public thievery by such 'upstanding' women also was a class violation; it starkly demonstrated codes of conduct which separated genteel classes and the undifferentiated masses who had not secured the privileges of consumer citizenship.

Observers concerned with the reproduction of consumer discipline and domesticity used the foil of the 'kleptomaniac' female shopper to outline the inverse of the ideal consumer. Ideologues ranging from store managers to ministers fostered consumer discipline by demonstrating its polar opposite, the uncontrolled middle-class female shopper. Physicians publicly situated shoplifting in women's essential nature, an illness which amplified the attributes lurking beneath the surface of all women. Ostensibly commentators were concerned with the reform of respectable women gone wrong, but the real target of such discourse was other consumers. The police columns, society pages, and community news in every local paper reported shoplifting religiously as a mechanism to display the opposite of the ideal disciplined consumer. Such discourses disciplined consumers not by outlining codes of conduct but instead displaying the inverse of that common-sense discipline. Advertising did the same thing by depicting ideal consumers, men and women who always were white and middle class, with women serving in domesticated roles and African–Americans appearing as service labourers (e.g., domestics, waiters, etc.) to 'real' consumers. Through such mechanisms, disciplined wage labourers with particular racial and social attributes were extended the potential promises of material affluence provided they internalized consumer discipline, a consumer discipline which ultimately served the state's interests in a disciplined workforce.

CONCLUSION: UNCOVERING THE MATERIAL CULTURE OF SURVEILLANCE

The archaeological consideration of baroque and panoptic architecture built in colonial contexts – be they North American, Spanish or Dutch – reveals the importance of surveillance in the construction and maintenance of expanding colonial states. In this chapter, we have touched upon several of the mechanisms through which state institutions have organized technologies of seeing and self-watching. The material manifestations of these mechanisms are often retrievable from the archaeological record. In this concluding section, we would like to suggest, first, how the material culture of surveillance can be found archaeologically, and, second, why such an enterprise should be undertaken. In doing so, we would like to reiterate that historical archaeology is really a composite, or interdisciplinary, enterprise through which scholars interpret the material remains of the recent past. As such, there are a number of data sets to which an archaeologist concerned with the material manifestations of colonial states can turn.

As the creation of a disciplined citizenry or subject population often requires the recreation of spatial logic or the imposition of landscapes of surveillance, and because these efforts are often preconceived, historical archaeologists should turn to the cartographic record of colonial expansion. Many colonizing states made meticulous maps of their conquests and colonies, on many different scales, from the continental to the individual estate. Such records often reveal the intended or actual layout of settlements, as we have demonstrated in our discussion of the landscapes of St Mary's City and Annapolis. Analysing such records can reveal the intentions and results of preconceived surveillance landscapes (Delle 1998; Shackel 1994). Similar cartographic sources can be examined in the interpretation of industrial urban landscapes (e.g., Mrozowski 1991; Mrozowski *et al.* 1996), as well as agricultural landscapes such as those incorporated on plantations (e.g., Delle 1996, 1998).

Historical archaeologists can, and should, turn to a variety of documentary sources in the effort to interpret the material culture of surveillance. Surveillance is carried out from towers. Many of the illustrations featured in this chapter depict external towers and façades which rise up over people, congregations, inmates, and students. Surveillance surrounds with a gaze from these peaks in a landscape. These are not small mechanisms for they can compose whole villages, factory towns, and the mountains of waste produced by mines and other extractive industries. These mountains all have ramps and roads on them, allowing a type of moving surveillance. Round and octagonal schools enclose, on the one hand, and pivot all bodies to the centrally placed master on the other. A careful inspection of Figures 28.4 and 28.10 will reveal houses and villages in view of the anthracite breaker and mission San Xavier, respectively. Each typifies the mechanisms of surveillance.

The internal side of surveillance is the creation of an individual who thinks he or she belongs to the watchful community. Benedict Anderson (1991) calls the result of such external and internal colonialism *Imagined Communities*. Anderson discusses the role of schools in producing colonial administrations, a special kind of cultural half-breed, who, once trained in bureaucratic techniques, becomes the kind of watcher who makes maps, takes censuses, writes dictionaries, and makes inventories of local ruins. Imagined communities can be created by printing, reading, and writing uniform scripts in languages defined as legitimate. This process automatically relegated other languages to illiteracy.

The negotiation of such imagined communities has resulted in what historical archaeologists typically call the documentary record. The analysis of both private and public papers held in various archival repositories will often reveal the social conditions which agents of colonial states hoped to transform, or to maintain. Such records can be found in national libraries in metropolitan colonial capitals (e.g., Library of Congress, British Library, Public Record Office), in the capitals of colonized states (e.g., the Jamaica Archives), in regional libraries and archives (e.g., state or county courthouses), and often in the private libraries of the descendants of colonialists. The archaeological record itself contains both subsurface and architectural evidence for the mechanisms of surveillance. While standing architectural remains can be complex, particularly in cases where buildings have been reconstructed one or more times, this class of record often provides the best evidence for the mechanisms of surveillance. Before excavations begin, historical archaeologists should examine the architectural remains of any buildings on the surface which might date to the colonial episode in which they are interested. The subsurface remains of buildings, including foundations, disused walkways and pavements, yards, and gardens, all can provide evidence for how individual houses or estates served as surveillance mechanisms. Similar features can be uncovered during the excavations of prisons, insane asylums, factories, missions, or other types of state institutions. Excavations of each of these latter examples will reveal features unique to the type of institution in question. However, once excavated, the architectural remains should be plotted on larger maps in order to interpret the relationships which existed between structures, which is a key to understanding the landscapes of surveillance.

Other types of material culture recovered from excavations can reveal how surveillance mechanisms worked. For example, the regularity of the individual conforming to a state-imposed order can be interpreted from the appearance of standardized ceramic assemblages. Diachronic studies of such small finds can reveal changing consumption patterns, and how those patterns of behaviour in turn created a consuming citizenry, disciplined in their participation as both producers and consumers in a national economy (Mullins 1996). While such studies have to date concentrated on refined earthenwares, interpretations of other types of material culture are possible, including locally produced earthenwares, opium pipes, and glass, to name just a few (Adams 1976, 1982; Mullins 1992; Riordan and Adams 1985; Spencer-Wood 1987; Turnbaugh 1985; Wylie and Fike 1993).

If, as most practitioners accept, the field of historical archaeology is concerned primarily with the expansion of European states and the impacts they have had on indigenous peoples (Deetz 1977, 1991; Orser and Fagan 1995), then a central focus of the enterprise should be on the mechanisms of state expansion and control. In this chapter we have outlined several of those mechanisms, particularly the mechanisms of surveillance of the individual, and how these have been interpreted archaeologically. We believe that when historical archaeologists use this approach they can produce studies of great interest, not only to other historical archaeologists but also to those interested in the political and social dynamics of complex societies in general. Matthew Johnson's *An Archaeology of Capitalism* (1996) is both such a book and an illustration of how to tie historical archaeology back to modern colonialism's European home. Johnson examines the ways, habits, and institutions that England used to create a nation out of itself. He describes landscapes of enclosure, building a national culture through the use of parish churches, house placement, the use of curtains and shutters for privacy, the building of inventories, maps, and the employment of the technical knowledge associated with the Renaissance. Johnson shows how the seemingly unrelated celebration of local histories, improvement of farming methods with how-to books, elimination of the category of witchcraft, and use of mould-made tablewares, were all employed in homogenizing a population – in creating a disciplined English citizenry.

Analyses such as Johnson's should be pursued, not only for their intrinsic scholarly interest but because each one of us in the modern world is still subject to increasingly powerful disciplinary mechanisms. By understanding how state power is reproduced at the level of the individual we can begin to reveal the processes through which individuals in the contemporary world are shaped by existing institutions, controlled today by both state and corporate powers. Quetzil Casteñada's *In the Museum of Maya Culture* (1996) provides an important description of how the state can use a rebuilt ruin, in this case Chichén Itzá, to contain and control a local population. While Benedict Anderson amply shows the colonial origins of ruin cataloguing and landscaping, Casteñada goes far beyond the building of tourist monuments into the state's negotiating of what is and is not authentic culture and thus the domestication of anthropology's central concept, culture, for state control. The physical site for surveillance is the tall ruin with its usually immaculate surrounding lawn. The inner world of self-monitoring involves both the tourists, who seek (and find) something each has learned is not yet in their lives, concerns, or resumés, and the guides and hawkers, who as residues of those who built the wonders can only sell the invented fragments which doubly prove they are incomplete individuals, subject not only to the eyes of the state but also to the gaze of the tourist.

As surveillance technologies become more sophisticated, each of us continues to be monitored in increasingly hard-to-detect ways by centralizing agents not only of the state, but of the evermore powerful gaze of multinational corporations. Both seek to create of us a fragmented, disciplined population of consuming individuals. It is well worth our time, as students of material culture, to examine how these mechanisms work to create and perpetuate the modern state.

REFERENCES

Abelson, E. S. (1989) *When Ladies Go A-Thieving: Middle-Class Shoplifters in the Victorian Department Store*, Oxford, New York.

Adams, W. H. (1976) 'Trade networks and interaction spheres: a view from Silcott', *Historical Archaeology* 10: 99–111.

Adams, W. H. (1982) 'Ethnography and archaeology of an American farming community: Silcott, Washington', in E. Tooker (ed.) *Ethnography for Archaeologists: 1978 Proceedings of the American Ethnological Society*, Washington, DC: American Ethnological Society: 43–62.

Adams, W. H. and Smith, S. D. (1985) 'Historical perspectives on black tenant farmer material culture: the Henry C. Long general store ledger at Waverly plantation, Mississippi', in T. Singleton (ed.) *The Archaeology of Slavery and Plantation Life*, San Diego: Academic Press: 301–34.

Agorsah, E. K. (1990) 'Archaeology of Maroon heritage in Jamaica', *Archaeology Jamaica* 2: 14–19.

Anderson, B. (1991) *Imagined Communities*, London and New York: Verso.

Armstrong, D. V. (1985) 'An Afro-Jamaican slave settlement: archaeological investigations at Drax Hall', in T. Singleton (ed.) *The Archaeology of Slavery and Plantation Life*, San Diego: Academic Press: 261–87.

Armstrong, D. V. (1990) *The Old Village and the Great House: An Archaeological and Historical Examination of Drax Hall Plantation, St. Ann's Bay, Jamaica*, Urbana: University of Illinois Press.

Armstrong, D. V. (forthcoming) *African-Jamaican Transformations at Seville*.

Arthur, D., Costello, J. and Fagan, B. (1975) 'A preliminary account of majolica sherds from the Chapel Site, Royal Spanish Presidio, Santa Barbara, California', *The Kiva* 41: 207–14.

Ascher, R. and Fairbanks, C. (1971) 'Excavation of a slave cabin: Georgia, U.S.A.', *Historical Archaeology* 5: 3–17.

Athearn, R. G. (1986) *The Mythic West*, Lawrence: University of Kansas Press.

Barbolla-Roland, D. (1983) 'Maiolica at the San Diego Presidio gateway search excavation: a preliminary analysis', *Journal of San Diego History* 29: 193–211.

Beaudry, M. C. (1989) 'The Lowell Boott mills complex and its housing: material expressions of corporate ideology', *Historical Archaeology* 23: 19–33.

Beaudry, M. C. and Mrozowski, S. A. (1987a) *Interdisciplinary Investigations of the Boott Mills, Lowell, Massachusetts, Vol. I: Life at the Boarding Houses*, Boston: Division of Cultural Resources, North Atlantic Region, National Park Service No. 18.

Beaudry, M. C. and Mrozowski, S. A. (1987b) *Interdisciplinary Investigations of the Boott Mills, Lowell, Massachusetts, Vol. II: The Kirk Street Agent's House*, Boston: Division of Cultural Resources, North Atlantic Region, National Park Service No. 18.

Beaudry, M. C. and Mrozowski, S. A. (1988) 'The archaeology of work and home life in Lowell, Massachusetts: an interdisciplinary study of the Boott Cotton Mills Corporation', *Journal of the Society for Industrial Archaeology* 14: 1–22.

Beaudry, M. C. and Mrozowski, S. A. (1989) *Interdisciplinary Investigations of the Boott Mills, Lowell, Massachusetts, Vol. III: The Boarding House System as a Way of Life*, Boston: Division of Cultural Resources, North Atlantic Region, National Park Service No. 18.

Beaudry, M. C., Cook, L. and Mrozowski, S. A. (1991) 'Artifacts and active voices: material culture as social discourse', in R. H. McGuire and R. Paynter (eds) *The Archaeology of Inequality*, Oxford: Basil Blackwell: 150–91.

Bond, K. H. (1989) ' "That we may purify our corporation by discharging the offenders": the documentary record of social control in the Boott boardinghouses', in M. C. Beaudry and S. A. Mrozowski (eds) *Interdisciplinary Investigations of the Boott Mills, Lowell, Massachusetts, Vol. III, The Boarding House System as a Way of Life*, Boston: Division of Cultural Resources, North Atlantic Region, National Park Service: 23–26.

Busbey, K. G. (1910) *Home Life in America*, London: Methuen.

Campbell, C. (1987) *The Romantic Ethic and the Spirit of Modern Consumerism*, Cambridge: Blackwell.

Candee, R. M. (1985) 'Architecture and corporate planning in the early Waltham system', in R. Weible (ed.) *Essays from the Lowell Conference on Industrial History 1982 and 1983*, Andover: Museum of Textile History: 17–43.

Carson, C., Barka, N. F., Kelso, W., Wheeler, G. and Upton, D. (1981) 'Impermanent architecture in southern American colonies', *Winterthur Portfolio* 16: 135–96.

Casteñada, Q. (1996) *In the Museum of Maya Culture*, Minneapolis: University of Minnesota Press.

Cheek, A. L. (1974) 'The evidence for acculturation in artifacts: Indians and non-Indians at San Xavier del Bac, Arizona', Ph.D. dissertation, University of Arizona, Tucson.

Cohen-Williams, A. G. (1992) 'Common maiolica types of northern New Spain', *Historical Archaeology* 26: 119–30.

Costello, J. (1998) 'The sporting life of 1890s Los Angeles parlor houses', Paper presented at the 31st Annual Meeting of the Society for Historical Archaeology, Atlanta.

Costello, J. (1991) 'Variability and economic change in the California missions: an historical and archaeological study', Ph.D. dissertation, University of California.

Costello, J. (1992a) 'Not peas in a pod: documenting diversity among the California missions', in B. J. Little (ed.) *Text-Aided Archaeology*, Boca Raton, Fla.: CRC Press: 67–82.

Costello, J. (1992b) 'Purchasing patterns of the California missions in ca. 1805', *Historical Archaeology* 26: 59–66.

Costello, J. G. and Walker, P. L. (1987) 'Burials from the Santa Barbara Presidio chapel', *Historical Archaeology* 21: 3–17.

Cotter, J. L., Moss, R. W., Gill, B. C. and Kim, J. (1988) *The Walnut Street Prison Workshop: A Test Study in Historical Archaeology Based on Field Investigations in the Garden Area of the Philadelphia Atheneum*, Philadelphia: The Atheneum of Philadelphia.

Cotter, J. L., Roberts, D. G. and Parrington, M. (1992) *The Buried Past: An Archaeological History of Philadelphia*, Philadelphia: University of Pennsylvania Press.

Craton, M. (1978) *Searching for the Invisible Man: Slaves and Plantation Life in Jamaica*, Cambridge, Mass.: Harvard University Press.

Craton, M. and Walvin, J. (1970) *A Jamaican Plantation: The History of Worthy Park, 1670–1970*, New York: W. H. Allen.

Dain, N. (1971) *Disordered Minds: The First Century of Eastern State Hospital in Williamsburg, Virginia, 1766–1866*, Williamsburg, Va.: Colonial Williamsburg Foundation.

De Cunzo, L. A. (1995) 'Reform, respite, ritual: an archaeology of institutions; the Magdalen Society of Philadelphia, 1800–1850', *Historical Archaeology* 29: 1–168.

Deagan, K. (1983) *Spanish St. Augustine*, New York: Academic Press.

Deetz, J. (1977) *In Small Things Forgotten: An Archaeology of Early American Life*, New York: Doubleday.

Deetz, J. (1988a) 'Archaeological investigations at La Purisima mission', in R. L. Schuyler (ed.) *Historical Archaeology: A Guide to Substantive and Theoretical Considerations*, Farmingdale, N.Y.: Baywood: 160–90.

Deetz, J. (1988b) 'American historical archaeology: methods and results', *Science* 239: 362–67.

Deetz, J. (1991) 'Archaeological evidence of sixteenth- and seventeenth-century encounters', in L. Falk (ed.) *Historical Archaeology in Global Perspective*, Washington, DC: Smithsonian Institution Press: 1–10.

Delle, J. A. (1989) 'A spatial analysis of sugar plantations on St. Eustatius, Netherlands Antilles', Unpublished Masters thesis, College of William and Mary, Williamsburg.

Delle, J. A. (1994) 'A spatial analysis of sugar plantations on St. Eustatius, Netherlands Antilles', in D. W. Linebaugh and G. G. Robinson (eds) *Spatial Patterning in Historical Archaeology: Selected Studies of Settlement*, Williamsburg, Va.: King and Queen Press: 33–62.

Delle, J. A. (1996) 'An archaeology of crisis: the manipulation of social spaces in the Blue

Mountains of Jamaica, 1790–1865', Ph.D. dissertation, University of Massachusetts, Amherst.

Delle, J. A. (1998) *An Archaeology of Social Space*, New York: Plenum Press.

Epperson, T. (1990) 'Race and the disciplines of the plantation', *Historical Archaeology* 24 (4): 29–36.

Epperson, T. (forthcoming) 'Panoptic plantations', in R. Paynter, J. Delle and S. Mrozowski (eds) *Lines that Divide: Historical Archaeology of Race, Class, Gender, and Ethnicity*, Knoxville: University of Tennessee Press.

Evans, W. S., Jr (1980) 'Food and fantasy: material culture of the Chinese in California and the West, circa 1850–1900', in R. L. Schuyler (ed.) *Archaeological Perspectives on Ethnicity in America: Afro-American and Asian American Culture History*, Amityville, N.Y.: Baywood Publishing Co.: 89–96.

Fagan, B. and Orser, C. E. (1995) *Historical Archaeology*, New York: HarperCollins.

Fairbanks, C. (1974) 'The Kingsley slave cabins in Duval County, Florida, 1968', *Conference on Historic Site Archaeology Papers* 7: 62–93.

Farnsworth, P. (1985) 'The archaeology of Spanish colonial sites in California', in S. L. Dyson (ed.) *Comparative Studies in the Archaeology of Colonialism*, Oxford: British Archaeological Reports, International Series 233: 93–114.

Farnsworth, P. (1986) 'Spanish California: the final frontier', *Journal of New World Archaeology* 6: 35–46.

Farnsworth, P. (1987) *The Economics of Acculturation in the California Missions: A Historical and Archaeological Study of Mission Nuestra Senora de la Soledad*, Los Angeles: University of California at Los Angeles.

Farnsworth, P. (1992) 'Missions, Indians, and cultural continuity', *Historical Archaeology* 26: 22–36.

Farnsworth, P. and Williams, J. S. (eds) (1992a) *The Archaeology of the Spanish Colonial and Mexican Republican Periods*, *Historical Archaeology* 26.

Farnsworth, P. and Williams, J. S. (1992b) 'Introduction', in P. Farnsworth and J. S. Williams (eds) *The Archaeology of the Spanish Colonial and Mexican Republican Periods*, *Historical Archaeology* 26: 1–6.

Ferguson, L. (1991) 'Struggling with pots in colonial South Carolina', in R. H. McGuire and R. Paynter (eds) *The Archaeology of Inequality*, Oxford: Basil Blackwell: 28–39.

Ferguson, L. (1992) *Uncommon Ground: Archaeology and Colonial African-America*, Washington, DC: Smithsonian Institution Press.

Foucault, M. (1979) *Discipline and Punish: The Birth of the Prison*, New York: Vintage Books.

Foucault, M. (1980) *Power/Knowledge: Selected Interviews and Other Writings, 1972–1977*, New York: Pantheon.

Fournier-Garcia, P. and Miranda-Flores, F. A. (1992) 'Historical sites archaeology in Mexico', *Historical Archaeology* 26: 75–83.

France, L. G. (1984) 'Sugar manufacturing in the West Indies: a study of innovation and variation', Masters dissertation, Williamsburg: College of William and Mary.

Friedlander, A. (1985) 'Establishing historical probabilities for archaeological interpretations: slave demography of two plantations in the South Carolina low country, 1740–1820', in T. Singleton (ed.) *The Archaeology of Slavery and Plantation Life*, San Diego: Academic Press: 215–38.

Gasco, J. (1992) 'Material culture and the colonial Indian society in southern Mesoamerica: the view from Chiapas, Mexico', *Historical Archaeology* 26: 67–74.

Gibson, E. S. and Meyer, M. D. (1998) 'Downtown Los Angeles, circa 1900: brothels, basques, and Chinatown', Paper presented at the 31st Annual Meeting of the Society for Historical Archaeology, Atlanta.

Gross, R. A. (1988) 'Culture and cultivation: agriculture and society in Thoreau's Concord', in R. B. St George (ed.) *Material Life in America, 1600–1800*, Boston, Mass.: Northeastern University Press: 519–33.

Hall, M. (1992) 'Small things and the mobile, conflictual fusion of power, fear and desire', in A. Yentsch and M. Beaudry (eds) *The Art and Mystery of Historical Archaeology*, Boca Raton, Fla.: CRC Press: 373–99.

Handler, J. (1979) 'Plantation slavery on Barbados, West Indies', *Archaeology* 32: 45–52.

Handler, J. and Lange, F. W. (1978) *Plantation Slavery in Barbados: An Archaeological and Historical Investigation*, Cambridge, Mass.: Harvard University Press.

Hardesty, D. L. (1986) 'Industrial archaeology on the American mining frontier: suggestions for a research agenda', *Journal of New World Archaeology* 6 (4): 47-56.

Hardesty, D. L. (1988) *The Archaeology of Mining and Miners: A View from the Silver State*, Special Publication Series, No. 6, Ann Arbor, Mich.: Society for Historical Archaeology.

Hardesty, D. L. (1994) 'Class, gender strategies, and material culture in the mining West', in E. Scott (ed.) *Those of Little Note: Gender, Race, and Class in Historical Archaeology*, Tucson: University of Arizona Press: 129-45.

Hartley, F. (1860) *The Ladies' Book of Etiquette, and Manual for Politeness*, Boston: G. W. Cottrell.

Henry, S. L. (1987) 'Factors influencing consumer behavior in turn-of-the-century Phoenix, Arizona', in S. M. Spencer-Wood (ed.) *Consumer Choice in Historical Archaeology*, New York: Plenum: 359–81.

Higman, B. W. (1974) 'A report on excavations at Montpellier and Roehampton', *Jamaica Journal* 8: 40–45.

Higman, B. W. (1988) *Jamaica Surveyed: Plantation Maps and Plans of the Eighteenth and Nineteenth Centuries*, Kingston: Institute of Jamaica Publications Ltd.

Hoover, R. L. (1992) 'Some models for Spanish colonial archaeology in California', *Historical Archaeology* 26: 37–44.

Hoover, R. L. and Costello, J. G. (eds) (1985) *Excavations at Mission San Antonio 1976–1978*, Los Angeles: Institute of Archaeology, UCLA.

Hudgins, C. L. (1990) 'Robert "King" Carter and the landscape of Tidewater Virginia in the eighteenth century', in W. M. Kelso and R. Most (eds) *Earth Patterns: Essays in Landscape Archaeology*, Charlottesville: University Press of Virginia: 59–70.

Isaac, R. (1982) *The Transformation of Virginia: 1740–1790*, Chapel Hill: University of North Carolina Press.

Johnson, M. (1996) *An Archaeology of Capitalism*, Cambridge: Blackwell Publishers.

Joseph, J. W. and Bryn, S. C. (1992) 'Socio-economics and trade in Viejo San Juan, Puerto Rico: observations from the Ballaja archaeological project', *Historical Archaeology* 26: 45–58.

Joseph, J. W., Ramos y Ramirez de Arellano, A. and Pabon de Rocafort, A. (1987) *Los Caficultores de Maraguez: An Architectural and Social History of Coffee Processing in the Cerrillos Valley, Ponce, Puerto Rico*, Atlanta, Ga.: Garrow and Associates.

Kelso, W. M. (1984) *Kingsmill Plantation, 1619–1800: Archaeology of Country Life in Colonial Virginia*, New York: Academic Press.

Kelso, W. M. (1986) 'The archaeology of slave life at Thomas Jefferson's Monticello: "a wolf by the ears"', *Journal of New World Archaeology* 6: 5–20.

Klingelhofer, E. (1987) 'Aspects of early Afro-American material culture: artifacts from the slave quarters at Garrison plantation, Maryland', *Historical Archaeology* 21: 112–19.

Kryder-Reid, E. (1994) '"As is the gardener, so is the garden": the archaeology of landscape as myth', in P. A. Shackel and B. J. Little (eds) *Historical Archaeology of the Chesapeake*, Washington, DC: Smithsonian Institution Press: 131–43.

Kulik, G. (1988) 'Pawtucket village and the strike of 1824: the origins of class conflict in Rhode Island', in R. B. St George (ed.) *Material Life in America, 1600–1800*, Boston, Mass.: Northeastern University Press: 385–403.

Lange, F. W. and Handler, J. (1985) 'The ethnohistorical approach to slavery', in T. Singleton (ed.) *The Archaeology of Slavery and Plantation Life*, San Diego: Academic Press: 15–32.

Langhorne, W. T., Jr (1976) 'Mill-based settlement patterns in Schoharie County, New York: a regional study', *Historical Archaeology* 10: 73–92.

Leach, W. (1993) *Land of Desire: Merchants, Power, and the Rise of a New American Culture*, New York: Pantheon.

Leone, M. P. (1973) 'Archaeology as the science of technology: Mormon town plans and fences', in C. Redman (ed.) *Research and Theory in Current Archaeology*, New York: John Wiley and Sons: 125–50.

Leone, M. P. (1984) 'Interpreting ideology in historical archaeology: the William Paca garden in Annapolis, Maryland', in D. Miller and C. Tilley (eds) *Ideology, Power and Prehistory*, Cambridge: Cambridge University Press: 25–35.

Leone, M. P. (1988) 'The Georgian order as the order of merchant capitalism in Annapolis, Maryland', in M. P. Leone and P. B. Potter, Jr (eds) *The Recovery of Meaning: Historical Archaeology in the Eastern United States*, Washington, DC: Smithsonian Institution Press: 255–61.

Leone, M. P. (1995) 'A historical archaeology of capitalism', *American Anthropologist* 97 (2): 251–68.

Leone, M. P. and Shackel, P. A. (1990) 'Plane and solid geometry in colonial gardens in Annapolis, Maryland', in W. M. Kelso and R. Most (eds) *Earth Patterns: Essays in Landscape Archaeology*, Charlottesville: University Press of Virginia: 153–68.

Lewis, K. (1984) *The American Frontier: An Archaeological Study of Settlement Pattern and Process*, New York: Academic Press.

Lewis, K. (1985) 'Plantation layout and function in the South Carolina low country', in T. Singleton (ed.) *The Archaeology of Slavery and Plantation Life*, San Diego: Academic Press: 35–66.

Lewis, M. ([1834]1929) *Journal of a West Indian Proprietor, 1815–17*, Edited with an Introduction by M. Wilson, Boston, Mass.: Houghton Mifflin.

McDougall, D. P. (1990) 'The bottles of the Hoff store site', in A. G. Pastron and E. M. Hattori (eds) *The Hoff Store Site and Gold Rush Merchandise from San Francisco, California*, Special Publication Series, No. 7, Ann Arbor, Mich.: Society for Historical Archaeology: 58–74.

McEwan, B. G. (1992) 'The role of ceramics in Spain and Spanish America during the 16th century', *Historical Archaeology* 26: 92–108.

McEwan, B. (ed.) (1993) *The Spanish Missions of La Florida*, Gainesville: University of Florida Press.

McGuire, R. H. (1991) 'Building power in the cultural landscape of Broome County, New York, 1880 to 1940', in R. H. McGuire and R. Paynter (eds) *The Archaeology of Inequality*, Oxford: Basil Blackwell: 102–24.

McKee, L. (1987) 'Delineating ethnicity from the garbage of the early Virginians: the faunal remains from the Kingsmill plantation slave quarters', *American Archaeology* 6: 31–39.

Menard, R., Green Carr, L. and Walsh, L. (1988) 'A small planter's profits: the Cole estate and the growth of the early Chesapeake economy', in R. B. St George (ed.) *Material Life in America, 1600–1800*, Boston, Mass.: Northeastern University Press: 185–201.

Miller, G. L. and Pacey, A. (1985) 'Impact of mechanization in the glass container industry: the Dominion Glass Company of Montreal, a case study', *Historical Archaeology* 19: 38–50.

Miller, H. M. (1988) 'Baroque cities in the wilderness: archaeology and urban development in the colonial Chesapeake', *Historical Archaeology* 22: 57–73.

Moore, S. M. (1985) 'Social and economic status on the coastal plantation: an archaeological perspective', in T. Singleton (ed.) *The Archaeology of Slave and Plantation Life*, San Diego: Academic Press: 141–62.

Mrozowski, S. (1987) 'Exploring New England's evolving urban landscape', in E. Staski (ed.) *Living in Cities*, Ann Arbor, Mich.: Society for Historical Archaeology: 1–9.

Mrozowski, S. (1991) 'Landscapes of inequality', in R. H. McGuire and R. Paynter (eds) *The Archaeology of Inequality*, Oxford: Basil Blackwell: 79–101.

Mrozowski, S. *et al.* (1996) *Living on the Boott*, Amherst: University of Massachusetts Press.

Mullins, P. R. (1992) 'Defining the boundaries of change: the records of an industrializing potter', in B. J. Little (ed.) *Text-Aided Archaeology*, Boca Raton, Fla.: CRC Press: 179–94.

Mullins, P. R. (1996) 'The contradictions of consumption: an archaeology of African America and consumer culture, 1850–1930', Ph.D. dissertation, University of Massachusetts, Amherst.

Mullins, P. R. (in press) *Race and Affluence: An Archaeology of African America and Consumer Culture*, New York: Plenum.

Myers, J. E., de Amores Carredano, F., Olin, J. S. and Pleguezuelo Hernandez, A. (1992) 'Compositional identification of Seville majolica at overseas sites', *Historical Archaeology* 26: 131–47.

Nassaney, M. S. and Abel, M. R. (1993) 'Political and social contexts of cutlery production in the Connecticut Valley', *Dialectical Anthropology* 18: 247–89.

Neiman, F. (1978) 'Domestic architecture at the Clifts plantation: the social context of early Virginia building', *Northern Neck of Virginia Historical Magazine* 28: 3096–128.

Noël Hume, I. (1982) *Martin's Hundred*, New York: Alfred A. Knopf.

Olson, A. P. (1985) 'Archaeology of the Presidio of Tucson', *The Kiva* 50: 251–70.

Orr, D. G. (1977) 'Philadelphia as industrial archaeological artifact: a case study', *Historical Archaeology* 11: 3–14.

Orser, C. E., Jr (1988a) *The Material Basis of the Postbellum Tenant Plantation: Historical Archaeology in the South Carolina Piedmont*, Athens: University of Georgia Press.

Orser, C. E., Jr (1988b) 'The archaeological analysis of plantation society: replacing status and caste with economics and power', *American Antiquity* 53: 735–51.

Orser, C. E., Jr (1988c) 'Toward a theory of power for historical archaeology: plantations and space', in M. P. Leone and P. Potter (eds) *The Recovery of Meaning*, Washington, DC: Smithsonian Institution Press: 235–62.

Orser, C. E., Jr (1989) 'On plantations and patterns', *Historical Archaeology* 23: 28–40.

Orser, C. E., Jr (1991) 'The continued pattern of dominance: landlord and tenant on the postbellum cotton plantation', in R. H. McGuire and R. Paynter (eds) *The Archaeology of Inequality*, Oxford: Basil Blackwell: 40–54.

Orser, C. E., Jr (1992) *Introdução à Arqueologia História*, Belo Horizonte: Oficina de Livros.

Orser, C. E., Jr (1993) *In Search of Zumbi*, Normal: Illinois State University, Midwestern Archaeological Research Center.

Orser, C. E., Jr (1996) *A Historical Archaeology of the Modern World*, New York: Plenum Press.

Orser, C. E., Jr and Nekol, A. M. (1985) 'Plantation settlement from slavery to tenancy: an example from a piedmont plantation in South Carolina', in T. Singleton (ed.) *The Archaeology of Slavery and Plantation Life*, San Diego: Academic Press: 67–94.

Otto, J. S. (1977) 'Artifacts and status differences: a comparison of ceramics for planter, overseer, and slave sites on an antebellum plantation', in S. South (ed.) *Research Strategies in Historical Archaeology*, New York: Academic Press: 91–118.

Otto, J. S. (1984) *Canon's Point Plantation 1794–1860: Living Conditions and Status Patterns in the Old South*, New York: Academic Press.

Pastron, A. G. and Hattori, E. M. (eds) (1990) *The Hoff Store Site and Gold Rush Merchandise From San Francisco, California*, Ann Arbor, Mich.: Society for Historical Archaeology.

Paynter, R. (1988) 'Steps to an archaeology of capitalism: material change and class analysis', in M. P. Leone and P. Potter (eds) *The Recovery of Meaning*, Washington, DC: Smithsonian Institution Press: 407–22.

Pogue, D. (1988a) *Archaeology at George Washington's Mount Vernon: 1931–1987*, Mt Vernon, VA: Mount Vernon Ladies' Association File Report I.

Pogue, D. (1988b) 'Spatial analysis of the King's Reach plantation homelot, ca. 1690–1715', *Historical Archaeology* 2: 40–56.

Potter, P. B., Jr (1991) 'What is the use of plantation archaeology?', *Historical Archaeology* 25: 94–107.

Praetzellis, A. and Praetzellis, M. (1989) ' "Utility and beauty should be one": the landscape of Jack London's Ranch of Good Intentions', *Historical Archaeology* 23 (1): 33–44.

Praetzellis, A. and Praetzellis, M. (1992) 'Faces and facades: Victorian ideology in early Sacramento', in A. E. Yentsch and M. C. Beaudry (eds) *The Art and Mystery of Historical Archaeology: Essays in Honor of James Deetz*, Boca Raton, Fla: CRC Press.

Pulsipher, L. and Goodwin, C. (1982a) 'A sugar and boiling house at Galways: an Irish sugar plantation in Montserrat, W.I.', *Post-Medieval Archaeology* 16: 21–27.

Pulsipher, L. and Goodwin, C. (1982b) *Galways: A Caribbean Sugar Plantation – A Report of the 1981 Field Season*, Boston, Mass.: Boston University, Department of Archaeology.

Purser, M. (1991) ' "Several paradise ladies are visiting in town": gender strategies in the early industrial west', *Historical Archaeology* 25 (4): 6–16.

Purser, M. (1992) 'Consumption as communication in nineteenth-century Paradise Valley, Nevada', *Historical Archaeology* 26 (3): 105–16.

Reinhart, T. R. (ed.) (1984) *The Archaeology of Shirley Plantation*, Charlottesville: University Press of Virginia.

Reitz, E. J. (1992) 'The Spanish colonial experience and domestic animals', *Historical Archaeology* 26: 84–91.

Reitz, E. J., Gibbs T. and Rathbun, T. A. (1985) 'Archaeological evidence for subsistence on coastal plantations', in T. Singleton (ed.) *The Archaeology of Slavery and Plantation Life*, San Diego: Academic Press: 163–91.

Riordan, T. B. and Adams, W. H. (1985) 'Commodity flows and national market access', *Historical Archaeology* 19: 5–18.

Sande, T. A. (1977) 'Industrial archaeology and the cause for historic preservation in the United States', *Historical Archaeology* 11: 39–44.

Sando, R. A. and Fenton, D. L. (1993) 'Inventory records of ceramics and opium from a nineteenth century Chinese store in California', in P. Wegars (ed.) *Hidden Heritage: Historical Archaeology of the Overseas Chinese*, Amityville, N.Y.: Baywood Publishing Co.: 151–76.

Saunders, R. (1996) 'Mission-period settlement structure: a test of the model at San Martin de Timucua', *Historical Archaeology* 30 (4): 24–36.

Savulis, E. (1992) 'Alternative visions and landscapes: archaeology of the Shaker social order and built environment', in B. J. Little (ed.) *Text-Aided Archaeology*, Boca Raton, Fla.: CRC Press: 195–203.

Schrire, C. (1991) 'The historical archaeology of the impact of colonialism in seventeenth century South Africa', in L. Falk (ed.) *Historical Archaeology in Global Perspective*, Washington, DC: Smithsonian Institution Press: 69–96.

Schrire, C. (1992) 'Digging archives at Oudepost I, Cape, South Africa', in A. Yentsch and M. Beaudry (eds) *The Art and Mystery of Historical Archaeology*, Boca Raton, Fla.: CRC Press: 361–72.

Schrire, C. (1996) *Digging Through Darkness: Chronicles of an Archaeologist*, Charlottesville: University of Virginia Press.

Schrire, C. and Merwick, D. (1991) 'Dutch–indigenous relations in New Netherland and the Cape in the seventeenth century', in L. Falk (ed.) *Historical Archaeology in Global Perspective*, Washington, DC: Smithsonian Institution Press: 11–20.

Schwartz, S. B. (1985) *Sugar Plantations in the Foundation of Brazilian Society: Bahia, 1550–1835*, Cambridge: Cambridge University Press.

Shackel, P. A. (1993) *Personal Discipline and Material Culture: An Archaeology of Annapolis, Maryland, 1695–1870*, Knoxville: University of Tennessee Press.

Shackel, P. A. (1994) 'Town plans and everyday material culture: an archaeology of social relations in colonial Maryland's capital cities', in P. A. Shackel and B. J. Little (eds) *Historical Archaeology of the Chesapeake*, Washington, DC: Smithsonian Institution Press: 85–100.

Shackel, P. A. (1996) *Culture Change and the New Technology: An Archaeology of the Early American Industrial Era*, New York: Plenum.

Shackel, P. A. and Larson, D. (forthcoming) 'Labor and racism in early industrial Harpers Ferry', in R. Paynter, J. Delle and S. Mrozowski (eds) *Lines that Divide: Historical Archaeology of Race, Class, Gender, and Ethnicity*, Knoxville: University of Tennessee Press.

Shackel, P. A. and Winter, S. E. (1994) 'An archaeology of Harper's Ferry commercial and residential district', *Historical Archaeology* 28: 16–26.

Shields, S. A. (1869) *Frost's Laws and By-Laws of American Society*, New York: Dick & Fitzgerald.

Singleton, T. (ed.) (1985a) *The Archaeology of Slavery and Plantation Life*, New York: Academic Press.

Singleton, T. (1985b) 'Introduction', in T. Singleton (ed.) *The Archaeology of Slave and Plantation Life*, San Diego: Academic Press: 1–14.

Singleton, T. (1988) 'An archaeological framework for slavery and emancipation, 1740–1880', in M. P. Leone and P. B. Potter, Jr (eds) *The Recovery of Meaning: Historical Archaeology in the Eastern United States*, Washington, DC: Smithsonian Institution Press: 345–70.

Singleton, T. (1990) 'The archaeology of the Plantation South: a review of approaches and goals', *Historical Archaeology* 24: 70–77.

Singleton, T. (1992) 'Using written records in the archaeological study of slavery, an example from the Butler Island plantation', in B. J. Little (ed.) *Text-Aided Archaeology*, Boca Raton, Fla.: CRC Press: 55–66.

Sisson, D. A. (1993) 'Archaeological evidence of Chinese use along the lower Salmon river, Idaho', in P. Wegars (ed.) *Hidden Heritage: Historical Archaeology of the Overseas Chinese*, Amityville, N.Y.: Baywood Publishing Co: 33-63.

Skowronek, R. K. (1992) 'Empire and ceramics: the changing role of illicit trade in Spanish America', *Historical Archaeology* 26: 109–18.

Spencer-Wood, S. (ed.) (1987) *Consumer Choice in Historical Archaeology*, New York: Plenum Press.

Spude, K. H. (1998) 'Brothels and saloons, families and priests: an archaeology of gender and the American West', Paper presented at the Society for Historical Archaeology, Atlanta.

Starbuck, D. (1983) 'The New England glassworks in Temple, New Hampshire', *IA: The Journal of the Society for Industrial Archaeology* 9: 45–64.

Staski, E. (1993) 'The Overseas Chinese in El Paso: changing goods, changing realities', in P. Wegers (ed.) *Hidden Heritage: Historical Archaeology of the Overseas Chinese*, Amityville, N.Y.: Baywood Publishing Co.: 125–49.

Stenger, A. (1993) 'Sourcing and dating of Asian porcelains by elemental analysis', in P. Wegars (ed.) *Hidden Heritage: Historical Archaeology of the Overseas Chinese*, Amityville, N.Y.: Baywood Publishing Co.: 315-31.

Szuter, C. (1991) 'A faunal analysis of home butchering and meat consumption at the Hubbel trading post, Ganado, Arizona', in P. J. Crabtree and K. Ryan (eds) *MASCA Research Papers in Science and Archaeology, Supplement to Vol. 8: Animal Use and Culture Change*, Philadelphia: University of Pennsylvania.

Thomas, D. H. (1993) 'The archaeology of Mission Santa Catalina de Guale: our first 15 years', in B. G. McEwan (ed.) *The Spanish Missions of La Florida*, Gainesville: University Press of Florida: 1-34.

Tomich, D. (1990) *Slavery in the Circuit of Sugar: Martinique and the World Economy, 1830–1848*, Baltimore, Md.: Johns Hopkins University Press.

Truettner, W. H. (1991) 'Ideology and image: justifying Western expansion', in W. H. Truettner (ed.) *The West as America: Reinterpreting Images of the Frontier, 1820–1920*, Washington, DC: Smithsonian Institution Press.

Turnbaugh, S. P. (ed.) (1985) *Domestic Pottery of the Northeastern United States, 1625–1850*, Orlando, Fla.: Academic Press.

Upton, D. (1986) 'Vernacular domestic architecture in eighteenth-century Virginia', in D. Upton and J. M. Vlach (eds) *Common Places: Readings in American Vernacular Architecture*, Athens: University of Georgia Press: 313–35.

Upton, D. (1988) 'White and black landscapes in eighteenth-century Virginia', in R. B. St George (ed.) *Material Life in America, 1600–1860*, Boston: Northeastern University Press: 357–69.

Upton, D. (1990) 'Imagining the early Virginia landscape', in W. M. Kelso and R. Most (eds) *Earth Patterns: Essays in Landscape Archaeology*, Charlottesville: University Press of Virginia: 71–86.

Upton, D. (1992) 'The city as material culture', in A. Yentsch and M. Beaudry (eds) *The Art and Mystery of Historical Archaeology*, Boca Raton, Fla.: CRC Press: 51–74.

Wheaton, T. R. and Garrow, P. H. (1985) 'Acculturation and the archaeological record in the Carolina Lowcountry', in T. Singleton (ed.) *The Archaeology of Slavery and Plantation Life*, San Diego: Academic Press: 239–59.

Williams, J. S. (1992) 'The archaeology of underdevelopment and the military frontier of northern New Spain', *Historical Archaeology* 26: 7–22.

Wurst, L. (1991) ' "Employees must be of moral and temperate habits": rural and urban élite ideologies', in R. H. McGuire and R. Paynter (eds) *The Archaeology of Inequality*, Oxford: Basil Blackwell: 125–49.

Wylie, J. and Fike, R. E. (1993) 'Chinese opium smoking techniques and paraphernalia', in P. Wegars (ed.) *Hidden Heritage: Historical Archaeology of the Overseas Chinese*, Amityville, N.Y.: Baywood Publishing Co: 255–303.

Zeier, C. (1987) 'Historic charcoal production near Eureka, Nevada: an archaeological perspective', *Historical Archaeology* 21 (1): 81–101.

SELECT BIBLIOGRAPHY

The corpus of literature on the historical archaeology of capitalism is massive and is quickly growing. However, there are a few key recent texts of particular interest. For those interested in a concise overview of the field, see the textbook recently published by Charles Orser and Brian Fagan titled *Historical Archaeology* (New York: HarperCollins, 1995). Orser also provides an interesting read on comparative historical archaeology in his *A Historical Archaeology of the Modern World* (New York: Plenum, 1996). Several recent anthologies contain articles which examine material expressions of inequality. See for example the volume edited by Randall H. McGuire and Robert Paynter, *The Archaeology of Inequality* (Oxford: Basil Blackwell, 1991) and Elizabeth Scott, *Those of Little Note* (Tucson: University of Arizona Press, 1994). Leone and Potter's edited volume, *The Recovery of Meaning* (Washington, DC: Smithsonian Institution Press, 1988) remains a classic, as does Robert Schuyler's *Historical Archaeology* (Farmingdale, N.Y.: Baywood, 1978), although the latter is somewhat dated. Charles Orser's edited reader, *Images of the Recent Past: Readings in Historical Archaeology* (Walnut Creek, Calif.: Alta Mira Press, 1996) provides a timely update. Other edited volumes of note include Barbara Little's *Text-Aided Archaeology* (Boca Raton, Fla.: CRC Press, 1992), Suzanne Spencer-Wood's *Consumer Choice in Historical Archaeology* (New York: Plenum Press, 1987), and Mary Beaudry's *Documentary Archaeology in the New World* (Cambridge: Cambridge University Press, 1988). Much of the recent work done in the Chesapeake has been summarized in a volume edited by Paul Shackel and Barbara Little titled *Historical Archaeology of the Chesapeake* (Washington, DC: Smithsonian Institution Press, 1994). Shackel directly addresses the question of surveillance institutions in the Chesapeake in *Personal Discipline and Material Culture* (Knoxville: University of Tennessee Press, 1993). A key collection of articles on New World plantations appears in *The Archaeology of Slavery and Plantation Life* (San Diego, Calif.: Academic Press, 1985) edited by Theresa Singleton. Important case studies of monograph length include Douglas Armstrong's *The Old Village and the Great House* (Urbana: University of Illinois Press, 1990), John Solomon Otto's *Cannon's Point Plantation, 1794–1860: Living Conditions and Status Patterns in the Old South* (Orlando, Fla.: Academic Press, 1984), and William Kelso's *Kingsmill Plantations, 1619–1800: Archaeology of Country Life in Colonial Virginia* (Orlando, Fla.: Academic Press, 1984). Several recent theme volumes of the journal *Historical Archaeology* provide good overviews of specific topics within the discipline, including a volume titled *Historical Archaeology on Southern Plantations and Farms* (1990) edited by Charles Orser, and one titled *Gender in Historical Archaeology* (1991) edited by Donna

Seifert. The latter was followed up by Diana Wall's monograph, *The Archaeology of Gender: Separating the Spheres in Urban America* (New York: Plenum Press, 1994). Studies surrounding the archaeology of industrialism can be found in Shackel's *Culture Change and the New Technology* and Mrozowski *et al.*'s *Living on the Boott* (Amherst: University of Massachusetts Press, 1996). A recent account of the British experiences of capitalism and modernity can be found in Matthew Johnson's *An Archaeology of Capitalism* (London: Basil Blackwell, 1996). Stanley South's *Method and Theory in Historical Archaeology* (New York: Academic Press, 1977) remains influential. Finally, a classic statement on culture change based on structuralism can be found in James Deetz's timeless *In Small Things Forgotten* (Garden City, N.Y.: Anchor Press/Doubleday, 1977). A recent feschrift dedicated to Deetz, *The Art and Mystery of Historical Archaeology*, edited by Anne Yentsch and Mary Beaudry (Boca Raton, Fla.: CRC Press, 1992), demonstrates the breadth of influence Deetz has had on the practice of historical archaeology in North America.

29

THE ARCHAEOLOGY OF INDUSTRIALIZATION

Marilyn Palmer

INTRODUCTION

Industrialization brought about a fundamental transformation in the social and economic structure of the western world in a very short space of time. Within a century, the adoption of sources of power other than human or animal muscle, together with the use of artificial lighting, meant that the lives of men and women need no longer be governed by the rhythm of the seasons, or even those of each day and night: they became subservient to the incessant demands of a machine which never slept. Traditional craft skills were no longer a valuable asset, since the machines could guarantee a standardized product which satisfied consumer demand, and speed of output was the main requirement. The nature of technological innovation meant that the production process was broken up into a number of discrete stages, since all processes were not mechanized at once: the yeoman clothier of Yorkshire in England, who had taken in wool and marketed his finished 'piece' in the cloth halls of Halifax or Leeds, was replaced by a spinner working in one place and a weaver in another. This fragmentation of the production process gave much greater powers of control to the capitalist entrepreneur, who could manipulate its different stages to satisfy market demand. His ability to control his workforce was assisted by its changing composition, since a man's strength was no longer a prerequisite for many of the tasks he had once carried out and these could now be undertaken by women and children. Of necessity, the workforce lived near the mill, factory or workshop, enabling the entrepreneur to exercise some surveillance over their domestic as well as their working lives. The settlement pattern was transformed, and the pace of urbanization quickened. Increased output demanded a change in the transport infrastructure, and within the same century tracks became paved roads and river navigation was supplemented by canals and railways. The construction of these still made use of human muscle, as machines were slow to replace a male workforce eager for employment when strength and persistence were the main requirements: technological innovation *per se* is a product of the twentieth rather than the nineteenth century, when manufacturers and employers were only too ready to spare their capital if people were available to undertake the tasks at a cheap rate. Such attitudes also prevailed in the extractive industries, where what was possible technologically was not necessarily employed when a cheap labour force was available.

What therefore characterizes the period of industrialization in Europe is not so much the power of the machine as the increasing ability of employers to exercise control over their workforce, whose proliferation in numbers was perhaps the dominant feature of the late eighteenth and early nineteenth centuries. In America, on the other hand, where industrialization was largely a nineteenth-century phenomenon, technological innovation was encouraged by the scarcity of labour, although immigration on an immense scale supplemented the indigenous workforce.

Since the purpose of archaeology is to ascertain changes in the human condition through analysis of the material record, the period of industrialization offers unparalleled opportunities because of the wealth of artefacts, standing buildings and alterations to the landscape which it brought about. But archaeology, like landscape history, has tended to stop short of the period of industrialization, perhaps overwhelmed by its enormity. The great landscape historian W. G. Hoskins resented the 'tide of industrialism' which overtook the rural communities in which he was interested, and regarded the whole process as the replacement of a qualitative by a quantitative culture. To him, it created 'landscapes of horror': between the new industrial towns, he says:

> stretched miles of torn and poisoned countryside – the mountains of waste from mining and other industries; the sheets of sullen water, known as 'flashes', which had their origin in subsidence of the surface as the result of mining below; the disused pit-shafts; the derelict and stagnant canals.
>
> (Hoskins 1955: 229)

The very unattractiveness of the material record, then, hindered its study. The process of industrialization was the province of the economic historian, who was protected from the realities of its human outcomes by the nature of the archive material. The social historian did become immersed in the conflicts generated by the changing relationships between employer and employee, but since most of the latter were illiterate, the written sources indicate what it was assumed they felt and are not firsthand accounts in most instances. This is where archaeology becomes important, since for all periods it has been concerned with explaining changes in the human condition and deducing reactions to those changes without the benefit of documentary material. Archaeologists also deal, in general, with the nameless and the faceless rather than the individual, and so it is an ideal discipline for understanding the workforce of the industrial period, as well as for analysing changes in the landscape. Until recently, however, few practising archaeologists have ventured into the period.

The wealth of standing buildings and even surviving machinery has, however, encouraged the growth of a rather separate discipline known as industrial archaeology. For reasons which will be explained below, both in Europe and America its practitioners have largely been concerned with the functional descriptions of sites and buildings and the elucidation of the technologies involved. The very wealth of material evidence has encouraged concentration on the processes of production and distribution, without much thought either for the products themselves or the people involved in making and selling them. Yet, in the early days of the discipline, a leading industrial archaeologist could write:

> Industrial archaeology is, of course, ultimately concerned with people rather than things: factories, workshops, houses and machines are of interest only as products of human ingenuity, enterprise, compassion or greed – as physical expressions of human behaviour. From whatever standpoint the subject is approached, man is the basic object of our curiosity.
>
> (Smith 1965: 191)

Few industrial archaeologists have, however, followed his lead, yet that is what must happen if industrial archaeology is to be synonymous with the archaeology of industrialization. It is now a well-established term in world-wide usage and should not be abandoned in favour, say, of historical archaeology. It is undoubtedly part of that discipline, but its parameters of interest are more closely defined. Industrial archaeology is the study of the physical evidence of past industrialization, but needs to embrace not only the workplace but also the workforce and the wider cultural context in which its members functioned.

The remainder of this chapter will look at the origins of the discipline of industrial archaeology and suggest how its scope could be widened so that it becomes the archaeology of industrialization. Its main focus will be Britain, but reference will be made to parallel developments in Europe, America and Australia.

ORIGINS

Industrial archaeology originated in Britain in the 1950s, after the post-war preoccupation with renewal had led to the destruction of much of the landscape associated with early industrialization. Its initial impetus was an attempt to catalogue and preserve selected relics of the period when Britain was the world leader in the process of industrialization. Industrial archaeology was a spontaneous growth, resulting in volunteer activity on a considerable scale in both preservation and recording. The Council for British Archaeology tried to give some shape to the latter by the introduction of record cards, which eventually grew into the National Record of Industrial Monuments (NRIM) based first at the University of Bath under R. A. Buchanan and later subsumed into the National Monuments Record (NMR) of the Royal Commission on the Historical Monuments of England (RCHME). The Commissions in England, Scotland (RCAHMS) and Wales (RCAHMW) have come to play an important role in industrial archaeology, undertaking specific surveys (for example: Douglas and Oglethorpe 1993; Giles and Goodall 1992; Hughes 1988, 1990) and spearheading attempts to ensure that sites and structures dating from as late as the twentieth century are included on both national and local Sites and Monuments Records. English Heritage has gone so far as to state that 'if there is one archaeological topic in which England can claim to have international pre-eminence, it is in the industrial archaeology of the post medieval period' (English Heritage 1995).

Concern with selection for preservation is no longer, therefore, entirely in the voluntary sector, and English Heritage, as part of its Monuments Protection Programme (MPP), commissioned the first comprehensive surveys of a range of industries so that priorities could be assessed and more industrial monuments included in the list of Scheduled (that is, protected) Monuments. The Association for Industrial Archaeology, which was set up in 1973 to represent the interests of industrial archaeology, still attempts to hold a balance between the volunteers, who have dominated industrial archaeology in the past, and the professionals, now the major players in the field, as well as publishing the major British journal in the field, *Industrial Archaeology Review*.

In Europe, the value of the physical remains of industry took rather longer to be appreciated. Although French historians had for a long time been interested in industrial history, little notice was taken of industrial sites until the 1970s and it was not until 1983 that the *Inventaire Générale* began to include industrial sites with the foundation of an industrial heritage group within it, the *Cellule du Patrimoine Industriel*. Various thematic surveys are being undertaken by this group and several regional publications have emerged (Belhoste 1988; Belhoste *et al.* 1984, 1994). A long-term project to create a national database of French industrial sites was initiated in 1986, and a similar database project has begun in the Netherlands where responsibility for the industrial heritage has now passed to the Projectbureau Industrieel Erfgoed (PIE), created in 1992. In Belgium, various categories of industrial building have been surveyed, particularly watermills and windmills, and a national survey published (Viaene 1986). The Scandinavian countries have an important industrial heritage which is increasingly being recognized by their governments. In Norway, buildings and sites of industrial interest have been recorded both by the Council for Culture and the Norwegian Technical Museum, while in Sweden the

1163

Central Office of National Antiquities is monitoring various recording initiatives. The ending of the Cold War has resulted in various east European countries having greater contact with western traditions and recognizing the wealth of their industrial heritage. Further afield, industrial archaeology has made rapid progress in Australia since the 1960s with National Trusts in each state including industrial sites and buildings in their registers (Donnachie 1981).

In the United States, the Historic American Buildings Survey (HABS) was created in the 1930s as a means of providing work for unemployed architects. Industrial buildings fell within their remit, but responsibility for recording them is now shared by the Historical American Engineering Record (HAER), established in 1969 under the aegis of the National Park Service, which itself dates back to 1916. The records are maintained by the Library of Congress in what is termed 'preservation by documentation', a concept similar to the British NMRs. Whereas the NRIM in England utilized amateur enthusiasts in the recording process, the HAER surveys are undertaken by university staff and students working under contract to the National Park Service. They have usually been architects and engineers: only after twenty-five years of activity did the National Park Service first employ an archaeologist on an HAER project, a survey of a hard-rock mining site in the Mojave Desert of California, and they envisage further cooperation between the various disciplines (Andrews 1994). Recording has not always ensured preservation and the HAER records form an invaluable inventory of the industrial built environment of the United States (Burns 1989).

At an international level, the General Council of UNESCO has adopted a policy of designating important cultural and ecological sites as World Heritage Sites (see Chapter 10). Around 300 have now been accorded this status, but only a handful are industrial sites. These range from the Ironbridge Gorge in Britain to the Potosi tin mines in Bolivia and a salt mine at Wieliczka in Poland. The International Committee for the Conservation of the Industrial Heritage (TICCIH) was established in 1973 and has led to increased awareness of the importance of the industrial past. It is seeking a more formal organization and consultation by UNESCO on further industrial World Heritage Sites. Many of its members have contributed to *The Blackwell Encyclopaedia of Industrial Archaeology* which seeks to set the discipline in its world context (Trinder 1992).

DEFINITIONS AND SCOPE

Industrial archaeology, then, unlike other period studies in archaeology, grew from concern about the future of standing structures rather than as an academic study concerned with deriving information from the tangible evidence of a period of the past. It has proved difficult to detach it from the complementary, but not identical, concept of industrial heritage, yet that is essential if it is to take its proper place as a component within the academic study of archaeology as the archaeology of industrialization.

Most early definitions of 'industrial archaeology' included elements of recording and preservation in their phraseology, and defined the period of interest as that of the Industrial Revolution (Buchanan 1972; Cossons 1975; Rix 1967). Other practitioners chose a less restrictive definition, arguing that the discipline was a thematic rather than a chronological one and could range from the prehistoric to the modern period (Hudson 1963; Raistrick 1972). This dilemma, frequently discussed (for example: Palmer 1990), needs resolution if industrial archaeology is to develop the necessary theoretical foundation it has so far lacked. If it is accepted that 'archaeology' can reasonably include the systematic study of standing as well as sub-surface structures, and few would now disagree with this, then it is the term 'industrial' which requires further analysis. It is generally taken to mean organized production of artefacts on a scale larger than a craft, but there are elements of this kind of production in most archaeological periods.

As suggested earlier, what perhaps characterizes the classic period of 'the Industrial Revolution' is capital investment on a large scale in both buildings and machinery and the consequent organization of the labour force to maximize production. It is with this development that industrial archaeology is largely concerned, although it must be recognized, first, that 'industrialization', in this sense, began earlier in some industries than others and, second, that the domestic method of production continued to coexist with factory production, albeit with many changes in the lifestyle of the workforce (Bythell 1978; Samuel 1977; Timmins 1993). Industrial archaeologists should therefore be concerned with interpreting the physical evidence of the vast social and economic changes which have overtaken society in the past 250 years or so. Within this period, like other archaeologists, they are contributing towards 'the basically anthropological task of understanding everyday life in the past and what accounts for its structure' (Leone and Potter 1988: 372).

INDUSTRIAL ARCHAEOLOGY AND HISTORICAL ARCHAEOLOGY

Since industrial archaeology began as a campaign to preserve, or at least to record, selected sites and structures deriving from the industrial past, it is hardly surprising that its practitioners were so concerned to assert the significance of their field evidence in the archaeological record that they tended to minimize the importance of other sources of evidence in giving meaning to those sites and structures, except in a technological sense. While some of the work has contributed considerably to a greater understanding of the typological development of particular structures (see

Palmer and Neaverson 1989; Patrick 1996; Sharpe *et al.* 1991), the relationship of these sites and structures to the social development of industrialized society has rarely been considered. The latter dimension has been regarded as the province of the economic historian, and British industrial archaeologists in particular have fought shy of making as much use of documentary sources as historical archaeologists in America and Australia. Yet, as Deetz has said, 'the combined use of archaeological and documentary materials should permit us to say something about the past that could not have been said using only one set of data' (Deetz 1996: 32). The combination of both types of evidence, for example, has made it possible to demonstrate the longevity of outwork alongside factory production in a number of nineteenth-century British industries (Palmer 1994). Industrial archaeologists are fortunate among archaeologists in the range of sources at their disposal for the interpretation of physical remains and should regard this as a strength rather than a weakness in their discipline.

Artefacts are the main component of the archaeological record, yet historical archaeologists and industrial archaeologists are at opposite ends of the spectrum in their consideration of these. To most historical archaeologists, artefacts comprise the main body of evidence from which information about the lifestyles of past societies is derived. Variations in the type and distribution of artefacts indicate material change and prompt investigation into its causes. Industrial archaeologists, however, have chronicled the development of the means of production in terms of textile mills (for example: Giles and Goodall 1992), pot-kilns (Baker 1991) and so on, but have paid little attention to the consequent effect of this development on the nature of the artefacts produced, and therefore of material change.

This is clearly a field in which the two disciplines need to work together, as has been done, for example, in aspects of the nineteenth-century glass industry in America. Here, archaeological work on production sites has produced typological sequences (for example: Lorrain 1968; Miller and Pacey 1985; Starbuck 1983) which demonstrate the progress of standardization in the products, and the increasing use of moulds and pressing machines rather than the traditional free-blowing techniques. The evidence prompts questions about the causes of technological change, for which changing levels of demand would be the traditional explanation: a rising population needing increased supplies of everyday items. However, technological change also implies a change in the nature of the labour force, with traditional skills less in demand and the speed of output the key element in production. The artefactual evidence therefore also prompts an enquiry into the changing nature of labour relations in the glass industry, which could be reflected in the design of the workplace and any associated housing. This kind of extrapolation from the nature of the artefacts to the labour force responsible for their production and to the physical nature of the environment in which they were produced is as essential for industrial as for historical archaeologists. The former have much to learn from the theoretical approach so powerfully advanced by American historical archaeologists (for example: Glassie 1975; Leone and Potter 1988).

AN ARCHAEOLOGY OF CAPITALISM?

The industrial archaeologist is therefore concerned with documenting and explaining the changes in material culture which took place in a period of rapid social and economic development. Patterns of mass consumption led to new systems of production involving considerable technological change, which in turn created new systems of discipline in the workplace. It is very tempting, therefore, to accept the Marxist model as a means of explanation, since undoubtedly in this period much social change was generated by the contradictions arising between the forces and the relations of production; that is, between a capitalist organization utilizing new technology and the social organization of the workforce which had to adapt to a new working and often also a new domestic environment. Looked at in this way, the introduction of a new steam engine into a previously water-powered mill, a common phenomenon in the nineteenth century which can be identified both from physical and documentary evidence, probably involved the workforce both in learning new skills and also in more rigorous shift work, since the owner would wish to recoup his capital expenditure by keeping the engine working on a continuous basis. Such shift work would have repercussions in the domestic environment and necessitate residence close to the place of work. The resolution of this conflict between the new technology and the social organization of the workforce which operated it would be, in Marxist terms, an example of the way in which society advanced.

Some European industrial archaeologists, especially those working on the textile industries, have accepted this mode of explanation, for example Manuel Cerda in Catalonia (Cerda 1991). In America, Paynter has argued that capitalist–worker conflicts underlie many of the innovations which appear in the archaeological record and that class models go a long way towards explaining change in the material world (Paynter 1988). But such a monocausal explanation is too restrictive: not all sites and structures of the industrial period, anyway, lend themselves to generalizations. Most industrial archaeologists are, in fact, content with what might be called a historical explanation of their site: that knowing as much detail as possible about the chronology of events accounts for the nature of the material record, without going beyond that to look at its general significance in accordance with any accepted models of explanation. This is obviously not sufficient if they are to contribute to a broader understanding of the development of human society, and a solution may well be to adopt the link between description and explanation offered by Hodder's definition of 'contextual archaeology'. He argues that description and explanation are indissolubly related as the whole network of associations and contrasts is followed through in order to arrive at a picture of the total context (Hodder 1986: 143). In industrial archaeology, these associations include not only labour relations but also sources of raw materials, methods of processing and transport networks: these are all part of the capitalist mode of production, but lead the archaeologist into a careful examination of changes in the landscape; that is, changes in spatial organization, which are linked to, but not identical with, changes in social organization. The Marxist model of explanation is useful but not all-embracing.

Matthew Johnson has argued that an important facet of capitalism is the placing of the individual at the centre of its ideological base (Johnson 1996: 203). This echoes Hodder's view of the active role of material culture: it is not a passive reflection of society but has been deliberately used by individuals to negotiate social position and bring about social change (Hodder 1982, 1986). The form of objects and structures is the result of deliberate choice rather than environmental

Figure 29.1 Individualism: the former carpet factory built for James Templeton in Glasgow, Scotland, in 1889. Designed by William Leiper, the polychrome brick and stone façade is in the Venetian Gothic style. Crown Copyright: Royal Commission of the Ancient and Historical Monuments of Scotland.

determinism. Of course, on industrial sites environmental factors like the presence of raw materials, the existence of a good water-power site and the immediate topography all influence its location, but human agency is ultimately responsible for the form (Palmer and Neaverson 1994: 1–17). Typological study of a series of structures may enable generalizations to be made about their development, and may also help to establish the position of a particular object or structure in a chrono-logical sequence, but the role of the individual cannot be omitted from the equation. The capitalist could design the structures he financed not only to maximize produc-tion along Marxist lines but also to emphasize his social position: for this reason, many nineteenth-century textile mills are models of polite rather than functional architecture. Josiah Wedgwood's personal interest in classical prototypes can be seen in Staffordshire pottery of the late eighteenth century, especially in the develop-ment of pastel-coloured, white-sprigged jasperware. The individual influence is discernible in the archaeological record: the industrial archaeologist is often fortu-nate in that the range of sources available for the period may enable the individual to be named, which is not often possible for earlier archaeological periods.

Industrial archaeology, therefore, is the study of a period dominated by the growth of capitalist organization in industry, and the archaeological record can add

Figure 29.2 Standardization: one of the many cotton spinning mills built in Lancashire, England, using Accrington brick. The only concession to individualism is the name of the company on the corner tower housing the water sprinkler cistern. Photograph: M. Palmer.

1169

much to an understanding of the influence of capitalism on society. It should not, however, be seen only as an adjunct to theoretical models of class analysis, although undoubtedly the material record can shed considerable light on the adaptations made by the workforce to new modes of production as well as their resistance to them. Capitalist organization can be detected in the landscape: in the large-scale development of extractive industry; transport networks on a scale never previously seen; and new kinds of settlement patterns, such as the model villages of the early cotton industry in Britain. The standardization of products is very obvious in the artefact patterns of the period, but equally so are the attempts to resist this – for example by the Arts and Crafts movement of the late nineteenth century. Buildings, too, exhibit a degree of standardization, but many indicate the individualism characteristic of many entrepreneurs: one only has to contrast the red-brick nineteenth-century textile mill characteristic of the Lancashire cotton industry with James Templeton's bizarre carpet factory in Glasgow built in polychrome brick and stone in the Venetian Gothic style to appreciate this point (Figs 29.1 and 29.2). Figure 29.3 illustrates how standardization and individualism could be combined in a single site, in this case a coal-mining complex in southern Spain.

Figure 29.3 Individualism displayed on a coal-mining complex in southern Spain. The functional pit head structures contrast with the bartizan-bedecked electricity transformer house on the right. Photograph: M. Palmer.

INDUSTRIAL LANDSCAPES

Landscape is, of course, often taken to mean natural scenery to which the onlooker reacts aesthetically and is therefore devoid of human interference. But to the historian and the archaeologist, landscape is the physical manifestation of changes wrought by people in both space and time. It therefore includes buildings, not as discrete entities but in their relationship to one another and to their topographical setting – in other words, their spatial distribution.

One of the major reasons for studying industrial landscapes is to transform a collection of individual structures into a coherent whole which has meaning in both technological and cultural terms. Technologically, the interrelationship of buildings and features in the landscape is usually determined by sequences of industrial production, as in the landscapes of metalliferous mining considered below (pp. 1186–91). Culturally, these interrelationships can reveal systems of industrial organization and social relationships, particularly those between the employer and his workforce as previously discussed. These spatial relationships are horizontal ones, manifested on the surface of the land. There are also vertical or sequential relationships which are equally components in the industrial landscape, the results of both technological and cultural change through time. The task of the industrial archaeologist is to analyse the industrial landscape in terms of both the spatial and the sequential relationships of structures and features in order to illuminate the process of industrialization.

Early definitions of industrial archaeology emphasized the importance of the industrial monument, an inevitable consequence of the need to protect selected examples of the industrial past, which in turn has led to the creation of inventories of sites and monuments in many countries. The site-specific tendency has been increased by volunteer participation, since few local groups possess the resources to undertake far-ranging studies. Increasing professional activity in the field has begun to reverse this trend, and most fieldwork and research programmes now reach beyond the structures of prime technological significance to consider their wider context, examining sources of raw materials, provision of power, transport systems, associated industry and accommodation (Crossley 1994; Palmer and Neaverson 1994: 13–17). Studies of industrial landscapes normally take one of two forms: extensive surveys of particular areas; or more limited surveys of features associated with a particular site or structure.

In Britain, foremost in the former category is the Nuffield-funded survey of the internationally important landscape of the Ironbridge Gorge, which sought to reveal change over time by means of detailed plot surveys (Alfrey and Clark 1993). The methodology may well be applicable to other landscapes, although few have survived so well as this World Heritage Site. The RCHME has developed a variety of strategies for extensive landscape survey, both to make good deficiencies in the

1171

NMR and to meet the needs of a variety of users. One such strategy made use of map evidence and aerial photographs to create a database of sites which could then be followed up by field enhancement. Three areas have been covered in this way: the Yorkshire Dales, the North Pennines (the part formally designated as an Area of Outstanding National Beauty) and the National Forest. The RCHME concluded that these rapid surveys had limited use (sites were not sufficiently considered in their historical context, so they revealed spatial but not sequential relationships) and that a balance needed to be struck between rapid survey and the creation of an intelligent, usable, record which reflected the linkages between sites (Lang 1995).

A different strategy has been to undertake ground-based field survey on landscapes known to be important, such as the early coal-mining area of Clee Hill in Shropshire or the Honister slate quarries in Cumbria, with their well-preserved tramway systems. Such field surveys have made minimal use of background research because of time constraints, but the complex nature of other landscapes has demanded a more integrated approach. This has been especially true where structures from the production process survive in the landscape, involving understanding of the sequence of a particular industrial activity. The ending of the Cold War has released many previously classified sites, some of which are in need of decontamination, and the RCHME has been involved in recording and researching sites and structures of the defence industries, including that of the Royal Ordnance Works at Waltham Abbey in Essex (Everson 1995; Everson and Cocroft 1996; Fig. 29.4). Fieldwork *per se* would not have been appropriate, since these sites clearly needed a historical context if their significance was to be appreciated: equally, the archaeological survey has revealed adaptations of buildings to contain new processes which were never recorded in writing.

Landscape surveys intended to give a context to structures of technological significance have not been carried out as frequently as they might have been. Few have attained the depth of the survey and excavation of Chingley Forge and Furnace in Kent (Crossley 1975), although the RCHME is currently attempting to document the sources of raw materials and fuel associated with the important charcoal iron furnaces of the southern Lake District. A similar study sought to set in context the historic charcoal kilns near Eureka in Nevada, which provided fuel for the silver mining industry of the late nineteenth century (Zeier 1987).

Transport systems such as railways and canals have usually been studied historically, but landscape surveys can elucidate their relationship to the sources of their cargo – mines, quarries, limekilns, ironworks and so on. Stephen Hughes of the RCAHMW has illuminated the relationship between the linear features of the Montgomeryshire Canal and the Swansea Canal, together with a system of tramways which eventually extended the hinterland of the latter into the Brecon Beacons, and the trading patterns and settlements which they both served and generated. The canals and their feeders were also used as sources of power for the

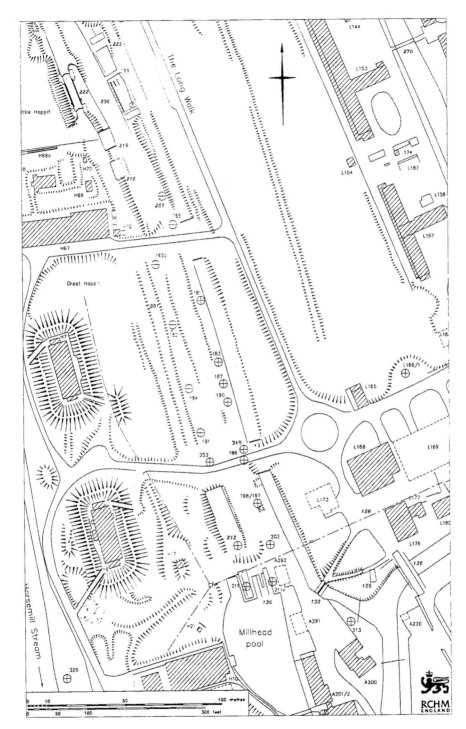

Figure 29.4 A complex industrial landscape: an extract from the Royal Commission on the Historical Monuments of England survey plan of Waltham Abbey Royal Gunpowder Factory. The plan shows both standing buildings and buried archaeology, the latter identified by numbered targets. Crown Copyright: Royal Commission on the Historical Monuments of England.

iron furnaces and foundries using water-wheels to drive bellows as well as a range of mills for corn-grinding, saw-milling and fulling. Limestone was an important cargo on the canals and recording work has been carried out on the limekilns to be found along the routes. The canals and tramways influenced settlement patterns, ranging from the isolated but complex depots at Sennybridge and Cnewr on the Brecon Forest Tramroad through the large warehouses at Newtown and Welshpool on the Montgomeryshire Canal to the many isolated houses at locks and wharves also to be found on the latter, many in a distinctive black and white patterned style (Hughes 1979, 1988, 1990). Studies such as these are the essence of industrial archaeology, revealing both the spatial links in the landscape and the social context of techno-logical development.

Industrial archaeology can undoubtedly contribute to the understanding both of the physical changes to the landscape and of changes to the fabric of society which have been brought about by the development of capitalist industry in the last 250 years or so. It needs to move beyond the description of the surviving physical evidence to an understanding of the significance of that evidence, making use of all available sources in doing so. The adoption of a theoretical model of change, such as the Marxist one of class conflict, may be appropriate in helping draw out the full meaning of the evidence, but not to the exclusion of other interpretations. The remainder of this chapter will explore how industrial archaeology has contributed to the debate over the nature and progress of industrialization in two major arenas: the production of textiles and the extraction and processing of coal and metals. These case studies have been chosen to illuminate the importance of both social context and spatial organization in the study of the archaeology of this period.

SOCIAL CONTEXT: THE TEXTILE INDUSTRIES

The manufacture of textiles is probably the most widespread of all industries, since provision of clothing was a fundamental necessity of life. In the medieval period, production on any scale was an urban craft dominated by the guild system, but gradually spinning, weaving and knitting became a rural activity. The first applica-tion of water power other than for corn milling was to the fulling of woollen cloth in the twelfth century, which further located the industry in the countryside. Techno-logical innovation came early, with the spinning wheel replacing the distaff and the horizontal loom the vertical loom: even more technologically significant was the invention in the late sixteenth century of the knitting frame (Palmer 1984; Wells 1972). All these devices could be used in the home, but nevertheless most of the industry was organized on a capitalist basis for the purposes of distribution and sale. It was, though, not until the eighteenth century that the further development of capitalism in the form of investment in power sources other than hand power revolutionized both the spatial and social organization of the textile industry. Individual entrepreneurs played a key role in this development, and it is in the textile industry above all others that new relationships had to be worked out between employer and employee.

Few of the standard histories of the textile industry make any use of material evidence, except as illustrations: Joseph Wright's painting *Cromford by Night* often serves to make the point about shift work by artificial light in the new cotton mills. Yet the industry created a completely new range of buildings and associated settlements which has hardly been subjected to social analysis. Ironically, it is the actual decline of the industry in both Europe and the United States in the late twentieth century and the consequent redundancy of large numbers of seemingly identical buildings which have prompted major studies of the material evidence of the textile industry. Once again, as in the 1950s and 1960s, it is the attempt to catalogue and preserve selected relics in the face of wholesale destruction which has prompted a re-evaluation of the contribution which the material culture of the textile industry can make to the historical debate over its development. Foremost among such studies in Britain have been those conducted by the RCHME at the request of various local authorities in the north of England. The large numbers of mill buildings in West Yorkshire prompted the development of a new methodology for investigation in industrial archaeology, using early twentieth-century 25-inch OS maps as a basis. A standard report form was used on brief site visits to over 1,800 sites, enabling comparisons to be made between mills which could be in the woollen, worsted, linen, silk, cotton, carpet, shoddy and mungo branches of the industry. This initial survey enabled a series of research questions to be framed, and the sites for more detailed study were chosen to demonstrate a range of criteria, including the development of the factory system, the structural evolution of textile mills and the effect of mills on the landscape: this resulted in detailed surveys of about a 10 per cent sample. The Greater Manchester survey followed a similar methodology, but, unlike in West Yorkshire, the mills were mainly for cotton and comparisons were simpler, resulting in a chronologically based typology in which size and layout, external details, methods of construction, internal organization and power systems were considered for each period of mill building. The East Cheshire survey concentrated on the housing and factories associated with both silk and cotton mills, and together these surveys provide a model for other large-scale surveys of industrial structures (Calladine and Fricker 1993; Giles and Goodall 1992; Williams and Farnie 1992; see also Watson 1990).

A similar decline in traditional textile industry prompted detailed studies of the Lower Merrimack Valley in Massachusetts, begun by HABS in 1968 and followed by the HAER survey of the water-power system at Lowell in 1974–75 (Molloy 1978). These were inventories of sites, concentrating on the industrial architecture and the water-power engineering, and can be contrasted with the more recent social analyses of material culture funded by the National Park Service, to whose care the city of Lowell passed following the work of HABS and HAER. These have been carried out by historical archaeologists (for example: Beaudry and Mrozowski 1988), and will be discussed in more detail below (p. 1183), but the two approaches provide an excellent illustration of the difference between industrial archaeology as usually defined and as possessing the wider meaning of the archaeology of industrialization.

Technological innovation in the textile industries is well documented, and numerous examples of both early and late machines survive in museum collections throughout Europe and the United States. Yet rarely has an overt connection been made between the machines and their products, possibly because of the lack of survival of textiles in the archaeological record. Museum textile collections focus on the unique, even the handmade, rather than the more mundane products of machines. One exception is the machine-made lace industry of Britain, where a clear relationship has been demonstrated between technical innovation and product design – for example in the provision of the lace curtains which graced so many Victorian homes (Earnshaw 1986). It is generally assumed that technological innovation in the textile industry was directed towards increased output, although the standardization of the product and quality control were part of the drive to meet the demands both of home consumers and the export trade. More investigation is needed into the relationship between investment in machines and the product they were intended for, as well as greater understanding of the way the machines were fitted into the workplace (see Calladine 1993; Markus 1993).

The pace of innovation varied considerably between different branches of the industry, and particular machines or sources of power remained in use long after more advanced versions were commercially available. Such technological inertia gives unique insight into past working practices: in Northern Ireland, for example, care has been taken to preserve examples of water-powered sites for scutching or breaking flax for the linen industry, while the National Trust cares for one of the last water-powered sites for beetling or imparting a shiny finish to linen cloth (see McCutcheon 1977). The Trust has also maintained a water-powered cotton spinning and weaving mill at Styal in Cheshire, while the National Park Service at Lowell, Massachussetts, maintains and runs the turbines which once powered the mills (Fig. 29.5). A visit to the steam-powered weaving shed of Queen Street Mills in Burnley, Lancashire, enables one to appreciate the intricacies of the power transmission systems as well as the human dimension of working in what is a noisy and dangerous environment by modern standards (Fig. 29.6).

The reasons for the longevity of a particular form of technology are as important as those for its first introduction, and bring into question the effectiveness of aggressive capitalism. In many instances, as can be seen throughout the archaeological record, if a tool did its job efficiently, it continued to be used in preference to

Figure 29.5 The textile complex of the Boott Cotton Mills Corporation in Lowell, Massachusetts, USA. Originally powered by water turbines, the mills have been converted to a variety of uses. Photograph: M. Palmer.

new-fangled versions not yet tried and tested – and sometimes well beyond that! Equally, a cheap labour force provided a viable alternative to investment in machinery if goods in demand could be manufactured at the right price. Technological inertia is a concept largely ignored by economic historians because their sources generally reveal change rather than continuity, but archaeology can assist in its elucidation and so make an original contribution to the continuing debate over the nature of industrialization.

In the 1780s and 1790s, a whole new range of buildings began to appear in the landscape, usually in a rural setting and many on a scale only comparable to the country seats of the aristocracy from which the people had been isolated by their formal settings. It is difficult to gauge the impact of the new textile mills on contemporary consciousness. Viscount Torrington in 1792 bemoaned the desecration of Aysgarth Falls in Wensleydale by the erection of:

> a great flaring mill, whose back stream has drawn off half the water of the falls above the bridge. With the bell ringing, and the clamour of the mill, all the vale is disturb'd: treason and levelling systems are the discourse; and rebellion may be near at hand.
>
> (Torrington [1790]1934, 3: 82)

Figure 29.6 The interior of the weaving shed at Queen Street Mills, Burnley, Lancashire, England, one of the last mills to be powered by steam. The tightly-packed looms and belt drives indicate the hazards experienced by the mill-hands. Photograph: M. Palmer.

But even he could not fail to be impressed by Arkwright's mills, one of which, in Wirksworth, 'seven storeys high and filled with inhabitants', reminded him of 'a first rate man of war, and when they are lighted up, on a dark night, look most luminously beautiful' (Torrington [1790]1934, 2: 196). Many of the earliest mills in Britain survive because their isolated location has saved them from later development, but their original cultural context can only be deduced with the aid of these contemporary reports. Both verbal and pictorial images of early industrialization are an invaluable source for the industrial archaeologist but, as an individual viewpoint, have to be used with caution.

The surviving structures help the industrial archaeologist to understand the aspirations of the capitalist entrepreneurs responsible for their construction. The recording work of the RCHME in Derbyshire has greatly enhanced our understanding of these early mills: Menuge has shown that Arkwright's well-documented obsession for the secrecy of his patented machines was reflected both in his choice of a site in Cromford, situated in a narrow valley in the Derbyshire Peak District, and the layout of the mill yard itself, hidden behind a high perimeter wall with no ground floor windows overlooking the road (Menuge 1993: 56–57). Equally,

Thomas Lombe's island site, closed off by iron gates, for his pioneering silk mill on the River Derwent in Derby, enabled him to protect the machines he had already pirated from Italy! (Calladine 1993). The employment of local masons and builders gave a certain standardization to the style of these early mills, with Georgian features of various kinds such as symmetrical fenestration, but the owners occasionally embellished them with something more dramatic. Arkwright took the opportunity afforded him by the front elevation of the stair and privy tower on his Masson Mill in the Derwent Valley to add surface details like Venetian and Diocletian windows arranged in a regular pattern beneath a bell cupola. He had just broken his partnership with Jedediah Strutt, and Masson Mill reflects the social aspirations which later led him to build Willesley Castle in a dominant position above the valley. The use of mill buildings to make a social statement was widespread among the gentleman-clothiers of southwest England in the early part of the nineteenth century (Stratton and Trinder 1997) and rather later in the more utilitarian cotton spinning districts of Lancashire, where specialist firms of architects made considerable use of Italianate features to indicate their employer's understanding of the classical traditions (Jones 1985).

The role of the capitalist entrepreneurs is therefore manifest in the material evidence they have left behind, but the primary function of these mills was to provide workspace for a rather more faceless labour force. The form of the buildings was governed by the need to provide unbroken spaces which could both house machinery and enable power to be transmitted from a remote source, at first a water wheel and later a turbine or steam engine. Two or more storeys housing machines enabled efficient use to be made of the power source, and the structure had to withstand not only the weight but also the vibration of the machines. Brick and timber remained the most common building materials for factories almost until the end of the Victorian period, both in Europe and the United States, despite the fire risk which was extreme in cotton mills: these burnt down with monotonous regularity. Examples remain of early cast-iron framing, including the first wholly iron-framed building, the Ditherington flax mill in Shrewsbury. The structural principles incorporated in this building remained more or less the same for the next half-century, to judge from surviving mid-Victorian examples such as Saltaire Mill near Bradford (Stratton and Trinder 1997: 66). The existence both of English-made textile machines and iron framing in European textile mills should help supplement the work on technological transfer carried out by economic historians such as Henderson once sufficient comparative studies have been carried out (see Gerber 1991; Henderson 1954). The reasons for the persistence of timber framing are worth investigation: cast iron could fail because of poor foundry practice and certainly did not make mills totally fire-proof, as can been seen from the number which did (and still do) burn down. Where timber was readily available, as in central Europe and the United States, timber-framed mills remained the norm.

Nevertheless, it was the textile mill, especially those where heavy machinery was used as in flax spinning, which pioneered the use of iron as a structural material, paving the way for the railway station canopies and great conservatories of the Victorian era. These linkages are important in understanding the impact of new technologies on related structures: the textile mill should not be studied in isolation.

Textile mills are therefore relatively well understood as a structural form, but far less attention has been paid to the buildings as spaces in which a whole new set of social relationships had to be worked out. This is generally assumed rather than analysed in any depth, although the source material exists not only in the buildings themselves but in engravings and documents such as fire insurance policies. The narrow, rectangular shape of each floor enabled daylight to penetrate to the machines, but also made the surveillance of the workforce a relatively easy task. The architectural historian Thomas Markus has made an attempt to apply the techniques of spatial analysis to some early Derbyshire mills, but has been more successful in his use of the concept of homology to explain the relationship between spatial structure and power transmission within a textile mill (Fig. 29.7).

Homology is the relation of corresponding parts forming a series in the same organism. Markus sees mill buildings developing to become like machines, with both static and dynamic systems within them. The static systems, that is the buildings themselves, changed over time, using different building materials and methods of construction. The machinery within the buildings, however, made them liable to movement, to become dynamic systems in themselves, and Markus shows how refinements were introduced to adjust them, such as the levelling devices on the basement supports in Strutt's Belper North Mill of 1804 (Markus 1993: 279). The other dynamic system within the buildings was for movement – of people, material substances and energy. The static systems for movement, such as staircase towers, were replaced by lifts and hoists, dynamic systems in which people and objects became static in moving space. With power transmission, he suggests that the early system of a wheel driving one horizontal shaft, which in turn drove several vertical shafts through all floors, did not result in a homologous whole, since the vertical structures of the power transmission system crossed those of social control and space, i.e. the machines and their attendants on each floor. In the more developed cotton mill, on the other hand, a single vertical shaft drove a horizontal shaft on each floor, which in turn powered belts to individual machines. Rope drives were later substituted for the vertical shaft, but the logic was the same and the homology now perfect, with power transmission in line with, rather than cutting through, the social and spatial structures of each floor (Markus 1993: 264). Commercially, this also made room and power systems possible, whereby the mill owner could let individual floors to separate firms who utilized the common power source. Markus's methods of analysis have not been pursued by other historians of

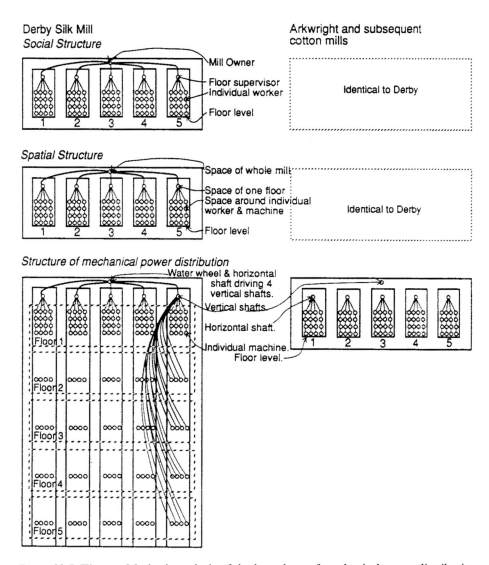

Figure 29.7 Thomas Markus's analysis of the homology of mechanical power distribution, social structure and spatial structure in some early textile mills in the English East Midlands. Source: Markus 1993.

industrial architecture (for example: Menuge 1993; Stratton and Trinder 1997), but they are a step towards an understanding of the spatial logic of a mill interior in a novel and challenging way.

The surveillance exercised over the workforce within the textile mill was echoed in the new communities created to house them. The isolated location of many early mills made provision of housing a necessity if shift work was to be efficiently carried out, enabling corporate paternalism to be manifested in the landscape. Employment of child labour in the late eighteenth century is revealed in the apprentice houses attached to many of the British mills, while the boarding houses which are such a feature of Lowell and Lawrence in Massachusetts provided a home for mill girls from country districts in the early nineteenth century. Rows of standardized houses were provided for families in late eighteenth- and early nineteenth-century Britain, occasionally, as in Cromford, revealing in their structure the provision of loomshops for outwork, since it was women and children who were primarily required in the spinning mill itself. In nearby Belper, the existence of numerous nailshops indicates alternative employment for men, and documentary research has shown that these were provided by the entrepreneur himself (Charlton, pers. comm.). Gender roles in industrialization have been investigated by economic historians such as Berg (1994), but careful analysis of the physical context of both mills and their communities would add substantially to the literature on the subject. The communities reinforced the hierarchy of the mill, with larger houses for the overlookers: this can be seen very clearly in the model settlement of Saltaire, near Bradford, laid out by Titus Salt in the 1850s. In Europe, large tenement buildings were preferred to the English-style villages, perhaps reflecting the later date of development and the generally urban location of many of the mills. In Lódz, for example, 'the Manchester of Poland', Prussian capital financed the development of large mills in the late nineteenth century, which have strong spatial and architectural links with the huge blocks of workers' flats in close proximity (Poplawska and Muthesius 1986; Fig. 29.8). As in southwest England, the construction of the owners' mansions alongside the mills enabled close surveillance both of the mill operations and of the workforce.

The vivid image of corporate ideology presented by the built environment of so many textile communities has been questioned as a result of the detailed interdisciplinary work carried out on the Boott Cotton Mills Corporation in Lowell, Massachusetts (Beaudry 1989; Beaudry and Mrozowski 1987a, 1987b, 1988, 1989). Excavation and documentary research have indicated that paternalism may have strongly influenced the lives of the workforce in the early days of the Corporation, but that its reality waned with time. Artefacts recovered from the backlots of the houses reveal that the mill girls shared their domestic premises both with male operatives and with the families of skilled workers from the outset, and considerable differences in ethnicity, status, diet, personal possessions and so on developed among the inhabitants in later years. While the American cotton industry made more use of immigrant labour that did its British equivalent in the nineteenth century, similar investigations at, for example, New Lanark in Scotland, might be illuminating on the extent of industrial paternalism in the post-Owen era. Many of the mill communities have been made Conservation Areas, terminating the natural

Figure 29.8 The blocks of tenement housing for the workers of the Schleiber mills in Lódz, Poland, built in the 1870s beside the huge factory. Surveillance of both mill and housing was guaranteed from the owner's nearby villa. Photograph: M. Palmer.

evolution of the landscape and thereby presenting a false image of the living conditions actually experienced by those for whom they were built.

The textile industry in the industrial period, therefore, appears to have been dominated by change – mechanization of processes, the construction of large numbers of new buildings, women and children employed outside the home, the establishment of mill communities where the discipline of the mill followed its workers home. The mechanization of spinning seems to have met with little resistance, possibly because the imbalance in the relationship between spinning and weaving following the invention of the flying shuttle was accepted, but also perhaps because spinning was a process carried out by women, who were less able to resist. Not so when it came to the more skilled aspects of textile production which were male preserves, such as weaving, machine knitting of both stockings and lace, cropping woven fabric and so on. These were the flashpoints of Luddism in the early nineteenth century, although the riots were as much about declining economic status as about new technology. Luddism was publicly defeated, but the archaeological evidence in fact charts a mute but dogged persistence in retaining old ways of working, which was far longer lasting than that which was expressed in open conflict.

The new textile mills were built for spinning from the 1770s onwards, but loomsheds for weaving were in most cases not added to them until the 1840s or later (Giles 1993; Giles and Goodall 1992). Where were the weavers who coped with the greatly increased output of spun yarn? Examination of the landscape has revealed the construction in this crucial period of large numbers of houses adapted for weaving by the inclusion of large windows to admit light. In most areas, these usually took the form of top-shops, which gave better light and could be given independent access: they were at once part of, but separated from, the domestic environment. They could be urban, as in the silk-weaving towns of Macclesfield, Congleton and Leek (Calladine and Fricker 1993), or rural, as in West Yorkshire where weaving shops were attached to isolated farmsteads as well as built in large numbers in villages, such as those grouped in the parish of Saddleworth (Caffyn 1986; Palmer and Neaverson 1994).

The physical provision for handloom weaving is less obvious in the cotton districts, where cellar or ground-floor workshops were more usual to provide the necessary damp conditions (Smith 1971; Timmins 1977, 1979). Such houses, however, do not indicate that the weaver lived the independent life noted by Defoe in the 1720s, but only that he retained the ability to work at home. The thread was no longer spun by his womenfolk, but supplied by merchants or master clothiers, who then marketed the finished cloth. Careful analysis of textile mill complexes has also revealed that some weavers accepted an even greater degree of discipline by working their handlooms in purpose-built loomshops within the mill area as early as the late eighteenth century (Giles 1993), thereby separating their work and home life (Fig. 29.9). This trend was intensified by the provision of sheds for power-loom weaving within the mills from the 1830s onwards. The most remarkable accommodation between the factory and domestic environment, however, took place in the ribbon-weaving town of Coventry, where houses with top-floor loomshops were grouped around a central steam engine, so that powered looms could continue to be used in a domestic environment (Palmer 1994; Prest 1960). These 'cottage factories' were built between 1830 and 1860, and represent a unique combination of artisan determination to retain independence and entrepreneurial attempts at control of the workforce. The system was not adopted in other weaving colonies with access to coal supplies, and the nearest equivalents are the powered workshops for jewellery and small metalwares crammed into areas of Birmingham and the Black Country, where the workers continued to live in cramped courts adjacent to their place of work. Capitalist entrepreneurs clearly could not force through total mechanization, and the reasons for their inability or unwillingness to do so are important in understanding the complex process of industrialization.

It is tempting to speculate that these efforts on the part of the workforce to retain what was in many ways an illusory independence were in fact highly beneficial to the employer, who was spared the cost of constructing workspace yet could retain control through provision of raw materials and marketing of goods. Nowhere was

Figure 29.9 A weavers' workshop in Rawtenstall, Lancashire, England. This building represents the first stage of the loss of independence, as the workforce was brought together under one roof for the purposes of supervision. Photograph: M. Palmer.

this more true than within the hosiery industry, which remained on a domestic basis until at least the 1870s. The surviving housing indicates three phases of the industry: the adaptation of existing buildings for knitting by the insertion of long windows from the seventeenth century onwards; the provision by speculative builders of purpose-built houses incorporating workshops from the late eighteenth century onwards; and the construction of workshops analogous to the loomshops of the cotton and woollen industries, where traditional skills could be preserved but surveillance practised by the master hosier (Palmer 1989, 1994). Some of the latter incorporated space for workshops within their own homes, but Campion has shown, by means of access analysis, that they were careful to preserve the distinction between private and public space by the provision of separate entrances and lack of physical communication between workshop and house (Campion 1996). However, most hosiery manufacturers were as anxious as the knitters themselves to maintain the domestic system, since they were not only spared the necessity of providing workspace but were also able to rent machines out to workers in their own homes. Not until the 1870s do any substantial numbers of powered factories appear in the landscape, indicating the longevity of a domestic system of production despite the technical advances made back in the sixteenth century.

1185

What an archaeological study of the textile industries indicates is that techno-logical innovation did not necessarily give rise to deterioration in worker–master relationships to the point of conflict. The latter is emphasized in documentary sources, which then as now concentrated on the newsworthy rather than the mun-dane. Careful analysis of the surviving physical evidence in the form of buildings, products and machinery, in conjunction with the documentary evidence, shows a much more gradual process of adaptation on the part of both employer and employee to the complex process of mechanization. Industrial archaeologists need to be as sensitive to the *continuing* use of well-established techniques as to the *first* use of particular technological innovations, whose social and spatial impact have commonly been overemphasized by historians.

THE SPATIAL CONTEXT: MINING AND METALS

The dramatic decline of heavy industry in the western world has, as in the textile industries, made redundant within a very short space of time large numbers of sites and structures whose sheer scale daunts attempts at archaeological recording. In Britain, the virtual disappearance of coal mining has led to efforts by all three Royal Commissions on Historical Monuments to carry out rapid surveys of surface remains, including the associated housing, since mining communities have been such an integral part of the coal-mining landscape (Gould and Ayris 1995; Hughes *et al.* 1995; Thornes 1994). The difficulty of interpreting large industrial sites from surviving remains encouraged the RCAHMW to experiment with process record-ing at operational sites, the results of which can illuminate the study of incomplete, damaged, or long defunct sites (Malaws 1997). Malaws argues that the study of the techniques and operations of industry has been overshadowed by the architectural and historical aspects of monuments and their industries, ignoring the fact that many important processes were carried out in architecturally undistinguished buildings; he also re-asserts the human dimension in industrial production. A further plea that the archaeologist should act as a witness has been urged by Richard Hayman, following the recording of a foundry making harness furniture: he emphasizes that a firsthand knowledge of manufacturing techniques enables the archaeologist to understand the empirical adaptations which took place, a know-ledge which can be utilized on sites where the techniques employed are now extinct (Hayman 1997). Such insights are a unique advantage enjoyed by the industrial archaeologist, who can make use of film and video to record working practices which elsewhere have to be deduced from physical remains alone.

The vast scale of many of these monuments of heavy industry has led to the preservation of a selected few for their tourist potential, and archaeological work has been carried out to provide an interpretative context. In Poland, recording programmes have been carried out on the numerous surviving headgears associated with the coal industry in the region around Katowice with a view to preserving the most important of these. In the United States, historical archaeologists have contributed to the Industrial Heritage Project in southwestern Pennsylvania, designed to interpret the remains of the important iron and steel industry of this area and particularly to look at its relevance to the labour movement, an aspect barely touched upon in British studies. In the southern states, the employment of negro labour in ironworks as well as in many other industries is a recurring theme in schemes of interpretation, and Congress in 1991 authorized a National Historic Landmark Theme study on American labour history, with a view to adding significant sites to those already in the care of the National Park Service. Exciting projects for the actual re-use of nineteenth-century steel-cased blast furnaces are already in place in Birmingham, Alabama, and in the Landschaftspark near Duisburg in Germany. In a world increasingly dominated by micro-technology, such preservation schemes will at least enable future generations to understand the impact of heavy industry on the consciousness not only of those who worked in it but also on the artists and writers who have left us contemporary accounts.

A further reason for accelerated programmes of archaeological recording and research on mining landscapes has been their threat from environmental improvement schemes designed to decontaminate or to rehabilitate what is perceived to be derelict land, thereby destroying a rich archaeological resource (Palmer 1993). In Cornwall, archaeological evaluation has usually preceded derelict land work, but accompanied by all the problems of developer-led archaeology: as Sharpe has said, 'not only the initiative, but the agenda belong to other organisations' (Sharpe 1995: 133). Nevertheless, Cornwall Archaeology Unit has produced what must be the most comprehensive set of field reports on the mining landscapes of any British county (for example: Sharpe 1993a, 1993b). Further east, in Devon, the Dartmoor Tin Mining Research Group has carried out extensive field survey and excavation on both tin-streaming sites and smelt mills, greatly enhancing understanding of the field archaeology of the post-medieval tin industry and giving some idea of its spatial organization (Gerrard 1994, 1996). A great deal of historical work on tin mining has been carried out by historians within the two counties, but the archaeological and historical data have yet to be brought together in any meaningful way.

Lead and copper mining landscapes have suffered on a greater scale because of the potentially contaminative effects of these minerals in the soil. The mines of Spain have been important in Europe since the prehistoric period, but although the earlier remains have received some attention (for example: Rothenburg and Blanco-Freijeiro 1981), the considerable physical survivals from the nineteenth century (Fig. 29.10) have been virtually ignored. In Britain, most of the work has been developer-led, and the archaeological evaluations have never found their way into accessible publications. Whole landscapes around Minera in North Wales and

Figure 29.10 The derelict headstocks and calcining furnace on the Cruz Chicita mine in the Murcian mining field of south-eastern Spain. Photograph: M. Palmer.

Snailbeach in Shropshire have been decontaminated and upstanding remains consolidated for their tourist potential, but without any real interpretation. There has been some interest in the archaeological potential of ore preparation sites, mundane structures usually ignored both by contemporaries and by historians of mining (for example: Cranstone 1989). Unfortunately, studies tend to be industry-specific (a trend encouraged by the Monuments Protection Programme) and few comparative studies have been carried out. Only these can really contribute to the debate over the nature and extent of industrialization, by revealing the contrasts between the effect of capital investment in mining technology in some areas and the extent of technological inertia in a great many others (Palmer and Neaverson 1989). Both spatial and sequential relationships need investigation in a wider context.

The difference between mining archaeology in Britain and in America is partly due to the long history of metalliferous mining in the former, where sites may reveal evidence of Roman and medieval as well as post-medieval activity, despite the destructive nature of extractive industry itself. In America, particularly in the West, mining was a phenomenon of the second half of the nineteenth century and characterized by the wholesale immigration of fortune-seekers, usually single males (Fig. 29.11). In Britain, the majority of metalliferous mines were comparatively small affairs and their workforce lived with their families in nearby villages, many of which are still populated and so not available for the kind of archaeological work on their domestic conditions which has been possible in America. As Hardesty has pointed out, surviving technology and buildings are not common on American mining sites, presumably because of the scrap value of the machinery, but rather they are rich in trash dumps, residential house foundations, privies and other remains of the miners themselves (Hardesty 1988: 17). Mining camps, which barely feature in European contexts, were a feature of the American West, and both archaeological and historical work have revealed the immense scale of immigration, not only of skilled participants such as the Cornish miners but of unskilled labour, notably the Chinese. The material culture reveals the contrast between the living conditions of individuals seeking their fortunes by panning for gold in the '49 Californian Gold Rush and those working in the heavily capitalized hard rock mines of both California and Nevada, who had rather greater security and later brought their womenfolk to join them. Stores provided necessities as well as luxuries, the range of which has been indicated not only from artefacts recovered from the mining settlements themselves but also from the intensive excavation of sites like the Hoff Store site in San Francisco. This burnt down on 3-4 May 1851 and, because of its position on the waterfront, the contents formed a sealed deposit which was not recovered until the late 1980s and so is invaluable in indicating the range of goods imported into San Francisco, the prime trading centre for the Gold Rush area (Pastron and Hattori 1990).

In Australia, the pioneering work of Judy Birmingham and Ian Jack did much to encourage the archaeological study of mining landscapes (Birmingham *et al.* 1979). The comparative isolation of many of the sites in this vast, underpopulated country has assisted the survival of a considerable number of both buildings and machinery, and so their approach was more that of traditional industrial archaeology than the more ethnographic approach favoured in America. An important theme, given Australia's colonial status, has been technological transfer, much of the machinery as well as mining skills being imported from Britain. Cornish-style engine houses are a feature of several sites, notably the Burra and Moonta mines of South Australia, and Methodist chapels are cheek by jowl with outback saloons. The physical

1189

Figure 29.11 A nineteenth-century image of prospectors seeking gold in California. Source: Malakoff & Co., California.

evidence provides information both about the adaptation of the imported techno-logy to cope with the environmental rigour of Australia, and about the pioneering frontier or zone of experimentation, often littered with evidence of failure. The archaeological work which has taken place on the settlements associated with the mines is even more redolent of isolation, with few imported luxuries compared with similar settlements in America (Holmes 1983). Historians have investigated the migration of skilled labour from Britain, often characterized as 'cousin Jack down under'. As in America, the tourist potential of mining sites has been exploited extensively, for example the Sovereign Hill Goldmining township at Ballarat in Victoria (Brown 1989; Donnachie 1981).

The archaeological investigation of mining landscapes has, like those of the textile industry, been prompted by their imminent destruction, and much of the work has been carried out in a 'rescue' context in which research strategies have not been strictly defined. In Europe, most studies have been concerned with the techno-logical elucidation of surviving sites and structures, unravelling the sequential rela-tionships inherent in the methods of extraction and processing of raw materials, but often not having the scope to consider the wider spatial linkages between mining, transport, industrial production, and use within the human sphere. Where, for example, did the raw material for the iron and glass used in the Crystal Palace of

1851 actually come from? Prehistoric, classical and medieval archaeologists use scientific methods to determine the origins of metals and other artefacts retrieved by excavation, and so discover trade patterns (see Chapter 9); industrial archaeologists have the advantage not only of scientific analysis but also of documentary sources in making such linkages. The latter also help in establishing the cultural context, which has figured largely in studies from Australia and America, where the effects of both technological transfer and human immigration are revealed in the archaeological record. The use of archaeology has, therefore, already added greatly to our understanding of the landscape of past extractive industries, despite the difficulties imposed by the circumstances in which much of the research has been carried out. The acceptance of wider research agendas would enable it to contribute even more effectively to this particular aspect of industrialization.

CONCLUSION

Industrial archaeology grew from the perceived need to record and preserve the fast-vanishing remains of early industrialization in Europe, America and further afield. A largely volunteer movement at first, the importance of the physical remains, especially in Britain, has prompted the intervention of the statutory recording bodies and more recently of mainstream archaeologists, especially those concerned with contract archaeology. The compilation of inventories of industrial sites and monuments for most of the industrialized countries means there is now an accepted corpus of significant structures and, despite significant losses, a tendency towards the preservation or re-use of industrial structures rather than their rapid demolition. We have moved towards a concept of sustainable development, aptly defined in the British context as 'development which meets the needs of today without compromising the ability of future generations to understand, appreciate and benefit from Britain's historic environment' (Clark 1993: 90). This has not yet been achieved everywhere, but it is at least a recognizable objective.

Industrial archaeology has not, however, just worked towards the preservation of the industrial heritage, but has begun to contribute towards the ongoing debate on the nature of industrialization. Archaeological work on derelict industrial landscapes threatened with rehabilitation has been extremely valuable in revealing the intricacies of past industrial activity, much of which was too mundane ever to be documented. Typological studies of buildings and structures have contributed not only to a fuller understanding of the development of particular industries but also to the realization of the importance of regional variation in the pace of change. Most important of all, perhaps, is the demonstration of continuity as well as change in the archaeological record, which prompts questions about the respective roles of the entrepreneur and the workforce in the take-up of technological innovations.

The future of industrial archaeology now lies in its practitioners adopting similar methodological approaches to historical archaeologists, and being ready to consider further the cultural as well as the technological significance of the physical evidence. They need to look more carefully at the relationship between the processes of production deduced from studies of sites or sequences of buildings and the artefacts which were generated: how were the latter transported, distributed, marketed and consumed? The work of Danny Miller and Matthew Johnson on the changing meanings of objects in different cultural contexts is relevant here (Johnson 1996; Miller 1987). Finally, they should not be reluctant to make use of the wealth of pictorial, documentary, and even oral sources available which can be used in conjunction with the physical evidence to arrive at a fuller understanding of the social as well as the economic and technological contexts of production. In these ways, industrial archaeology – while not changing its name – would mature into an archaeology of industrialization.

REFERENCES

Alfrey, J. and Clark, C. (1993) *The Landscape of Industry: Patterns of Change in the Ironbridge Gorge*, London: Routledge.

Andrews, D. (1994) 'Written in rock and rust', *Federal Archeology* 7 (2): 16–23.

Baker, D. (1991) *Potworks: the Industrial Architecture of the Staffordshire Potteries*, London: RCHME.

Beaudry, M. C. (1989) 'The Lowell Boott mills complex and its housing: material expressions of corporate ideology', *Historical Archaeology* 23: 19–33.

Beaudry, M. C. and Mrozowski, S. A. (1987a) *Interdisciplinary Investigations of the Boott Mills, Lowell, Massachusetts, Vol. I: Life at the Boarding Houses*, Boston: Division of Cultural Resources, North Atlantic Region, National Park Service No. 18.

Beaudry, M. C. and Mrozowski, S. A. (1987b) *Interdisciplinary Investigations of the Boott Mills, Lowell, Massachusetts, Vol. II: The Kirk Street Agent's House*, Boston: Division of Cultural Resources, North Atlantic Region, National Park Service No. 18.

Beaudry, M. C. and Mrozowski, S. A. (1988) 'The archaeology of work and home life in Lowell, Massachusetts: an interdisciplinary study of the Boott Cotton Mills Corporation', *IA. Journal of the Society for Industrial Archeology* 14: 1–22.

Beaudry, M. C. and Mrozowski, S. A. (1989) *Interdisciplinary Investigations of the Boott Mills, Lowell, Massachusetts, Vol. III: The Boarding House System as a Way of Life*, Boston: Division of Cultural Resources, North Atlantic Region, National Park Service No. 18.

Belhoste, J.-F. (1988) *Les Ardoisières en Pays de la Loire*, Nantes: Inventaire Général des monuments et des richesses artistiques de la France.

Belhoste, J.-F., Bertrand, P. and Gayot, G. (1984) *La Manufacture de Dijonval et la Draperie Sedanaise 1650–1850*, Paris: Inventaire Général des monuments et des richesses artistiques de la France.

Belhoste, J.-F., Claerr-Roussel, C., Lassus, F., Philippe, M. and Vion-Delphin, F. (1994) *La

Métallurgie Comtoise, Xve–XIXe Siècles: Etude du Val de Saône, Besançon: Inventaire Général des monuments et des richesses artistiques de la France.

Berg, M. (1994) *The Age of Manufactures, 1700–1820: Industry, Innovation and Work in Britain*, London: Routledge.

Birmingham, J., Jack, I. and Jeans, D. (1979) *Australian Pioneer Technology: Sites and Relics*, Richmond: Heinemann.

Brown, I. (1989) 'Mining and tourism in Southern Australia', *Industrial Archaeology Review* 12 (1): 55–66.

Buchanan, R. A. (1972) *Industrial Archaeology in Britain*, Harmondsworth: Penguin.

Burns, J. A. (ed.) (1989) *Recording Historic Structures*, Washington: The American Institute of Architects Press.

Bythell, D. (1978) *The Sweated Trades*, London: Batsford

Caffyn, L. (1986) *Workers' Housing in West Yorkshire, 1750–1920*, London: HMSO.

Calladine, A. (1993) 'Lombe's Mill: an exercise in reconstruction', *Industrial Archaeology Review* 16 (1): 82–99.

Calladine, A. and Fricker, J. (1993) *East Cheshire Textile Mills*, London: RCHME.

Campion, G. (1996) 'People, process and the poverty-pew: a functional analysis of mundane buildings in the Nottinghamshire framework-knitting industry', *Antiquity* 70: 847–60.

Cerda, M. (1991) 'Industrial archaeology and the working class', in M. Cerda and J. Torro (eds) *Arquelogia Industrial*, València: Diputació de València: 403–22.

Clark, C. (1993) 'Archaeology and sustainable development', in H. Swain (ed.) *Rescuing the Historic Environment*, Hertford: RESCUE: 87–90.

Cossons, N. (1975) *The B.P. Book of Industrial Archaeology*, Newton Abbot: David and Charles.

Cranstone, D. (1989) 'The archaeology of washing floors: problems, potentials and priorities', *Industrial Archaeology Review* 12 (1): 40–49.

Crossley, D. (1975) *The Bewl Valley Ironworks*, London: Royal Archaeological Institute.

Crossley, D. (1994) 'Early industrial landscapes' in B. Vyner (ed.) *Building on the Past*, London: Royal Archaeological Institute: 244–63.

Deetz, J. (1996) *In Small Things Forgotten*, New York: Doubleday (revised edition; 1st edition New York: Anchor, 1977).

Donnachie, I. (1981) 'Industrial archaeology in Australia', *Industrial Archaeology Review* 5 (2): 96–113.

Douglas, G. and Oglethorpe, M. (1993) *Brick, Tile and Fireclay Industries in Scotland*, Edinburgh: RCAHMS.

Earnshaw, P. (1986) *Lace Machines and Machine Laces*, London: Batsford.

English Heritage (1995) *Industrial Archaeology: a Policy Statement*, London: English Heritage.

Everson, P. (1995) 'The survey of complex industrial landscapes', in M. Palmer and P. A. Neaverson (eds) *Managing the Industrial Heritage*, Leicester: University of Leicester, School of Archaeological Studies: 21–28.

Everson, P. and Cocroft, W. (1996) 'The Royal gunpowder factory at Waltham Abbey: the field archaeology of gunpowder manufacture', in B. Buchanan (ed.) *Gunpowder: the History of an International Technology*, Bath: Bath University Press: 377–94.

Gerber, P. (1991) 'The flax spinning mill in Myslakowice, Poland', *Industrial Archaeology Review* 13 (2): 142–51.

Gerrard, S. (1994) 'The Dartmoor tin industry: an archaeological perspective', *Proceedings of the Devon Archaeological Society* 52: 173–98.

Gerrard, S. (1996) 'The early south-western tin industry: an archaeological view', in P. Newman (ed.) *The Archaeology of Mining and Metallurgy in South-West Britain*, Matlock Bath: Peak District Mines Historical Society: 67–83.

Giles, C. (1993) 'Housing the loom, 1790–1850: a study of industrial building and mechanisation in a transitional period', *Industrial Archaeology Review* 16 (1): 27–37.

Giles, C. and Goodall, I. (1992) *Yorkshire Textile Mills 1770–1930*, London: HMSO.

Glassie, H. (1975) *Folk Housing in Middle Virginia: a Structural Analysis of Historical Artifacts*, Knoxville: University of Tennessee Press.

Gould, S. and Ayris, I. (1995) *Colliery Landscapes: an Aerial Survey of the Deep-mined Coal Industry in England*, London: English Heritage.

Hardesty, D. (1988) *The Archaeology of Mining and Miners: a View from the Silver State*, Ann Arbor, Mich.: The Society of Historical Archeology.

Hayman, R. (1997) 'The archaeologist as witness: Matthew Harvey's Glebeland works, Walsall', *Industrial Archaeology Review* 19: 61–74.

Henderson, W. O. (1954) *Britain and Industrial Europe 1750-1870: Studies in British Influence*, Leicester: Leicester University Press.

Hodder, I. (1982) *Symbols in Action*, Cambridge: Cambridge University Press.

Hodder, I. (1986) *Reading the Past: Current Approaches to Interpretation in Archaeology*, Cambridge: Cambridge University Press.

Holmes, K. (1983) 'Excavations at Arltunga, Northern Territory', *Australian Journal of Historical Archaeology* 1: 78–87.

Hoskins, W. G. (1955) *The Making of the English Landscape*, London: Hodder and Stoughton.

Hudson, K. (1963) *Industrial Archaeology*, London: John Baker.

Hughes, S. (1979) 'The Swansea Canal: navigation and power supplier', *Industrial Archaeology Review* 4 (1): 51–69.

Hughes, S. (1988) *The Archaeology of the Montgomeryshire Canal*, Aberystwyth: RCAHMW.

Hughes, S. (1990) *The Brecon Forest Tramroads: the Archaeology of an Early Railway System*, Aberystwyth: RCAHMW.

Hughes, S., Malaws, B., Parry, M. and Wakelin, P. (1995) *Collieries of Wales: Engineering and Architecture*, Aberystwyth: RCAHMW.

Johnson, M. (1996) *The Archaeology of Capitalism*, Oxford: Blackwell.

Jones, E. (1985) *Industrial Architecture in Britain, 1750–1939*, London: Batsford.

Lang, N. (1995) 'Rapid desk-based recording of industrial landscapes', in M. Palmer and P. A. Neaverson (eds) *Managing the Industrial Heritage*, Leicester: University of Leicester, School of Archaeological Studies: 15–20.

Leone, M. P. and Potter, P. B. (eds) (1988) *The Recovery of Meaning*, Washington, DC: Smithsonian Institution Press.

Lorrain, D. (1968) 'An archaeologist's guide to nineteenth century American glass', *Historical Archaeology* 2: 35–44.

McCutcheon, W. A. (1977) *Wheel and Spindle*, Belfast: Blackstaff Press.

Malaws, B. (1997) 'Process recording at industrial sites', *Industrial Archaeology Review* 19: 75–98.

Markus, T. A. (1993) *Buildings and Power*, London: Routledge.

Menuge, A. (1993) 'The cotton mills of the Derbyshire Derwent and its tributaries', *Industrial Archaeology Review* 16 (1): 38–61.

Miller, D. (1987) *Material Culture and Mass Consumption*, Oxford: Blackwell.

Miller, G. and Pacey, A. (1985) 'Impact of mechanization in the glass container industry: the

Dominion Glass Company of Montreal, a case study', *Historical Archaeology* 19 (1): 38–50.

Molloy, P. M. (ed.) (1978) *The Lower Merrimack River Valley: an Inventory of Historic Engineering and Industrial Sites*, North Andover: Merrimack Valley Textile Museum.

Palmer, M. (1984) *Framework Knitting*, Aylesbury: Shire.

Palmer, M. (1989) 'Houses and workplaces: the framework knitters of the East Midlands', *Knitting International* 96 (1150): 31–35.

Palmer, M. (1990) 'Industrial archaeology: a thematic or a period discipline?', *Antiquity* 64: 275–85.

Palmer, M. (1993) 'Mining landscapes and the problems of contaminated land', in H. Swain (ed.) *Rescuing the Historic Environment*, Hertford: RESCUE: 45–50.

Palmer, M. (1994) 'Industrial archaeology: continuity and change', *Industrial Archaeology Review* 16 (2): 135–56.

Palmer, M. and Neaverson, P. A. (1989) 'The comparative archaeology of tin and lead dressing in Britain during the nineteenth century', *Bulletin of the Peak District Mines Historical Society* 10 (6): 316–53.

Palmer, M. and Neaverson, P. A. (1994) *Industry in the Landscape, 1700–1900*, London: Routledge.

Pastron, A. G. and Hattori, E. M. (eds) (1990) *The Hoff Store Site and Gold Rush Merchandise from San Francisco, California*, Ann Arbor, Mich.: The Society for Historical Archaeology.

Patrick, A. (1996) 'Establishing a typology for the buildings of the floor malting industry', *Industrial Archaeology Review* 18 (2): 180–200.

Paynter, R. (1988) 'Steps to an archaeology of capitalism: material change and class analysis', in M. P. Leone and P. B. Potter (eds) *The Recovery of Meaning*, Washington, DC: Smithsonian Institution Press: 407–33.

Poplawska, I. and Muthesius, S. (1986) 'Poland's Manchester: 19th-century industrial and domestic architecture in Lódz', *Journal of the Society of Architectural Historians* 45 (2): 148–60.

Prest, J. (1960) *The Industrial Revolution in Coventry*, Oxford: Oxford University Press.

Raistrick, A. (1972) *Industrial Archaeology: an Historical Survey*, London: Eyre Methuen.

Rix, M. (1967) *Industrial Archaeology*, London: Historical Association.

Rothenburg, B. and Blanco-Freijeiro, A. (1981) *Studies in Ancient Mining and Metallurgy in South-west Spain*, London: IAMS.

Samuel, R. (1977) ' "The Workshop of the World": steam power and hand technology in mid-Victorian Britain', *History Workshop Journal* 3: 6–72.

Sharpe, A. (1993a) *Geevor and Levant: an Assessment of their Surface Archaeology*, Truro: Cornwall Archaeological Unit.

Sharpe, A. (1993b) *Geevor and Levant: a Consideration of the Archaeological Potential of Geevor and Levant Mines, West Penwith*, Truro: Cornwall Archaeological Unit.

Sharpe, A. (1995) 'Developments under derelict land grants: the potential, the problems', in M. Palmer and P. A. Neaverson (eds) *Managing the Industrial Heritage*, Leicester: University of Leicester, School of Archaeological Studies: 133–36.

Sharpe, A., Lewis, C., Massie, C. and Johnson, N. (1991) *Engine House Assessment: the Mineral Tramways Project*, Truro: Cornwall County Council.

Smith, D. (1965) *Industrial Archaeology of the East Midlands*, Dawlish: David and Charles.

Smith, W. J. (1971) 'The architecture of the domestic system in south-east Lancashire and the adjoining Pennines', in S. D. Chapman (ed.) *The History of Working Class Housing*, Newton Abbot: David and Charles: 250–75.

Starbuck, D. R. (1983) 'The New England Glassworks in Temple, New Hampshire', *Industrial Archeology* 9: 45–64.

Stratton, M. and Trinder, B. (1997) *Industrial England*, London: Batsford/English Heritage.

Thornes, R. (1994) *Images of Coal*, London: RCHME.

Timmins, J. G. (1977) *Handloom Weavers' Cottages in Central Lancashire*, Lancaster: Centre for North-West Regional Studies.

Timmins, J. G. (1979) 'Handloom weavers' cottages in central Lancashire: some problems of recognition', *Post-Medieval Archaeology* 13: 251–72.

Timmins, J. G. (1993) *The Last Shift*, Manchester: Manchester University Press.

Torrington, Viscount ([1790]1934) *The Torrington Diaries, containing the Tours through England and Wales of the Hon. John Byng* (4 volumes), edited by C. B. Andrews, London: Eyre and Spottiswoode.

Trinder, B. (ed.) (1992) *The Blackwell Encyclopaedia of Industrial Archaeology*, Oxford: Blackwell.

Viaene, P. (1986) *Industriële Archeologie in België*, Gent: Stichting Mens en Kultur.

Watson, M. (1990) *Jute and Flax Mills in Dundee*, Tayport: Hutton Press.

Wells, F. A. (1972) *The British Hosiery and Knitwear Industry: its History and Organisation*, Newton Abbot: David and Charles.

Williams, M. and Farnie, D. A. (1992) *Cotton Mills of Greater Manchester*, Preston: Carnegie Publishing.

Zeier, C. D. (1987) 'Historic charcoal production near Eureka, Nevada: an archaeological perspective', *Historical Archaeology* 21: 81–101.

SELECT BIBLIOGRAPHY

Two classic books which demonstrate the original thematic approach to industrial archaeology in Britain are Buchanan (1972, reprinted 1980) and Cossons (1975, reprinted 1993). Raistrick (1972) deals with a longer time-span and includes a thematic scheme for industrial archaeology which has been used by English Heritage as the basis for their industrial Monuments Protection Programme. Methods for recording buildings and machinery are described by M. Palmer and P. A. Neaverson, *Industrial Archaeology: Principles and Practice* (London: Routledge, 1998). The development of industrial landscapes is described historically in B. Trinder's *Making of the Industrial Landscape* (1982), and thematically by Palmer and Neaverson (1994). Alfrey and Clark (1993) used detailed plot surveys for their in-depth study of the important Ironbridge Gorge, and the archaeology of transport systems is dealt with by Hughes (1988, 1990), whilst Crossley (1994) argues for wider spatial analysis of post-medieval industrial landscapes. Industrial buildings were first examined by J. M. Richards in his classic *The Functional Tradition in Early Industrial Buildings* (1958); Jones (1985) deals mainly with textile mills, whilst Stratton and Trinder (1997) attempt to look at buildings in relation to the people they accommodated. The more structured analysis of Markus (1993) on issues of freedom and surveillance has been better worked out for public institutions than for industrial buildings.

The literature on industrialization is vast, but the best recent book to examine the world of work is Berg (1994), which also contains a comprehensive bibliography. Trinder (1992) provides the best introduction to the international scene, largely from the point of view of the industrial heritage. The theoretical stance taken by east coast American historical archaeologists is best demonstrated in R. Paynter's powerfully argued 'Steps to an archaeology of capitalism' in Leone and Potter (1988), while the value of an interdisciplinary approach can be seen in the work of Beaudry and Mrozowski in Lowell, Massachusetts (1987a, 1987b, 1988, 1989) and Hardesty's 1988 study of mining. Much site-specific work is included in journals such as *Historical Archaeology* and *IA: Journal of the Society for Industrial Archeology* in the United States and *Industrial Archaeology Review* in Britain. Many British and Irish archaeological journals now include reports on sites of industrial interest and are usefully abstracted in the Council for British Archaeology's British and Irish Archaeological Bibliography.

INDEX